MORE
CORNWALL RAILWAYS REMEMBERED

This book is dedicated to the late Jim Renshaw,
who was a well known railwayman in the Stockport Area.

More CORNWALL RAILWAYS REMEMBERED

UNIQUE PHOTOGRAPHS OF CORNWALL'S HISTORIC RAILWAY INFRASTRUCTURE

Stephen F. Heginbotham

First published in Great Britain in 2013

British Library Cataloguing-in-Publication Data
A CIP record for this title is available from the British Library

ISBN 978 0 85704 207 1

HALSGROVE
Halsgrove House,
Ryelands Business Park,
Bagley Road, Wellington, Somerset TA21 9PZ
Tel: 01823 653777 Fax: 01823 216796
email: sales@halsgrove.com

Part of the Halsgrove group of companies
Information on all Halsgrove titles is available at: www.halsgrove.com

Printed in China by Everbest Printing Co Ltd

CONTENTS

Introduction 7

The Author 9

Acknowledgements and Reference Sources 10

Foreword 11

Signalman 13

Chapter 1: **Penzance to Truro** 15

Chapter 2: **Truro to Par** 53

Chapter 3: **Par to Plymouth** 69

Chapter 4: **St Blazey** 81

Chapter 5: **The Branches** 97

Chapter 6: **Signalling** 110

Chapter 7: **Mishaps** 141

Chapter 8: **The HSTs** 153

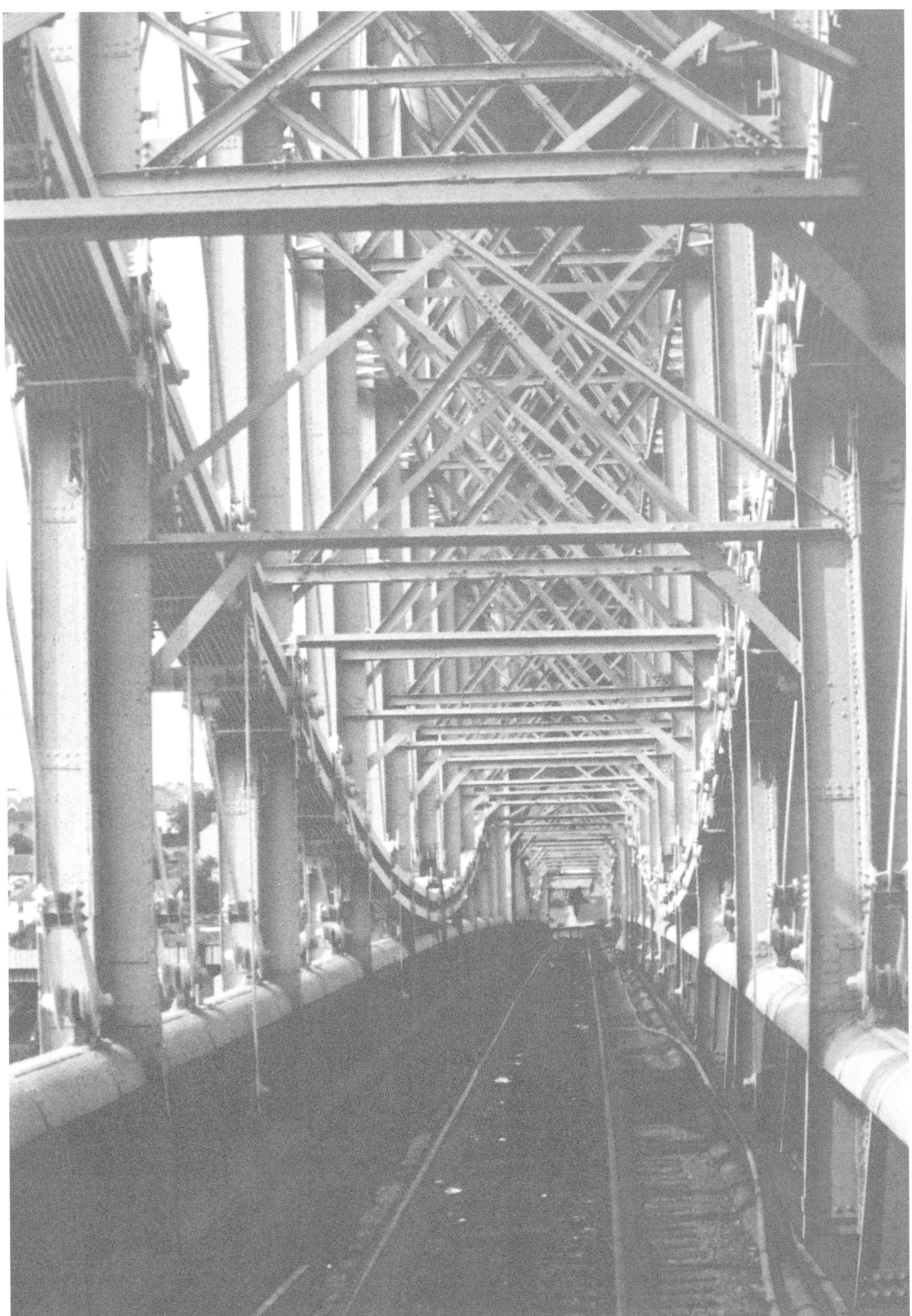

INTRODUCTION

FOLLOWING ON from my very successful previous book, *Cornwall's Railways Remembered* which catalogued the life and times of Signalling Technician Frank Sperritt, I was invited to write a sequel based around my career, life and times in public transport. This will include my long career working for the railway, and also include contributions and photographs from colleagues past and present.

As a MOM (Mobile Operations Manager) for Railtrack, which became Network Rail in 2002 I have been, and I am still, privileged to witness many unusual, rare and out of course events during the day-to-day running of the national railway network. In 1994, when Railtrack was formed by the then Conservative Government as a privatised version of British Railways, my title was Signalling Inspector (SI), a job which involved primary responsibility for keeping the railway running in times of disruption or emergency, but in between these events I managed the daily tasks, including assessing and certifying competence of Signalmen and Signalwomen, rostering, checking level crossings, ordering stores, tending the signal lamps (which were still paraffin lamps) and a myriad of other duties.

My job as a MOM (ASI – Area Signalling Inspector) was, and still is, very unpredictable, and it is this factor that makes the job, for me most enjoyable, in that you never know what each day will bring; but when called-out on a "shout" there is a great job satisfaction when you get the railway running again promptly and most importantly of all, safely.

The travelling public are aware and rightfully expect, that punctuality is core to the success of the railway, but in times of disruption or failure, we as the "operators" have to be sure we have done all the checks and balances before we allow trains, conveying either thousands of tons of freight, or hundreds of passengers, to move safely.

Without the integrity of the signalling, the MOM has an extremely responsible job to ensure that each movement will be done with the utmost safety and when he or she says those familiar words "Driver – please pass this signal at danger" that this is the only train on that section of railway and each set of points and each crossing is set correctly and any other staff working near the line, on stations or in the signalbox knows exactly what is occurring.

Of course the MOM cannot achieve this alone, and liaises closely with the Signal(wo)men (Signallers), Permanent way (track), Signalling Technicians (S&T) and Control. In other emergency situations the MOM acts as a Railway Incident Officer and in this case liaises with all the emergency services, undertakers, local councils, the Environment Agency, the military and other specialists.

Wherever the railway interfaces with the public there is always a risk that something will occur by accident or deliberately – that can be an over-height truck hitting a bridge, a vehicle running a red light at a level-crossing, vandalism, cable theft, animals on the line, flooding, a line-side fire or fire close to the line or someone threatening suicide or actually committing it.

MOMs are called to attend almost anything on the railway, not only as a first and rapid response, but to investigate, assist and help with any third party.

With regards to the privatised railway that we all now know, the following comments on this are those of my opinions only, but I am confident that my colleagues would support my views unreservedly, and probably even managers within the industry would agree if they were allowed to.

The Conservative Government of the day had a mind that the only good and well run business has to be privatised and any state owned public utility or public transport provider was inefficient and badly run. In 1994 when Railtrack was formed, investment in the railway became driven by shareholders and profit. The labour Government in 2002 decided, rightly or wrongly, to bankrupt Railtrack and form a 'Not for Profit' company called Network Rail. This was an arm's-length nationalised company, which is as close to BR as we are probably ever likely to get. The money that has been and still is wasted is staggering and had a fraction of that money actually been invested in BR, we would now have a railway that would be truly world-class. In 2002 the company were encouraging their own employees to buy shares in the company right up to the hour it was wound up.

Thousands of hard working employees of Railtrack were lost out at the hands of a government that had given little thought to what might happen and who might be affected when this political decision was taken.

Since then Network Rail has invested in the infrastructure, but there are many areas, Cornwall included, that are still operating with Victorian signalling and infrastructure designed and built in early BR or late GWR days.

Network Rail is a publicly owned company that gets its funding from the British Tax payer. It is not a Private company and it is not a Business.

There is a delay attribution system which I believe is fundamentally flawed and is counter-productive, in that staff are so obsessed with preventing very minor delays, because of the governments passenger performance regime, that it employs countless staff chasing signallers and train crew trying to allocate blame for a couple of minutes or even a couple of hours delay. This costs the industry millions of pounds each year.

If a train broke down in BR days, it would be assisted and replaced quickly, because BR owned everything on the railway. Nowadays, hours can pass while the train companies argue who will rescue it, or who has the correct coupling to attach to it.

If a train runs late, it will be terminated short of its destination, not for the benefit of the passengers, but to meet its government passenger performance measure, in other words, to keep the figures looking good. In BR days, although it was perceived as always late, it always endeavoured to get you home and turning people out short of their destination was unthinkable. The train terminated short will either run to its final destination non-stop and empty, or turn around and start back right time.

I will not say any more, as I could fill this book with facts about everything that is wrong with the railway now. Rest assured, dear reader, all those professional staff that still operate the railway from one day to the next, whether or not they started with BR, are still applying the same professional dedication of the past. BR wasn't perfect, that is certainly true, but it was far more efficient and caring than any company that has tried to emulate it since.

This book will try and give an insight into the recent history of railway in Cornwall and by showing a collection of photographs from friends and colleagues I hope illustrate a bygone era and explain some of the many incidents my colleagues and I have attended over the years. I hope you as the reader find it interesting and informative.

THE AUTHOR

I WAS BORN in 1951 and raised in Stockport Cheshire and after working for The National Bus Company for many years, I joined British Railways as a Signalman at Furness Vale in Derbyshire, transferring to Lostwithiel, Cornwall in 1992. In 1994, with the creation of Railtrack, I was promoted to Signalling Inspector in Cornwall, joining the Operations Team at St Blazey, where I still work as an MOM in the Old Station House, which was the one time GWR ticket office for the long defunct St Blazey Station. I have a lifelong interest in all things transport, including many years studying railway accidents and incidents that have lead to the signalling systems and rules we use today.

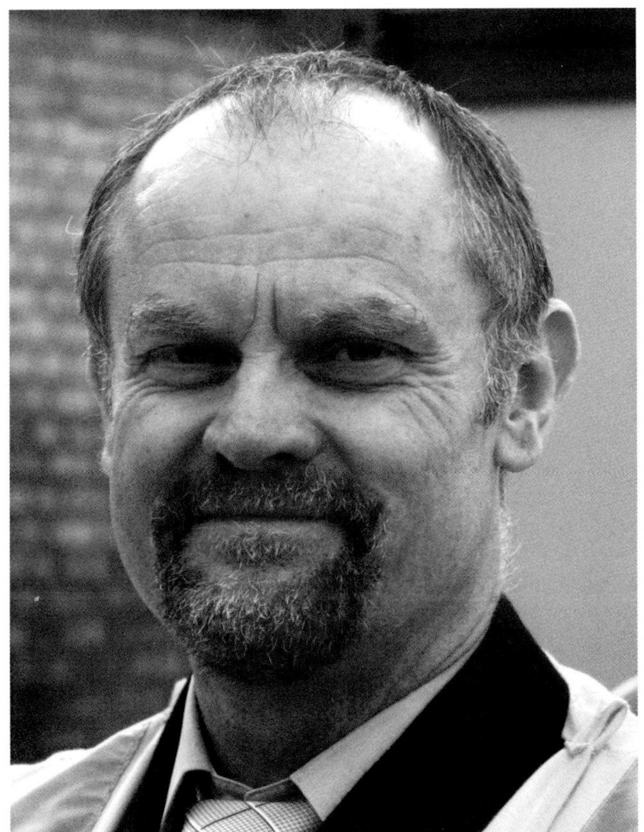

Stephen Heginbotham.

I have been fortunate to work in an industry which is both my hobby and my career, though I feel that changes in recent years within the industry have fragmented the 'big family' that was once BR. I sit on the Area Council as the Rep for the RMT Union. I have been married for forty-three years and have one daughter and four grandchildren.

Born in an age of steam, I well remember the transition from steam to diesel and electric, and was 'fortunate' enough to see steam to its demise in August 1968, Stockport (9B) being one of the very last steam sheds. As a child I watched named trains with named locos thunder past my school, and at weekends or school holidays I watched the Woodhead Electrics at Reddish, the trolleybuses in Manchester, or Pacifics on the West Coast or at Crewe, making the journey there by either steam train or pre-war bus. Once a year there was a family holiday in Blackpool, which meant passing the engine sheds at Preston, and many hours watching the trams both along the promenade or at the depot, where I was allowed to roam freely.

I was a member of the preservation movement for many years from the mid 1960s and was actively involved in helping to save some important vehicles for our heritage.

ACKNOWLEDGEMENTS

My thanks go to my wife for her support in compiling the second book on Cornwall's Railways. My thanks also go to Simon Butler of Halsgrove.

The credit for all photographs is as shown below, unless otherwise stated. My thanks and my apologies also go to any other photographers, if any of the photographs are incorrectly credited, or credit omitted.

SFH	Author or Authors collection
GP	Graham Pearse
JR	Jim Renshaw
MD	Martin Duff
PE	Peter English** (GP Collection)
PM	Peter Moore* (MD Collection)
RKM	Roger Matthews
RW	RAILWAYANA
SL	Shaun Lethbridge Collection

My special thanks to Roger K Matthews, signalman extraordinaire, for writing the Foreword.

REFERENCE SOURCES

Signalbox Diagrams of the Great Western & Southern Railways Vols 14 & 16. G.A.Pryer
The Great Western Railway in East Cornwall & The Great Western Railway in Mid Cornwall. Alan Bennett. Runpast.
The Great Western Railway in West Cornwall. Alan Bennett. Kingfisher Railway Publications
Branches & Byways – Cornwall. John Vaughan. OPC
The Newquay Branch and Its Branches. John Vaughan. OPC
BR Diesel & Electric Locomotive Directory (2010). Colin J. Marsden. OPC
BR Combined Volumes 1961, 1962 and 1968. Ian Allen
My own notebooks and files which date back to 1959

FOREWORD

I WAS FLATTERED when author Stephen Heginbotham asked me to write the Foreword for this, his second book on Cornwall's railways.

I started my career on the railway with British Railways, like so many others of my age who still work in the industry. My first job was as a Telephonist at St Blazey Shed (the Roundhouse) in July 1969, moving on to be a Guard at St Blazey for two years. After various other jobs, including Shunter and Checker, I transferred into the signalling grade and my first box was at Newquay in December 1975, becoming a Relief Signalman in March 1977, working at most of the signalboxes then still open between St Germans and Penzance.

I am presently the longest serving Signaller in Cornwall and, as mentioned earlier, I have worked all over the Duchy, but being both an enthusiast and traditionalist I have only worked in purely mechanical locations, so have avoided the two signalboxes than have mini-panels to supplement the lever-frames.

As a teenager I wanted to be a driver, but my eyesight let me down; however a neighbour of mine, who was a Signalman, let me work St Austell Signalbox and this fuelled my interest in signalling before I left school and somewhat ironically, in March 1980 I was the last signalman to work this box.

Other highlights of my long career on the railway are such things as working on, and signalling the Royal Train, and many other unusual events and special trains, all of which are unique and happy memories.

If this book turns out be as good as the first one, I am sure everyone who has even the smallest interest in railways and recent local history will find this book both a good read and excellent reference.

The railway in general has changed almost beyond belief since I started forty-three years ago, and the only constants are the track and the fact trains still run over much of what I remember. But of course Cornwall does still have one thing that is almost extinct on the wider network, and that is extensive semaphore signalling, and mechanically operated points. The trains are still signalled from box to box using apparatus designed in the Victorian era and this authentic equipment is still maintained to a high standard, with its polished brightwork and nostalgic noises.

One could say it is a working museum, but of course it is primarily still a working railway and a business, which is endeavouring to deliver a safe, prompt and regular service to the travelling public and freight operators.

The trains are not as interesting as when I started, and the standardisation and uniformity of locomotives, modern coaches and Multiple-Units, including the Cross Country Voyagers, does leave me yearning for the early days when Western Region Hydraulics, class 37s, 46s and first generation DMUs, to name but a few, traversed the tracks of this historic railway.

I have had a great life on the railway, I have made many good friends, some of whom are no longer with us and I would do it all again without question, but until I retire in just a few years time, I hope that I manage to see out the old system before it disappears under a new regime of computer driven technology.

Roger K. Matthews
Relief Signalman

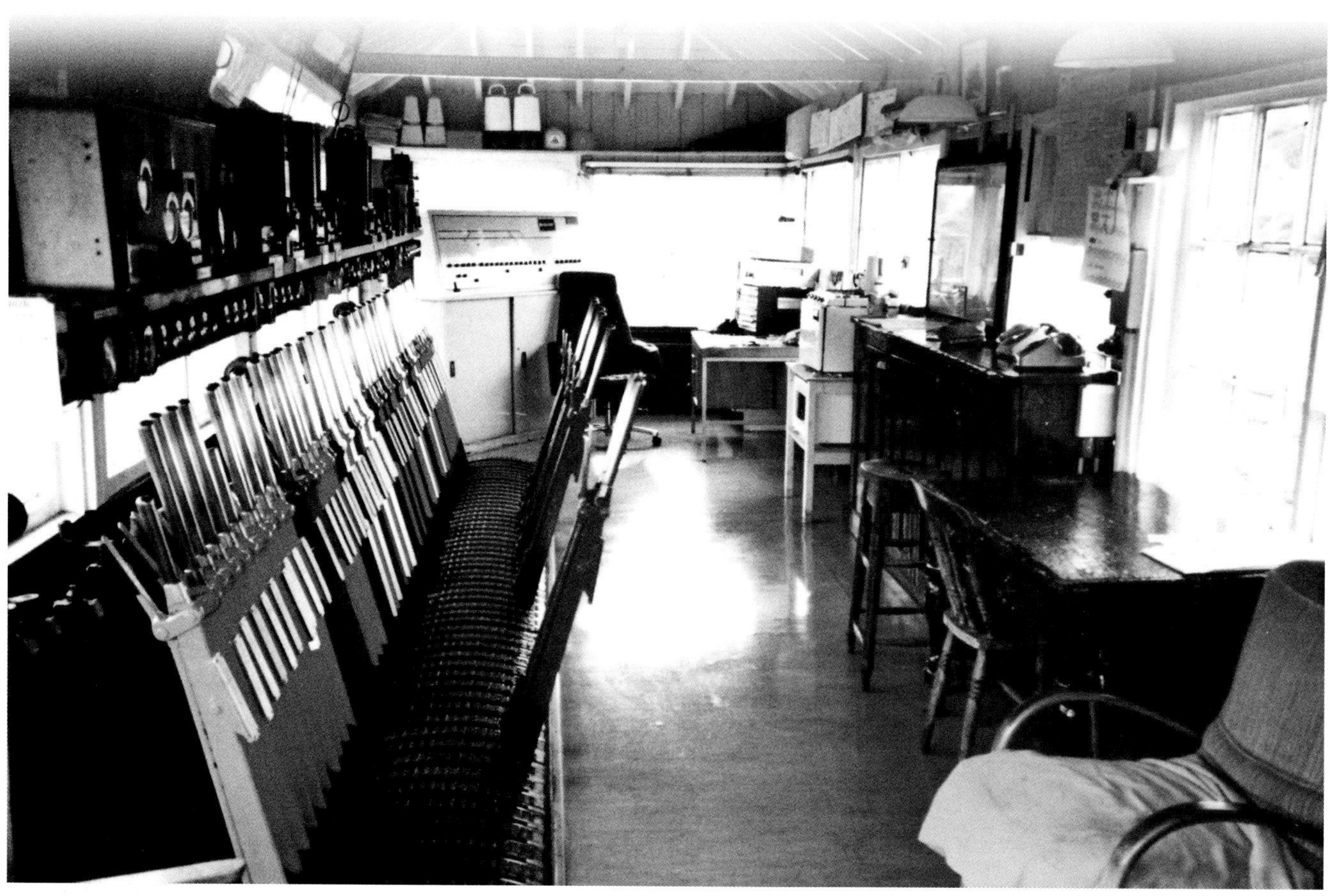

SIGNALMAN

MY CAREER AS a Signalman (Signaller) started with British Railways at the BR Training College in Webb House, Crewe. This lovely building, resembling a stately home, was actually built to house orphans, primarily of those employees that once worked for the LNWR (London & North Western Railway). Situated in several acres of its own grounds which formed the gardens, and close to the Crewe Electric Depot, it was a self contained centre for railway training and vocational learning, but ostensibly functioned for teaching trainee signal(wo)men, on six week, classroom-based courses, using practical and theory methods.

Though not actually owned by BR, it was leased from the trustees of the orphanage and was a warm and pleasant place to learn a railway vocation. Reputed to be haunted, it was steeped in history and the inside had been tastefully converted into bedrooms, lounges, bars, recreation rooms, restaurants and of course, classrooms. Each classroom was

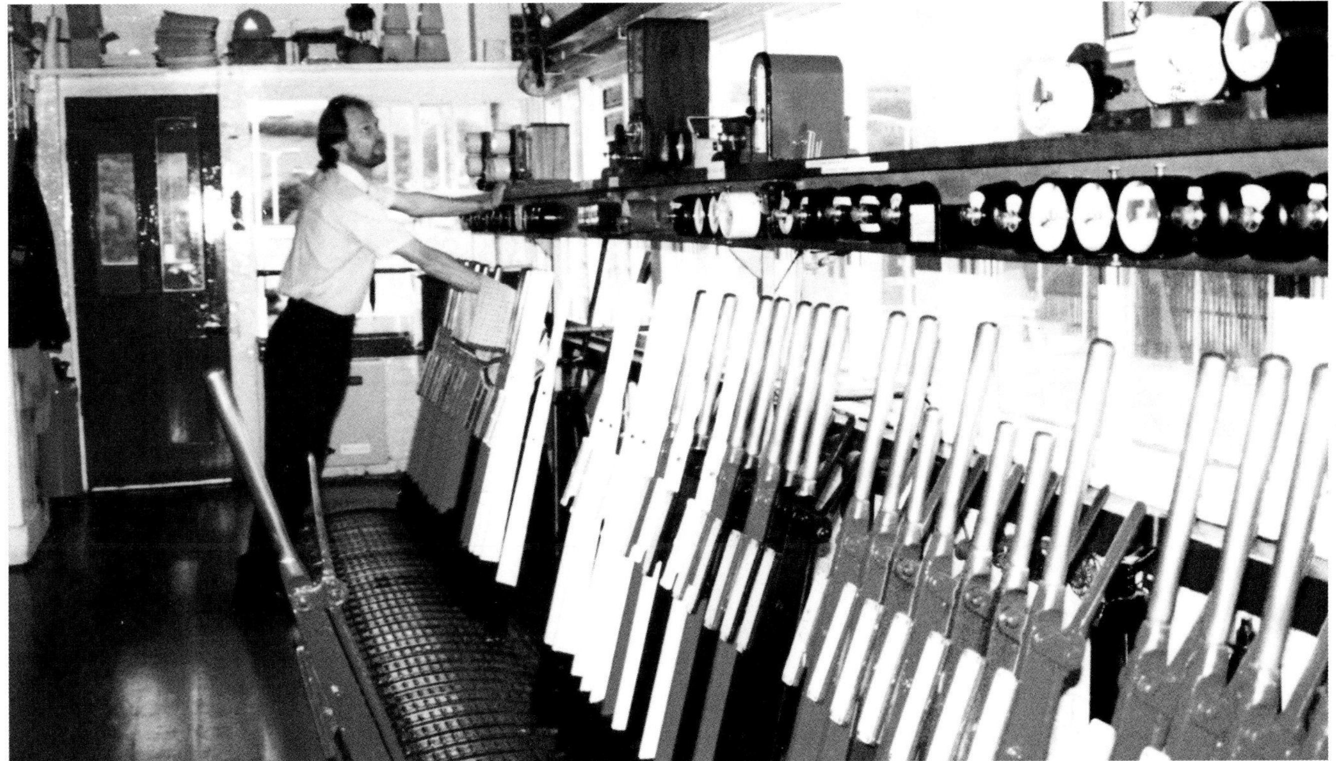

Lostwithiel box in 1993 sees the author operating the frame at this busy location. The ensuing twenty years or so, have taken their toll on both the author and the signalbox. There is now less traffic, though more passenger services, the yard hardly ever used, the 'Cattle Pens Sidings' out of use more than in use, regular point failures, and the Milk Sidings disconnected and Ground-Frame removed. (JR)

partially equipped with signalbox instruments, and there was a simulator for training on lever-frames and modern and semi-modern panel signalling types.

The trainers were either ex-inspectors or former signalmen who had opted to transfer to the training establishment by choice, and they delivered a modular based course, with assessments and exams interspersed within the course, and a final exam to assess whether or not you were competent enough to be sent out for practical training with existing signalmen at the location you had been allocated when you had applied for the original job. During each assessment a few more candidates either dropped out by failure or voluntarily left after finding the course too arduous. The fourteen or so that my course started with, were eventually thinned out to about eight.

My interview to join the railway was at Manchester Victoria Station, which is another grand building, now only a shadow or its former self, but then was still intact. I had been told about the job by a very good friend of mine, who had been on the footplate during steam days at Macclesfield, in Cheshire. Ron Dyer was then working in the Red Star office at Macclesfield due to ill health, and had regularly travelled as a passenger on one of our frequent summer outings on our restored vintage ex-Blackburn Corporation Leyland Tiger PS1.

Ron was an enthusiast and fount of railway knowledge; his voluminous records of locomotives he had seen being one of complete envy to my meagre records. There were not many locos that had evaded his gaze over a spotting career going back to pre BR days. I will remain eternally grateful to Ron and the Oldfields, for their friendship and faith in me, and for that priceless bit of knowledge of just who to ask when applying for a job in that monolithic organisation that was once BR.

To digress for a moment here, Ron Dyer lived near the top of one of the few high rise blocks of flats in Macclesfield. He had served in the RAF (National Service I think) and was meticulous in his housekeeping and record keeping. His flat was spotless and I visited him only once at home and whilst perusing his vast collection of written records of his career on the railway, I had to ask him why he had no curtains at any window. He reply was not only funny, but practical: "who is going to look in at this height – why waste money on something I don't need". There were not many people he did not know on the railway in that area, and when he retired through ill health, he regularly travelled into Manchester for a pub lunch. It was this pub lunch that finally was his downfall. He had been missing for days, and only when the police contacted his friends about a John Doe they had had for several days in the morgue, did his friends finally find out what had happened to poor Ron. He had collapsed on the way out of the pub and, typical of Ron, had no ID on him as everyone knew him and no one ever asked him for his pass! Ron's ashes are scattered on the Severn Valley Railway, a favourite of his.

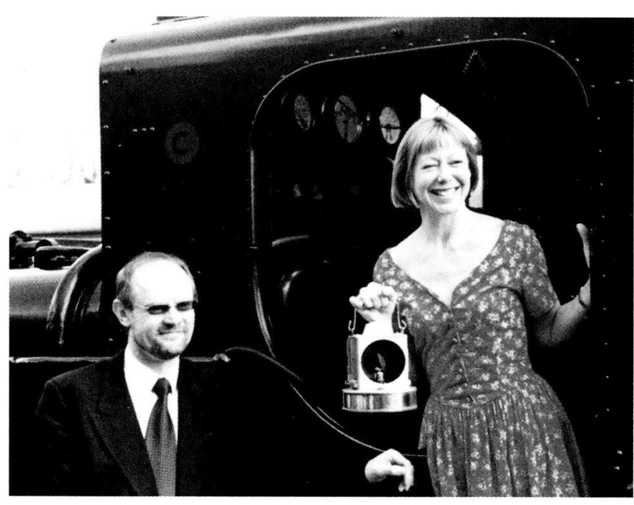

On 30 March 2002 I was joined at Bodmin General Station by the famous actress Jenny Agutter, of *The Railway Children* fame amongst many other roles. The reason was that I had invited her to present cheques to four charities which were benefiting from £2000 each, plus company matching, after I auctioned off the old paraffin signal lamps that had recently been withdrawn, after electricity had at last made its way into Cornwall signalling. As a thank you, I restored a lamp especially for Jenny and had a commemorative plaque fitted. A funny story about this great day, was that surreal moment when my mobile phone rang and Jenny Agutter's number showed up. On answering the call, she said that her car had broken down at Redruth and she was catching a train, and could I pick her up at Bodmin Parkway. I will never forget the strange looks I got from passengers on the platform at Bodmin when Jenny alighted and I asked her to accompany me to the Response Vehicle. She is a lovely person, who was charming and very pleasant. She made the day very enjoyable and memorable. (SFH)

CHAPTER 1

PENZANCE to TRURO

THIS FIRST CHAPTER covers the area from Penzance to Truro over the Cornish main line, and the collections of photographs cover a period from the 1970s onwards, but ostensibly they are from the British Rail 'Blue' era, though not exclusively. The line from Plymouth downwards to Penzance is still host to long-distance passenger trains from London and other parts of the UK. The only things that have changed from the era covered by this book is the demise of loco-hauled trains in favour of HST (High Speed Trains) and modern long distance DMU (Diesel Multiple Units) and the local DMUs being replaced by second generation DMUs. The only loco-hauled passenger train still running in Cornwall in 2013 is the Night Riviera, which is the domain of the refurbished class 57 locos, which are rebuilt class 47s, with new more efficient power units and equipment.

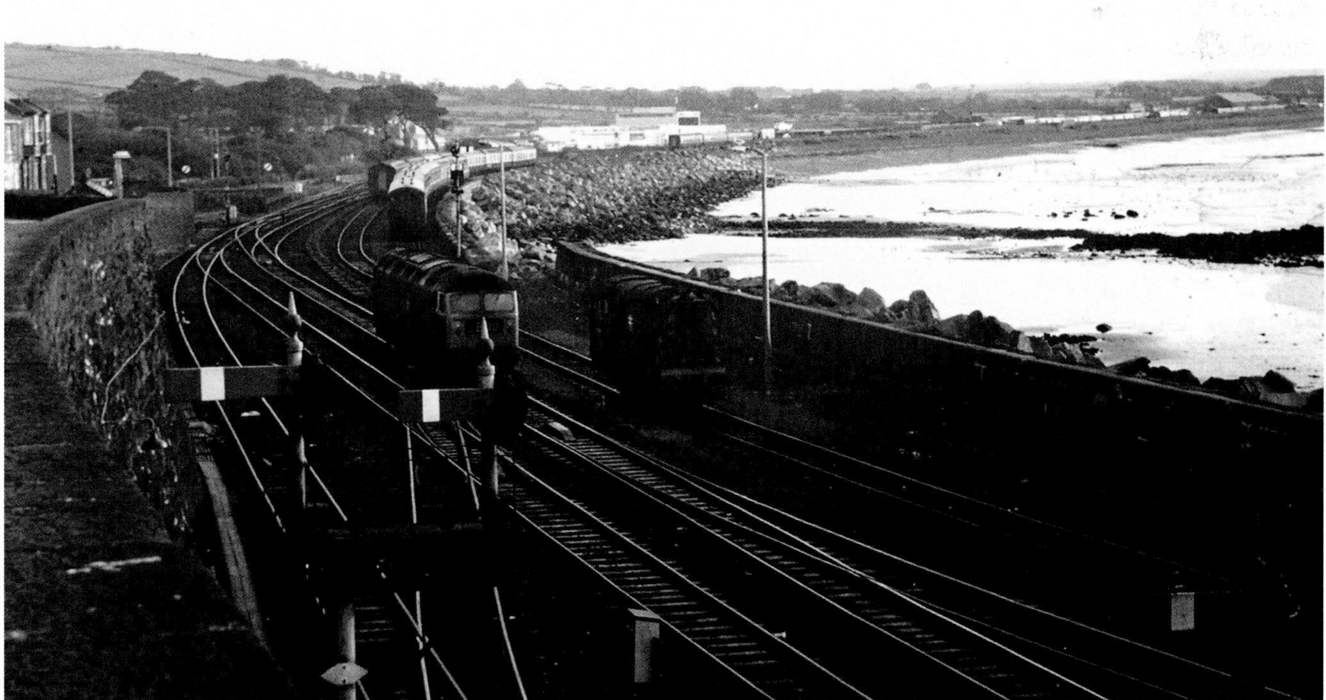

Penzance in 1975 shows a different layout than today, with the Sea Sidings now reduced to one road, the 08 shunting loco being kept on Long Rock Depot and the trackwork altered to coincide with the TCB signal alterations which will see fully electro-hydraulic points, track circuiting and axle-counters, and full LED colour-light signalling, replacing the mechanical points and semaphore signals. The class 47 appears to be shunting or in transit to the depot for fuel. (JR)

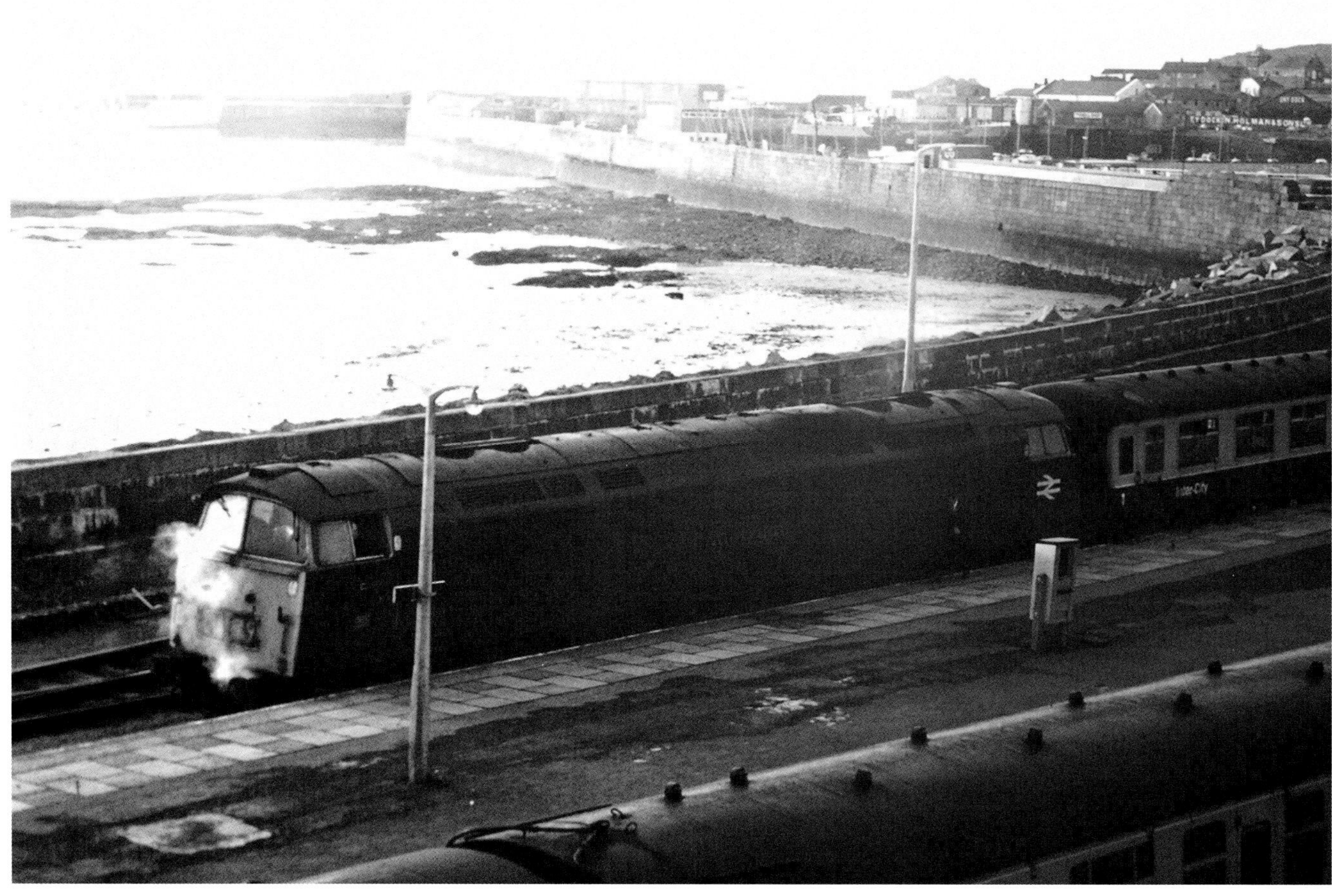

Platform 4 at Penzance in 1975 sees D1064 *'Western Regent'* at the head of an express train carrying headcode 1A79. (JR)

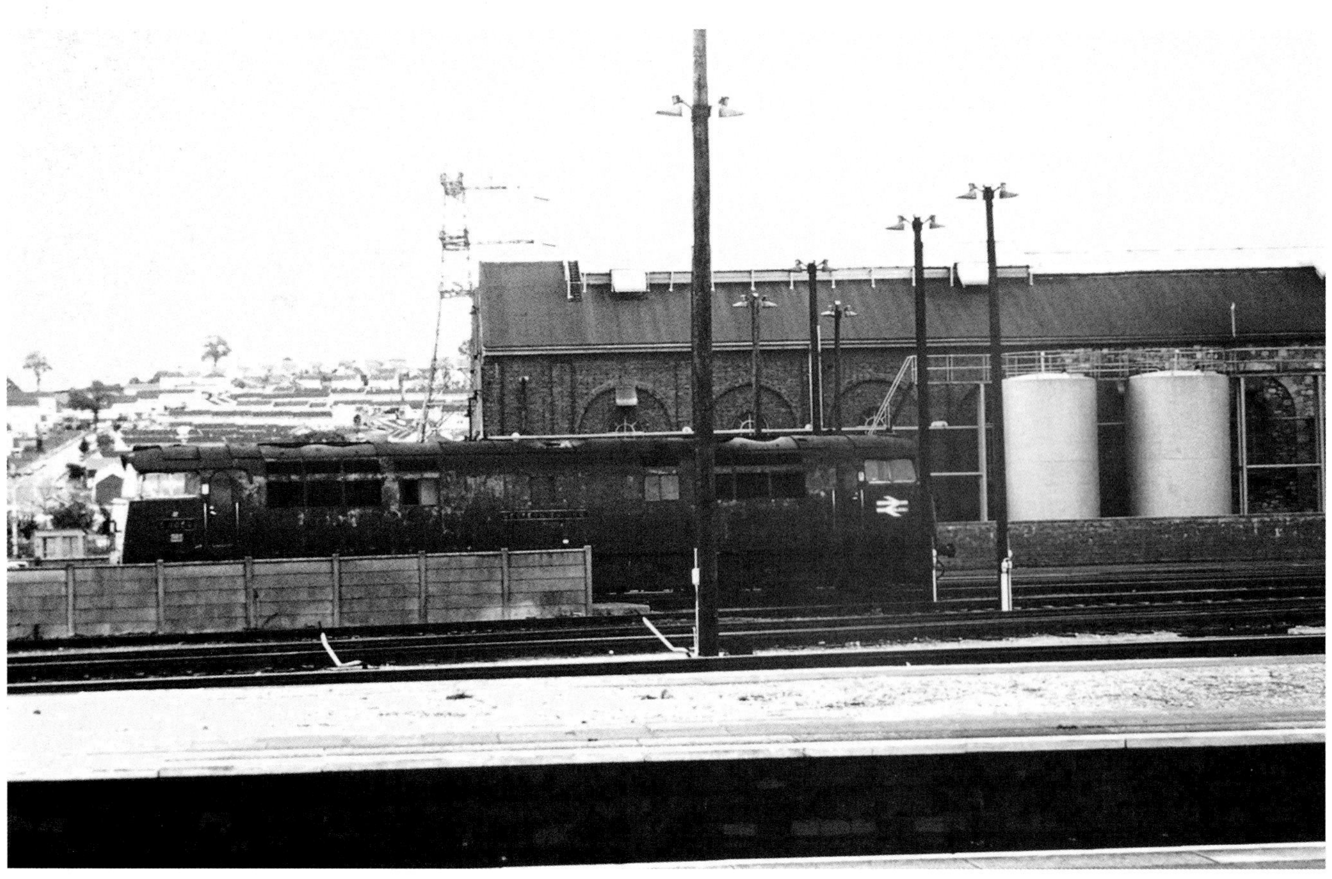

Long Rock Depot is host to D1059 *'Western Empire'* on a sunny day in 1975. (JR)

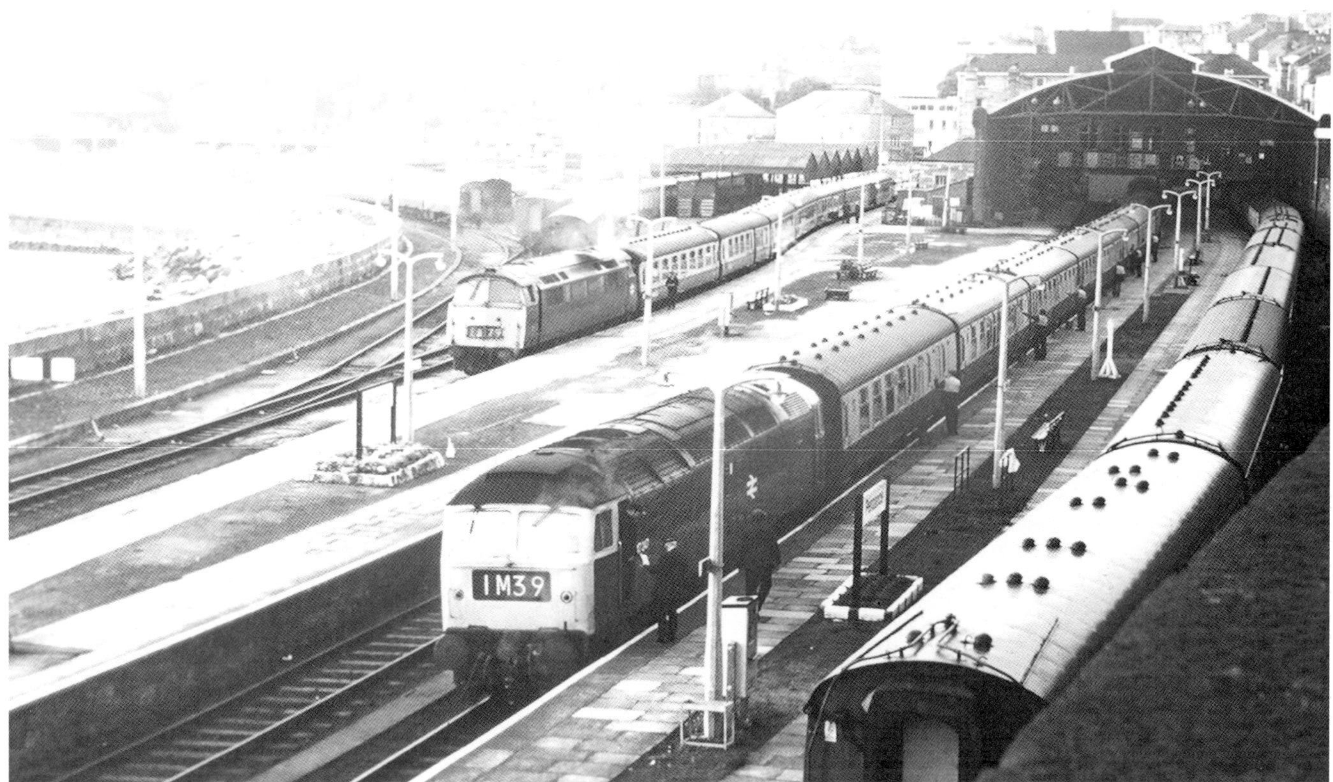

A busy scene in Penzance sees platform 1 occupied with Mk 1 stock, platform 2 with 1M39, a class 47 hauled cross-country train, which is receiving a remarkable amount of attention from platform staff cleaning windows etc., and platform 4 occupied with D1064 as shown elsewhere. Of note, is the yard, which still stretches around the sea wall and has coaching stock stabled in it. This area is now occupied by the Bus Station and cycle-path. The goods depot is now no longer and the station car park, taxi rank, and bus station offices have replaced it. (JR)

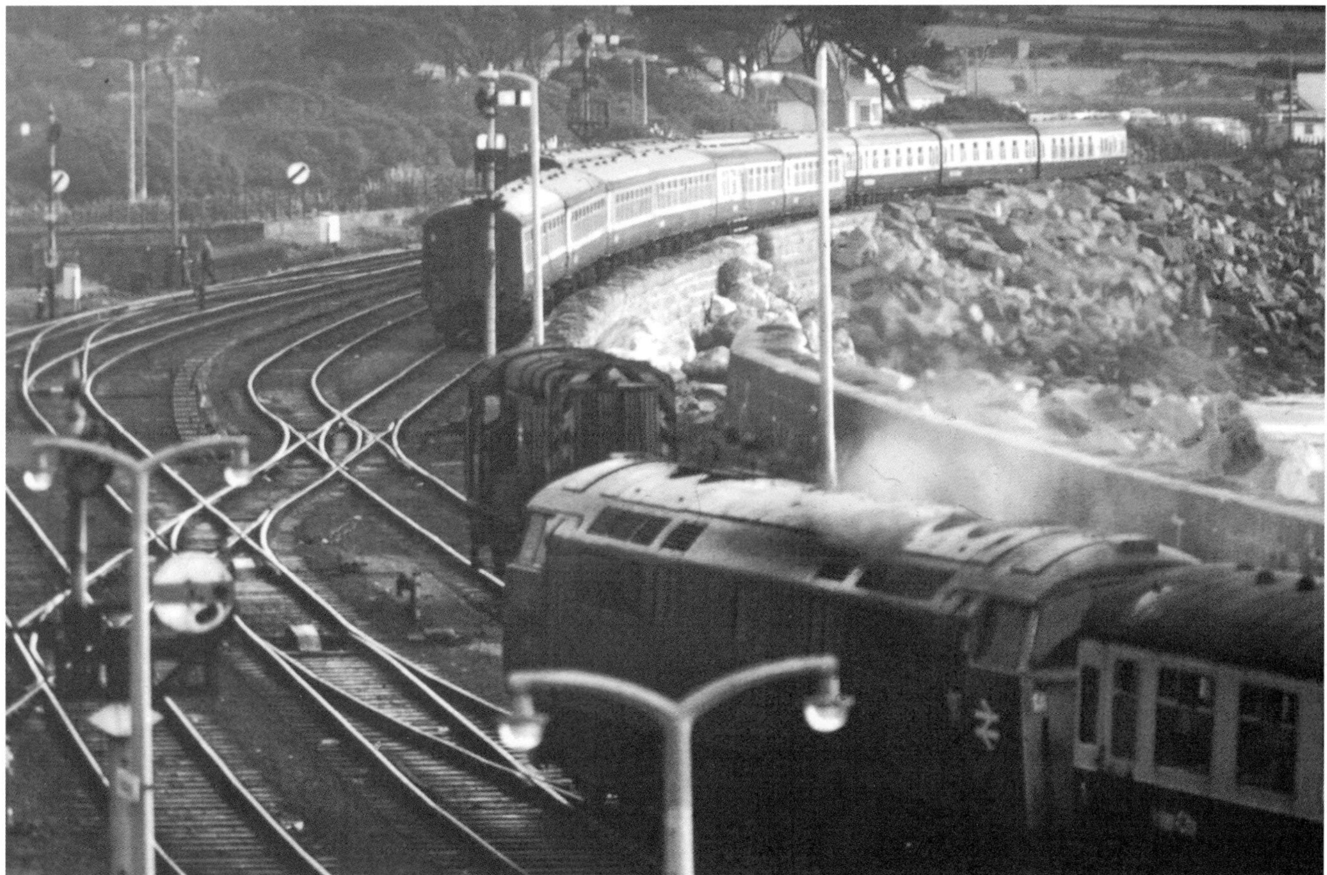

This is 1A79 departing Penzance from platform 4 in 1975. (JR)

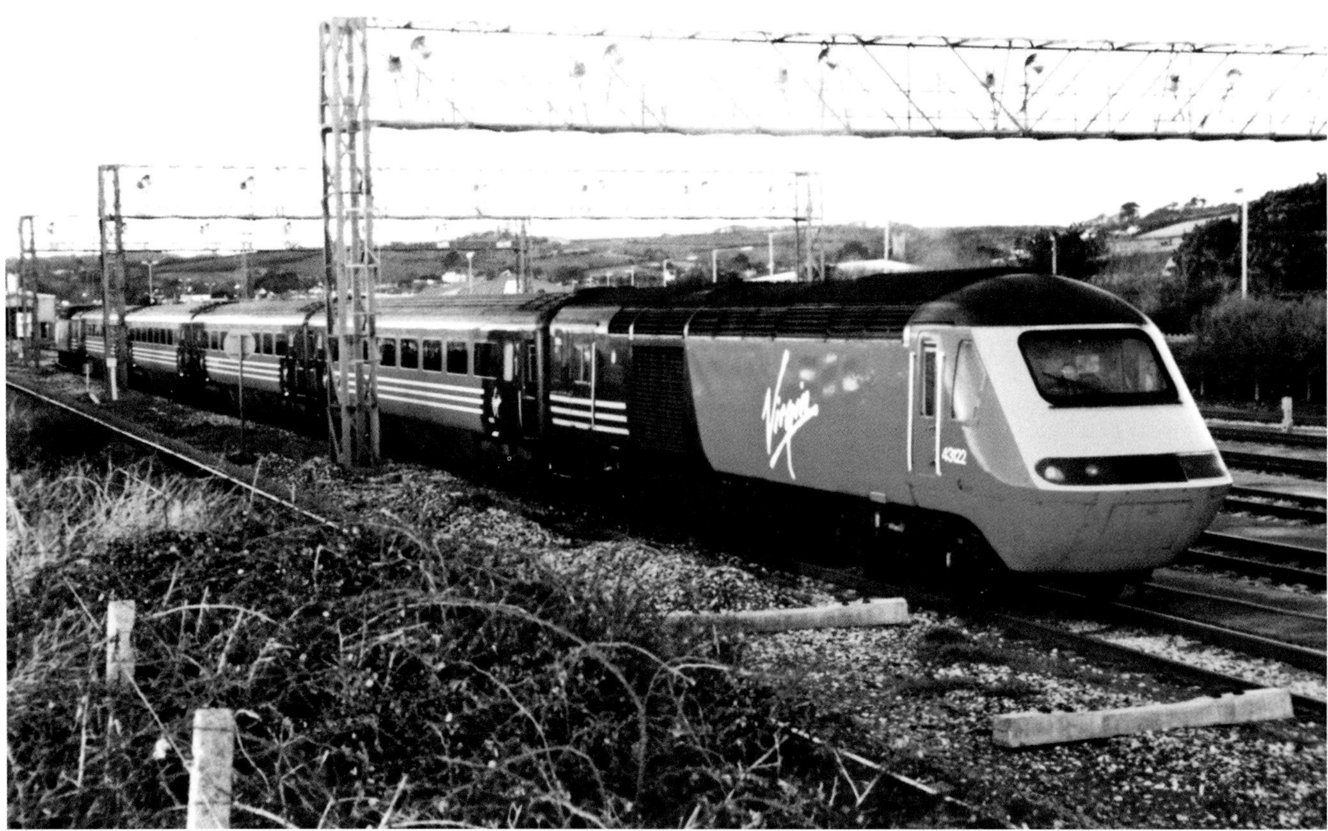

Virgin HST power car 43122 is set to depart from Long Rock Depot on an ECS trip to Plymouth as 5E65 on 8 January 2001. Built by BR at Crewe in April 1979, it is still in service with First Great Western. (MD)

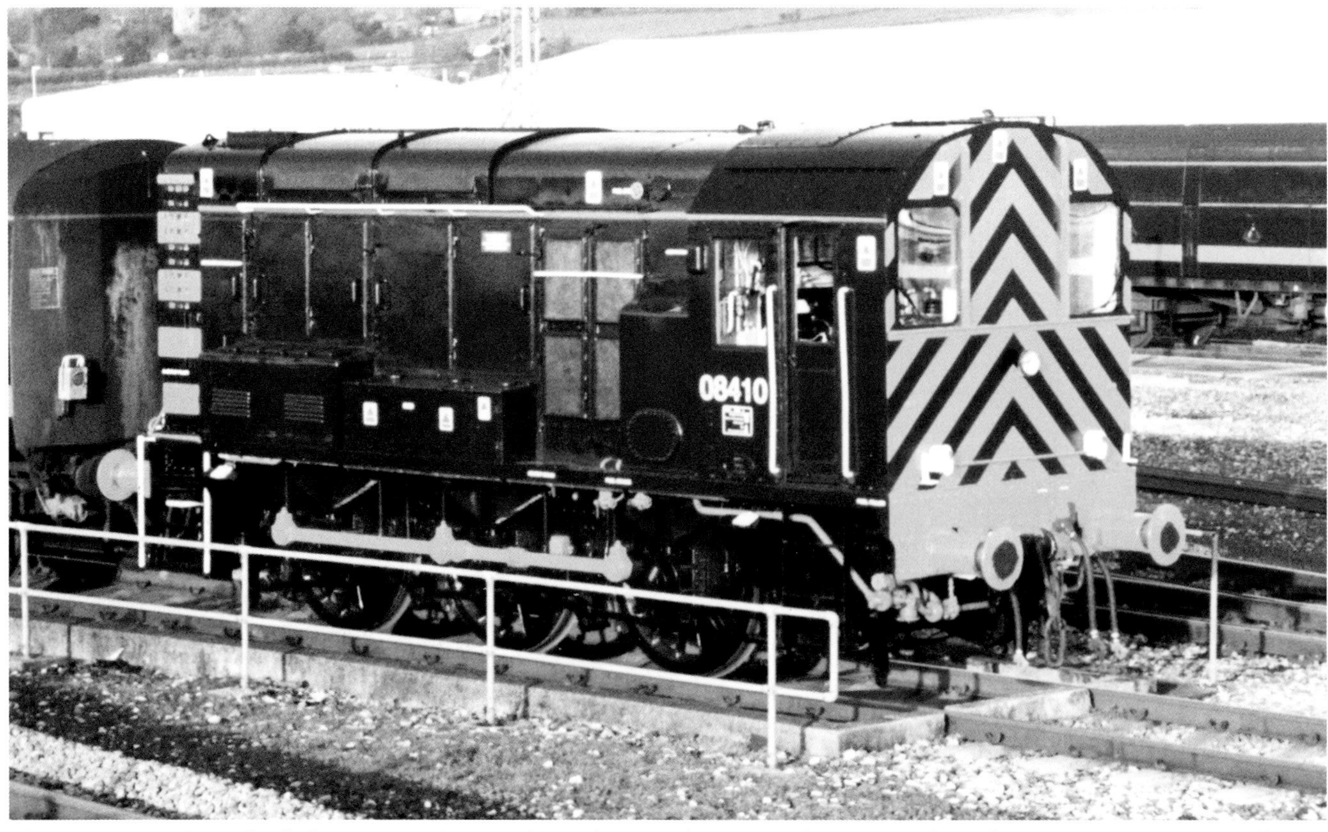

08410 is seen at Long Rock Depot on 19 January 2002 shunting the Motorail empty stock. Built in June 1958 as D3525 by BR at Derby Works, it is still in service today with First Great Western at Laira Depot. (MD)

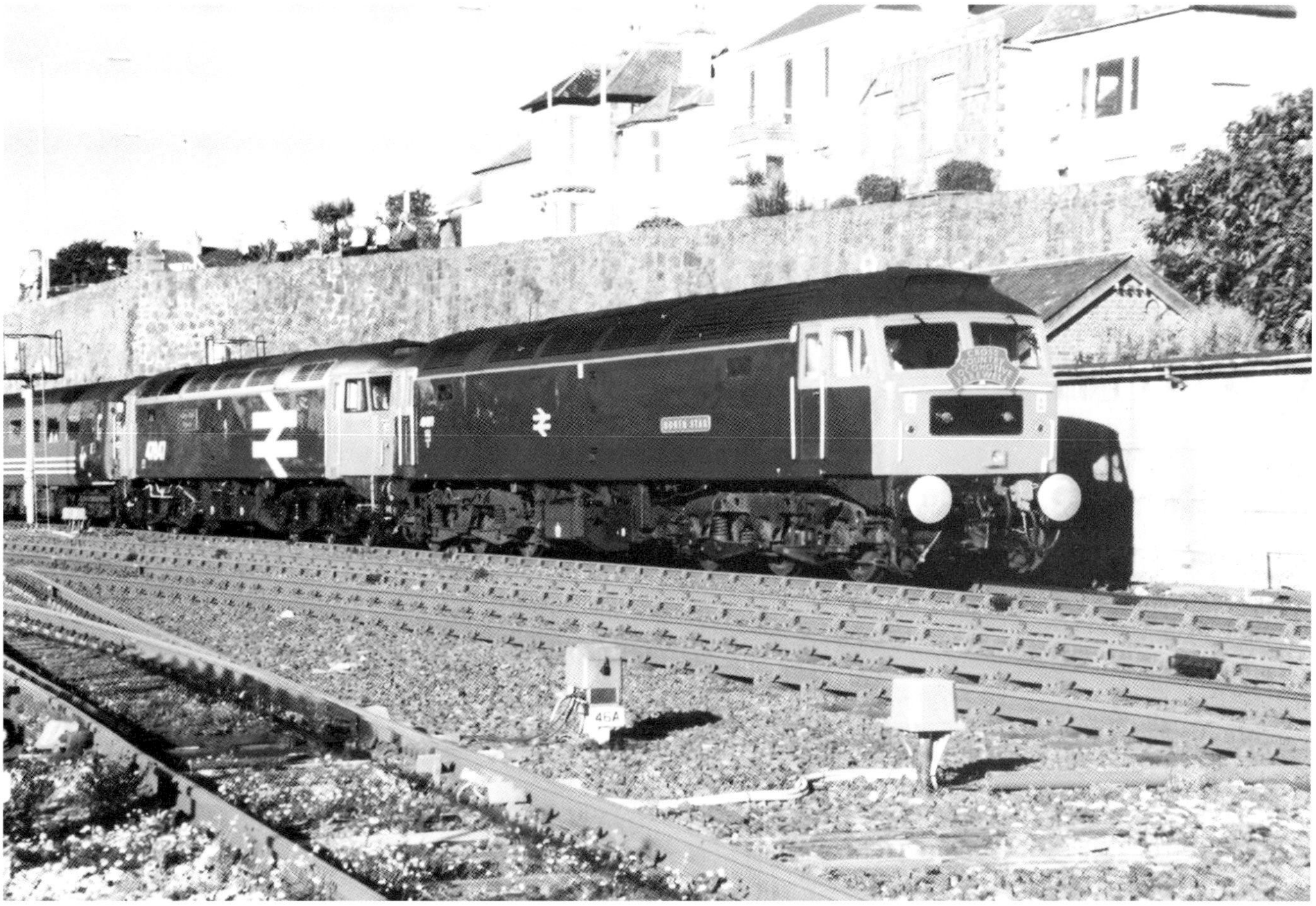

Virgin Cross-Country did things in style when the last of their loco-hauled trains left Penzance, it was double-headed by immaculately turned out, BR blue liveried, 47077 *'North Star'* and 47847 *'Benjamin Gimbert G.C.'*. The date was 19 August 2002 and the train was the last 1M56 engine and stock for Birmingham New Street. I turned out to see this train hammering through Burngullow. The former was withdrawn in May 2007 and is now owned by the D&EPG on the West Somerset Railway; the latter was withdrawn in January 2008 and now works for Riviera Trains at Eastleigh. (MD)

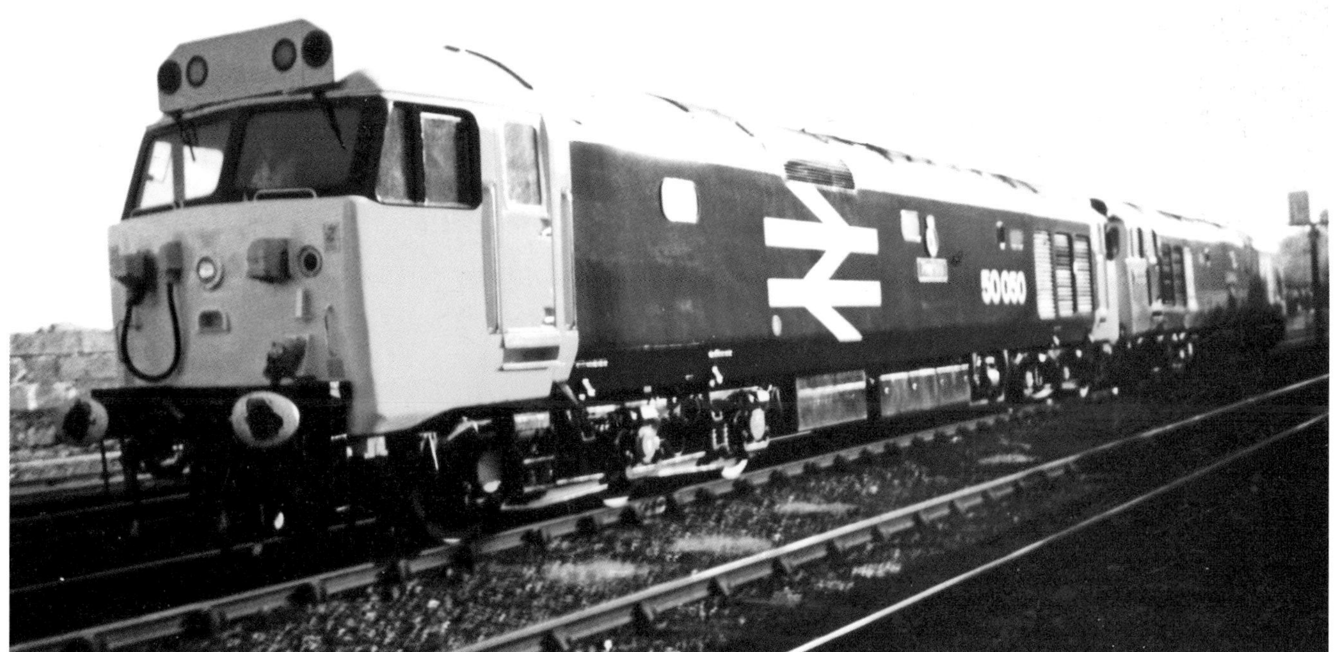

Although this picture dates from after the class 50s had finished as front line locomotives and had passed into preservation, it is worth including, because it features 50050 (D400) and 50007 (D407), both of which were celebrity locos before their respective retirements. Here they are shunting in Penzance after bringing in an enthusiasts special. (SFH)

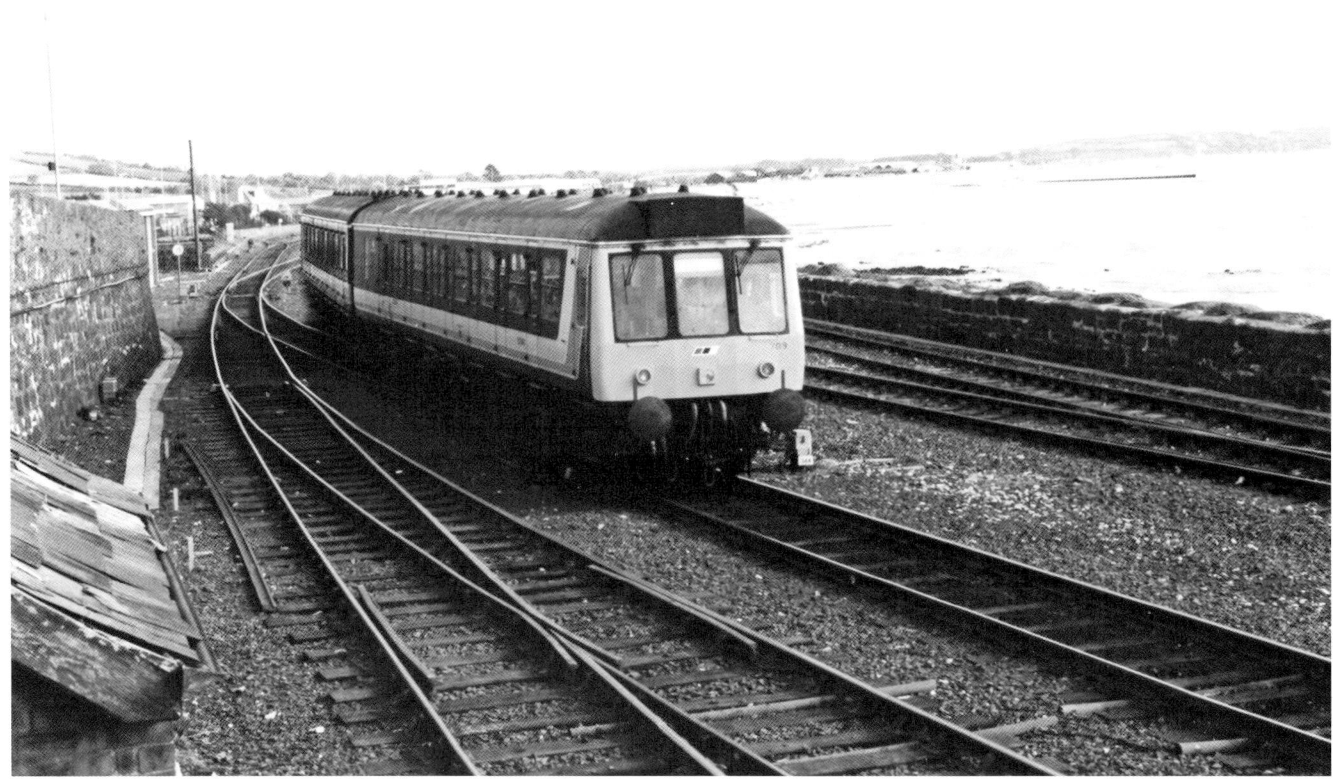

Network South East liveried 117709 is seen here approaching Penzance during the late 1980s. Prior to the transfer of Second Generation DMUs in the shape of class 150, 153 and 158, these units were the mainstay of local services in Devon and Cornwall. (GP)

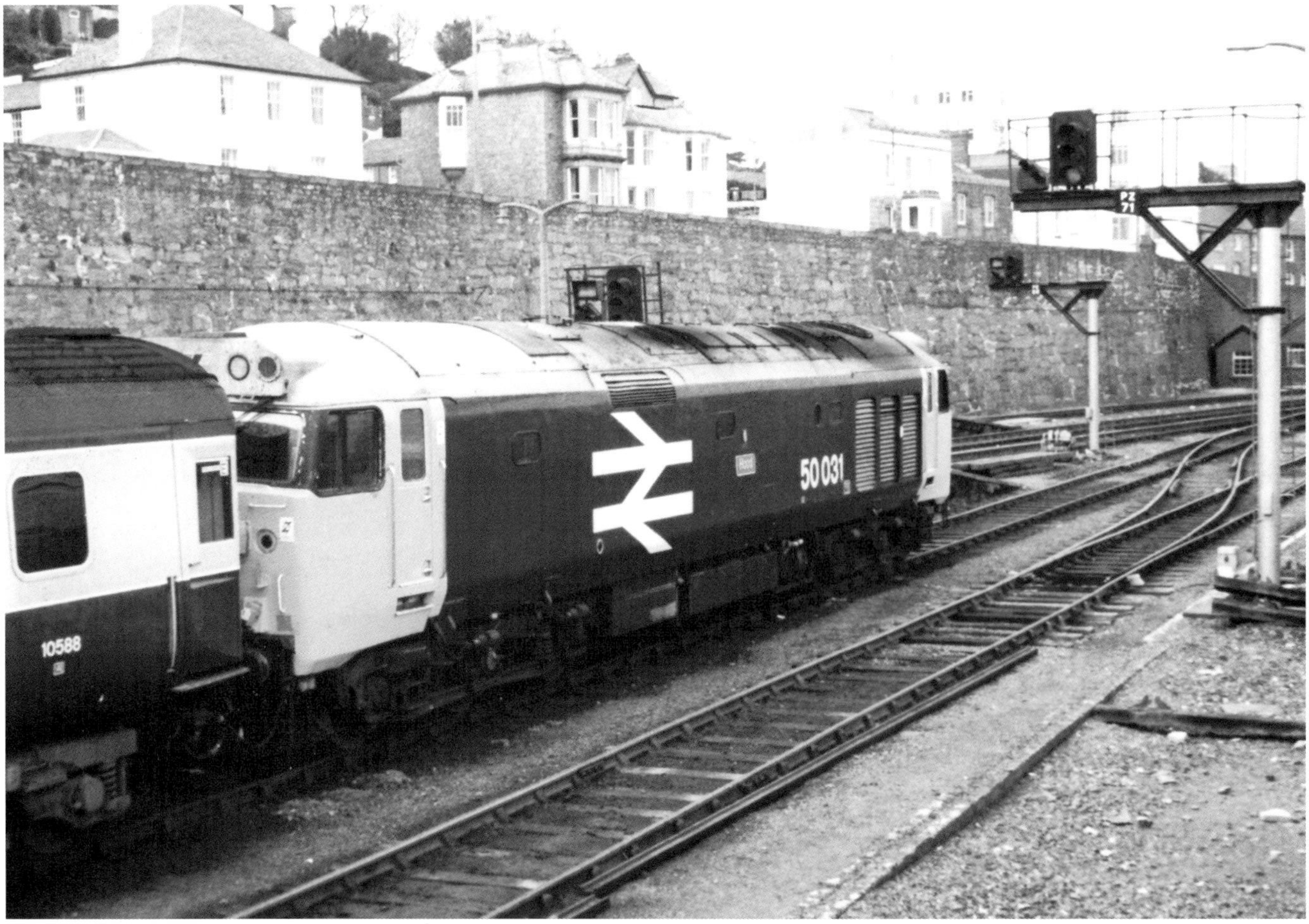

Large Logo liveried 50031 *'Hood'* in platform 4 at Penzance. The class 50s ostensibly took over from the Western Hydraulics, and filled in until the HSTs started to take over in large numbers. It survives in preservation. (GP)

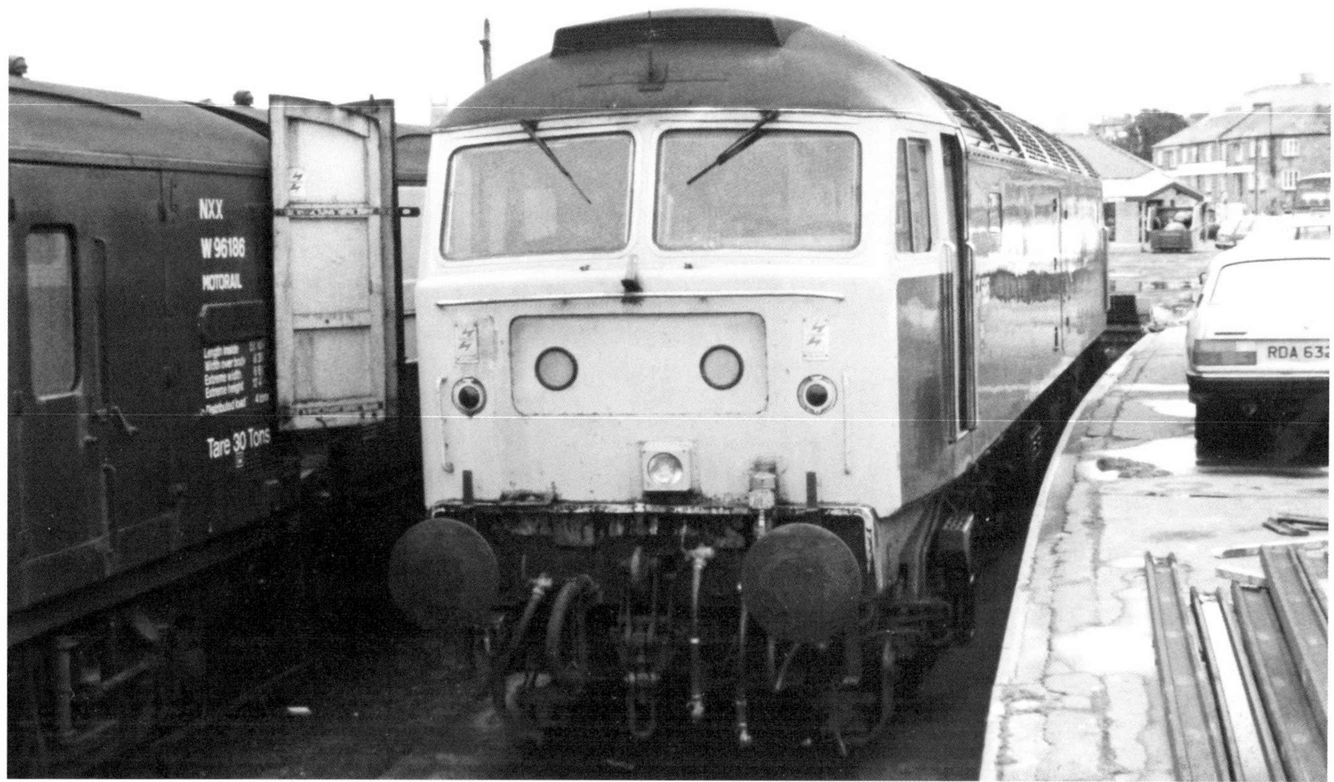

In the bay siding at Penzance on 30 April 1989, we see 47565 stabled. It had probably brought in the Motorail train, which can be seen on the adjacent siding. Built by September 1964 by Crewe Works as D1620, it also carried the number 47039. Cut up in February 2004 by C.F. Booth of Rotherham. (GP)

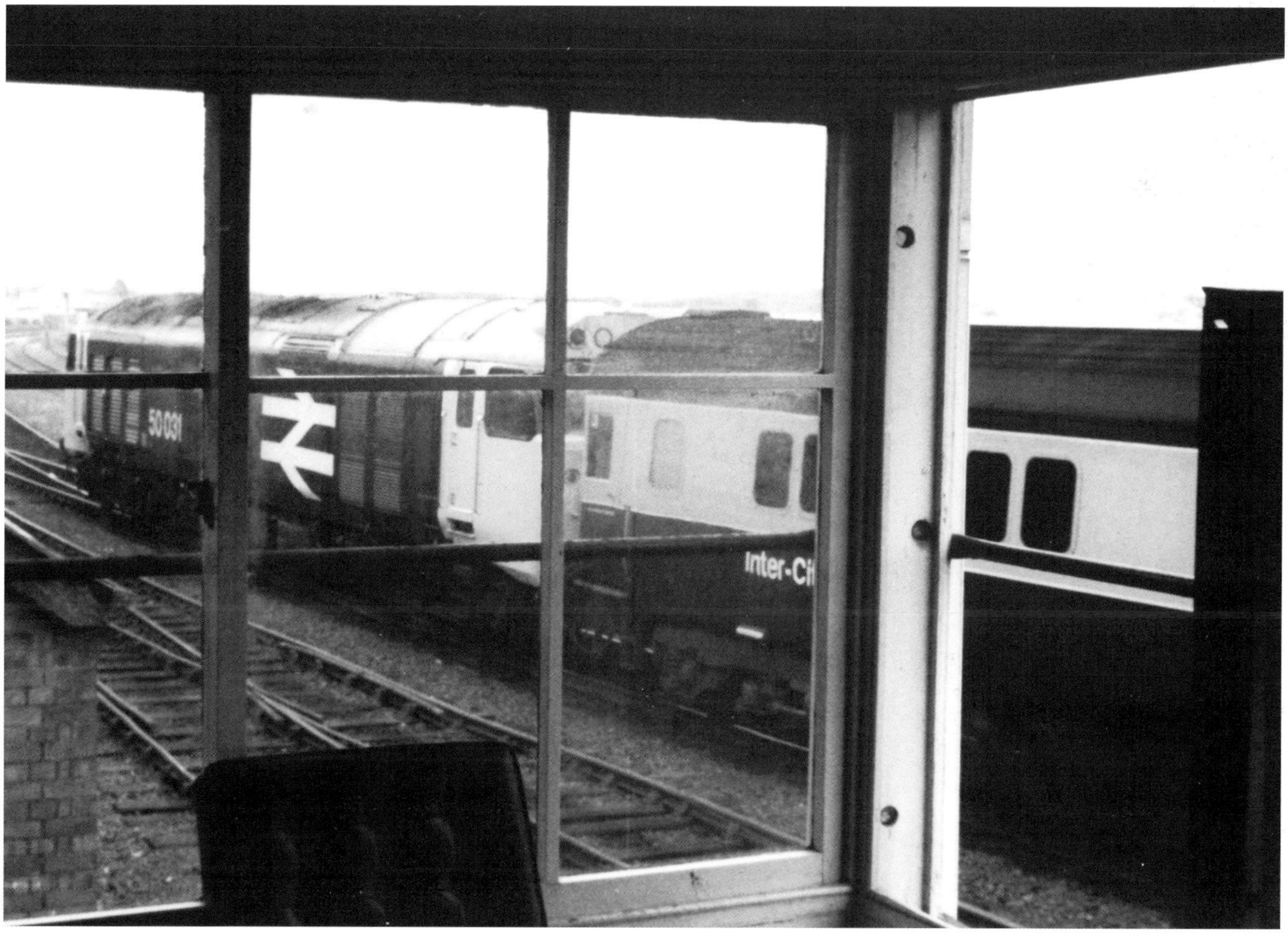

This is a Signalman's view of 50031 *'Hood'* departing Penzance on 30 April 1989. (GP)

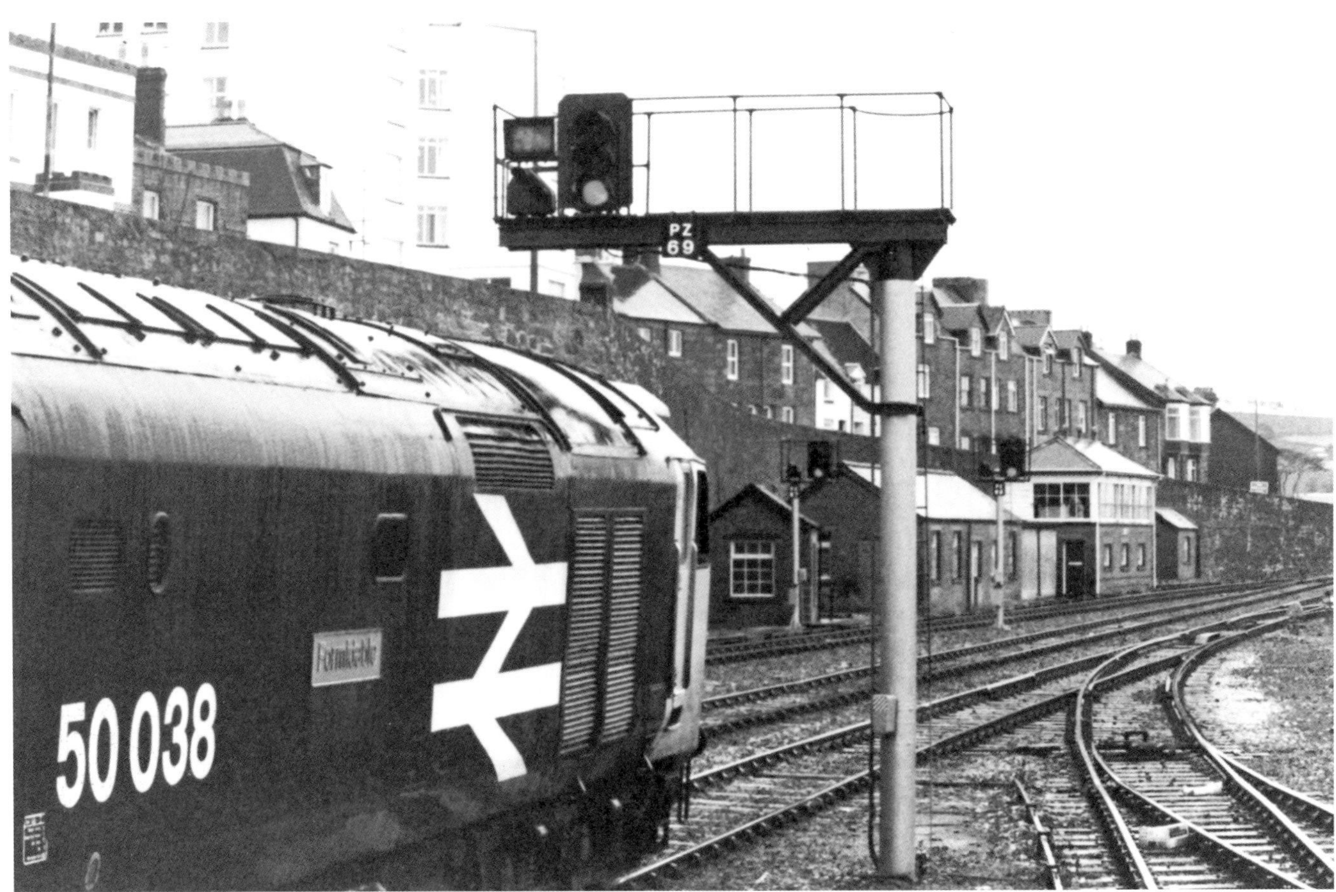

50038 *'Formidable'* is awaiting departure from platform 3 at Penzance in October 1987. It was cut up in August 1989 at Old Oak Common. (GP)

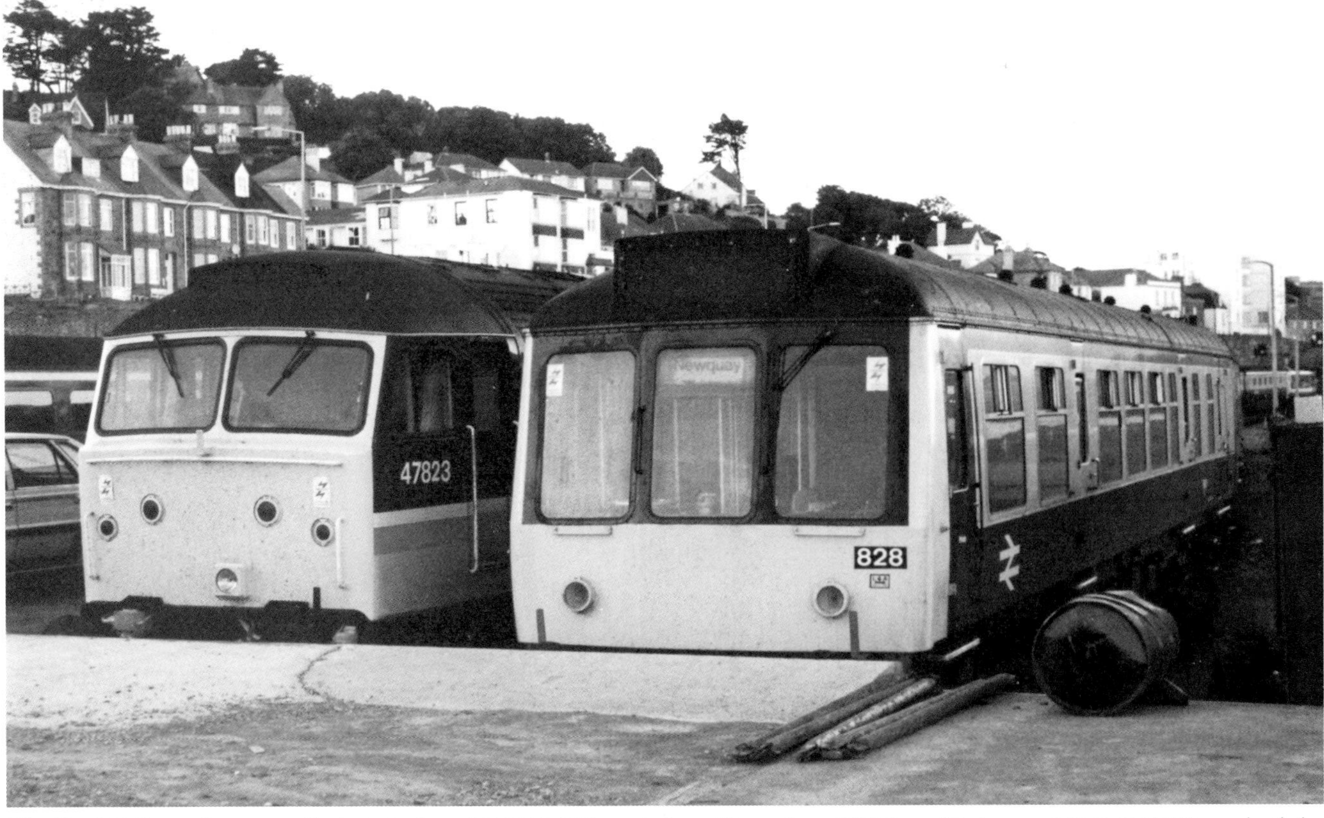

The Yard Siding at Penzance finds Laira based DMU, 828, and class 47 number 47823 on 19 August 1989. D1757 was built by Brush in September 1964, but was renumbered 47163, 47610, and lastly 47787 in September 1994. It carried three names; *'SS Great Britain'*, *'Victim Support'* and a previously used royal name of *'Windsor Castle'*, though it was never a 'Royal Engine'. It is still in service with WCR, Carnforth. (GP)

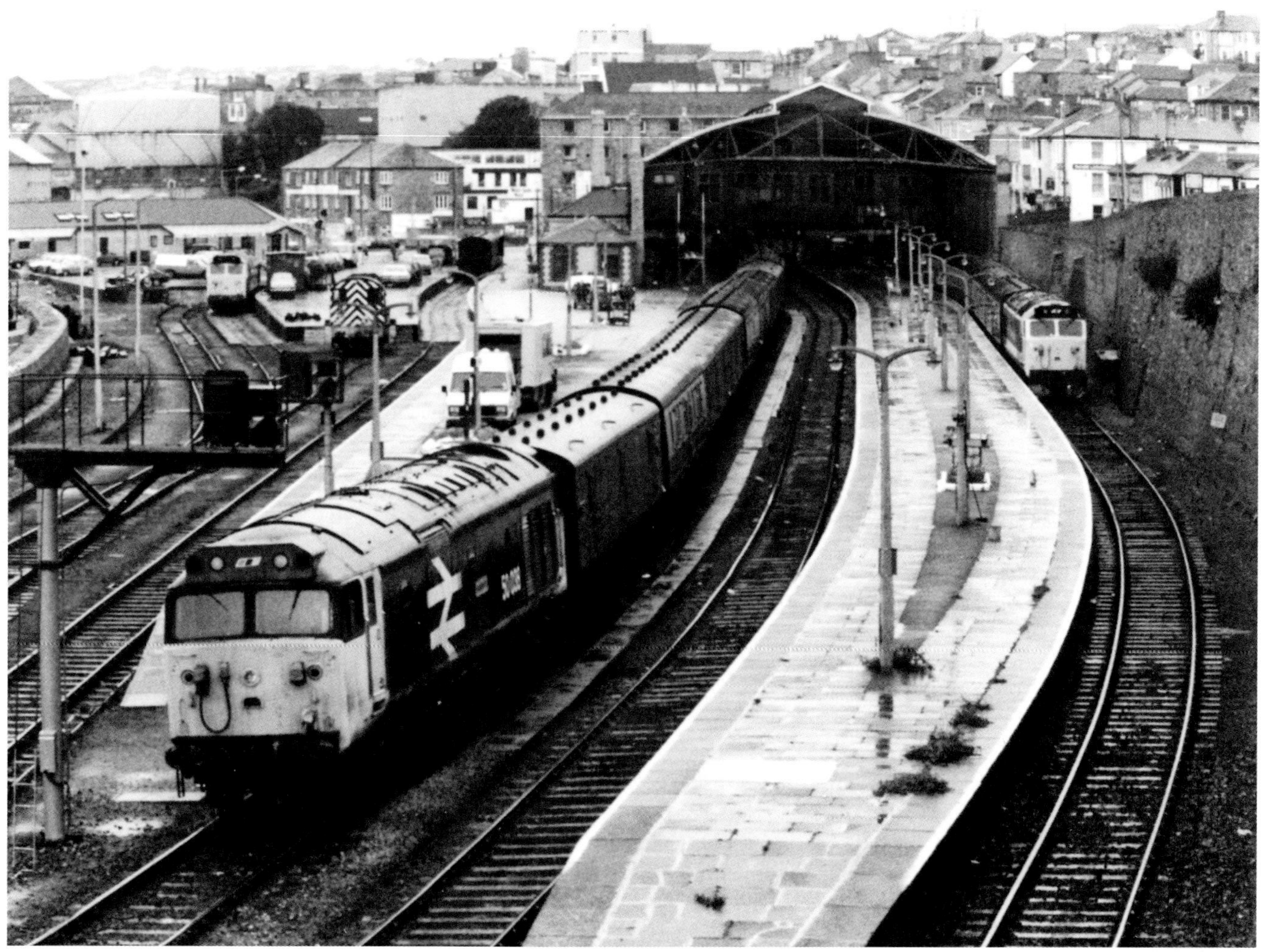

The date is October 1983 and the location is Penzance platform 3. The class 50 is 50038 *'Formidable'* is ready to depart with an Up Postal Train. It is in company with two other class 50s and a class 08 shunting loco. This October 1968-built English Electric loco was originally D438 and was withdrawn in September 1988 and cut up in August 1989 at Old Oak Common. (GP)

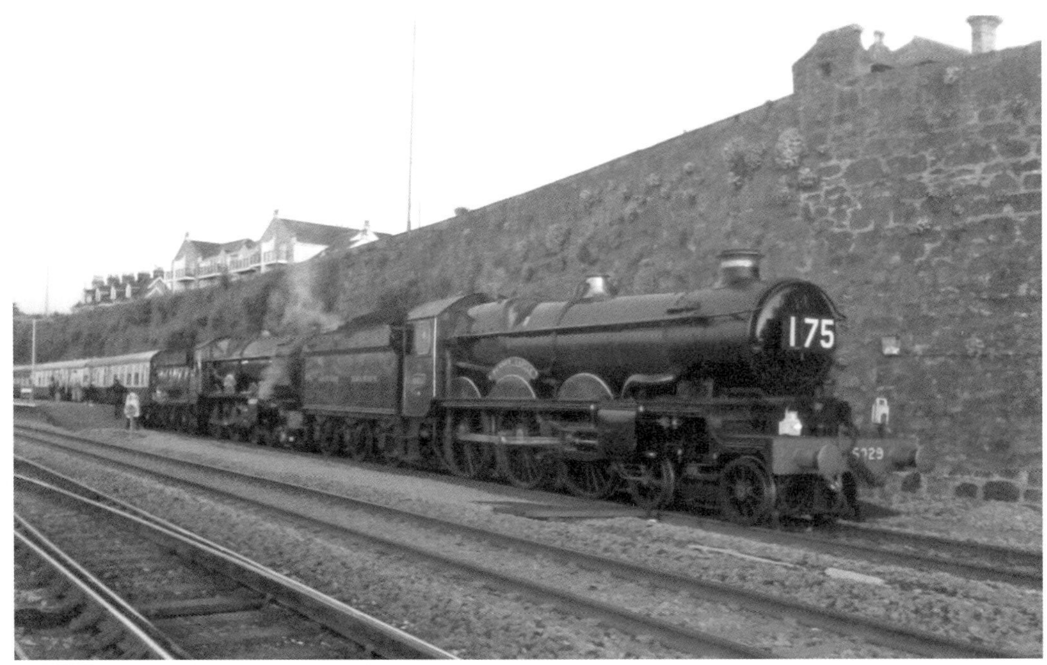

One of most memorable days in my career was being asked to be Pilotman for Single-Line Working to position the GWR 175 celebration train in Penzance for its departure on 28 June 2010. The reason for S.L.W. being required was because the King locomotive was 'tight to the loading gauge' when passing under a couple of bridges in the Hayle area due to the cant of the track on the curves. The Up line had plenty of clearance, so it was decided to form the train at St Blazey and run it down to Truro, cross it over and run it wrong road to Penzance which of course requires a Pilotman. The Steam locomotives were on the rear and at the front was D1062 *'Western Courier'* which looked stunning and sounded great. So, after the last service had passed through Cornwall on both Up and Down lines the train left Par at approximately 0200 hours. I met the train at Truro and arranged for it to be crossed over to the Up line. With everything ready and all staff briefed, at 0300 we set off for Penzance with the *'Western'* making a spirited start from Truro, up towards Highertown Tunnel. There is no way that anyone in that part of Truro could have slept through the fantastic noise of those Maybachs pulling fourteen coaches and two steam locos. It took an hour to complete the journey, which was made easier by me clipping up all facing points earlier that evening and briefing the crossing attendants and signallers. The picture is at 0408 at Penzance after just arriving in Platform one, with the sun rising. A truly memorable day. (SFH)

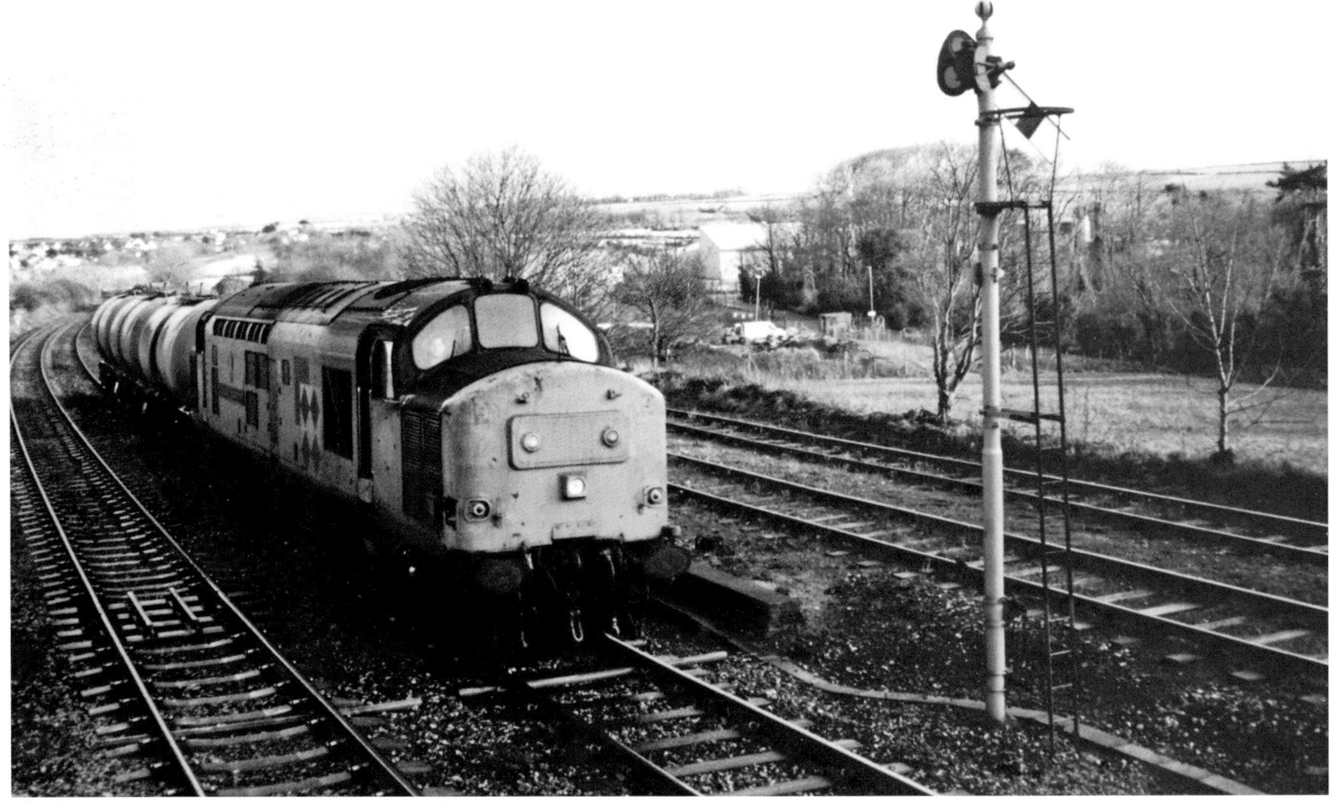

St Erth Down line is the location of this picture from 30 December 1998. It shows the St Blazey–Ponsandane Fuel Tanks, which still runs in 2013, though with a class 66. Class 37 number 37692 *'The Lass O'Ballochmyle'* was built by E E Robert Stephenson & Hawthorn in May 1963 and was withdrawn in December 2000, but it was August 2009 before it was broken up by C.F. Booth. (MD)

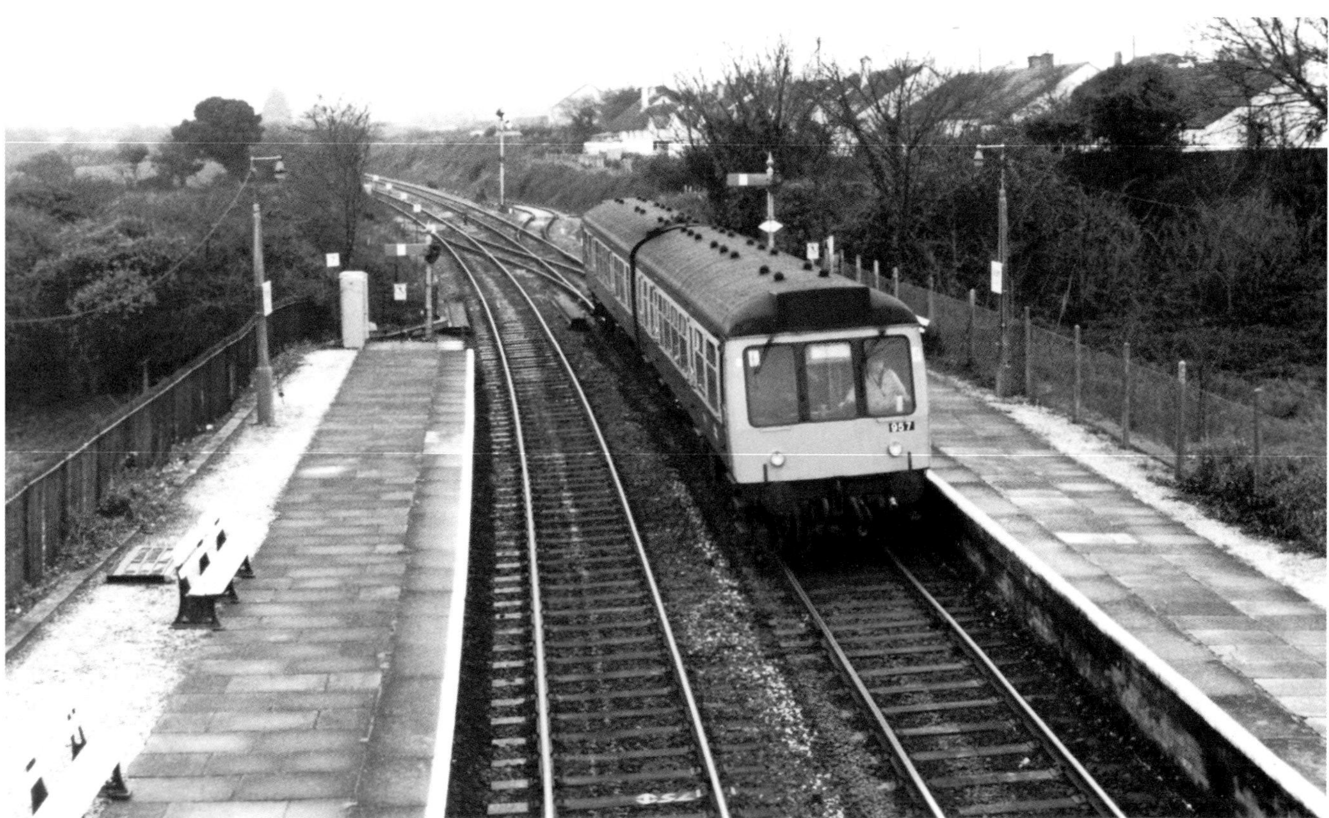

Class 108 unit number 957 is seen here entering the Up platform at St Erth in March 1989. In the background the long removed Up Refuge Siding is seen still intact and connected. (GP)

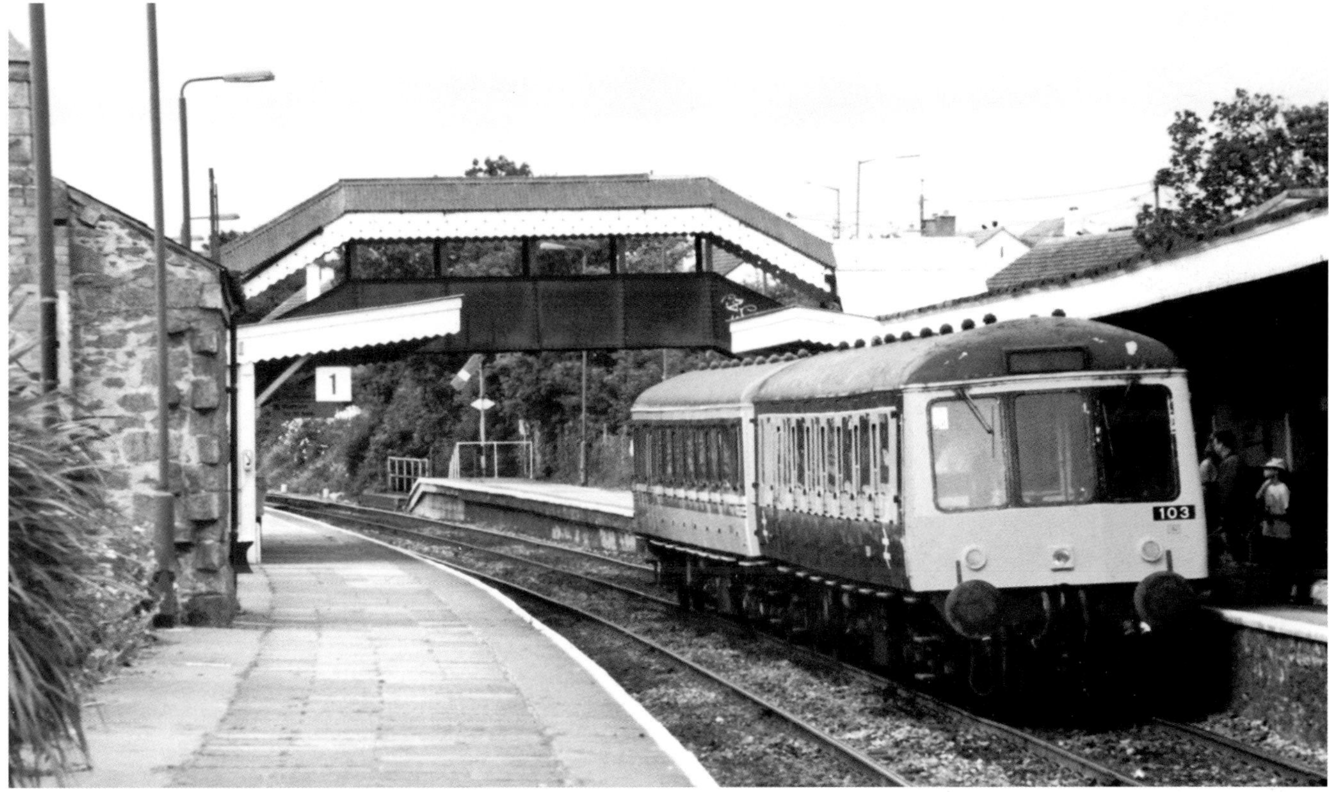

St. Erth Up platform is the location of Penzance bound, ex St Ives, class 122s number 103 (55003) and probably 100 or 112 (55000/55012) in July 1992. After remodelling of the layout in 1964, Penzance bound trains from the St Ives Branch had to traverse the Up line and cross over to the Down line at the west end cross-over using main arm signal SE54 (seen 'off' in the background), which utilised the lever previously controlling a disc shunting signal. (GP)

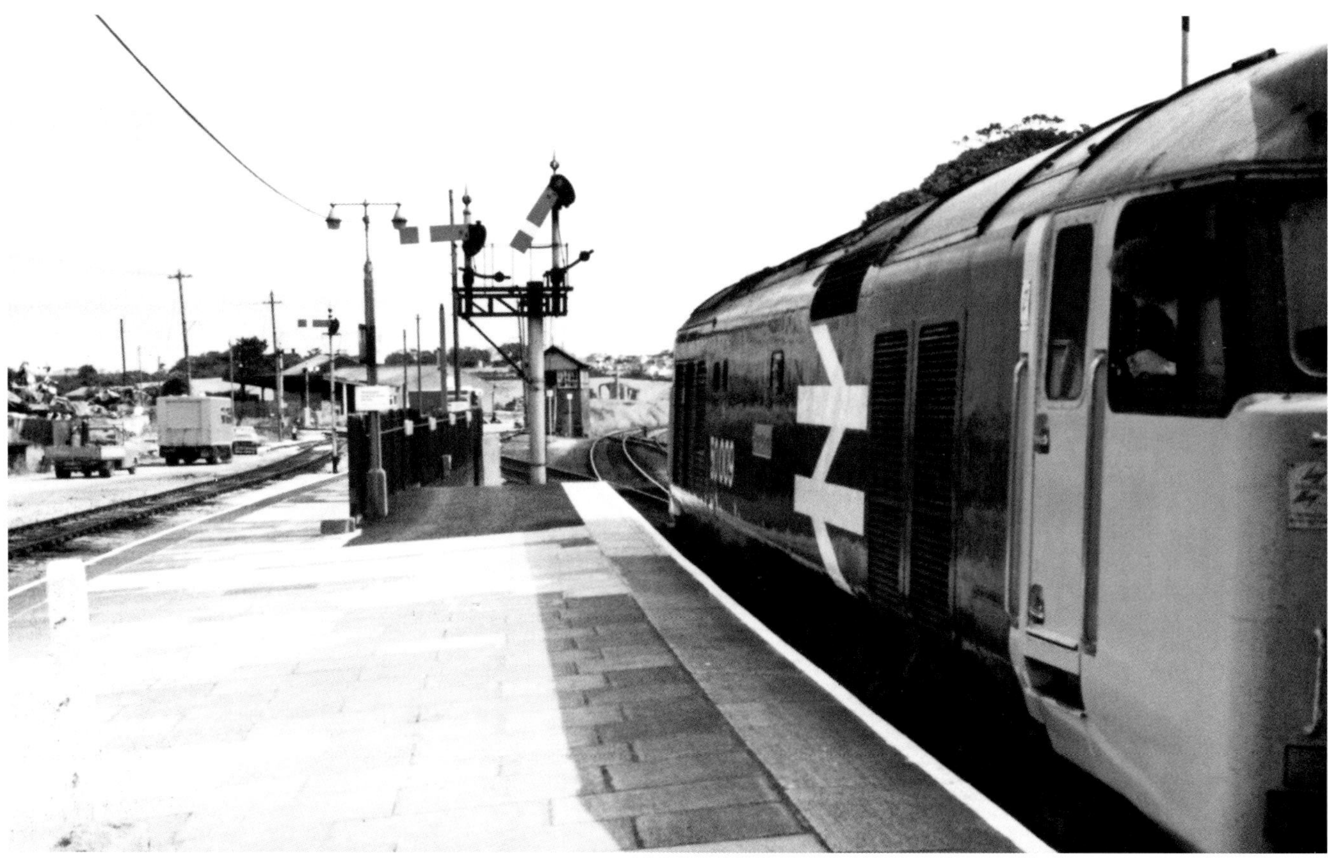

Large Logo liveried 50009 *'Conqueror'* is seen here in the Up platform at St Erth in August 1983. Built by English Electric in March1968 as D409, for the West Coast Main Line, it was transferred to Laira Depot at Plymouth, from where it was withdrawn in January 1991 and subsequently sent to Old Oak Common for disposal and was cut up in February of the same year. (GP)

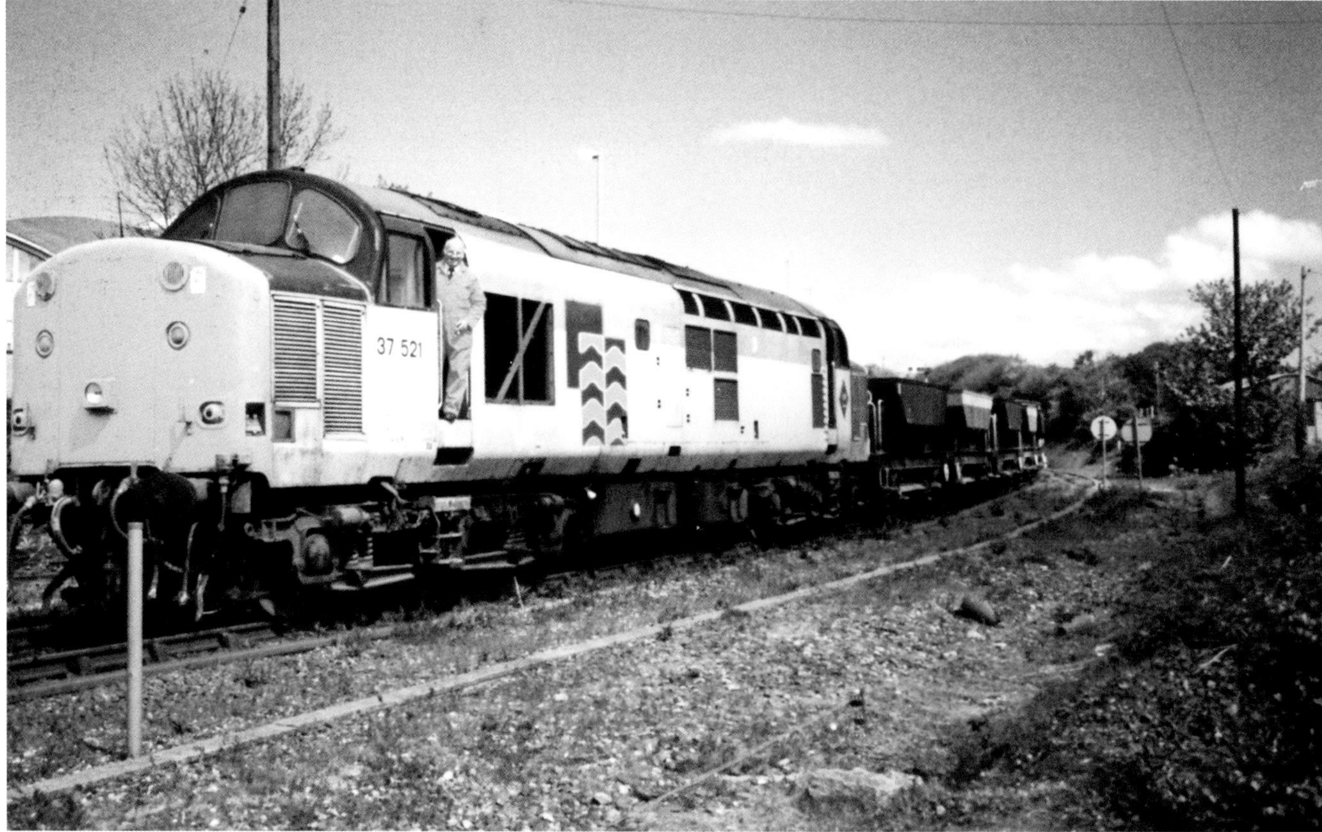

37521 was Top & Tail with 37678 on engineering duties when photographed coming off the St Ives Branch at St Erth in May 1992. Built as D6817 by English Electric in 1963, it was renumbered 37117 first, but when numbered 37521 it became the highest numbered 375XX. It is still in service with HNRC. (GP)

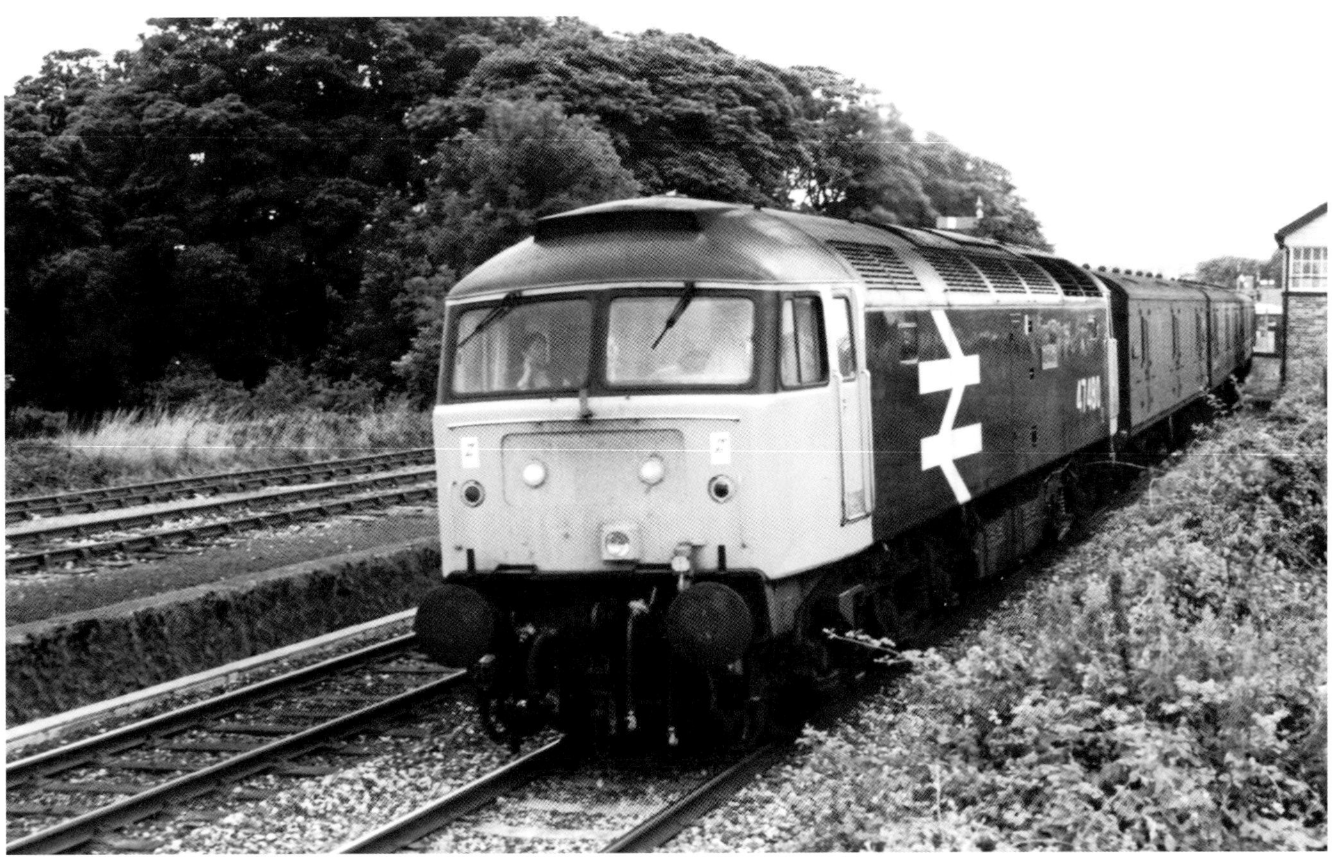

47480 seen leaving St Erth on an Up Parcels train in July 1988. Built in September 1964 at BR Crewe Works as D1616 it became Departmental loco 97480 in September 1988, but was then was renumbered again in July 1989 as 47971 and reinstated back into the operational fleet. It was named *'Robin Hood'* in November 1979. It was cut up in November 1991. (GP)

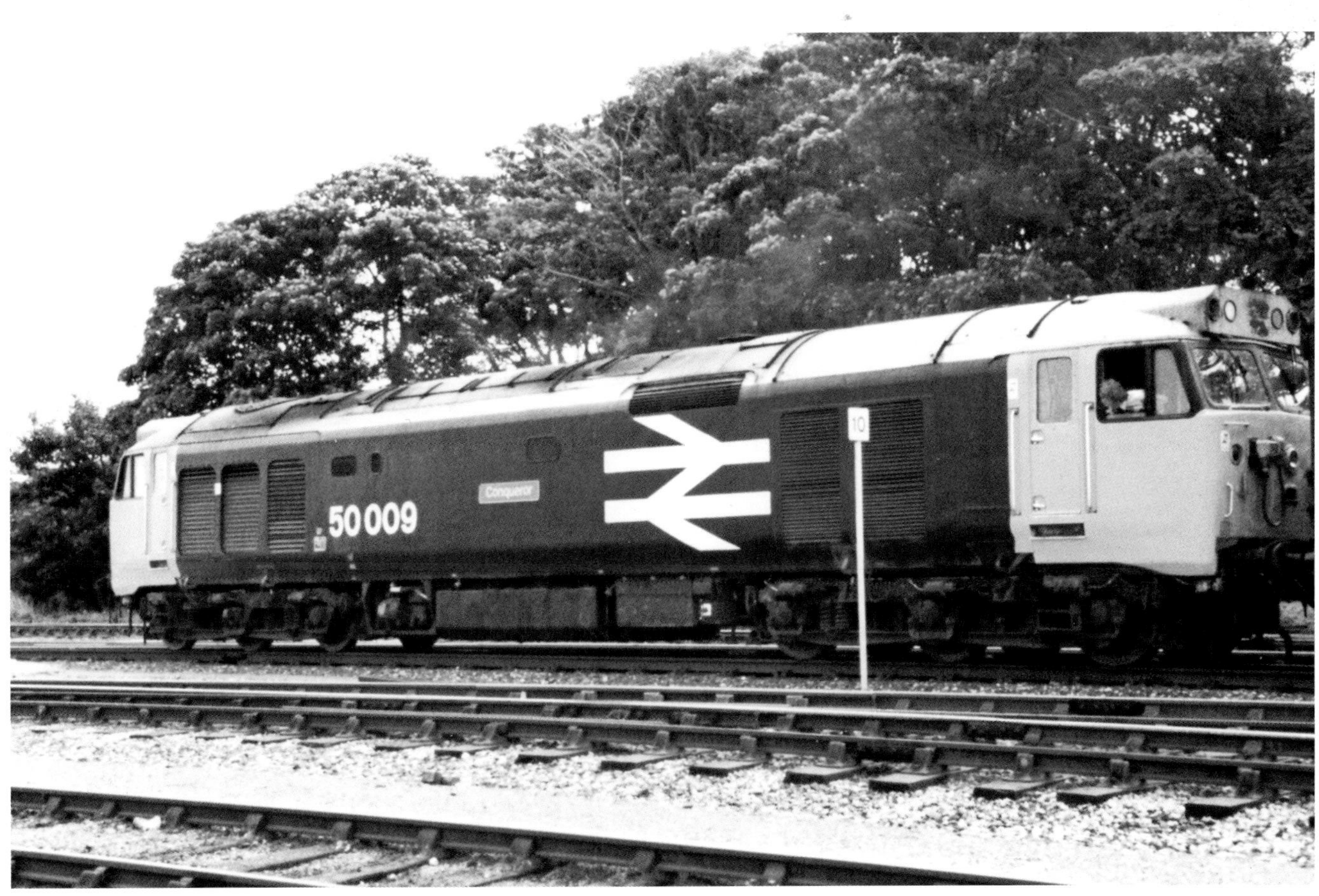

Another view of 50009 *'Conqueror'* departing St Erth on the Up line. (GP)

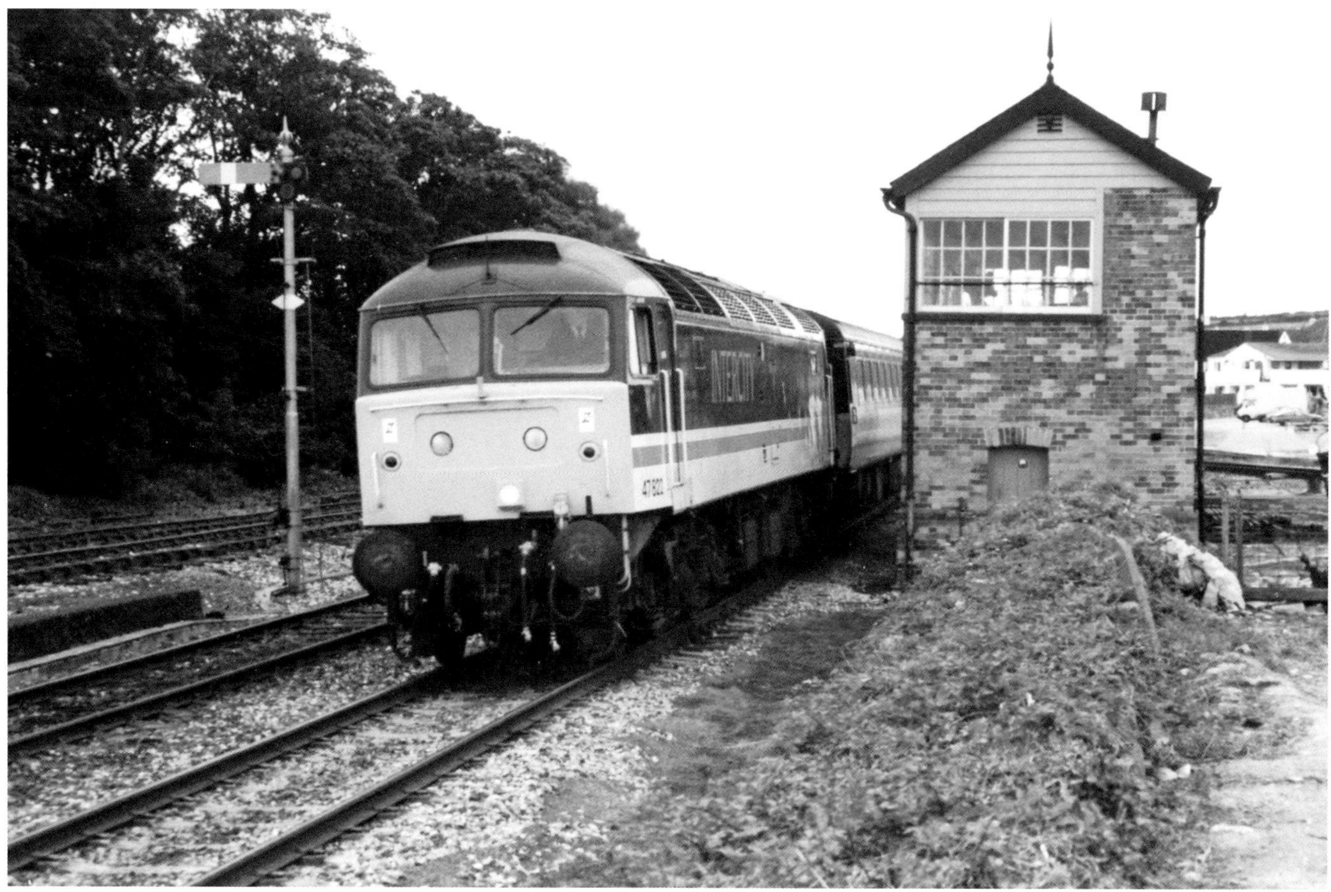

Intercity liveried 47822 is passing St Erth Signalbox in July 1992. Built by Brush in May 1964 as D1758, it was renumbered 47164 and 47571 prior to its final number. Rebuilt as 57305 and operated by Network Rail as a rescue loco. (GP)

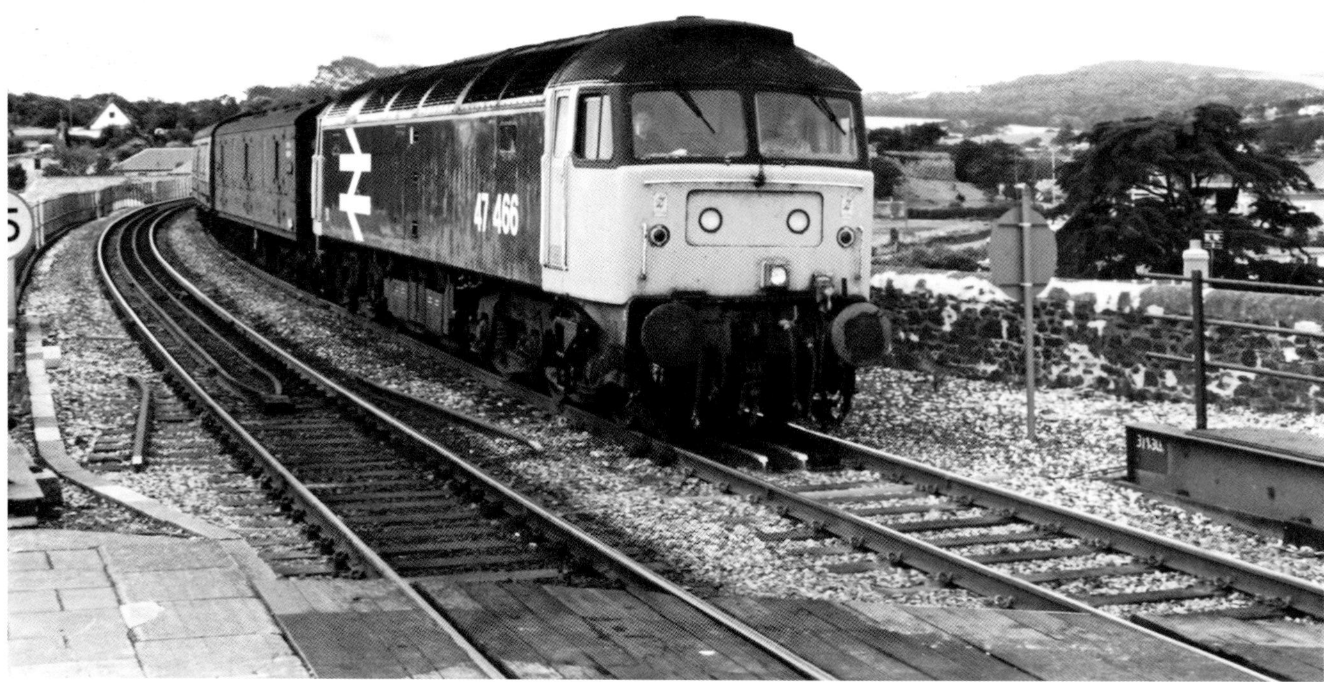

47466 started out as D1590 at BR Crewe Works in 1964 and is seen here on an Up train passing over Hayle Footpath Crossing in July 1990, having just traversed Hayle Viaduct and about to pass through Hayle Station. The former branch line to Hayle Wharf is visible on the loco's nearside. It was cut up at Crewe in March 1997.(GP)

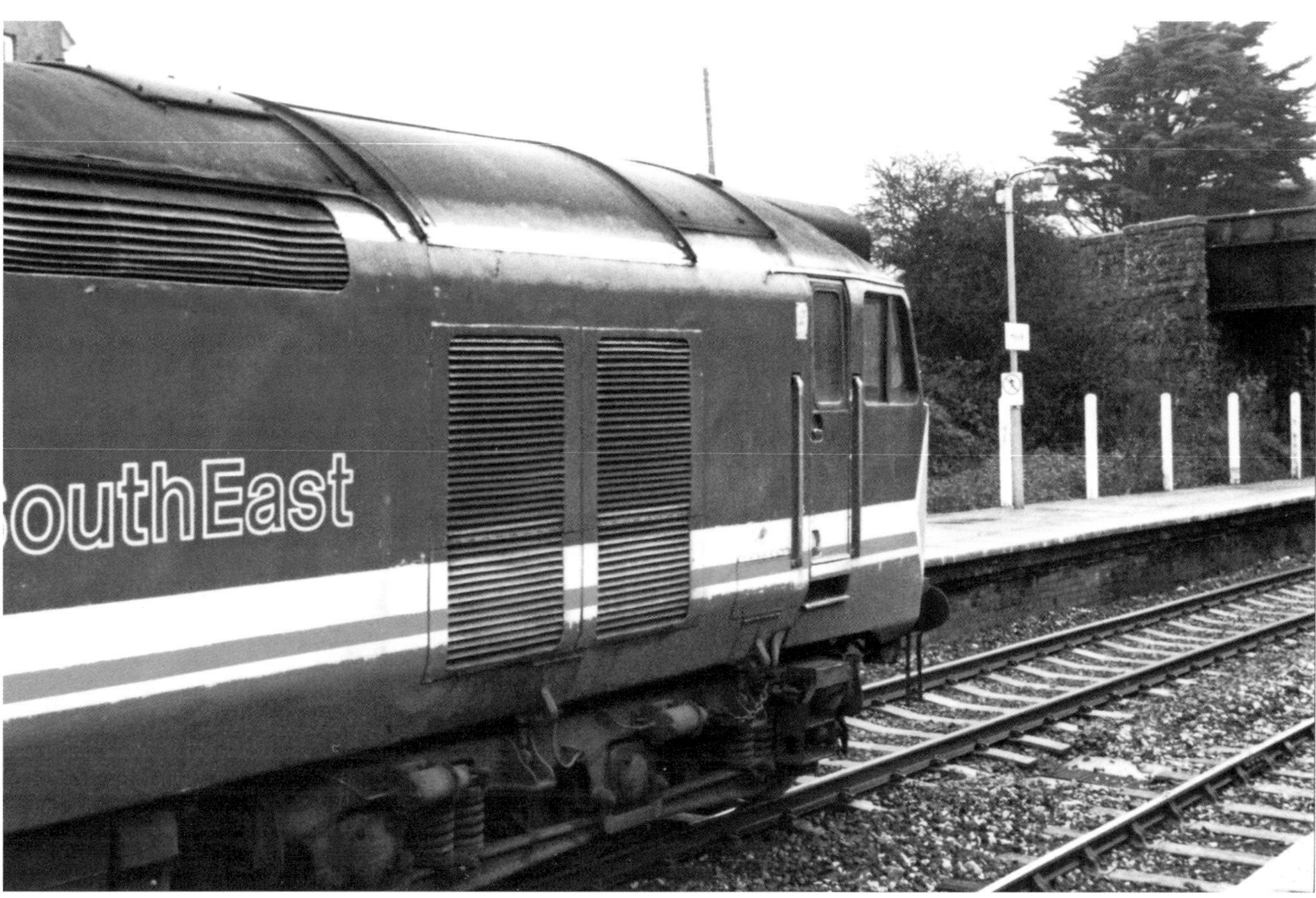

Hayle Up Platform is host to a Network South East liveried class 50 in March 1989. (GP)

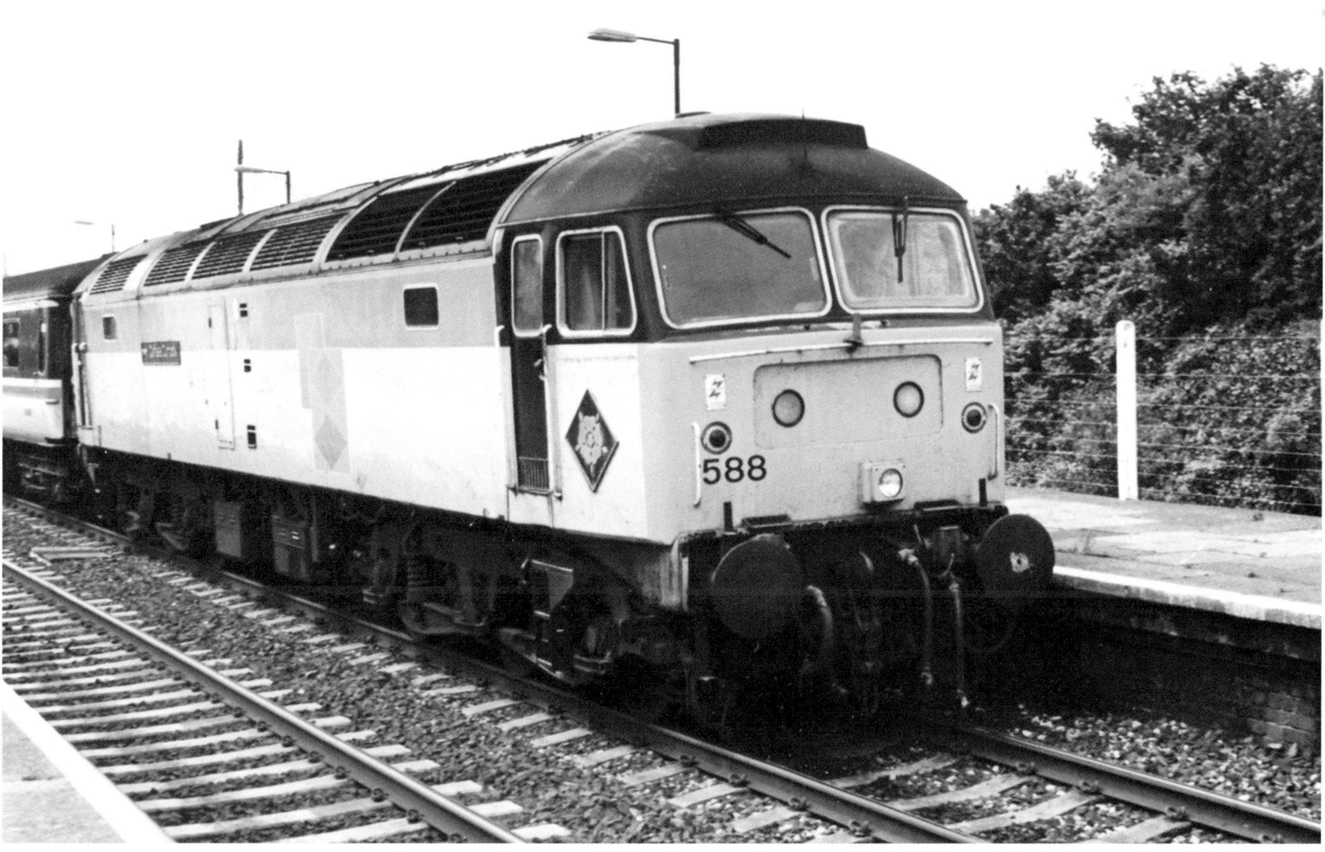

The Up platform at Hayle finds Railfreight Distribution Sector 47588 drafted in for passenger duties, on a train for Paddington in July 1990. D1773 was the first number carried by 47588 when it was built by Brush in September 1964. Transferred to the Freight Sector in June 1983, it was named *'Carlisle Currock'* in July 1988, after carrying 47178 from 1974. It was cut up in August 2008. (GP)

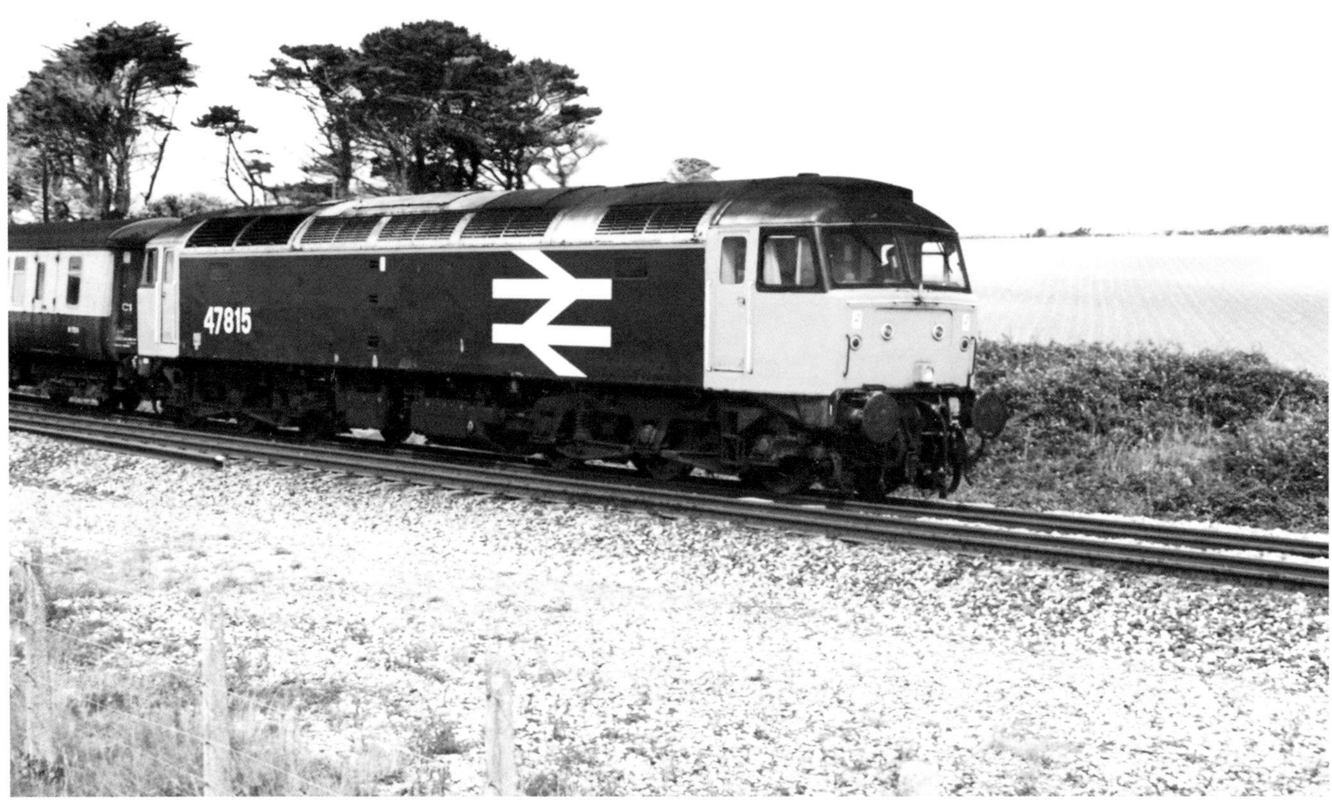

Class 47, 47815 in Large Logo livery, on the Up Cornish Main Line at Gwinear in July 1990. Built in 1964 by Brush as D1748, it became 47155 then 47660. (GP)

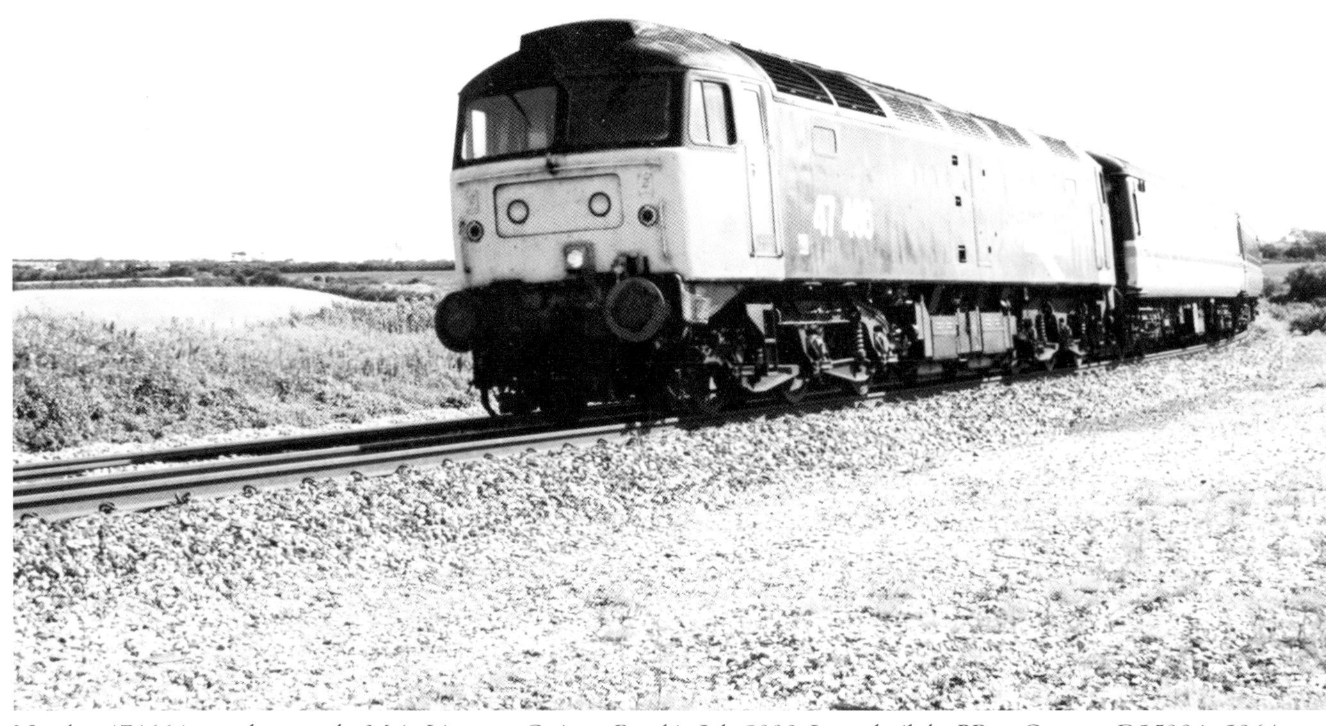

Number 47466 is seen here on the Main Line near Gwinear Road in July 1990. It was built by BR at Crewe as D1590 in 1964. (GP)

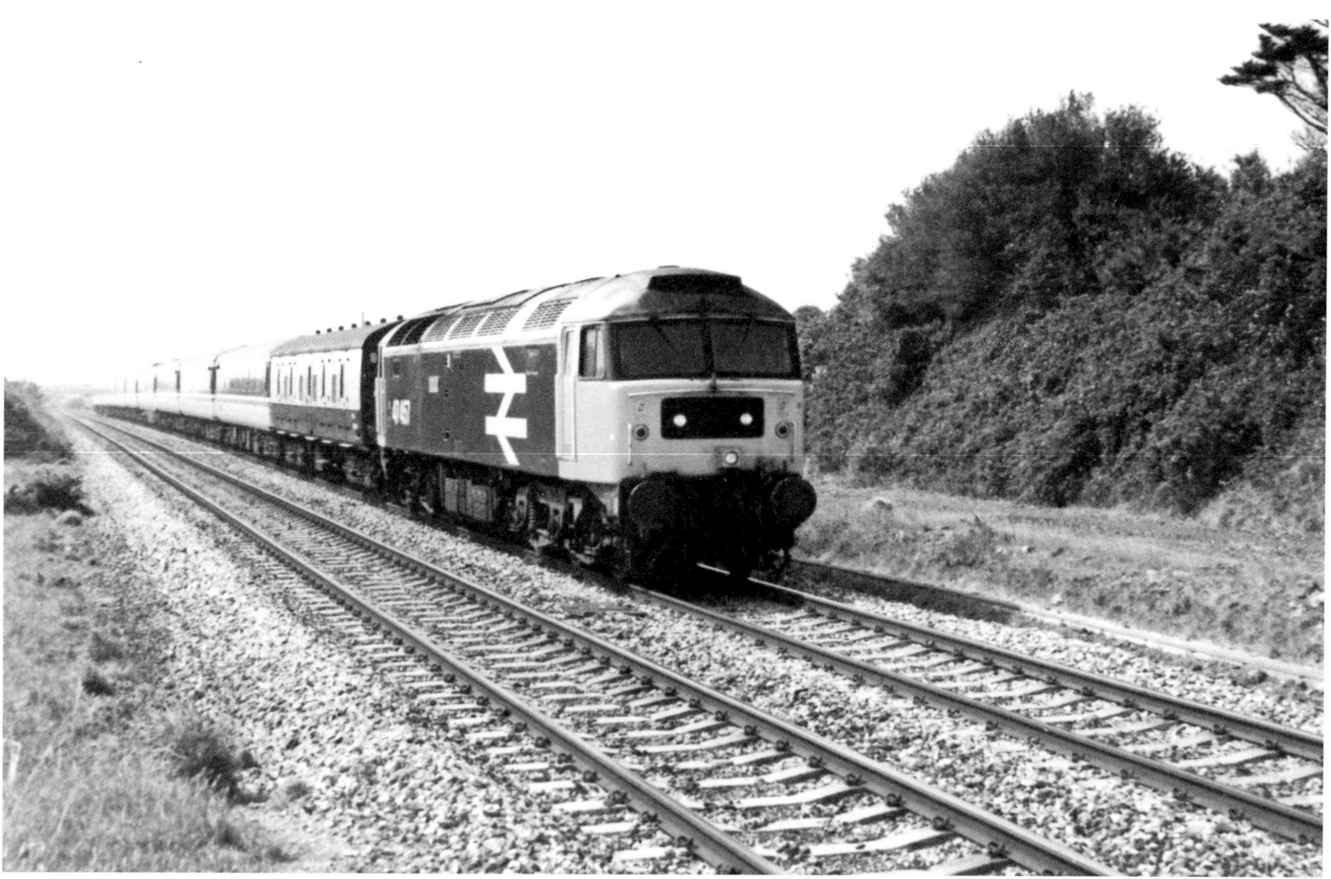

47457 is seen here on the Cornish Up Main Line approaching Gwinear Road in June 1989. It was built by BR at Crewe Works in April 1964 as D1577 and was broken up in May 1997 at Old Oak Common. (GP)

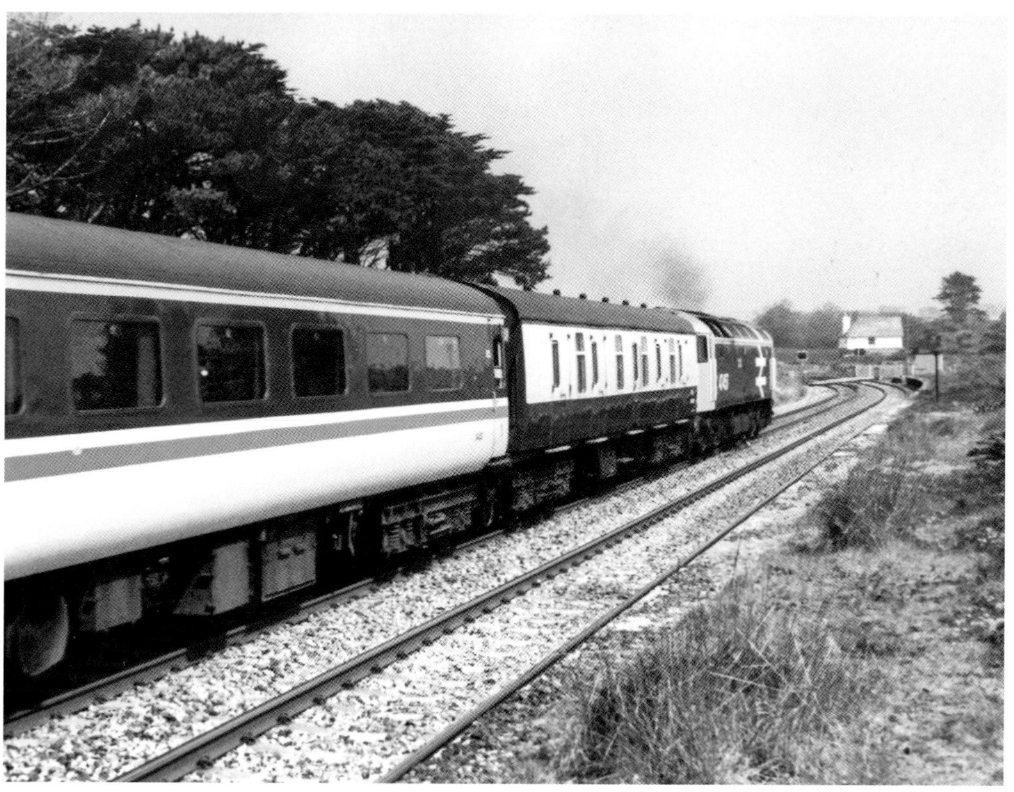

The location is Gwinear Road on the Up line, at the point where the station used to stand. The loco is large logo liveried 47457 *'Ben Line'* and the train, an unidentified Up express in June 1989. This loco started out as D1577 in April 1964 at BR Crewe Works. It was withdrawn in February 1992 and cut up at Old Oak Common in May 1997. (GP)

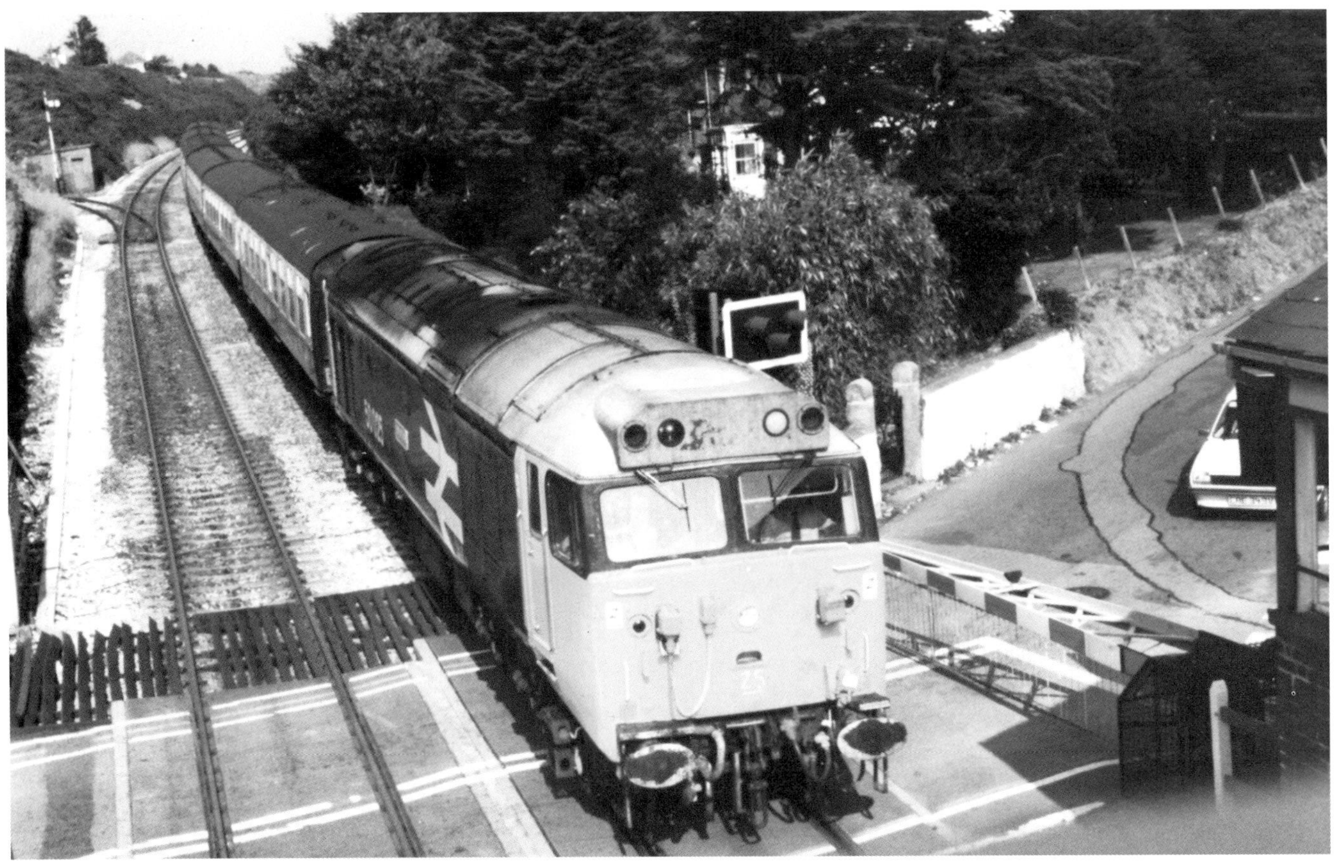

English Electric built 50025 *'Invincible'* is seen here passing Roskear Junction Signalbox on the Down line in August 1983. Roskear was a true junction then and the short branch line from the Up line can be seen in the background. Aside from the branch line going and the lever frame removed, the box and area remain much the same today. It entered service in July 1968 as D425 and was cut up at Old Oak common in October 1989. (GP)

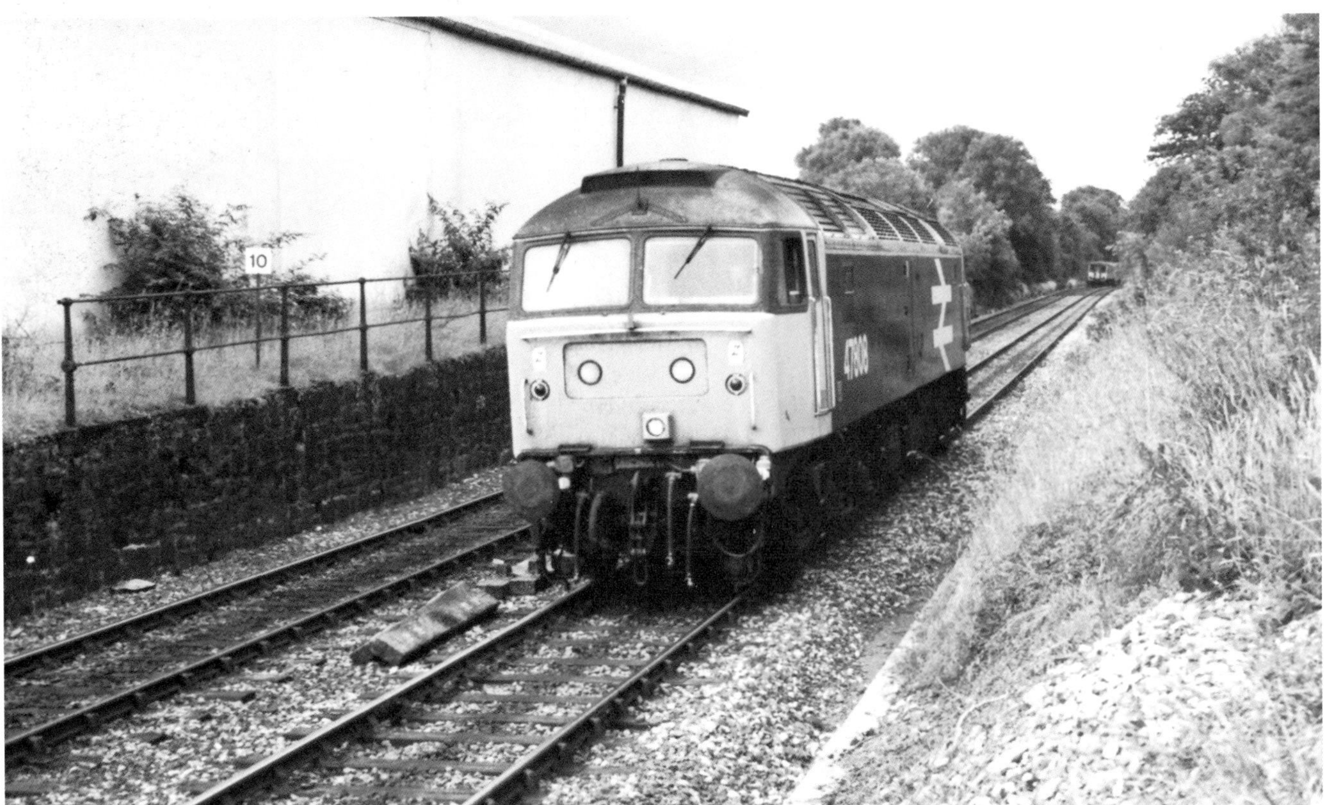

The Up line approaching Camborne Station sees 47808 running light loco in August 1989. Built as D1674 by Crewe Works in May 1965, it was subsequently renumbered 47088 and 47653. It was named *'Samson'* in September 1965 and was cut up in April 2007. In the background on the Down line is Sprinter 155311, which became two separate class 153 'Bubble Cars' in 1991/2. (GP)

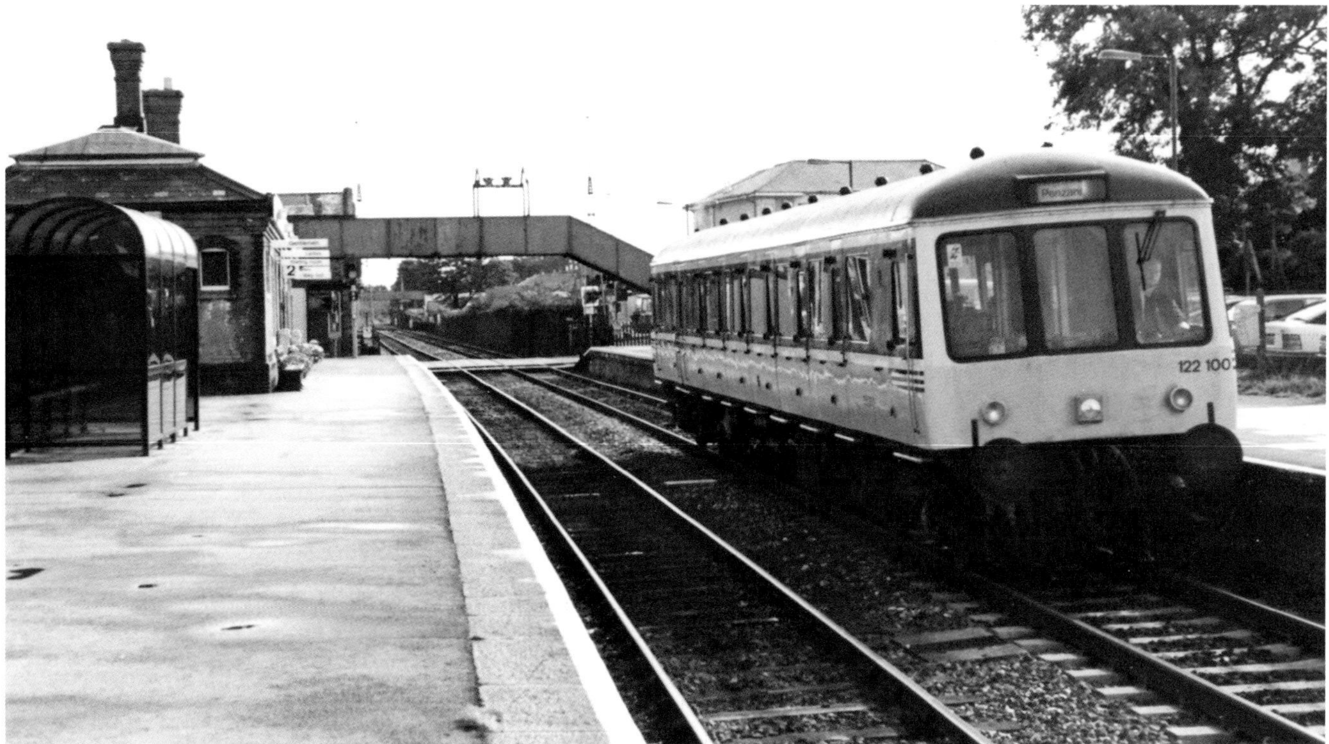

Camborne Down platform is the location of this picture from c.1992 and shows class 122100 number (55000) which was the first numbered 'Bubble-Car' in that class. These popular, useful and robust units were common in Cornwall when I was a signalman at Lostwithiel and there were up to seven of these units operating on every branch line and the main line. They survived well into the privatisation period, and many went on to serve minor branches elsewhere until fairly recently, some even surviving as Departmental units for applying Sandite during the autumn. Here the unit is in Regional Railways livery. (GP)

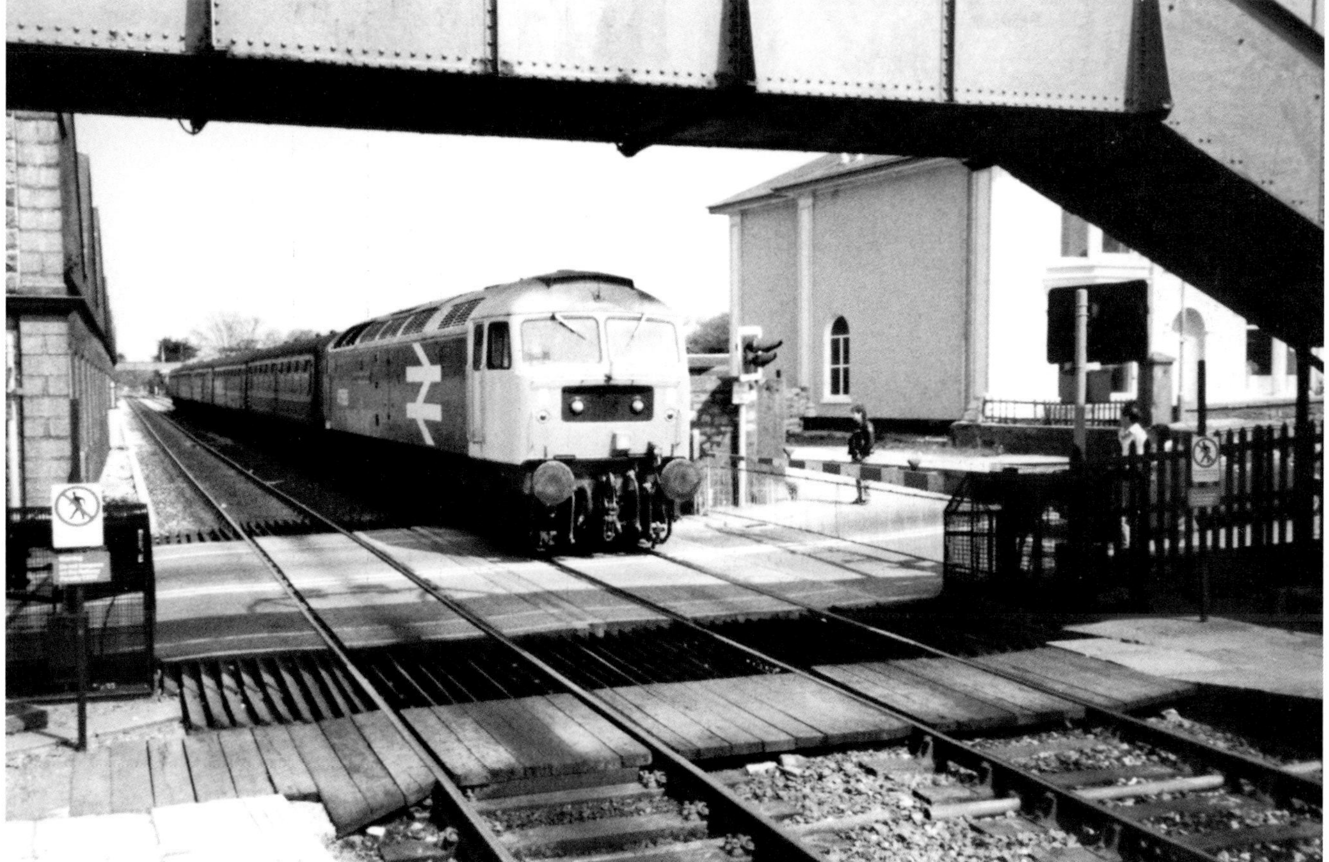

47585 with large logo livery, on the Down line at Camborne in April 1989. Named 'County of Cambridgeshire' in May 1979, it was built as D1779 by Brush in October 1964, and carried 47184 as its first TOPS number. It was cut up in March 2006 at Stockton-on-Tees. (GP)

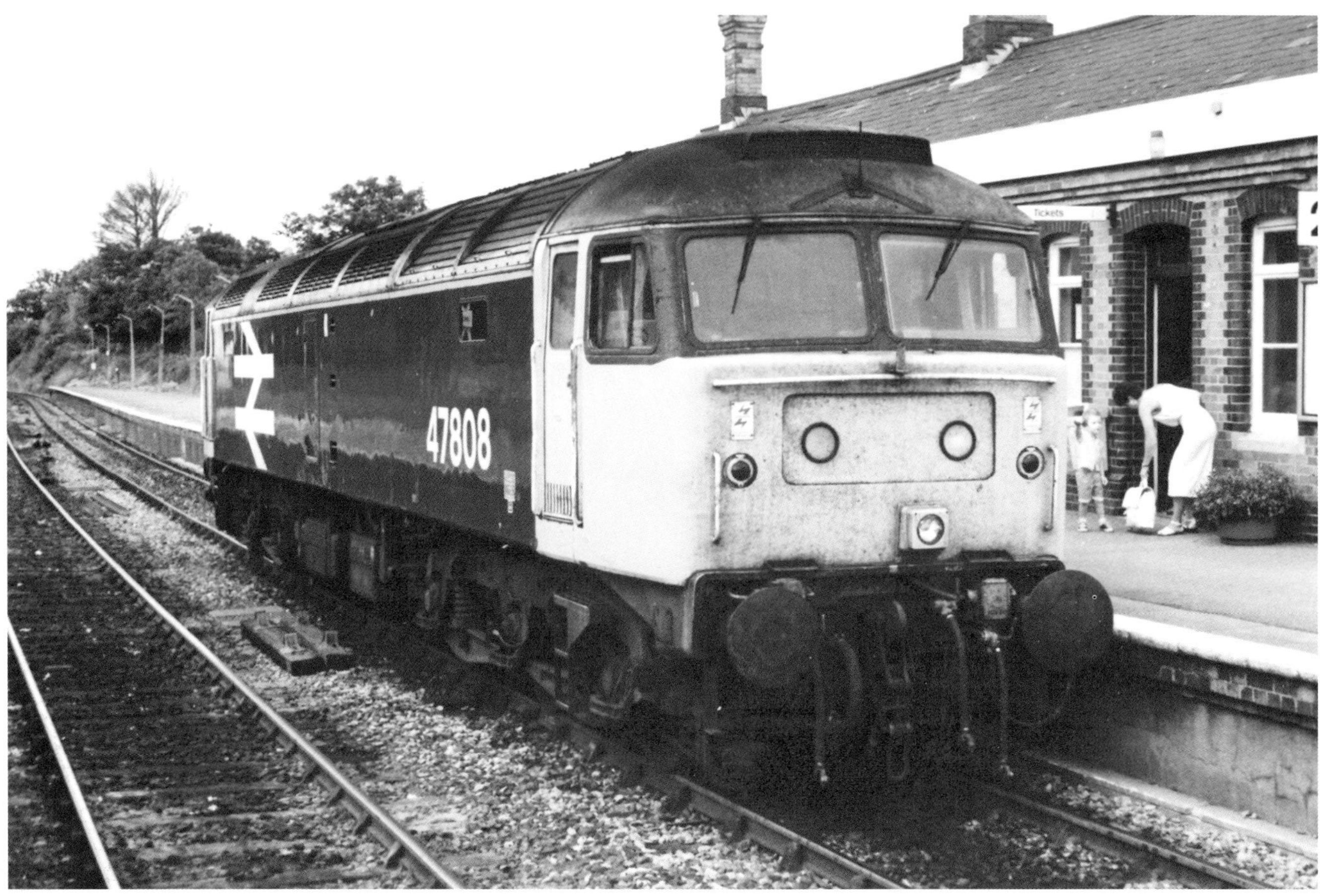

Large logo livery 47808 is seen here in Camborne Up platform in August 1989, probably awaiting the signal (R4) to clear towards Truro. 47808 was built in 1965 by BR at Crewe as D1674, becoming 47088 and then 47653. It was named *'Samson'* four months after entering service. (GP)

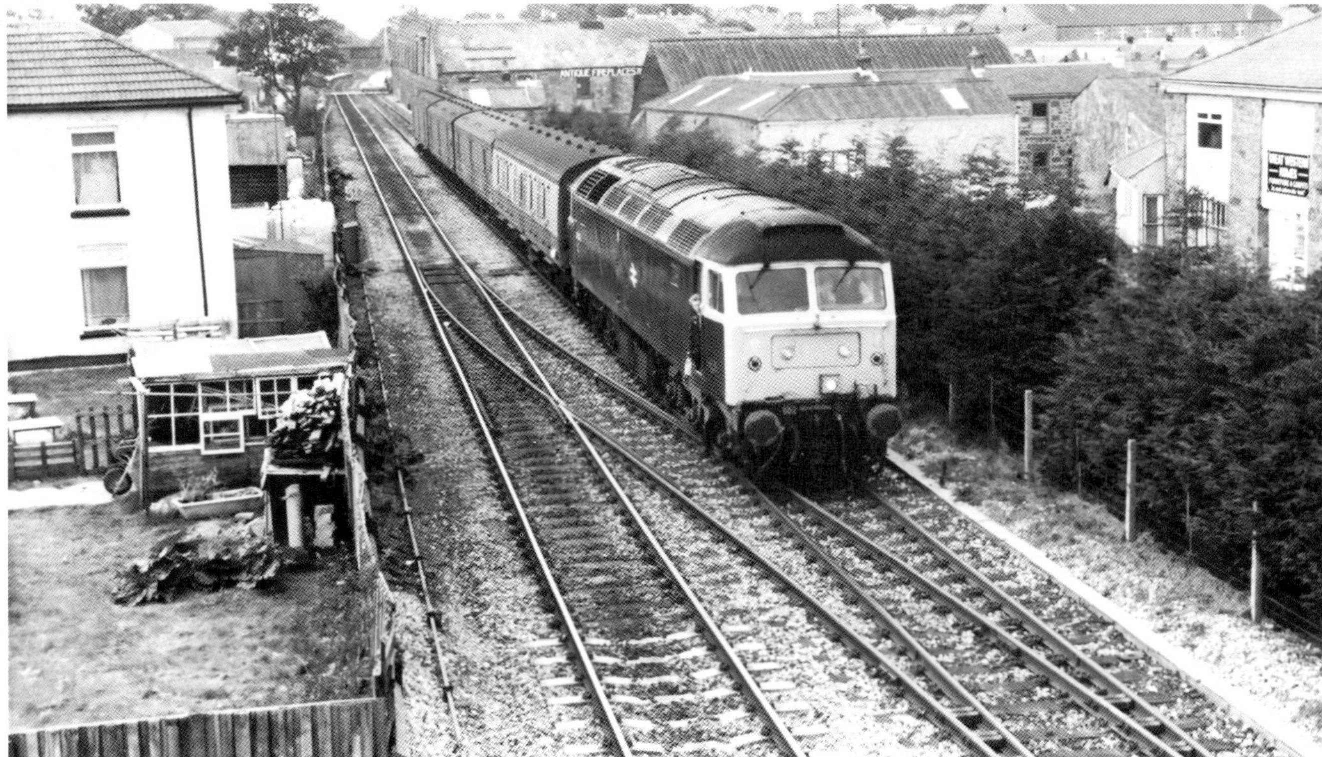

An unidentified class 47 is here seen approaching Roskear Junction Signalbox in October 1989 with an Up parcels train. The Secondman is preparing to drop off a letter or parcel as it passes the signalbox, something that would not happen now, for three reasons, firstly, there are no longer any secondmen, the trains do not carry company mail for Network Rail and there could be no risk assessment for dropping off a parcel! (GP)

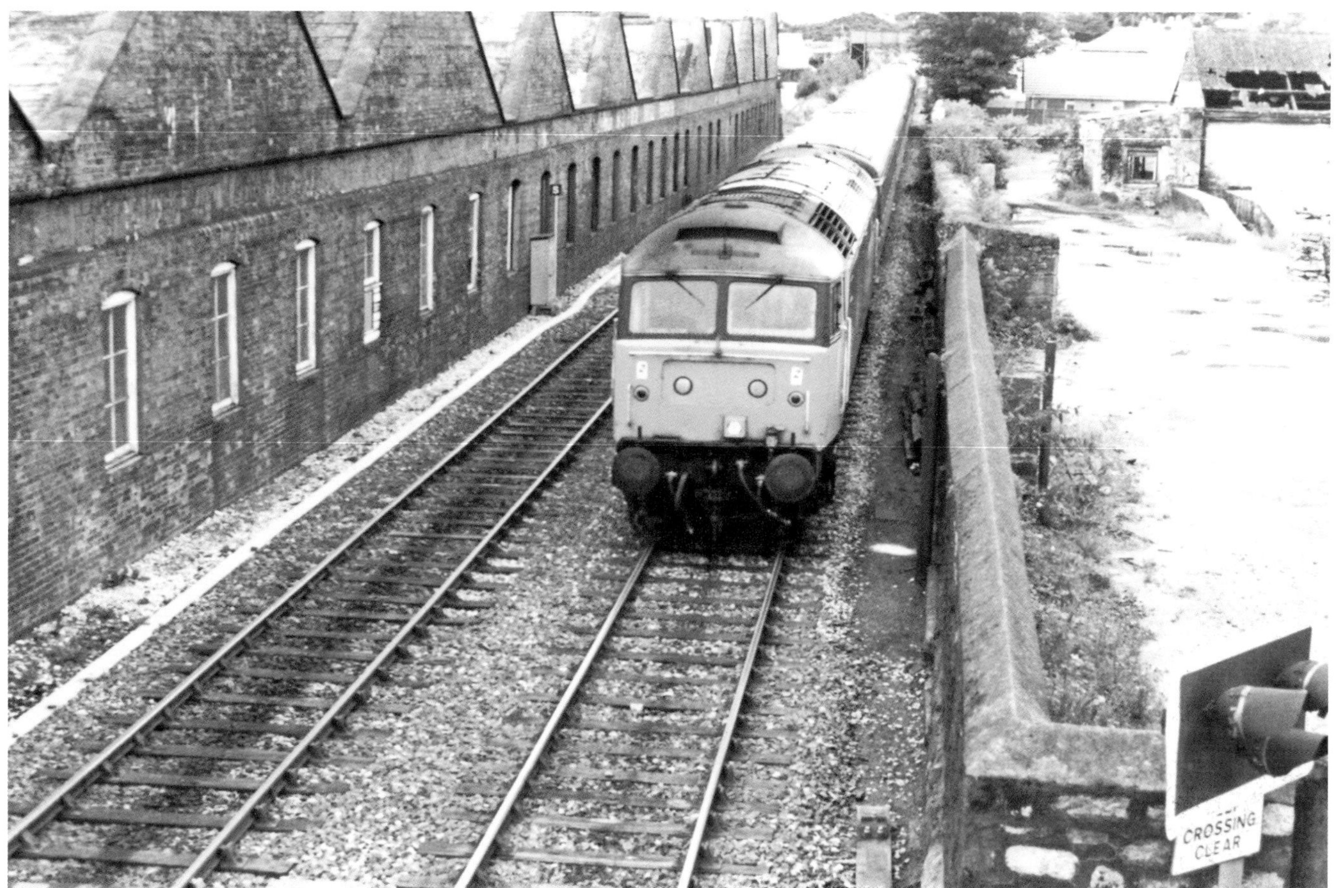

An unidentified class 47 is seen here at speed approaching Camborne on the Down with a passenger train that may not be booked to stop there. The date is 22 July 1988. (GP)

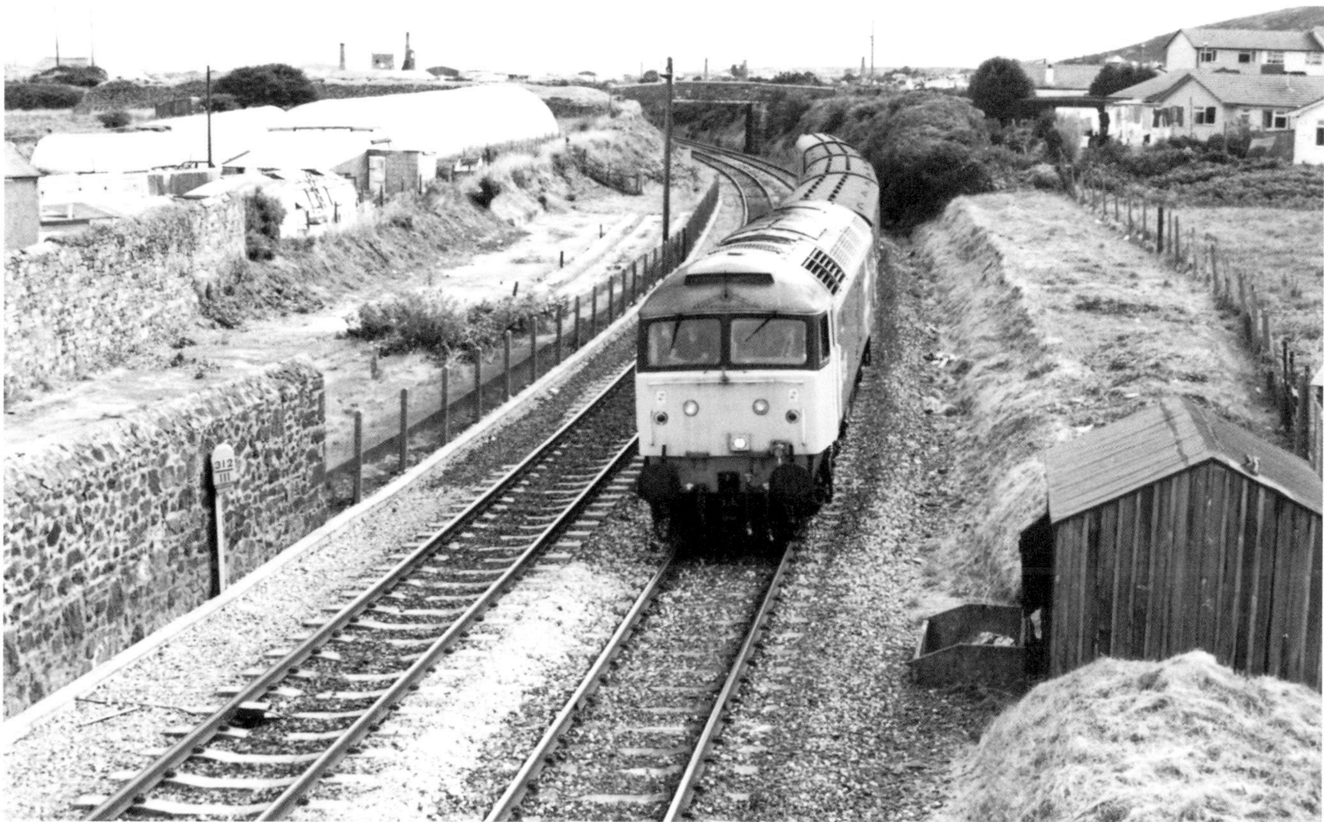

An unidentified class 47 on a short down parcels train is seen here approaching Dolcoath Crossing in August 1989. Dolcoath Area was famous for its Copper Mine, but in BR days was also the site of a milk factory, the siding for which was still in situ at this time, on the Up side. (GP)

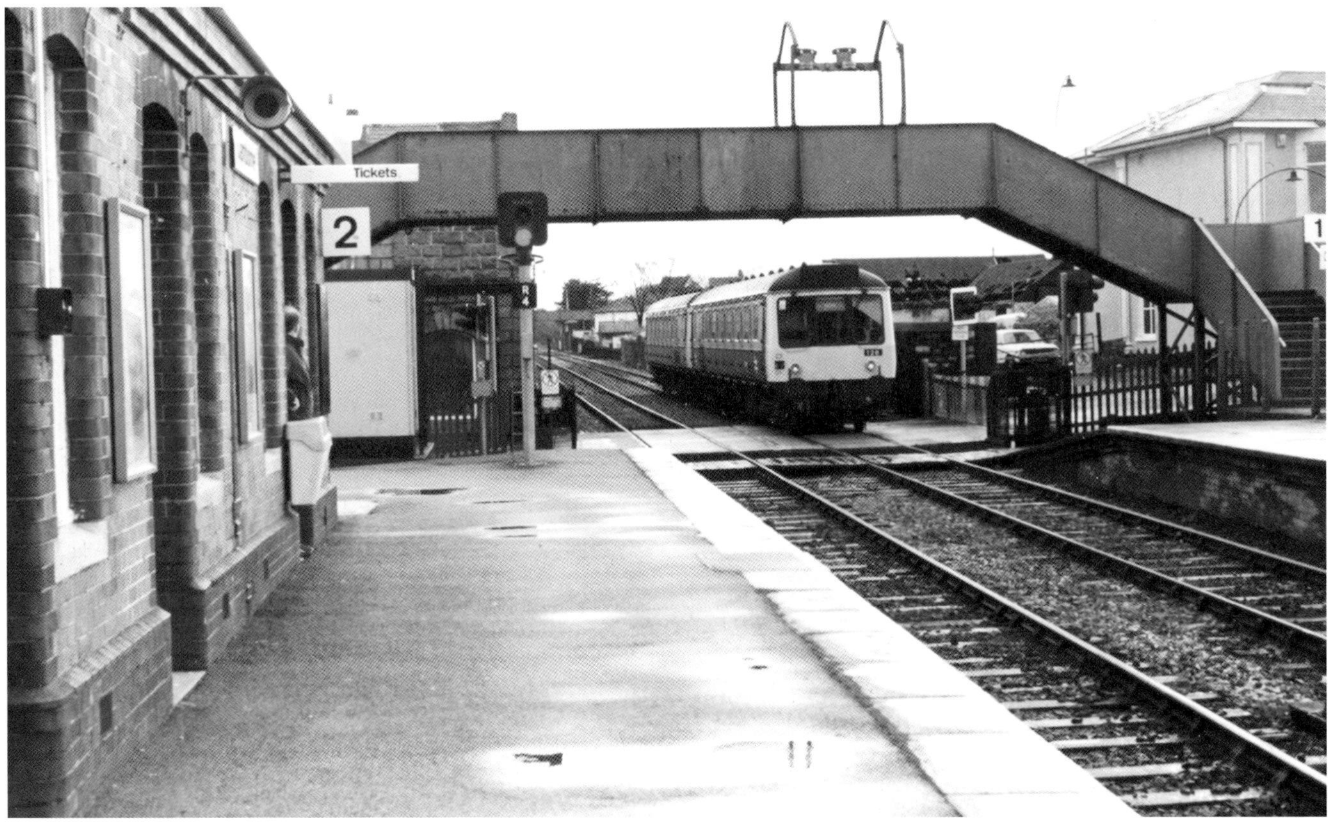

An interesting photo of class 121 and 122 units approaching Camborne Down platform in November 1989. Laira Depot only had one class 121 by this time. The class 121 was almost identical to the 122, except for the four character headcode box (disused) but they were built by Pressed Steel Ltd and had two 150 hp Leyland engines instead of the A.E.C engines in the 122s. (GP)

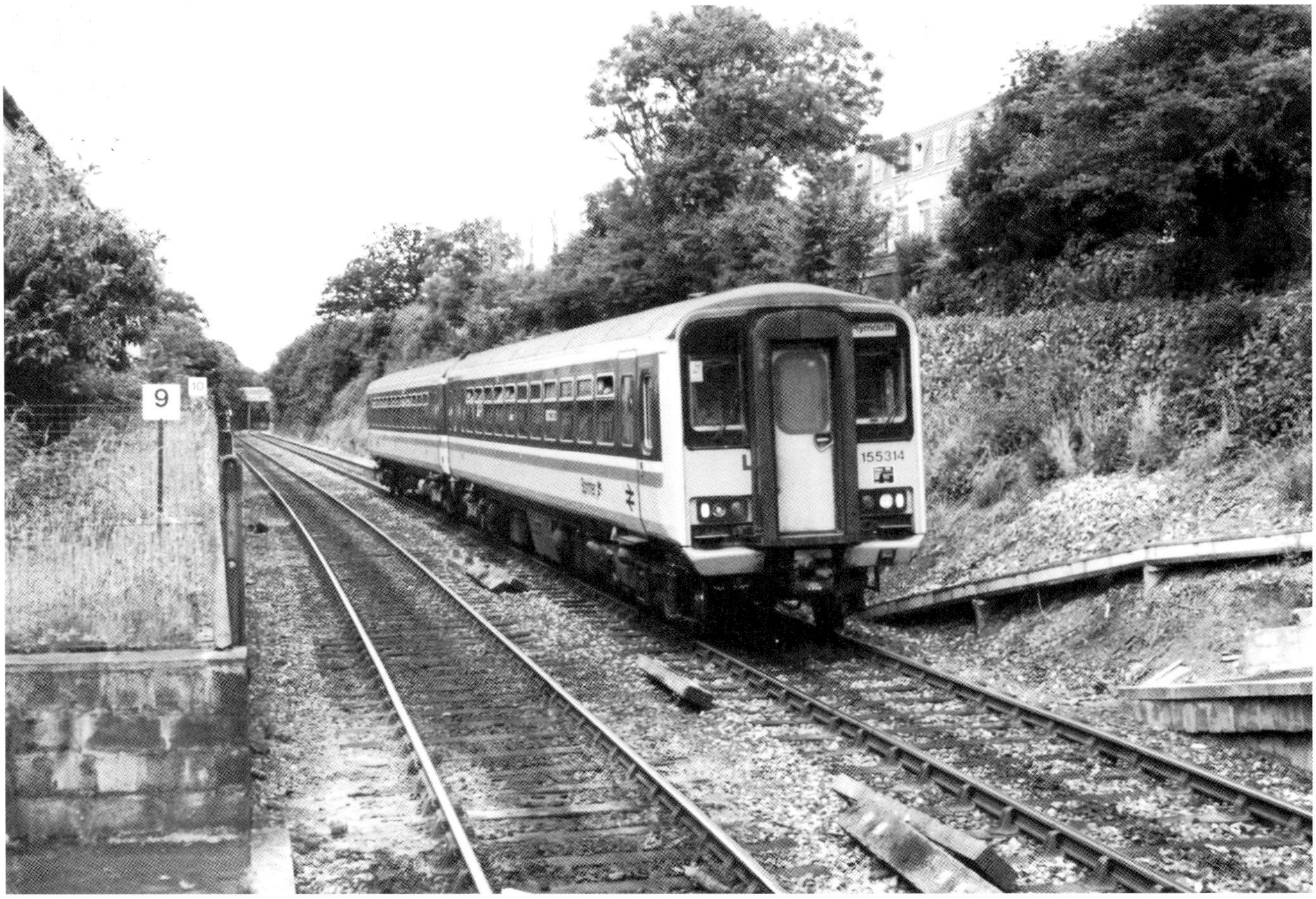

Sprinter 155314 is entering Camborne on the Up line in August 1989. This unit was split into 153314 and 153364. (GP)

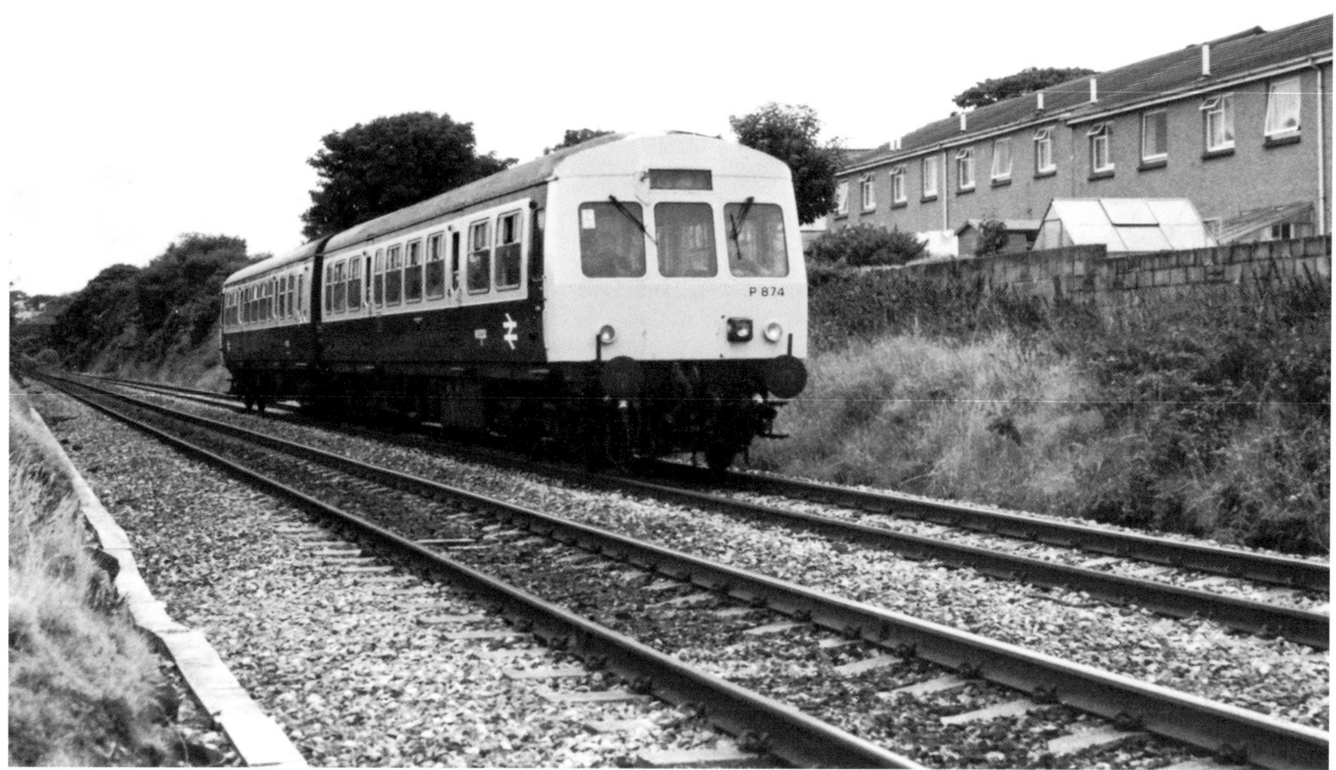

A nice picture of class 101 unit number 874 traversing the Down main line near the site of the former Redruth Junction in August 1989. (GP)

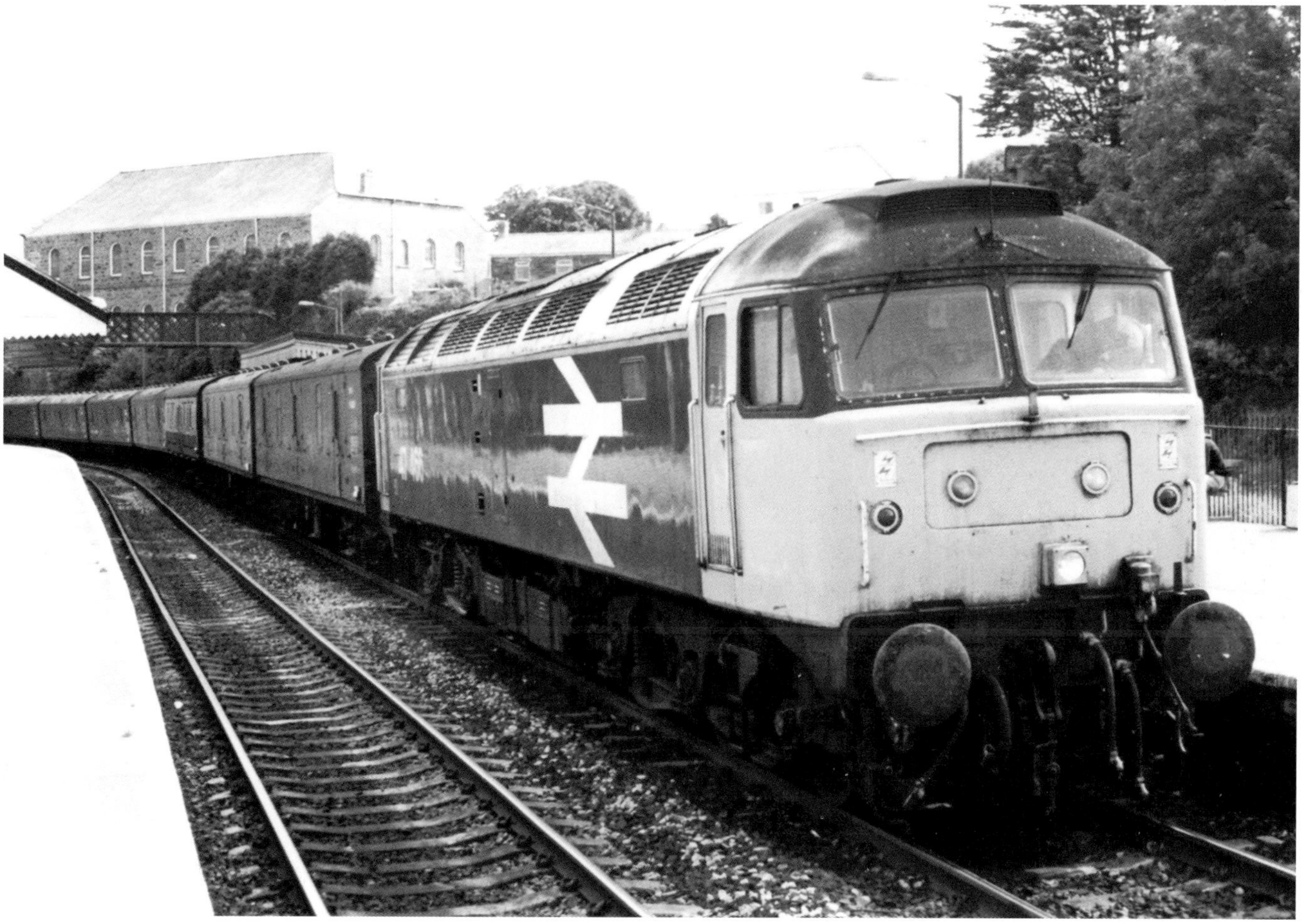

Redruth Station Down Platform is host to 47466, on a Down Postal/Parcels Train on 25 July 1990. It was built in May 1964 by BR at Crewe Works as D1590 and was cut up in March 1997 at Crewe. (GP)

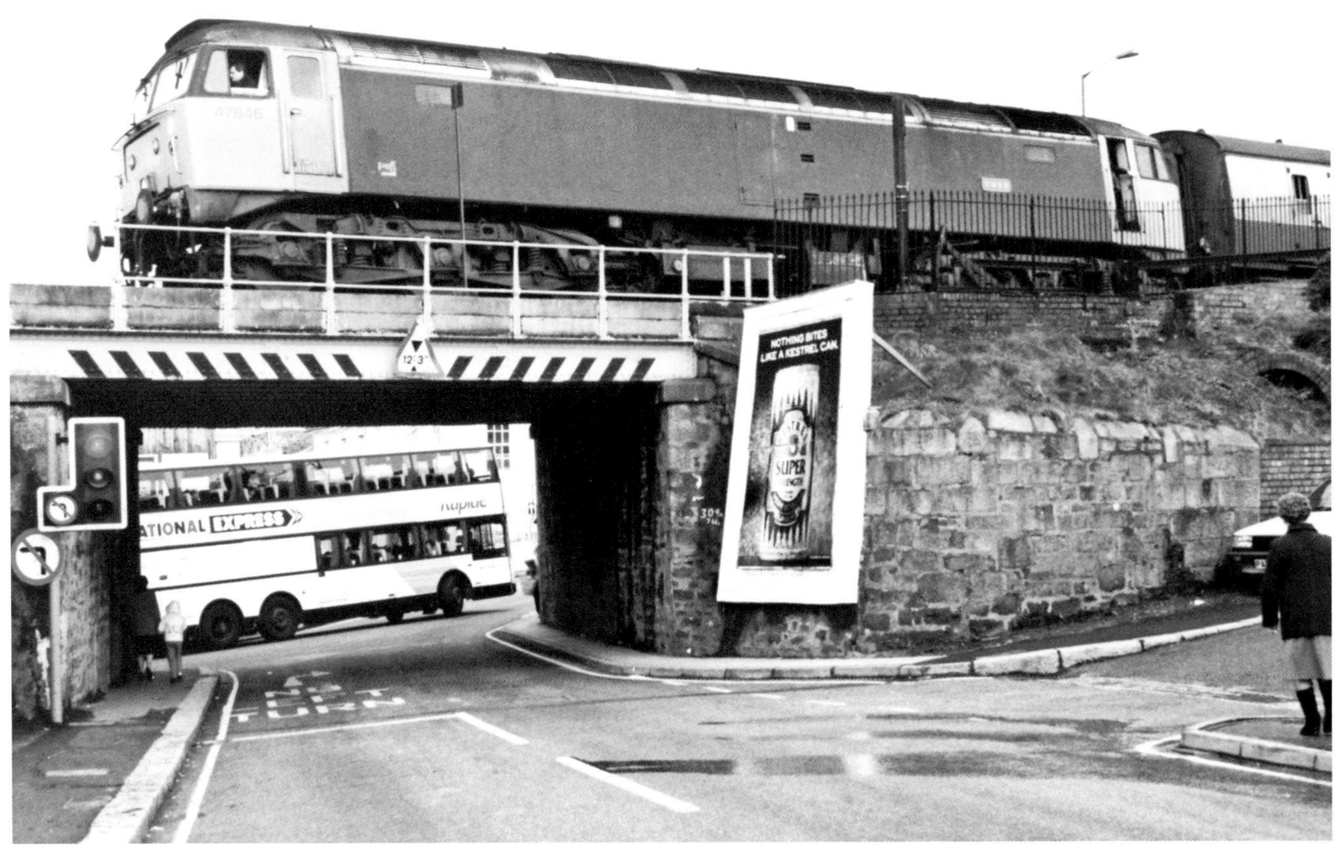

47846 *'Thor'* is seen here standing on Bond Street Bridge, Redruth on the Down line with a parcels train. As D1677 it started life at BR Crewe Works in 1965, becoming 47091 then 47647, being named in 1966. The coach in the background is a National Bus Company 'Rapide' and is probably on the 500 service from Penzance to London. The loco was rebuilt as 57308 and still in service with Virgin Trains and named *'Tin Tin'*. Picture dated December 1989. (GP)

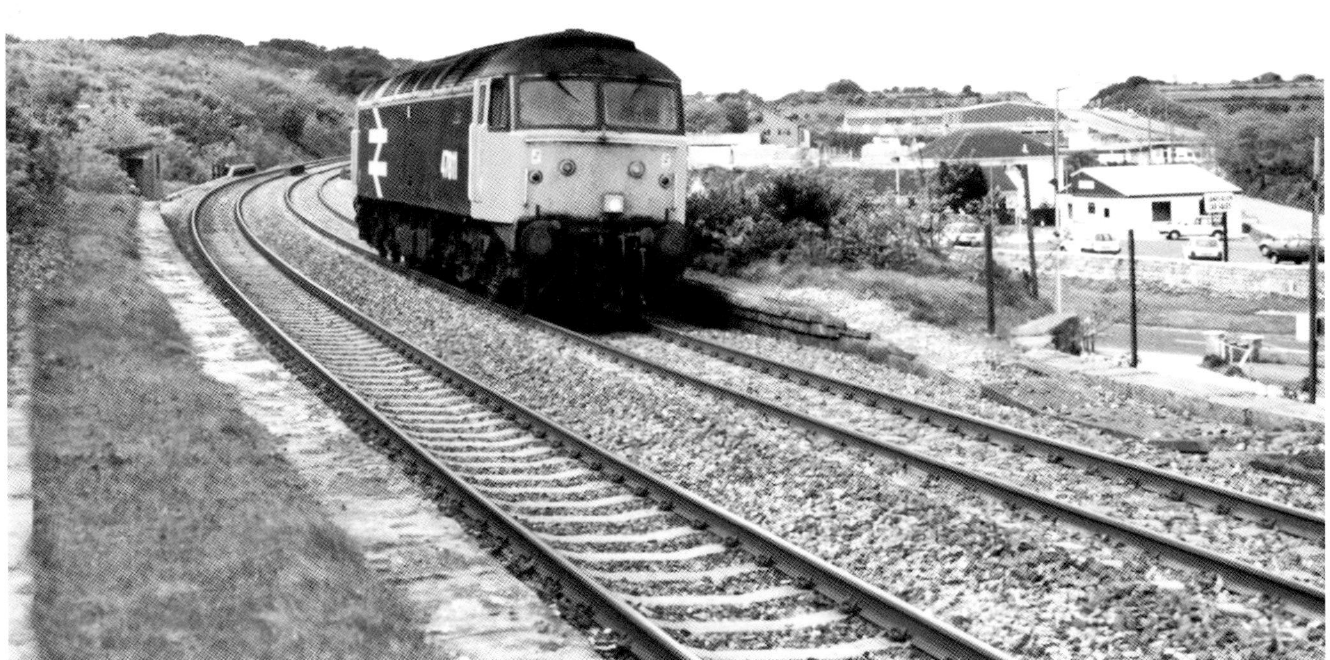

47811 is seen here running light along the Up line at Scorrier passing through the site of the former station in May 1990. D1719 was the number it carried first when built by Brush in February 1964. It is still in service. (GP)

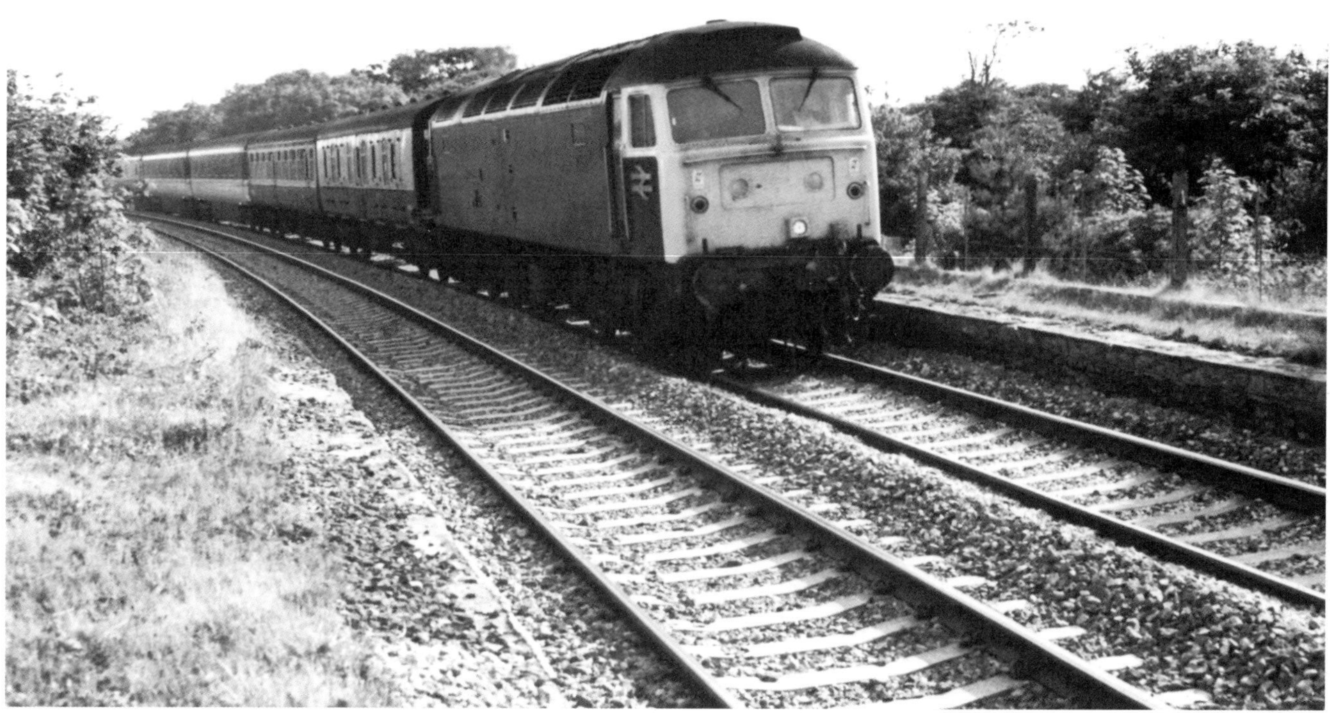

Celebrity loco, 47500 *'Great Western'* is seen here at Scorrier on 19 August 1989. Built in June 1966 by Brush, as D1943, it was repainted in GWR Brunswick Green and lined out. It survives in service with West Coast Railways. (GP)

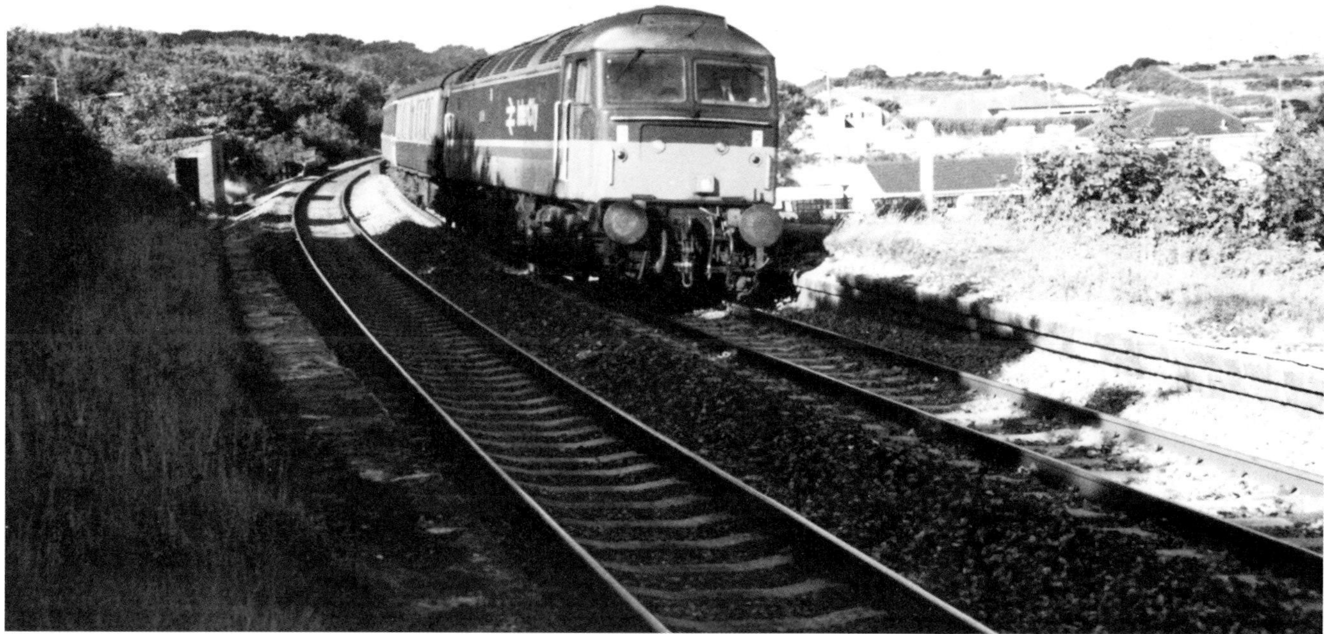

A Mainline liveried but unidentified class 47 is seen here passing the site of the former Scorrier Station, with an Up express on 19 August 1989. (GP)

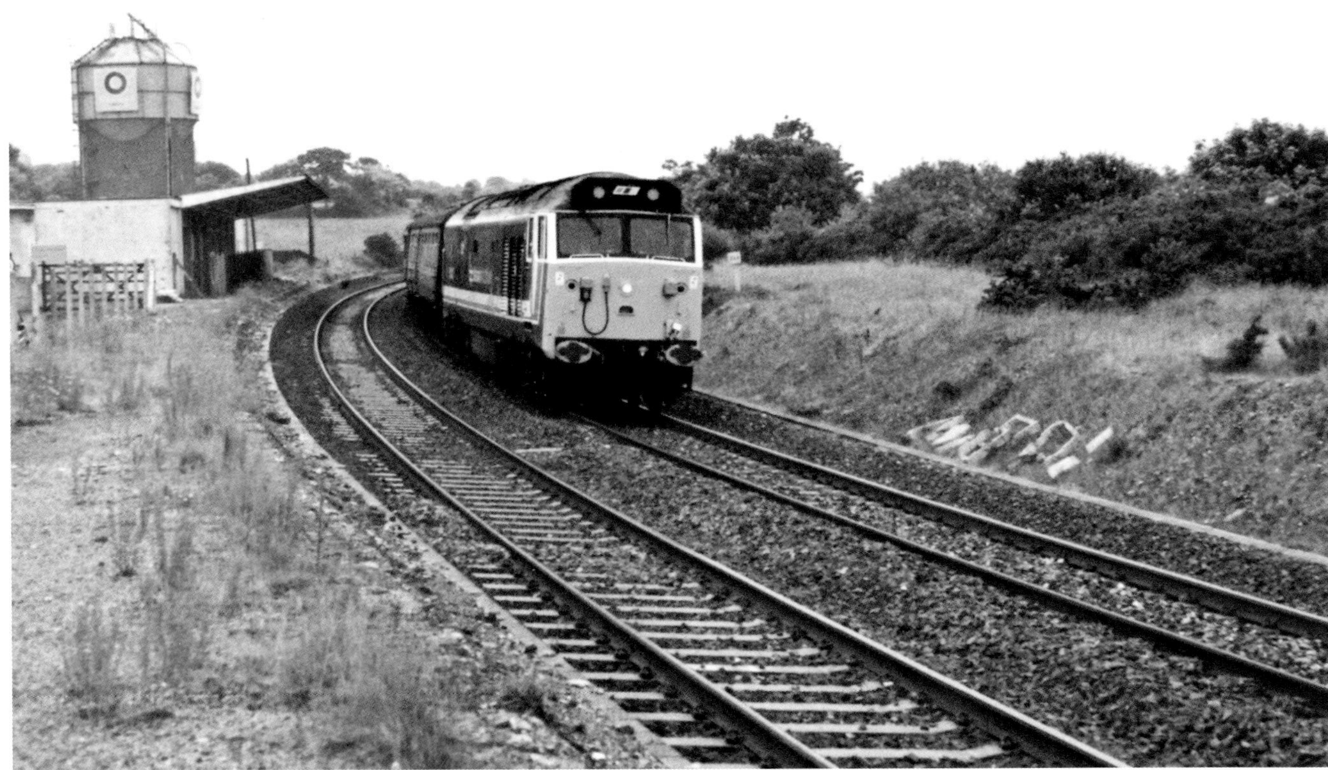

The old station at Chacewater is the location for this June 1989 picture of an unidentified class 50 in Network South East livery with an Up train. Chacewater was once a busy junction station where three tracks were laid westwards towards Blackwater (triangular) Junction. Here trains could turn right and take coastal route through St Agnes, Perranporth, and Shepards to Tolcarn Junction near Newquay. This route was also a useful diversionary route if there was a problem on the line between there and Par. The junction at Blackwater is still visible from the realigned A30 where it sliced through it. (GP)

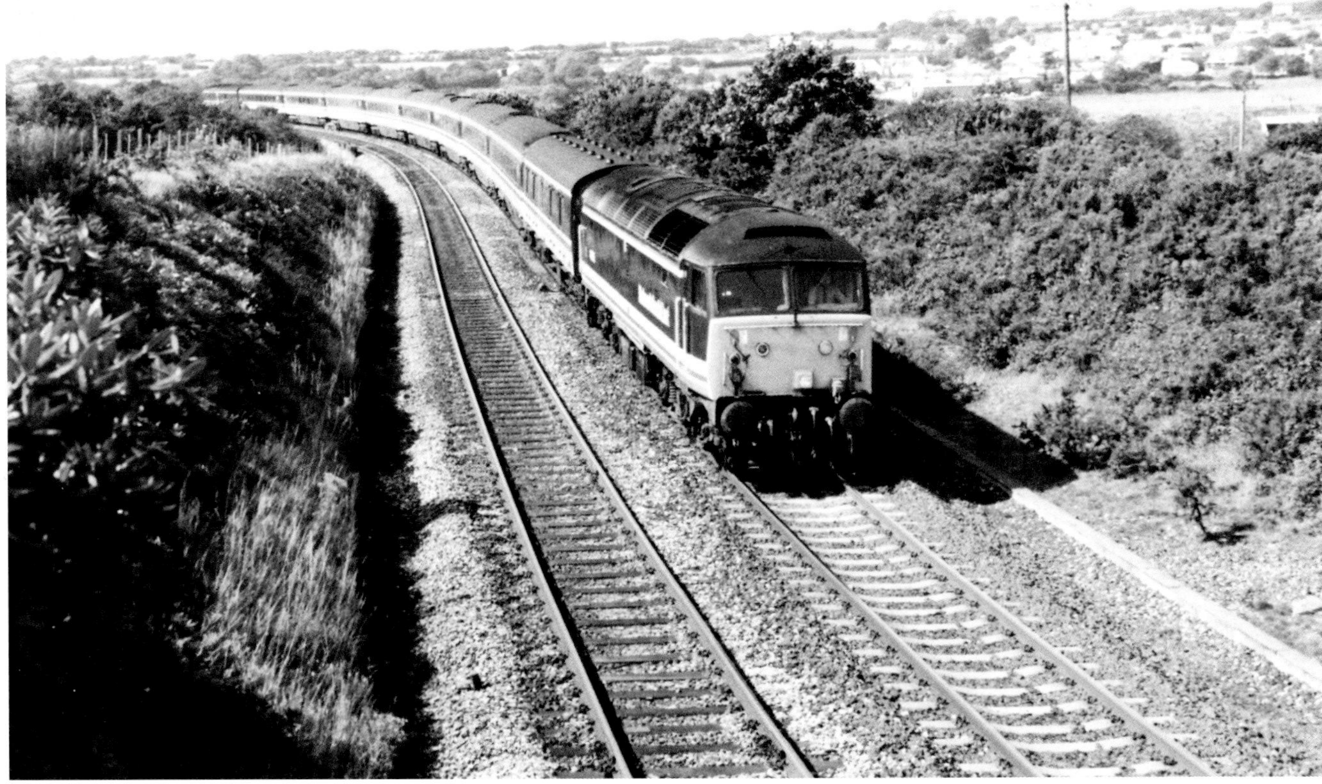

Chacewater in September 1991 sees an unidentified class 47 in Network South East livery, speeding along the Up line. (GP)

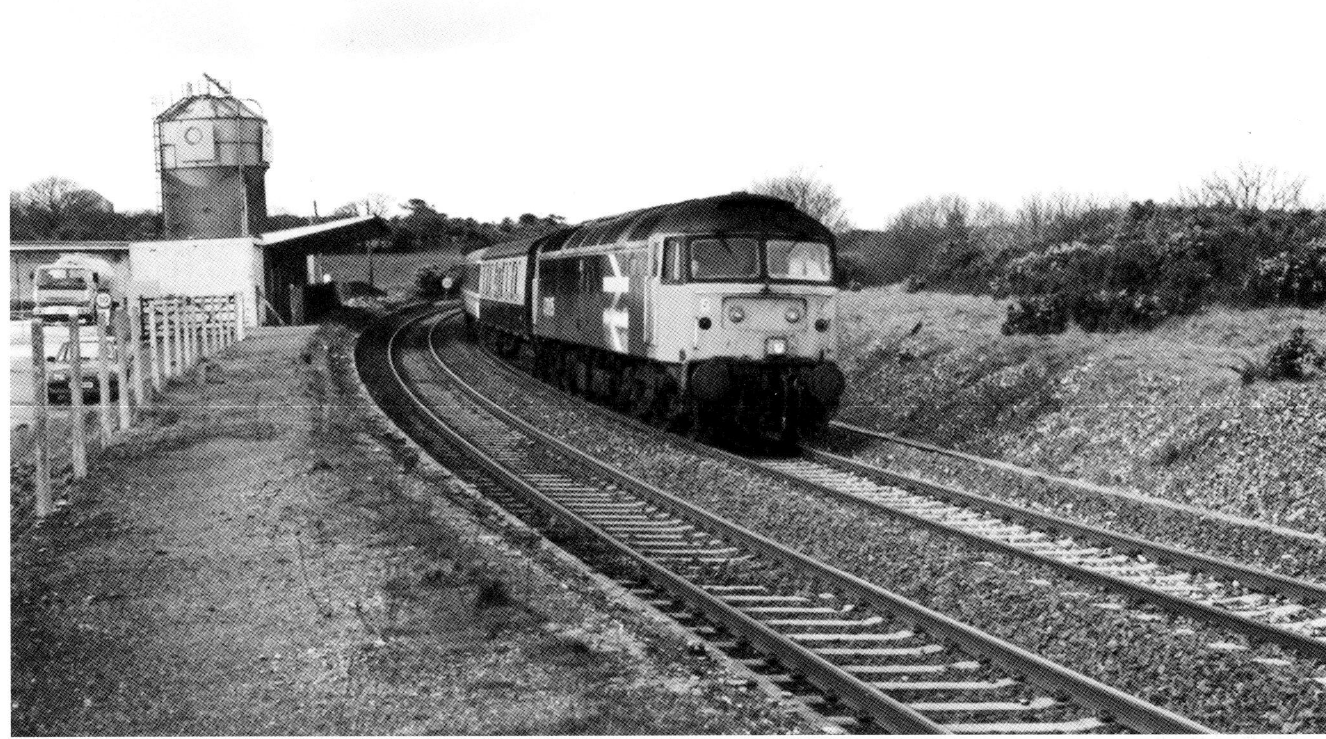

Large logo liveried 47815 is seen here passing Chacewater on the Up line in March 1990, with a semi-fast to Bristol. The Ground Frame giving access to the Down-side former milk sidings is still in place at this one busy junction for the Newquay line. Built by Brush as D1748 it was renumbered to 47155, and 47660, before receiving 47815. It is still in service and now carries the name *'Great Western'* which was lifted from 47500. (GP)

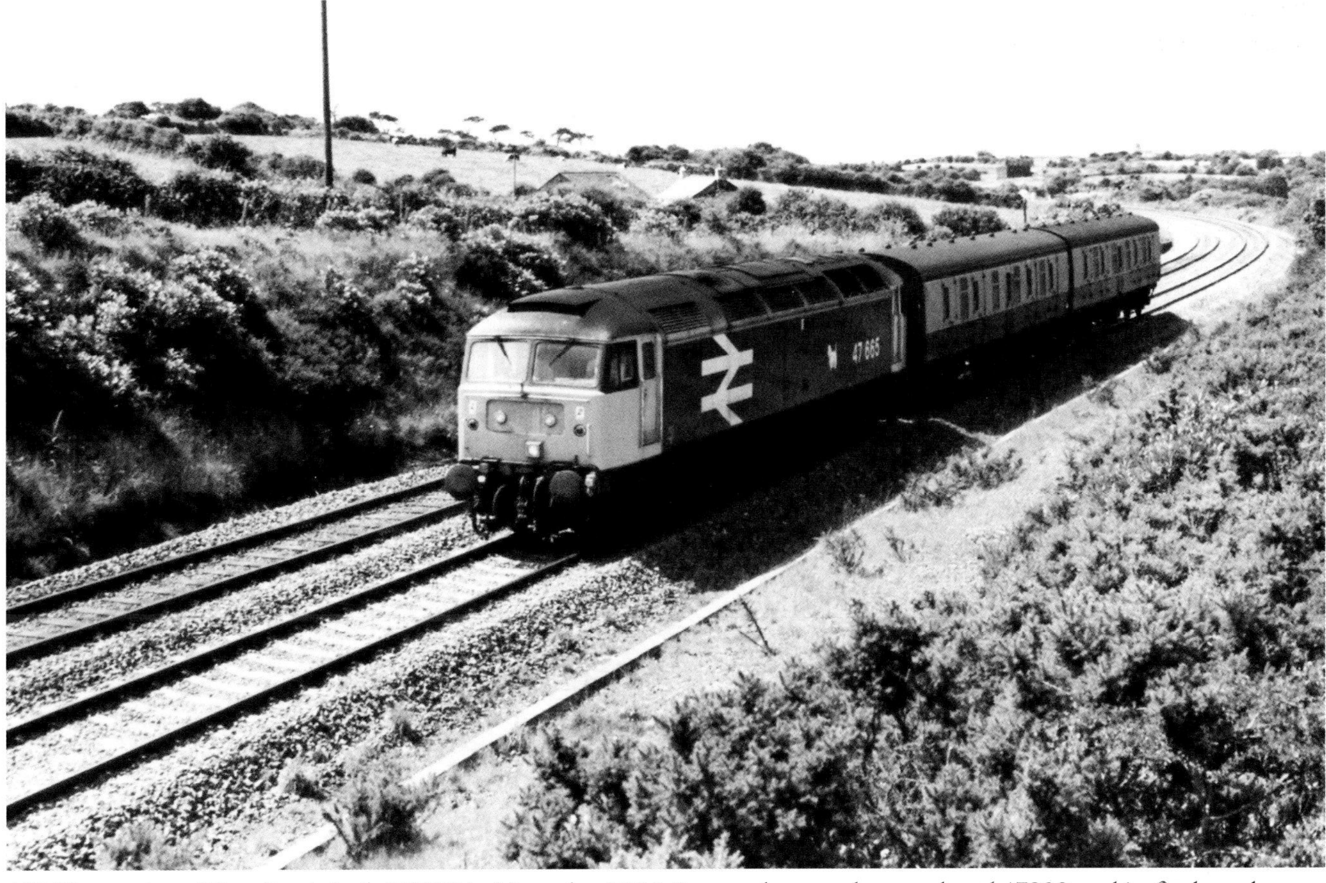

47665 started out life as Brush-built D1909 in November 1965. It was subsequently renumbered 47232, and its final number was 47820 in 1989. It is seen here approaching the site of the former Chacewater Station in July 1988. It is privately preserved at Kirkby Stephen. (GP)

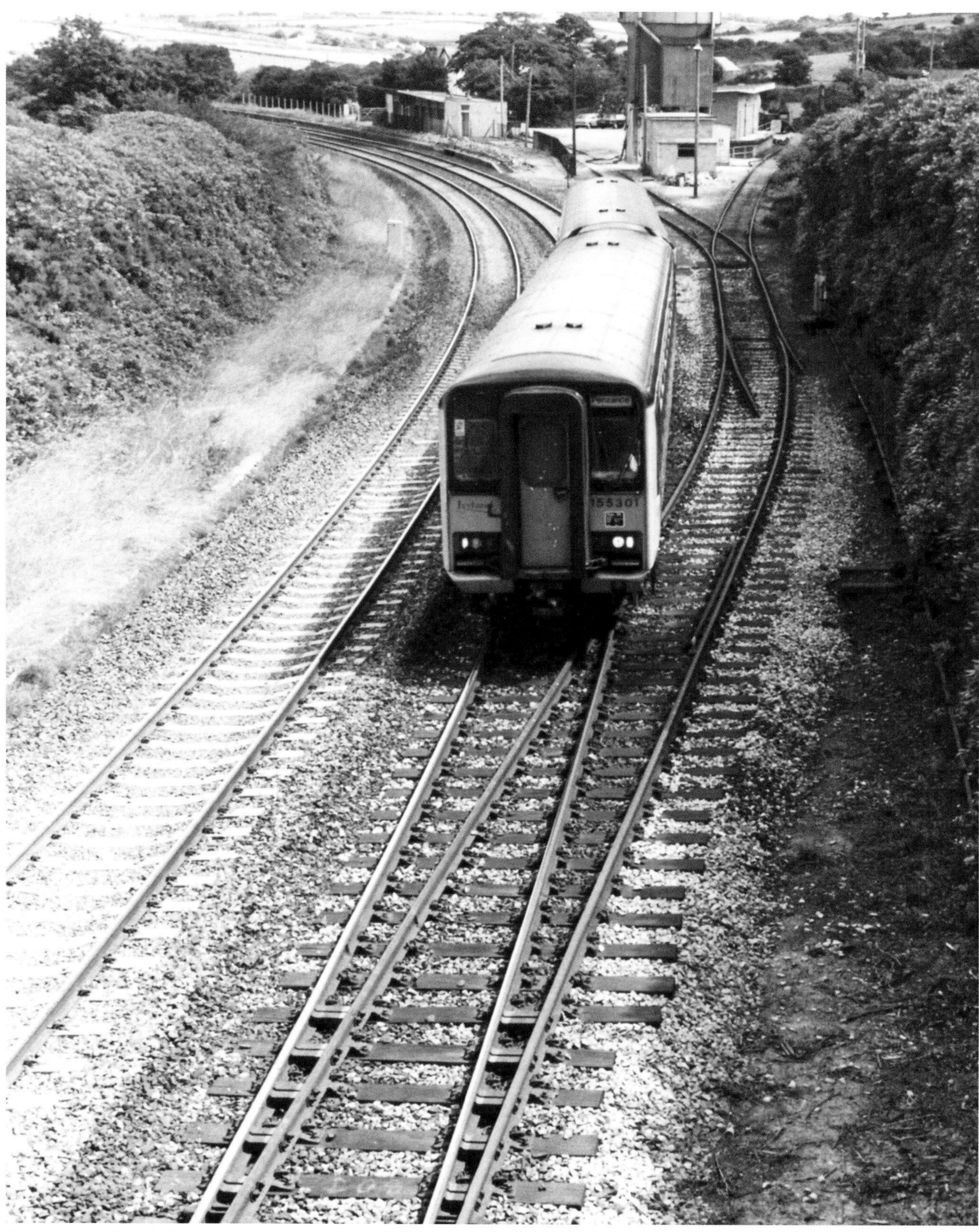

Sprinter number 155301 is almost new when seen here passing Chacewater old station on the Down line in July 1988, with a local train for Penzance. The sidings and ground-frame is still in situ, giving access to the businesses still in the station yard. The Ground frame was removed in the early 1990s, but the disconnected controls remained in Truro signalbox until relatively recently. Of particular note is the 'Leyland' logo on the front of the unit and the fact that this is numerically, the first of the 155s. It became 153301 and 153351 when subsequently rebuilt as 'Bubble Cars'. (GP)

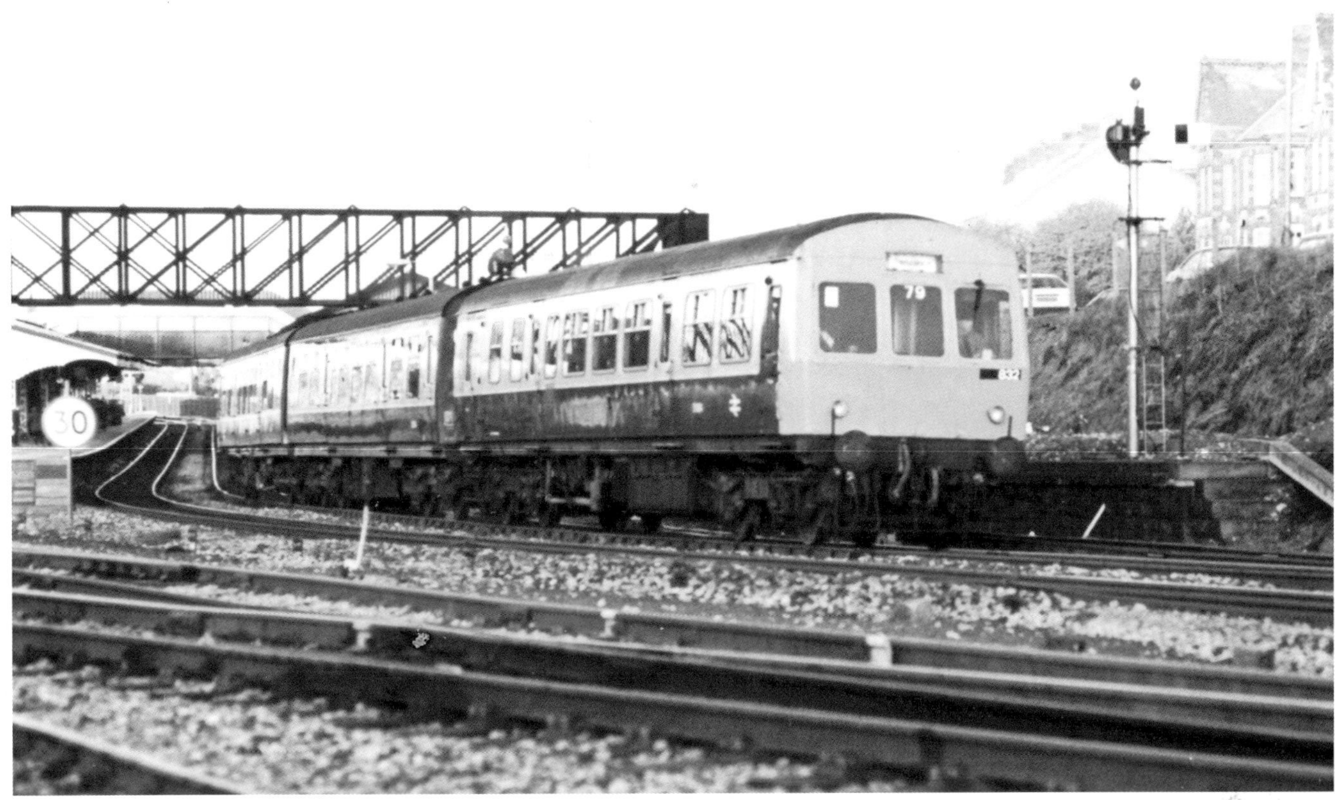

In Summer 1990 we see another highbred unit departing Truro on the Down line. This unit appears to be two parts of a class 108 and a class 101 power car leading. (MD)

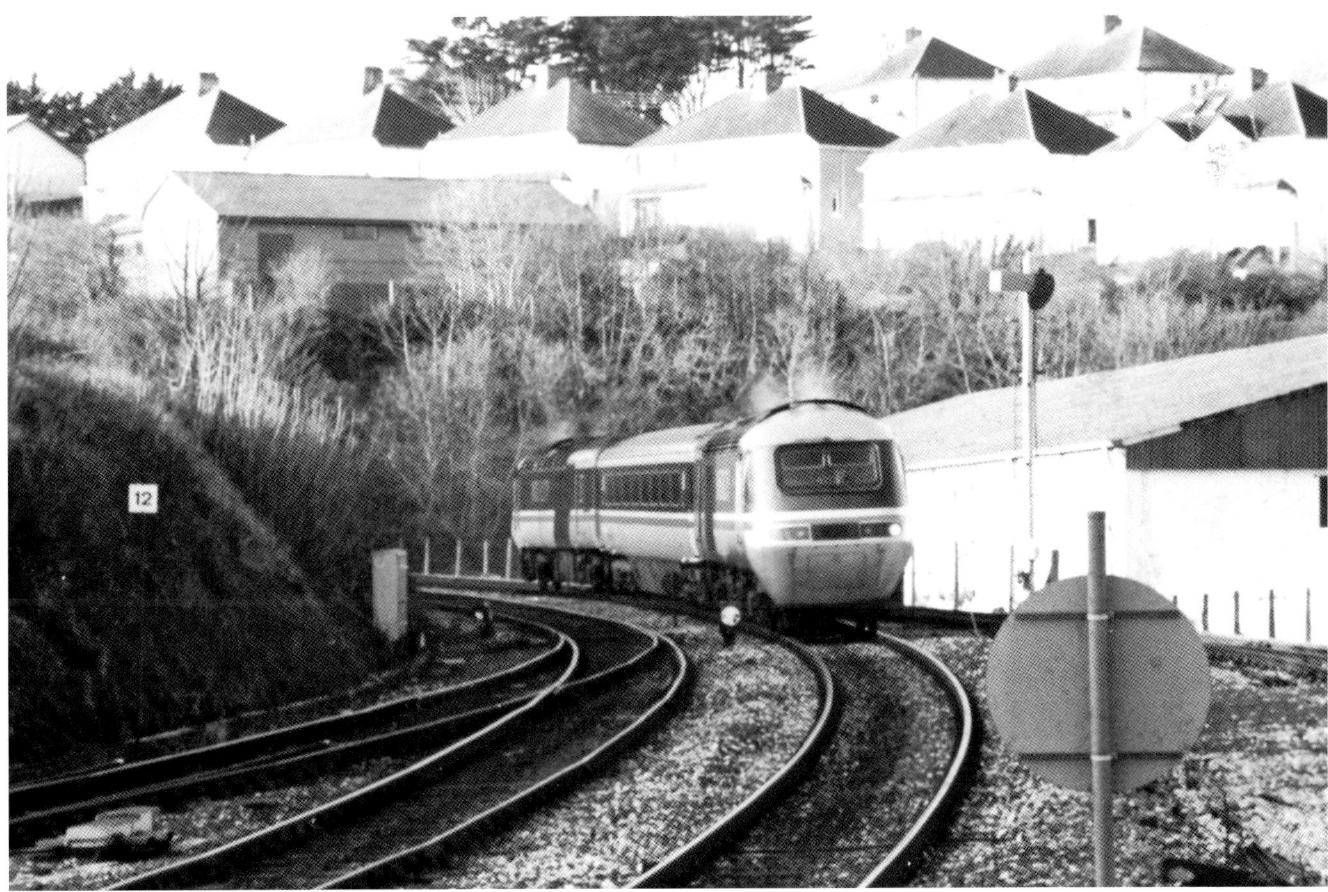

A fun-sized HST is seen here approaching Truro on the Up line on 12 January 1993 whilst enroute to Laira Depot from Long Rock Depot. In those days HST power cars were always moved with a barrier coach in between. (MD)

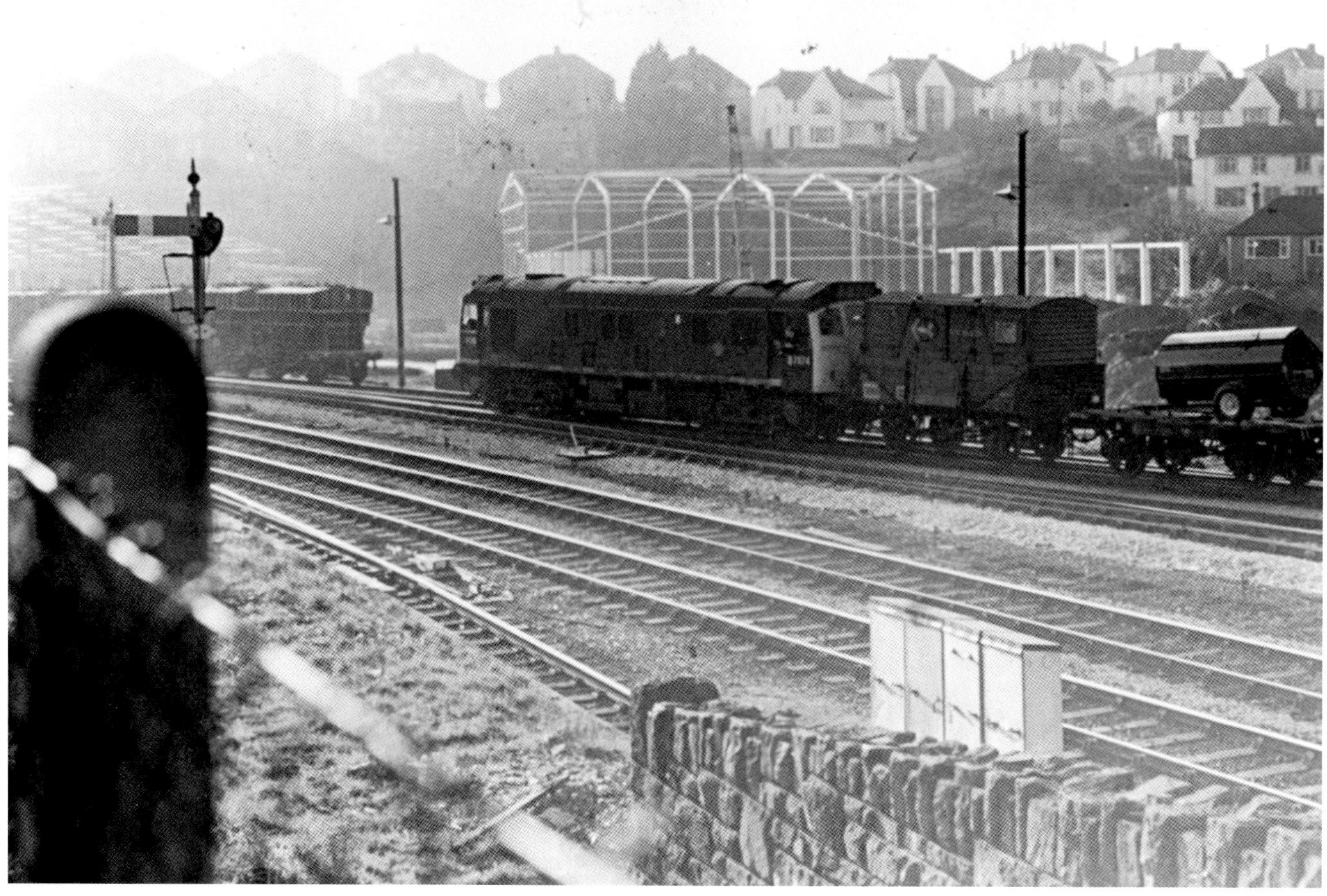

This interesting photo dates from circa 1973 and shows D7574 shunting a train at Truro Yard, which had originated from Holman's on the Roskear Branch. The class of loco were reclassified 25 and thus became 25224 in February 1974. It was built by BR at Darlington Works in October 1963. It was scrapped by Vic Berry of Leicester in March 1987 after being withdrawn the previous May. It was originally withdrawn in January 1983, but reinstated in the March. (PM)*

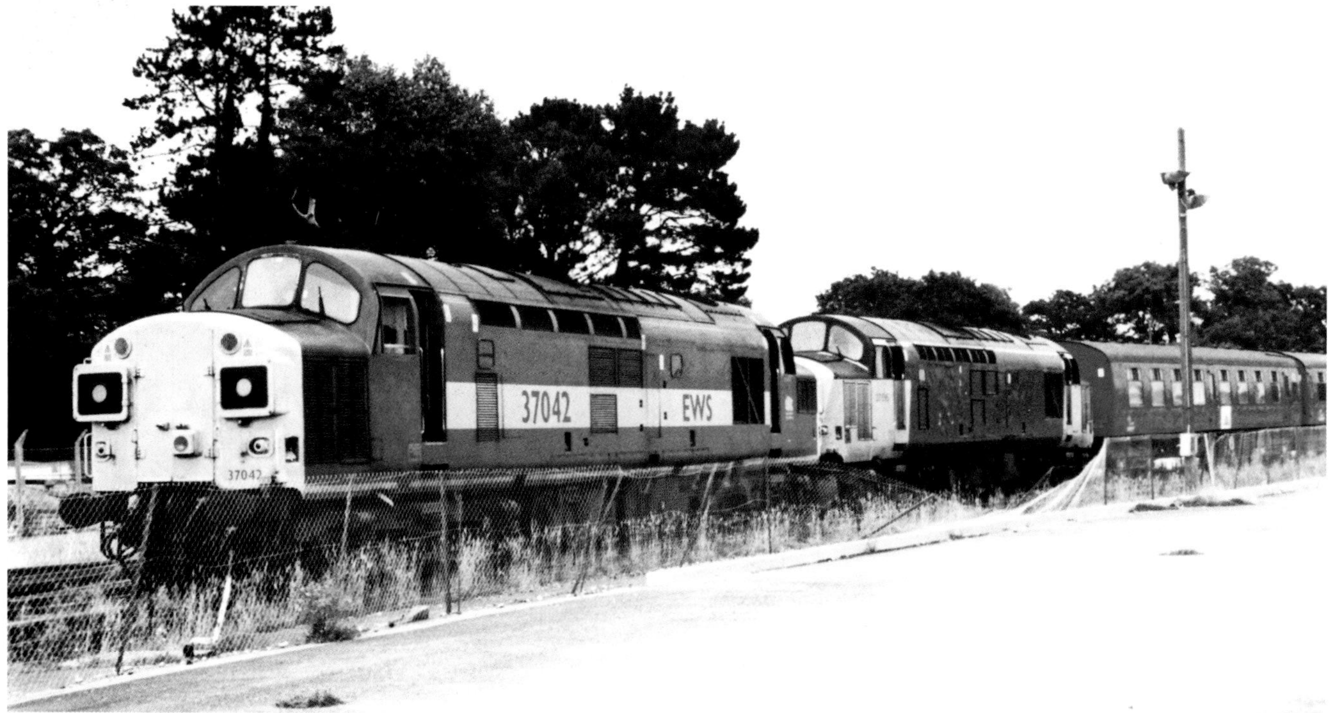

The Weed Killing Train (7Z07 Truro – Exeter via Newquay) visited Cornwall on 11 August 2000, and is seen here in Truro Yard with 37042 and 37516 in charge. Both are English Electric products dating from June and December 1962 respectively. Vulcan and Robert Stephenson & Hawthorns were the two works and both survive. 37042 was originally D6742 and is now on the Eden Valley Railway, 37516 was built as D6786, then 37086 and now works for the West Coast Railway Company. (MD)

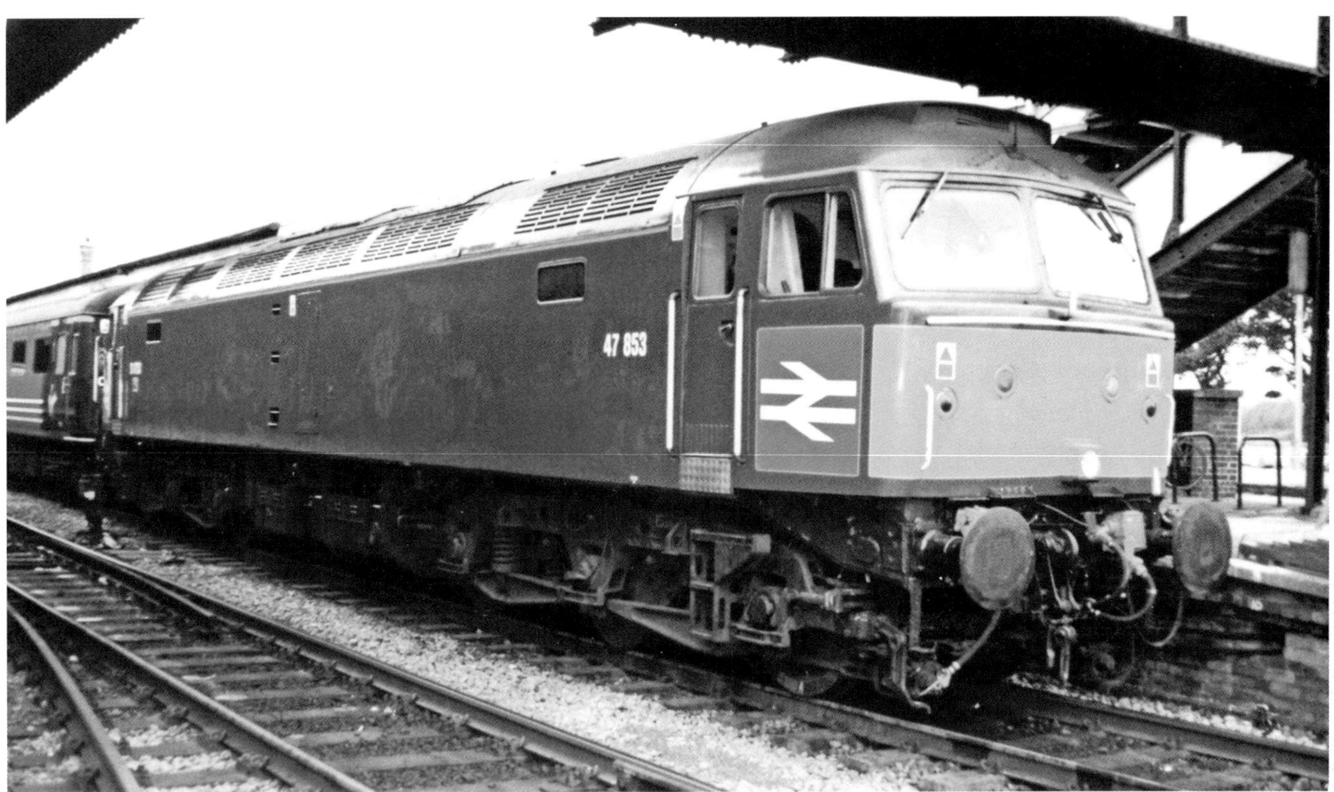

The Up platform at Truro finds 47853 on 6 March 2002 with 1M56, the 0846 Penzance to Manchester Piccadilly train. This loco is still carrying this experimental livery of XP64 Blue with red cab-sides and its original number of D1733. Built in June 1964 by Brush, it was renumbered to 47141 then 47614 and is still in service with DRS at Crewe. (MD)

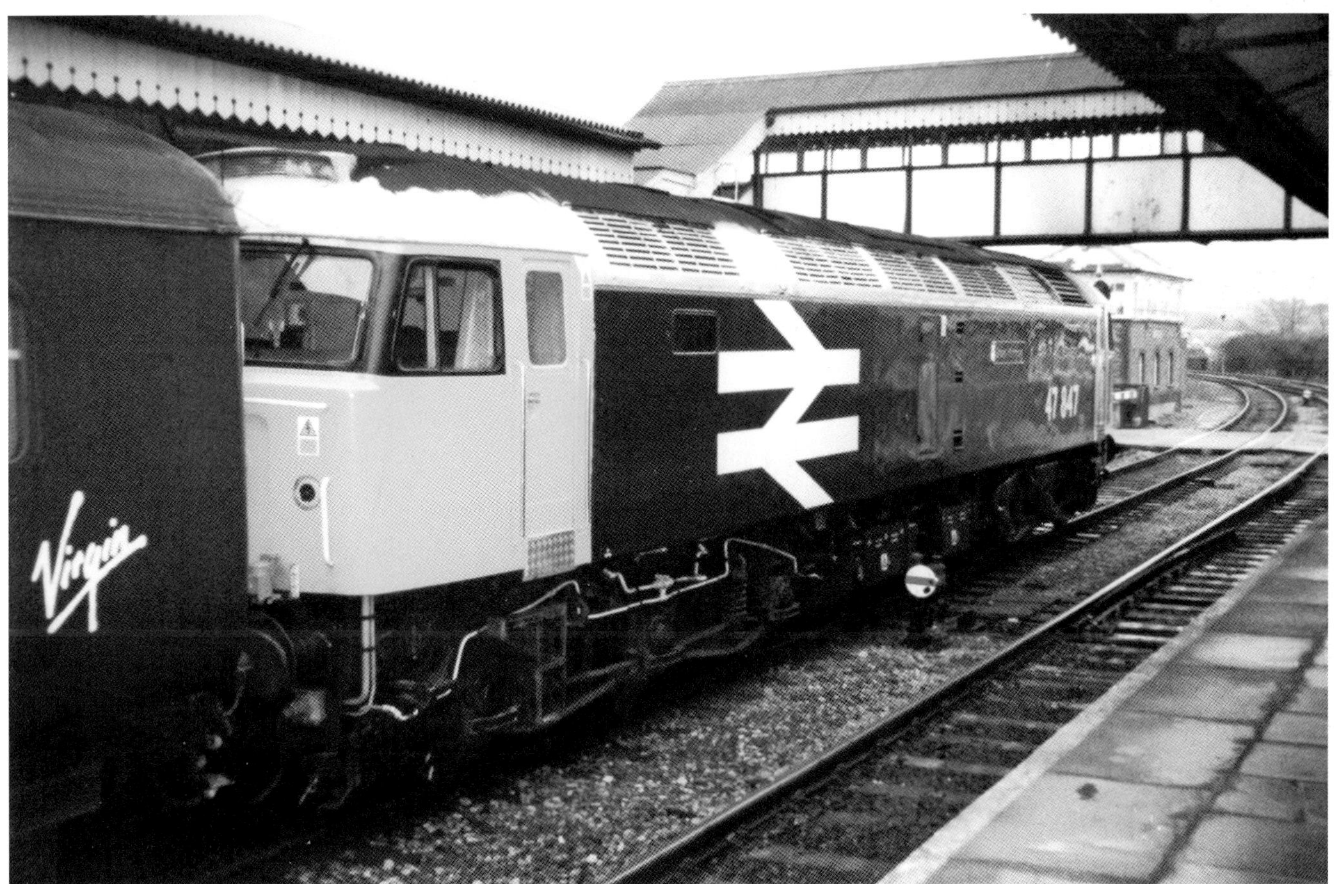

The large logo livery of British Rail was without doubt one of the best they ever designed. Here 1M56 is in the Up platform at Truro with 47847 in charge on 14 January 2002. Built by Brush in September 1964 it carried the name *'Benjamin Gimbert GC'* until May 1987, and two other numbers, 47179 and 47577. It is still in service with Riviera Trains at Eastleigh. (MD)

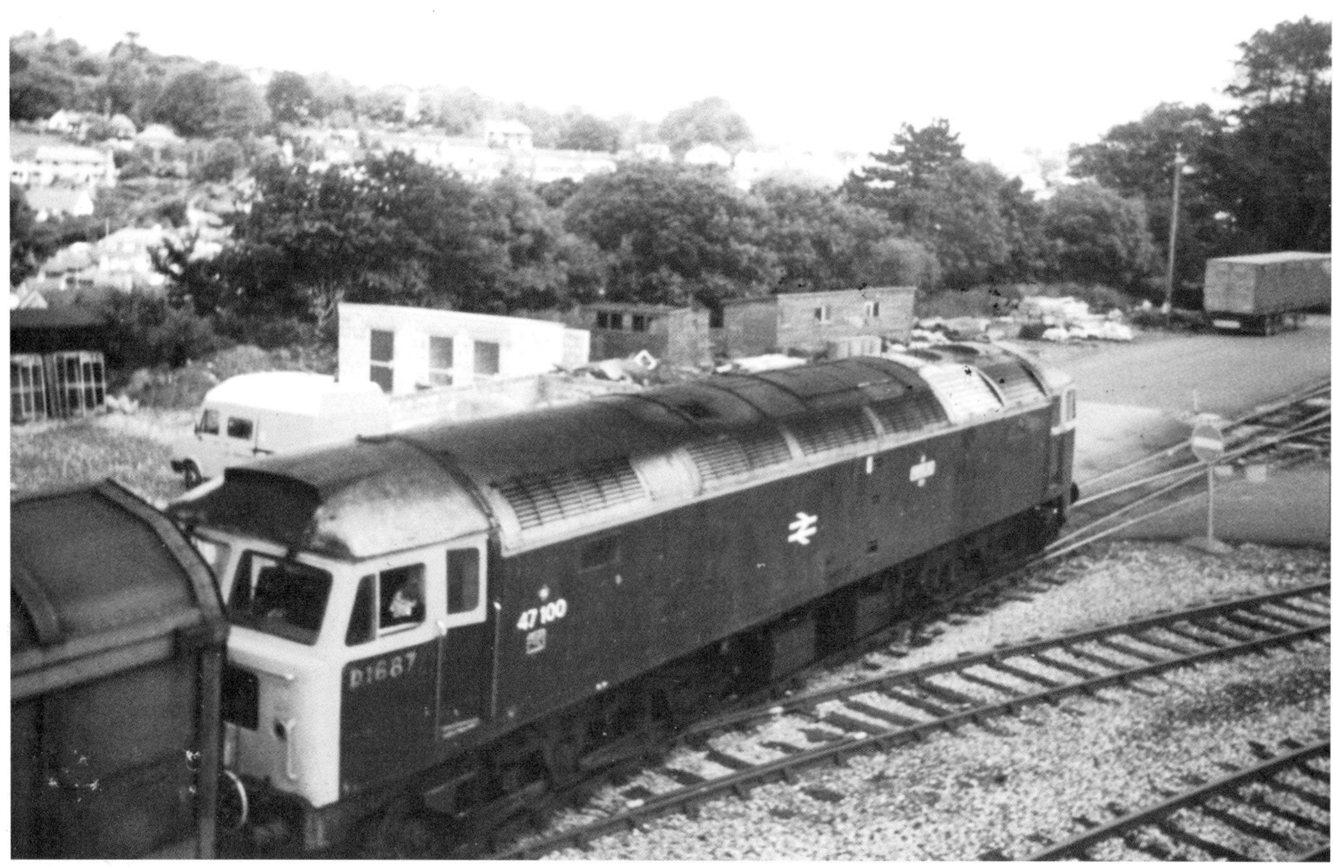

The Ince & Elton UKF Fertiliser Train (6M22) is backing out of Truro Yard with 47100 in June 1991. Built by Brush in November 1963 as D1687 it was withdrawn in one month after this picture was taken and cut up by C.F. Booth in February 1994. (MD)

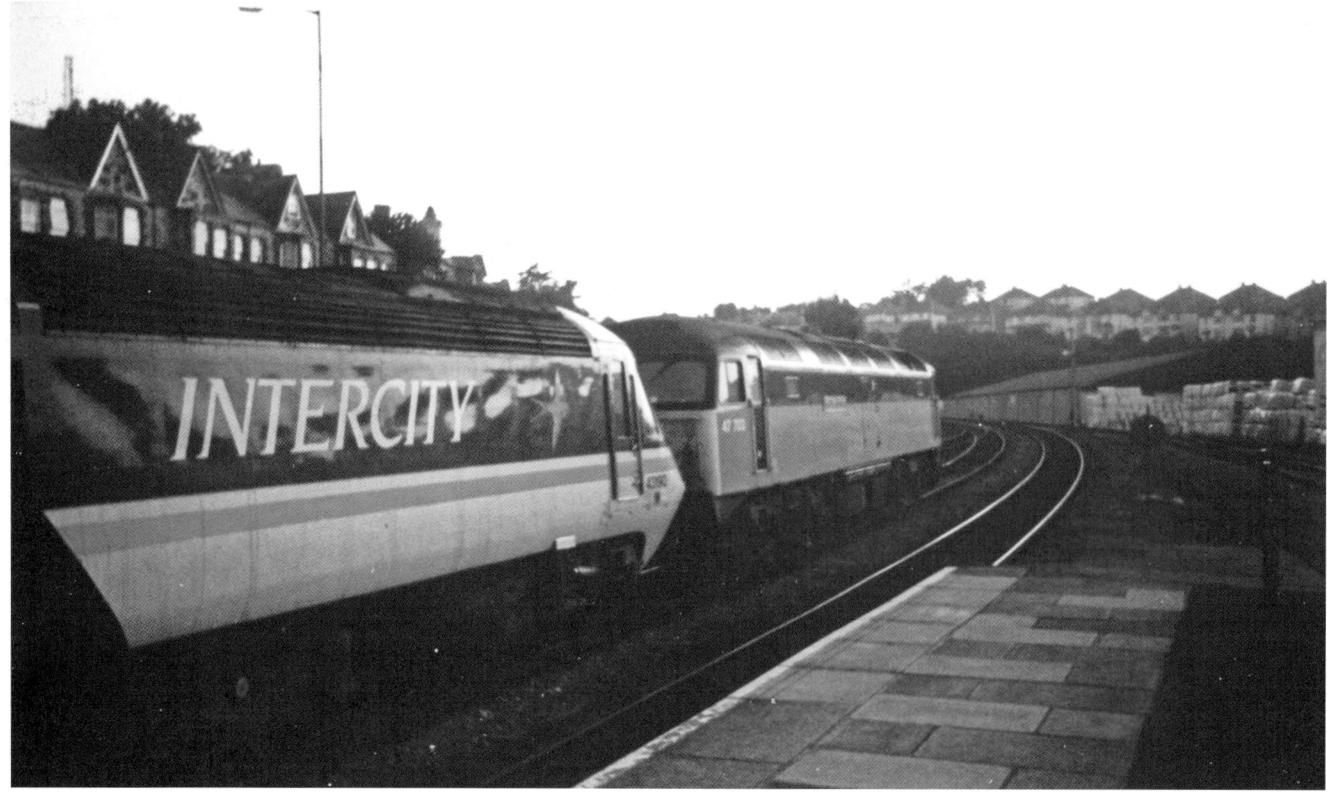

Pictures of HSTs being rescued by any locomotive are rare these days since the majority have been re-engined and their noisy, dirty, Paxman Valenta engines have been consigned to the scrapyard. The picture of the Cross-Country Intercity in the Down Platform at Truro dates from August 1991. 47703 *'The Queen Mother'* dates from July 1967, a product of Brush, as D1960, but later carried 47514 and a remarkable five names, this one being from March 1991 to March 1995. It is preserved on the Wensleydale Railway after being withdrawn in December 2007. 43190 is still in service with First Group. (MD)

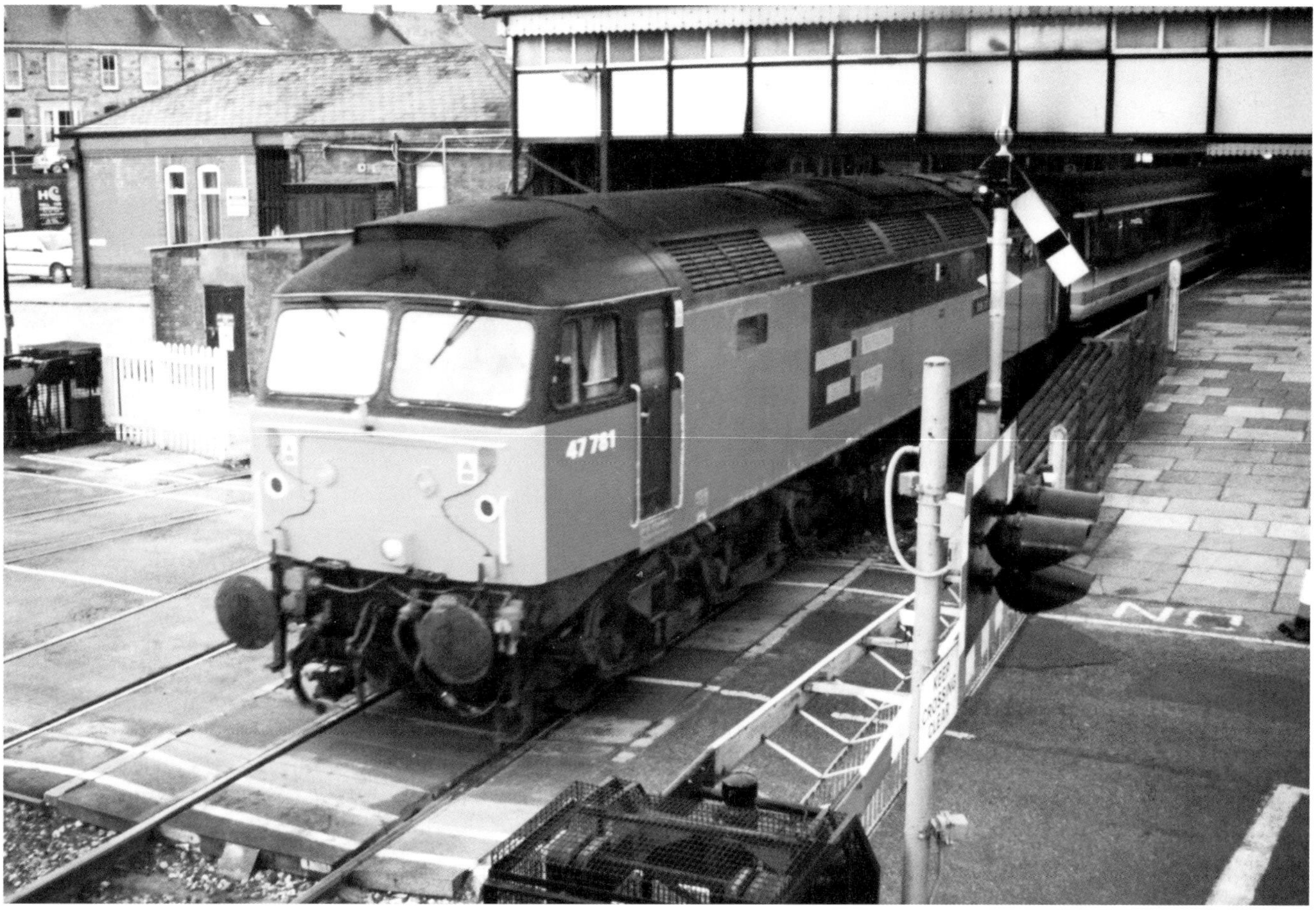

On 18 January 2002, the 0820 Penzance to Paddington (1A45) was hauled away from Truro by a borrowed Res loco, number 47781 *'Isle of Iona'*. Formerly *'Samson'* and D1674, 47088, 47653 (twice) and 47808, it was built by BR at Crewe in May 1965 and was withdrawn in September 2003 and cut up in April 2007. (MD)

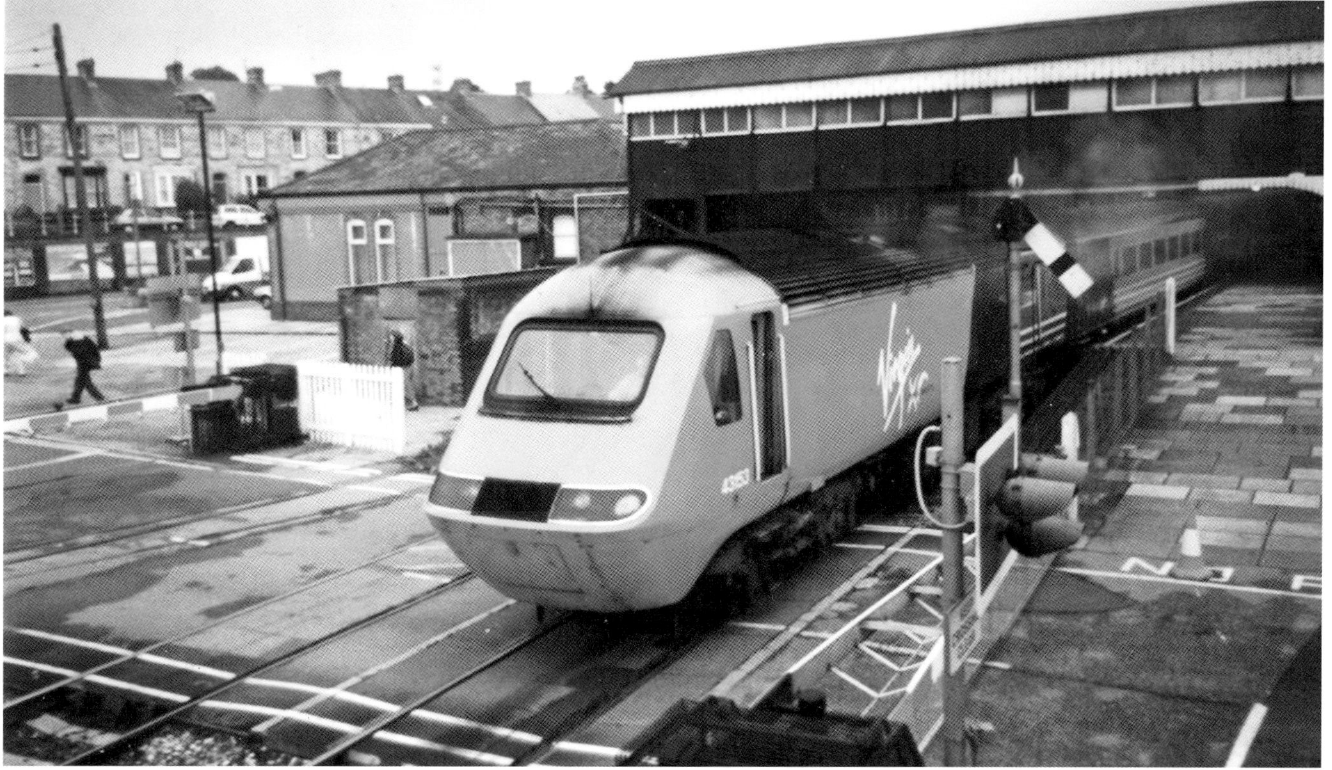

The Penzance to Edinburgh Virgin Cross-Country service is seen here pulling away from Truro in summer 1997 with HST power car 43153 leading. Built in January 1981 by BREL at Crewe, it went on to serve First Great Western after Virgin lost the franchise and is owned and operated by them in 2013. (MD)

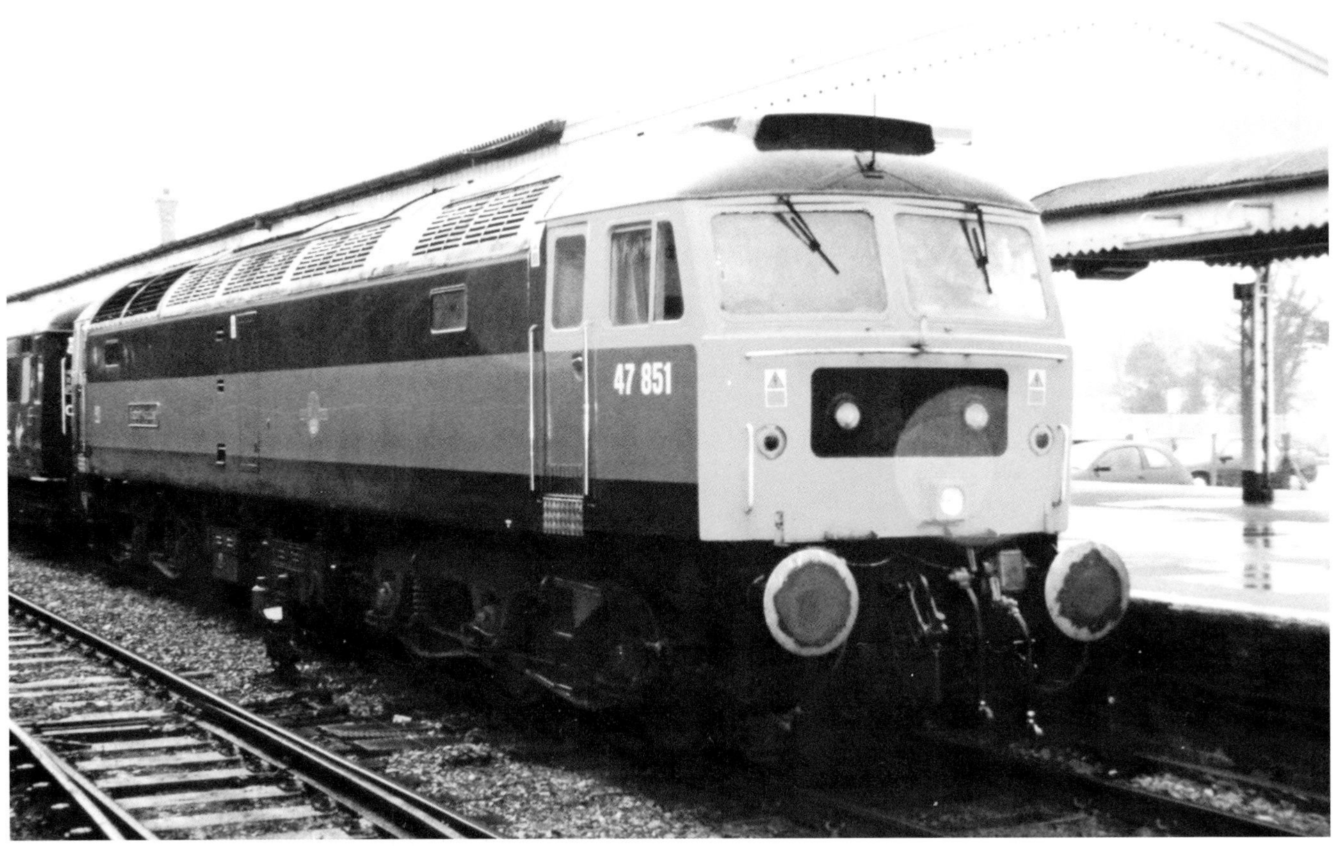

In Truro Up platform on 19 March 2002, we find 47851 in original style of livery as applied by Virgin Cross-Country. Built by BR Crewe in January 1965 as D1648, it went on to become 47064 and 47639 and is still in service with West Coast Railways at Carnforth. (MD)

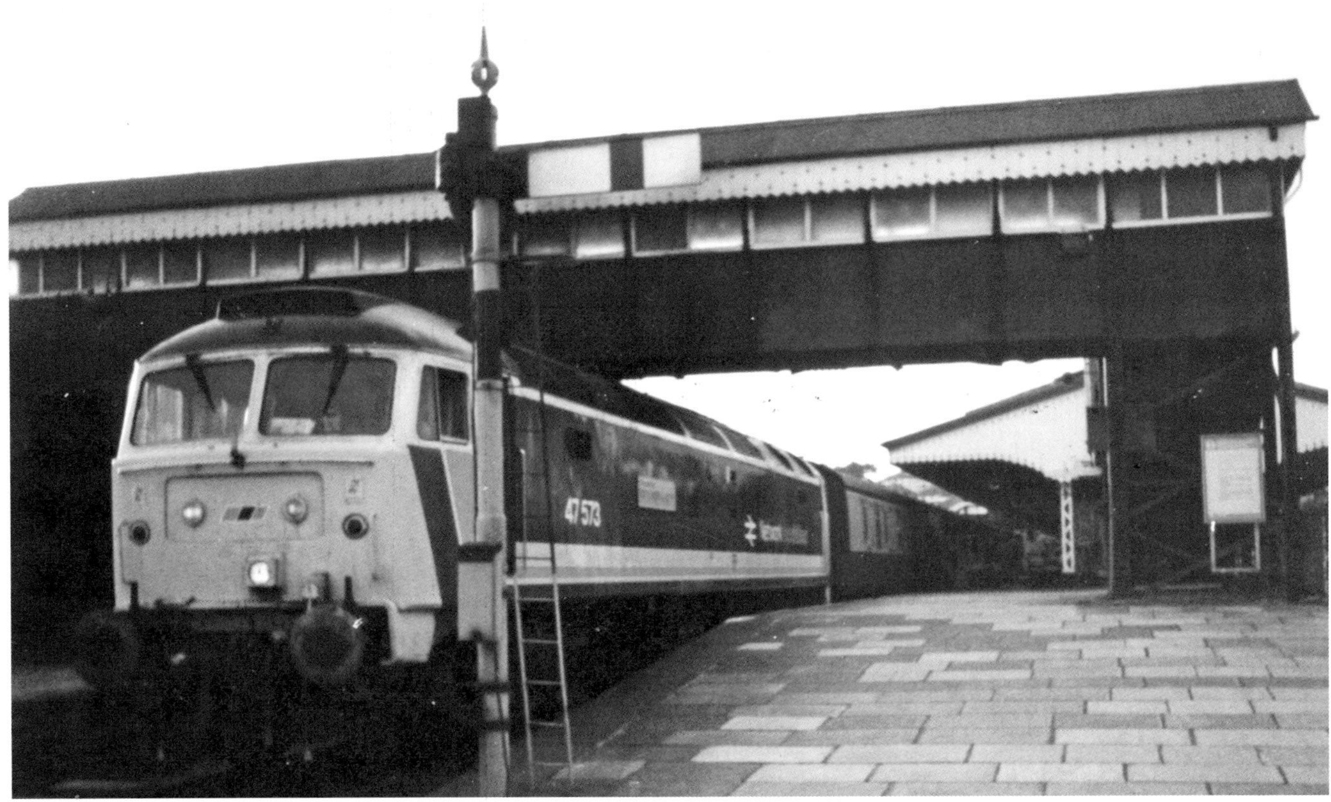

Network-South-East liveried 47573 *'London Standard'* on the 1348 Penzance to Bristol Temple Meads Postal Train on 17 December 1989. It is awaiting 'the road' at Truro, which will be given after all the mail bags are loaded. In January 1994 it was repainted into Res livery and renumbered in the Res series as 47762. Built by Brush in October 1964 as D1768, it became 47173 and was withdrawn in May 2001 and stored until cut up in June 2005 by C.F. booth. (MD)

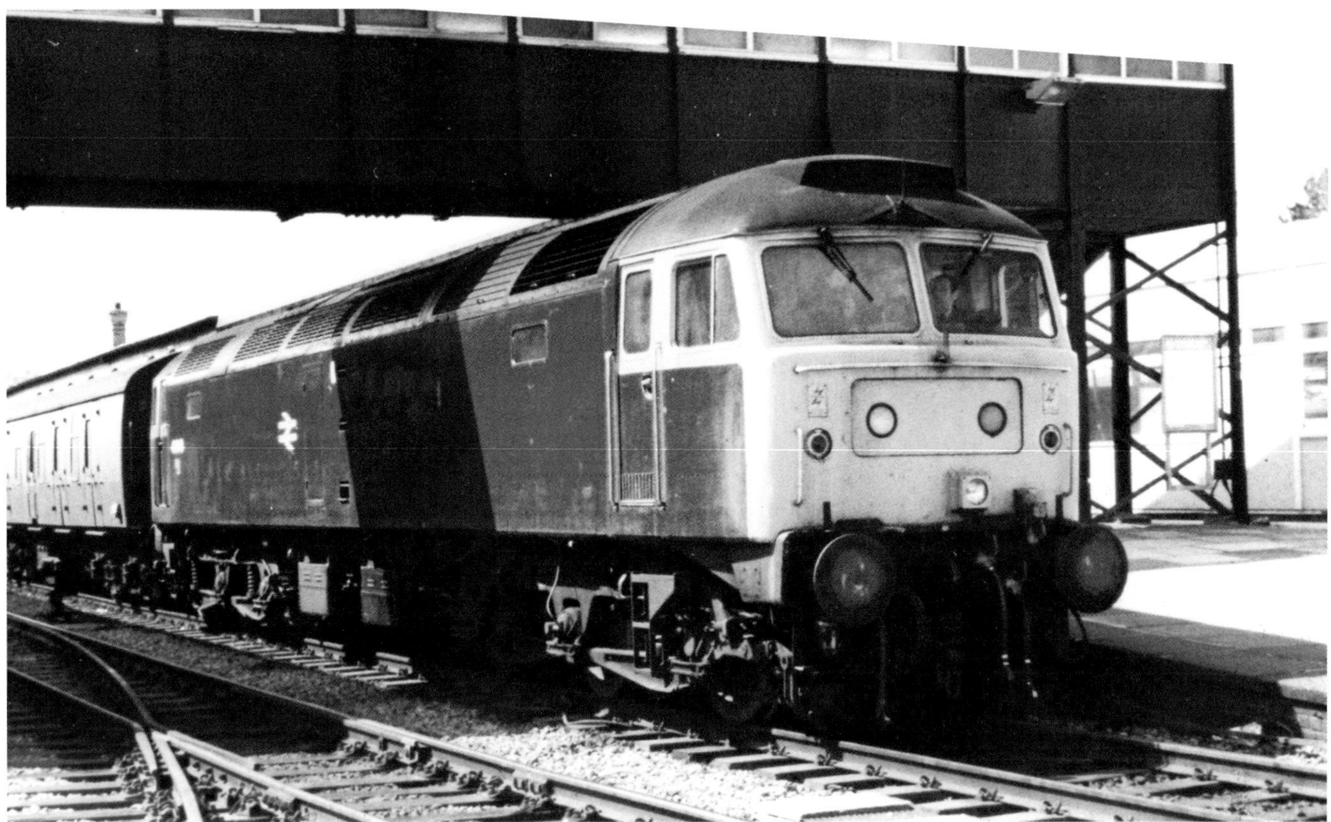

Blue 47543 at Truro on the up line on 29 April 1989. In the foreground can be seen the points leading to the Down Yard sidings, which were left in even after the sidings were fenced in and covered over by Vospers Cars. In the middle of Vospers yard were two ground disc signals numbered 30 and 31. During the 1990s a signal at Liskeard was damaged during engineering work and it was these signals that were then recovered to replace the Liskeard one, after having several cars moved first! 47543 was built by BR at Crewe, as D1588 in May 1964, it was subsequently renumbered 47023. Cut up in April 1998 by C.F. Booth of Rotherham. (GP)

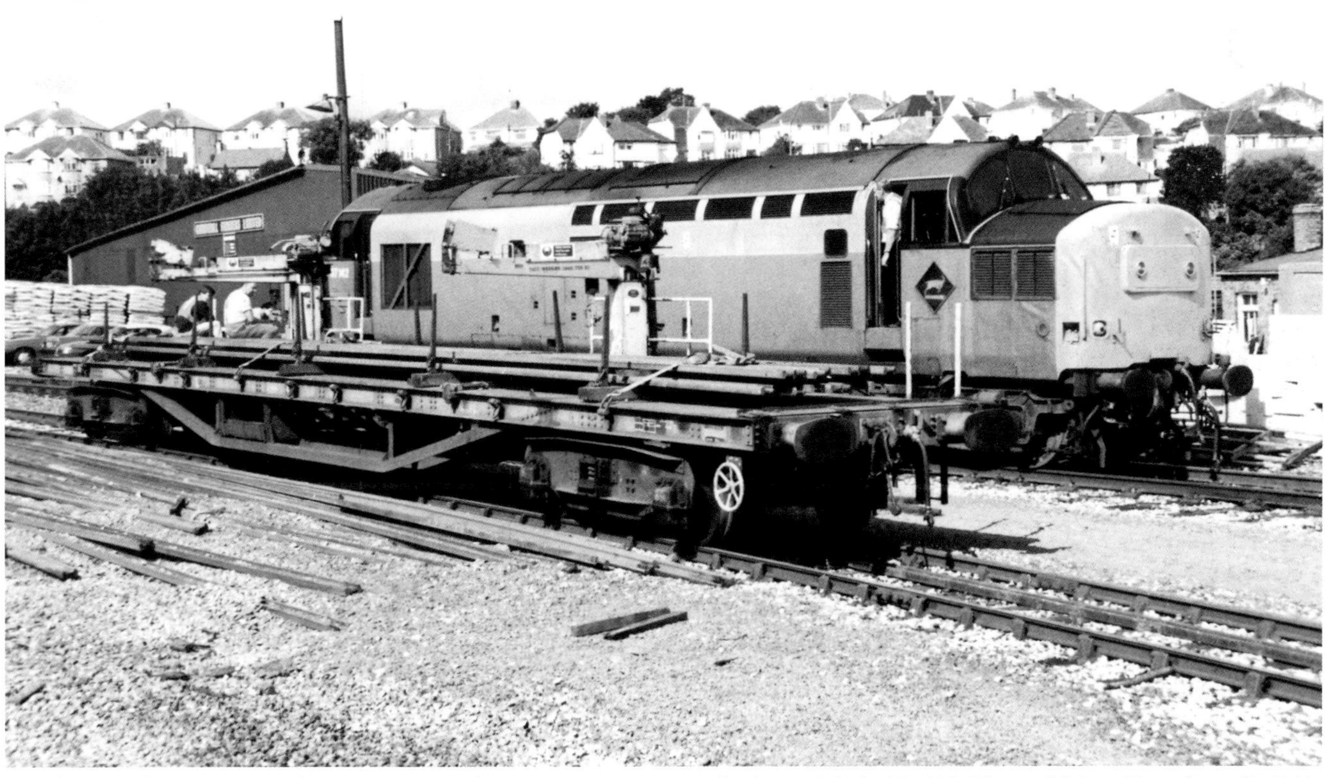

Dutch liveried 37142 is seen here in Truro Yard in August 1992. It was built in 1963 by English Electric Vulcan Foundry as D6842. It survives on the Bodmin & Wenford Railway. (GP)

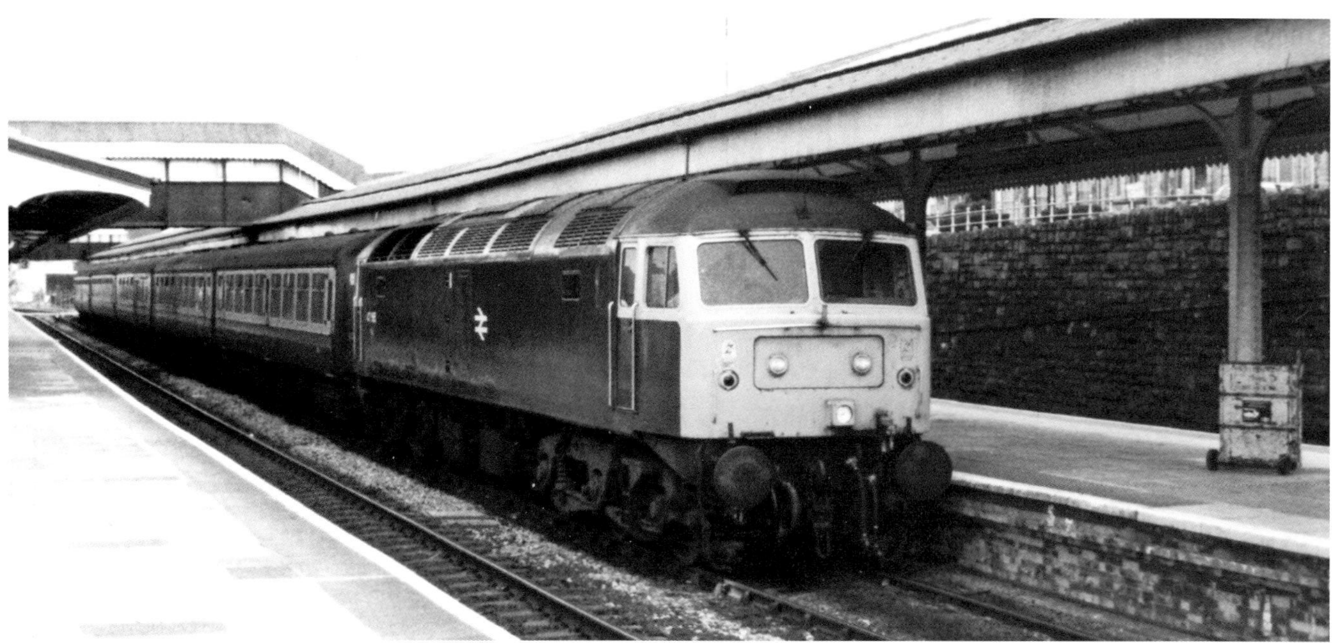

Class 47 number 47565 stands in Truro Down platform in August 1983. Built in September 1964 as D1620 it was renumbered to 47039 under the TOPS scheme. Cut up in Feb 2004 by C. F. Booth of Rotherham. (GP)

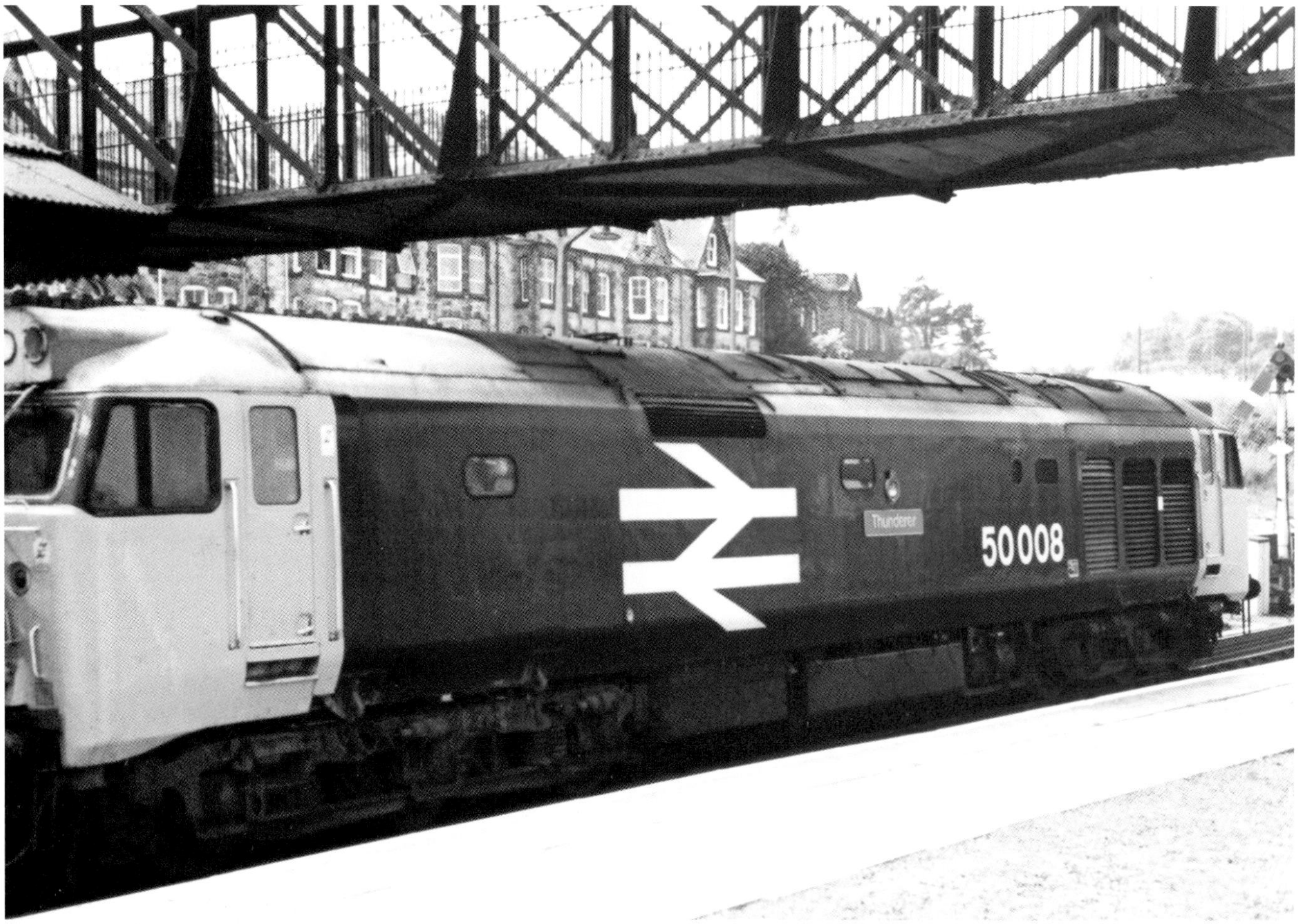

Large logo liveried Class 50 number 50008 *'Thunderer'* stands on the Down at Truro on a fast train for Penzance in August 1983. Built by English Electric in 1968 as D408, it was one of just 50 class 50s built for the West Coast main line but subsequently, they were all transferred to the 'Western' though frequently worked on the South-Western line to Waterloo. The interesting fact concerning these locos was that they were direct descendants of a 1962 built experimental loco numbered DP2, which looked like one of the Deltic class and shared many components. DP2 suffered a serious accident as was withdrawn in 1967 and cut up in 1968. I saw it just once when travelling through London. 50008 is preserved privately. (GP)

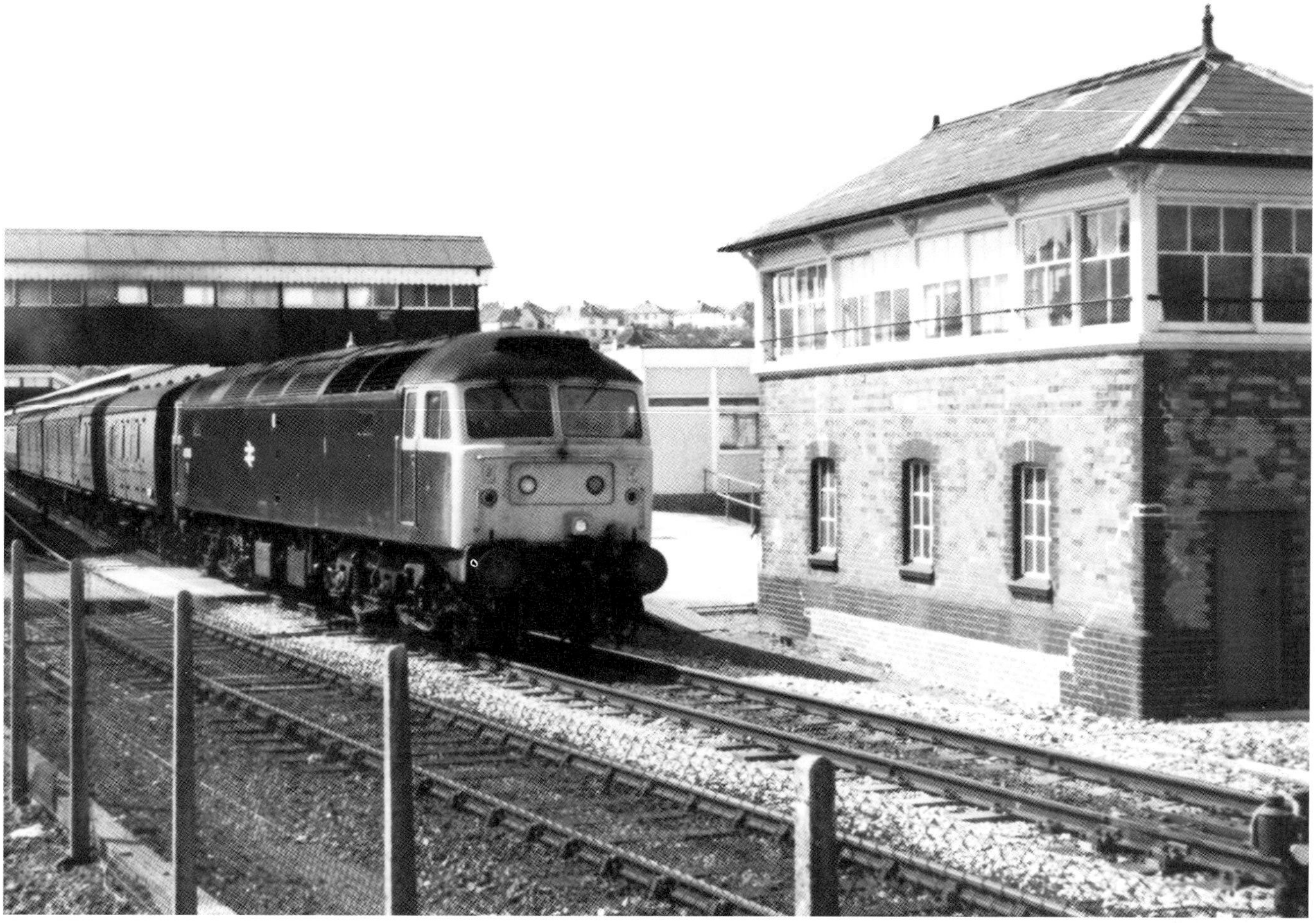

Blue liveried 47543 is seen again, departing Truro past the former (East) signalbox on the Up line in April 1989 on a van train. (GP)

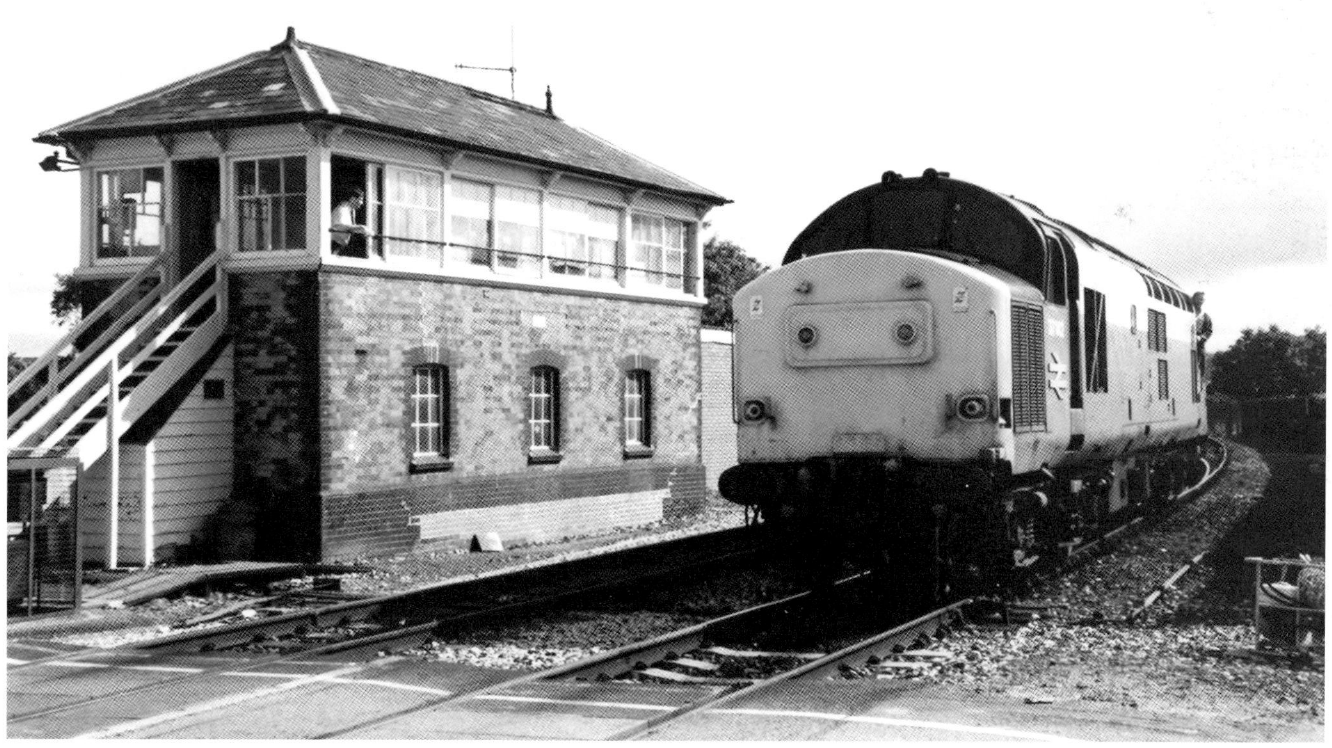

Another picture of 37142, this time standing on the Down line at Truro whilst running round its train in August 1992. The signalman is a very young Dave King, who is still a Relief Signaller in Cornwall in 2013. (GP)

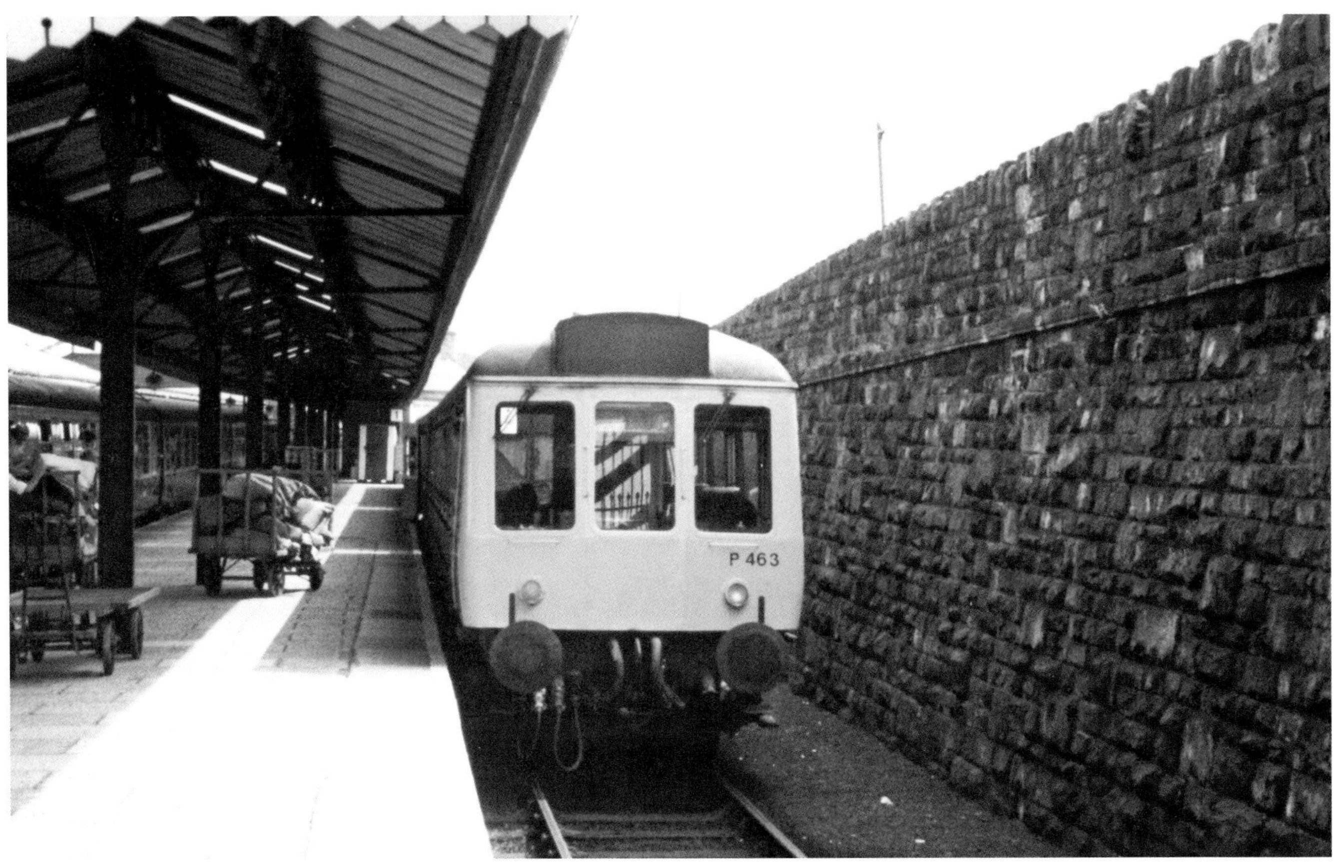

The Bay platform at Truro is still the departure point for trains to Falmouth, although since 2010 all platforms are signalled for trains to depart from but only the Up and Bay platforms are signalled for arrivals from Falmouth. This first generation DMU is seen in company with a Down express that is being unloaded with mail bags and parcels. Truro is now even busier than when this picture was taken in August 1983. (GP)

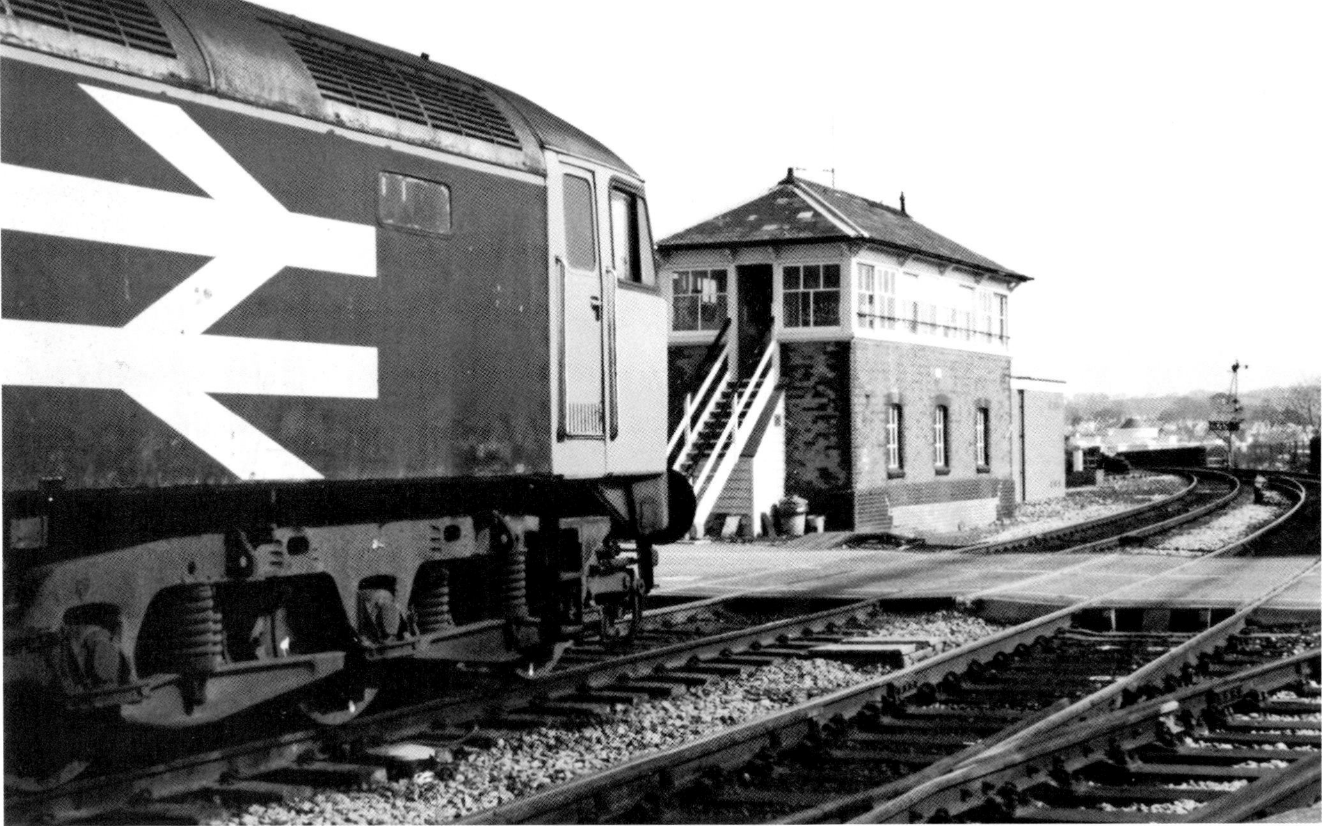

A nice study of the good looking Large-Logo livery on a class 47 in the Up Platform at Truro in March 1990, with the signalbox in view on the opposite side of the level crossing. (GP)

CHAPTER 2

TRURO to PAR

I HAVE SEPARATED this part of the main line as an individual chapter because, as from 2004 it was redoubled at some considerable expense, so as to remove the single-line section from Probus to Burngullow, which had become an ever increasing operational bottleneck since the years when the double line was removed to save the cost of repairing, replacing and maintaining it. It was a short-sighted economy and the saving was negligible compared to the enormous cost of putting it back. All the photographs cover the period when the single line was still in situ.

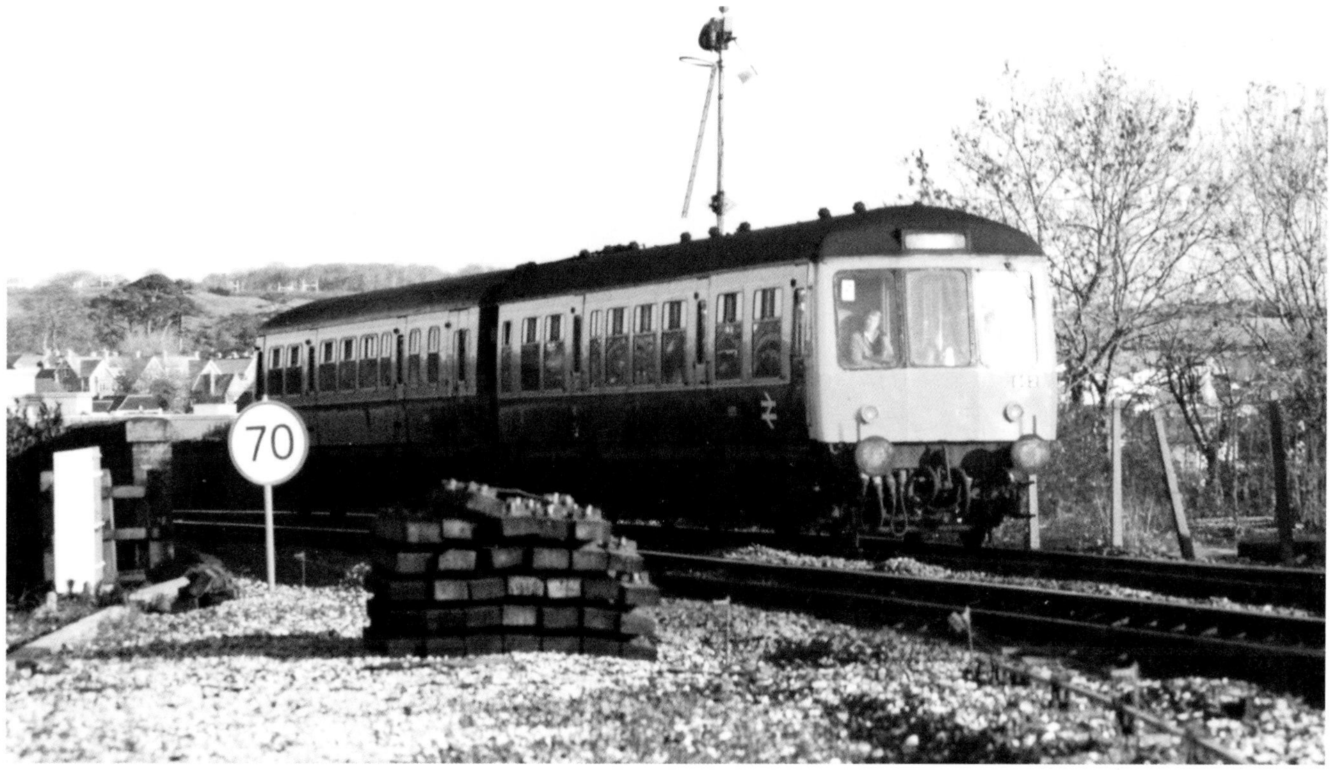

The summer of 1989 sees highbred unit 862 approaching Truro on the Down line. It is made up of half of a 108 and half of a 101. (MD)

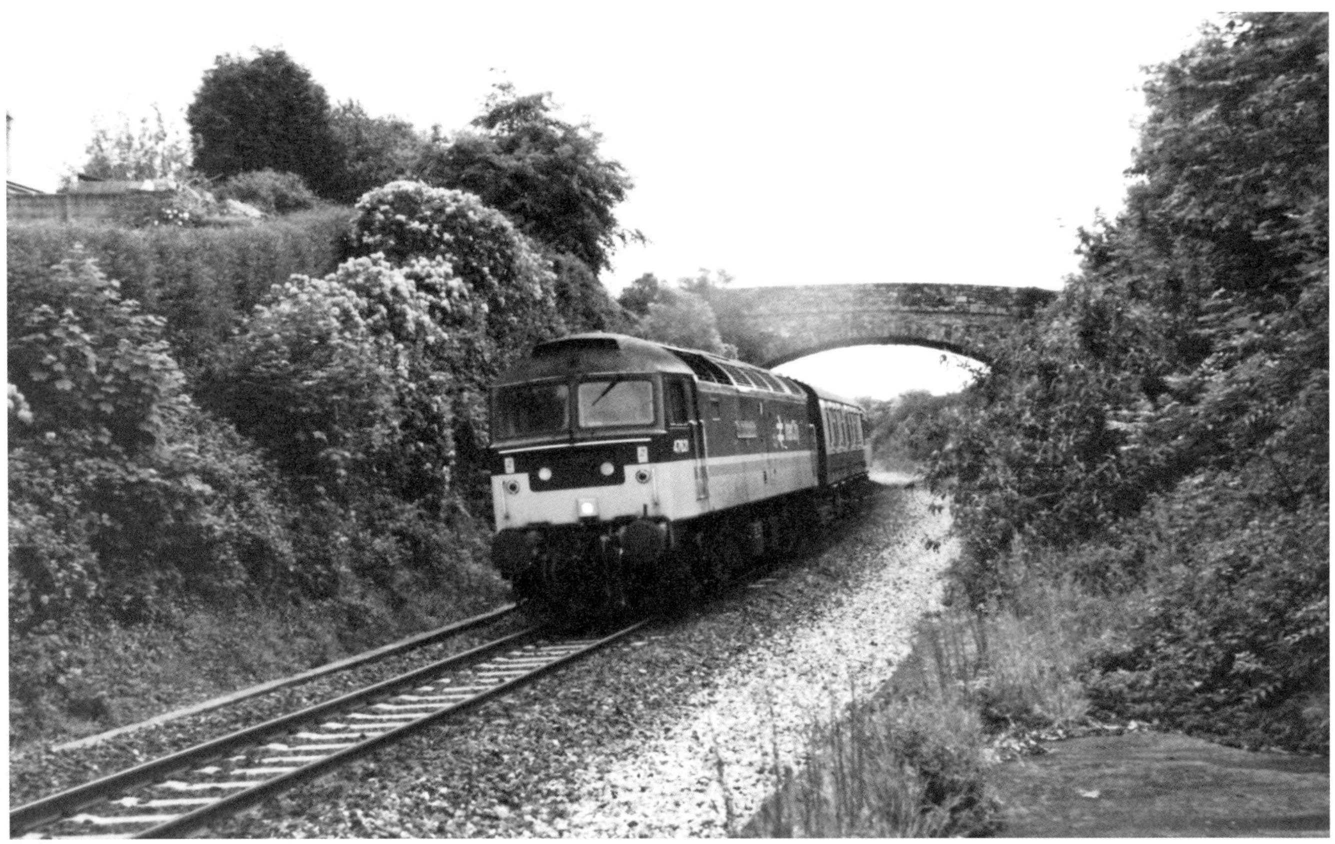

Intercity livery is carried by 47621 in July 1988 as it passes the site of the old Grampound Road station with an Up train. Built in 1964 by Brush as D1728, it was named *'Royal County of Berkshire'* between June 1985 and December 1989. Its first renumber was in 1974 as 47136, then the number it carries here from September 1984, and finally it was renumbered 47839 in October 1989. It is still in service. (GP)

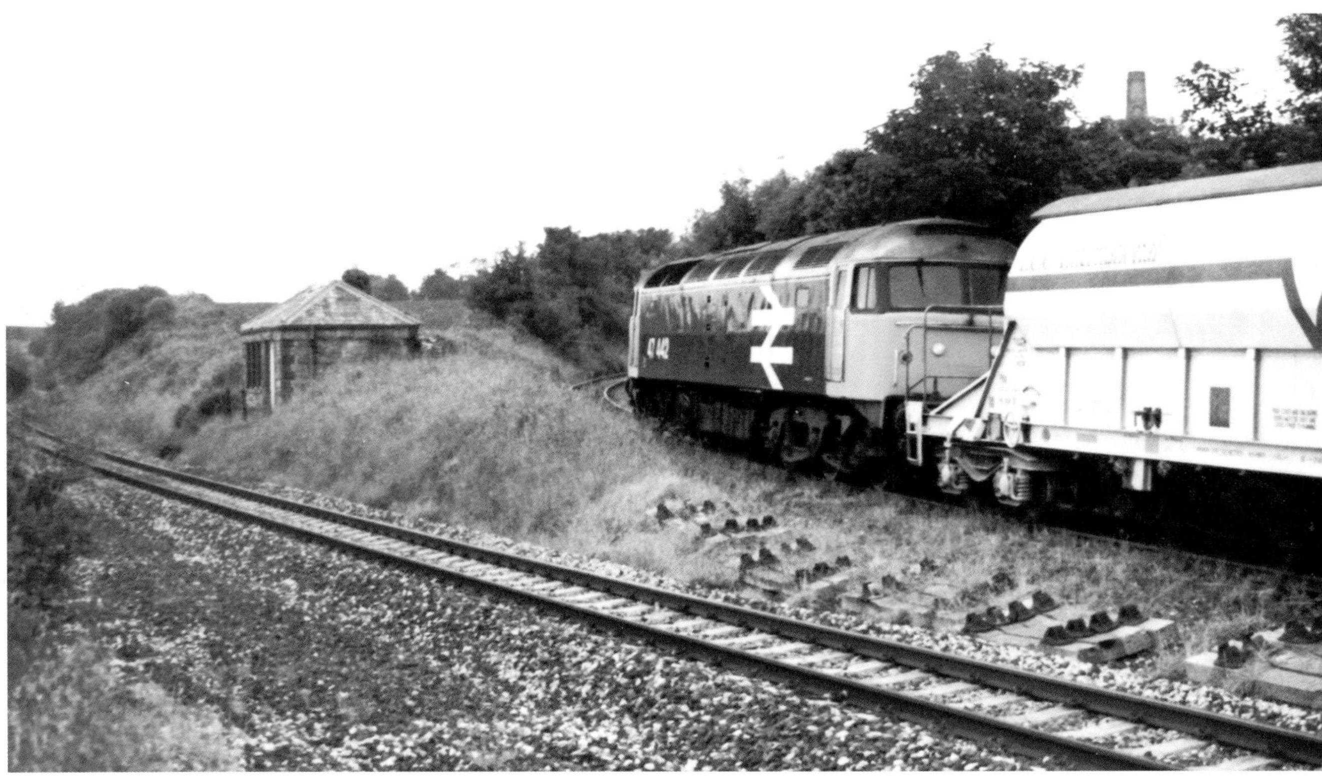

D1558 was the first number carried by 47442, which is seen here climbing the Parkandillack Branch from Burngullow with empty bogie wagons. It was built in 1964 by BR at Crewe Works. Plans still exist to convert this line to passenger status, with a view to running the Newquay trains this way and combine it with the Falmouth service, which would involve a reversal at St Austell and the provision of a bay platform. It was scrapped in March 1997 at Crewe. Picture dated June 1988. (GP)

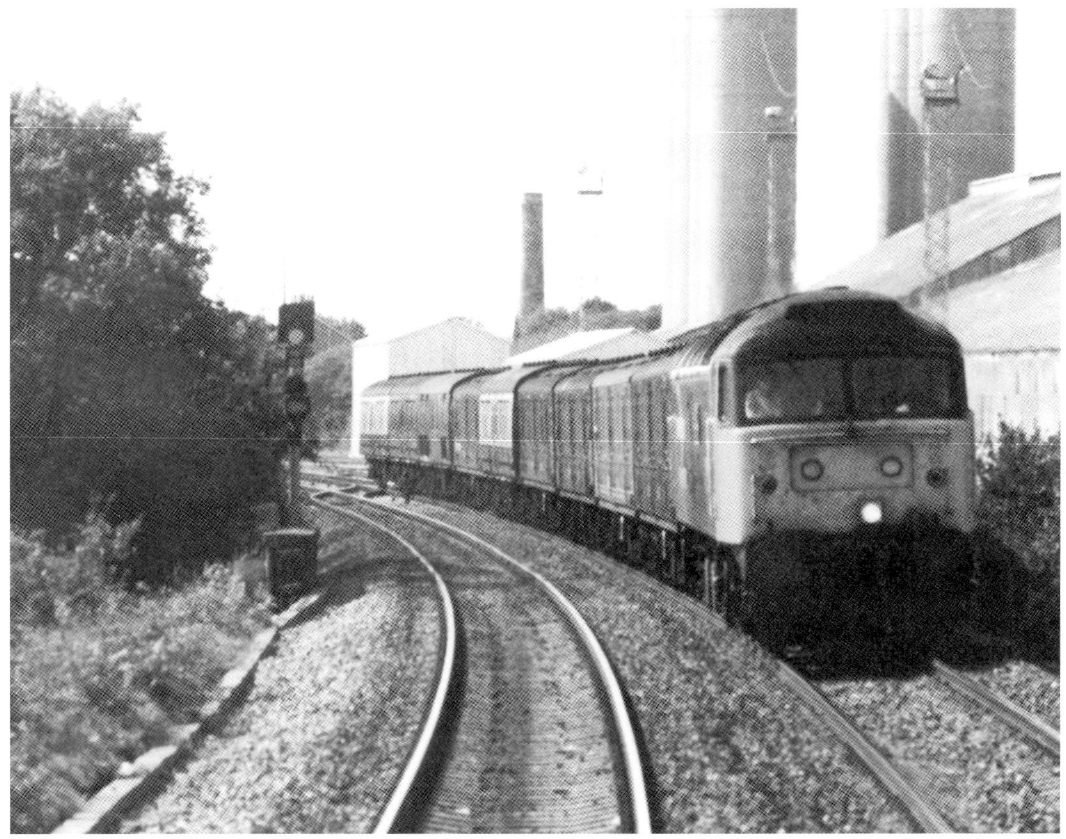

An Up Postal/Parcels Train at Burngullow and just about to Pass PR106 signal with an unidentified class 47 in Large-Logo livery. The picture was taken from the cab of a DMU. (GP)

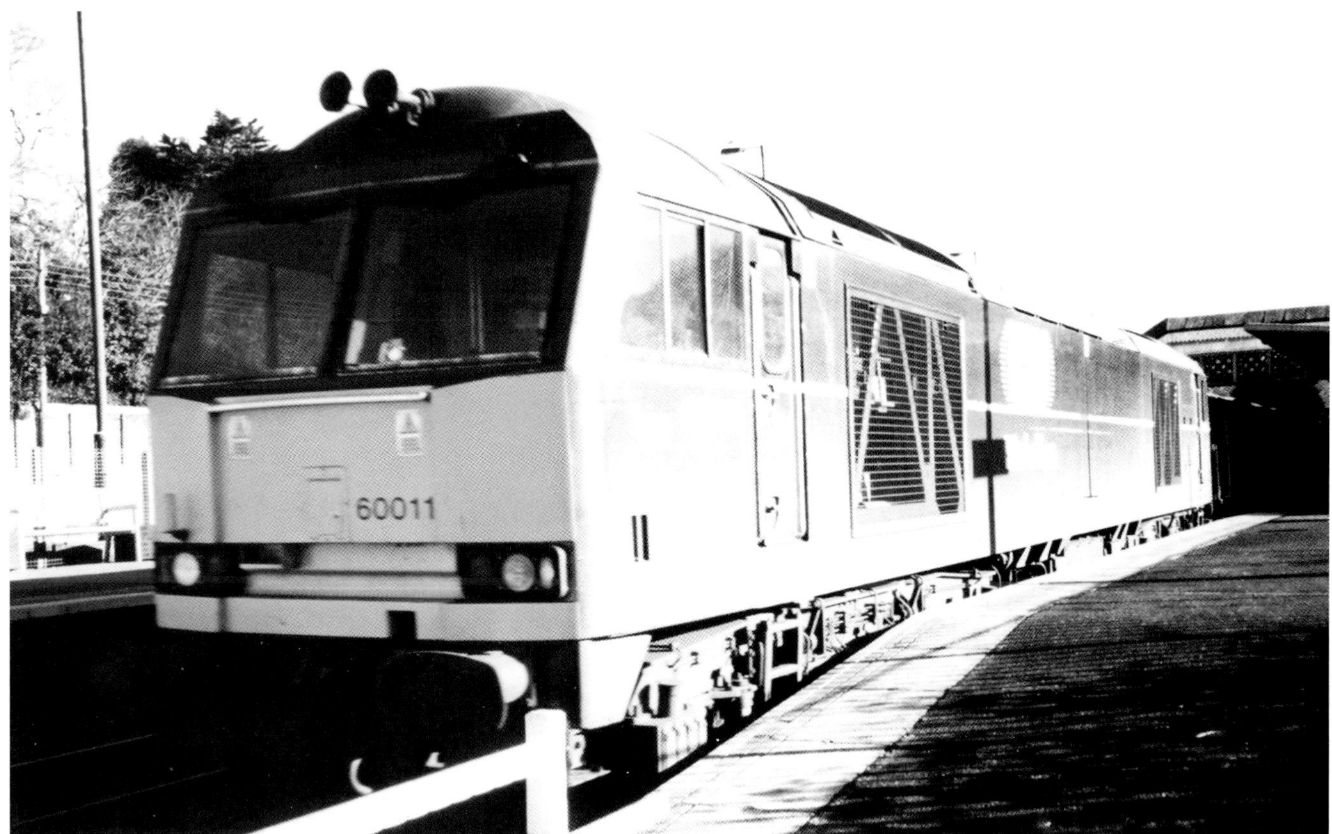

On Sunday 16 January 2004, during the Burngullow-Probus double-track reinstatement, 60011 is seen here waiting on the Down line at St Austell, to take an engineering train into the possession. Built by Brush in February 1990 it was then stored for twenty months and previously carried the name *'Cader Idris'*. It is still in service with D.B.S. though no longer named. (MD)

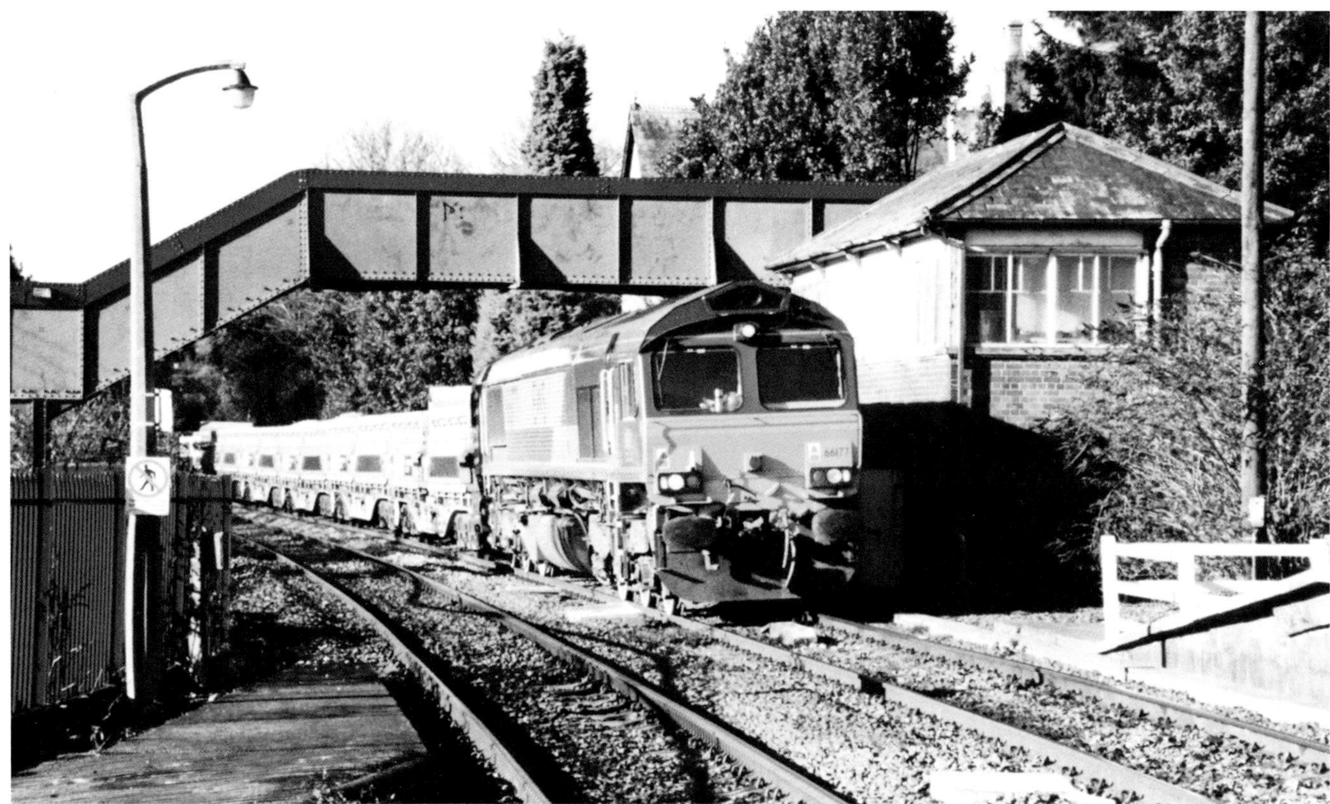

66177 is here passing the now derelict St Austell Signalbox on 16 January 2004 with a Sunday Permanent-way train. Built by General-Motors-EMD in London, Canada, and delivered on 17 November 1999, this now numerous class of loco is the most common to be found on the national network. (MD)

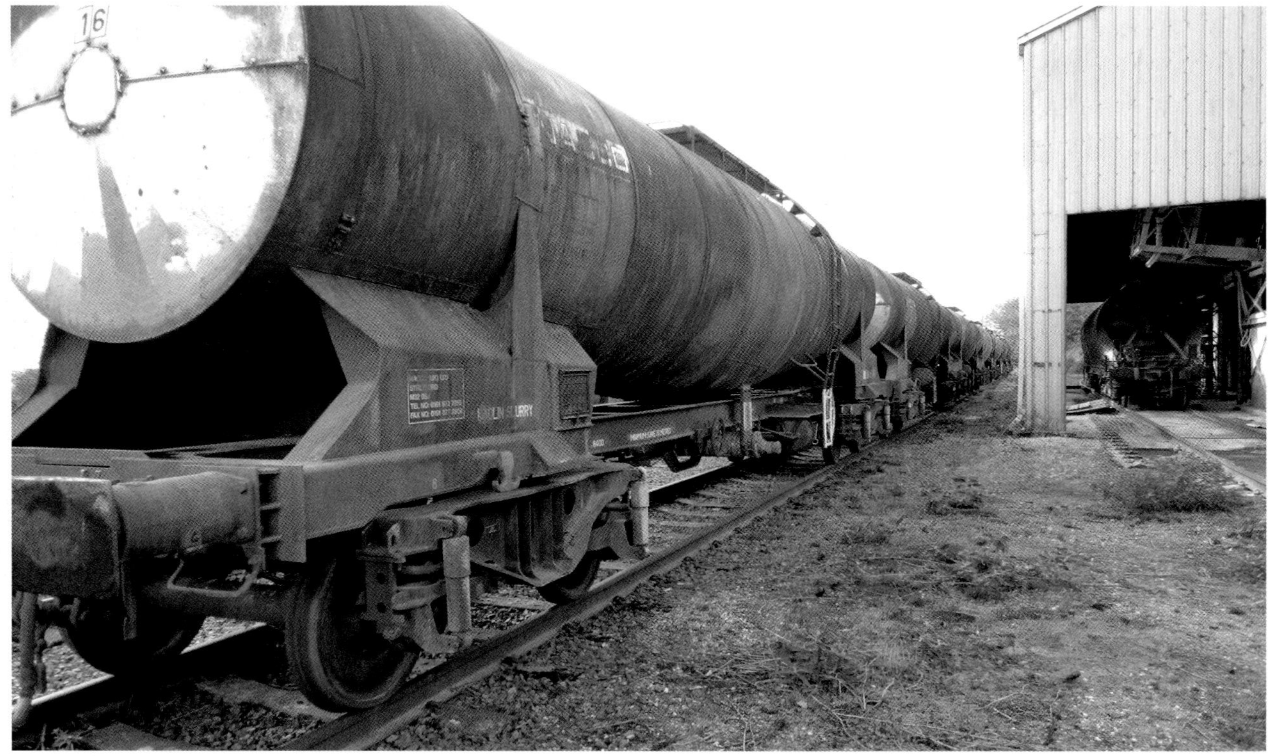

The location is Burngullow in 2012, where the new fleet of 'Silver Bullets' had been stored for the last five years or so, after the clay slurry traffic for Irvine ceased operation. These hardly-used tanks were stored on five roads at Burngullow, including one on blocks minus its bogies and one minus its wheels. Over the course of a month, West Coast Railways moved the whole fleet to Stoke-on-Trent for refurbishment for a new traffic flow from the east coast to Scotland. Vintage 56302 and 47375 double-headed the three trains, which initially complained about being dragged from their long time resting place and covered in rust and growth from being stored so close to the sea. (SFH)

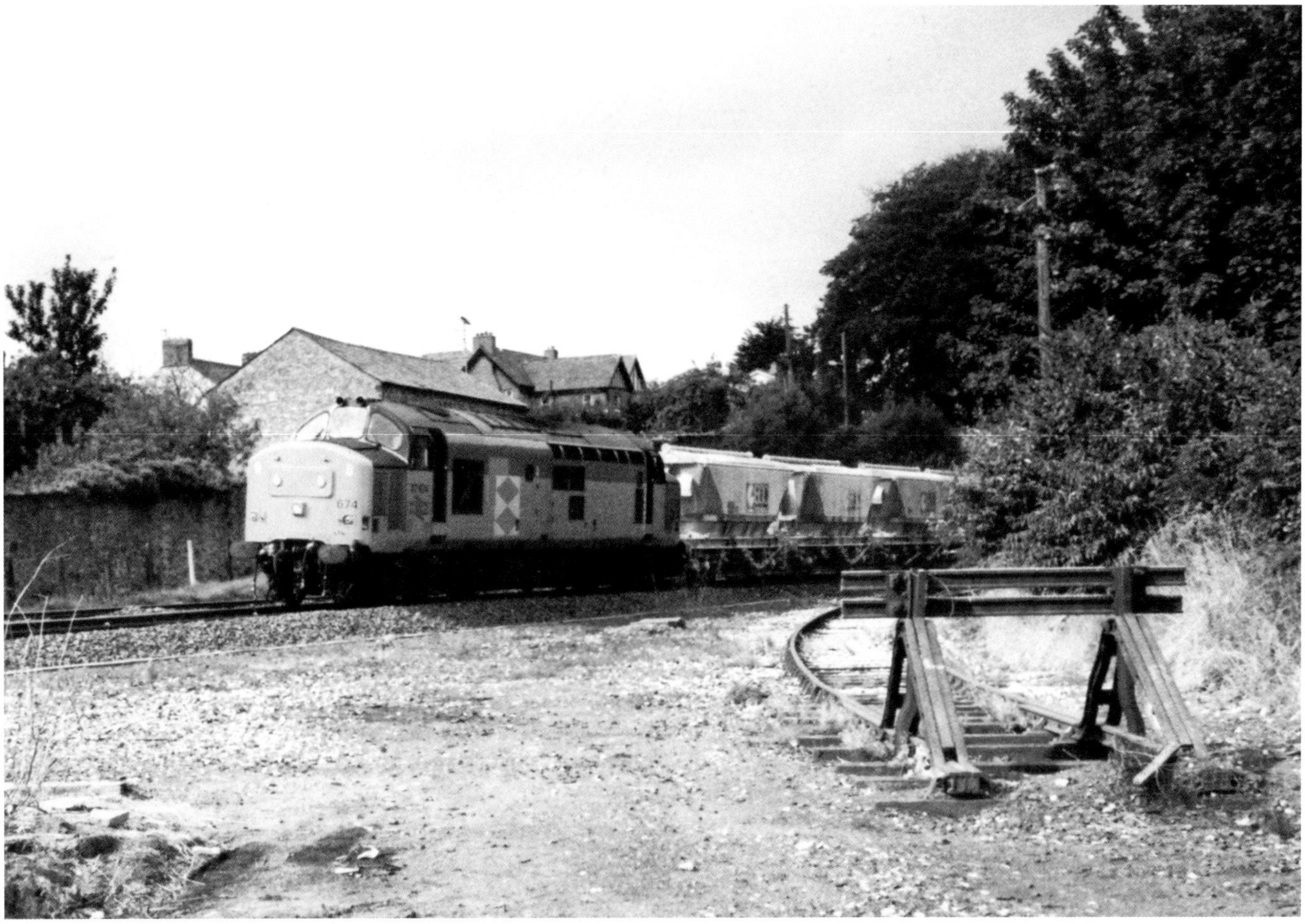

37674 is seen here on the Up line, passing the truncated line that once served St Austell Good Yard. Enroute to Fowey via Lostwithiel with modern CDA type clay wagons from the Parkendillack Branch. Picture dated September 1990. (GP)

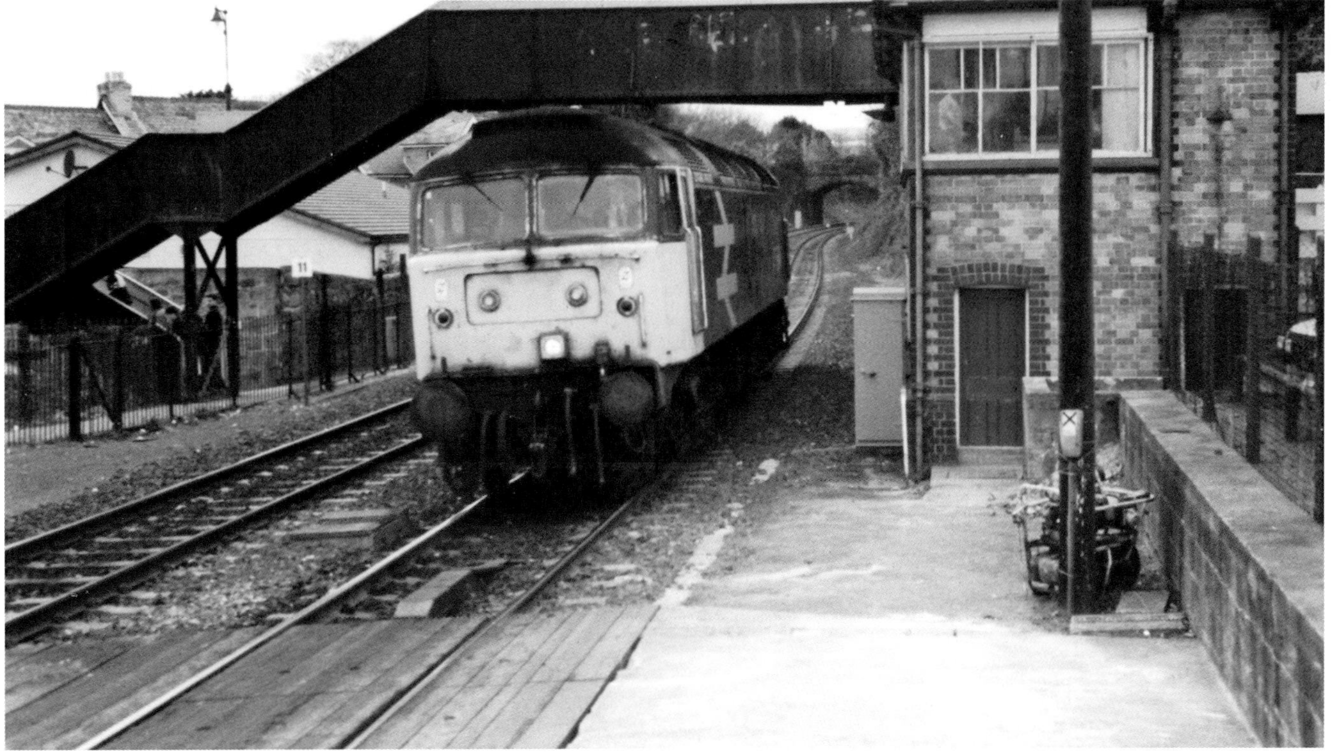

An unidentified Large Logo liveried class 47 running 'light engine' is seen here passing the closed signalbox at St Austell in April 1992. (GP)

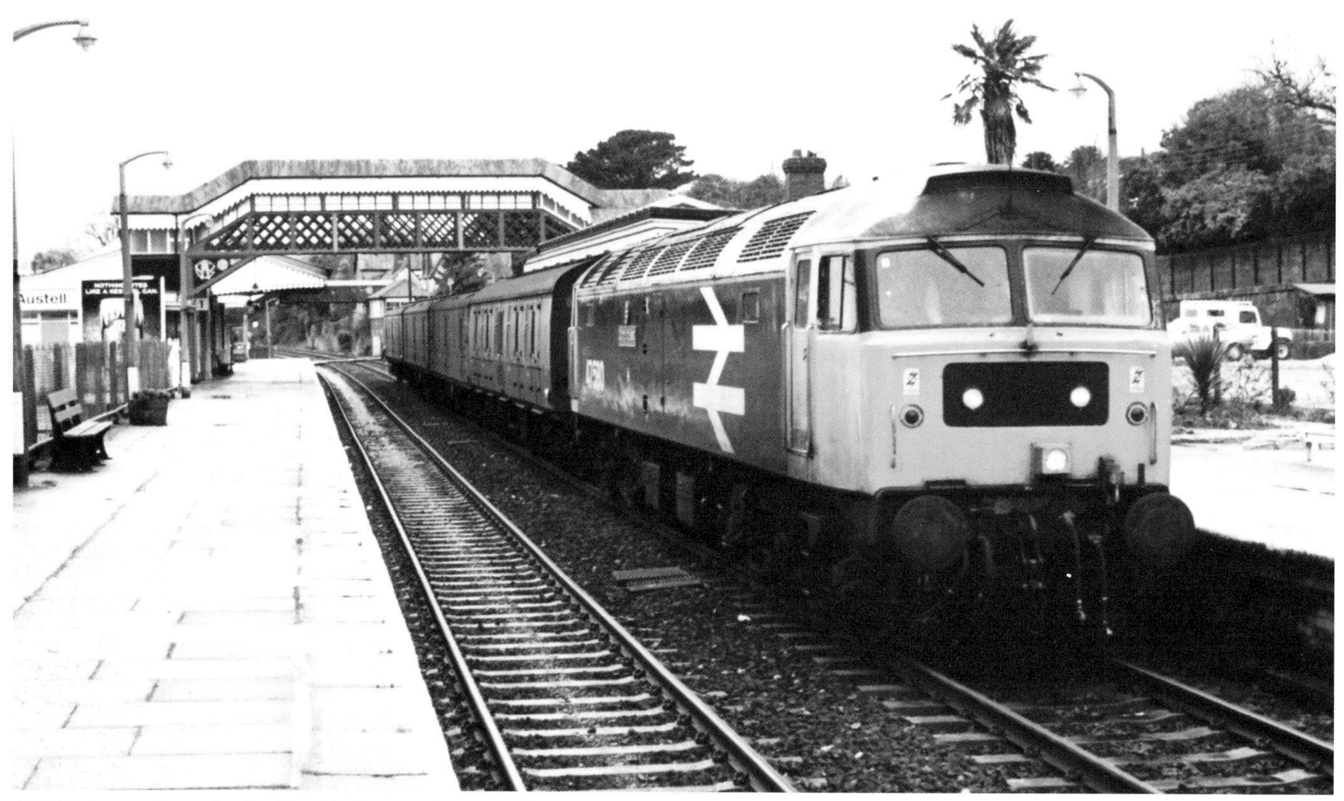

47580 is seen here in the Up platform at St Austell in January 1990, on a parcels van train. Built by Brush as D1762 in 1964 and named *'County of Essex'* in 1979 when carrying the number 47167. It survives in preservation on the Mid Norfolk Railway. (GP)

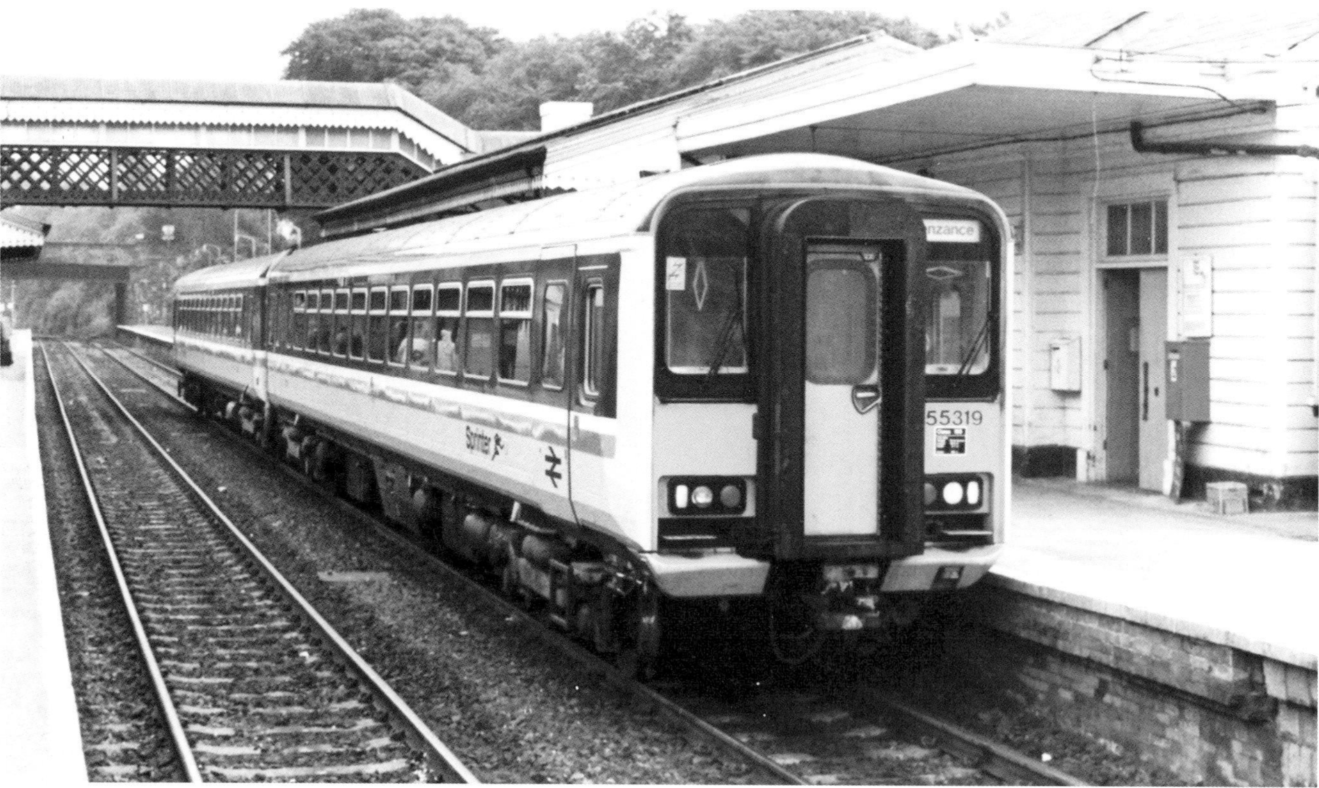

A second generation unit is seen here in the Down platform at St Austell with a local train for Penzance in June 1988 when still quite new. The class 155 'Sprinters' were not the best design BR ever made and became even more unpopular after they were split and converted to form a new fleet of 'Bubble Cars' in the class 153. Built using parts from the Leyland National Bus, the windows are too high to comfortably see out of and the redesigned cabs on the converted 153s are so cramped, that they were 'blacked' by the unions at some depots. They are still in use today and still suffer the same problems. 1987/8 built 155319 here became 153319 and 153369 during the 1990s. (GP)

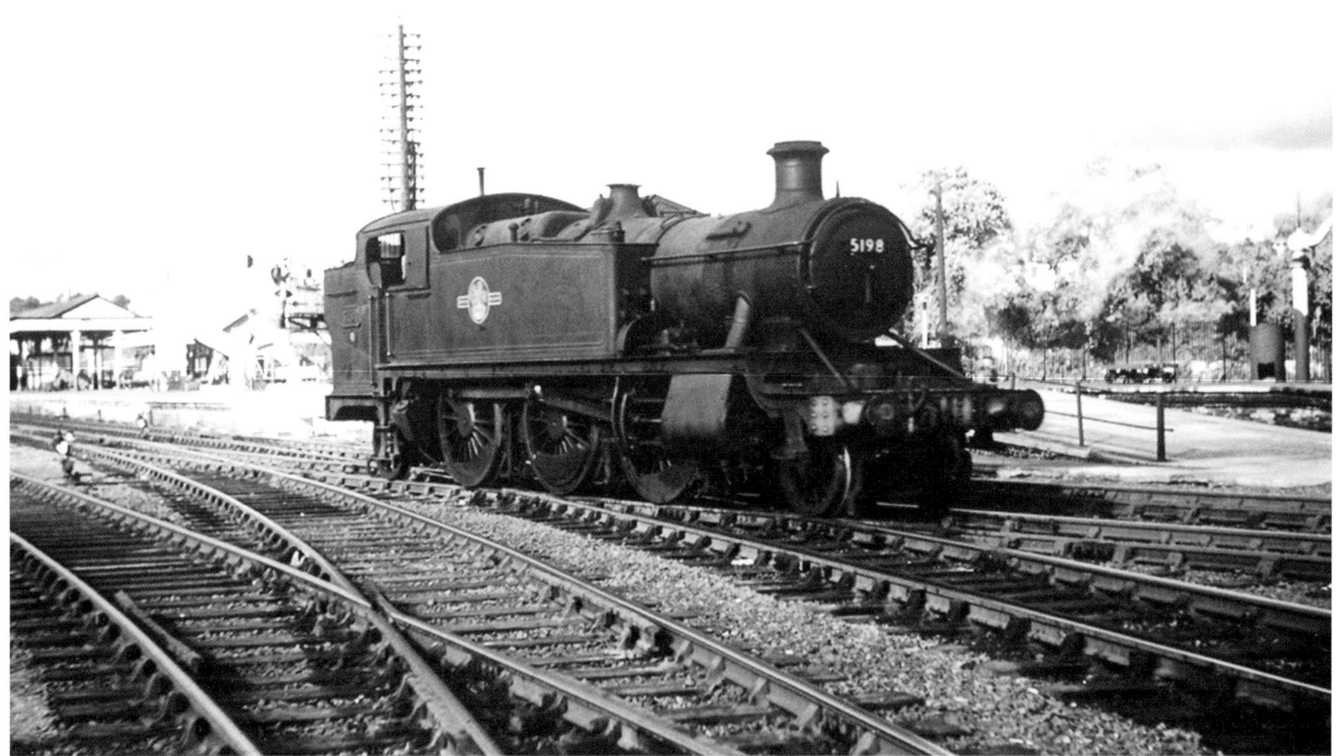

Sometimes referred to as 'Large Prairies', these powerful locomotives were a Churchward design, and this one is the penultimate of the class, being built in Swindon in 1934. All were withdrawn by 1965 but 4141 and 5164 survive. It is seen here at Par in the 1950s, adjacent to the signalbox, which is hidden from view by the loco. (RW)

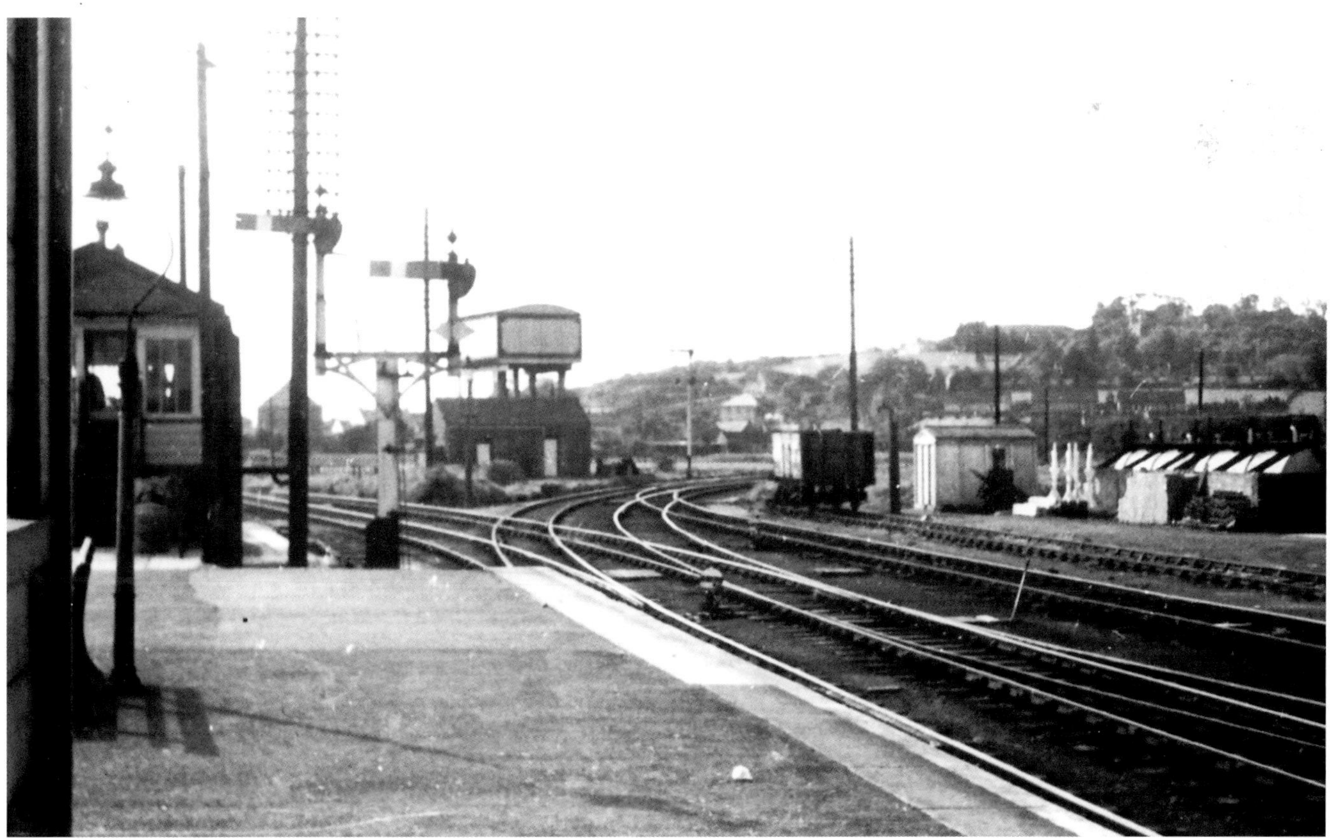

This interesting view of Par is circa 1950, but shows how vegetation has altered the view today. The track layout is more complex here, but although some rationalisation as taken place, it is not hugely different today. The water-tower has gone, as indeed have a couple of the buildings, but the main signals, although replaced, are still in the same place today. (RW)

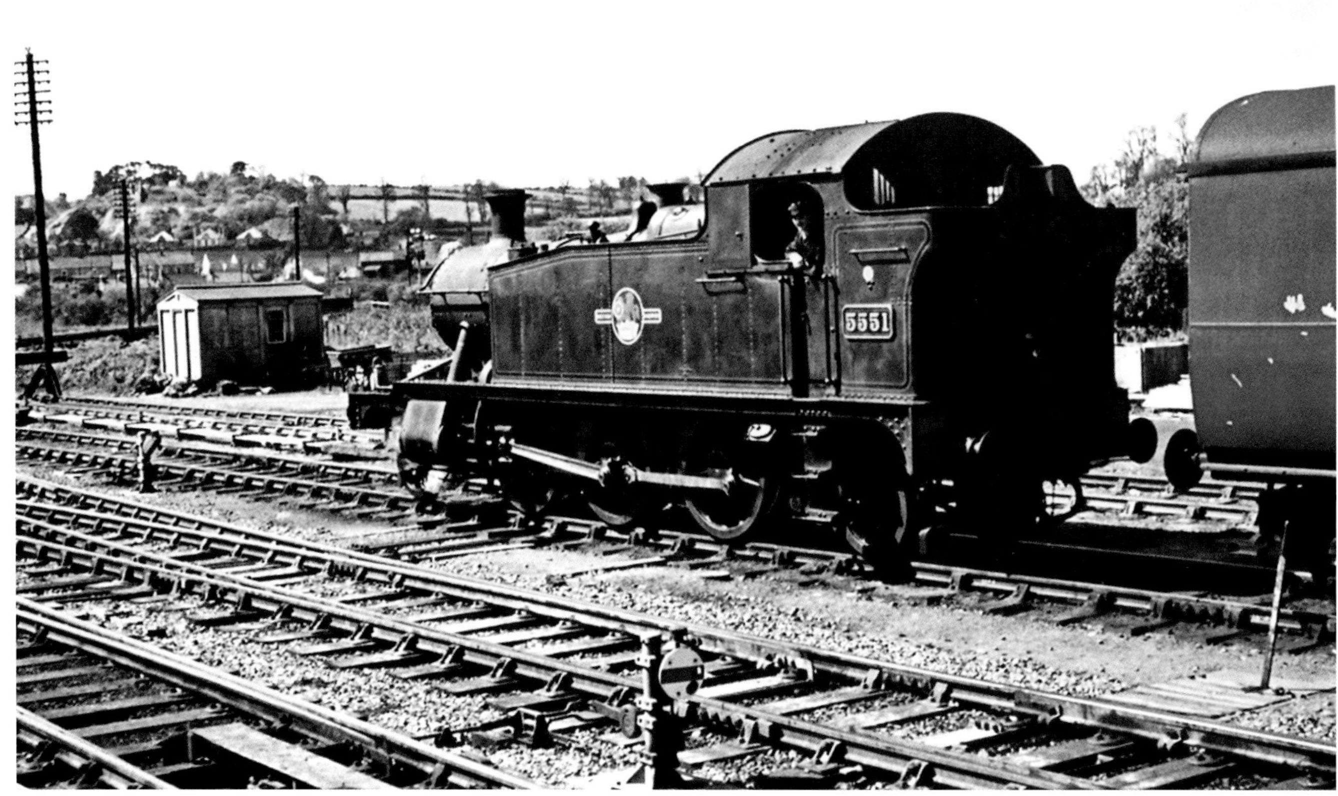

Another 1950s picture depicting 5551 shunting coaching stock at Par. Several of this successful and useful class of engine have survived into preservation, including sister 5552. (RW)

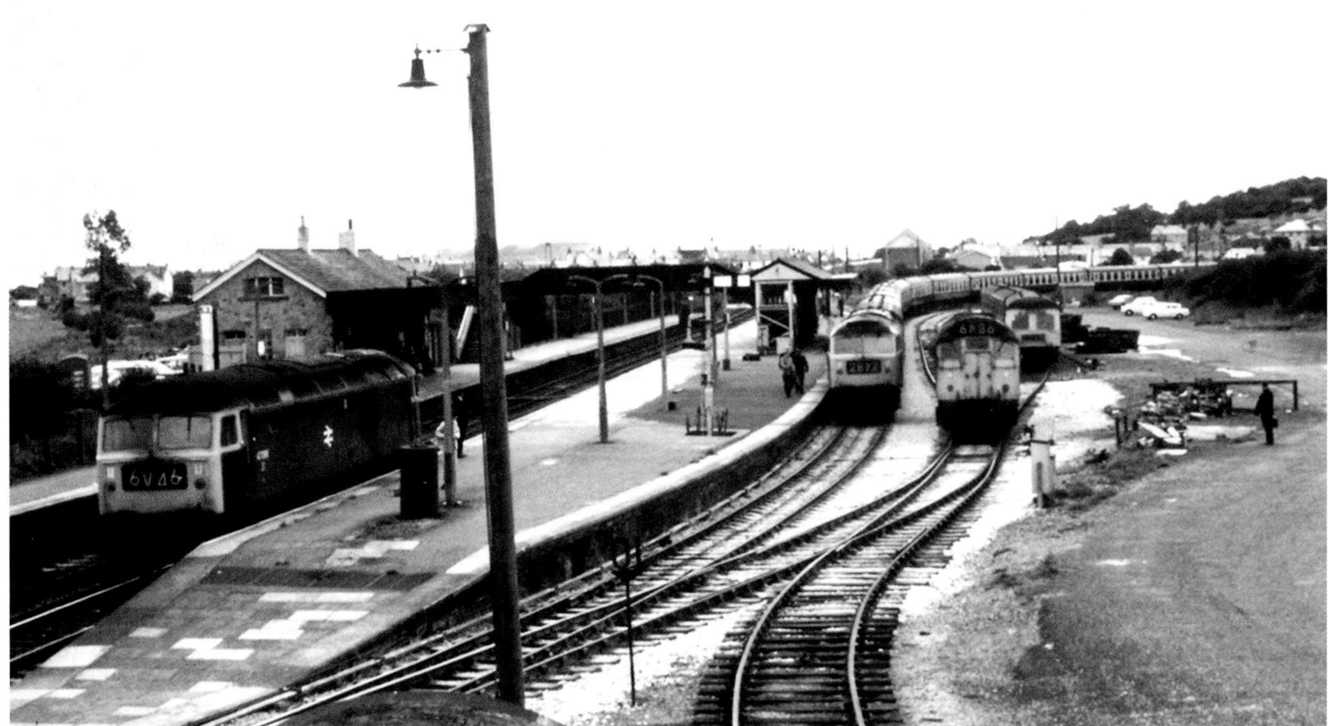

A nice period picture of the BR 'Blue Era' at Par, with a Class 47 light engine on the Up line and another 47 bringing a train of Mk I stock from the Newquay direction. Next to it is a Class 25 light loco, probably waiting for the first two to clear the section towards Lostwithiel. In the siding is a class 120 Swindon built, three car Cross-Country DMU. (RW)

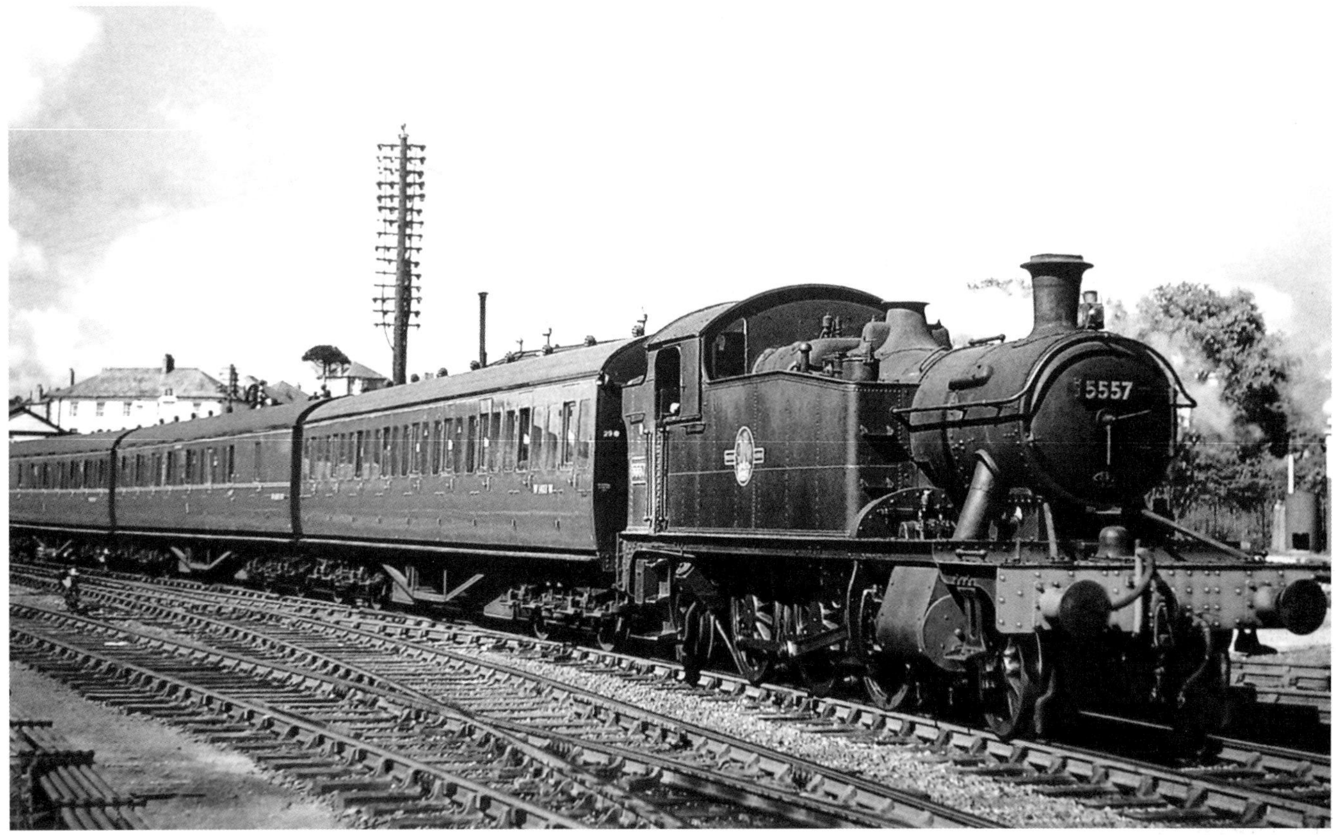

Prairie Tank 5557 is seen here departing Par from Platform 3, probably bound for Newquay with a local train circa 1960. The loco is missing from the 1961 stock lists, but has the later style totem, so must have been close to the end of its life when this photo was taken. (RW)

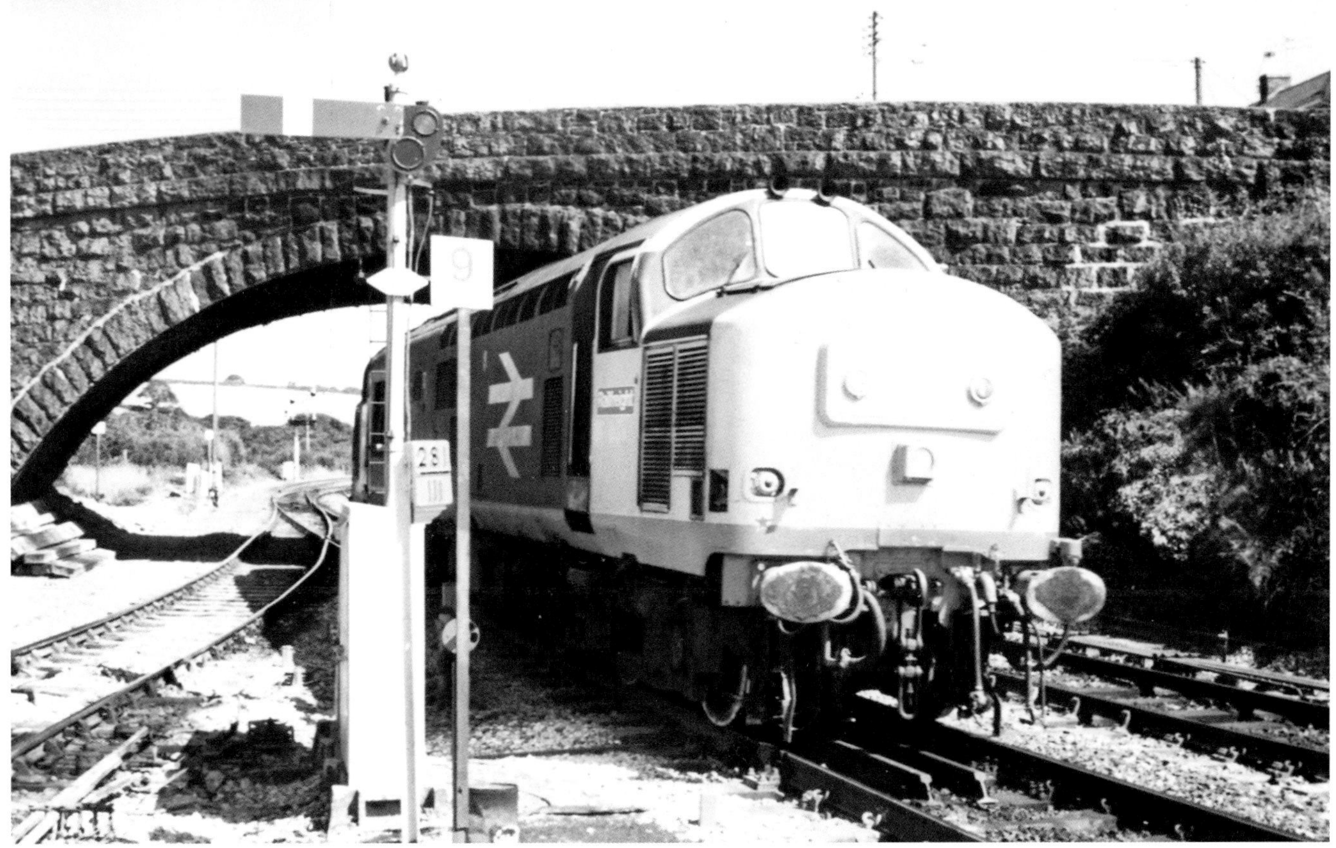

37675 *'William Cookworthy'* is at Par on the Up line running around its train from Burngullow Junction and is destined for St Blazey yard. Built as D6864 in August 1963 by English Electric, Robert Stephenson & Hawthorns it was first renumbered to 37164. It was cut up in October 2010. This picture dates from 9 August 1988. (MD)

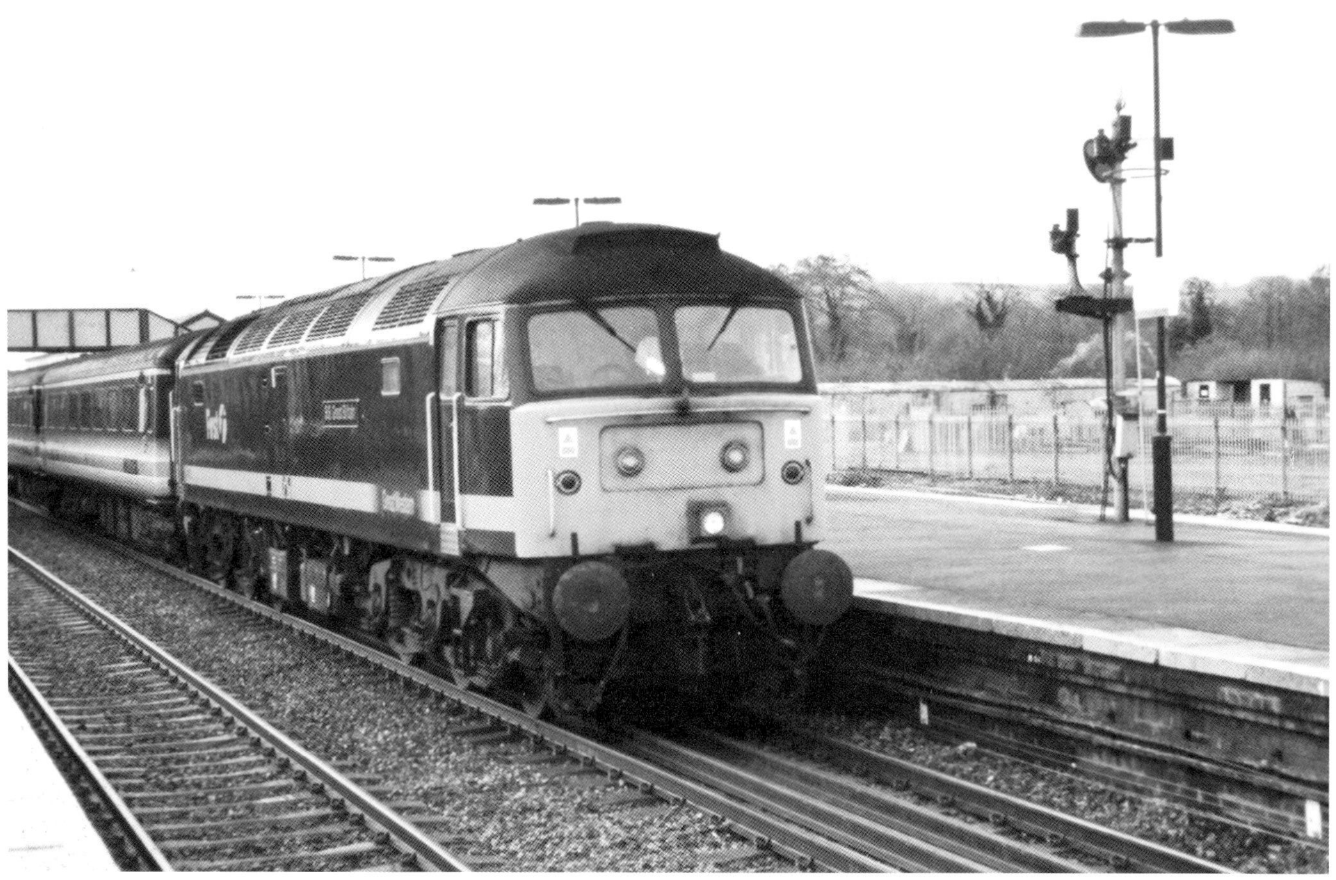

Par is the location of 1A45 the 0846 Penzance to Paddington, with 47813 *'SS Great Britain'* at the front on 12 January 2002. This livery was the first 'First Great Western' livery used. Built as D1720 by Brush in March 1964 it also carried the numbers 47129 and 47658. It lost its name in May 2003 and received the name *'John Peel'* from October 2005 to March 2009. It is still in service with DRS. (MD)

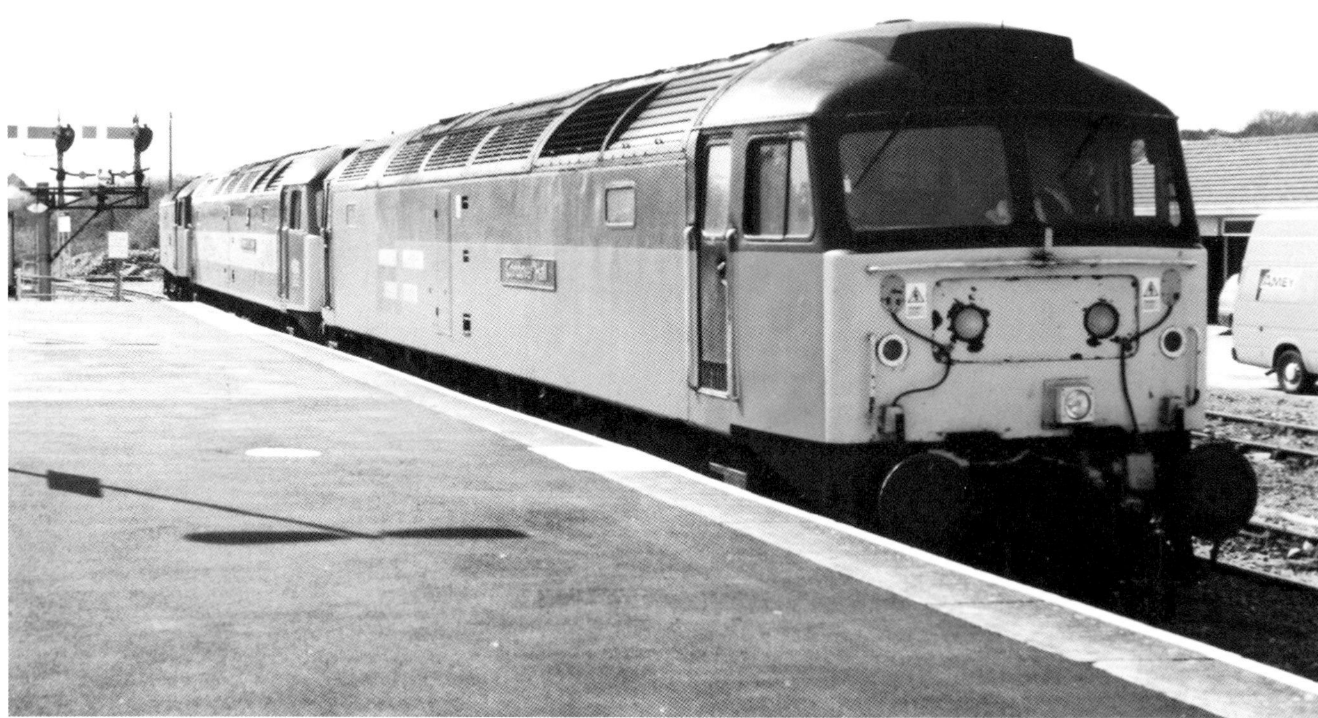

0C06 is the reporting number for three class 47s heading from St Blazey Depot to Plymouth in Spring 2003. Res liveried 47784 *'Condover Hall'* leads the trio through Par Branch Platform (3). It actually carried five different numbers at various dates, namely, D1727, 47135, 47664, 47819 and finally 47784. Built in March 1964 by Brush it was withdrawn in April 2004 and sold to Ron Hull Junior of Rotherham who broke it up In December 2007. (MD)

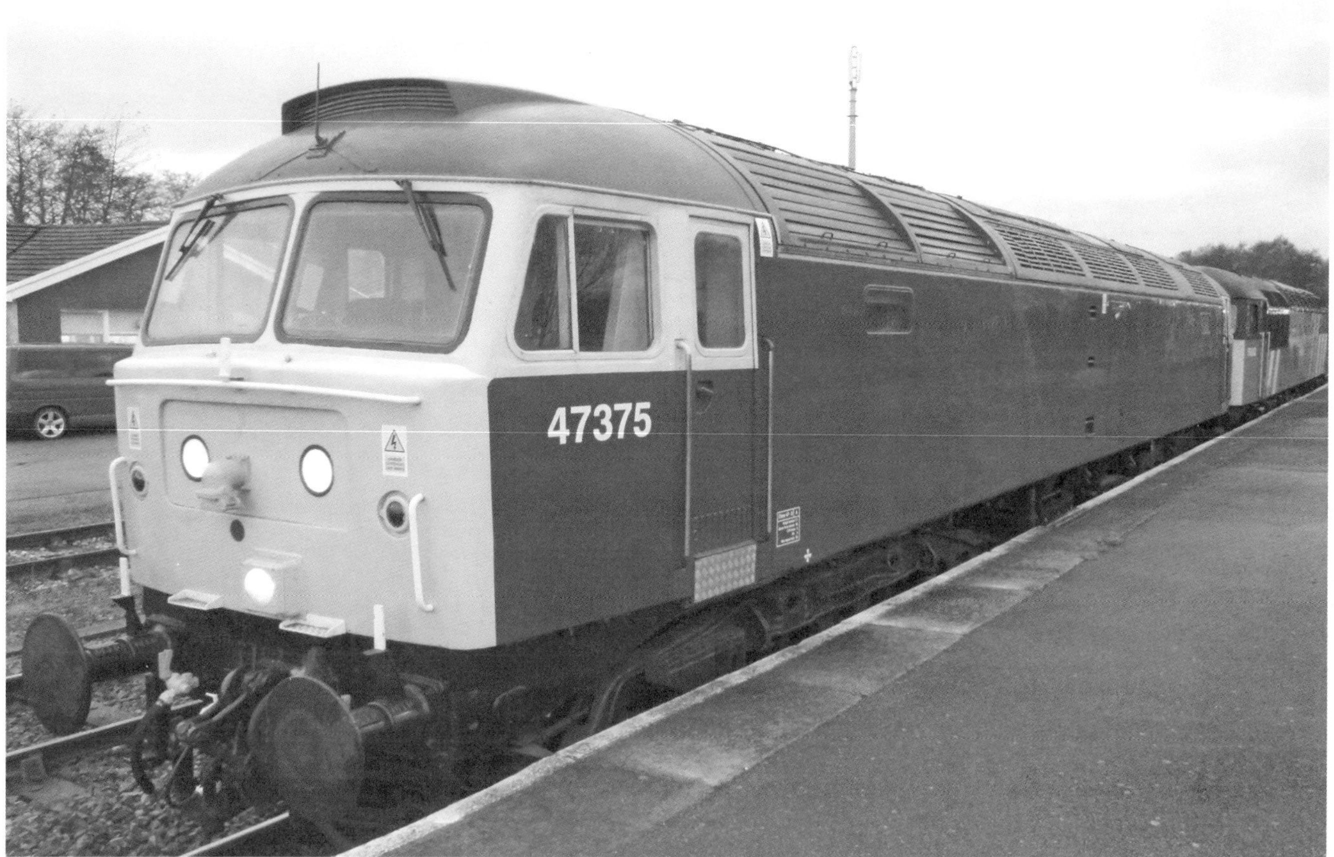

One of the two locomotives used to move the 'Silver Bullets' was 47375 (D1894), which was built by Brush in December 1965 and after being withdrawn in March 2009 was stored for while before being repainted in Rail blue livery and hired to WCR. It is seen here at Par platform 3 in company with the 56 and about to depart for Burngullow, on 29 November 2011, after residing in Par's Chapel Siding overnight. (SFH)

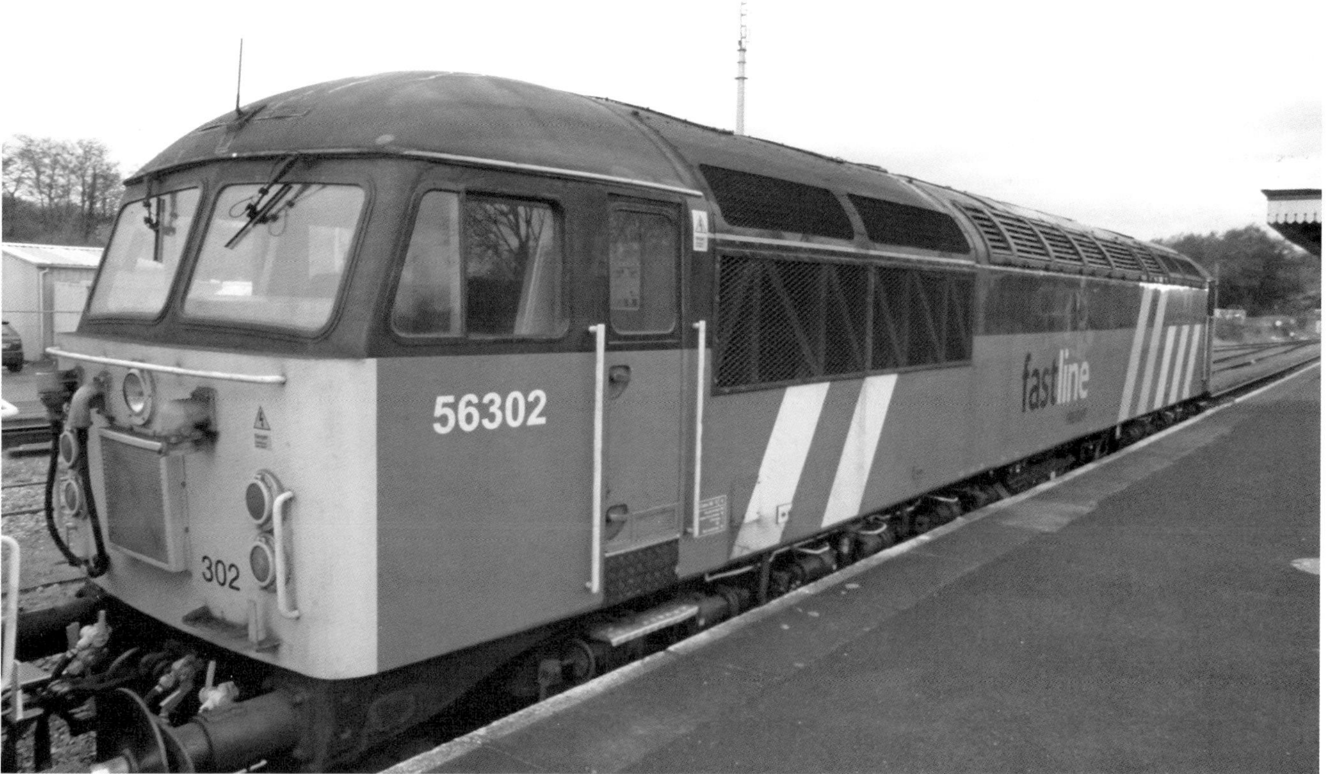

The other loco used to move the 'Silver Bullets' was 56302 (56124) which is another product of BREL at Crewe and was built in September 1983 and withdrawn in October 2009. It was stored at Nemesis Rail at Burton until hired by WCR along with 47375. (SFH)

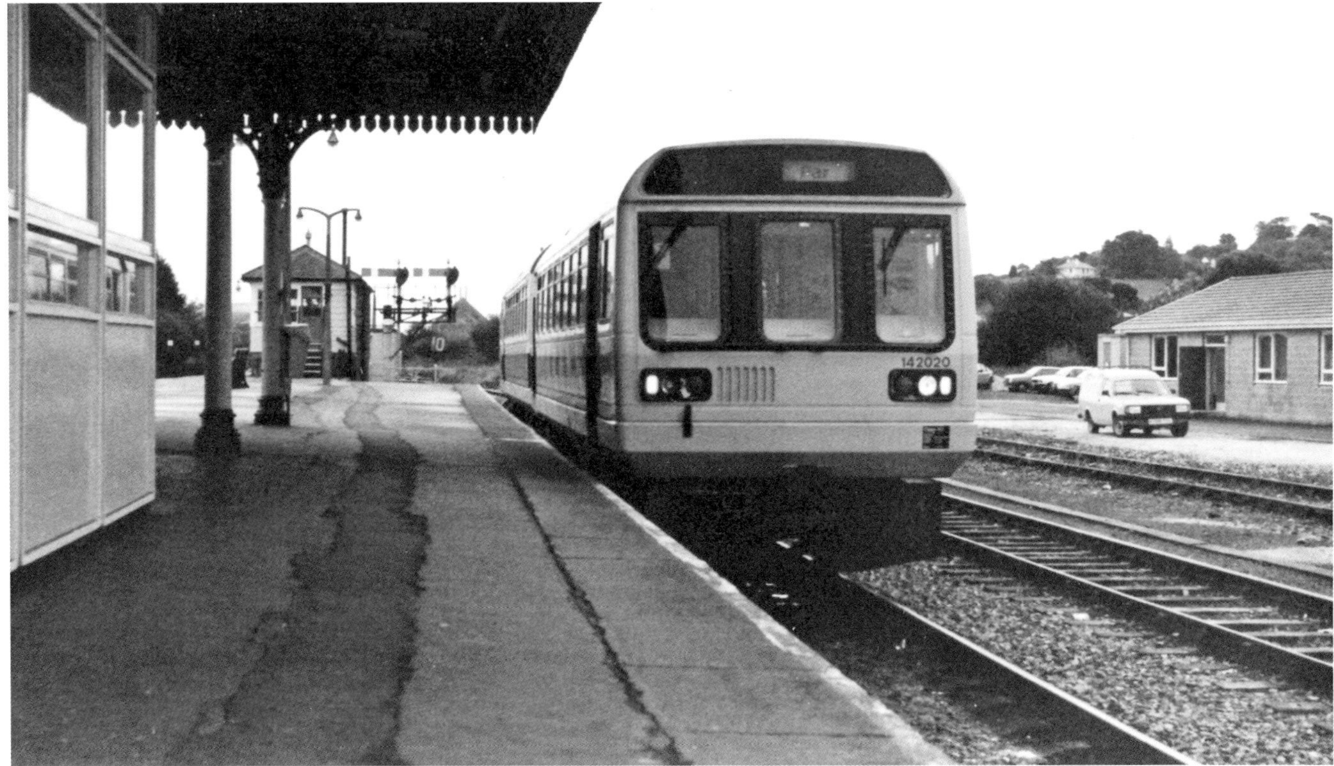

The ubiquitous and notorious class 142 units (Skippers) were sent new to Cornwall and were painted in a pseudo Western Region livery of Chocolate and Cream. Sometimes known as 'Nodding Donkeys' because of their lively ride, they were used as a direct replacement for first generation DMUs, but were unpopular with both public and crews. Noisy, uncomfortable and with poor riding qualities, they were soon transferred out of the county and replaced with old first generation units again. Their long wheel-base, with only two axles meant they screeched and squealed on the sinuous curves of Cornwall. Many survive in 2012 in everyday service, though they are now being withdrawn, and many are being sold abroad. (GP)

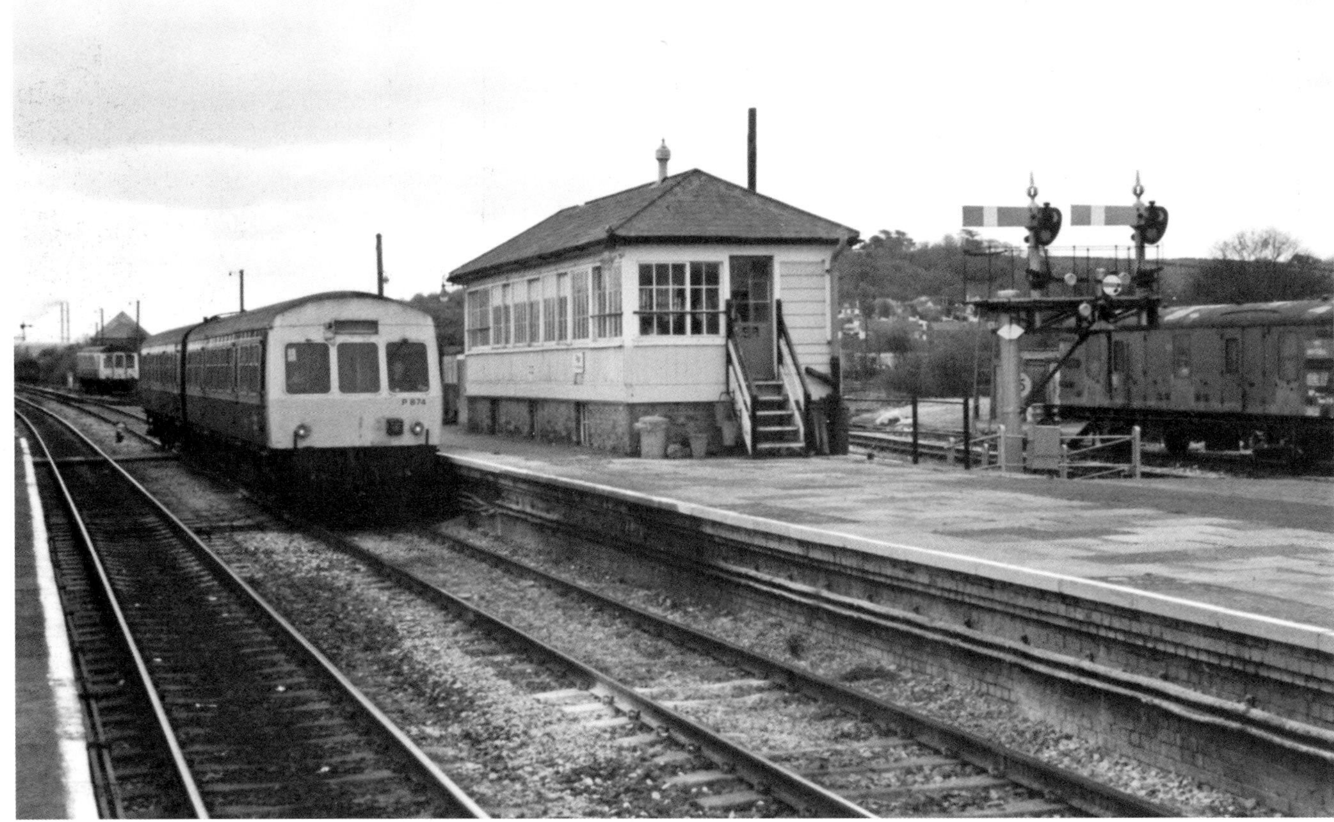

Metro-Cammell built Class 101 unit P874 was a regular performer in Cornwall, and is seen here entering Par Up platform in April 1992. (GP)

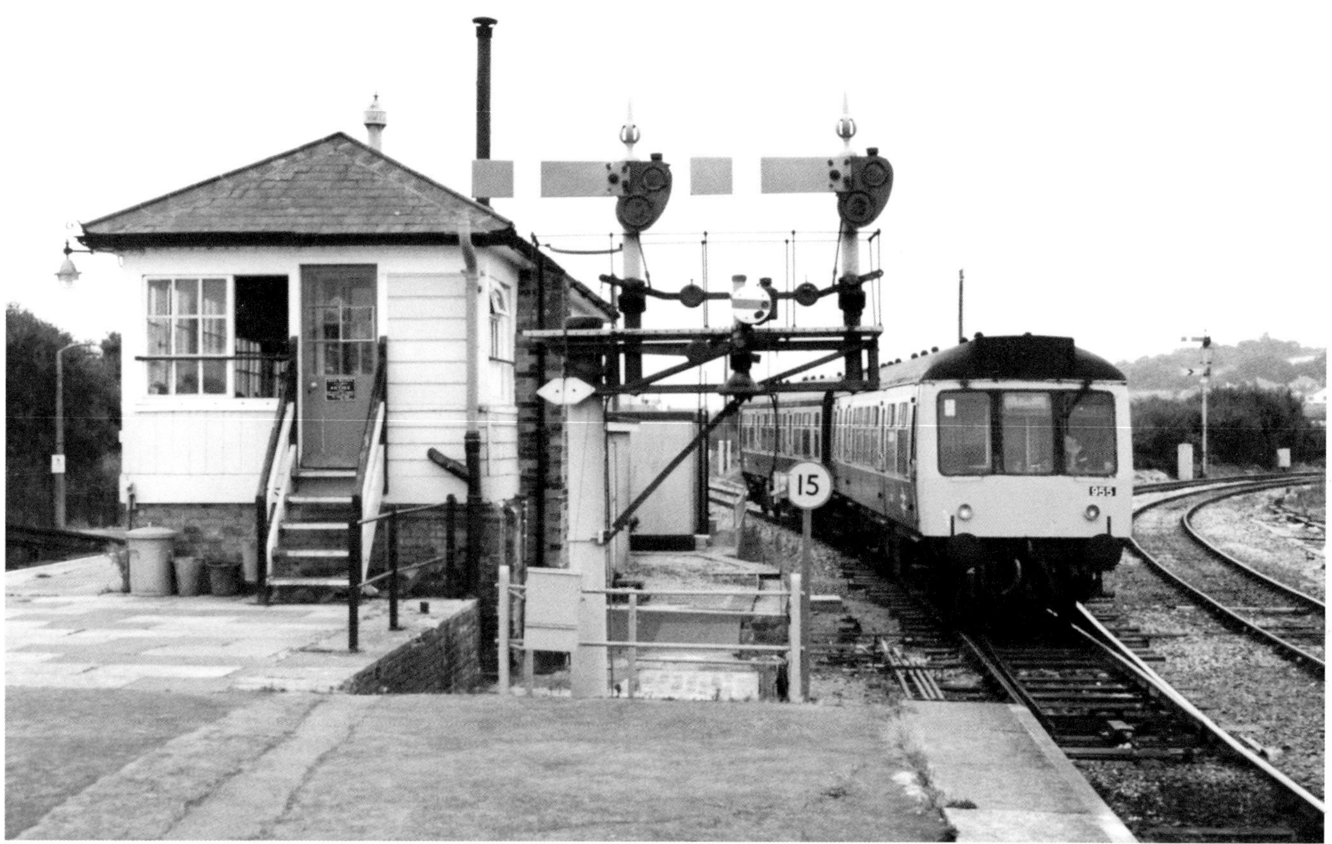

Class 108 unit P955 is seen here entering Par Branch platform (3) in September 1991. Built by BR Derby with Leyland O680 engines, they could be found almost anywhere on the network. (GP)

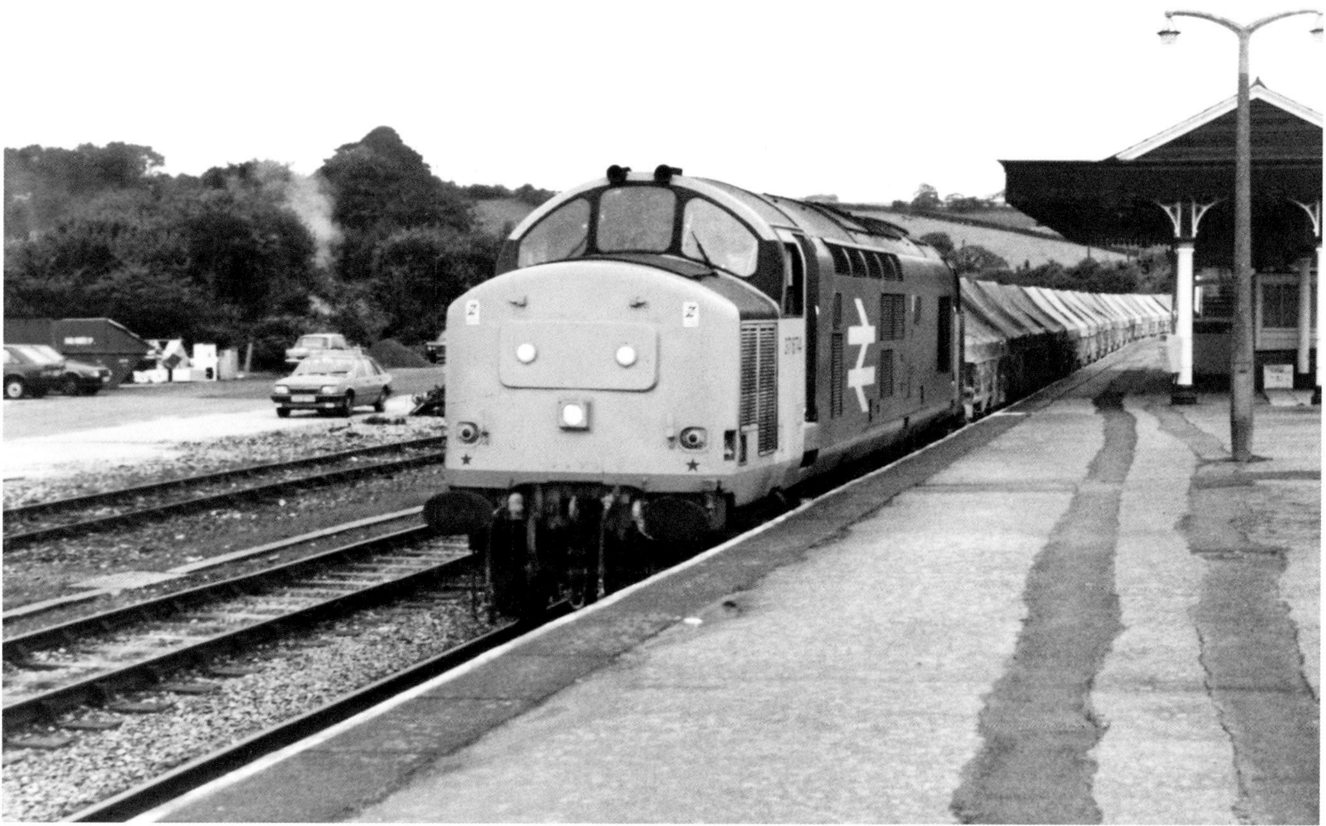

37674 is seen here traversing the Branch Platform line at Par enroute to Goonbarrow in August 1983, with a train of original wooden bodied clay hoods. As D6869 it was built by English Electric Vulcan Foundry in 1963, and carried the number 37169 before it was renumbered as seen here. It survives in preservation. (GP)

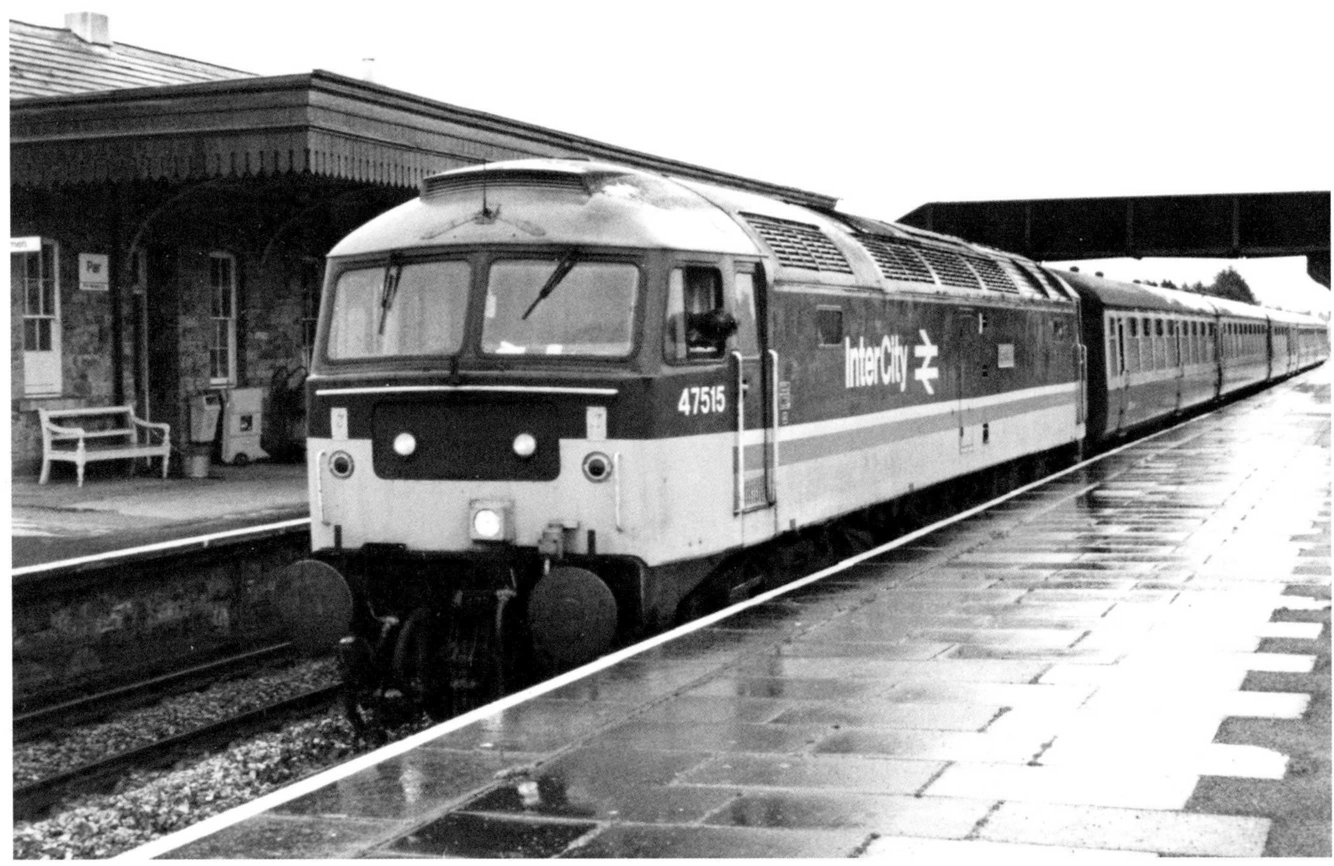

47515 is seen here at Par in the Up platform on a cross country train on 18 March 1989. A product of Brush and built in January 1968 as D1961 and subsequently named *'Night Mail'* in 1986, it was, according to the records, the final class 47 built by Brush and the final one to enter service for BR. Unfortunately it was cut up in May 2006 at Crewe. (GP)

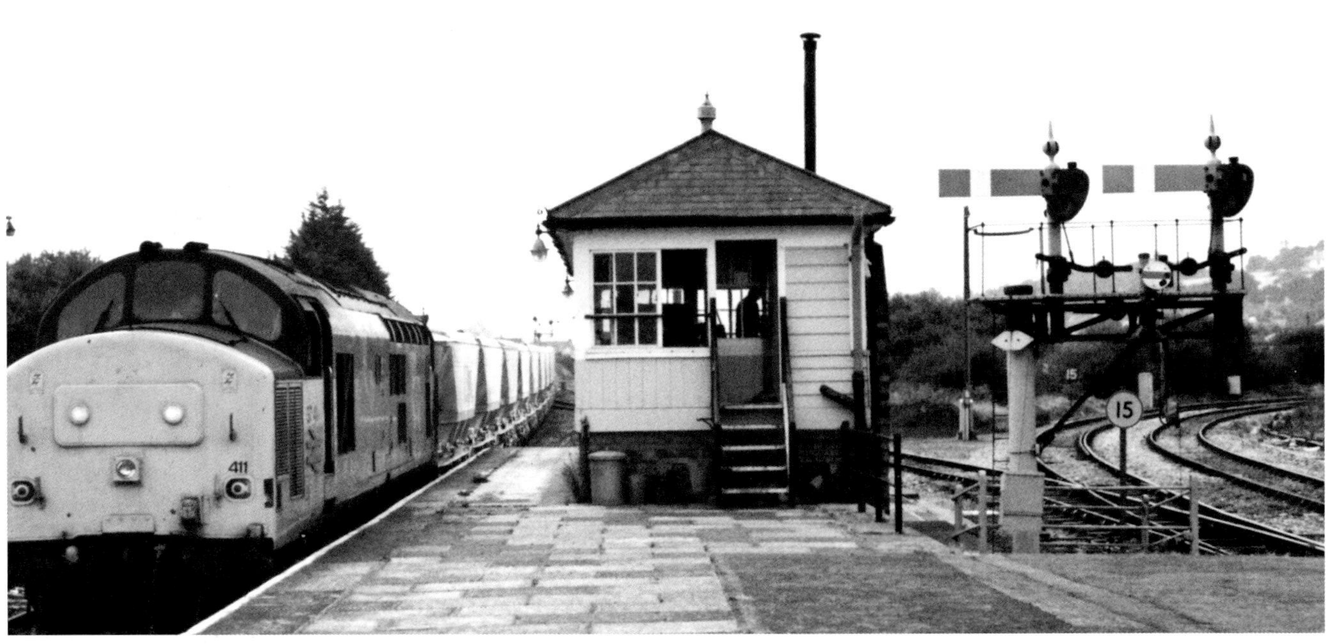

37411 is seen here passing Par Signalbox on an Up train from Burngullow to Fowey via Lostwithiel. The train would have originated from Parkendillack, Treviscoe, Drinnick, Crugwallins or Burngullow (Blackpool), all of which are on the Branch line from Burngullow to Parkendillack. Built in June 1965 as D6990, it was renumbered 37290 in 1974 and named *'Institute of Railway Signal Engineers'* between 1986 and 1990 after receiving its final number in 1985. It is still in service with DRS. Picture dated September 1991. (GP)

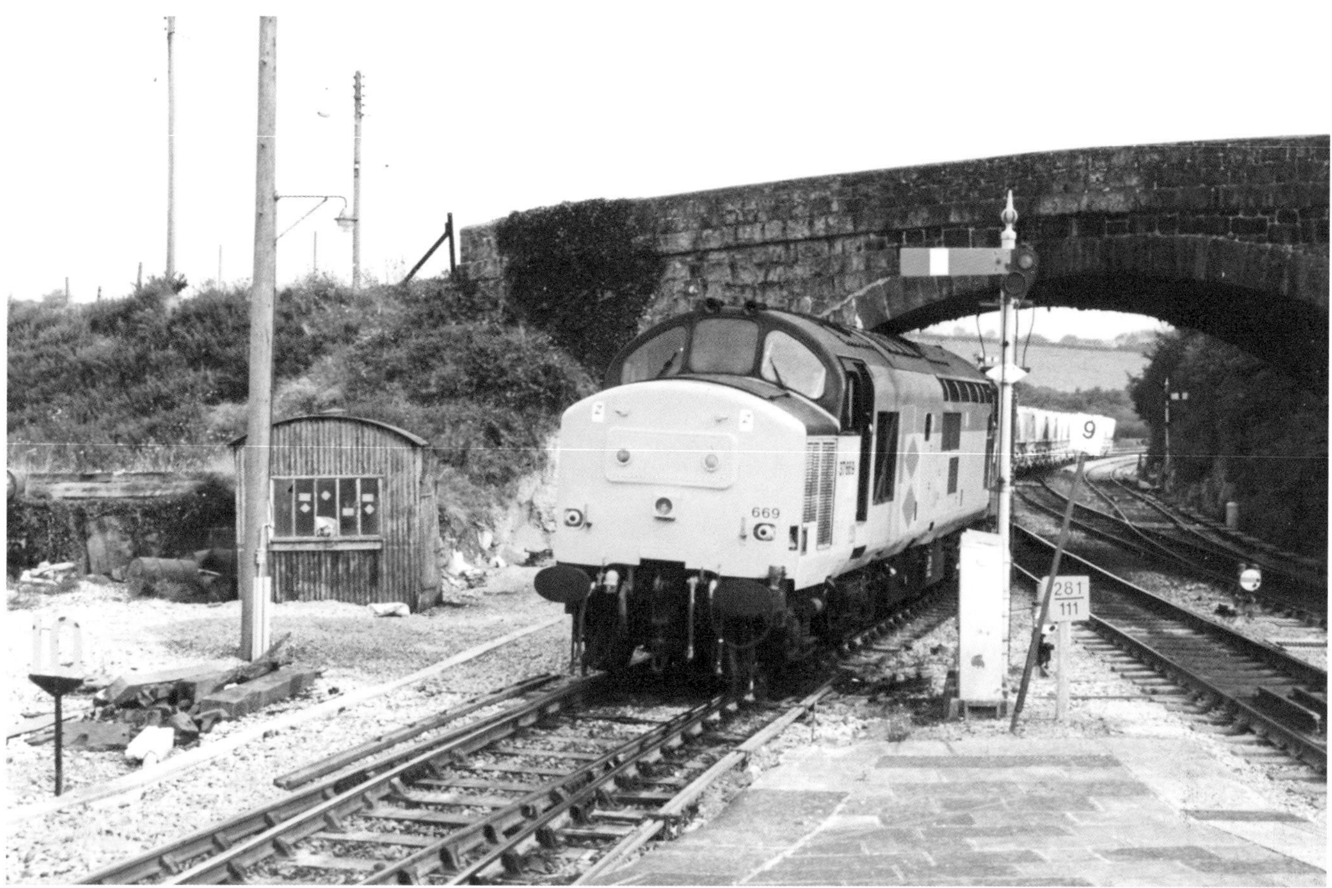

37669 at Par, having crossed over with a train of empties (usually 19) from the Down line to the Up and then taken the Branch line for St Blazey and subsequently Goonbarrow (Rocks). Picture dated September 1991. (GP)

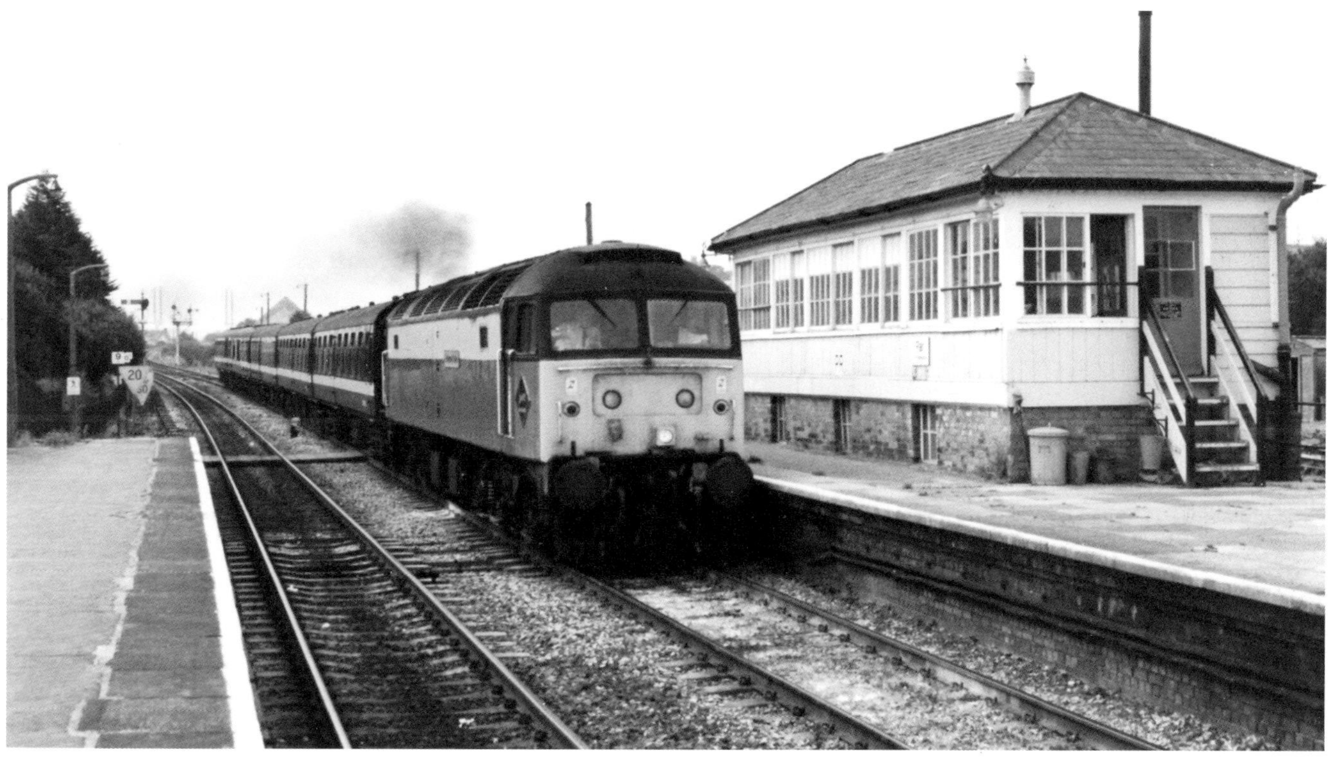

An unidentified, Dutch liveried, class 47 is seen here passing Par on the Up line in September 1991, with the test train. (GP)

Par is the location for this September 1994 picture of 37411 on a clay train for Lostwithiel and after reversing will traverse the branchline to Fowey Docks. Built in June 1965 as D6990 by E E Vulcan, it was renumbered 37290 and carried several names, but was eventually withdrawn in October 2010 but stored by Direct Rail Services at Carlisle. It carries its original number and BR Brunswick Green livery. (GP)

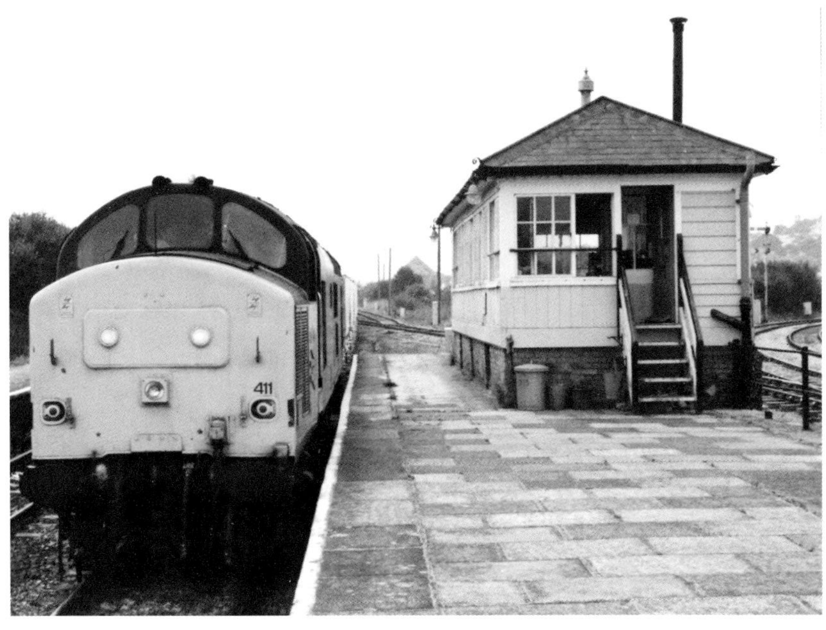

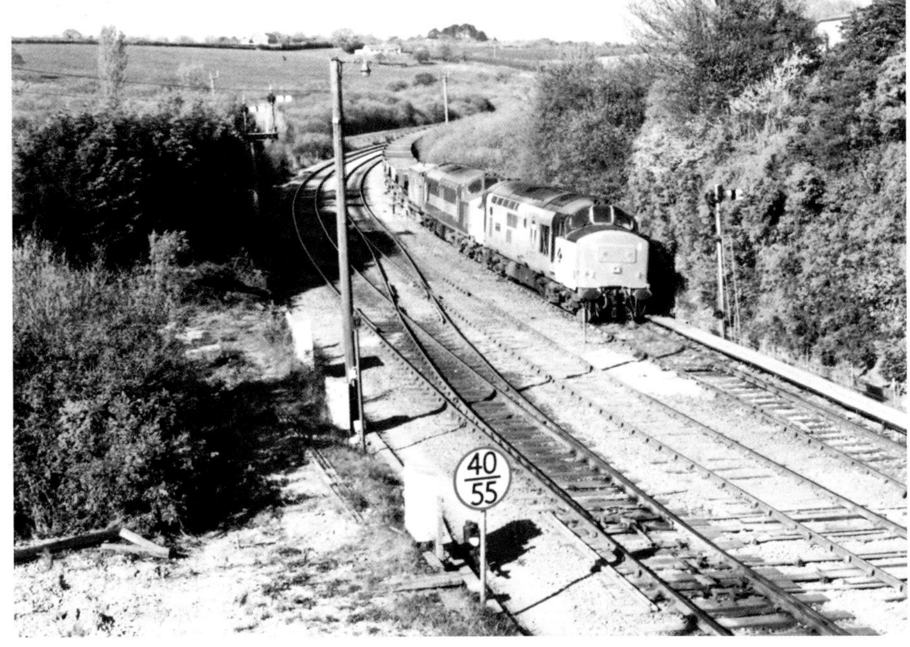

A pair of unidentified class 37s are at the head of a ballast train in Par Down Goods Loop, in early E.W.S. days. The leading loco is in the short-lived Transrail livery. (GP)

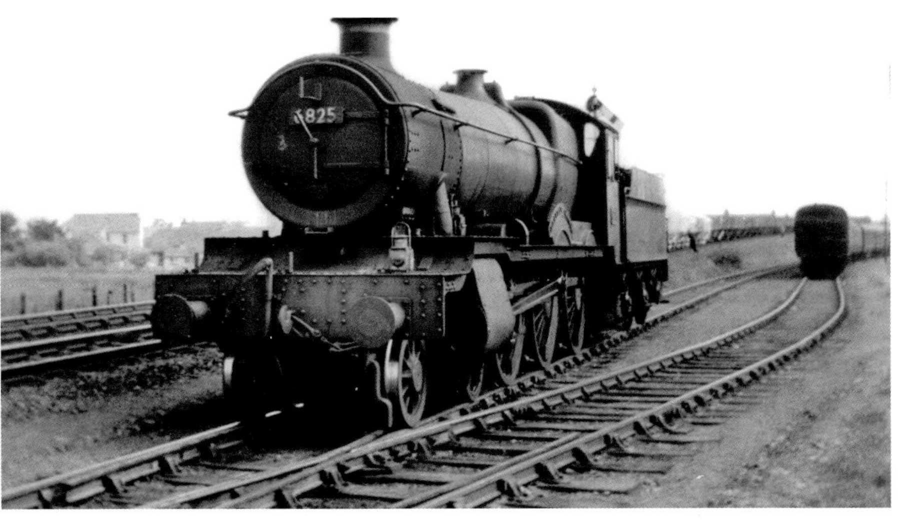

Grange class 6825 *'Llanfair Grange'* is seen on the Chapel Sidings at Par, which, in circa 1960 was a double siding. The siding is still there, but only one track is now in place. Only eighty Granges were built and none survived. (SL)

CHAPTER 3

PAR to PLYMOUTH

THE SECTION OF LINE from Par upwards to Plymouth is interesting in that it shares the tracks with regular and scheduled freight movements along with movements during the summer months of holiday trains from all over the UK, for Penzance and Newquay. This varied traffic sometimes brings unusual and rarely seen locomotives and rolling stock.

During the era that this book covers, St Blazey Depot and Yard were far busier than the trickle of movements to and from the main line that use the yard in 2013, and freight to and from the Newquay, Fowey and Moorswater Branches was more frequent than these days. Clay no longer leaves Moorswater, though cement traffic is still carried over the line by the Freightliner Company.

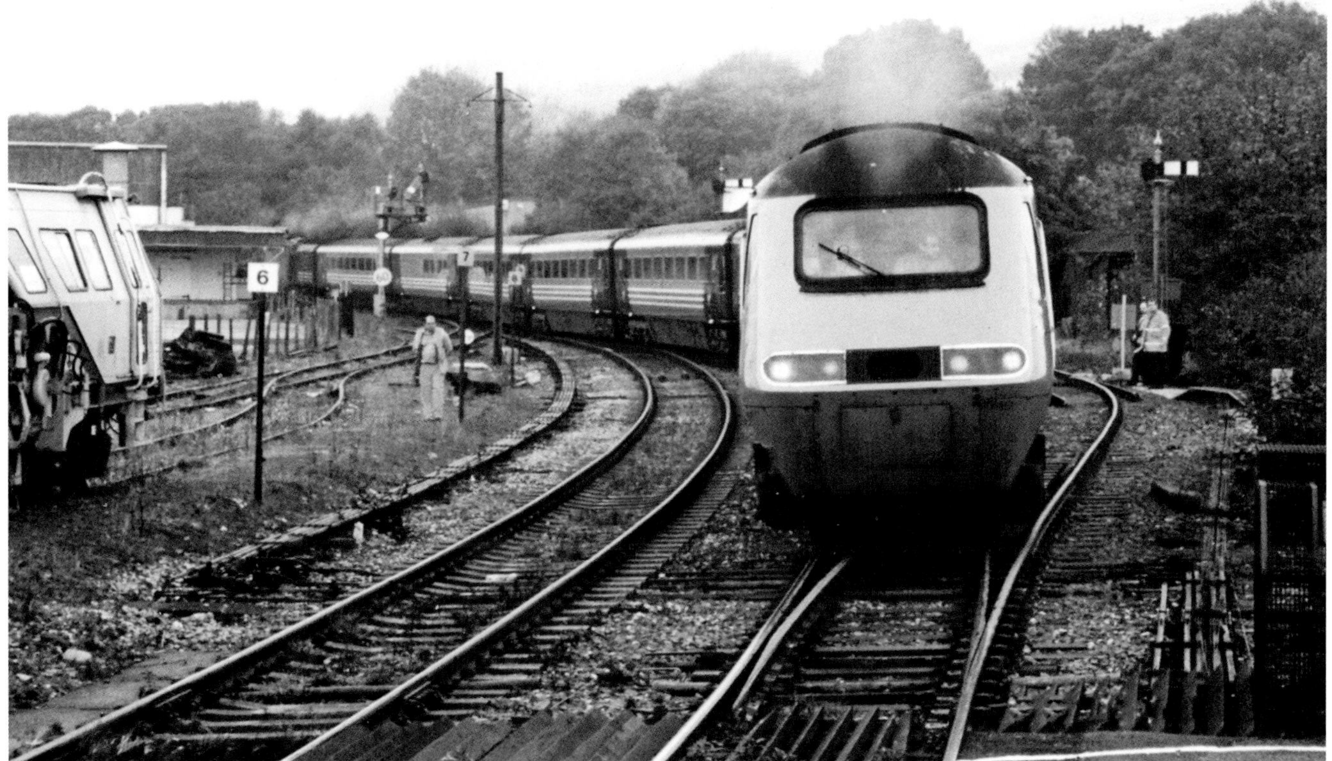

On 28 October 2001 Single-Line Working (SLW) was in operation between Lostwithiel and Par over the Up line, and the Virgin HST set is seen shunting over the cross-over with the Pilotman on board. The Pilotman escorts or sends the train over the one remaining line and acts as a human token, ensuring that no train can enter the single-line without the Pilotman (name applies to both sexes) authorising it in person. (MD)

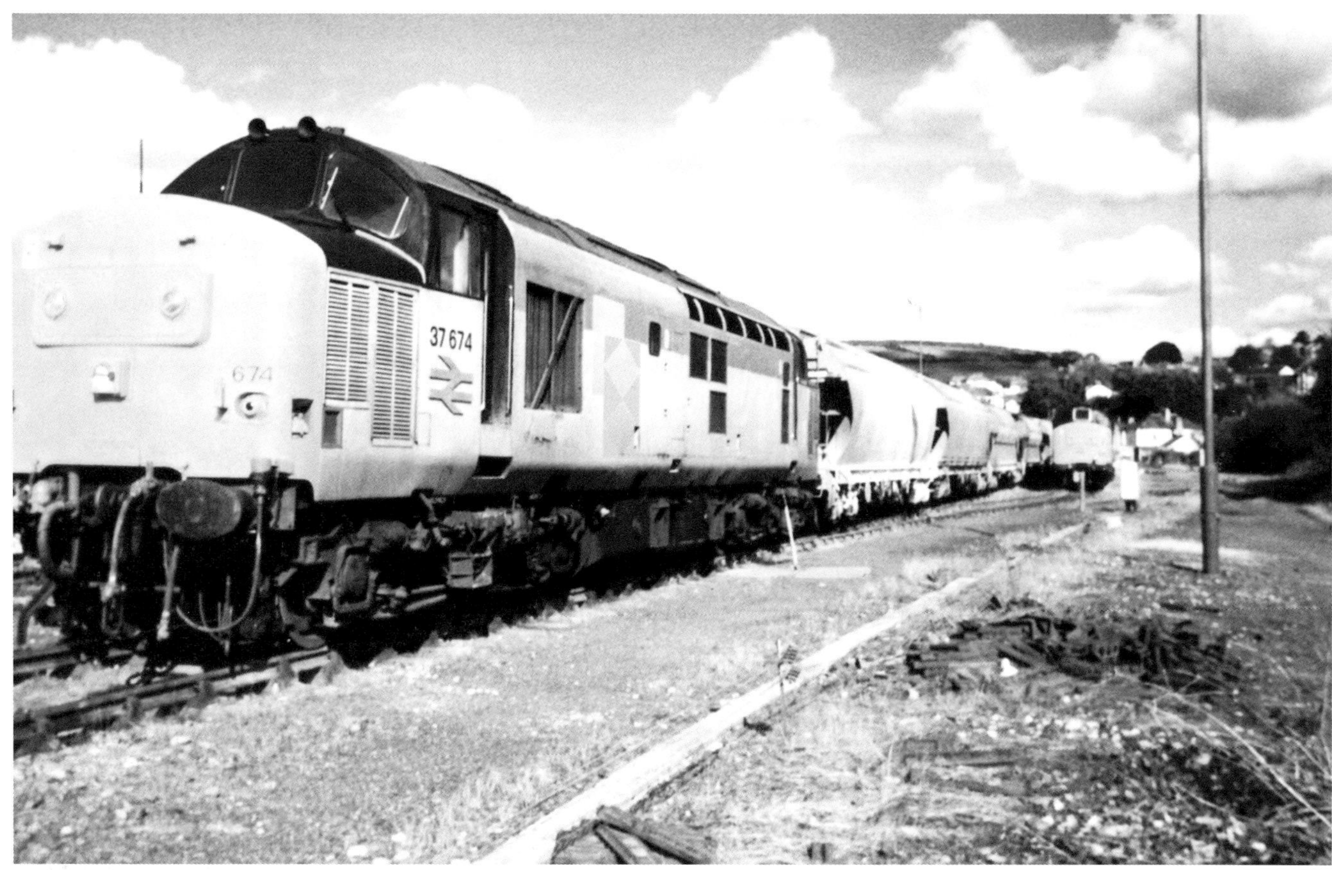

37674 is seen here with main-line wagons stabled in Lostwithiel yard, the reason for which escapes me now, but can only assume it was because of a failure ahead between there and Par on the down line, which required it to be shunted to one side, for either an HST or DMU to proceed to rescue the failed train. The proliferation of coupling types is another failure of the privatisation of the railways, along with the arduous bureaucracy of getting various train companies to agree to move other companies' failed trains, aside from the huge cost incurred in doing so and for the resultant delay whilst a deal is reached. (SFH)

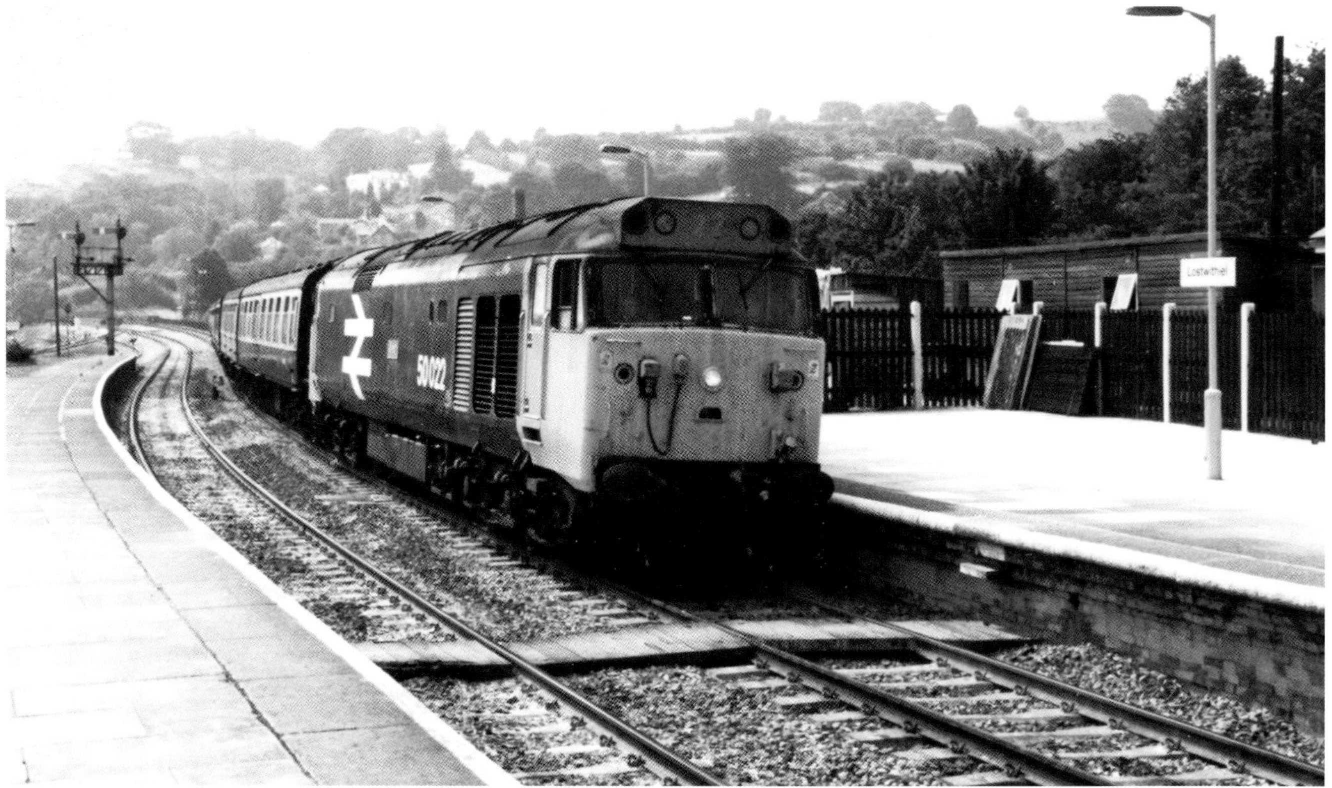

50022 *'Anson'* is seen here entering Lostwithiel Up platform in August 1983 with a local train. Built by E E in May 1968 as D422, it was withdrawn in September 1988 and was cut up by V. Berry of Leicester in May 1989. (GP)

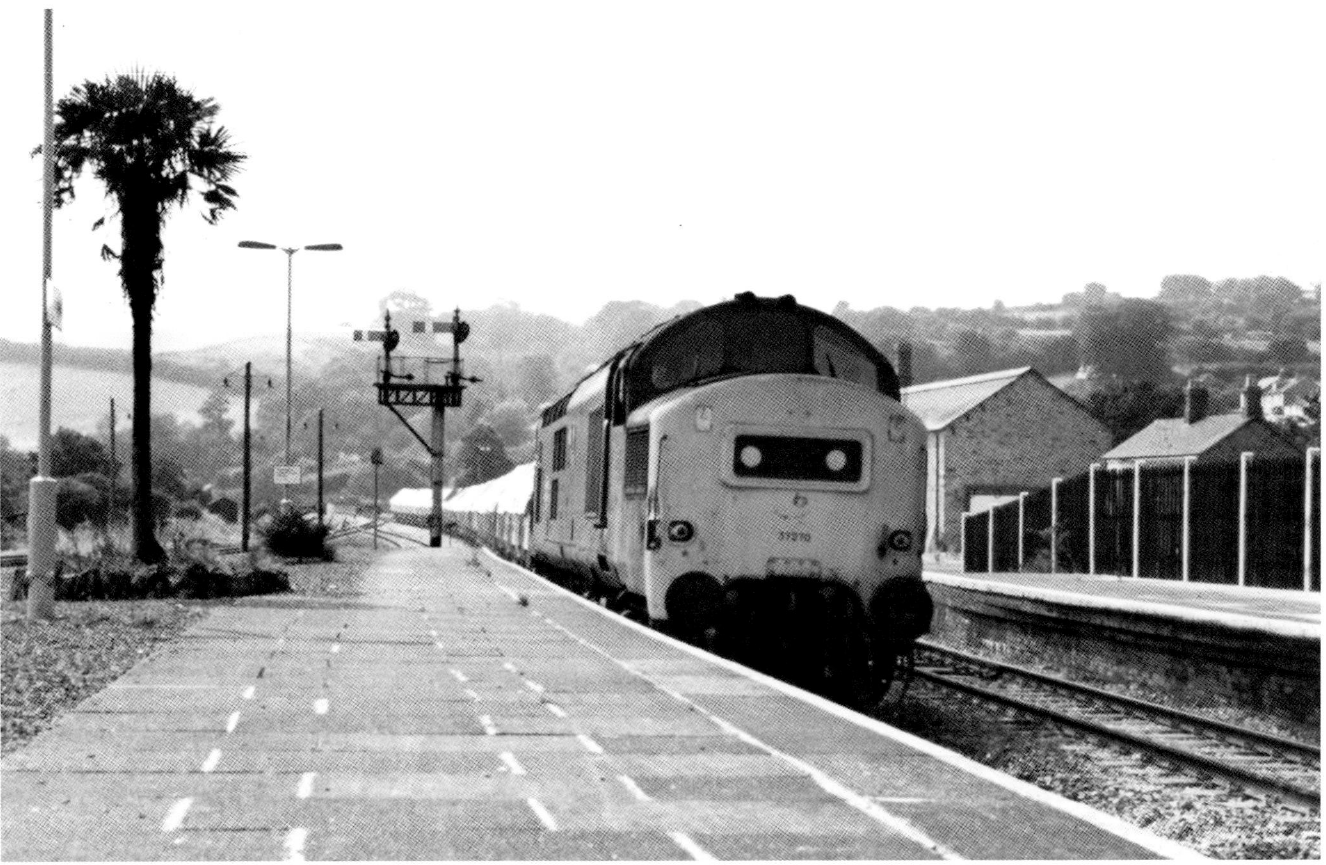

37270 is seen here traversing the Down Platform at Lostwithiel, after coming off the Fowey Branch with a string of clay hoods, which could be bound for any of the numerous clay sidings then still operated by English China Clays (ECLP) which became ECC Ltd and eventually Imerys. The picture dates from August 1983 and the loco, previously D6970, became 37409 and was built in March 1965 but still survives today on the Bo'ness & Kinneil Railway. (GP)

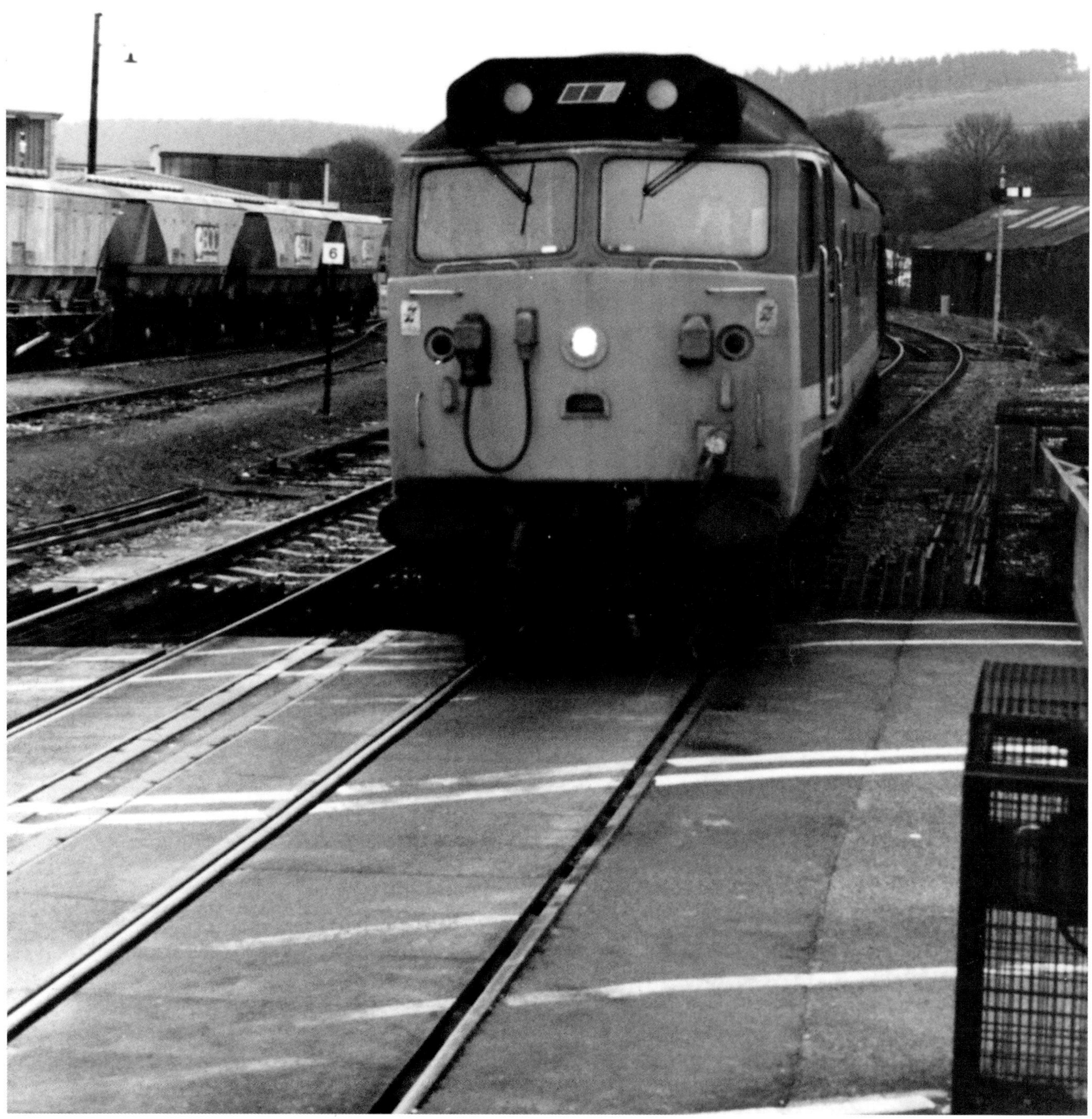

A Network South East liveried class 50 approaching Lostwithiel level crossing on the Down line in December 1987. The 'Cattle-Pens' has some CDA wagons stored in the two roads, which in those days was regularly used for the odd wagon and frequently for locomotives, standing by. Now sadly they are no longer used and are in poor condition. (GP)

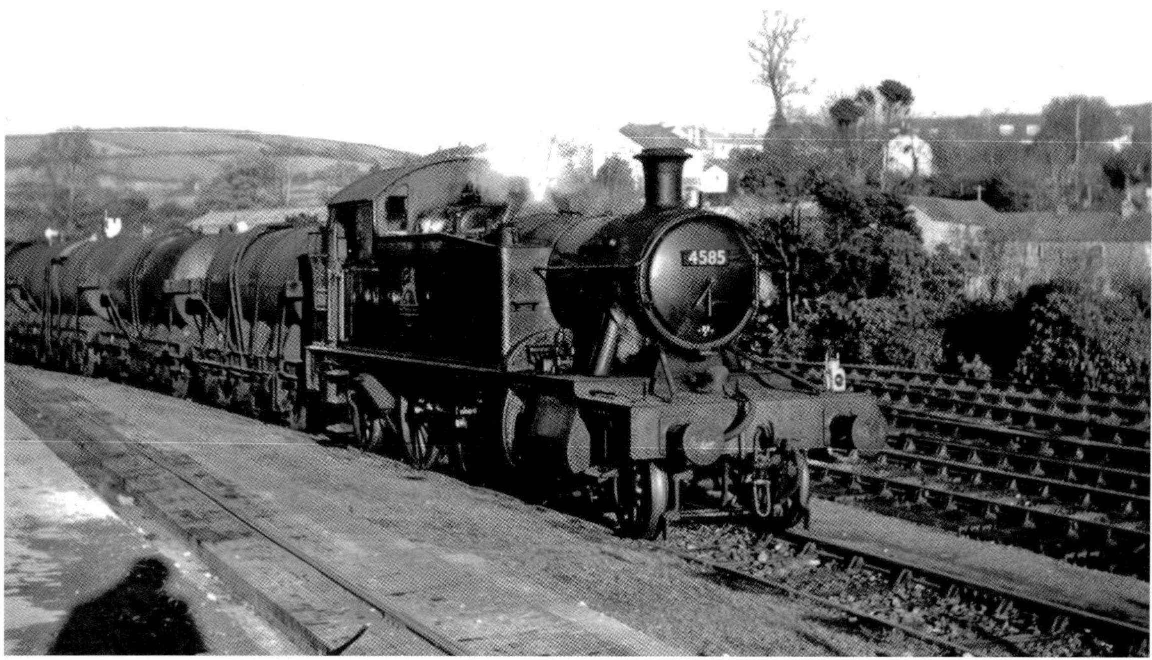

Prairie Tank number 4585 is seen here at Lostwithiel shunting six-wheeled milk tanks in the Up Loop. The concrete apron is adjacent and although disconnected, is still in situ in 2013, though the ground-frame at the north end of the milk siding was removed a few years ago. (SL)

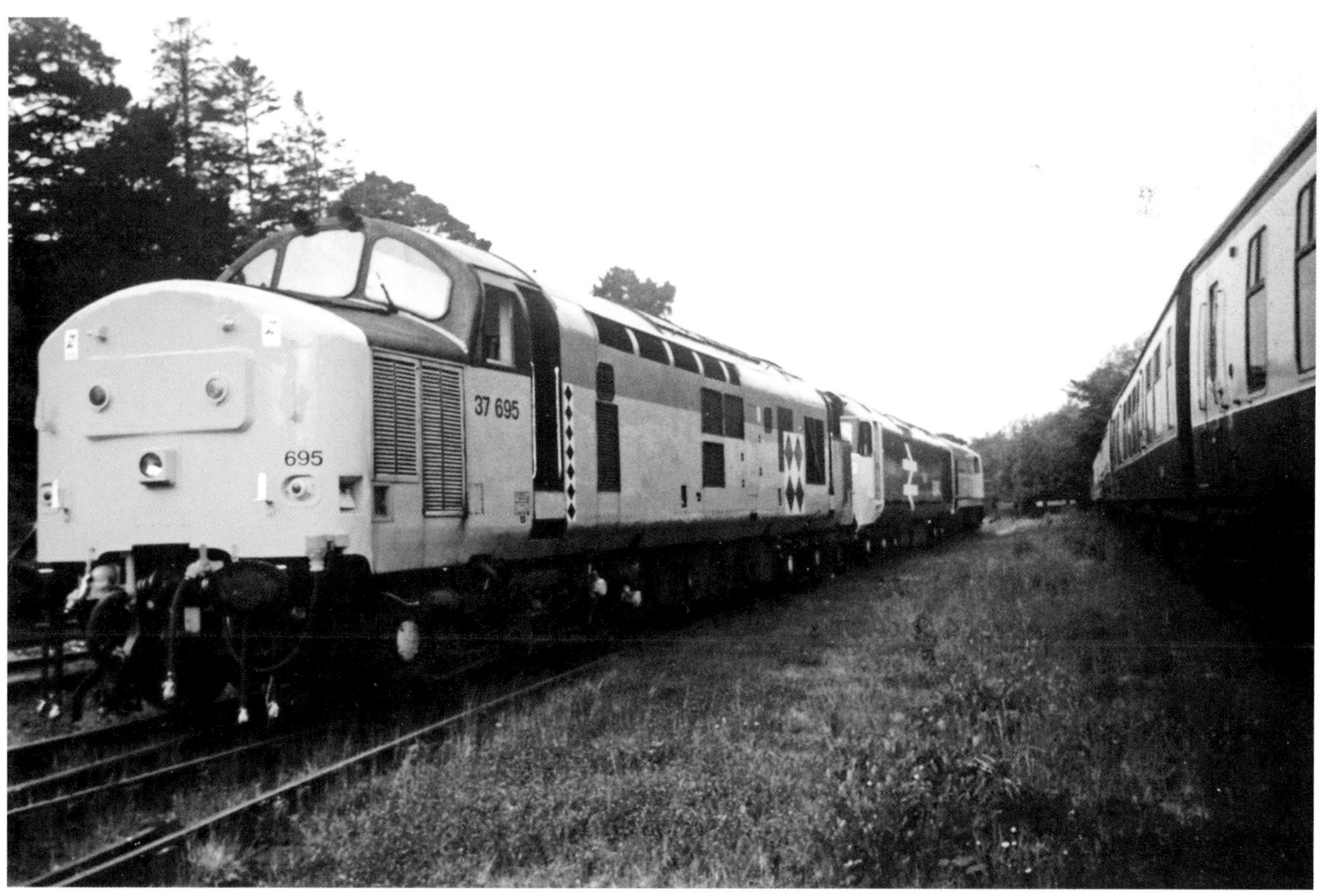

37965 is seen here having just propelled 50042 *'Triumph'* and RFS 2015 a class 20 hire loco, previously used in the building of the Channel Tunnel, into the Exchange Sidings at Bodmin Parkway. The locos were hired in for a Diesel Gala Day on the Bodmin & Wenford Railway, and I was there to operate the ground-frame, giving access from the Up main line. (SFH)

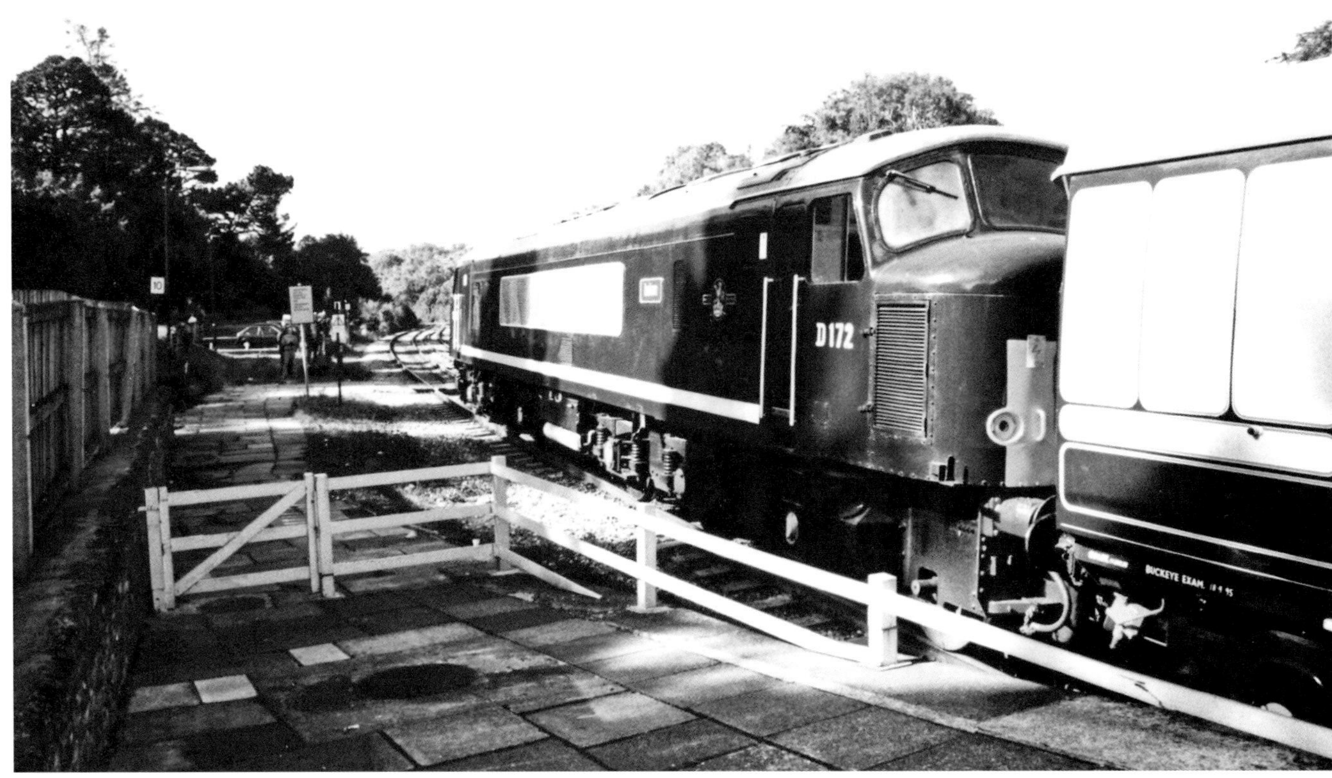

In 1995 a charter train is seen in the Down Platform at Bodmin, with class 46 D172 *'Ixion'* in charge. Built by BR at Derby in July 1962 it was withdrawn in January 1991 as 97403 in Departmental stock. It was renumbered to 46035 when in BR capital stock. At the date of the photo it was kept at the Crewe Heritage Centre. (SFH)

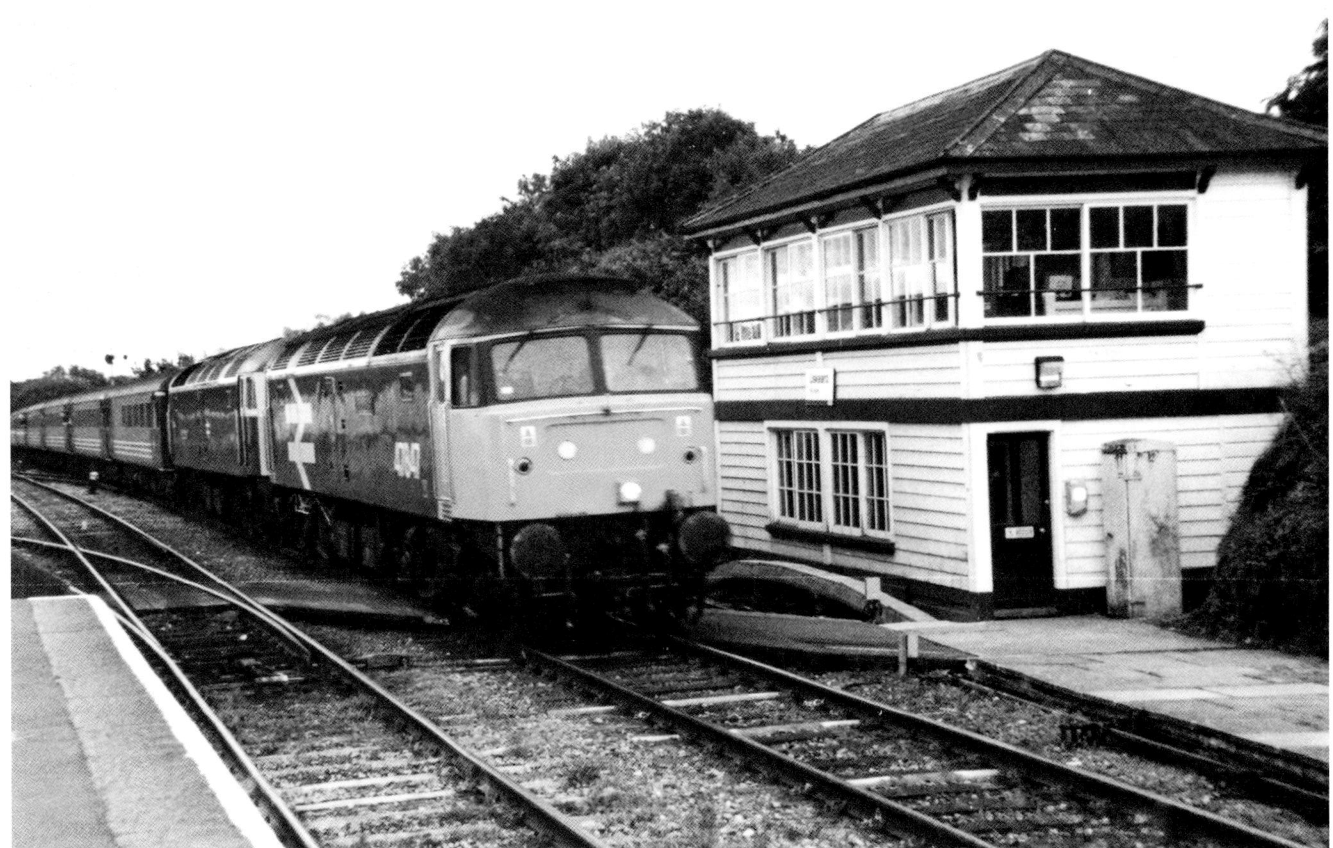

On the day before the final loco hauled Virgin Cross-Country train, the Down train is seen passing Liskeard Signalbox with 1V84, the 1003 Glasgow to Penzance train. (MD)

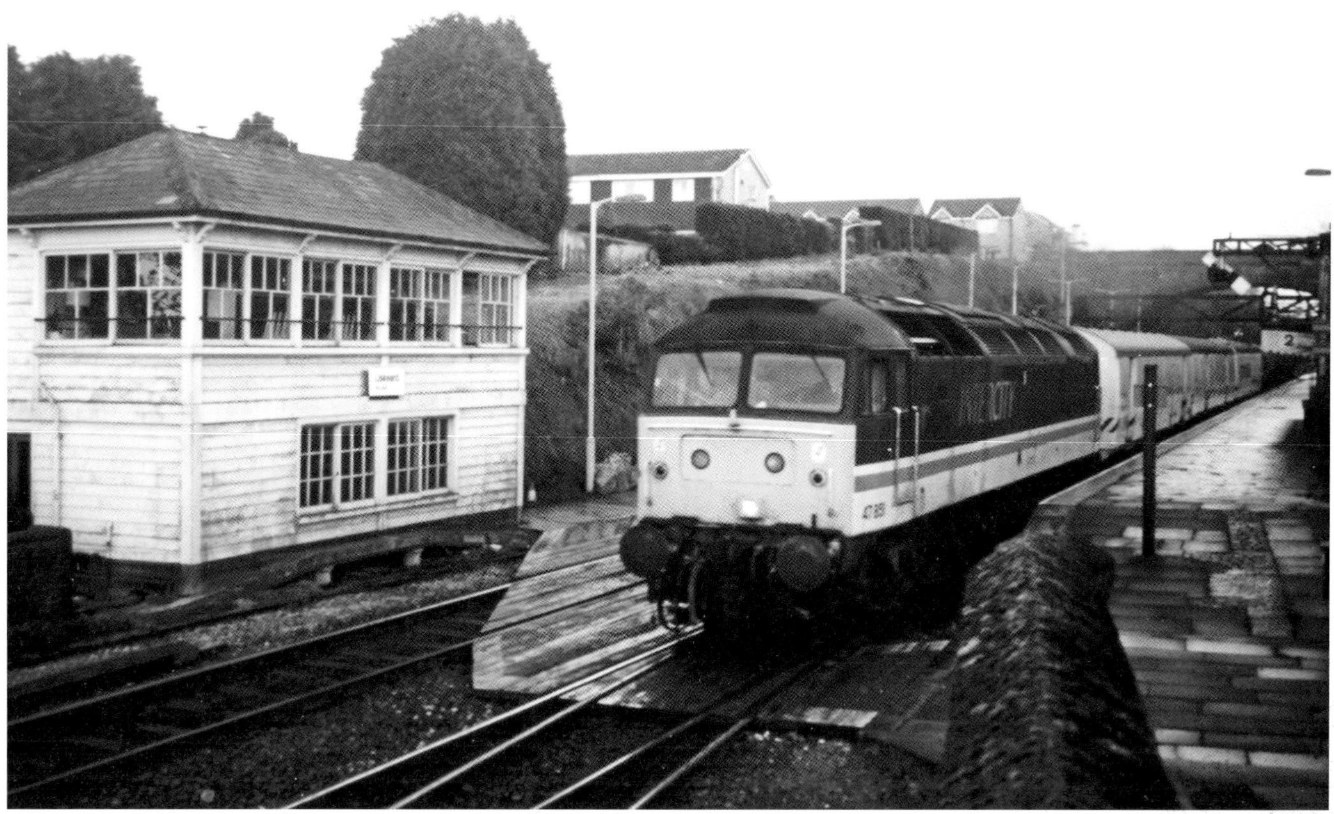

The Up line at Liskeard is the location of Intercity liveried 47851at the head of the Breakdown train returning to Laira, where it was kept until Network Rail reorganised the locations where they were based. This loco started life as D1648 in Crewe Works in January 1965. It went on to become 47064, 47639 and is still in service with WCR. (SFH)

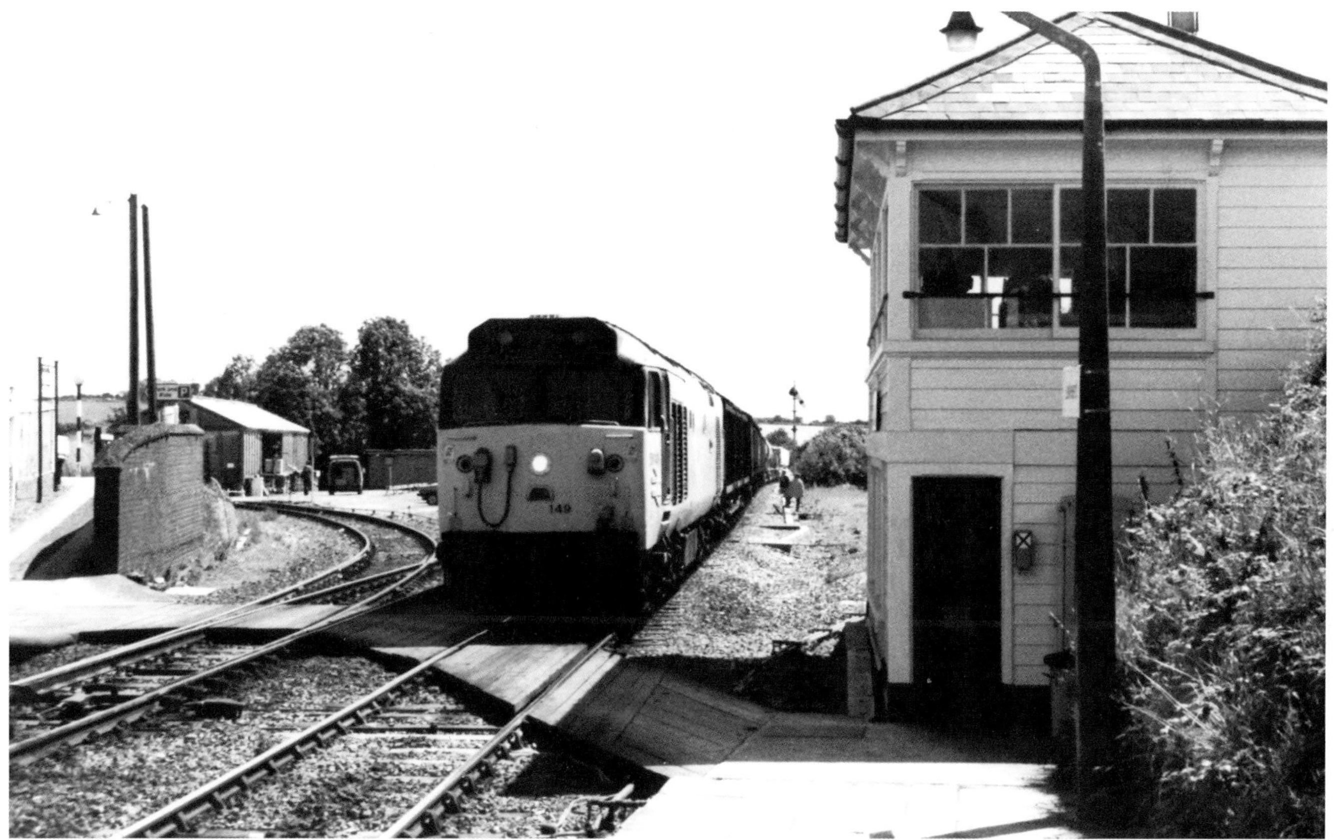

50149 was another celebrity loco, but this time because it was the only one of the class to carry Freight Sector livery and re-gearing for freight work. It operated in this guise only between August 1987 and February 1989, when it returned to passenger stock. It is seen here passing Liskeard Signalbox on the Down line, with a train for St Blazey Yard in July 1988. It survives in preservation by 'The Fifty Fund'. (GP)

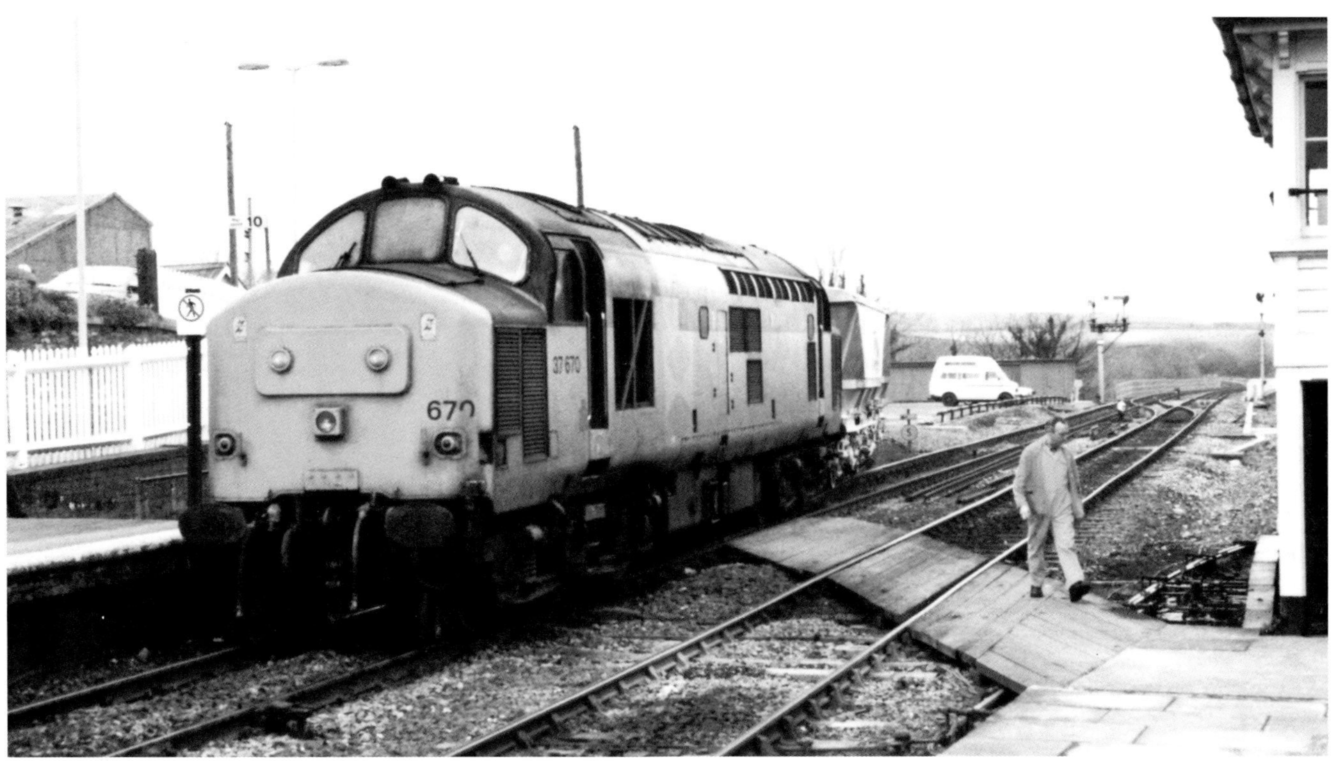

An excellent picture of 37670 about to bring its train of china clay off the branch connection at Liskeard and onto the Up main line, shortly after it will cross over to the down line and the West End of the station and thence to Lostwithiel and Fowey Docks, with a load from Moorswater. Built as D6882 in October 1963, it was renumbered 37182 in 1974 before taking its final number in August 1987. The date is April 1991. It is currently owned by HNRC. (GP)

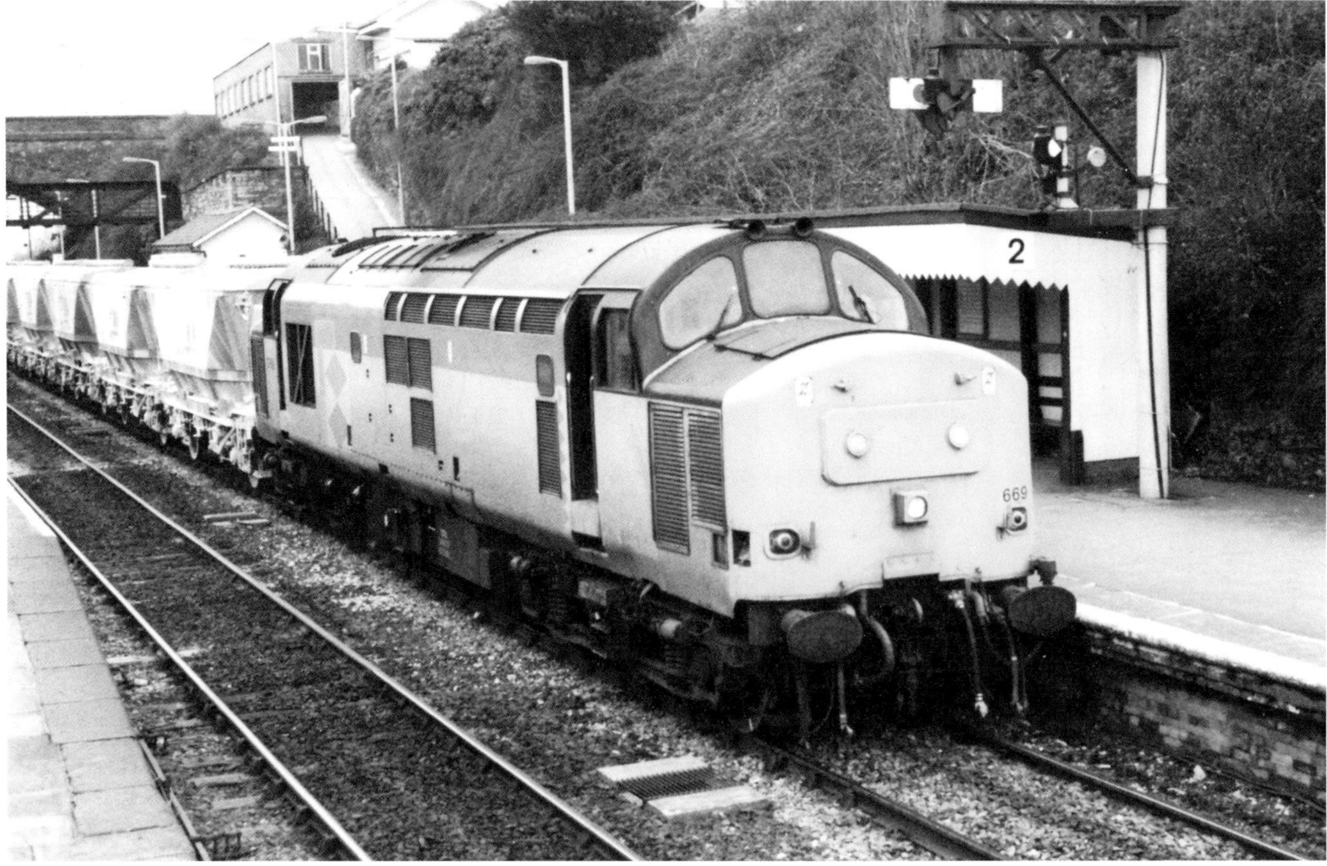

April 1991 sees 37669 with a train of empties for Moorswater Clay Works. The disc signal number 17 is in the 'off' position for the slow move onto the tight curve through the yard and to the ground frame for access to the line to Coombe Junction. Built in March 1963 by English Electric at their Vulcan Foundry as D6829 it was renumbered 37129 eleven years later. It is currently owned by West Coast Railways at Carnforth. (GP)

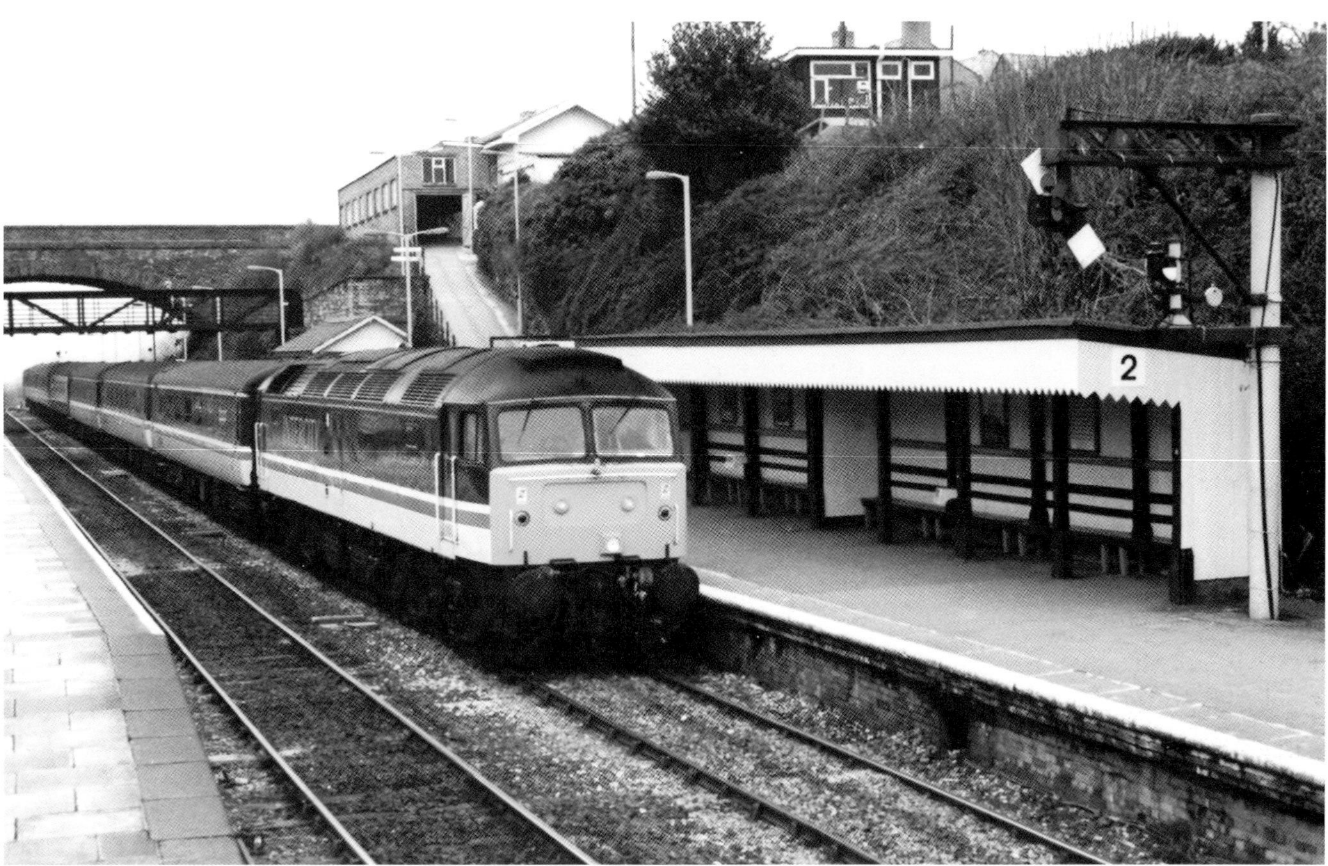

This picture is taken from Liskeard signalbox on 9 April 1991 and shows an unidentified 'Intercity' liveried class 47 on an Up train to Bristol. Of particular note is the up somersault signal LD3 which is wooden and is still in use in 2013. (GP)

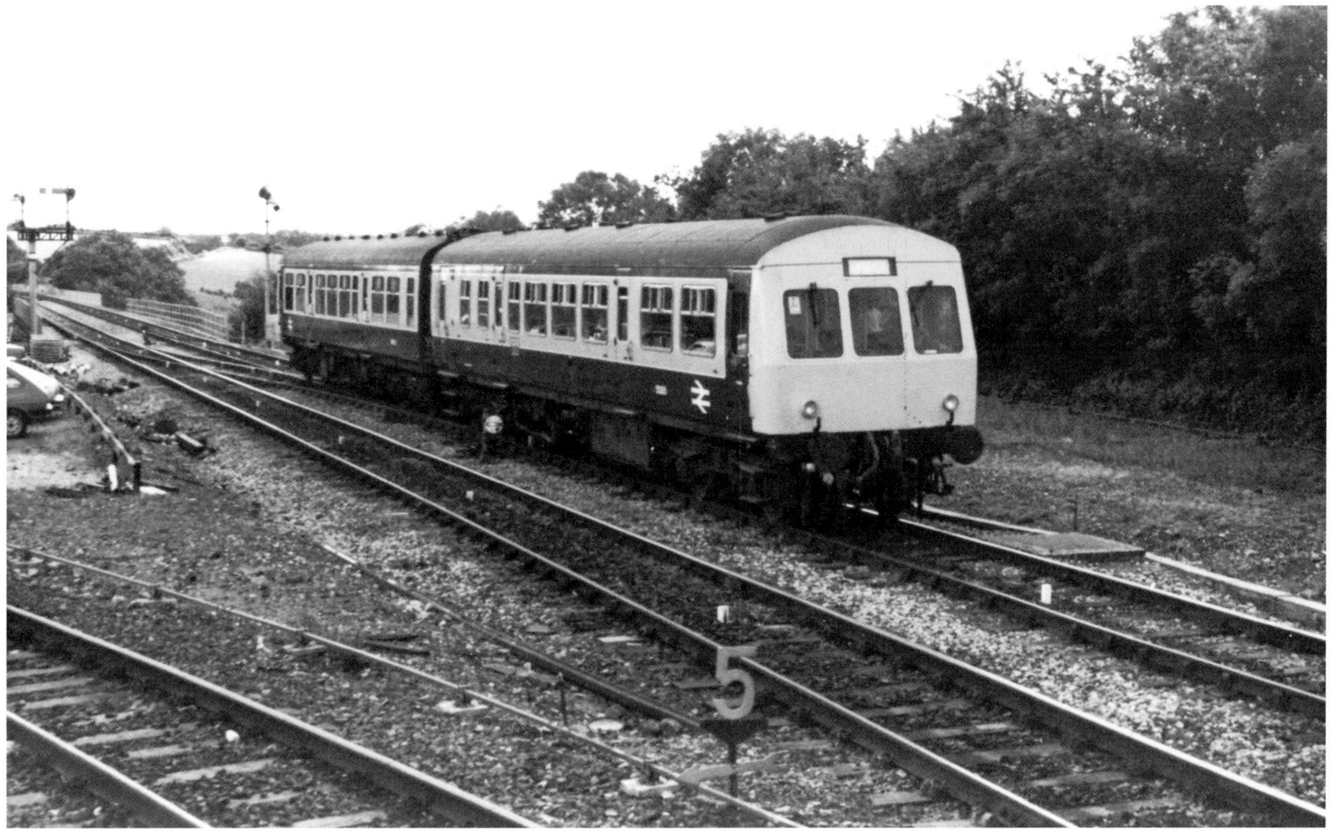

Another hybrid unit (101 & 108) is here entering Liskeard on the Down line in June 1988 with a local train from Plymouth to Penzance. The Up line bracket signal (LD4 and 5) on the left of the picture is now on the Bodmin & Wenford railway after being removed when St Germans signalbox was closed and the signalling system changed to Track-Circuit-Block to Plymouth Panel. The short arm is the former LD 5 'Shunt Ahead' signal, which after being thrown away, I (SFH) recovered and have since presented to the B&W. (GP)

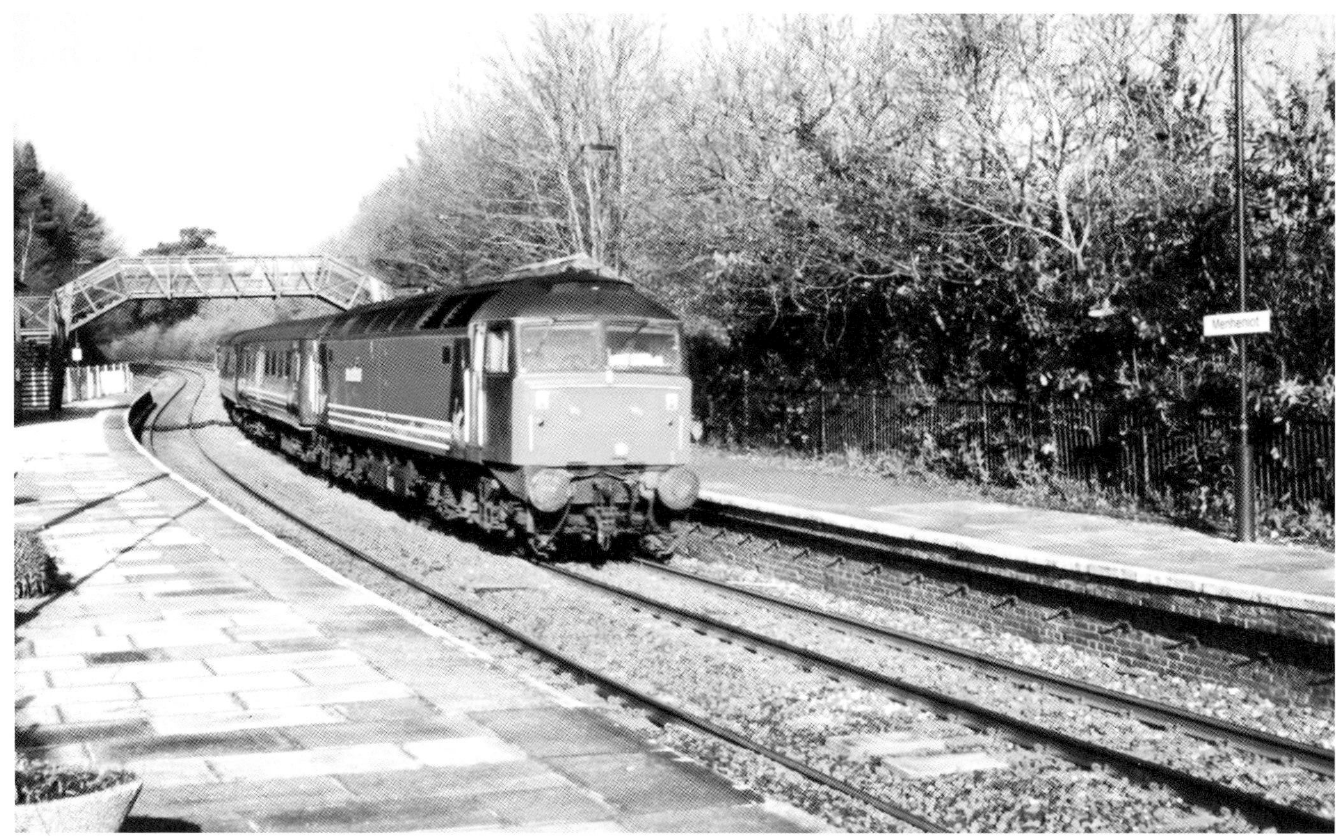

On 16 February 2002 an unidentified Virgin class 47 passes over the Up line at Menheniot, with 1M56, the 08:46 Penzance to Manchester. (MD)

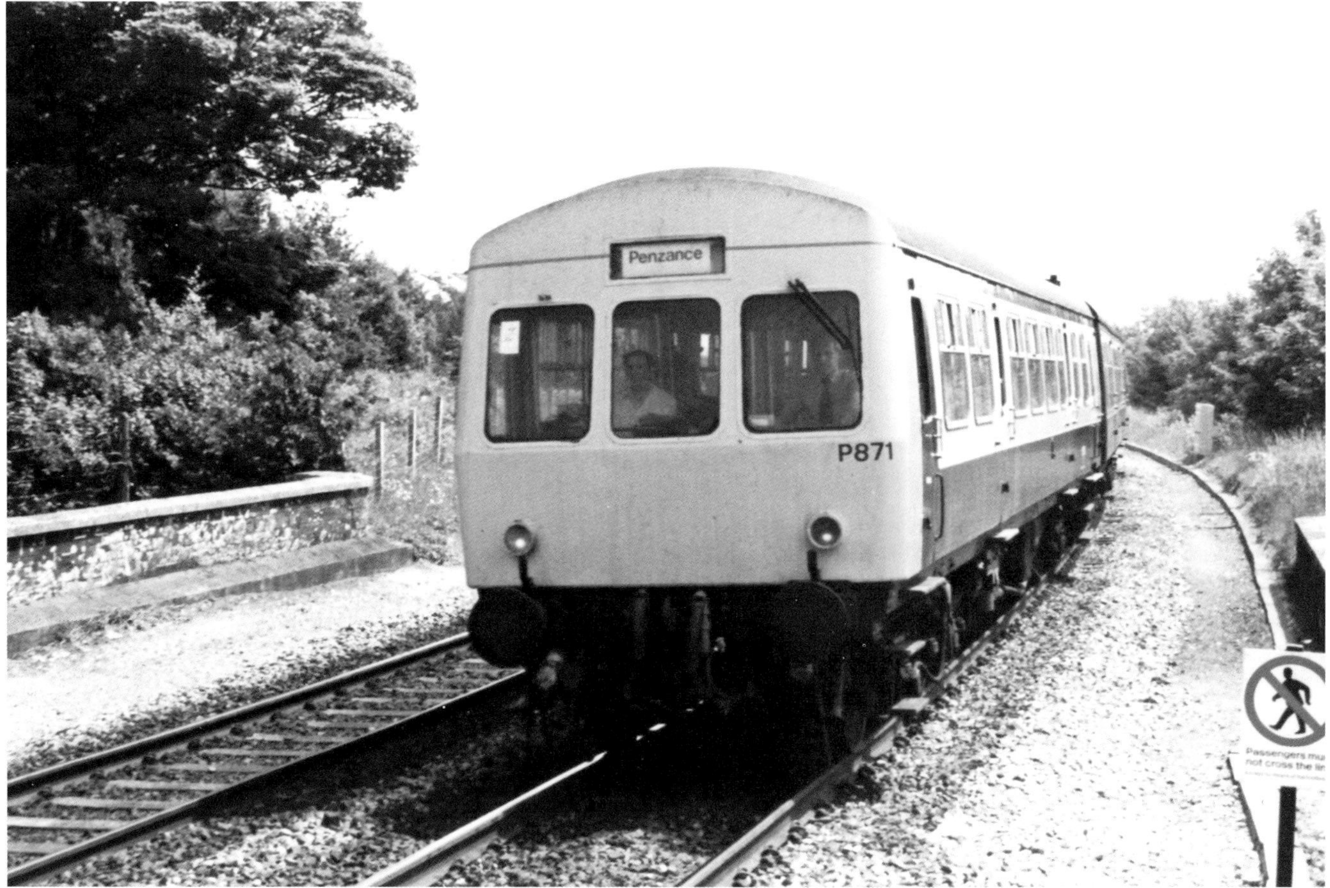

St Germans Station is the location here for this picture of a Penzance bound class 101 unit on a local trip from Plymouth in June 1988. (GP)

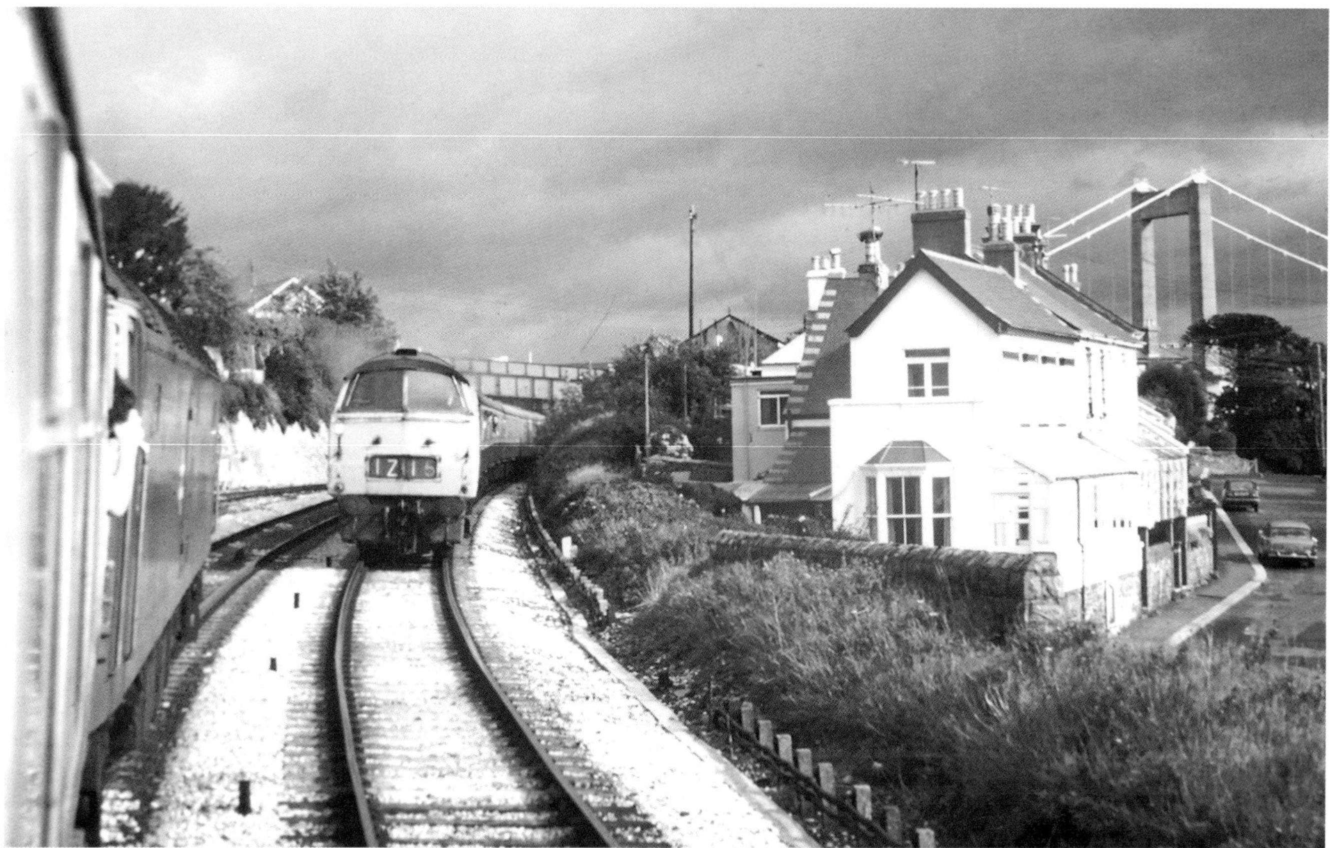

This is an unusual shot of an unidentified Western on the Down line, about to pass a Class 47 hauled Up train just outside Saltash Station in 1975. (JR)

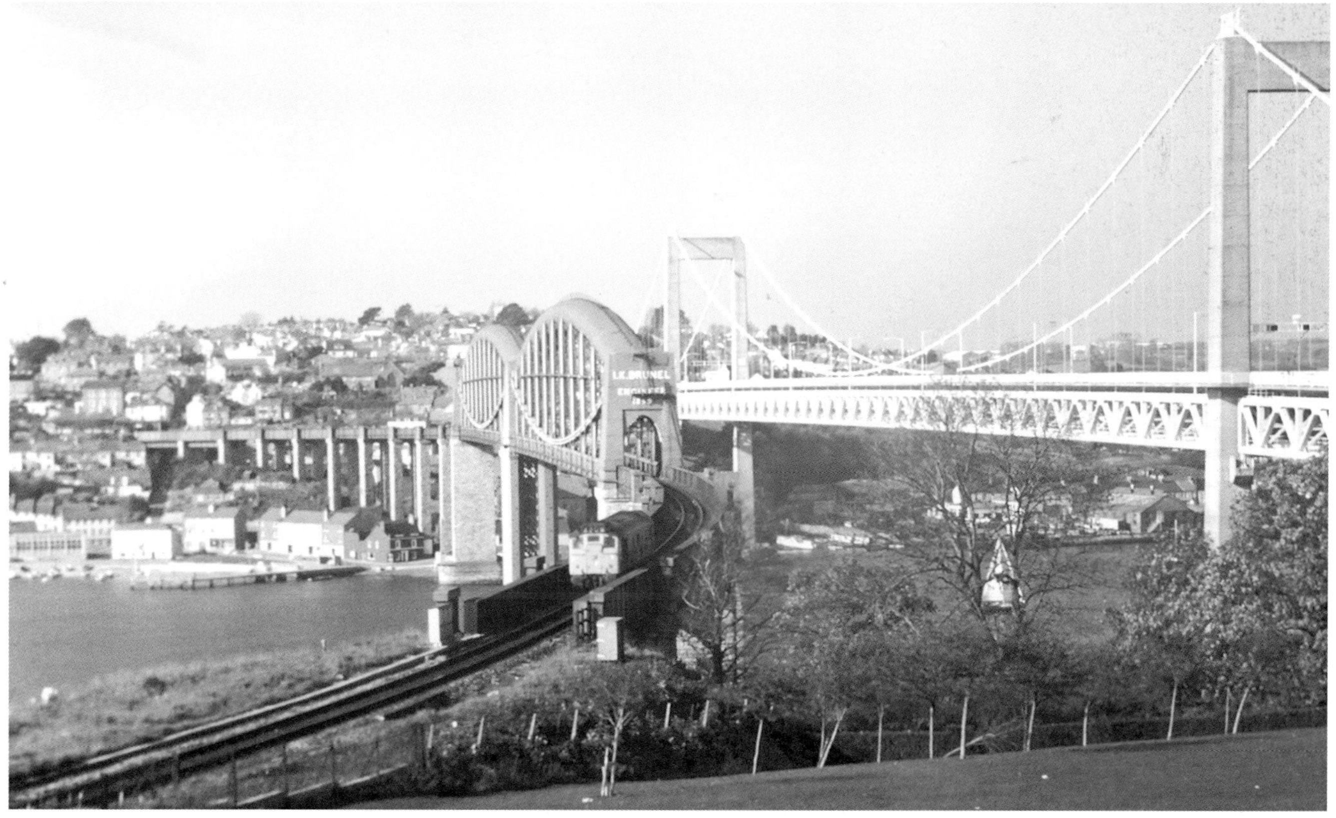

A lovely sunny day in 1975 sees a light loco class 25 on the RAB (Royal Albert Bridge). Thirty-eight years later will see the ugly steps and ironwork that had defaced the 'I.K.Brunel' name removed, the trackbed and sleepers replaced with the original design Baulk Road and the structure swathed in sheeting and scaffolding whilst it undergoes its most thorough refurbishment and repaint in over fifty years. (JR)

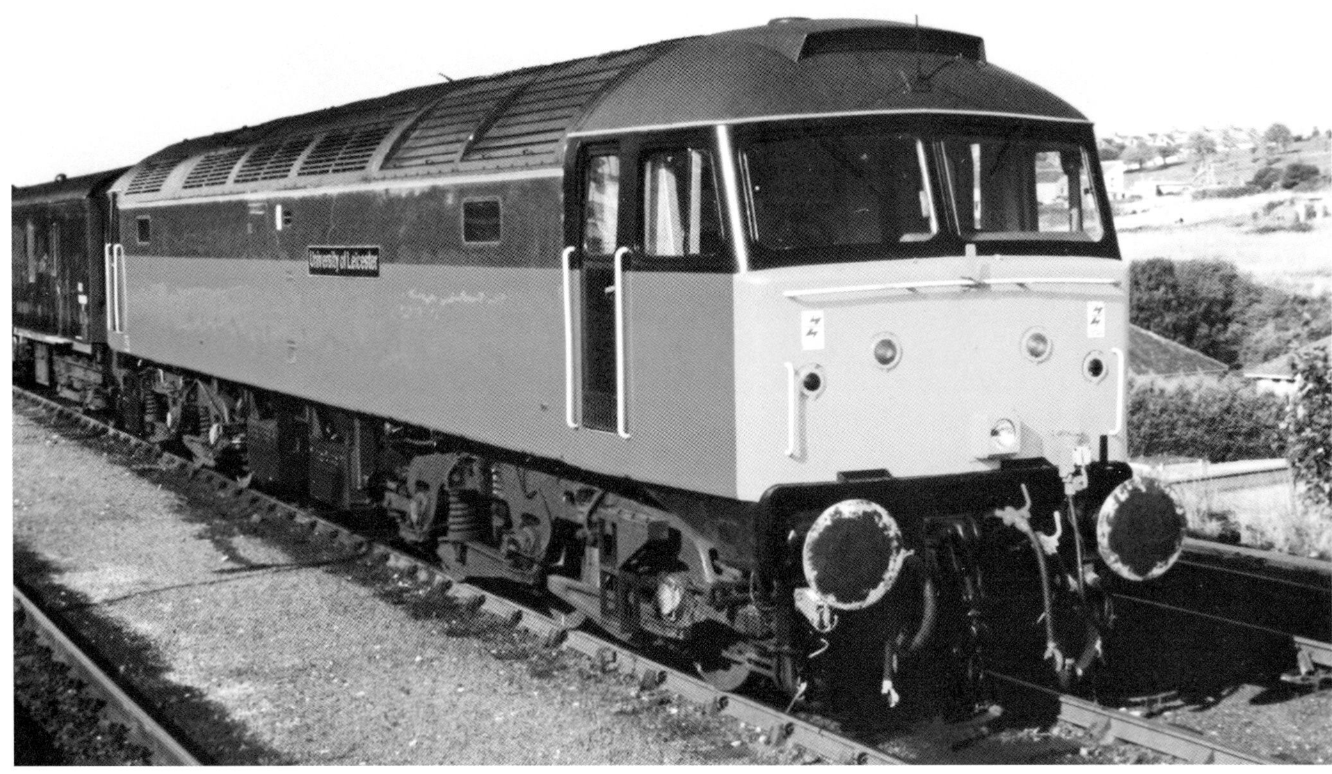

The date is September 1990, and the location is the Up Sidings at Plymouth, which finds an apparently unnumbered *'University of Leicester'* stabled with vans, probably for the next Postal Train. Built as D1649 in January 1965 by BR at Crewe, it became 47065 and is actually 47535 here. It was withdrawn in February 1999 and scrapped by HNRC at Old Oak Common (OOC) depot in April 2004. (GP)

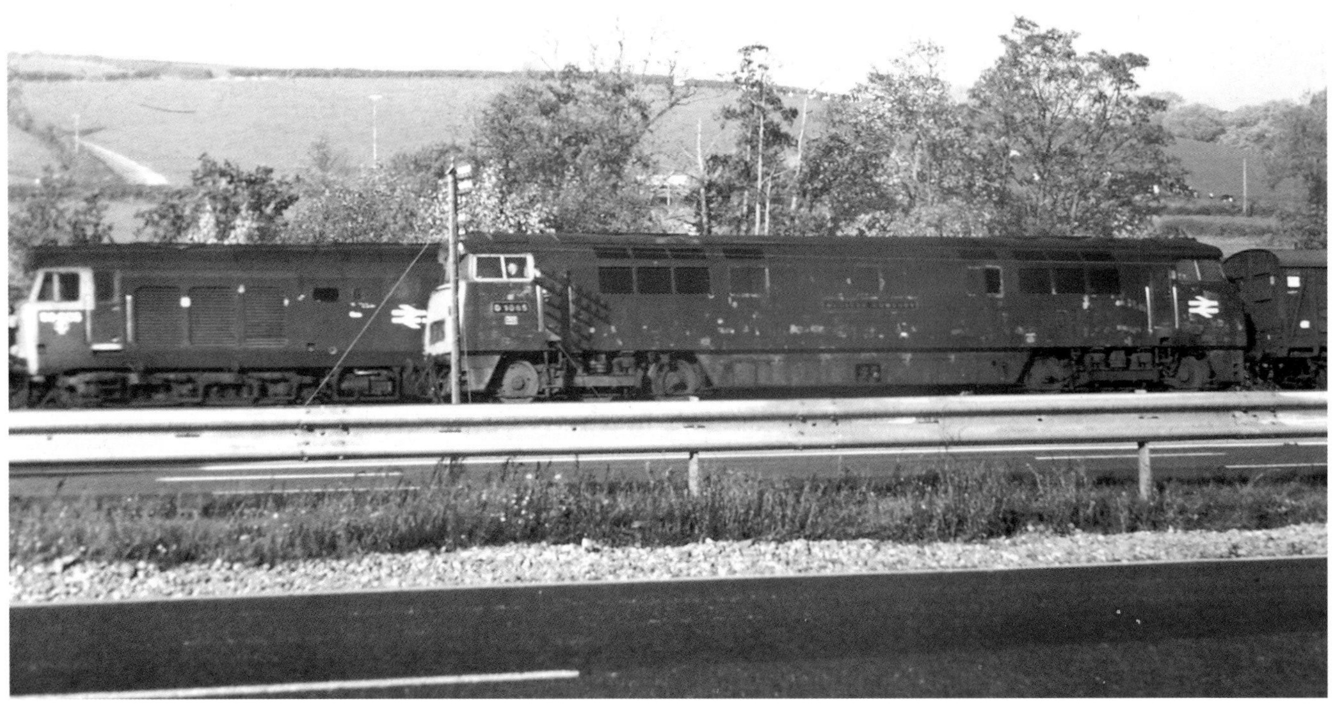

D1065 *'Western Consort'* is seen here on the Down line passing an unidentified class 50 in Devon where the M5 motorway passes close to the railway for several miles. (JR)

CHAPTER 4

ST BLAZEY

THE ST BLAZEY AREA has always been an interesting place to watch trains, though of course there is very little to see these days. The photos included in this chapter will focus on the days in previous decades when traffic around this area was prolific and varied. Aside from the maintenance and servicing that once took place there, the depot was home to a dozen or so locomotives throughout its life, and the local DMU fleet was both kept here and received daily servicing.

The Postal Trains were kept here during the weekdays and the locomotives that used to haul them were also serviced here every day, and during shortages or failures of main line locos or freight locos, they could find themselves being seconded to hauling clay trains, or assisting an express.

Engineering trains also stabled in the long sidings that St Blazey still has, as well as being shunted onto the old 'Ballast Siding' opposite the signalbox.

St Blazey was once a thriving and important location and the pictures in this chapter hopefully will reflect that bygone, but not too distant, period when traffic was plentiful.

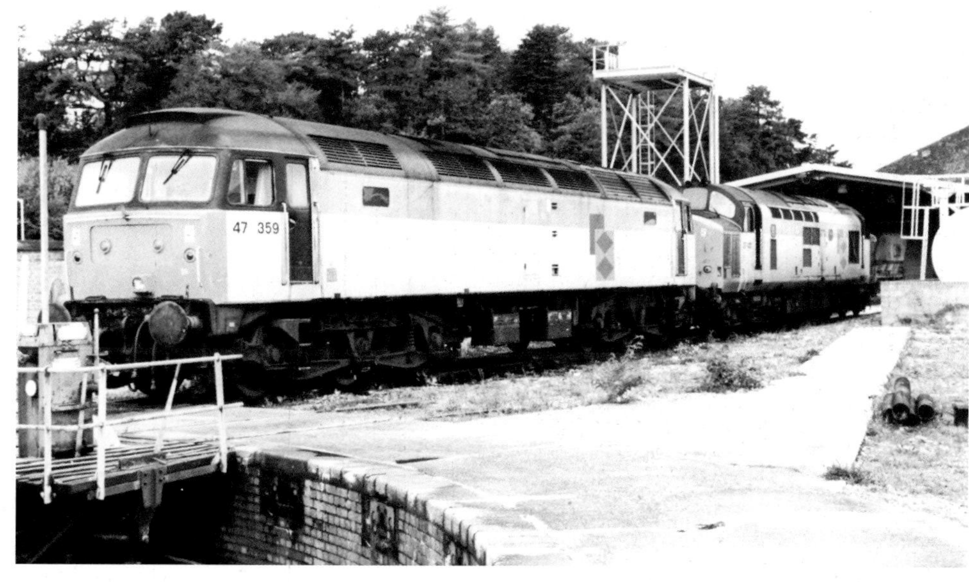

37412 and 47359 are seen here stabled adjacent to the turntable at St Blazey in 1989. 37412 was built as D6601 by English Electric at the Vulcan Foundry in September 1965 and was renumbered to 37301 first, but in 1994 was named *'Driver John Elliot'* after a driver at St Blazey, who unfortunately was killed in the depot in Christmas Eve 1993. I was at Lostwithiel as Signalman the day before when John had broken down on the Fowey Branch. This tragic accident sent a shock wave through the depot and railway in Cornwall and further afield. The loco survives as a source of Spares for DRS at Barrow Hill. 47359 was built by Brush as D1878 in June 1965 and was cut up in February 1998 by C.F. Booth. (MD)

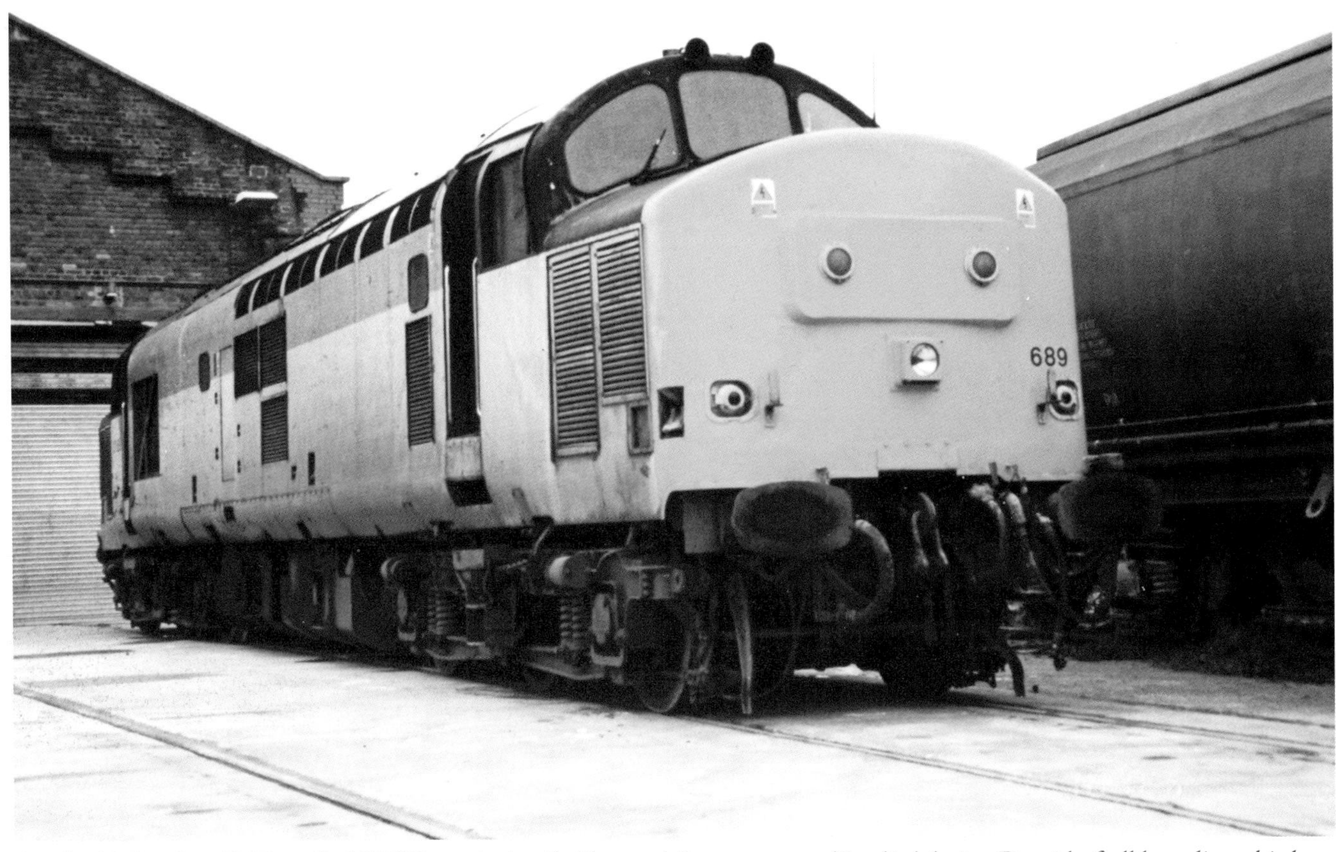

On the 28 October 2001 we find 37689 on shed at St Blazey whilst on autumn 'Sandite' duties. Devoid of all branding, this loco started out life as English Electric D6895 in March 1964 and became 37195. Never named, it was withdrawn in September 2007 and cut up in February 2011. (MD)

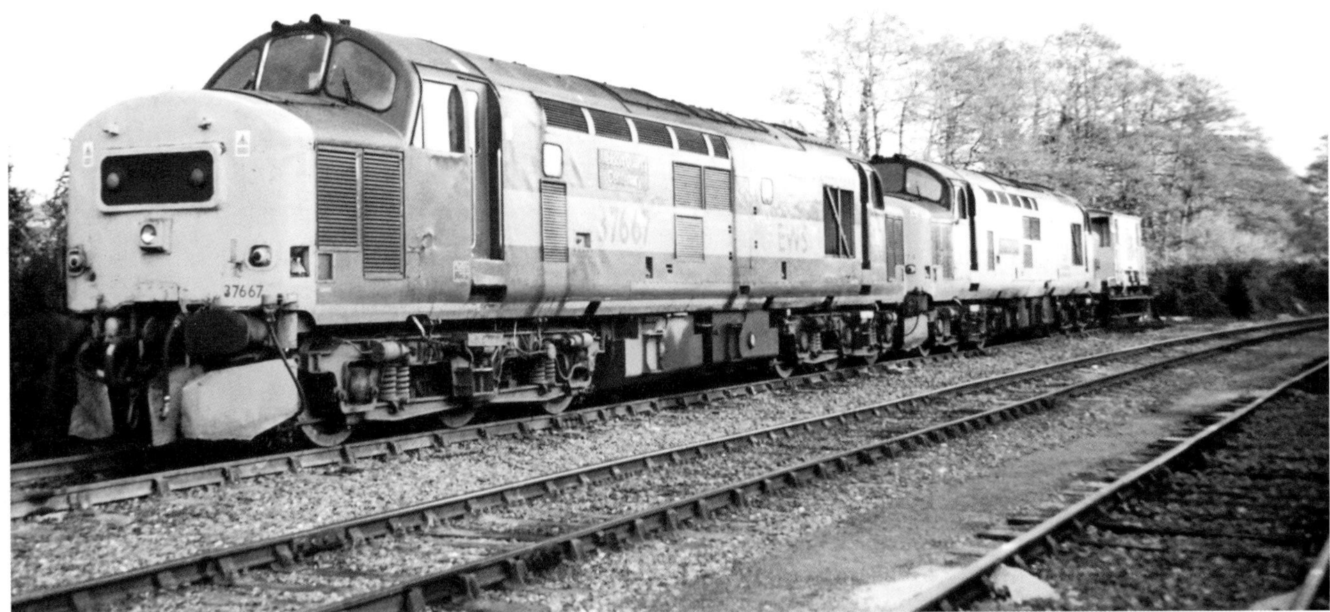

The 9 March 2004 finds 37667 and 37674 stabled in 'River Siding' at St Blazey. It is hard to believe now, but this siding and one other were laid due to shortage of room whilst I have worked in the St Blazey Operating Department Office since 1994. Both were built at the EE Vulcan Foundry in July and August 1963 respectively. 37667 *'Meldon Quarry Centenary'* was formerly D6851 then 37151 and now works for Direct Rail. 37674 was formerly D6869 and 37169 and was named *'St Blaise Church 1445-1985'* between December 1995 and January 2005. (MD)

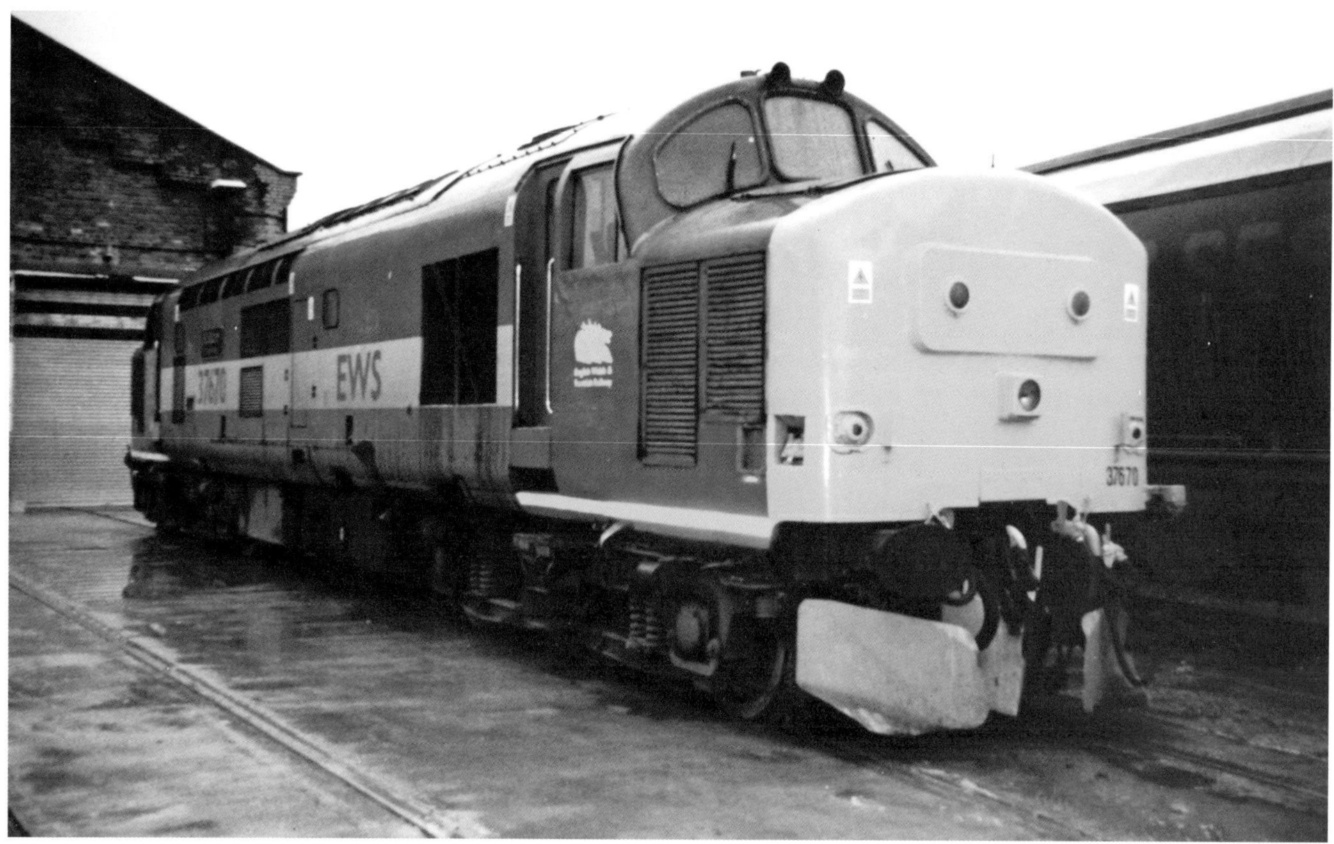

37670 *'St Blazey T&RS Depot'* is on St Blazey Shed in between 'Sandite' duties on 10 November 2002. Built by E E Robert Stephenson & Hawthorn in October 1963 as D6882 and renumbered under the TOPS scheme to 37182, it was withdrawn in September 2007 and sold to HNRC and is operated from Barrow Hill. (MD)

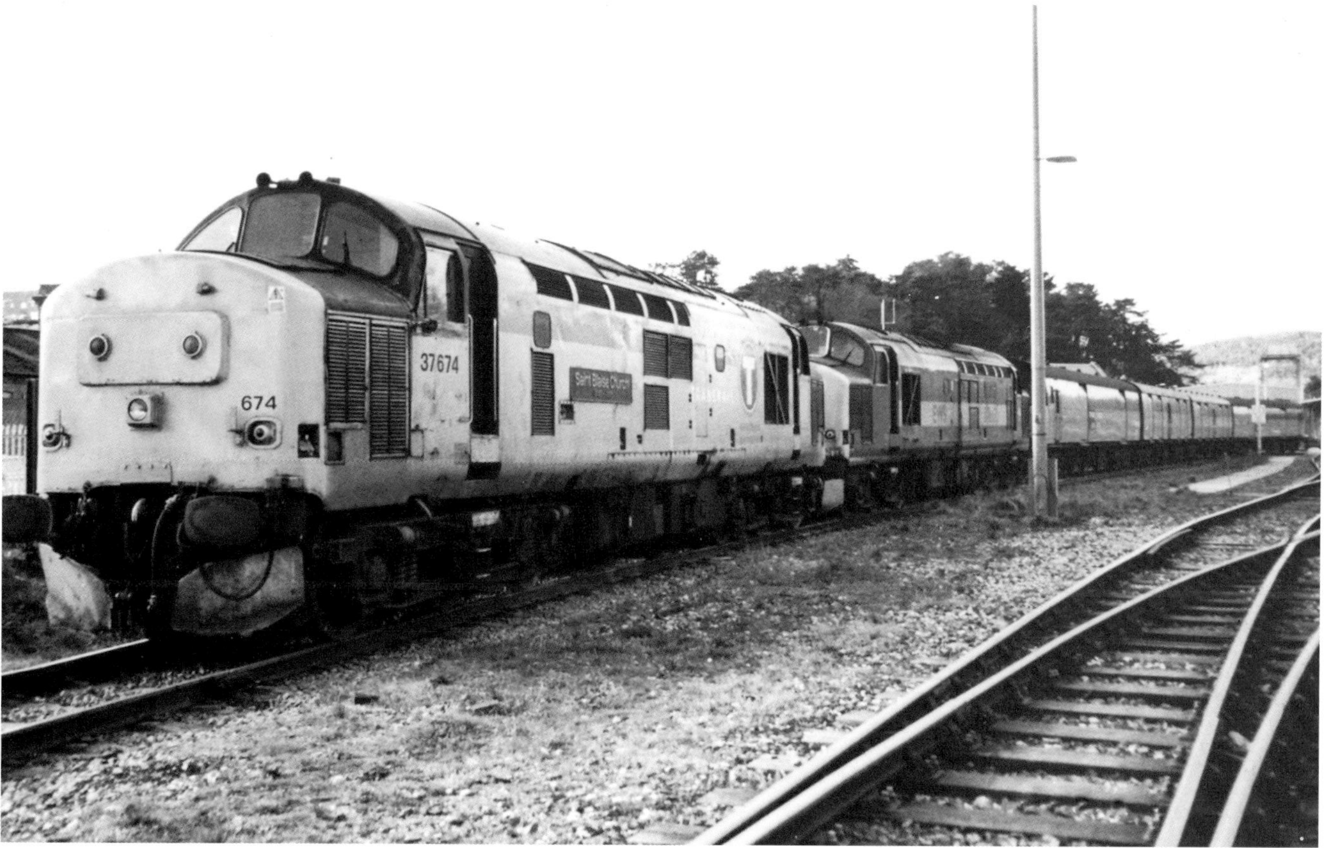

37674 *'St Blaise Church 1445-1985'* and an unidentified class 37 shunting the Postal Train in the 'Coal Siding' at the south end of the yard at St Blazey on 23 March 2004. It is unlikely the 37s were used on the actual Postal Train, though not impossible if there had been a failure of the booked 47s. (MD)

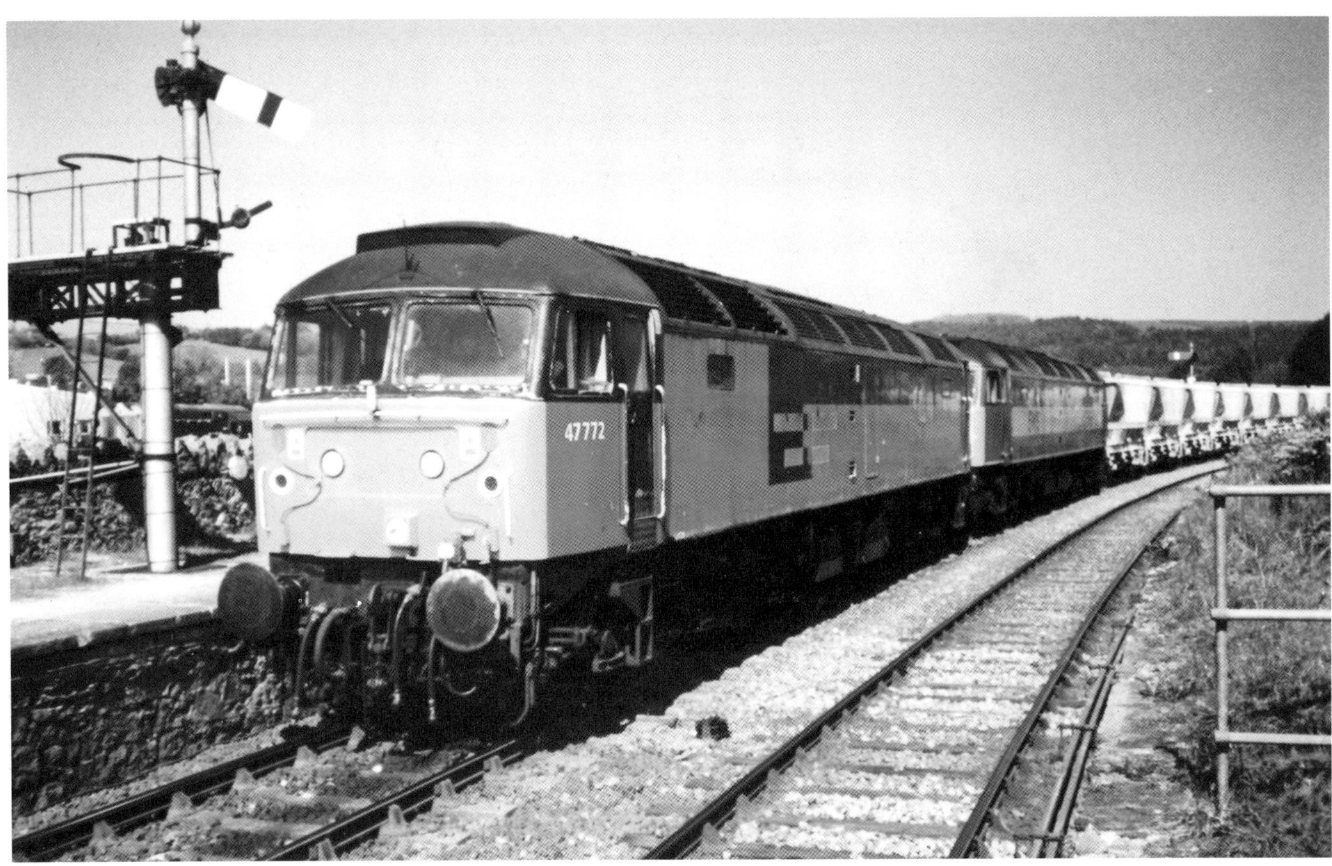

Another unusual working was for class 47s, probably the Postal locos, to be used on clay movements. Here 47772 and 47760 are backing out of the yard at St Blazey in March 2003 with 6C06 to Tavistock Junction. 47772 was built in February 1965 by BR at Crewe and carried the numbers D1657, 47073 and 47537 before its current number. 47760 *'Ribblehead Viaduct'* was also built at Crewe in September 1964 and carried a total of five numbers, the others being; D1617, 47036, 47562 and 47672. Both survive and work for West Coast Railways (WCRC) at Carnforth. (MD)

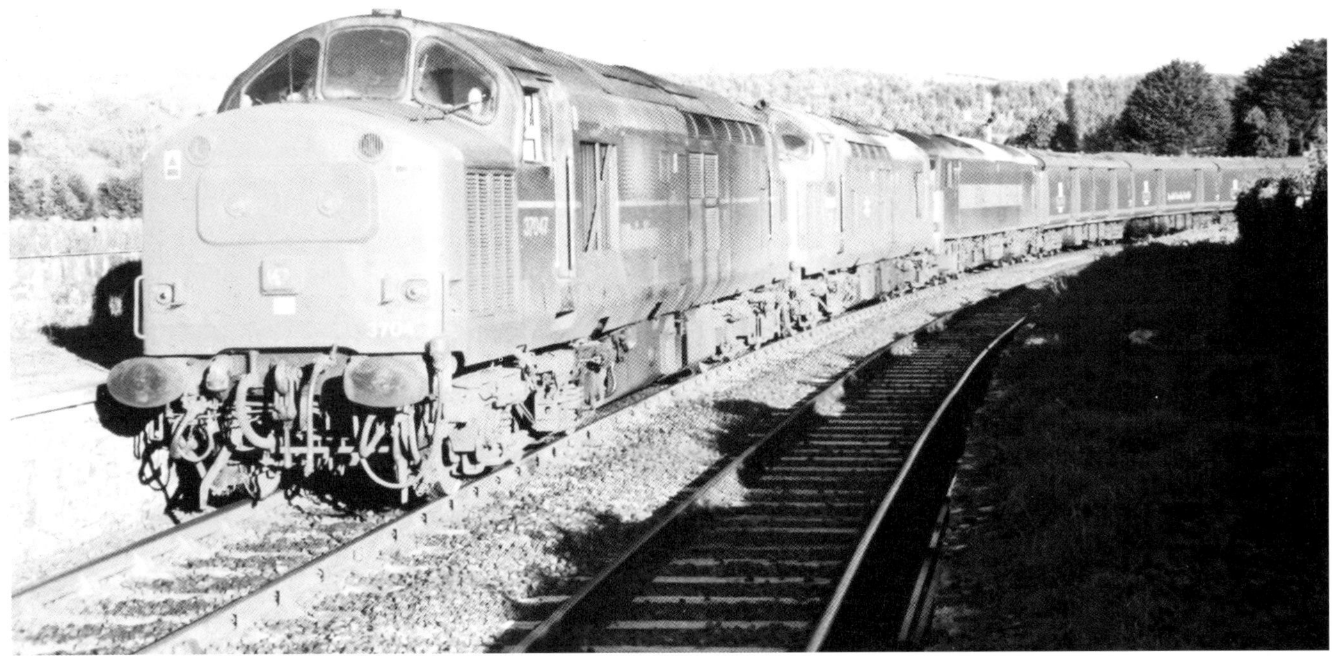

The 0850 St Blazey Yard to Exeter Riverside Yard on 18 February 2004 was hauled by 37047, 37308 and 60041. The leading loco was built in February 1962 at E E Vulcan Foundry as D6747, along with 37308 in November 1965 as D6608. They were both withdrawn in January 2005 and 37308 is privately preserved at Cardiff Canton Depot, but the former was scrapped in May 2008. 60041 was built in February 1992 and named *'High Willhays'* until October 1996. It was withdrawn and stored in December 2009 at Toton. (MD)

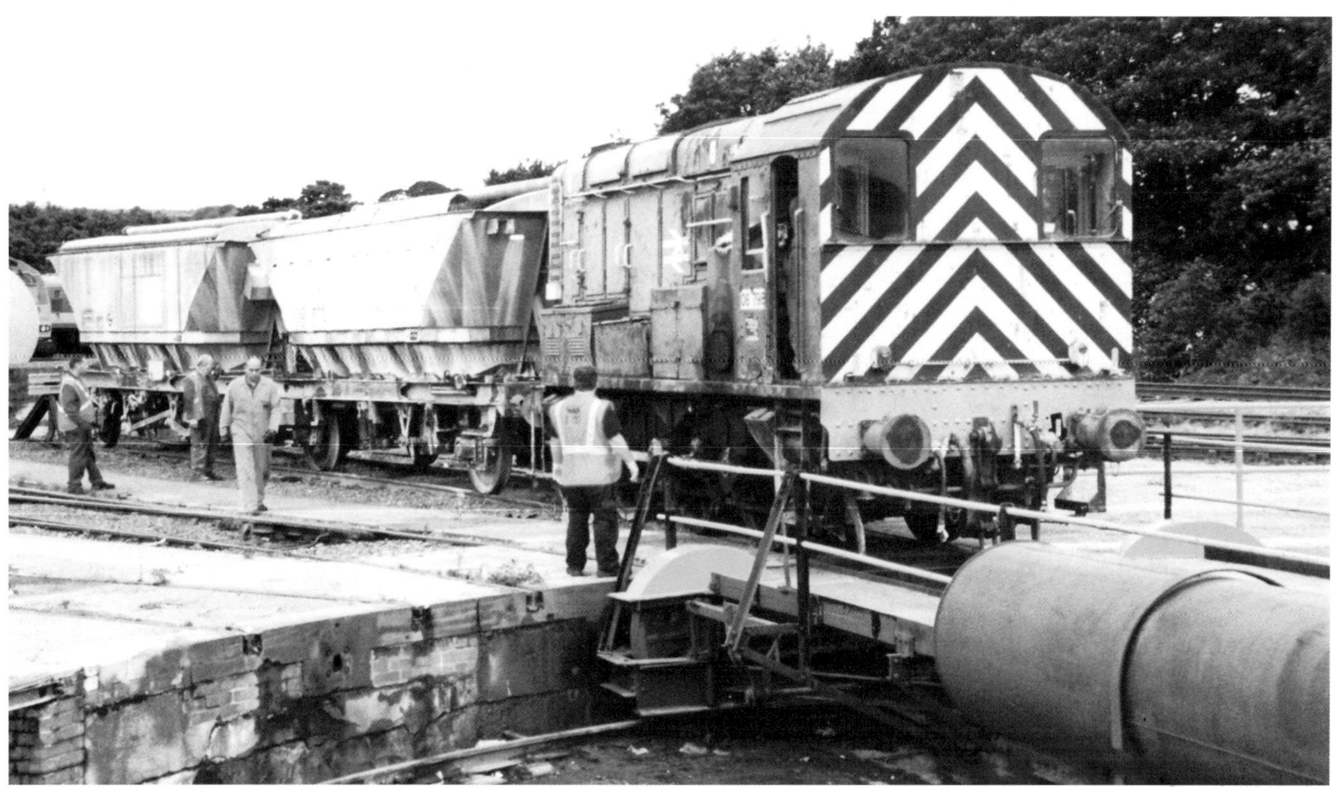

An interesting picture of 08798 on the turntable road at St Blazey on 18 August 2002. The two CDA wagons had been stored here for several years after being casualties of the Lostwithiel derailment on the cross-over from Down to Up in 1998. They were deemed beyond repair and were used as a source of spares, until they were dragged around to the 'Mileage Siding' near my office, and broken up by Henry Orchard scrap dealer along with other redundant stock. The '08' was built at Derby in May 1960 and withdrawn in April 2011 and cut up. (MD)

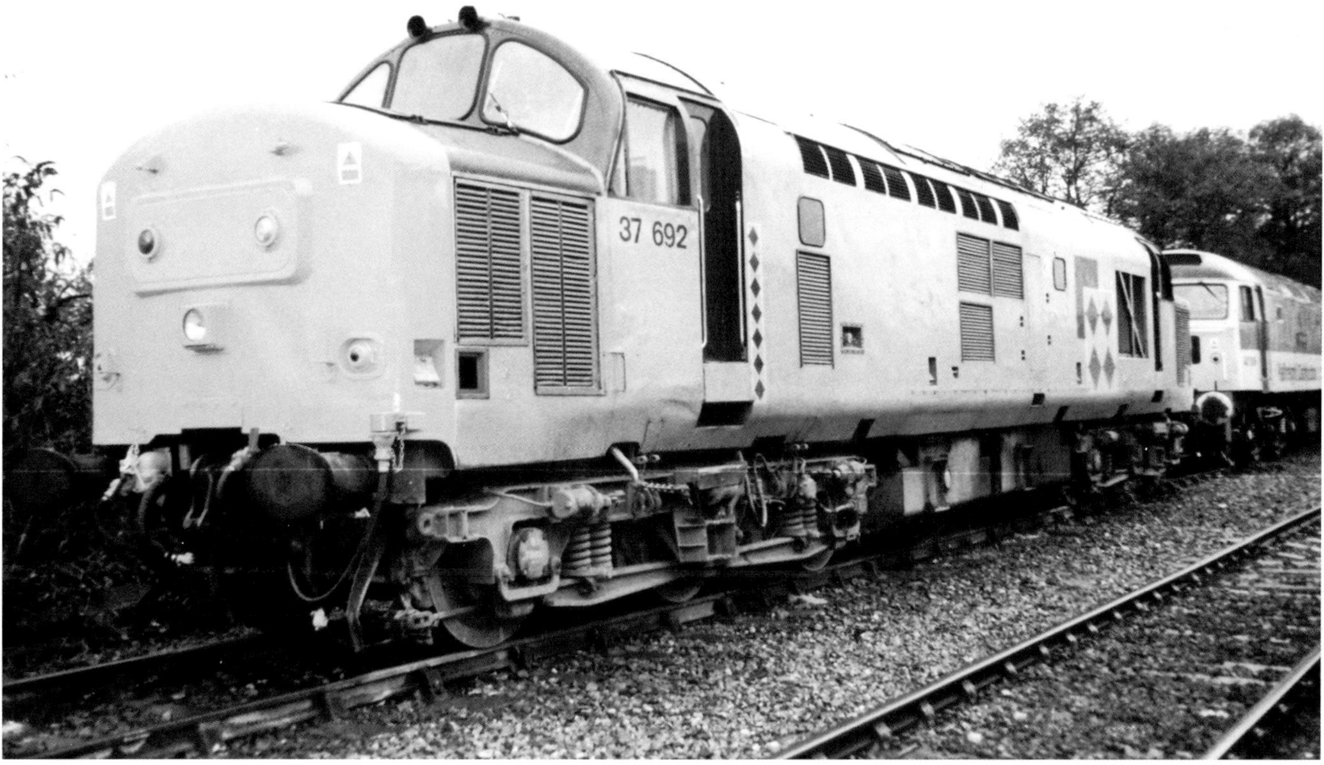

The River Siding at St Blazey is the location of 37692 and 47306 on 10 November 2002. Both were unallocated at the time, 47306 *'The Sapper'* did eventually find a home on the Bodmin & Wenford Railway after spending several years in store at St Blazey. I personally let this loco off Network Rail metals and into the private railway at Bodmin Parkway Groundframe. It was built as D1787 by Brush and was withdrawn in March 2000. 37692 was built by Robert Stephenson & Hawthorn in May 1963 as D6822, becoming 37122 under the TOPs system. It was withdrawn in December 2000 and cut up in August 2009 by C.F. Booth. (MD)

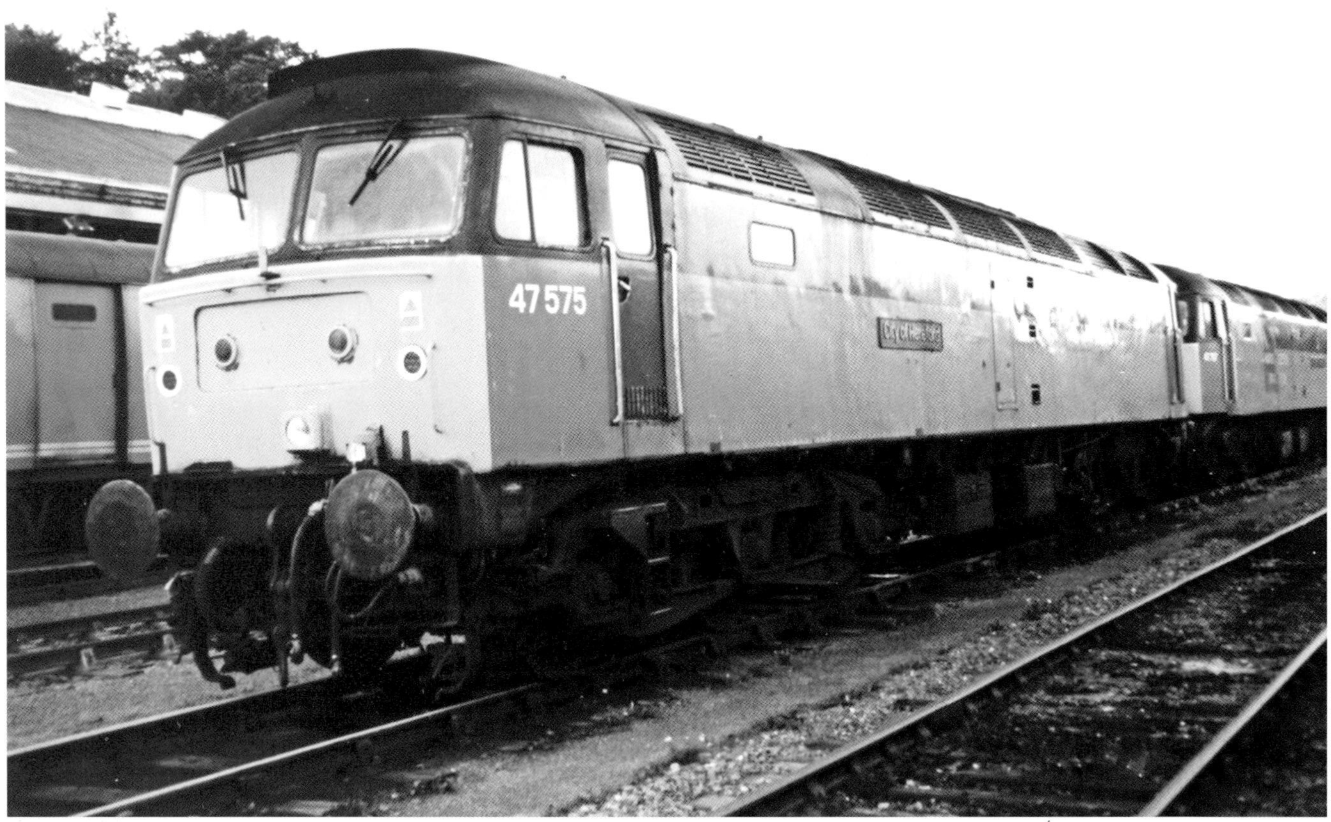

In the days when Postal Trains were stabled in St Blazey every weekday, it was a busy yard and depot, with up to six class 47s, the odd class 60 and of course up to a dozen class 37s on clay, freight and engineering trains. What a different place it is today. On 4 November 2000, 47575 *'City of Hereford'* stands in company with others. It was another Brush product from October 1964, when it was numbered D1770. It became 47175 and after 47575 was allocated 47730 but never carried it. Withdrawn in January 2001, it was kept in store until May 2010 when it was cut up by C.F. Booth. (MD)

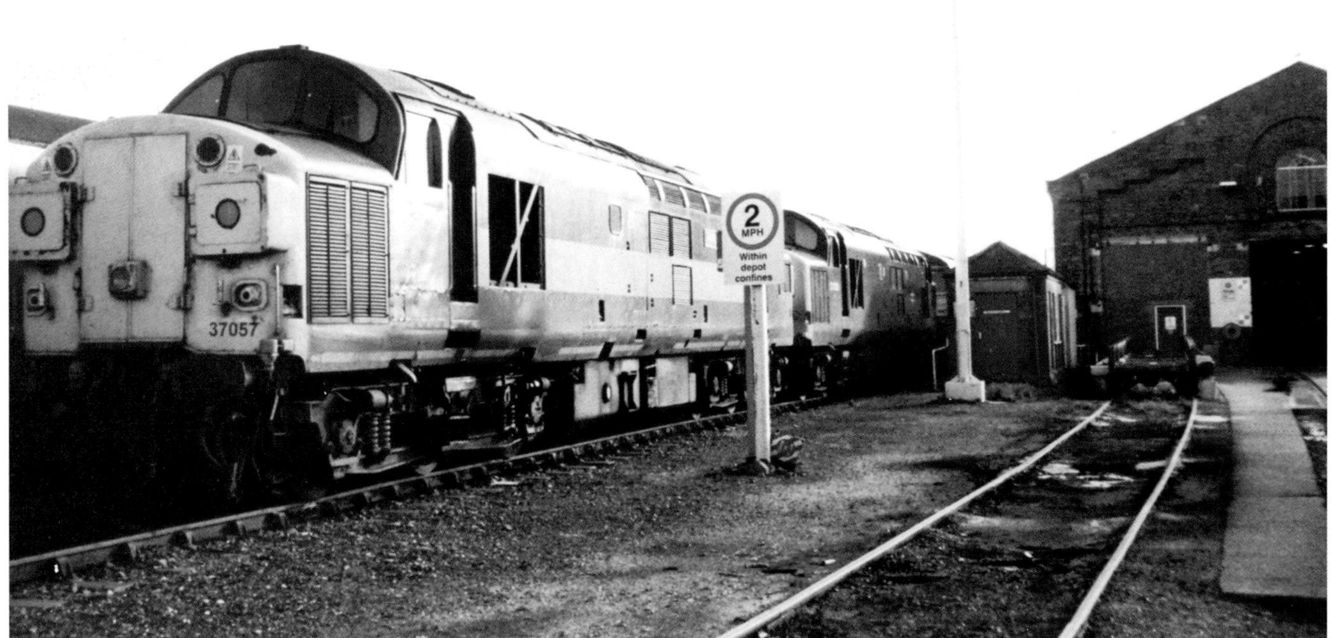

On shed at St Blazey on 29 November 2002 is split headcode 37057 *'Viking'* and 37308, which will later take 6M72 to Cliffe Vale. These two English Electric, Vulcan Foundry, products, date from October 1962 and September 1965 respectively and were originally D6757 and D6608. The latter carried 37274 and was withdrawn in January 2005, but privately preserved at Cardiff Canton, whilst the former is owned by HNRC as a source of spares after being withdrawn in August 2008. (MD)

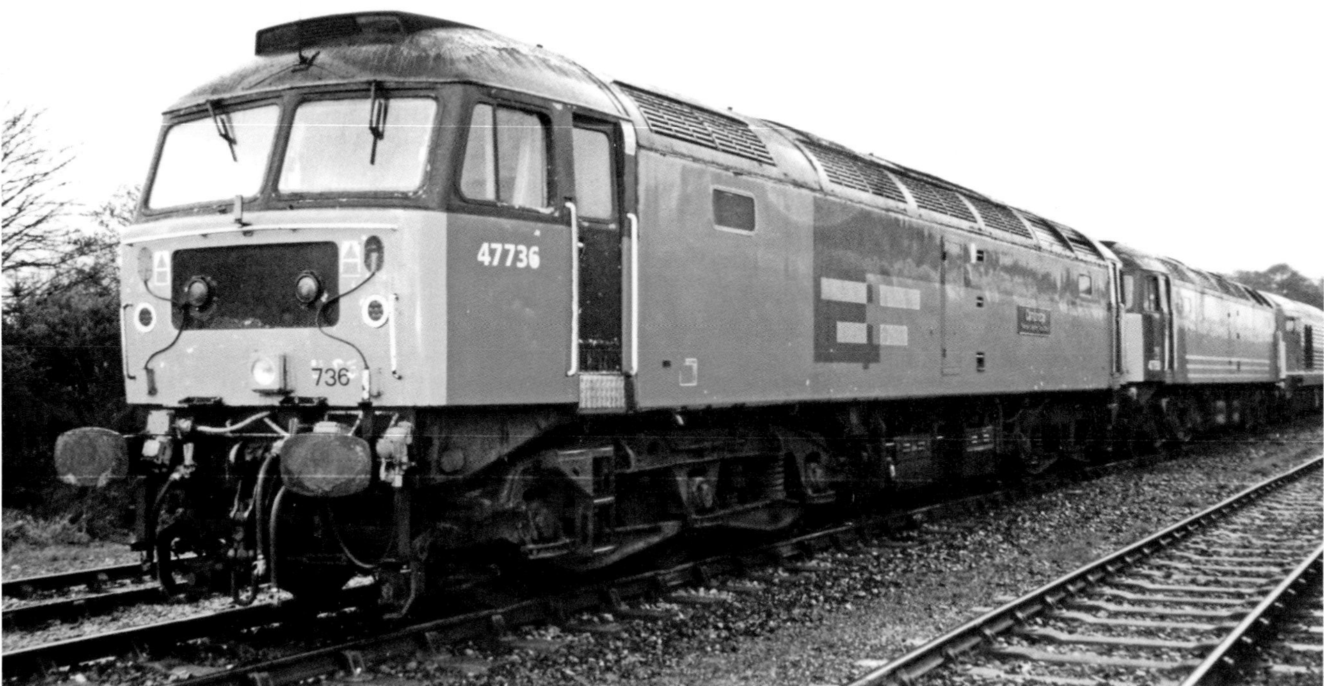

Another photo of St Blazey Yard, this time on 10 November 2002, and showing Res liveried 47736 which was built by BR in Crewe in September 1965 as D1963, before becoming 47263 and 47587. Here it carries the name *'Cambridge Traction & Rolling Stock Maintenance Depot'* but was withdrawn in August 2003 and scrapped by Ron Hull Jnr of Rotherham in November 2007. Behind it, is 47750 in former Virgin livery. This class 47 was built in March1965, also at Crewe, as D1667, becoming 47082 and 47626 and carrying the name *'Atlas'* twice. It was withdrawn in June 2004 and broken up by European Metal Reprocessing (EMR) in May 2008. Behind that is a class 67. (MD)

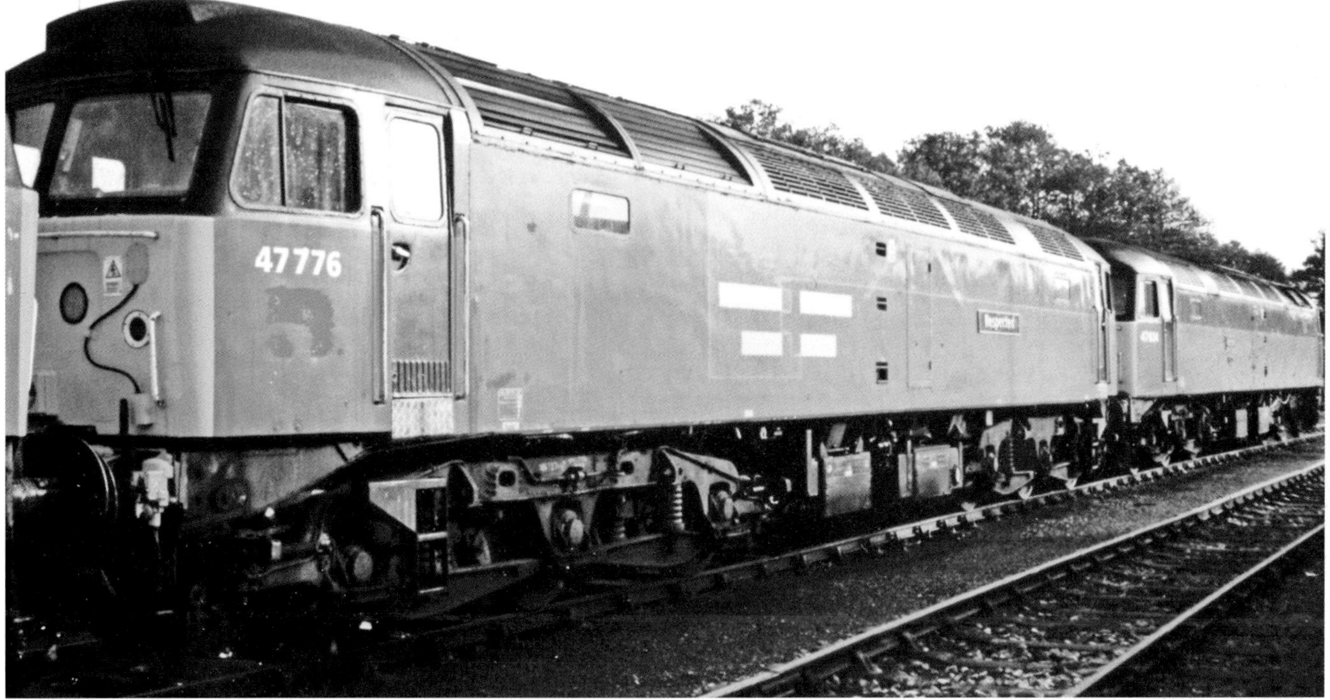

St Blazey on 11 November 2002, is also host to 47776 *'Respected'* and 47634 *'Holbeck'* stabled before their next trip on the Up Mail. It was not unusual to find double-heading on the Mail trains, the second loco being an insurance measure against failure, especially when cash was carried. A careful eye was kept on the trains progress by each signalman, and if it was a 'long time in section' without good reason, emergency procedures where quickly put in place. I worked the Mail trains several times over the single-line sections as Pilotman, after failures of the signalling systems, usually due to lightning strikes. This meant keeping the train at a remote location until I got there, and Control were on tenterhooks until it was moving again. Both were built by Brush in October and July 1964 respectively and were withdrawn in March 2004, March 2001. 47776 (D1776, 47181, 47578) is stored by WCRC at Carnforth, and 47634 (D1751, 47158, and 47753-which was not carried) was broken up by HNRC at Kingsbury for EMR. (MD)

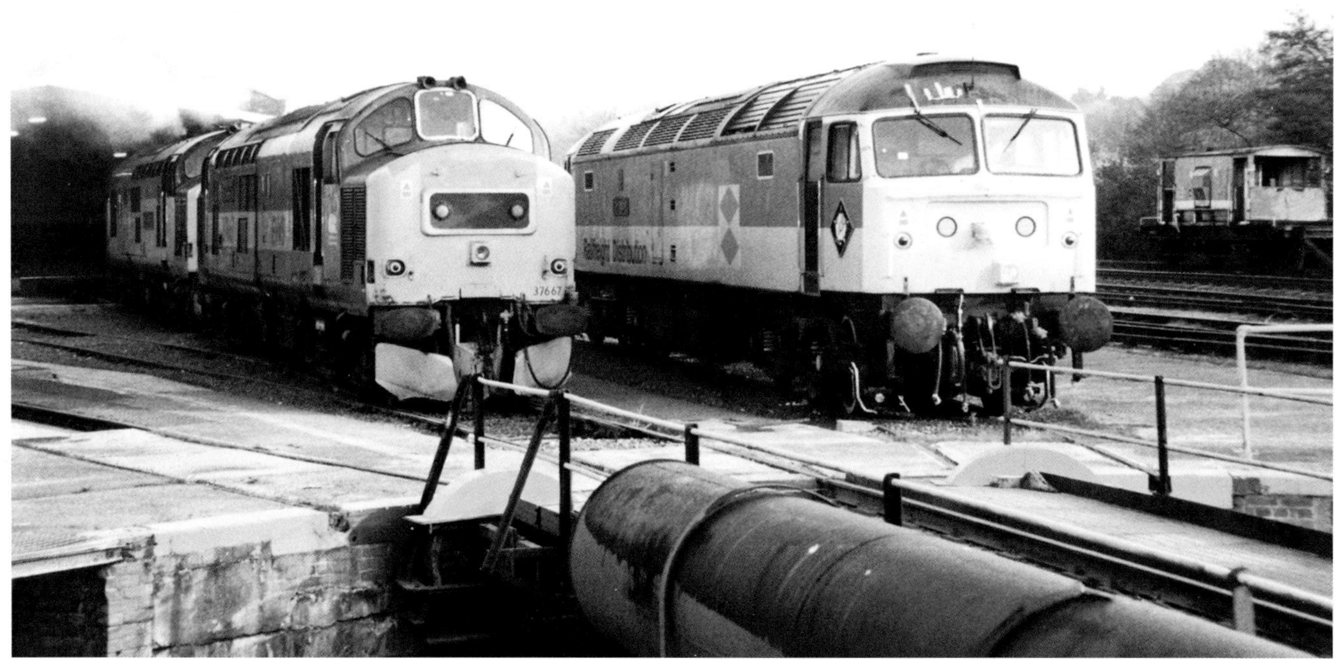

Adjacent to the turntable at St Blazey on 28 March 2004 is seen 37667, 37674 *'St Blaise Church 1445-1985'* and 47306 *'The Sapper'*. (MD)

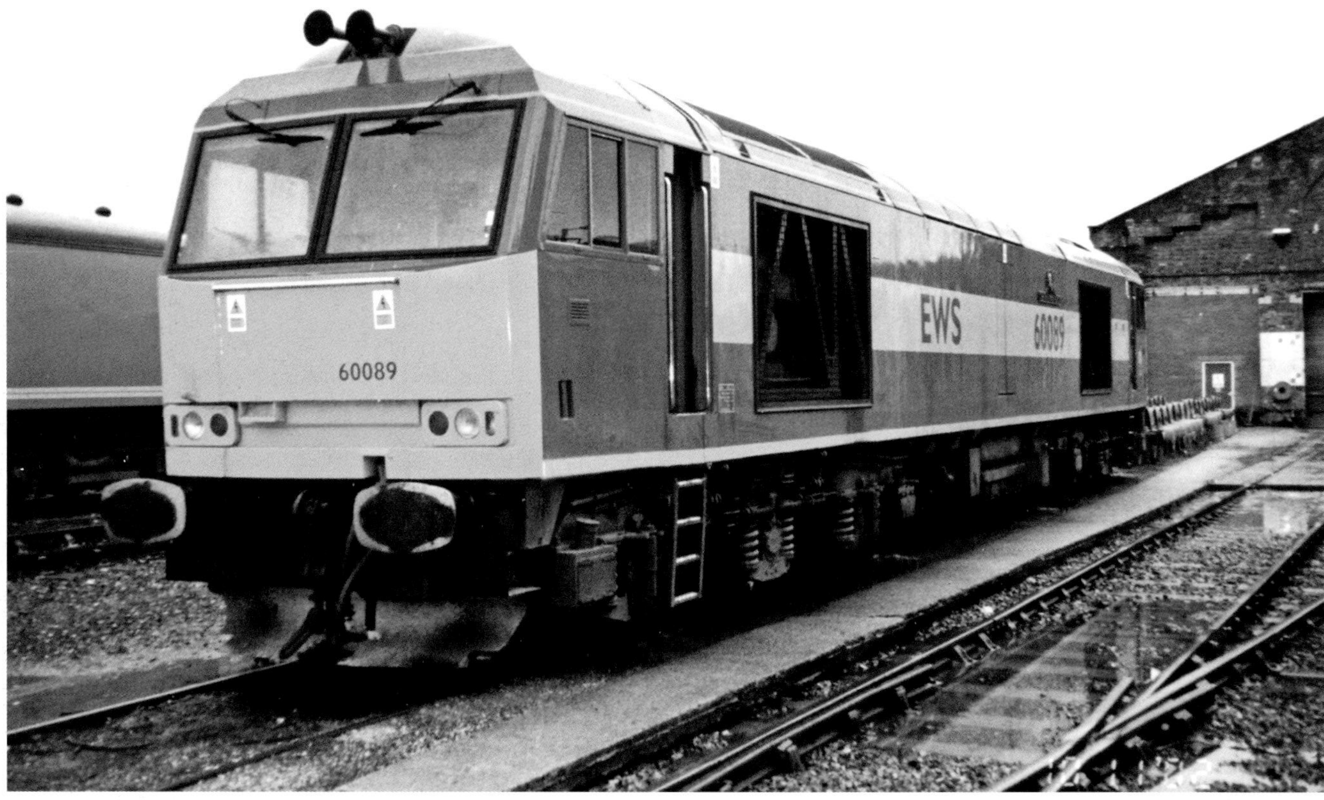

60089 *'The Railway Horse'* is seen here on 10t November 2002 having arrived on St Blazey with 6V70 the previous Friday. This Brush product was built in December 1991 and entered service in January 1992, but was withdrawn in August 2008 and is currently stored at Toton. (MD)

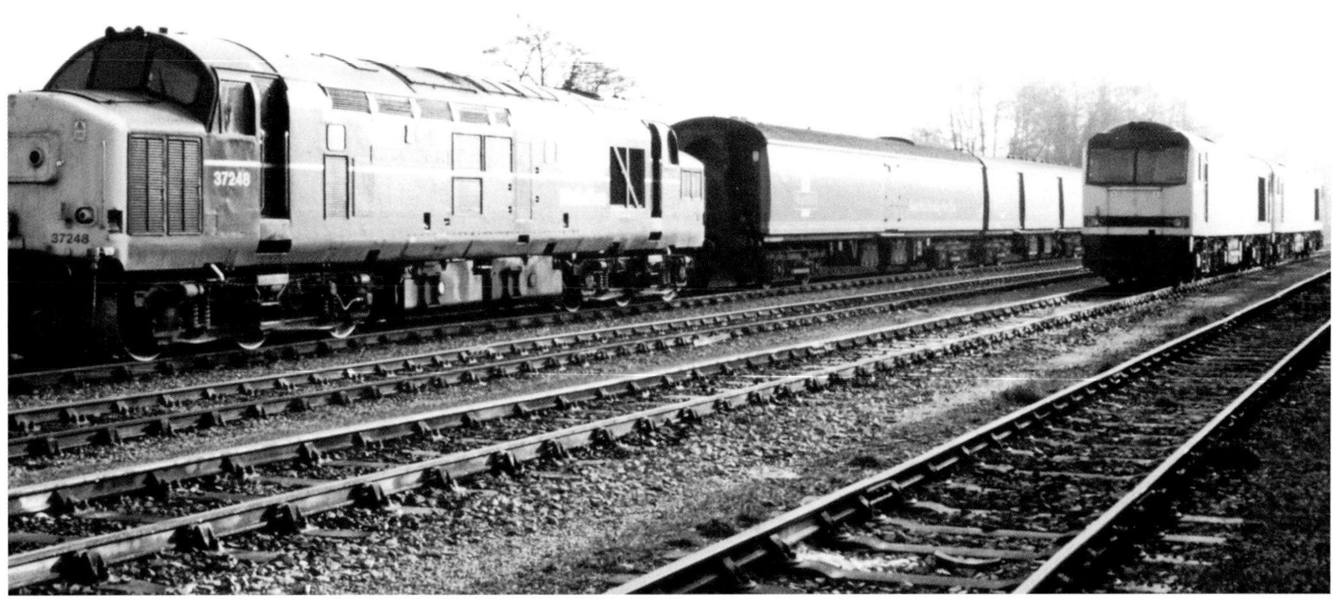

On Millennium Day we see the shed at StBlazey is home to 37248 *'Midland Railway Centre'*, 60047 and 60074. The 37 was built by EE in October 1964 and withdrawn in February 2009 and is preserved on the Gloucester Warwickshire Railway. The Brush-built class 60s were previously named from new and date from 1991. The former was withdrawn in October 2008 and is stored at Crewe, the latter is still in service. (MD)

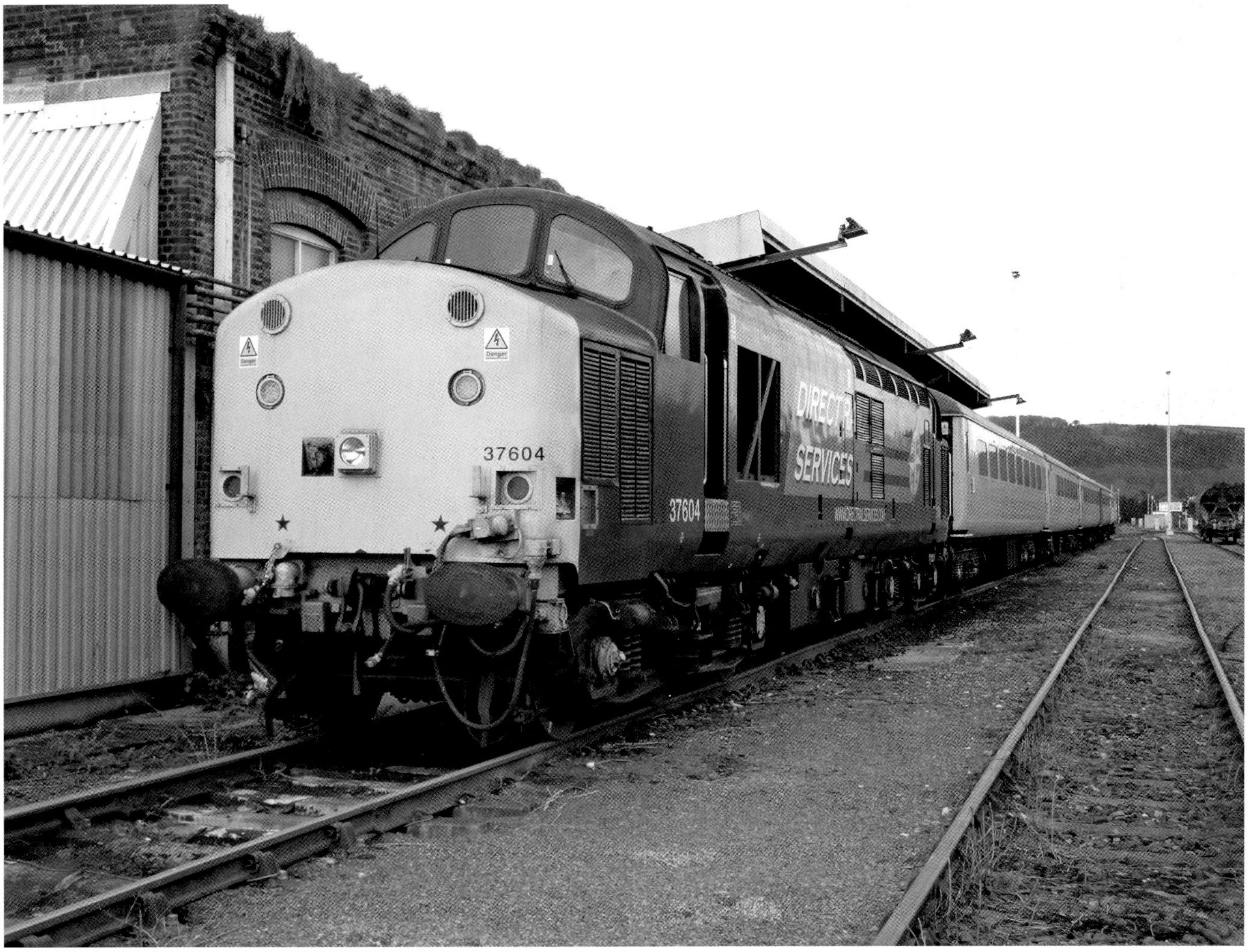

On 7 February 2012 I found the Network Rail Measurement Train stabled in St Blazey on the Fuel Road. Direct Rails 37604 had been hired in for this occasion. This E E loco started out as D6707 in February 1961 before becoming 37007 and 37506. (SFH)

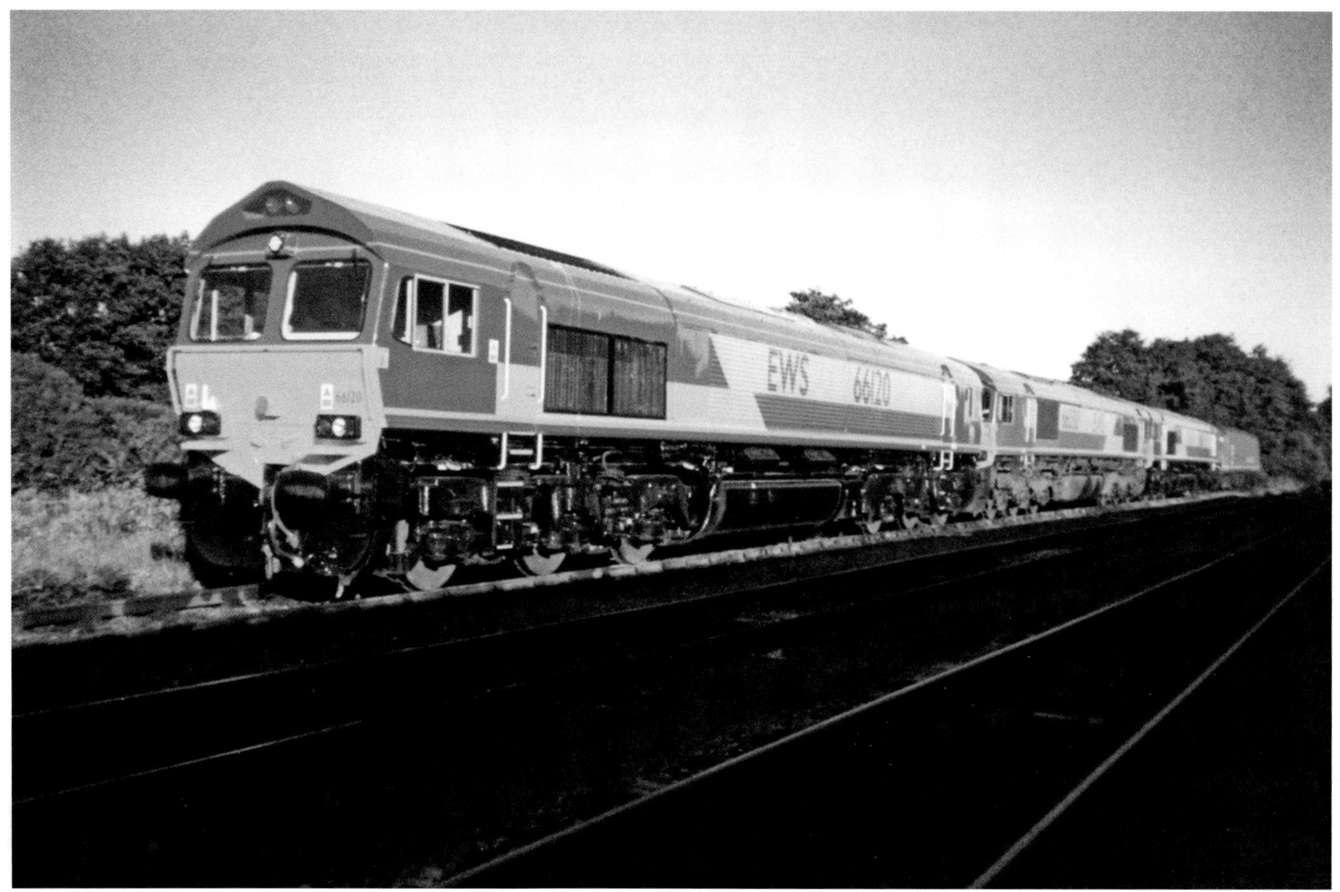

66120 is seen here in 1999, brand new and stored in River Siding pending post delivery inspection, in company with two others and a mail coach. (SFH)

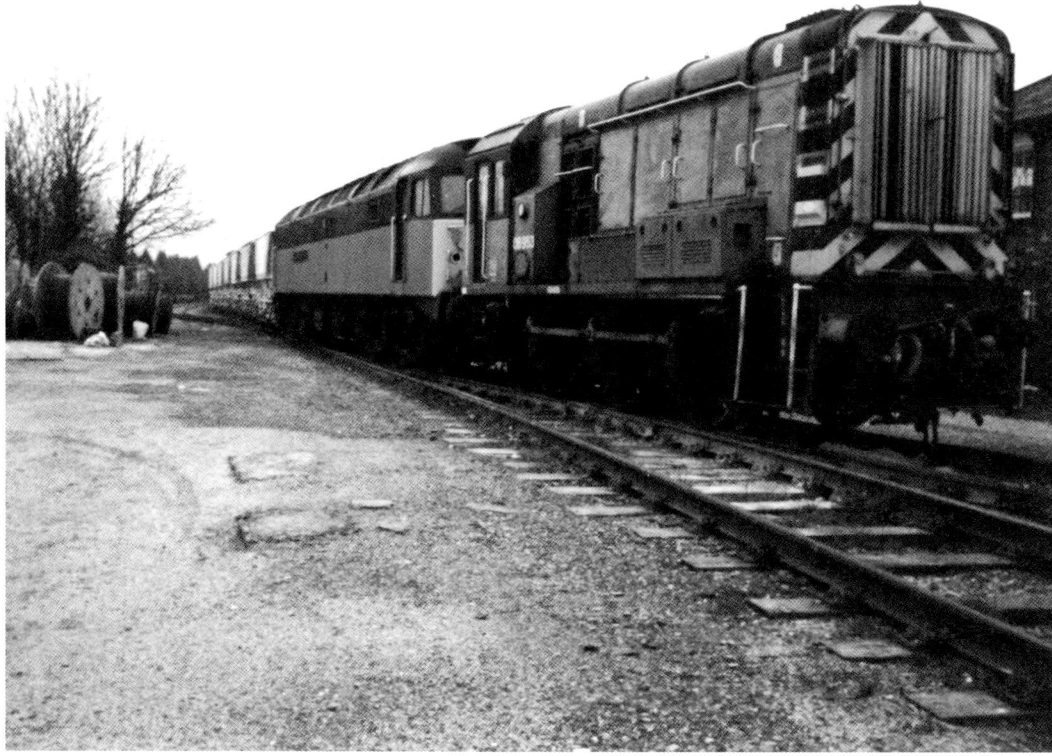

08953 is seen here shunting a clay train headed by 47640 *'University of Strathclyde'* after it had failed whilst enroute from Goonbarrow to Fowey. The 08 had travelled up to Ponts Mill to rescue the train and drag it back to St Blazey. The RES loco was itself deputising for a failed class 37. 47640 started life as Brush-built D1921 in January 1966, and went on to become 47244, before it was renumbered again to the one it carries here. Interestingly, it was allocated 47755 but never carried it. It was withdrawn in June 2000 and survives on The Battlefield Line. (SFH)

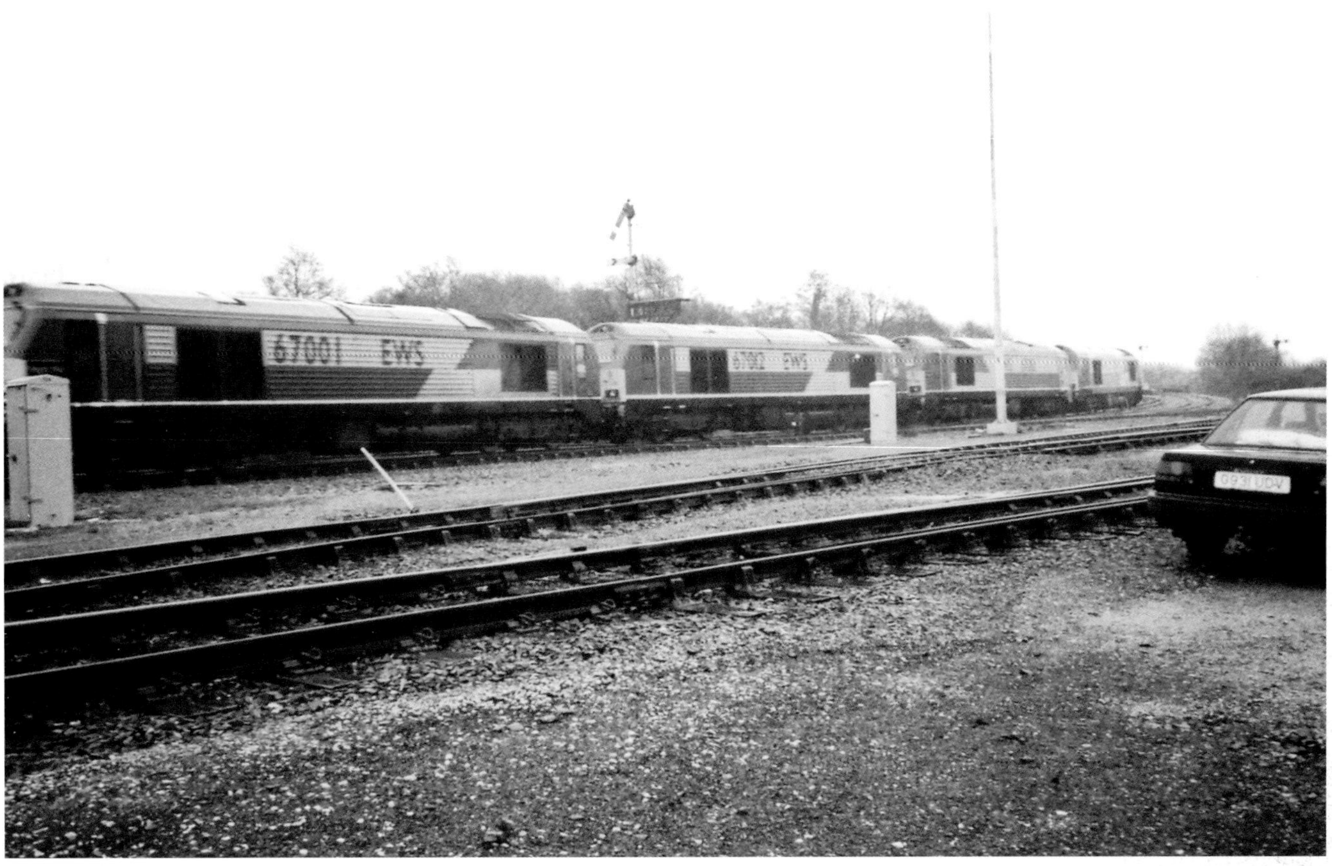

A rake of four class 67s with pioneer 67001 at the rear are seen here leaving St Blazey for Par. As the Travelling Post Office was hauled by a pair of 67s and both trains were stabled in St Blazey each weekday, this was not an uncommon sight, but it was uncommon for them to depart St Blazey together and without their respective trains. (SFH)

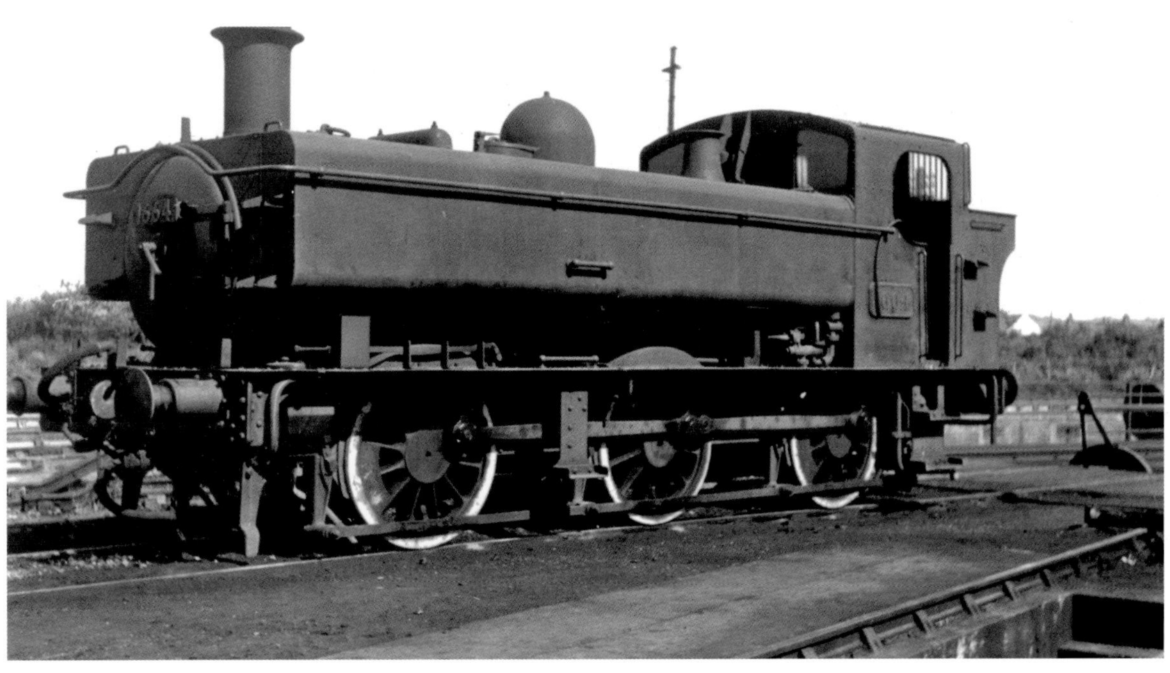

1664 is seen here on shed at St Blazey in the 1950s and is adjacent to the turntable, which is still functional today. Built in 1949 under BR from an earlier design by Hawksworth, the class of seventy locos were started to be withdrawn in 1959, when only ten years old and all, except one, were gone by 1966. 1638 survives. (SL)

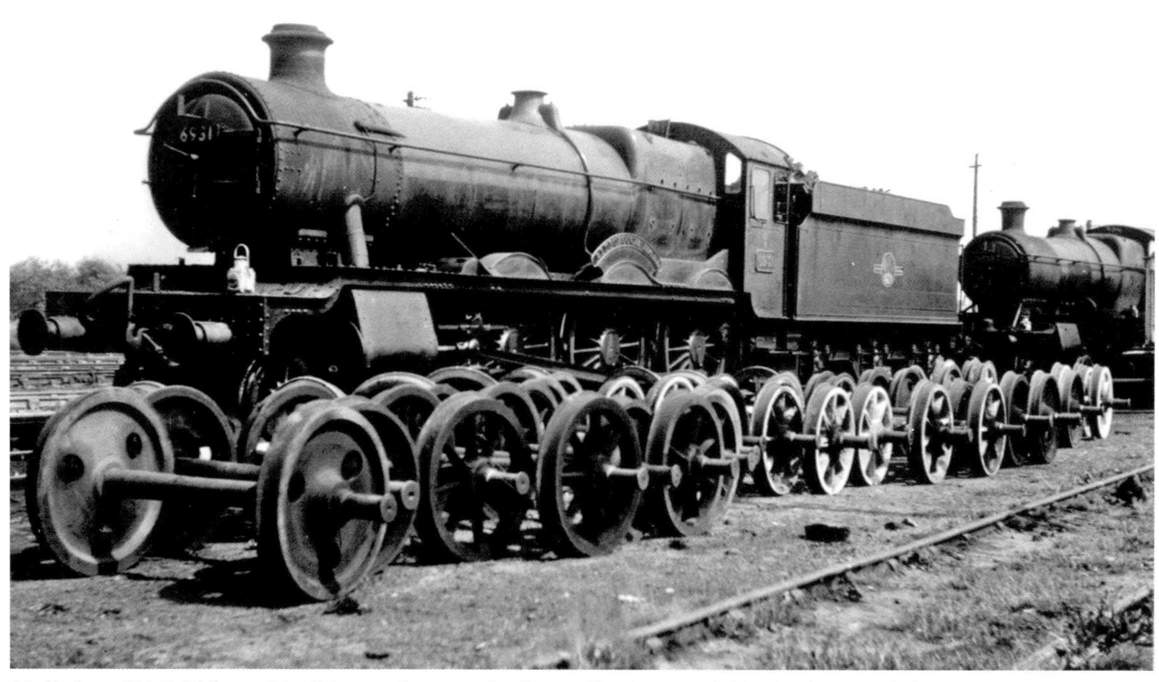

Hall class 6931 *'Aldborough Hall'* is seen here on St Blazey Shed circa 1960. Scrapping of this once numerous class began in 1959 and most were gone by 1965, although several has survived into preservation. (SL)

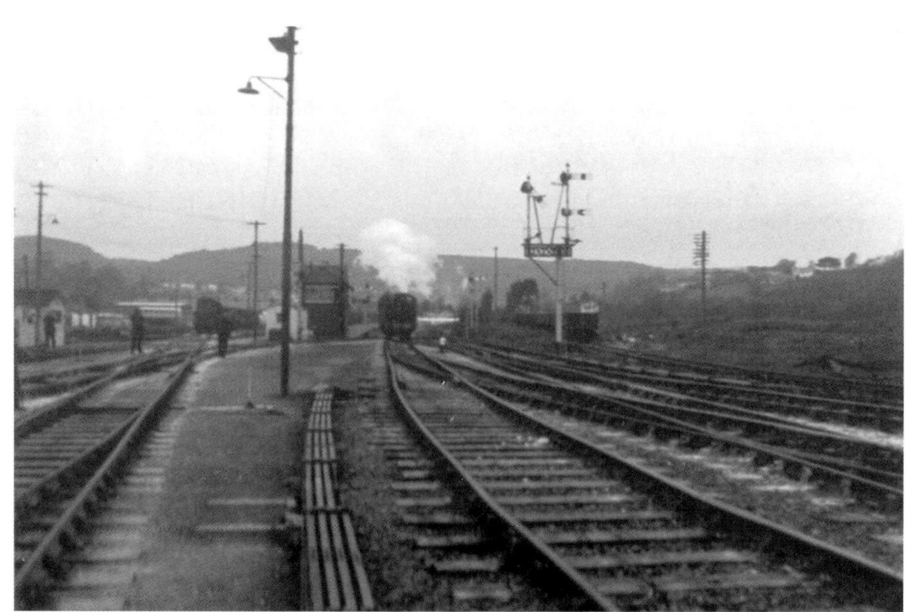

St Blazey Yard in the early 1960s finds a train signalled from the down line to the 'Fowey Main' with a train for Fowey Docks or Par Harbour. The double junction is still in place as indeed is the original yard junctions and a yard far busier than it is now. (SL)

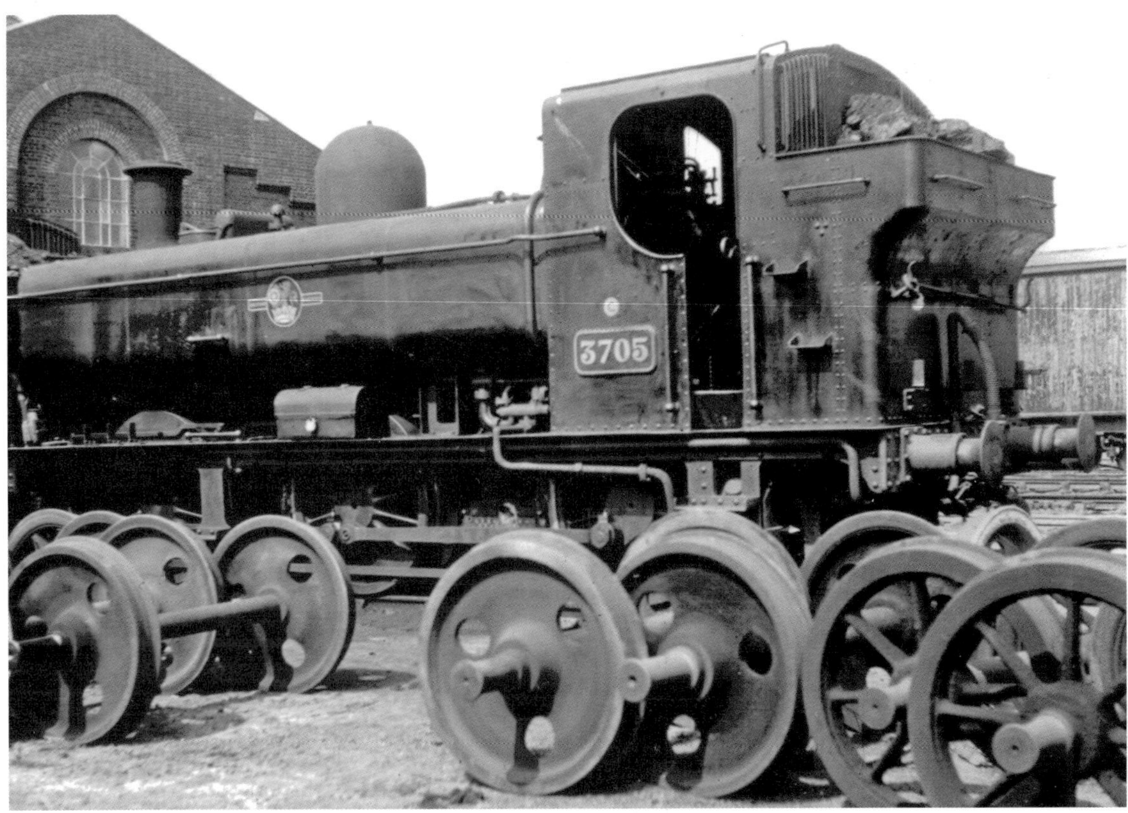

Pannier Tank 3705 is seen on shed at St Blazey circa 1960. (SL)

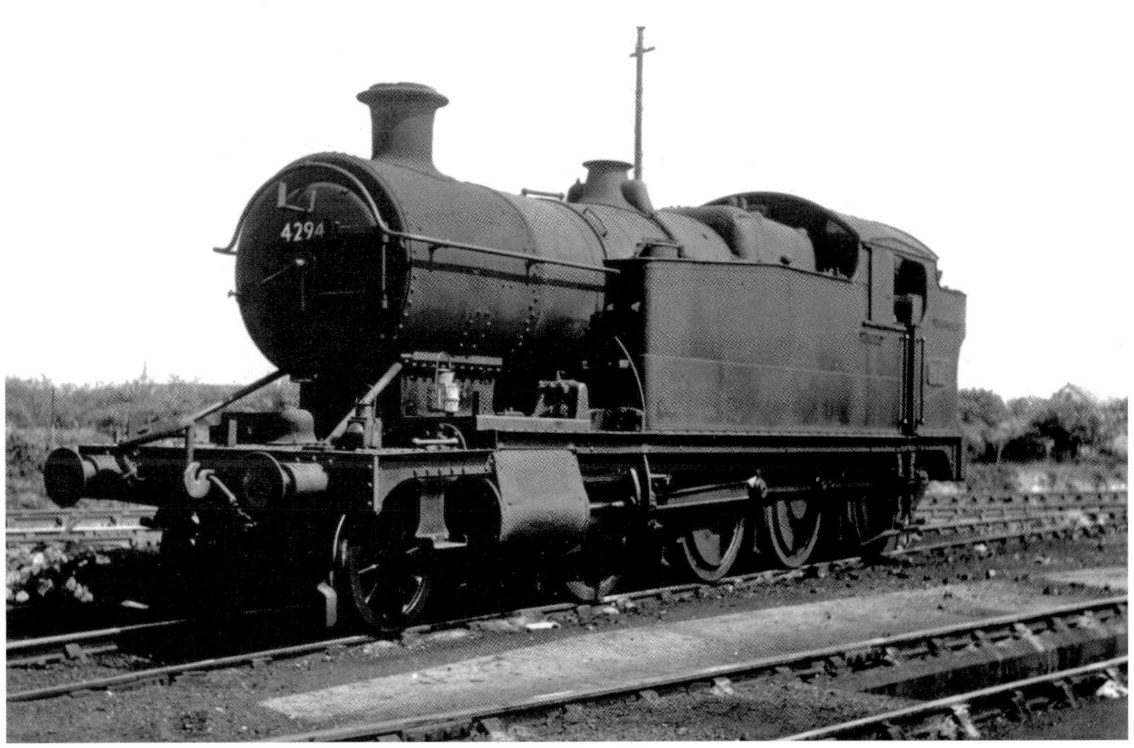

Large Prairie Tank number 4294 is reposing on shed at St Blazey circa 1960. (SL)

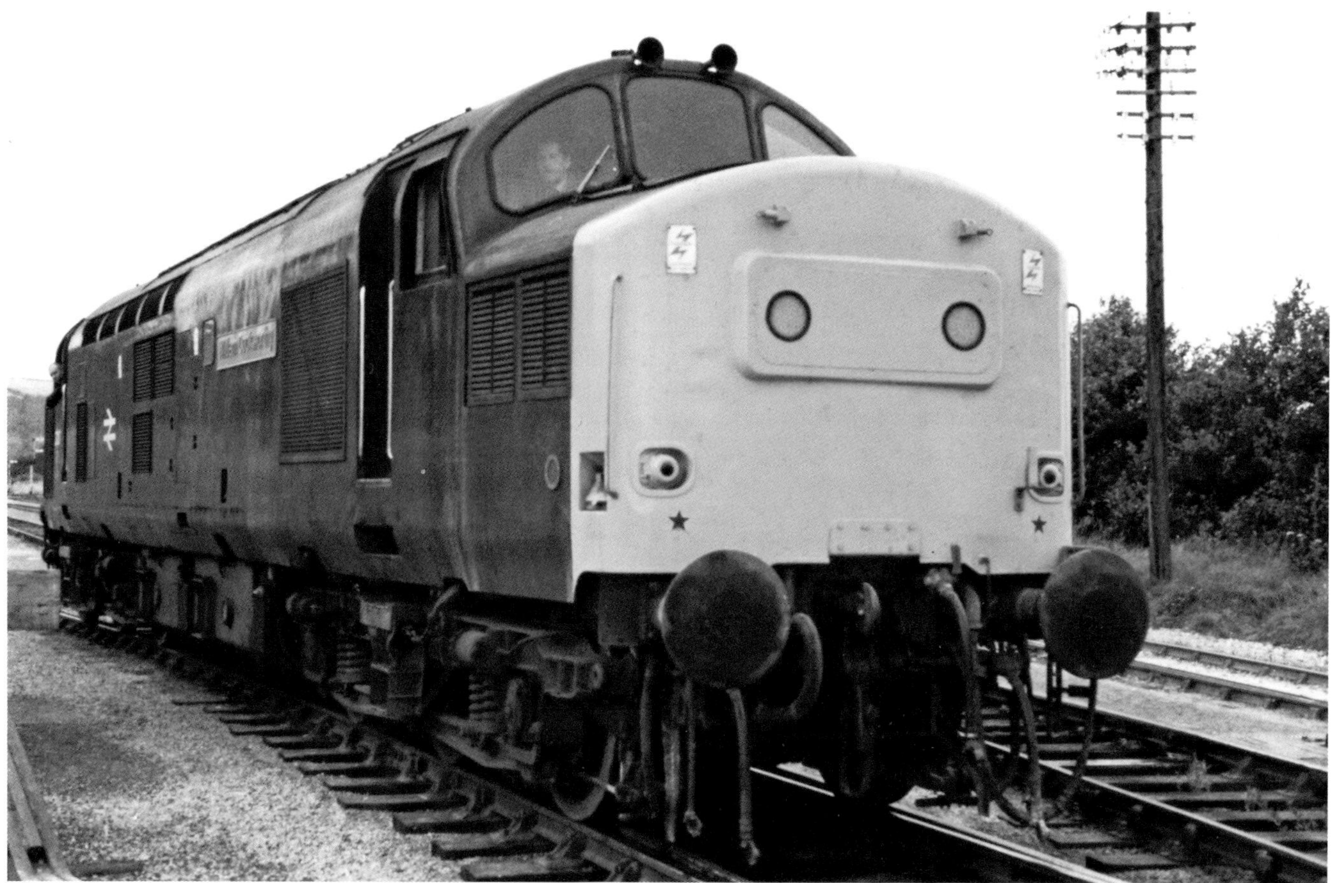

Celebrity Class 37 number 37207 *'William Cookworthy'* passing St Blazey Shed in August 1983. Built in November 1963, by English Electric at their Vulcan Works as D6907, it was renumbered in May 1974. It carried its name from May 1982 to May 1987. The name was then transferred to 37675. It is preserved on the Plym Valley Railway. (GP)

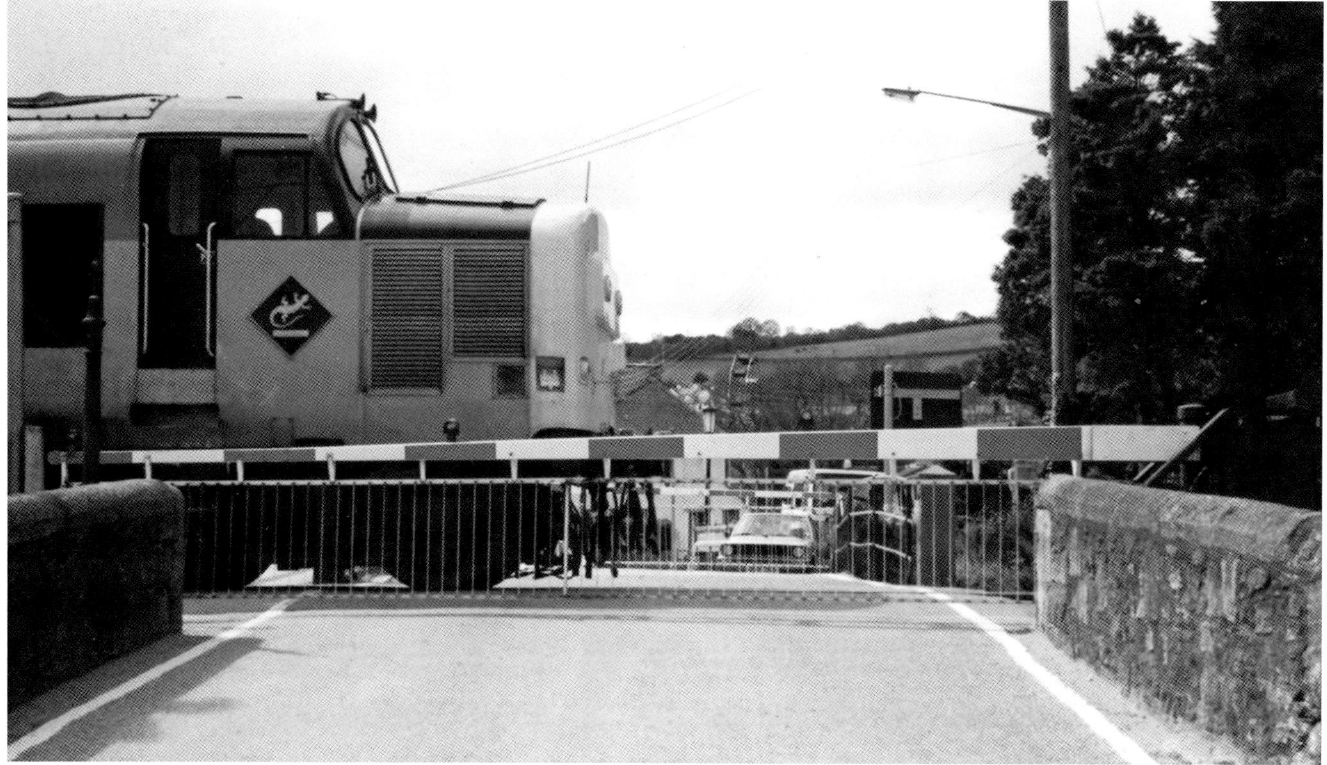

37670 is traversing Middleway level crossing in April 1992, running 'light'. The St Blazey Depot identifier can be clearly seen, and the Lizard is reputed to represent the six branch lines in Cornwall (tail, legs and head) joined by the body of the main line. Of course Lizards are common in Cornwall and Cornwall has 'The Lizard' Peninsular, but St Blazey Depot was always colloquially known as 'Snake Pit'. (GP)

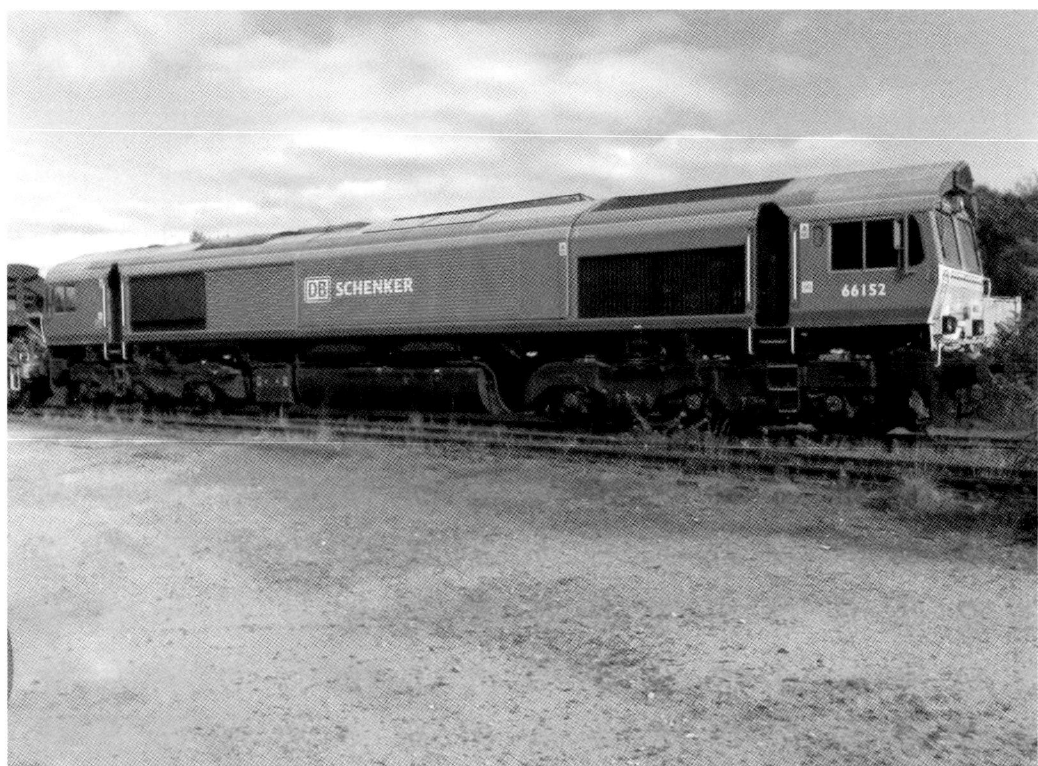

Although quite new, this is an important picture in that it depicts the first of the new livered class 66 locos 66152, which had been brought to Cornwall to take part in the Michael Portillo program on railway journeys using the original Bradshaw's Guide. The location is outside my office in St Blazey in September 2009. (SFH)

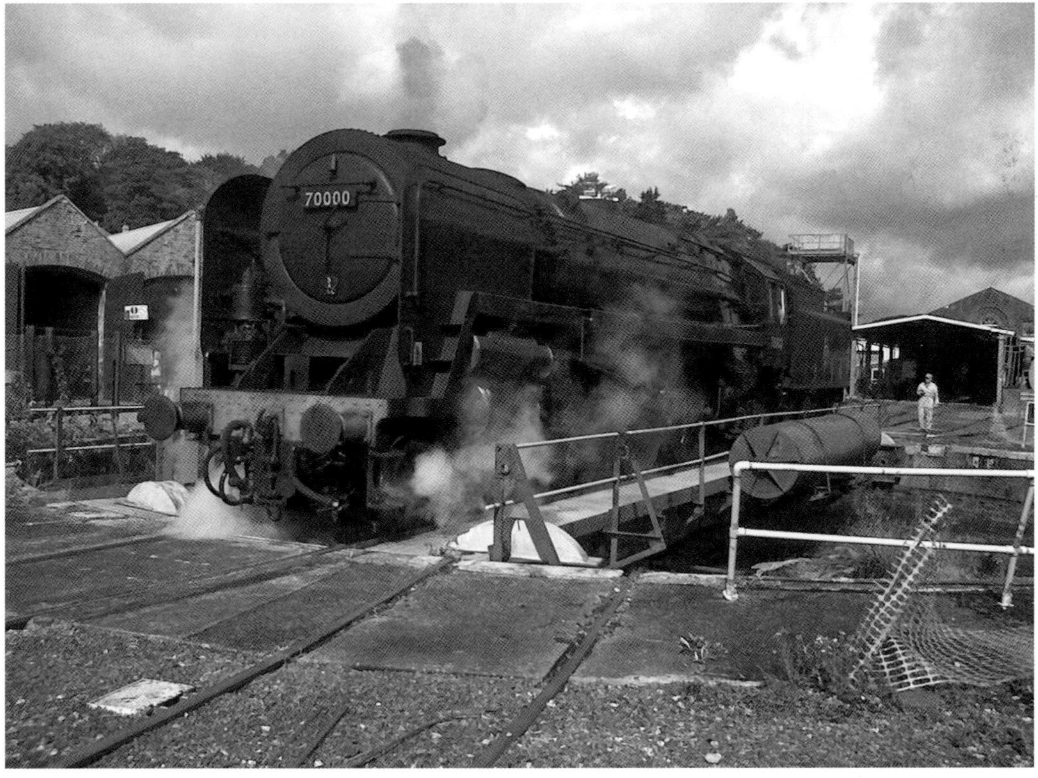

In September 2011 70000 *'Britannia'* made another journey into Cornwall and stabled as usual at St Blazey. In all black livery and unnamed, as she would have appeared when new in 1951, she made a memorable sight, and was reminiscent of how many of her class appeared in the run up to the end of steam in the 1960s. Here *'Britannia'* is seen being turned on the only working turntable still on the Western Route, at St Blazey. (SFH)

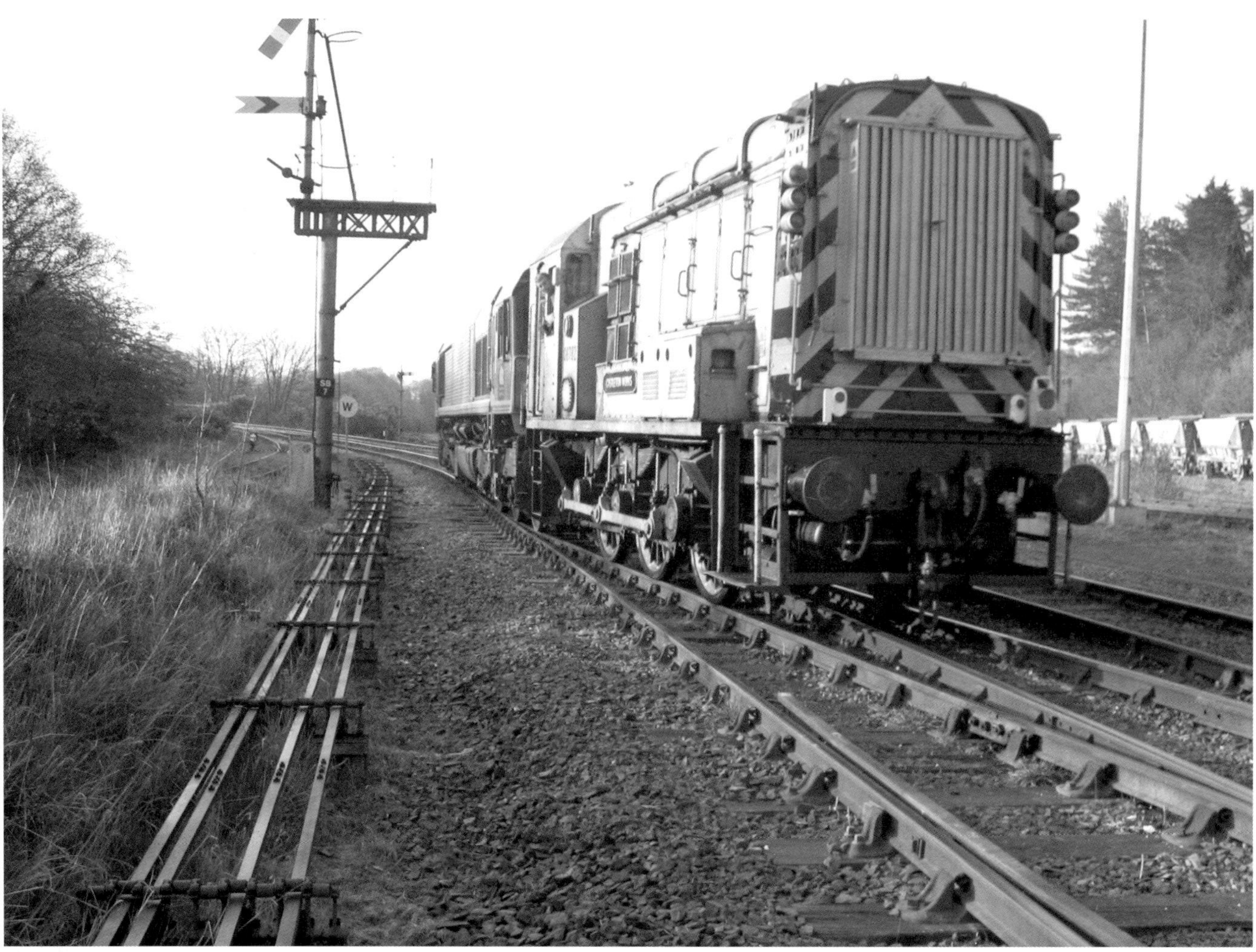

St Blazey Yard has been progressively cleared of redundant stock, and much of it mothballed until recently when class 60s were started to be stored pending decisions on their futures. In April 2010 08782 *'Castleton Works'* was towed away by 66171. It was built as D3950 in April 1960 at BR Derby Works.

CHAPTER 5

THE BRANCHES

IN RECENT TIMES the branch lines serving Cornwall have had somewhat of a renaissance in terms of passenger use. The beautiful St Ives line enjoys a very good service throughout the day, and the line to Falmouth has been an unprecedented success since the loop was reinstated at Penryn and the daytime service increased to half hourly. The line to Newquay is still popular, but one still wonders what could be achieved on this line if a little investment was forthcoming and maybe the proposed line is diverted up the Parkandillack route through to St Dennis Junction from St Austell.

The line to Fowey is less busy than in previous years as the clay industry in the UK is not producing the amounts previously seen in past years, and of course the class 66 locos can haul much heavier trains, so less trains are required to move the clay. The line to Looe is still popular and well patronised, as is the line to Gunnislake from Plymouth. The line from Liskeard to Coombe Junction still carries cement traffic to and from the Moorswater works, and this intersperses with the passenger service.

Finally, the nicely restored and preserved line from Bodmin Parkway to Bodmin General and Boscarne still carries passengers in authentic and nostalgic rolling stock hauled by steam and vintage diesel locomotives, and operated by the Bodmin & Wenford Railway.

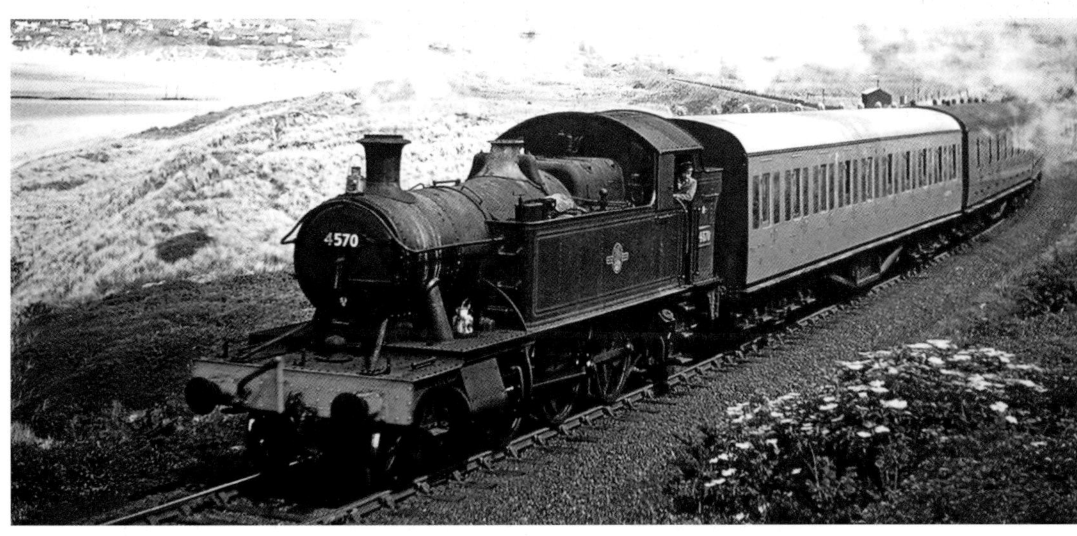

Prairie Tank 4570 is seen here traversing the Towans with a train from St Erth to St Ives circa 1960. This beautiful and unspoilt line is little changed today, although the motive power is much less inspiring, as it is usually a 150 unit (x2 in summer) or a 153. This photo must have been after 1959 as the loco is still shown as in capital stock in the winter 1961/62 Combined Volume, but it did not receive the later BR totem style emblem until after that date. Several of the class have survived into preservation. (RW)

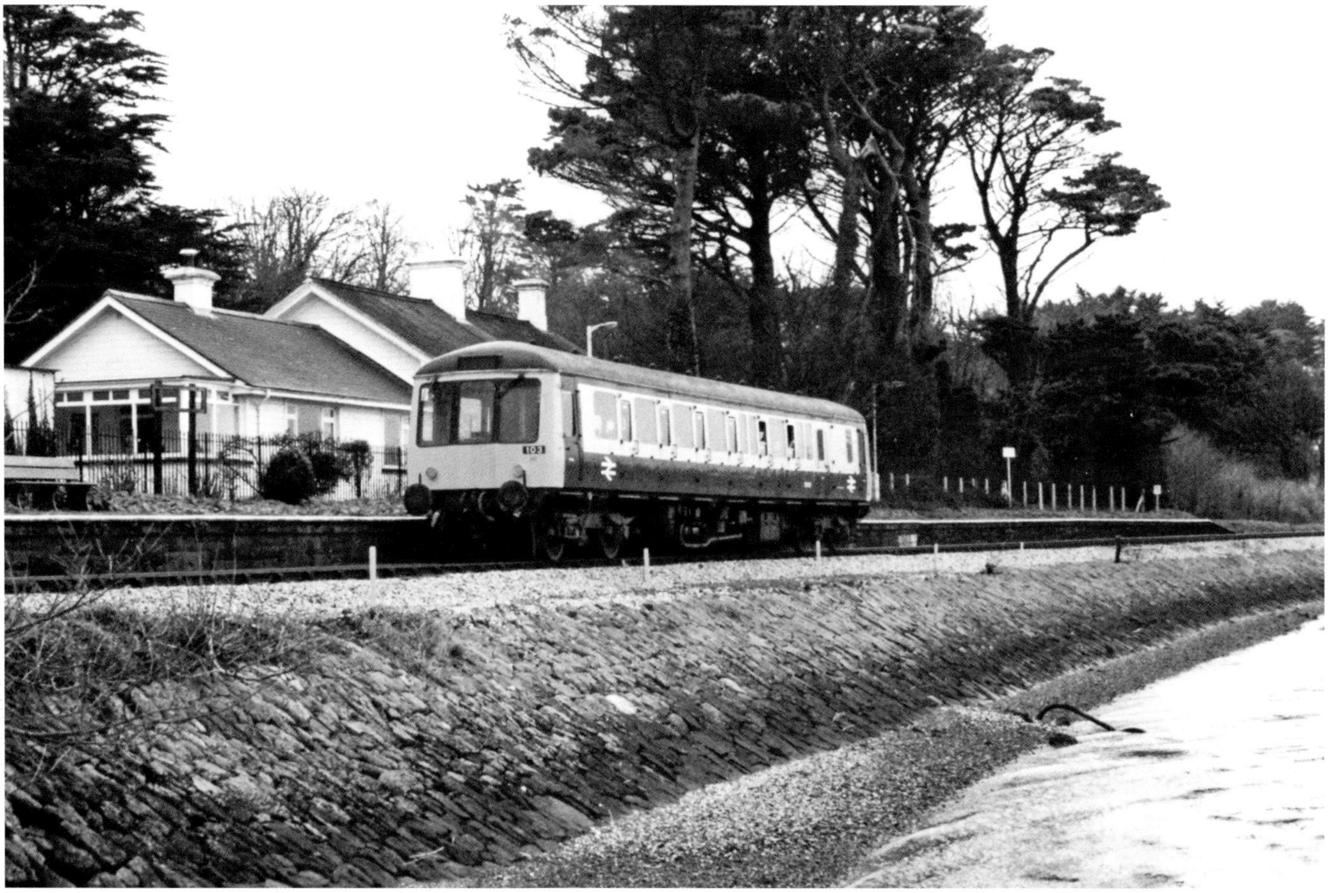

Gloucester Railway Carriage & Wagon, 1958 built Class 122 number 103, later renumbered 122103 (55003) is seen here on the St Ives Branch at Lelant platform. These AEC engined DMUs were popular units and regular performers on this route. (GP)

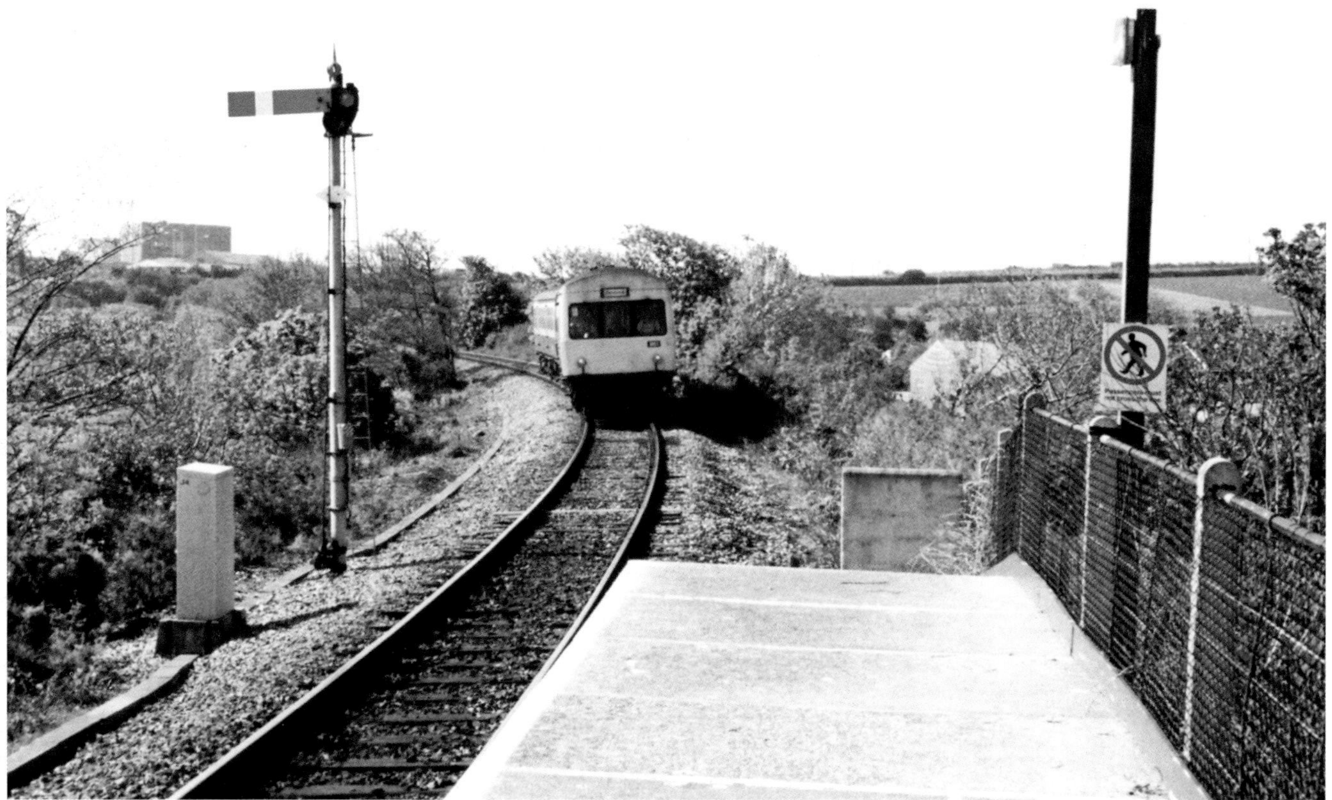

Another class 101 unit, but this time on the scenic St Ives Branch from St Erth. The location is Lelant Saltings Station (Park & Ride) and the train is heading in the Down direction for St Ives in April 1990. The signal is the 'Home' signal for the Up direction. (GP)

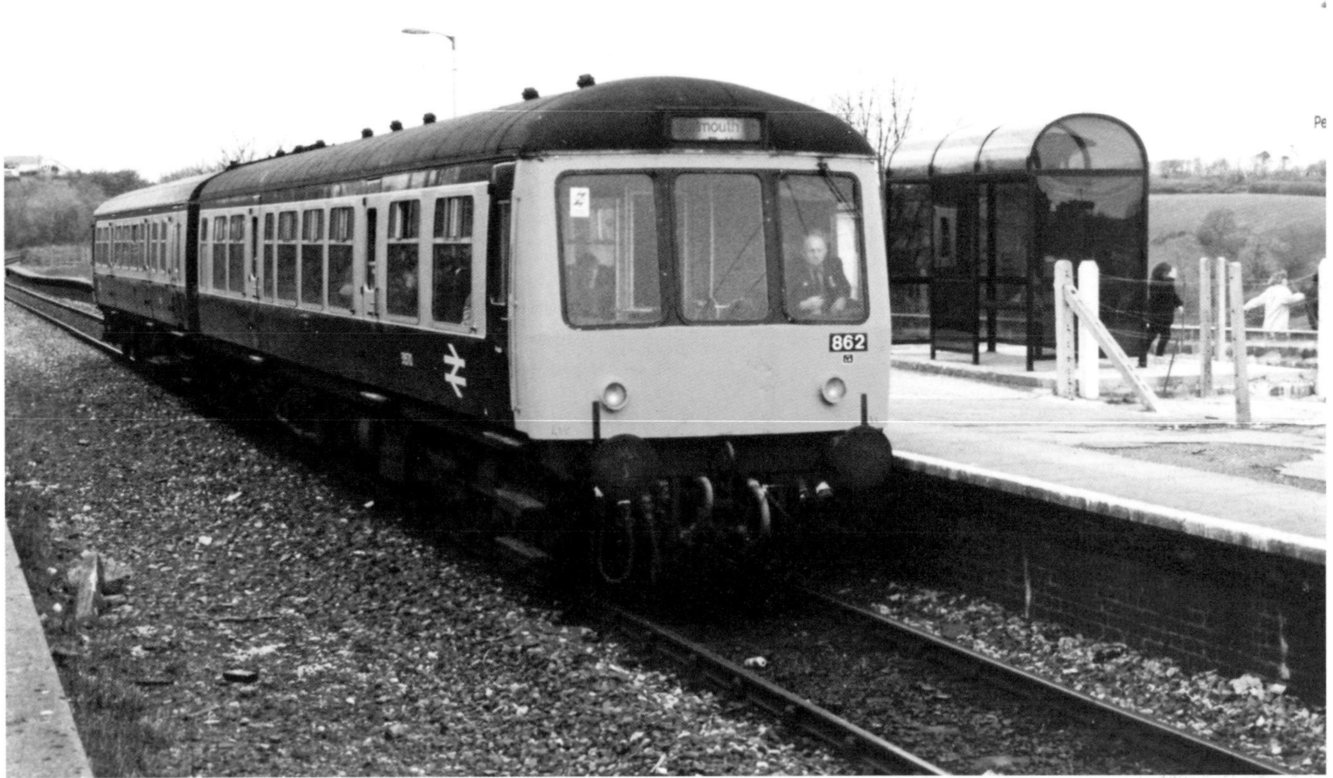

DMU 862 is made up of half a class 108 and half of a 101 and is seen here in Penryn enroute to Falmouth. Penryn is now a very different place, with the loop line reinstated and state of the art signalling and points. This station is now the busiest on a branch line in Cornwall, being busy all year round, although Newquay and St Ives are very busy, they have very seasonal patronage. Picture dated March 1980. (GP)

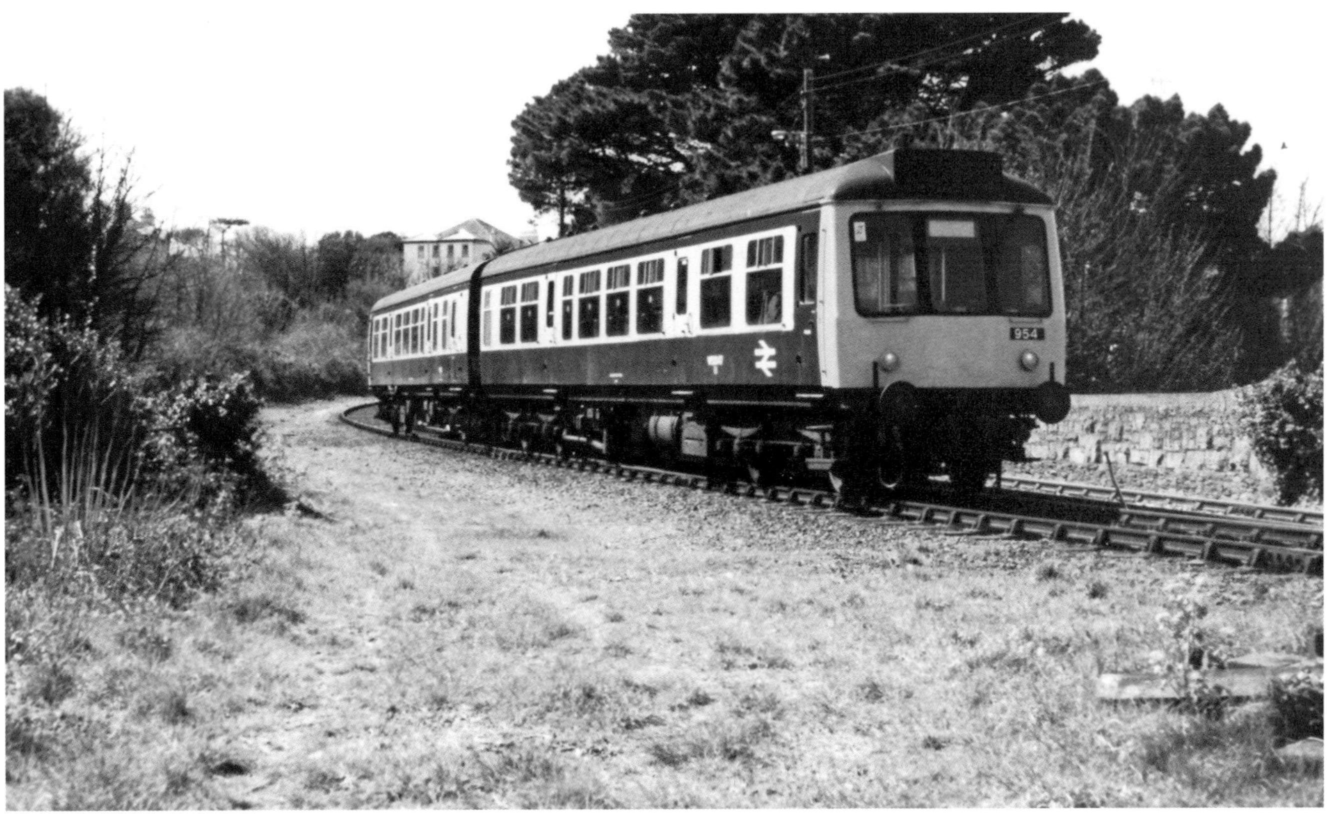

Class 108 unit number 954 is seen here leaving Falmouth for Truro, passing the still intact Ground Frame number 2, which still gives access to the loop, yard and docks, although not used for several years. The picture is dated April 1989. (GP)

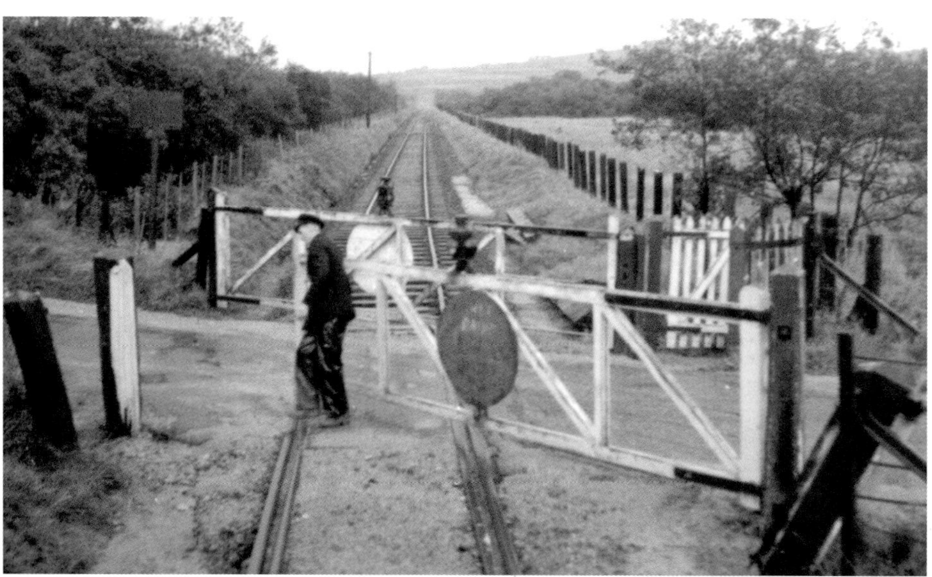

The guard of a train on the Retew Branch is opening the gates across the road, which is probably the road between the A30 and Treviscoe. The crossing point on this road is still visible if you look carefully. (SL)

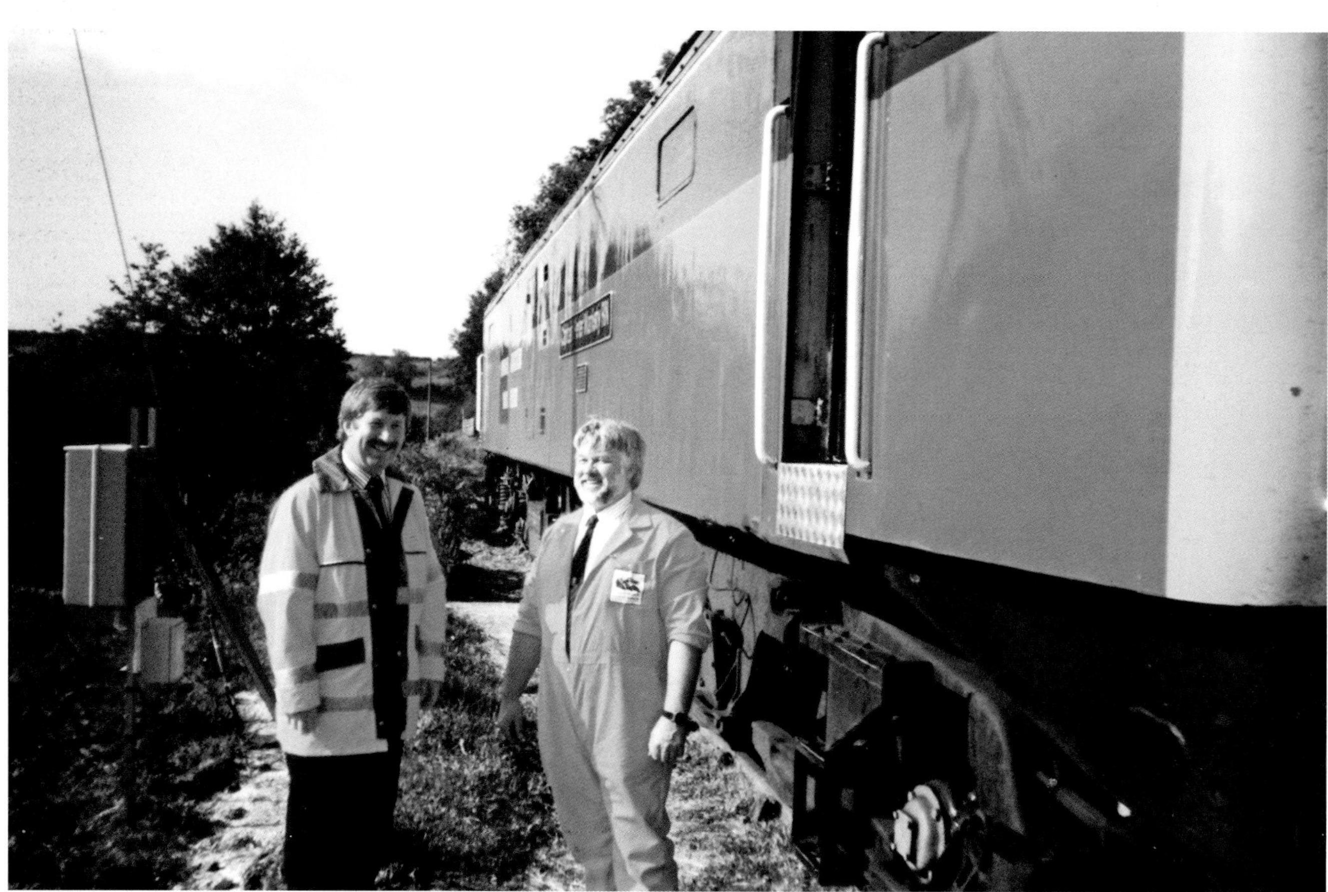

47788 *'Captain Peter Manisty RN'* is seen here in an historic move that found it traversing the little used siding at Ponts Mill. The reason for the move was in connection with a forthcoming trip by the Royal Train, which on this occasion was planned to be stabled in this remote siding. E.W.S. Depot Manager Hugh Phillips and Driver Leader (the late) Derek Aston are seen here posing for my photograph. The Permanent Way Dept had de-weeded the track, applied a few tie-bars and fettled it here and there, whilst the S&T (Signal & Telegraph) Dept had serviced the very old ground-frame giving access from the single line. The track groaned and complained bitterly at having such a heavy loco traverse this siding, especially after such a long time out of use. The Royal Train was successfully stabled there, but it was never put in there again nor in fact was anything else, except for a removal of some equipment from the closed works, after which it was decommissioned, and the ground-frame and pointwork removed. (SFH)

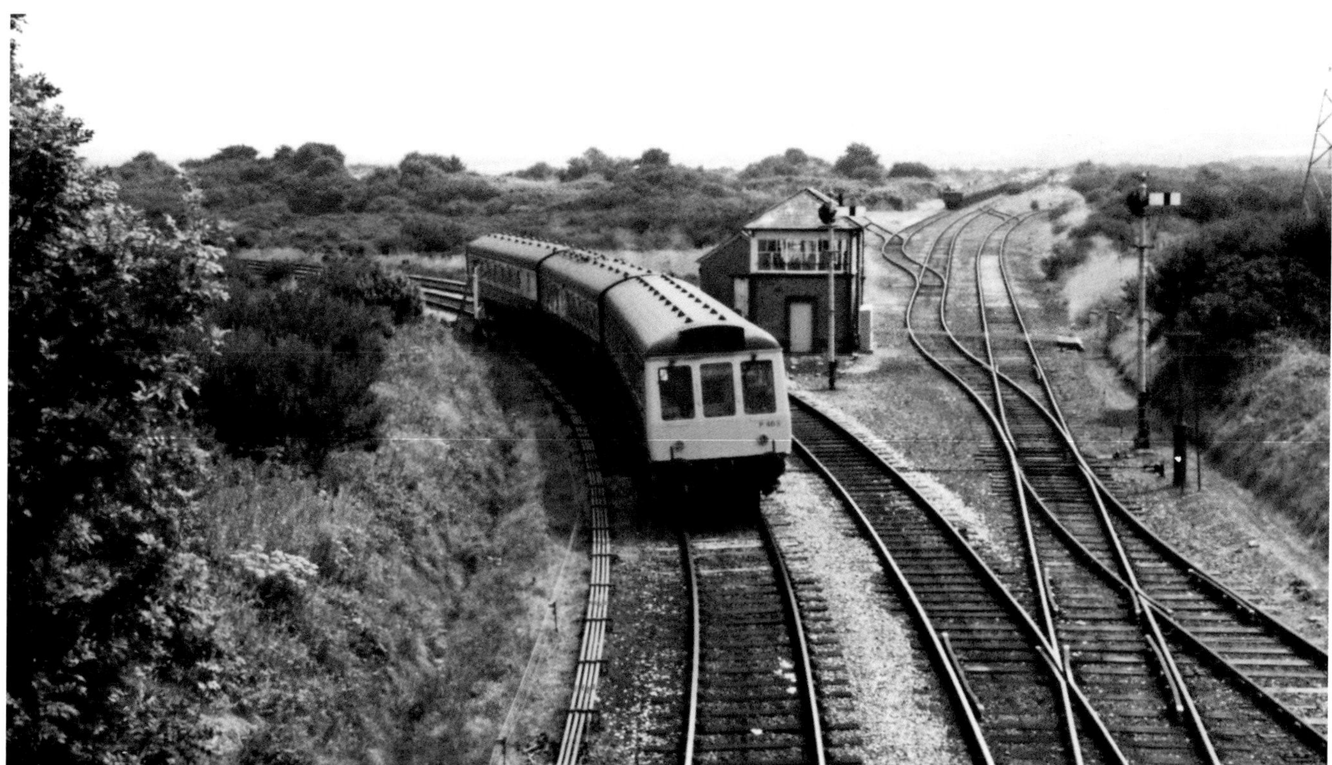

An interesting photograph of class 117 unit numbered 457 at St Dennis Junction in August 1983 The unit is on the Up line and is bound for Par, having just exchanged single line tokens with the signalman, the Newquay token being exchanged for the Goonbarrow token. Built in 1959/60 by Pressed Steel Ltd, which was a subsidiary of BMC (British Motor Corporation) which went on to become the ailing British Leyland. They had Leyland 0680 engines, and were primarily for suburban work. In the background can be seen the sidings at St Dennis Junction and in the distance the line to Retew branches off to the right. If the plans go ahead there could be trains from Newquay travelling over the line towards Parkendillack once again. The infrastructure is ostensibly still intact and mostly still owned by Network Rail Property Board. (GP)

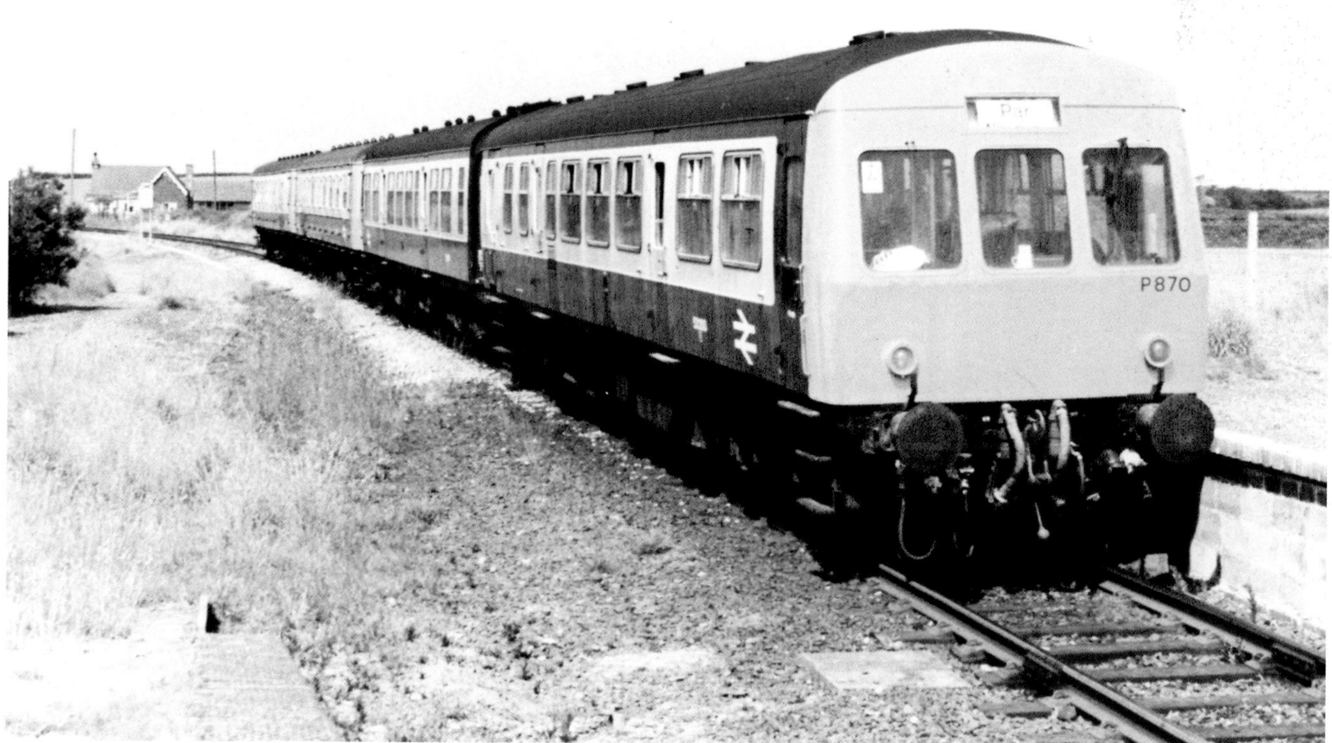

This mixed up set is at St Columb Road Station, apparently enroute to Newquay in June 1988. The set comprises a class 101, 108 and what appears to be two class 122 units. Each unit is a power car, so there certainly is no shortage of horsepower. (GP)

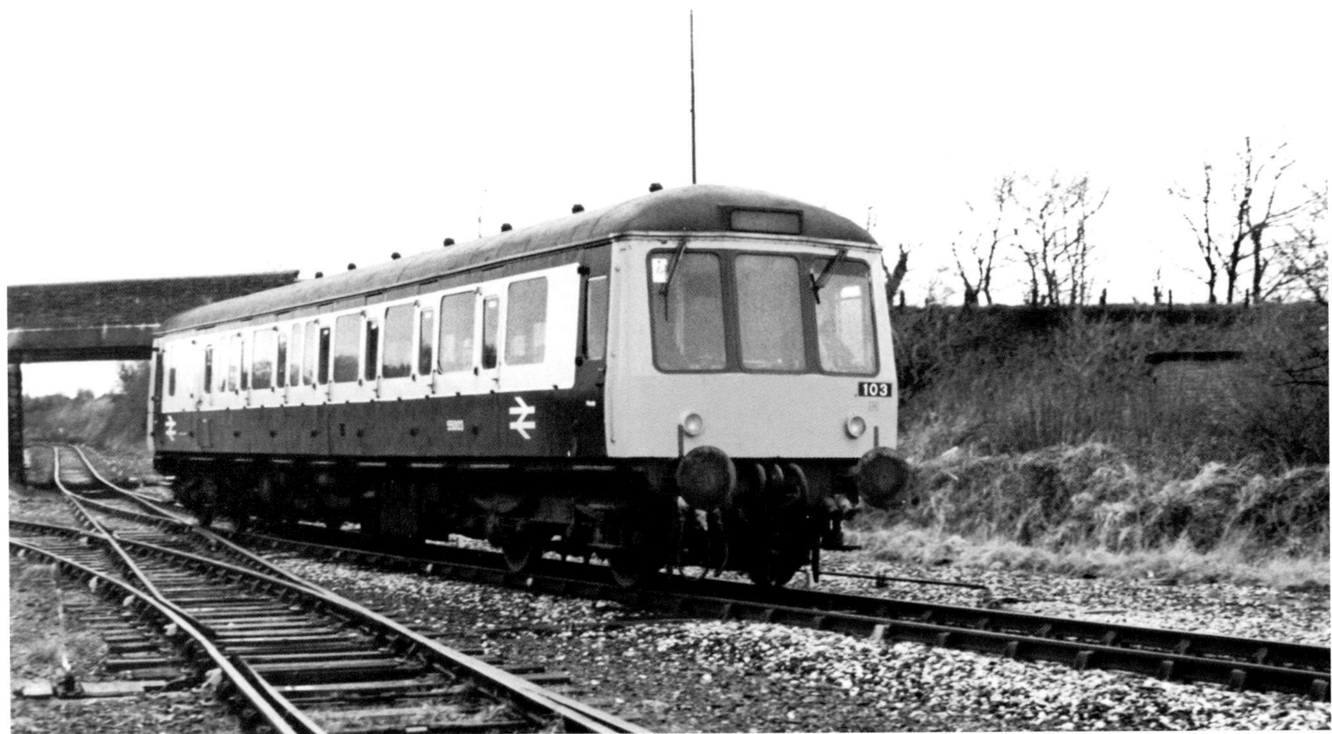

The picture here is located at St Dennis Junction and shows class 122 unit number 103 (55003) enroute from Newquay to Par. The line is already singled towards Tregoss, so the junction into the yard will be operated by a Ground Frame, which is behind the unit, near the bridge, the signalbox having been closed in 1986. The A30 is carried on the bridge in the background, but the area now has the massive bridge carrying the A30 Indian Queens Bypass crossing the line where number103 is shown. Built by Pressed Steel Ltd in 1958 they were powered by AEC engines and it is pictured here in January 1990. (GP)

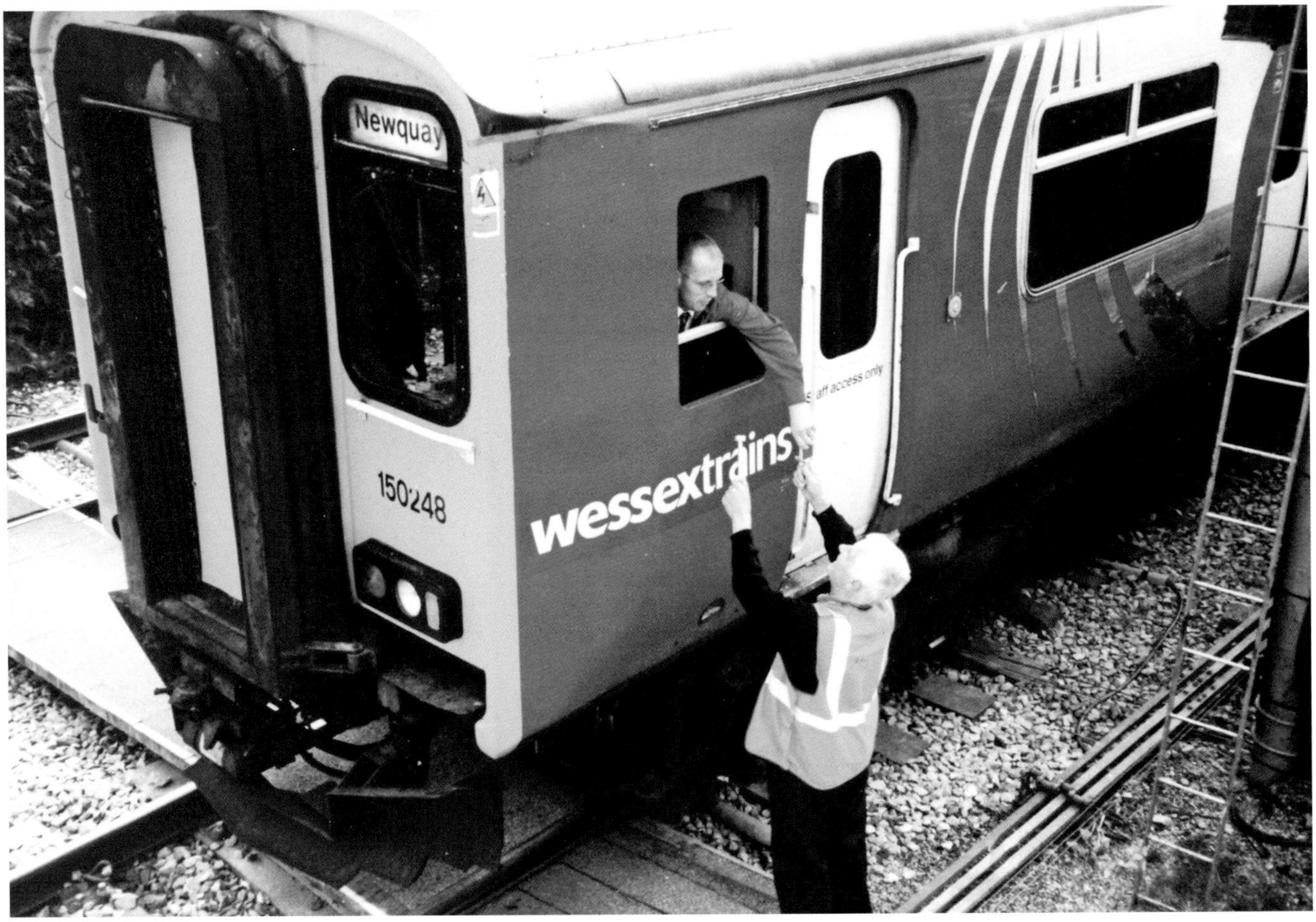

Second generation DMU 150248 in Wessex Trains livery is stopped at Goonbarrow Junction Signalbox to exchange tokens with the Signalman, Brian Coad. The driver is giving up the St Blazey token and receiving the Newquay one. (MD)

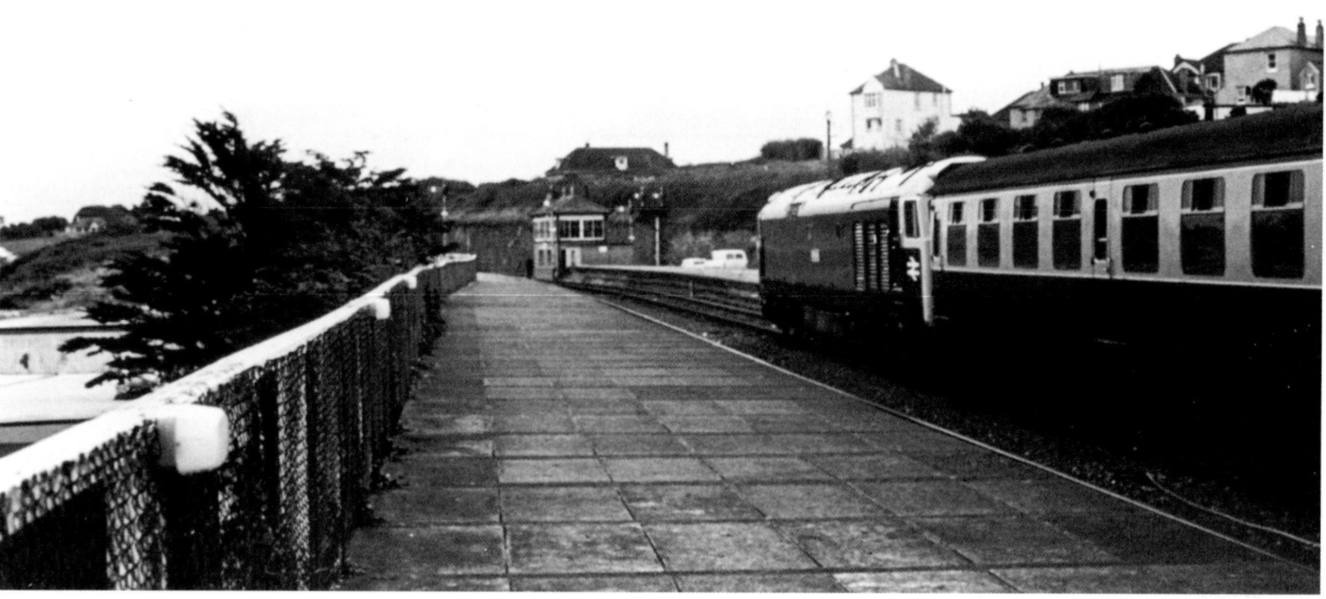

In June 1980 a class 50 is seen at the head of a train awaiting departure. The picture shows the signalbox is still open and full semaphore signals prevail, though this scene is no longer possible as the signalbox was destroyed by fire after a vandal attack and the station is now reduced to a single platform, with no station buildings. It is hard to believe that Newquay is the premier resort of Cornwall yet has the worst train service and fewest facilities. (PM)*

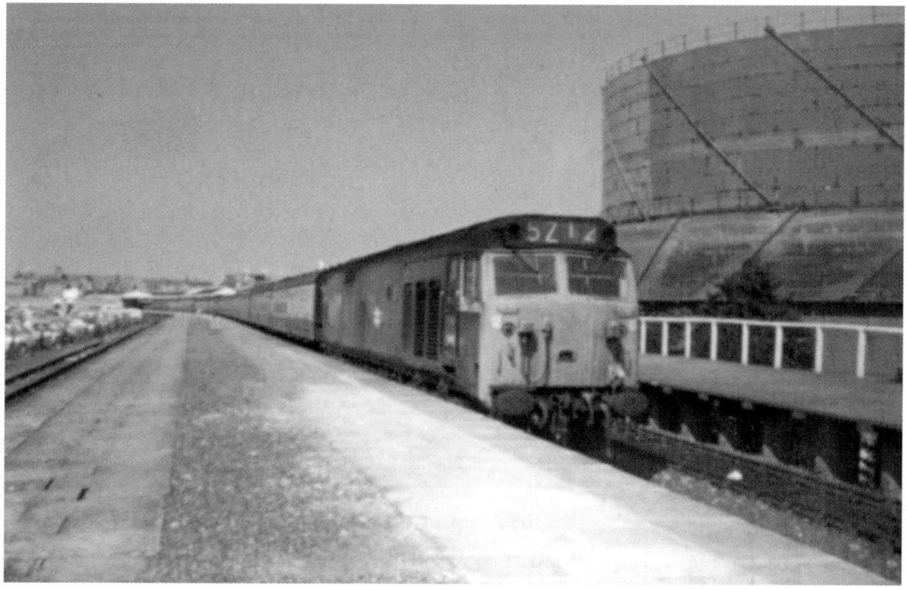

Newquay platform is the location of this unidentified class 50 on a empty stock movement. (SL)

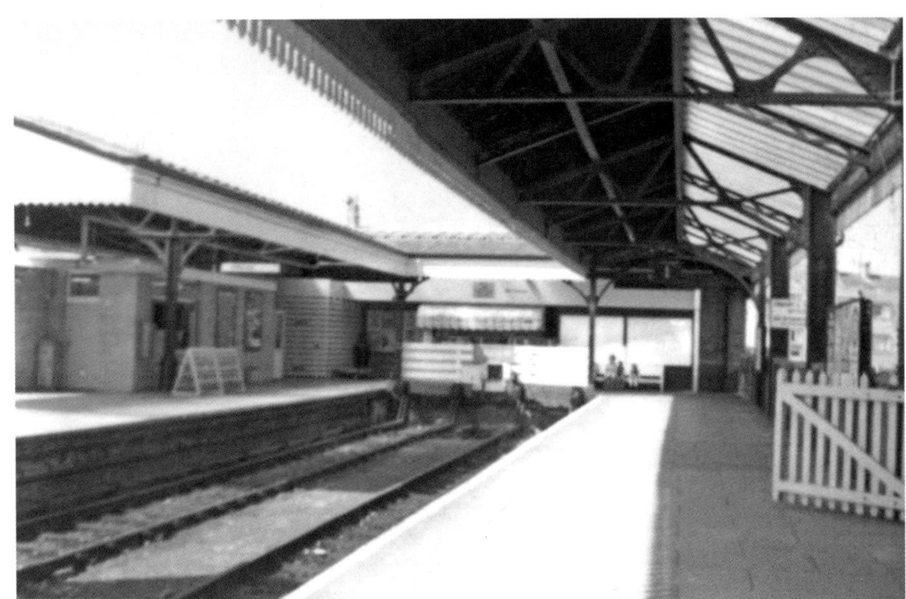

Newquay Station as it used to look like before its demolition and downgrading to a single platform and one-train working line. (SL)

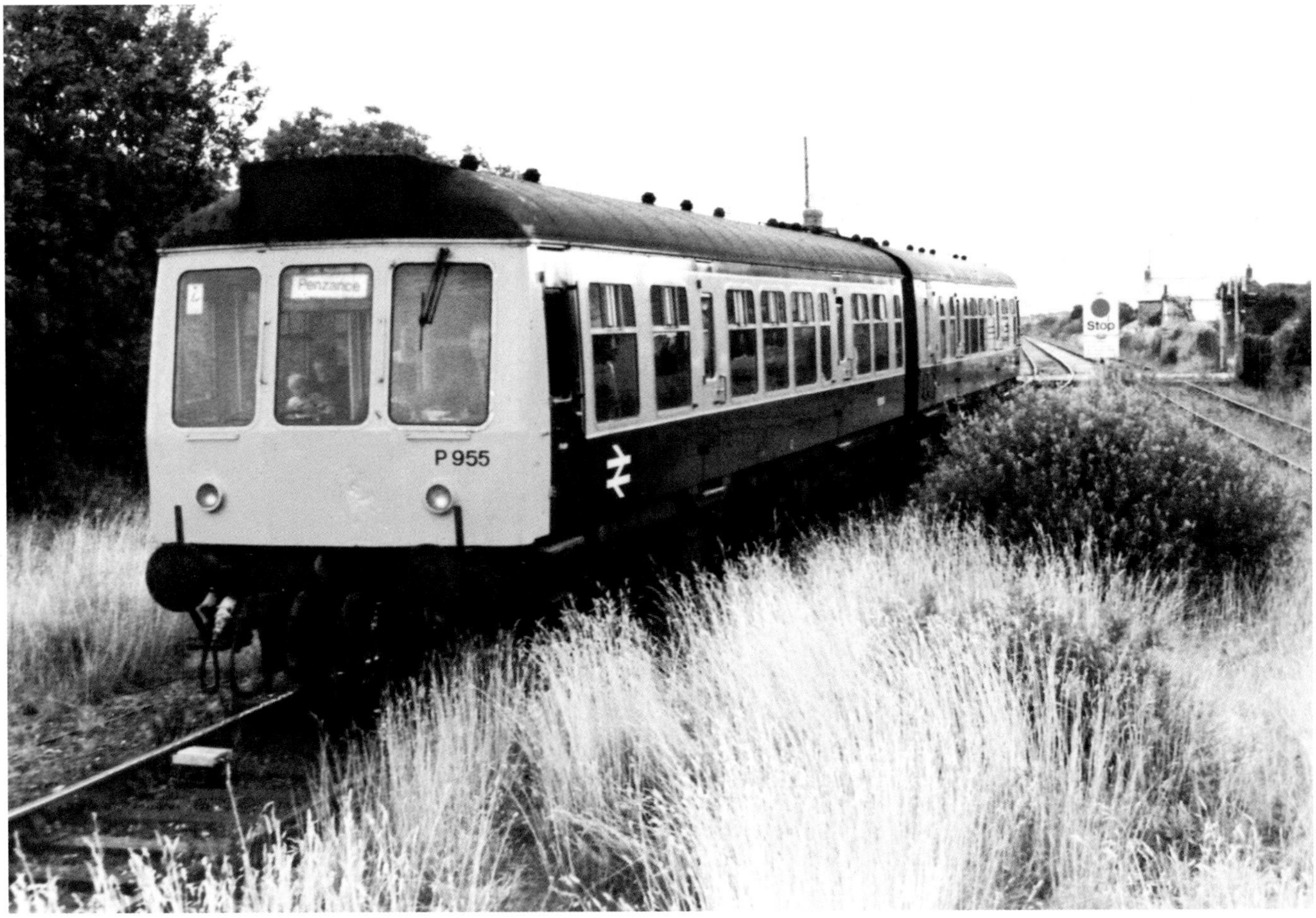

Set P955 is a 1960/1 BR built 'Derby Lightweight' class 108 unit, seen here allegedly destined for Penzance but actually enroute to Newquay and passing through Bugle in the Down direction. The branch line to Carbis is seen here still in situ, which dates the picture to October 1988. (GP)

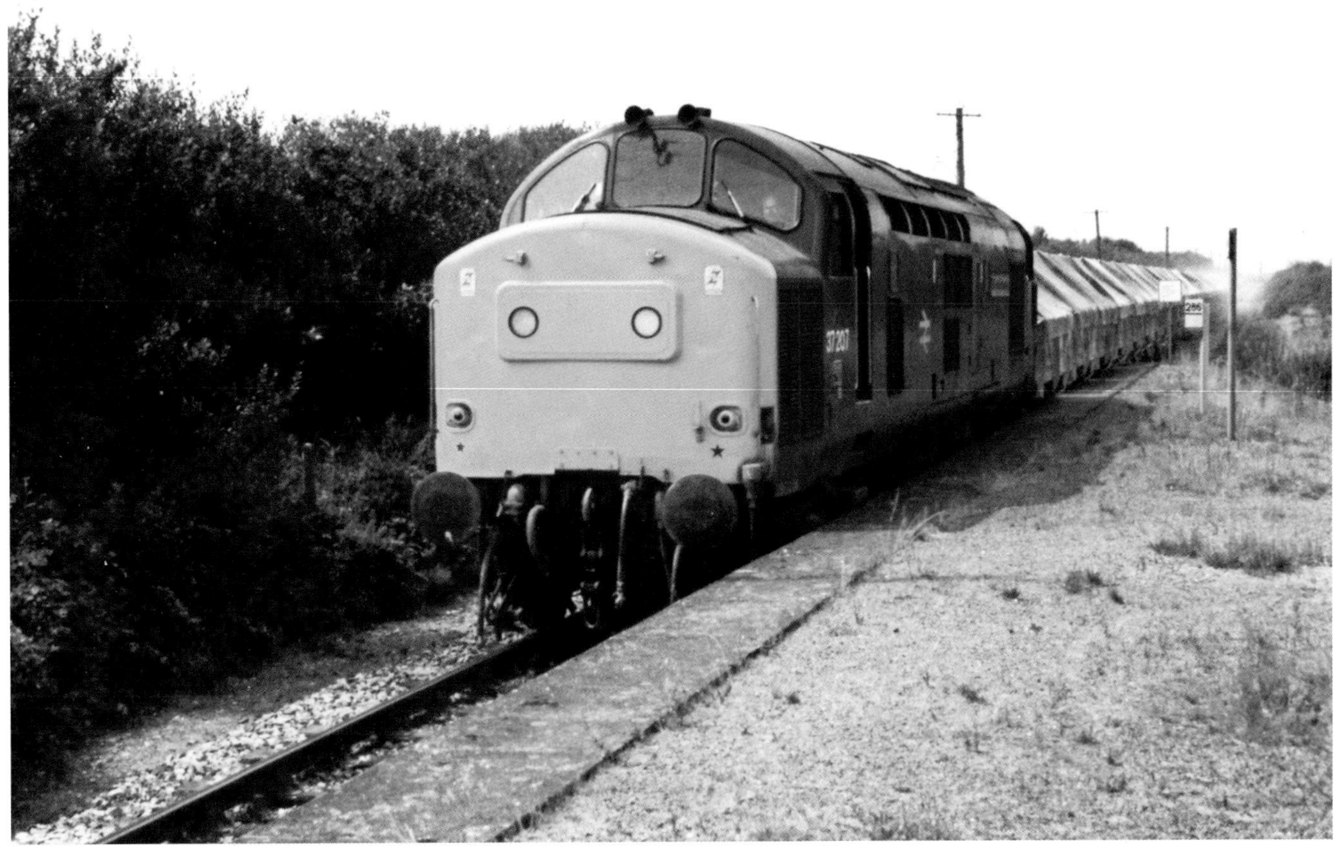

37207 again, but this time traversing Luxulyan Station with a train of China clay hoods from St Dennis to St Blazey in August 1983. (GP)

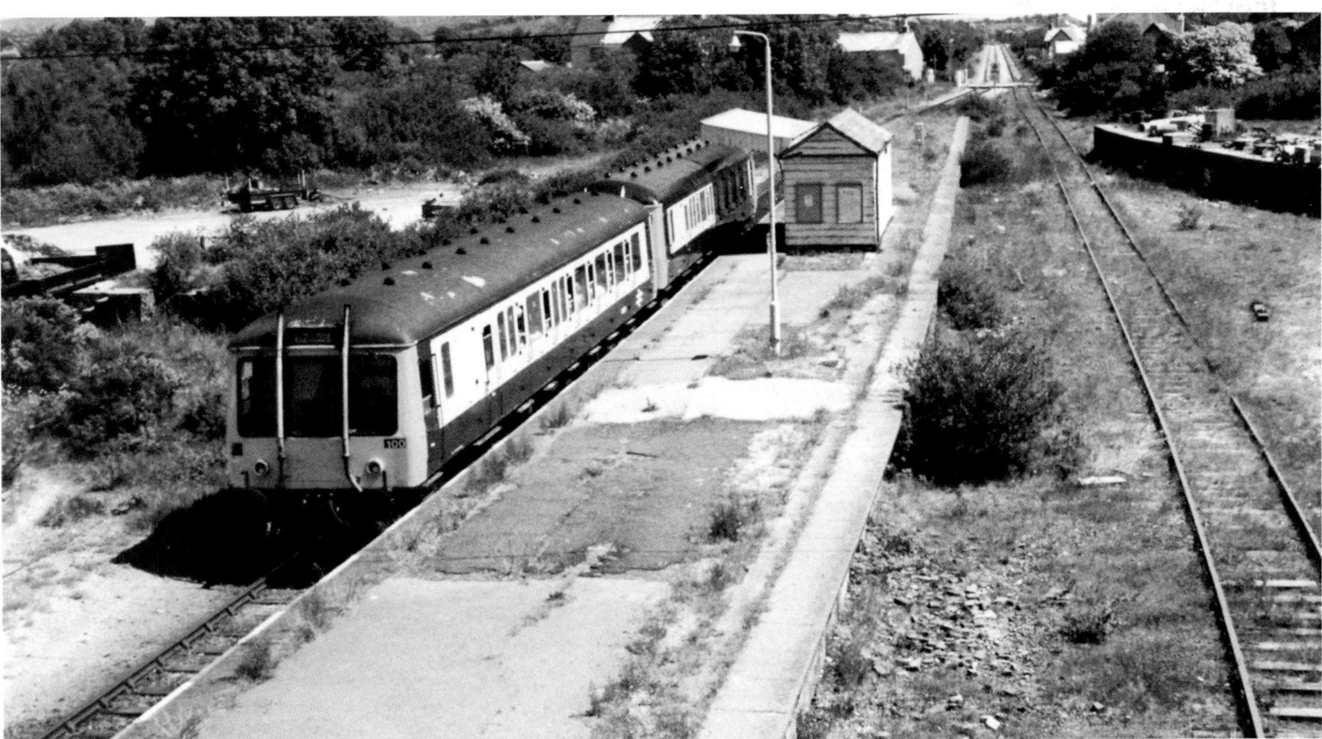

Bugle Station in May 1990 finds two Class 122 'Bubble Cars' enroute back to Par from Newquay. The rearmost unit is the first of the class, 55000 (122100) which was built in 1958 by Gloucester Carriage and Wagon. The remains of the branch to Carbis Wharf is still in situ. (GP)

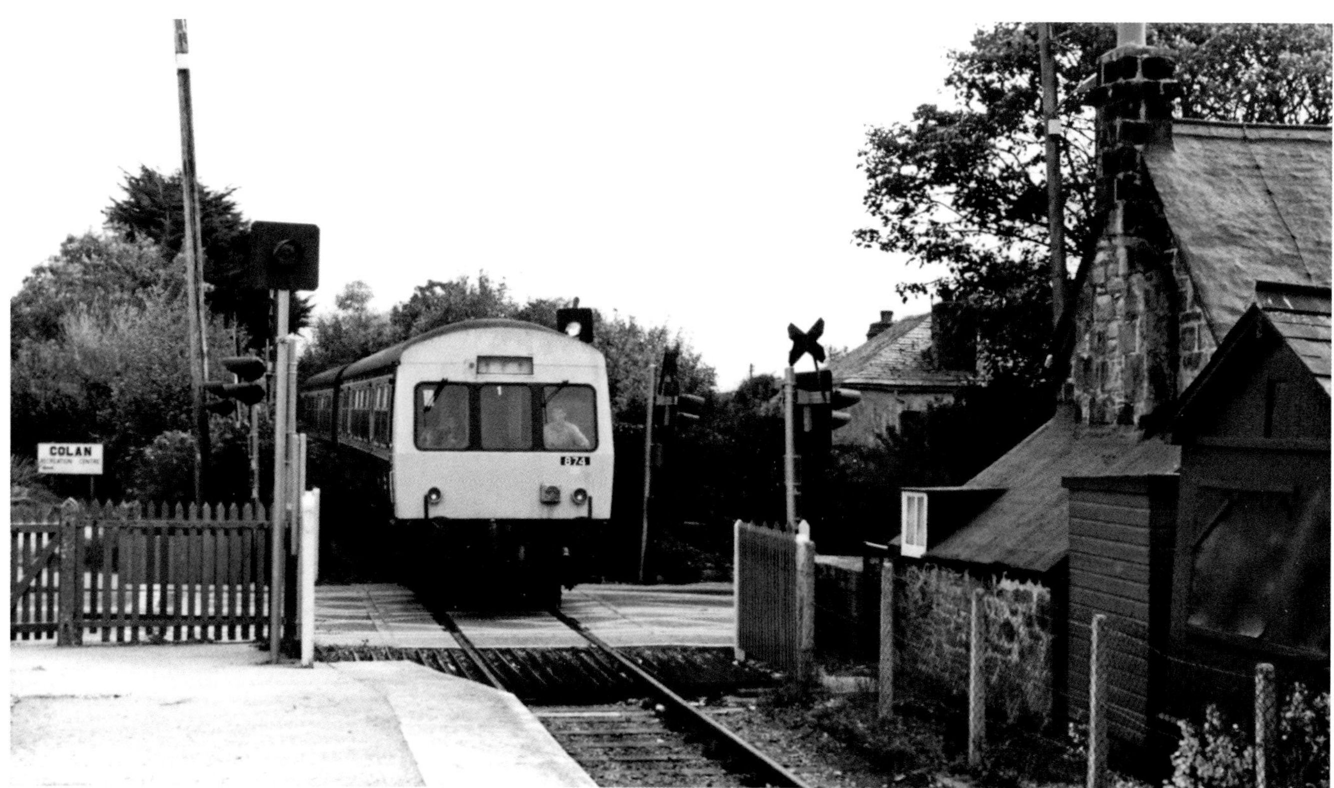

The location is Quintrell Dows AOCL Crossing in October 1989 and sees a class 101 unit enroute to Newquay. Quintrell Downs has seen a couple of serious accidents during my time as MOM for Cornwall, and the last one resulted in a reassessment of the risk on this main road to and from Newquay. Although the road speed over the crossing is only 30 m.p.h, it was thought that fitting barriers would improve safety, although hugely expensive to install. Today the crossing is of the ABCL type with half barriers and emergency controls. (GP)

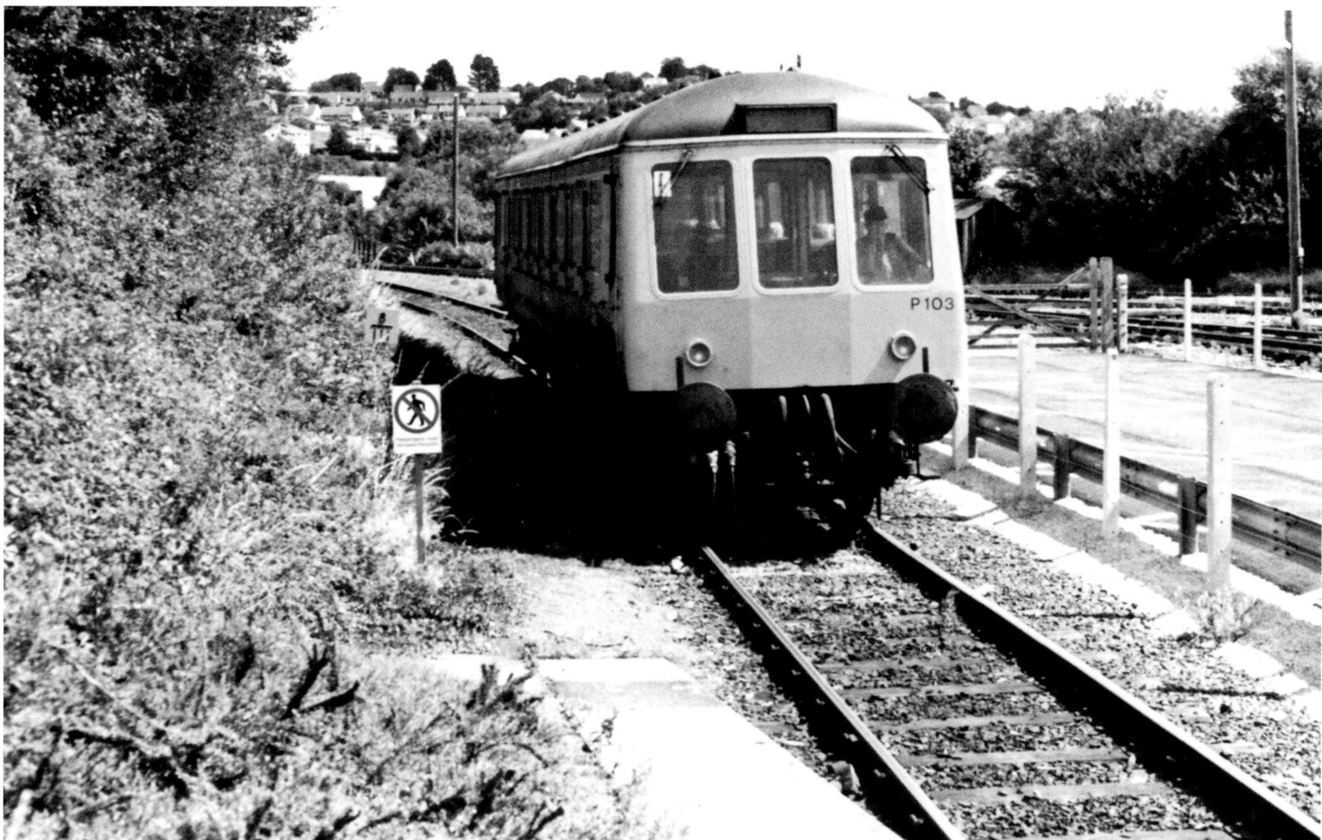

This 1980s view of 55003 (122103) shows the Bubble-Car approaching Liskeard (Looe Branch) platform. These units worked on every branch line and during peak summer loadings, especially on the St Ives Branch, they could be found working in multiple or added on to a class 101, 108 or 117 unit. (GP)

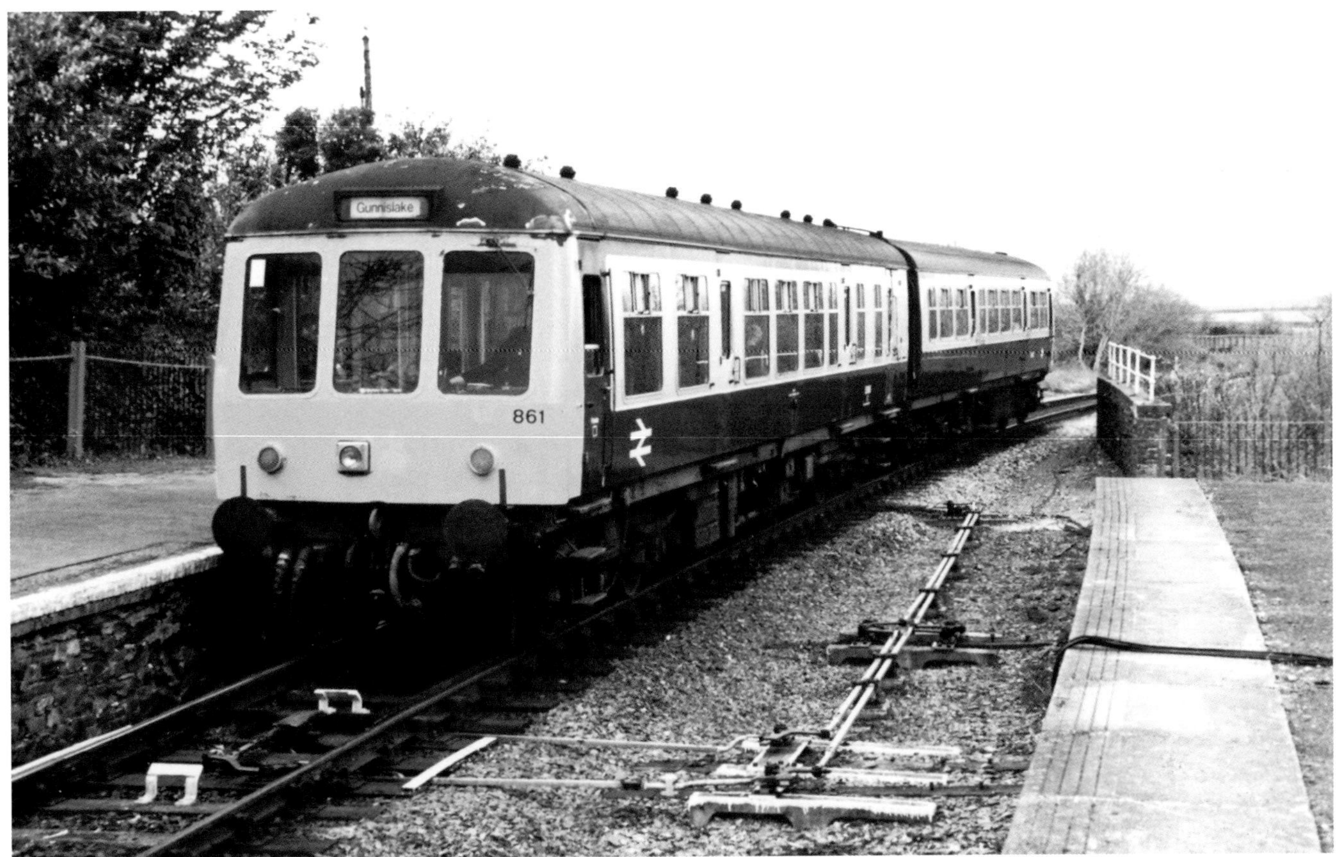

This photograph from April 1992, shows a highbred DMU (Diesel-Multiple-Unit) arriving at Bere Alston. The unit is made up of a 108 (nearest) and 101. This type of mismatching became increasingly common during the last years of the first generation DMUs. (GP)

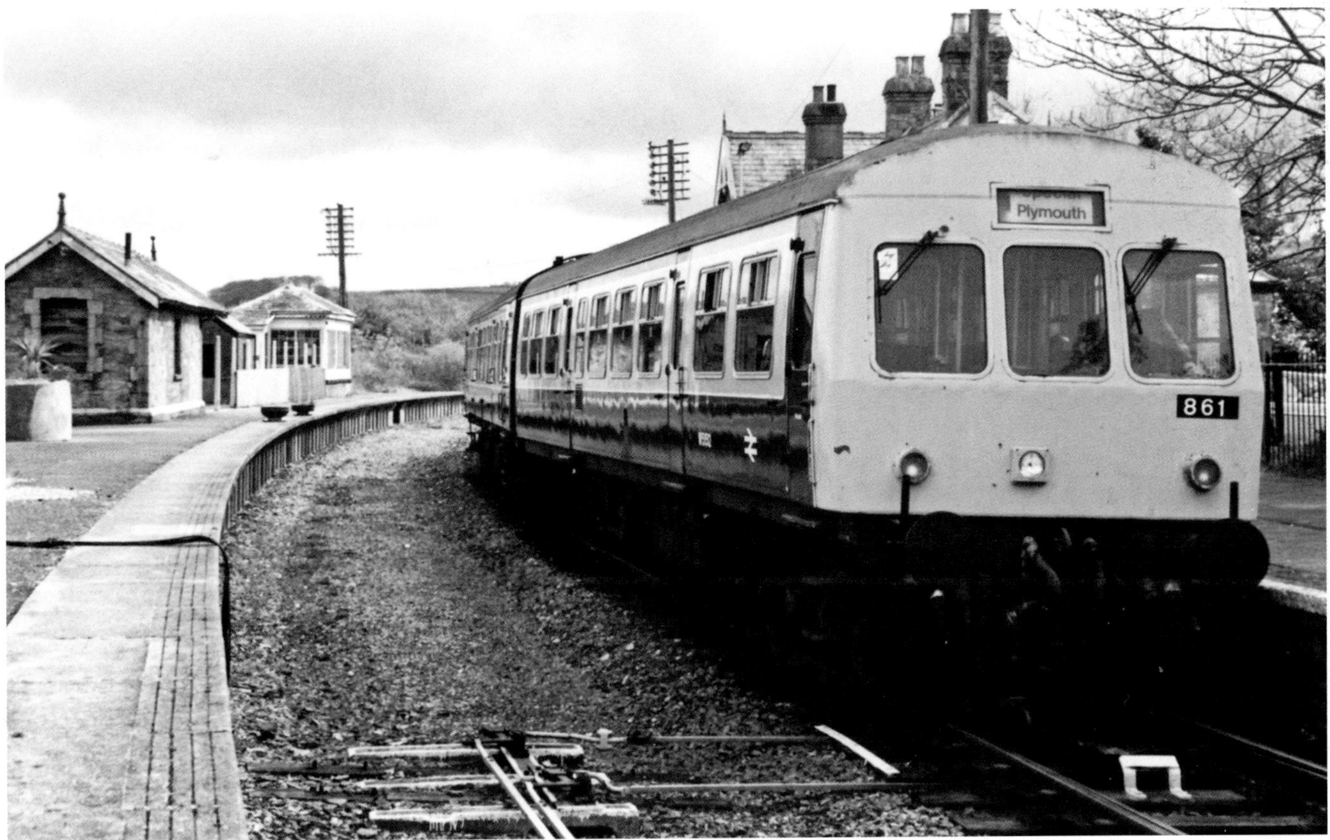

Bere Alston Station is the location of a hybrid unit (101 and 108) heading for Plymouth, having just reversed from Gunnislake in April 1992. The Ground-Frame is directly in front of the train, and is operated by the train-crew, using the staff (token) as a release for the instrument. (GP)

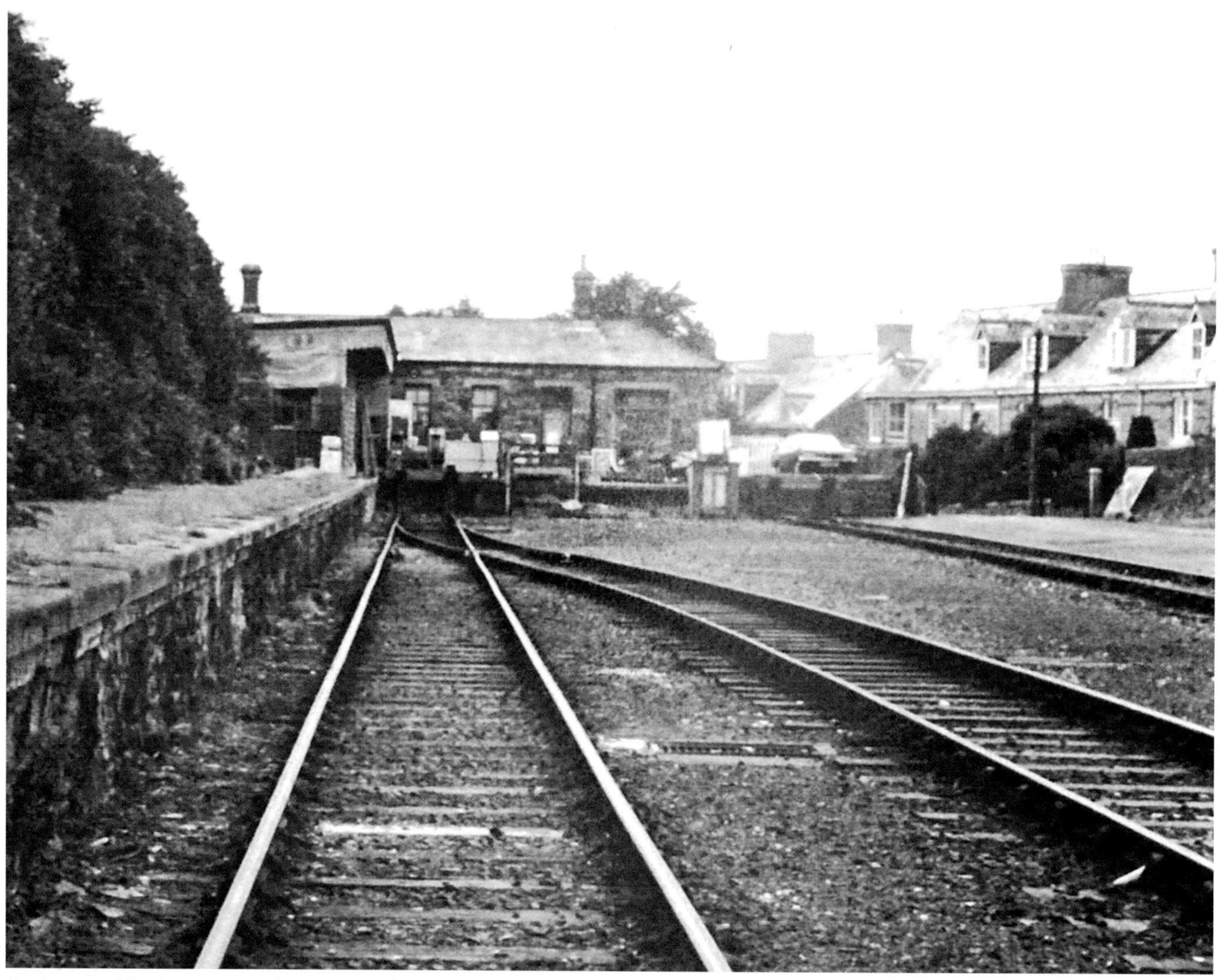

A picture of Bodmin General Station in the transitional period between BR selling it and the Bodmin & Wenford taking it over as a Heritage Railway. How much better it looks today, with reinstated track, and signalling, a new, authentic signalbox, and heritage trains running to Boscarne and Bodmin Parkway (Road). (SFH)

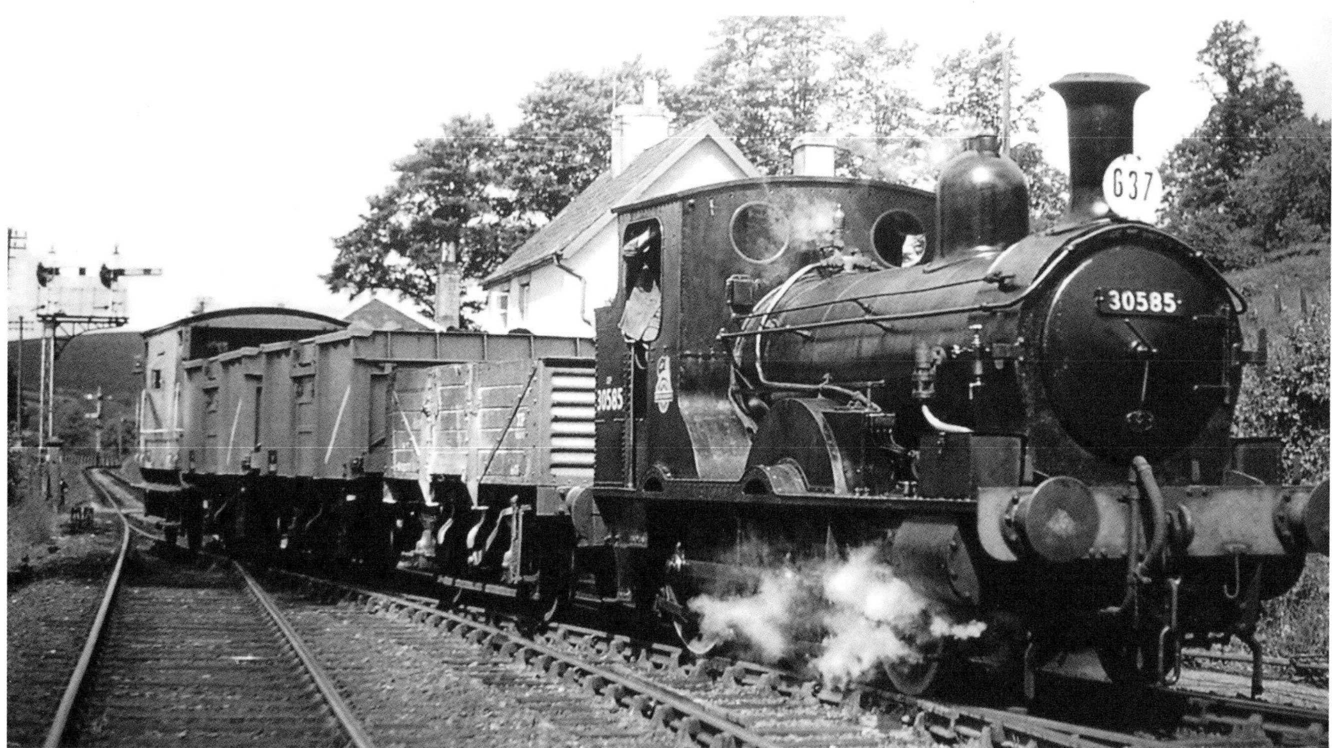

One of the ubiquitous Beattie Well Tanks dating from 1874 and built by the London South Western Railway. Number 30585 was one of only three that survived into BR days and all were used on the Wadebridge, Wenford Bridge and Bodmin sections of the old LSWR route. The three locos (30585-7) were particularly suited to the sinuous curves of the lightly laid section of line from Boscarne Junction to Wenford Bridge. It is seen here circa 1960 approaching Boscarne Junction from the Wadebridge direction, with a short goods train. (RW)

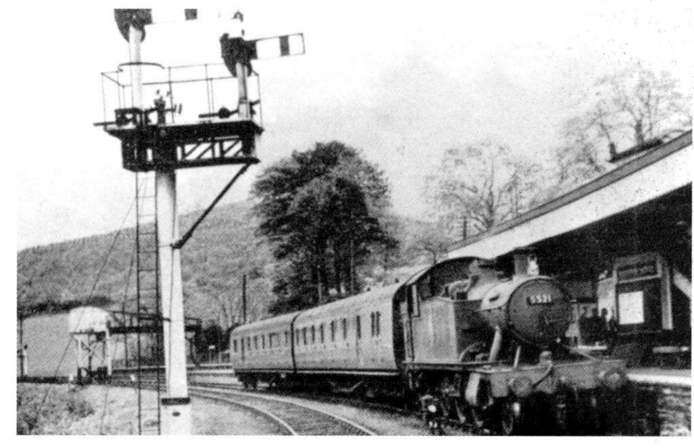

The 45XX class Prairie Tank 5521 is in the Branch Platform at Bodmin Road Station (Parkway), circa 1960, with a train for Bodmin General. This platform is now used by the trains on the Bodmin & Wenford Railway, though the platform canopy, water tower and semaphore signals were consigned to history decades ago. The B&W does have a plan to build a signalbox here and reinstate the signalling and modify the layout to reflect how it used to be. (SL)

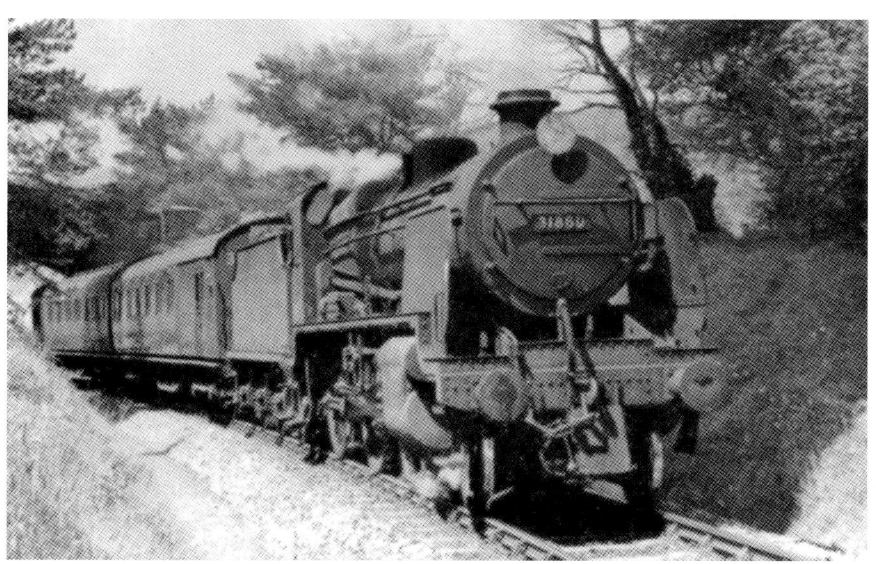

'Lord Nelson' class 30860 *'Lord Hawke'* is seen somewhere on the line between Wadebridge and Bodmin with a train of suburban stock. This ex-Southern Railway loco was built between 1926-29 and all were withdrawn between 1961 and 1962, but 30850 (850) *'Lord Nelson'* is preserved. (SL)

CHAPTER 6

SIGNALLING

It is appropriate that I have compiled this volume now, in 2013, as it is only recently that Network Rail has announced its plan to modernise the signalling throughout England, Scotland and Wales over the next several decades or so.

Some would say, "about time too" and others will mourn the passing of a piece of history, as the remnants of mechanical signalling and early electronic signalling will be swept away and new regional signalling centres will open, which in turn will give way to National Signalling Centre(s).

For the West Country, including Devon and Cornwall, this is planned to take place in just seven short years from now, though the sceptics amongst us, might speculate that that date might slip. I am not so sure, as this modernisation is driven by politics as well as money. The fewer centres there are, the fewer staff required to operate the signalling and although some might say that having fewer 'signalboxes' is a higher risk of disruption by attack or failure, the security surrounding these new centres is strong.

For us down here in sunny Cornwall, the signalling centre will, initially be in Didcot. Delivered by state of the art IT, electronic and fibre-optic technology, this centre will initially replace the nine signalboxes in Cornwall, Plymouth Panel and those still left in Devon, though the date of Exeter Panel Box closing is still in flux at present. The 'Southern' signalling centre is based in Basingstoke and this will probably take over Exmouth Junction. Didcot will take over Bristol Panel by 2015, and likewise the 25 KV electrification of the West of England main line from Paddington into Bristol and South Wales will also be completed.

In the past one-hundred-and-fifty years or so, Cornwall has had over one hundred signalboxes, though not all at the same time, and now we are down to just nine. The signalboxes at Penzance (PZ) and Roskear (R) are all colour-light signalling, but the boxes at Liskeard (LD), Lostwithiel (LL), Par (PR), St Blazey (SB), Goonbarrow (GN), Truro (TR) and St Erth (SE) are still mainly mechanical though LL and PR have mini-panels controlling areas where once other boxes existed, and all, except GN have some colour-light signals.

During my time in Cornwall I have worked all the signalboxes, including the now closed St Germans (SG), both as a Signalman, Relief Signalman and MOM. They have changed very little in the last twenty years or so, and although rationalisation of the track layouts and signalling has taken place piecemeal over their whole period of existence, only Par is as close to its original GWR layout. Par has a 56 lever frame (formerly 57) of which 50 still work, but there was once two additional levers (A&B) for the Detonator Placers on the London end of the frame. All detonator placers were removed in the 1990s.

Signalling types in Cornwall are of a varied and historic pattern. All systems work on the principle of only one train in each section at any one time, either controlled by the signaller or the passage of trains.

The main system used is called Absolute Block (AB), which is a nineteenth century system using bells, tappers, commutators and needles to signal trains by bell codes between two adjacent signalboxes. The signaller at box B gives an electrical release to box A, which releases the signal controlling the entrance to the next section. Next most common is the Track-Circuit-Block (TCB) system, in which the passage of trains passing along the track uses low voltage circuits to alter the signals. The single line branches use Electric-Token-Block (ETB), No-Signalman-Token (NST) and One-Train-Working-with-Train-Staff (OTWwTS).

ETB uses a metal token drawn from a Tyers Machine, which is released by the signaller at the other end of the section (box B) and is given to the driver by the signaller at the end where the train is proceeding from (box A). This, and the associated signals, are the authority to proceed. There can only be one token out of the system between two adjacent signalboxes at any one time.

NST uses a system similar to ETB but the signaller gives a token release from one machine to the train crew at a remote location, so they can release a token from the machine at the other end. This token is frequently associated with the working of Ground Frames (small remote single junctions usually operated by the train crew).

OTWwTS uses a piece of wood or metal (a form of token but called a Train Staff) inscribed with the limits of the section. Given directly, or released remotely by telephone or plunger, this 'Staff' is inscribed with the signal section and is the authority for the train to proceed. A signal or Stop-Board controls the entrance to this section and only one train is allowed in each section in at any one time.

(2988)

(Form referred to in Rule 193, clause (c).)

GREAT WESTERN RAILWAY.

SINGLE LINE WORKING DURING REPAIRS OR OBSTRUCTION.

.... *Station,*

.... 194

The.............................line being blocked between.................................

and.., all traffic will pass between these two places on the.............................line.

....will act as Pilotman, and no train must be allowed to pass on to the single line, except as provided in Rule 200, clause (*f*), unless he is present and personally orders the train to start.

*(*a*) Block working or Block Regulation 25, clause (*a*/iii), is in operation.
(*b*) Block working is suspended.

* *Strike out sentence (a) or (b) not applicable.*

This order is to remain in force until withdrawn by the Pilotman.

† Catch points, spring points or unworked trailing points exist at..................................
and arrangements have been made for working as directed in Rules 195 and 196.

† *Strike out sentence if no such points exist.*

(Signed) ....

To..

		TIME.
Noted by..............................	at..............................	....
Noted by..............................	at..............................	....
Noted by..............................	at..............................	....
Noted by..............................	at..............................	....
Noted by..............................	at..............................	....
Noted by..............................	at..............................	....

Noted by.. Pilotman.

10,000 Est. 618. 9/47. (8) S

A G.W.R. Single-Line-Working form as issued then by the Station Master. A modern day form is still used today, though dictated by the Pilotman to the Signalman. (SL)

SOUTHERN RAILWAY.

Stock. (1269 / 4-37.)

(10 / 43)

PILOTMAN'S TICKET.

To be used when it is necessary to work the traffic of a single line by Pilotman owing to failure of the Electric Tablet, Staff or Key-token Apparatus, or when the Electric Tablet, Staff or Key-token, or Ordinary Train Staff has been lost or is defective.

To the GUARD AND DRIVER of the ________ Train

From ________ *To* ________

You are authorised to proceed from ________

to ________ Pilotman following.

Signature of Pilotman ________

Date ________

[SEE OVER.

This pre-1948 Southern Railway S.L.W. Ticket was issued to the driver of a train that was sent through the section if there was more than one train in the same direction, the Pilotman travelling on the last train and then brings or sends one (or more) back the other way. This procedure still exists, though the modern form has more information recorded. (SL)

(1190)

Form referred to in Rules 175, *clause* (*c*), 183, *clauses* (*f*) *and* (*g*), 184 *and* 203.

GREAT WESTERN RAILWAY.

(A supply of these Forms must be kept in each Signal Box).

WRONG LINE ORDER FORM D.
SIGNALMAN TO DRIVER.

To Driver of Engine No..................... *working*.. *train.*

I authorise you to travel with your train on the *.......................... line in the wrong direction to this signal box.

Catch points exist at..............................

Signed.. *Signalman.*

at.............................. signal box.

Date.......................... 19...... Time issued.........m.

† Countersigned.. *Signalman.*

at.................................. signal box.

* *Insert name of line, for example, Up or Down Main, Fast, Slow or Goods*
† *If necessary.*

3 000 Bks., 12 lvs. and cover—Est. 693—(11)—11/32.—S.

A Wrong Direction movement needed a form in those days, even if the train was a failure and requested assistance. But of course with better communications, especially GSMR, commissioned in 2012, all trains and signalboxes are now in direct communication and trains disappearing into 'black holes' of no communications, are relegated to the past. (SL)

PINK

Form referred to in Rule 183, clause (f).

GREAT WESTERN RAILWAY (1188)

(A supply of these forms must be kept by each Guard).

WRONG LINE ORDER FORM **A.**
GUARD TO SIGNALMAN.

To the Signalman at.. *signal box.*

Allow an engine or breakdown van train to travel in the wrong direction to my train which is stationary on the*.. line at..

I will prevent my train being moved until the engine or breakdown van train arrives.

Catch points exist at..

Date.............................. 194....... Signed.. *Guard.*

† Countersigned.. Time issued.........m.

† Countersigned.. *Driver of engine assisting in rear.*

Signalman.

at.. signal box.

* *Insert name of line, for example, Up or Down Main, Fast, Slow or Goods.*
† *If necessary.*

750 bks., 12 lvs. and cover—B.M./26/2. 1944. (8) S.

The Guards form to request assistance in the wrong direction. (SL)

There are other systems, though not in Cornwall, namely Radio-Electric-Token-Block (RETB) which uses a virtual token released remotely by electronics and radio. Other systems still in use are, One-Train-Working-without-Train-Staff, which is similar to that above but the authority to proceed is by signal or verbal authority only. C2 working is very similar. In Devon there is another system used on the ex-Southern section on the Exmouth Junction line to London Waterloo, which uses a system called Tokenless-Block, where trains are released into the next section by the signaller at box B releasing the equipment at box A electrically, and thus the associated signalling allows the train to proceed to box B.

SIGNALBOXES

As mentioned elsewhere in this volume, Cornwall currently has nine signalboxes (2013) still extant. Penzance ((PZ) - the most southerly and westerly signalbox in Britain), St Erth ((SE) – is junction for the line to St Ives), Roskear ((R) – formerly Roskear Junction controlled the branch line to Roskear and South Crofty mines), Truro ((TR) – is junction for the line to Penryn and Falmouth), Par ((PR) – is junction for Newquay Branch and Par also controls the remote junction at Burngullow for the Parkandillack Branch, St Blazey ((SB) – is junction for the short branch to Par Harbour and the former line to Fowey), Goonbarrow Junction ((GN) – is no longer the junction for the Goonbarrow Branch), Lostwithiel ((LL) – is junction for the line to Fowey, Liskeard ((LD) – is junction for the line to Coombe Junction and either Moorswater or reversing for the line to Looe).

Starting with PZ box I will give a brief description of the box and the area of operation of each signalbox in Cornwall in 2013. As a general rule Down trains work away from London and Up trains work towards London.

PENZANCE

This box was built in 1938 and is of a pattern 12B. It has 75 levers or lever spaces although the highest number is 71 of which 46 are still used and controls the line from SE on the Down line and up to Marazion on the Up line. Partially TCB signalling and AB signalling, all the signals in PZ control are of the colour-light type, controlled from traditional levers which are slightly shortened, as they are all converted to electro-mechanical for operation of both signals, points and the level- crossing at Long Rock.

ST ERTH

Built in 1899 and is of a type 5 pattern. It has a frame containing 69 levers or spaces where levers once existed of which 31 still work and is AB signalling to both PZ and R, but controls the branch to St Ives by OTWwTS. It is ostensibly mechanical, but has one electro-mechanical crossover from up to down and four colour-light signals, amongst mainly semaphore signalling.

ROSKEAR (JUNCTION)

Built in 1895 and is of the type 5 pattern and has no levers now, but has switches controlling three colour-light signals on the down line and only one on the up line. It works AB to SE and TR boxes. When the area between Camborne and Truro was rationalised under BR during the 1970s and 1980s, the rationalisation was overdone and consequently there is only one signal on the up line between SE and TR, which causes both problems structuring the timetable and delays when trains run late for any reason.

TRURO (EAST)

The only remaining signalbox in Truro, it was previously known as Truro East until 1971, but now just Truro. Built in 1899 at a type 7A, it has been reframed and now has the 51 lever frame at the rear, the original frame being at the front. Forty levers still work.

There is an Intermediate Block Section (IBS) on the Down line where there was once a signalbox at Baldu.

(Intermediate Block Signalling – (IBS) is just a couple of colour-light signals that replace a signalbox previously closed and that split the section and is operated by the signalbox in rear.

PAR

This signalbox is still on the same site as it was when constructed in 1879, though it has been extended over the years. It is an unclassified type with 56 levers, (formerly 57 plus AeB Detonator placers) of which 50 still work. It still controls the once busy junction for the Newquay line, including China Clay trains to Goonbarrow, Rocks, Bugle and Carbis branches and for trains and locomotives traversing to St Blazey Depot and yards and of course, Par Docks.

On the west end of the box there is a mini-panel controlling the line between Par and Probus. This is of the TCB signalling type, but the section between Probus and Truro is still AB with special operating instructions.

At Burngullow is the junction for Parkandillack, Treviscoe and the numerous small branches that fed the clay works, including the former Drinnick Mill Junction.

AB signalling applies to and from SB and LL and the main line to LL has an Intermediate Block section at Treverrin for the up and down lines, shared with LL. The Line to Parkandillack is the One-train-Working method of signalling.

The junction at Par is not as busy as it once was, and the amount of china clay is less than in the past, but still significant, nonetheless. The introduction of the far more powerful class 66 locos, from the ubiquitous class 37XXX locos and the subsequent lengthening of the clay trains from nineteen CDA wagons to 38 wagons has more than halved the amount of freight trains passing through Par. Each CDA wagon weighs sixteen tons empty, and forty-six tons loaded. The loss of the Postal Trains in 2004 and the removal of depot maintenance facilities for the local DMU trains has also seen less traffic traversing the short loop around to St Blazey.

ST BLAZEY

Built in 1908 as a type 7D, it controls the single line token section to Goonbarrow junction and subsequently Newquay. It also controls the junction to Par Harbour and the yard and depot at St Blazey as well as the Up and Down line to Par. A mere shadow of its former self in terms of traffic and layout. It has a 41 lever frame of which 23 still work and it still serves a useful function being unique in the current Western Route for two things. Firstly, it retains the only authorised token catcher on the up line, which is used for catching the hoop containing the token from Goonbarrow Junction, when used by heavy Up freight trains, and secondly, it is now the only location that has never had a box between it and an adjacent box, in this case, Par.

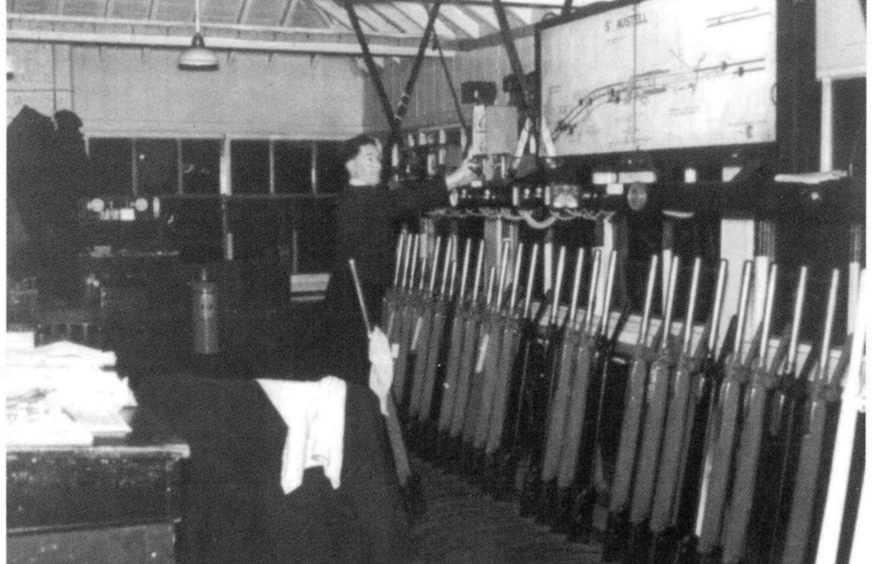

This mid 1960s view of the inside of St Austell Signalbox, shows signalman Lethbridge operating the block instrument. (SL)

GOONBARROW

Built in 1909 as a type 7D, it remains open in 2013, but with re-signalling of the West Country now looming ever nearer, its days are plainly numbered. It has 25 lever frame of which 21 still work. It controls the entrance to the sidings at Imerys Rocks Works, and the truncated siding to Carbis Wharf. The Up refuge is intact but disused. The Electric Token Block system is used for train to and from St Blazey and the line to Newquay is One-Train-Working-With-Train-Staff system, though an ETB type token from a second Tyers machine is used for the purpose. During the summer months, usually on busy Saturdays, the trains are crossed here, but due to the cost of replacing the worn out track, signalling, and Signalbox, there is a plan to 'plain-line' Goonbarrow, remove the track and fittings and just leave a two-lever Train Crew operated, Ground-Frame.

LOSTWITHIEL

This is a type 5 box, built in 1893, with a 1923, 63 lever frame of which 38 still work. It controls the Intermediate Block Section to Par on the Absolute Block signalling system, and since 1991 it controls the line to Liskeard via a Mini-Panel covering the Bodmin and Largin areas. It also controls the single-line to Carne Point, Fowey, for the movement of China Clay trains using the One-Train-Working-With-Train-Staff system.

LISKEARD

Here we find the last signalbox in the County of Cornwall before reaching Devon. Liskeard is a rare operational wooden construction box built in 1915 to a type 27C pattern. The box controls the line to Plymouth on the Track-Circuit-Block system, using a Train-Describer, and in the other direction it interfaces with the Mini-Panel at Lostwithiel, the boundary being around Doublebois. It has a 36 lever frame of which 19 still work. The entrance into the yard leads to the line used for freight traffic to Moorswater (currently cement from Hope) and the passenger line from Platform 3 to Looe via (reversing) Coombe Junction. To Coombe it is signalled on the No-Signaller-Token system, and from Coombe to Looe the One-Train-Working-With-Train-Staff system is used.

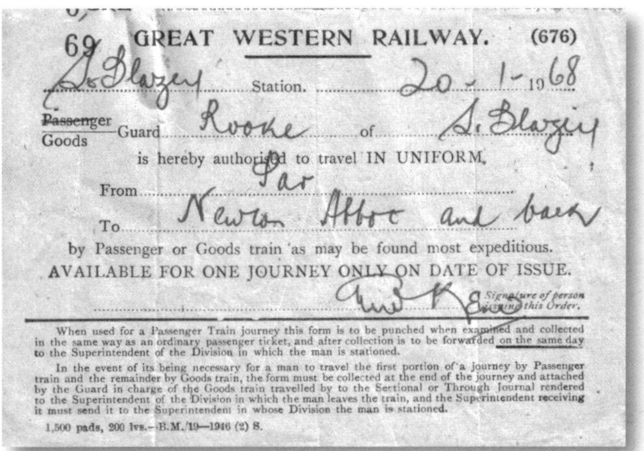

69 GREAT WESTERN RAILWAY. (676)

St Blazey Station. 20-1-1968

~~Passenger~~ / Goods Guard Rooke of St Blazey

is hereby authorised to travel IN UNIFORM,

From Par

To Newton Abbot and back

by Passenger or Goods train as may be found most expeditious.

AVAILABLE FOR ONE JOURNEY ONLY ON DATE OF ISSUE.

Signature of person issuing this Order.

When used for a Passenger Train journey this form is to be punched when examined and collected in the same way as an ordinary passenger ticket, and after collection is to be forwarded on the same day to the Superintendent of the Division in which the man is stationed.

In the event of its being necessary for a man to travel the first portion of a journey by Passenger train and the remainder by Goods train, the form must be collected at the end of the journey and attached by the Guard in charge of the Goods train travelled by to the Sectional or Through Journal rendered to the Superintendent of the Division in which the man leaves the train, and the Superintendent receiving it must send it to the Superintendent in whose Division the man is stationed.

1,500 pads, 200 lvs.—B.M./19—1946 (2) S.

A very interesting travel warrant from 1968, issued from St Blazey Station (closed), but obviously issued from the depot, for a Guard to travel to Newton Abbot and back, using any train available, including a goods train. Since privatisation such journeys require a ticket for the relevant train company and the only time I (as an employee) can travel without a ticket is in the course of my duties, such as examination of the track, or as Pilotman. A backward step one might say, and just another piece of bureaucracy that has mushroomed since 1994. (SL)

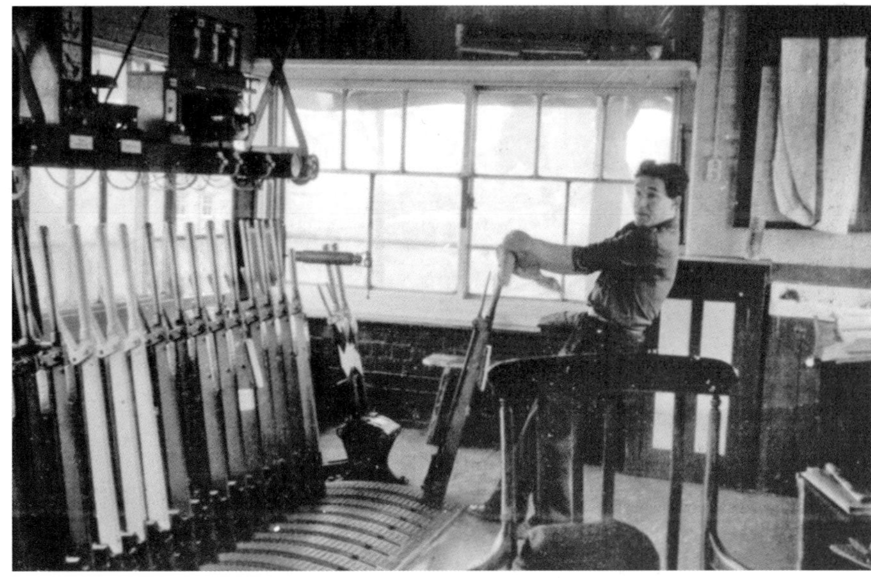

Another view of Signalman Lethbridge working St Austell Signalbox. (SL)

GREAT WESTERN RAILWAY. (4981)

Time Interval Working—Block Regulation 25.

From the Signalman at Cattewater Junc Signal Box. | To the Signalman at Mount Gould Junc Signal Box.

As I am unable to obtain communication from you on :—

the * Block Instruments and Bells / ~~Block Instruments~~ / ~~Bells~~ for the † up & down main Line

and the Speaking Instruments are not available, the Train which left here at 10.0 am worked by Engine No. 4918 is the first to work on the Time Interval System. Trains will be allowed to follow at intervals of not less than Three minutes.

Signature [signature]

Date 23rd March 54.

* Delete words which do not apply. † Insert description of line.

The Driver to whom this form is given must stop at the Signal Box to which it is addressed and hand it to the Signalman there.

IN THE EVENT OF BELL COMMUNICATION ONLY BEING AVAILABLE TIME INTERVAL WORKING MUST BE PUT INTO OPERATION.

20,000—B.M. 1947/59—(11)—S

This form is a remarkable insight into emergency working arrangements in the early years of British Railways and the previous 'Big Four' companies. Time Interval Working was only finished as I started on the railway, more than thirty years after this form was made out. Time Interval Working was a method whereas the trains were allowed to continue running between each signalbox after a failure of the communication instruments, by the issue of a ticket and a set time which had previously been worked out as long enough to be safe. It is also interesting to note that, the form was printed by the G.W.R., yet was still in use by BR almost ten years after the G.W.R. ceased to exist. Also of interest is the reference to 'Speaking Instruments' which is a colloquial term used as a reference to the 'Single-Needle-Telegraph' (Morse type code) and/or telephones. (SL)

GREAT WESTERN RAILWAY. (4810)

Cancellation of Time Interval Working—Block Regulation 25.

From the Signalman at Cattewater Junc Signal Box | To the Signalman at Mount Gould Junc Signal Box

The* Speaking Instruments / ~~Speaking Instruments and Bells~~ / ~~Speaking Instruments and Block Instruments~~ / Block Instruments and Bells for the † up & down line are now in working order and the train which left here at 5-0 pm worked by Engine No. 6901 is the last to work on the Time Interval System.

* Delete words which do not apply. † Insert description of line.

Signature [signature]

Date 23rd March 54

The Driver to whom this form is given must stop at the Signal Box to which it is addressed and hand it to the Signalman there.

The Signalman receiving this notice must give the "Train out of Section" Signal in accordance with the Regulation 10 and ordinary working must then be resumed.

500 Pads, 50 lvs.—L.C.1947(22) S

The cancelling form for the previous issue. (SL)

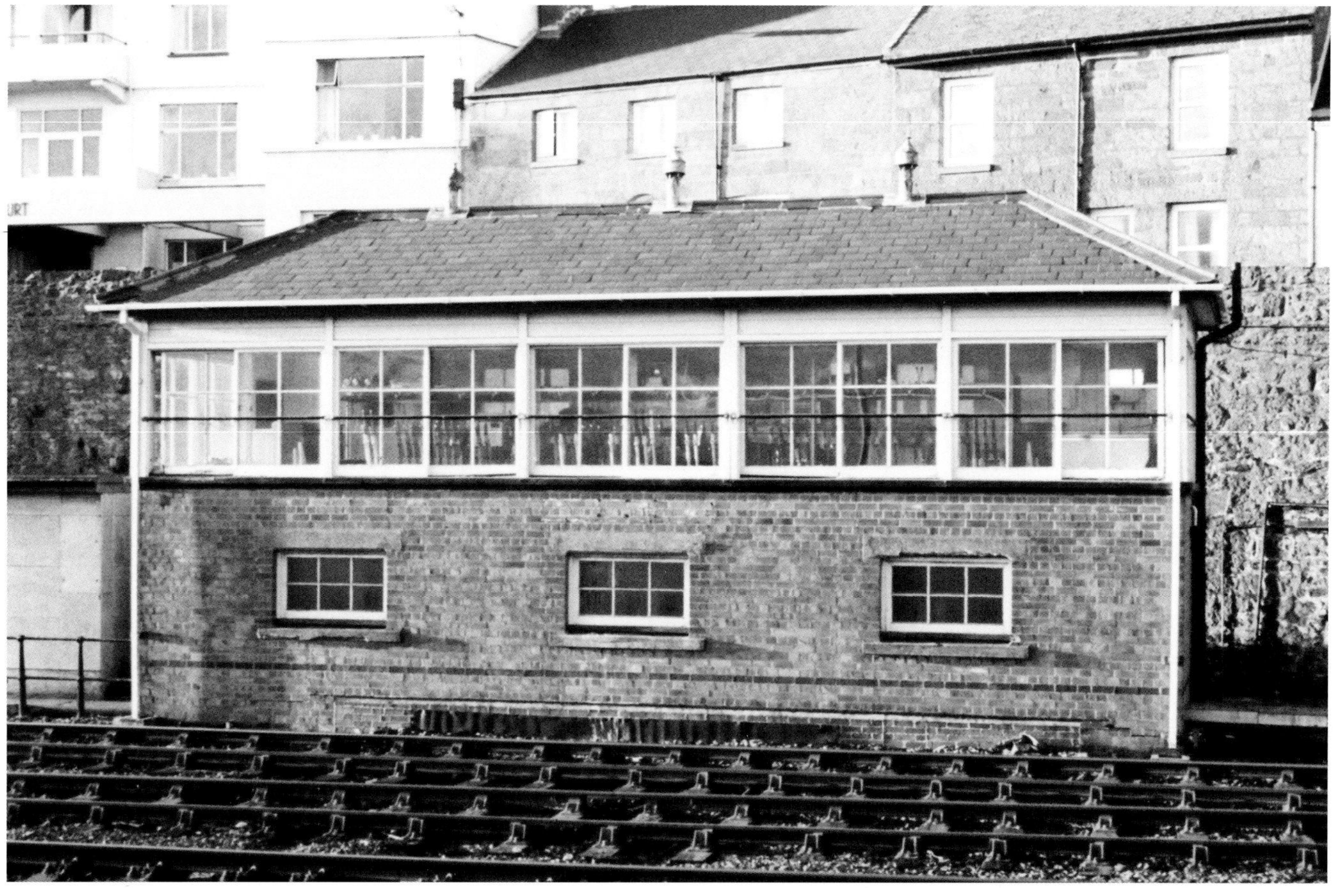

Penzance Signalbox is seen here in January 1990, before relaying of the station throat had occurred. Built in 1938 to replace an earlier structure and when the station was remodelled. A type 12B box, it still retains its levers although all are 'short' type as all signalling is LED colourlight type and points are all motorised with clamp-locks. It interfaces with St Erth using the Absolute Block regulations, but the area between the station and Marazion is Track-Circuit-Block. Always considered as 'dead men's shoes' with regards vacancies arising for working there, it has a spectacular view over St Michael's Mount and the bay. (GP)

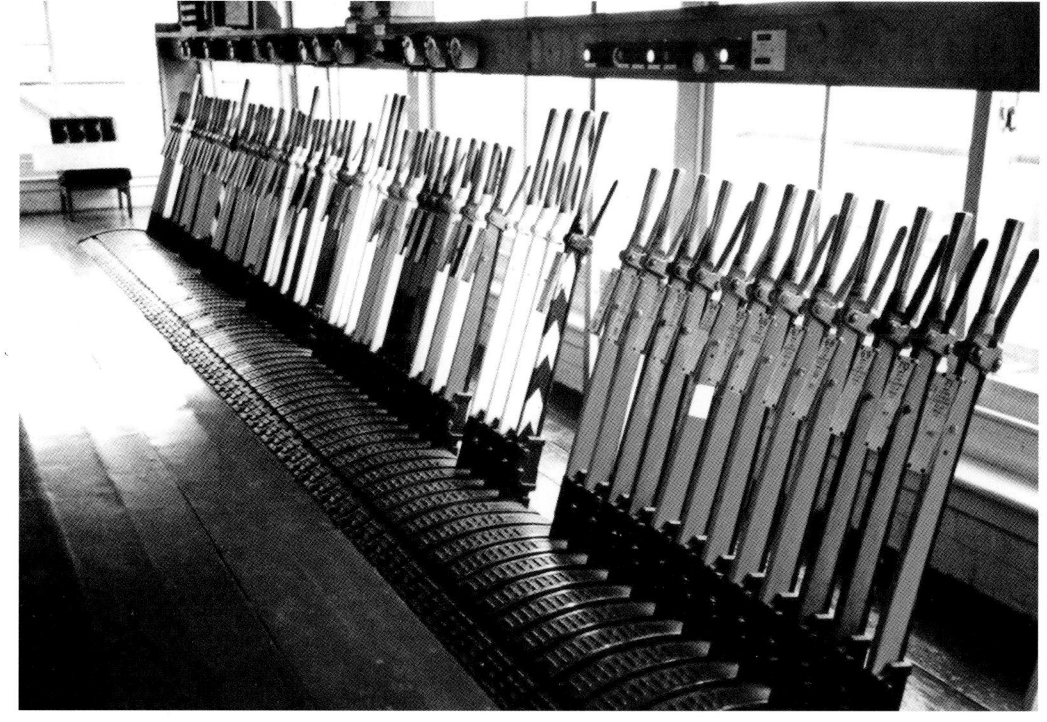

Penzance frame has 75 lever slots but as it is now all power operated the 46 remaining levers that are still used are cut down to short levers as they do not require much effort to operate them. (GP)

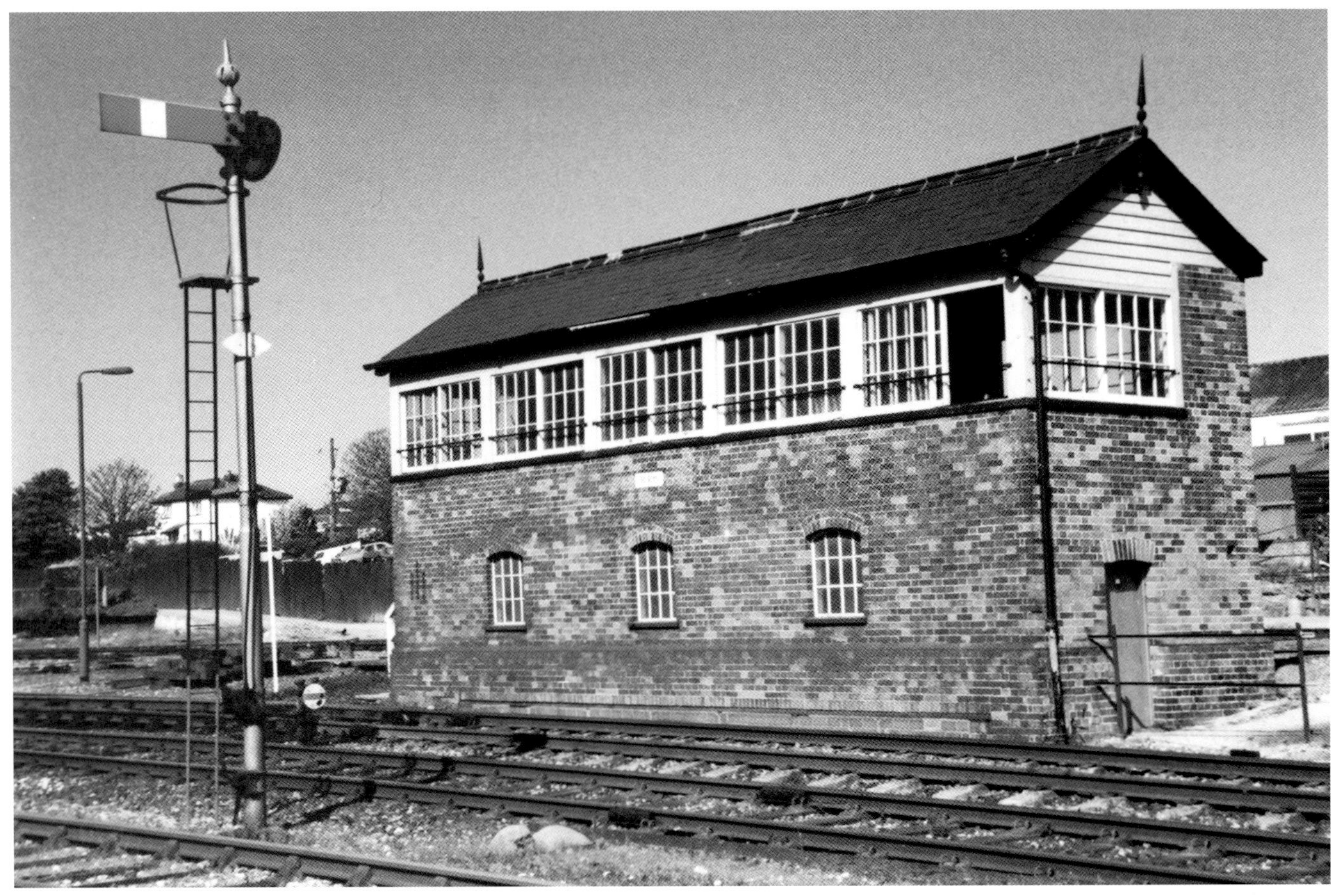

The type 5 box at St Erth is still open in 2013, but like the remaining boxes in Cornwall, its days are numbered. Opened in 1899, it controls the branch line to St Ives and the main line to Penzance at Marazion and in the Up direction to Roskear. This photograph is from May 1993. (GP)

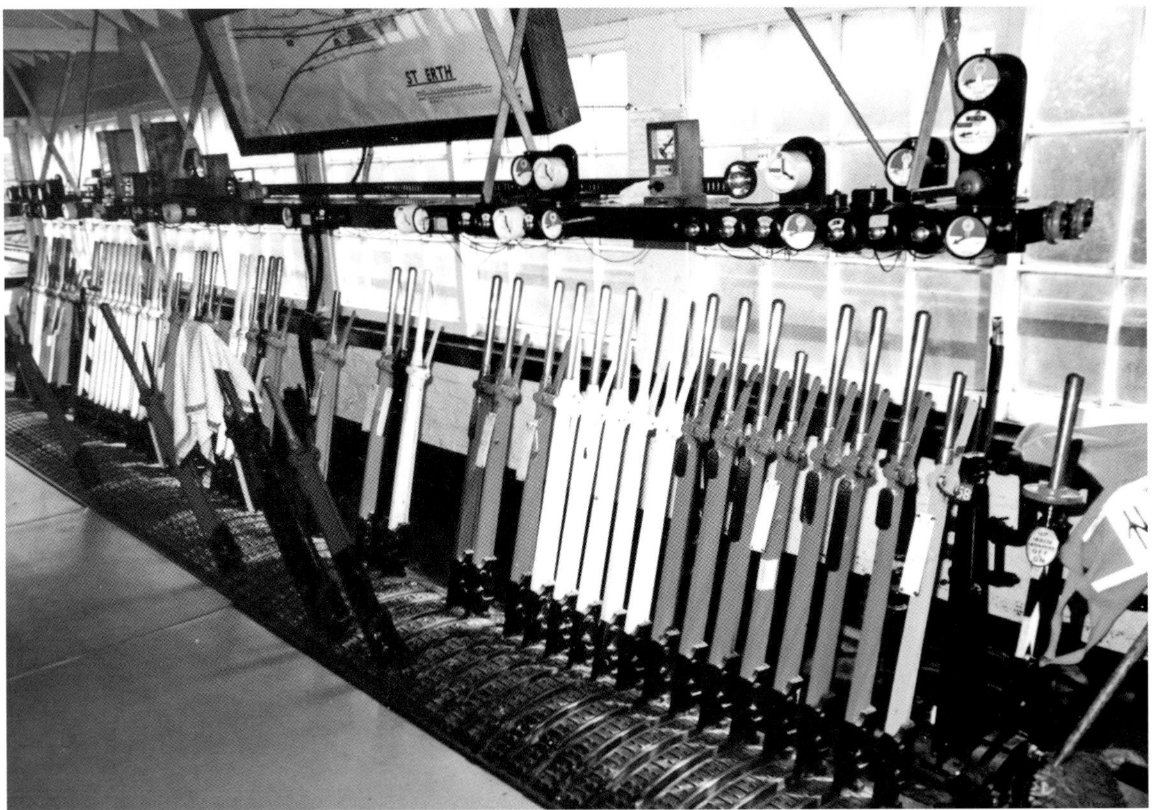

St Erth Frame has 69 levers of which 31 still work. Five of those levers are shortened, because they operate electrically as well as mechanically. (GP)

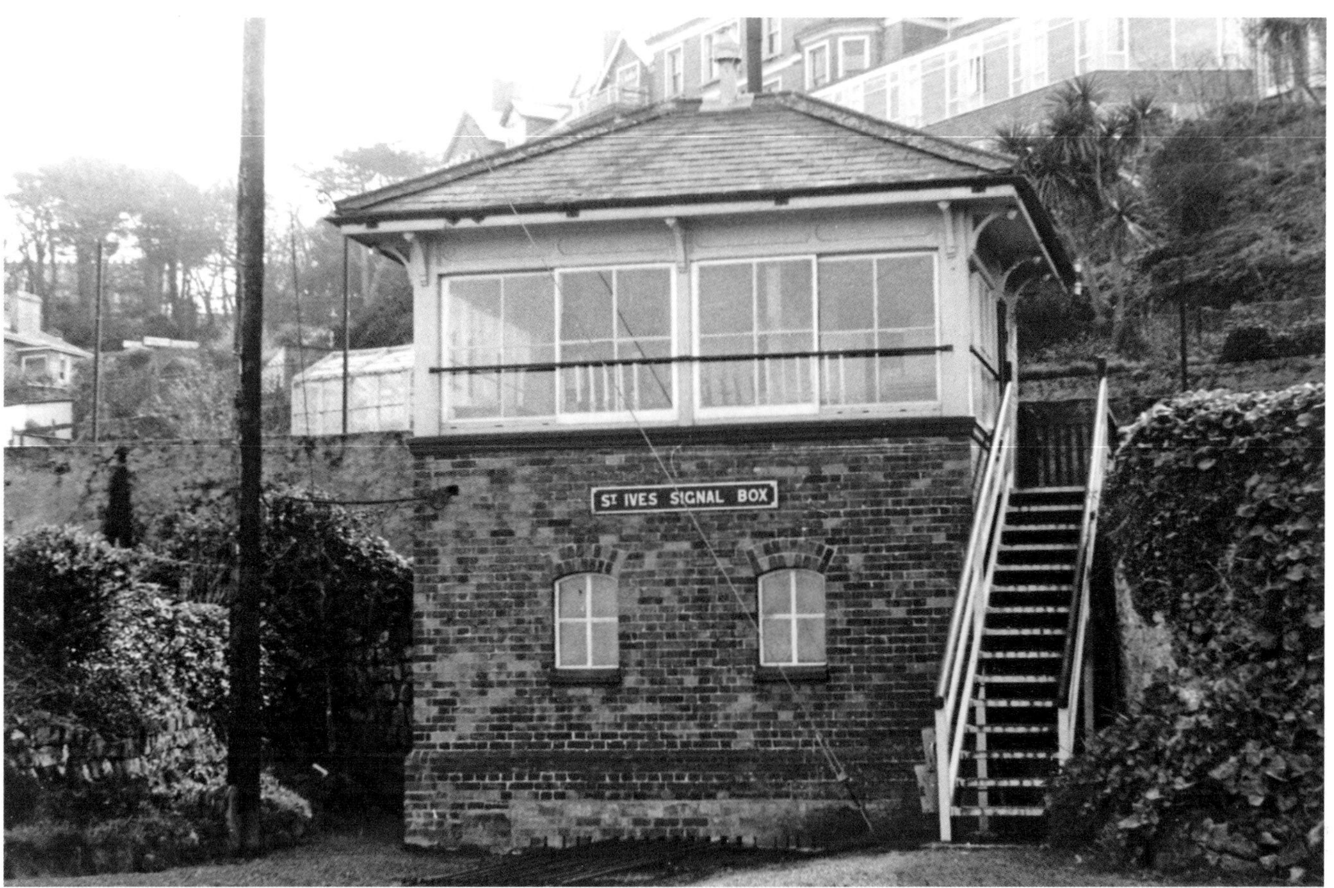

St Ives box opened pre 1884 and was a Saxby & Farmer design. Reduced to a ground-frame on 8.9.63, it survived until 10.3.65, after which the station layout was rationalised. (GP)

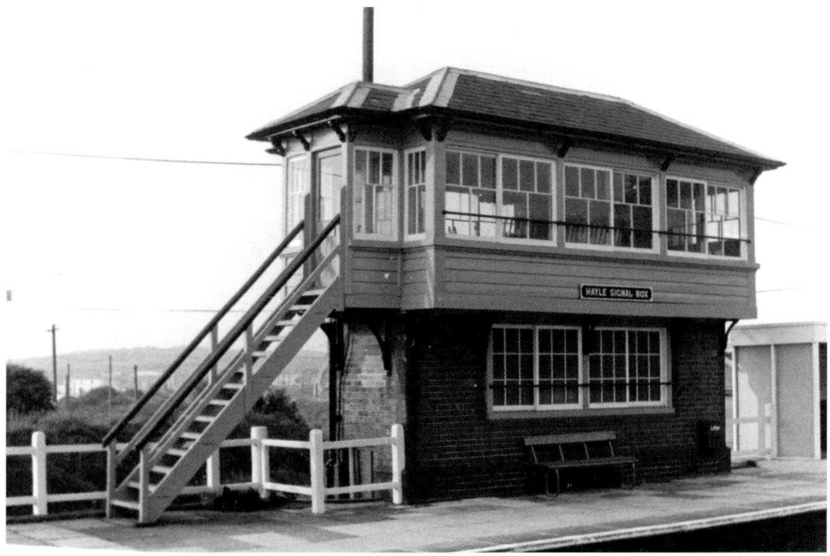

Hayle Signalbox was another type 27C, but on a narrow base due to a lack of room. Opened in October 1912, to replace two older boxes, it survived to 7 July 1982 when the branch to Hayle Wharves was taken out of use. (GP)

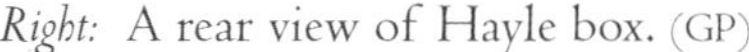

Right: A rear view of Hayle box. (GP)

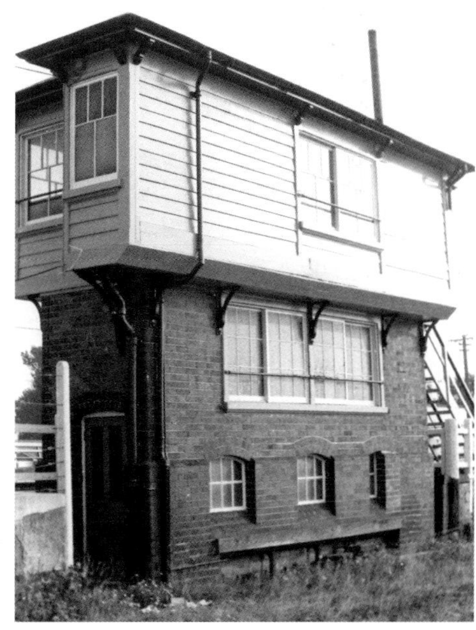

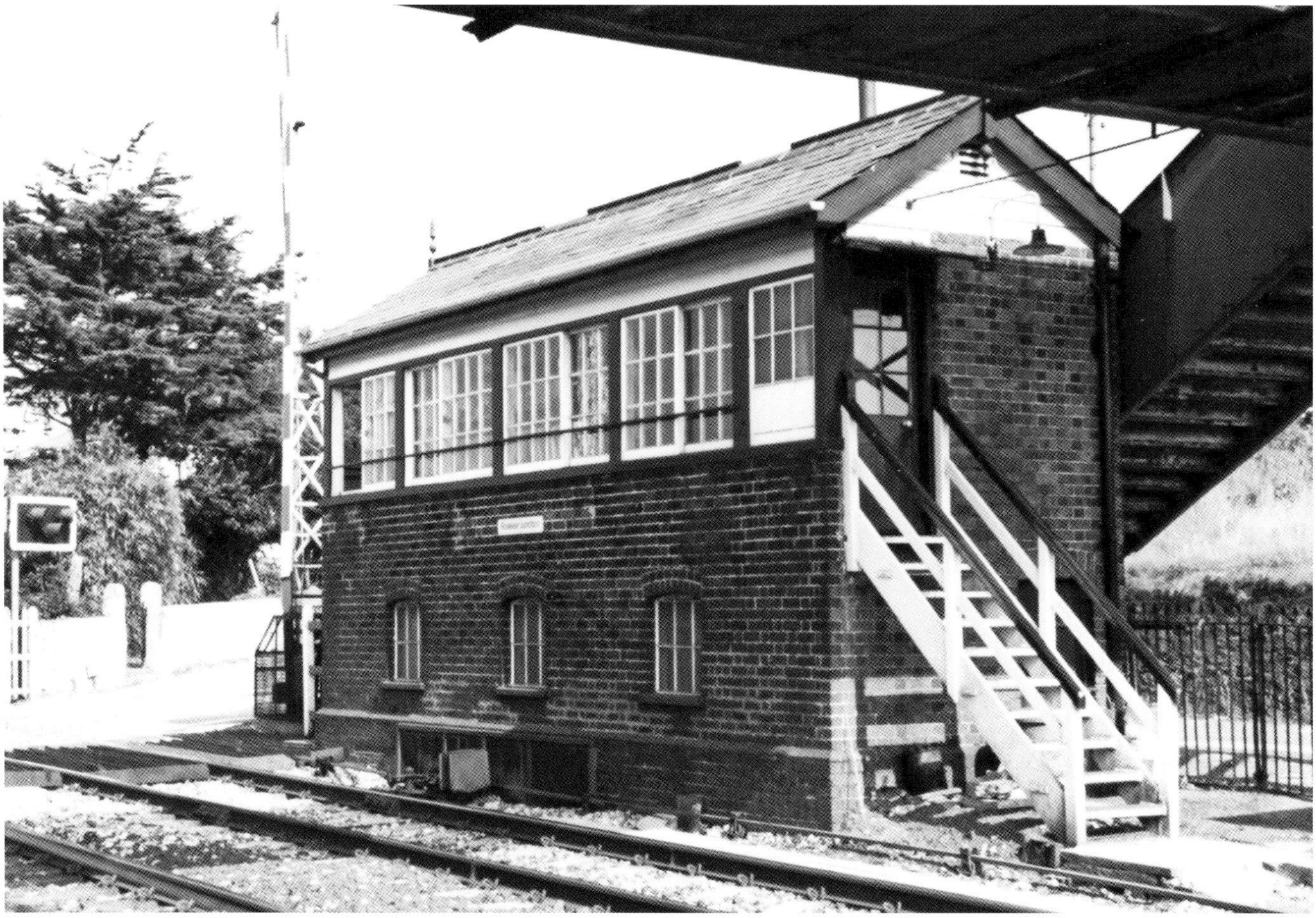

Roskear Junction Signalbox is a type 5 and dates from 1895. It is squeezed into a rather narrow gap, being only 9'6" (2700mm) wide and very narrow on the inside. It ceased to be a junction in July 1985 when the North Roskear Branch was closed. This picture dates from August 1983 when the frame was still in situ and although the box is still in use in 2013, it only has switches for the signals, barrier controls for Camborne and Roskear with CCTV. The cross-over is out of use and has now been removed in 2013 but I have taken trains across this several times in the 1990s, during emergency single-line-working. (GP)

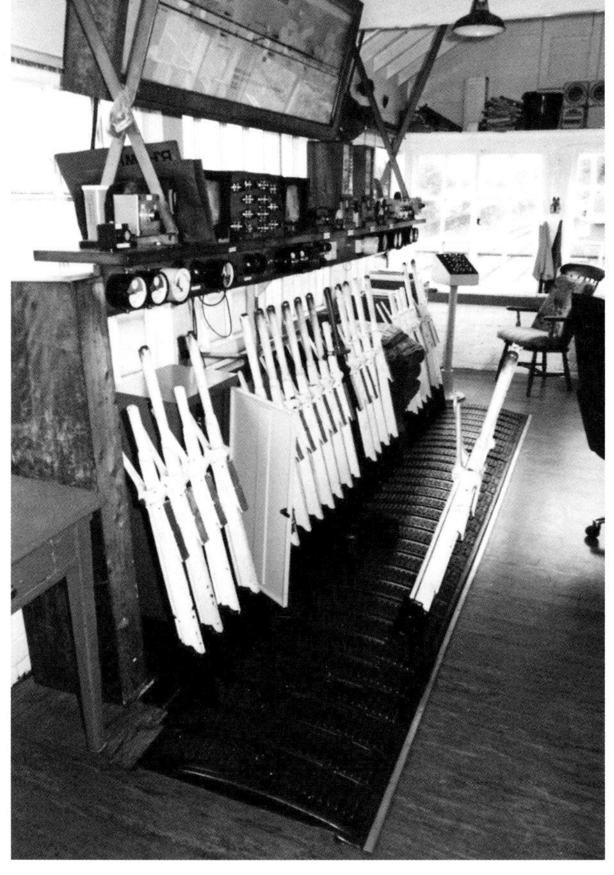

Roskear (with frame still in situ and 15 points still connected in August 1992). Roskear now has no levers and the frame was removed during the early 1990s, and replaced with three switches controlling the colour-light signalling. Number 15 Ground-Frame lever was placed outside and was released by the S&T if the emergency cross-over was required, which has not been for many years now, due to the complex operational constraints required to be carried out at the three level crossings and the handsignalmen required for the protecting signals. (GP)

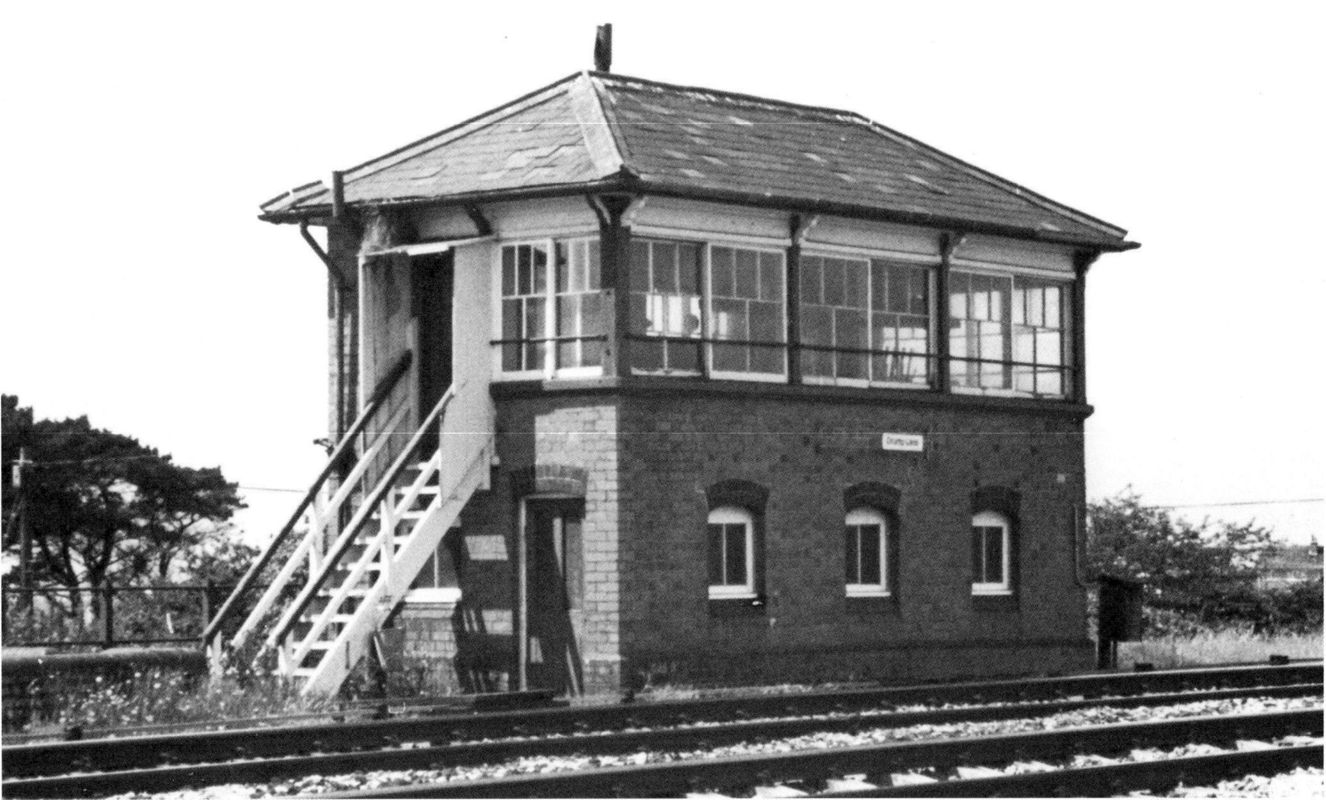

Drump Lane box opened in December 1911 and was a type 7D design. The layout was progressively rationalised from 1955 to 1973 after which it remained in use until 12 January 1986. (July 1989). (GP)

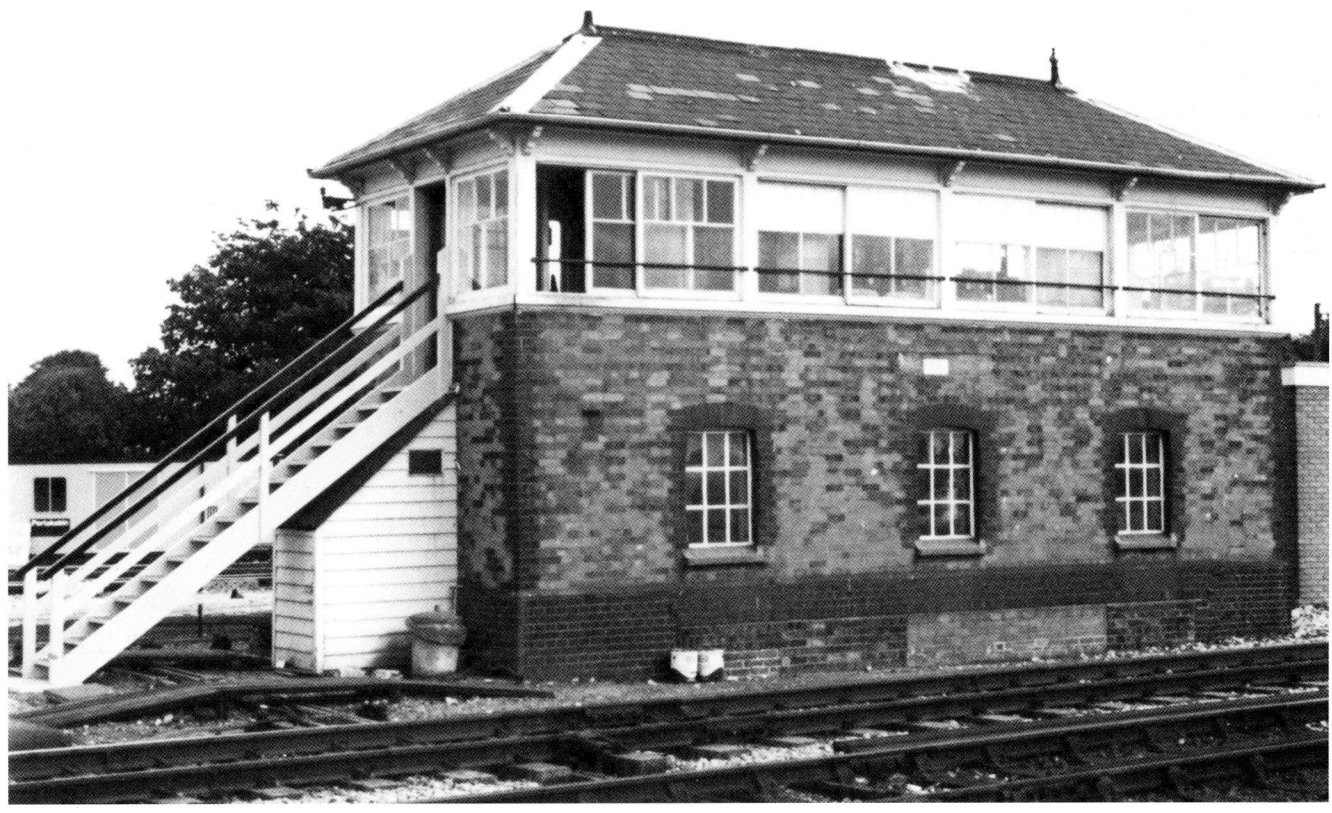

Truro was formerly Truro East until November 1971, when Truro West closed and the track layout was rationalised. Opened in 1899 to replace an earlier box, it is of a type 7A. Now Cornwall's busiest box, it had the new Penryn Loop added in 2009 and because of a shortage of spare levers, redundant levers were taken from other boxes to provide the eight additional levers needed to operate the upgraded Falmouth Branch and alteration to the signalling at Truro to allow passenger trains to depart from the Up platform in the down direction. Truro box layout was changed in 1971 and the domestic layout has been extensively upgraded in 2012. This picture dates from August 1983. (GP)

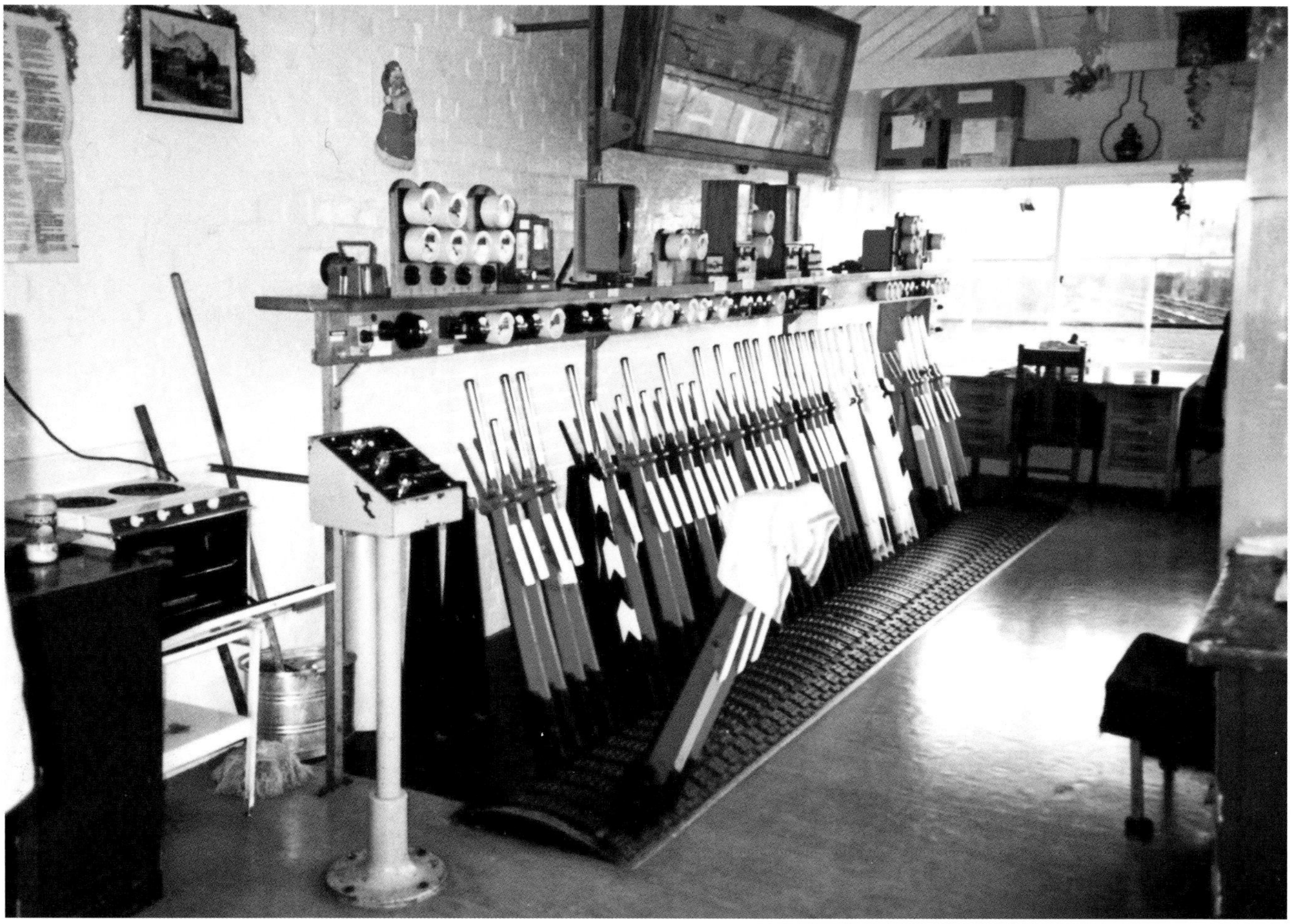

Truro Signalbox frame is the one fitted new in 1971, as shown elsewhere, but has had some levers replaced in the gaps, from an old signalbox in the Cotswolds, that had closed. These eight extra levers formed the core of the new signals and points at Penryn, but unfortunately they are scattered throughout the frame. This photograph is taken pre 2009 before the Penryn Scheme was commissioned showing the levers that work in the original 51 lever frame. (GP)

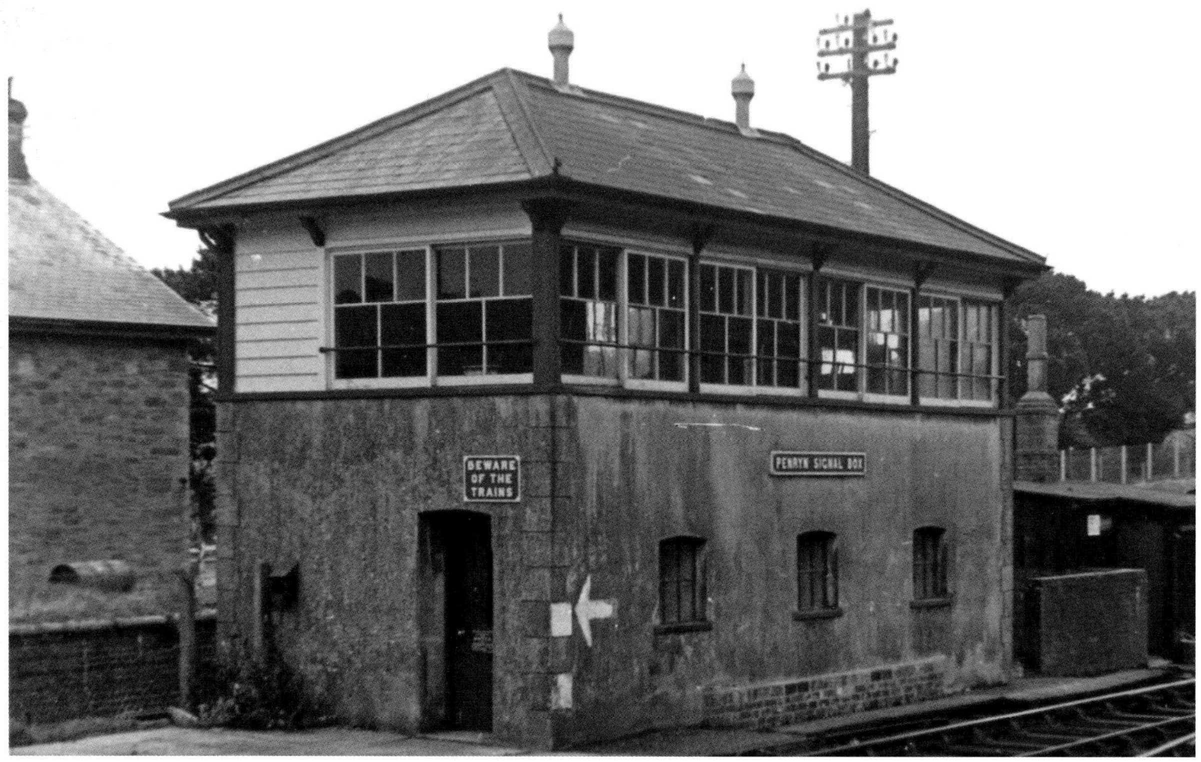

Penryn Signalbox was a type 27C and opened on 24.6.1923. The box closed on 7.11.71. (GP)

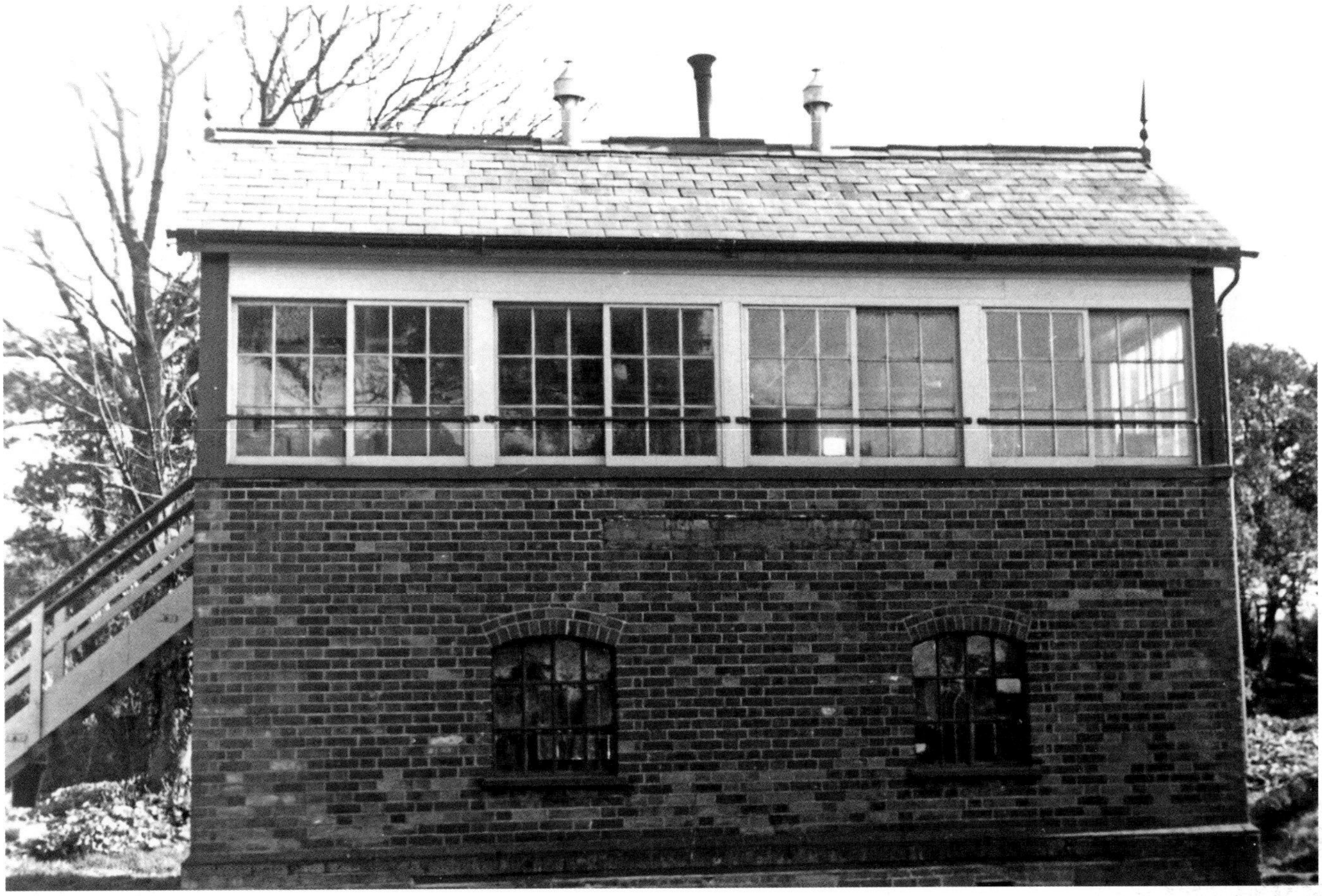

Falmouth GWR type 5 box was built in 1894. The box closed on 27.2.66. (GP)

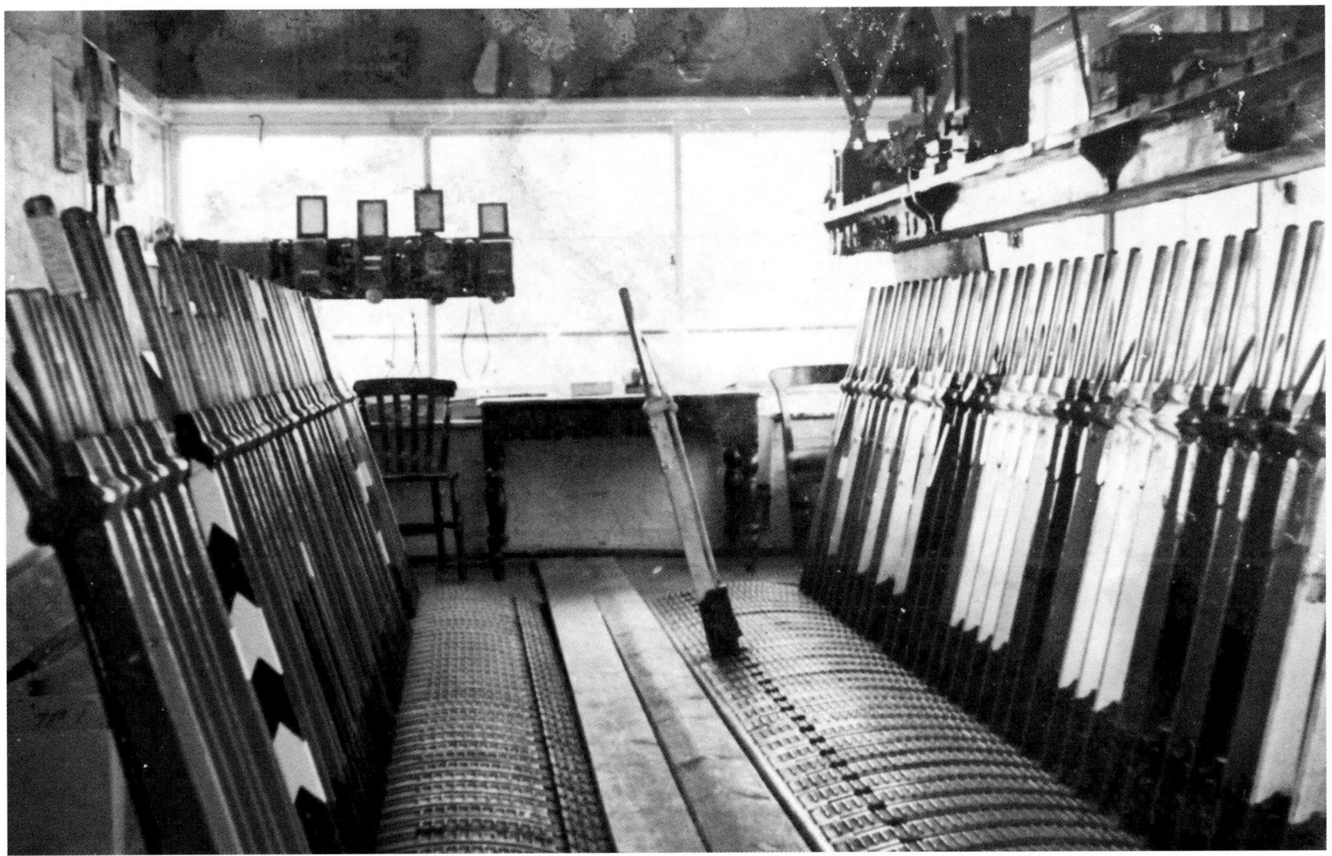

Truro (East) signalbox in 1971, when the frame was replaced with a new one at the rear of the box. During the interim period both frames were in situ, but the signalling was being carried out in a temporary shed outside. (RKM)

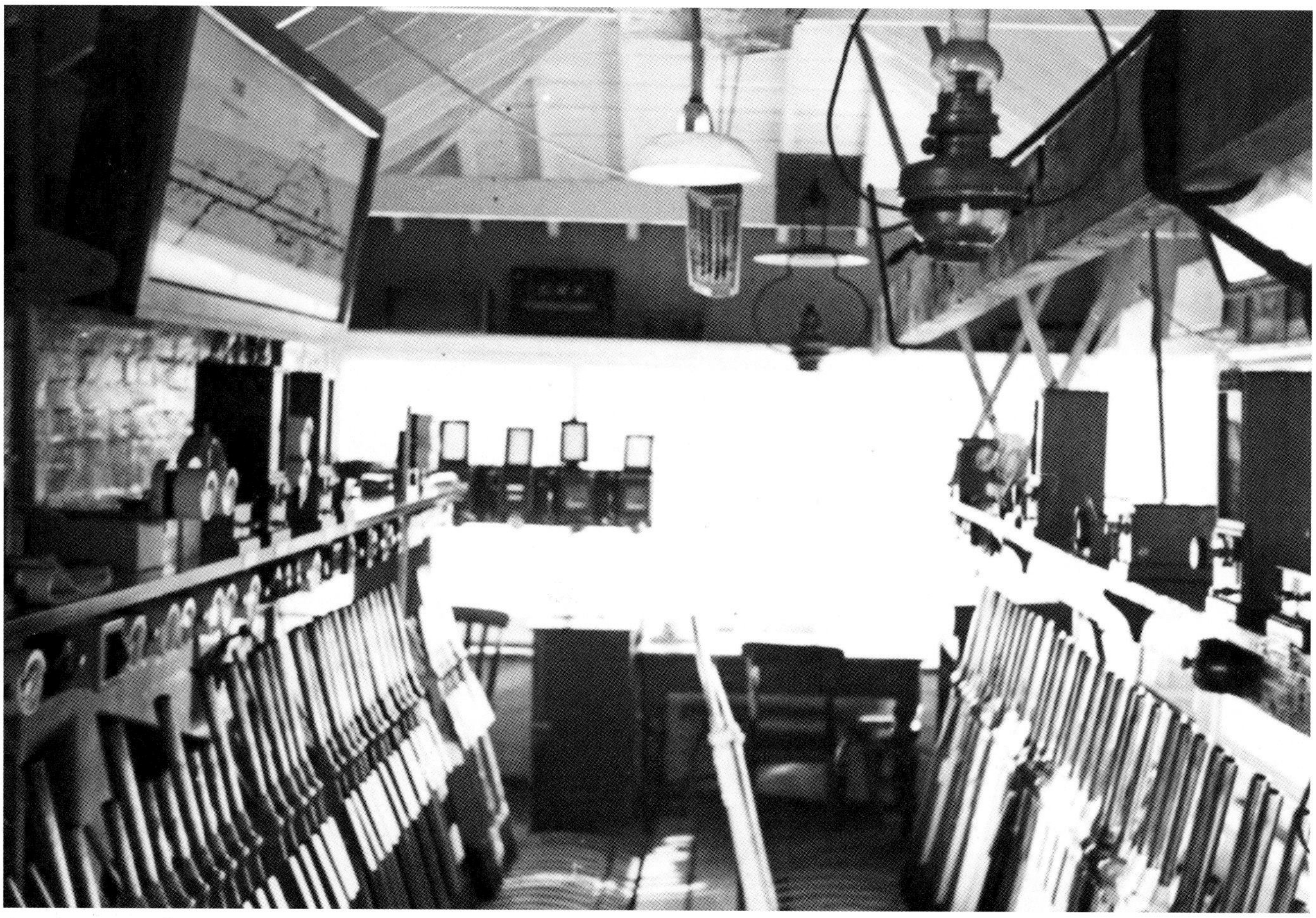

Another view of Truro (East) in 1971. (RKM)

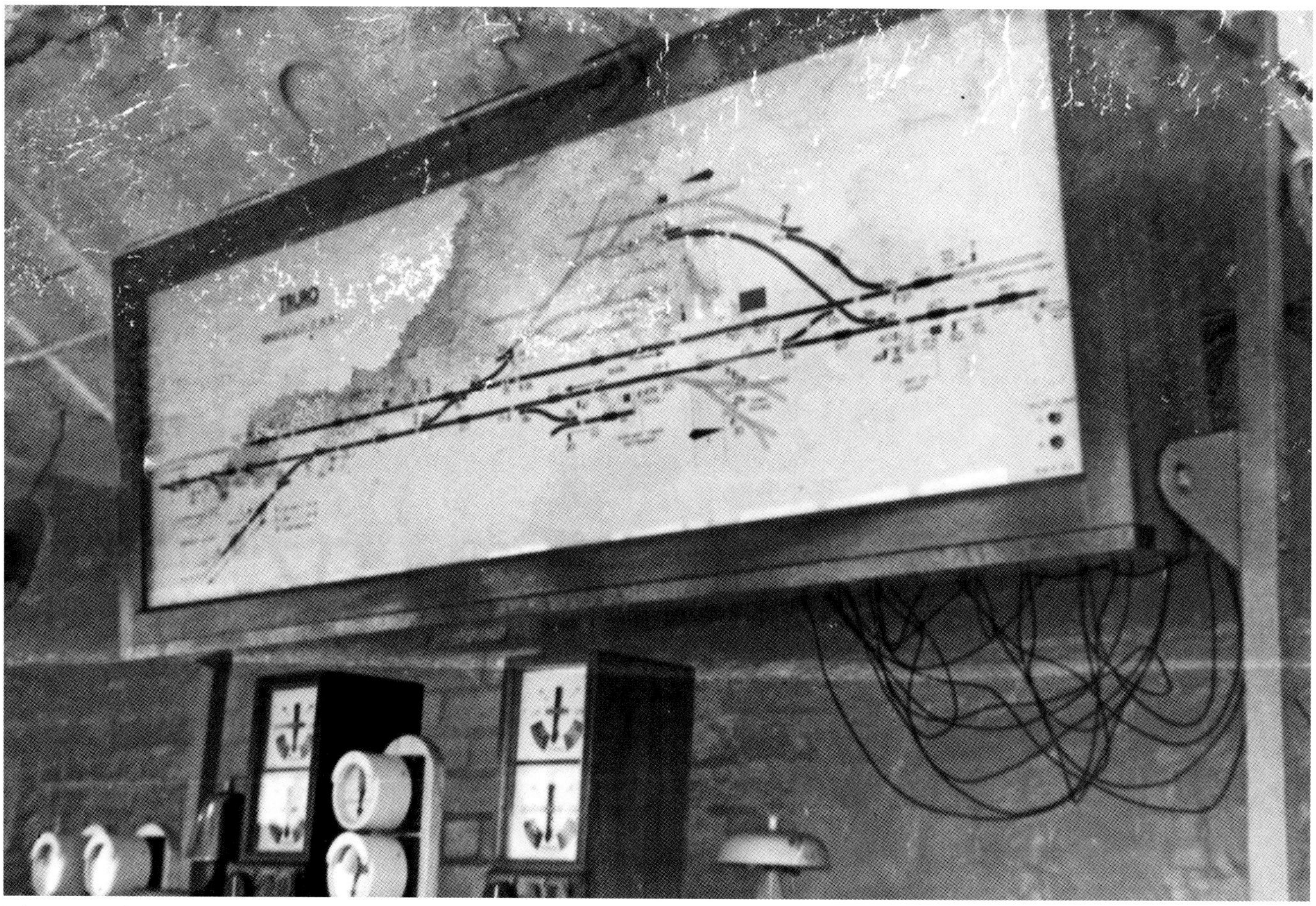

The Truro (East) diagram in 1971. (RKM)

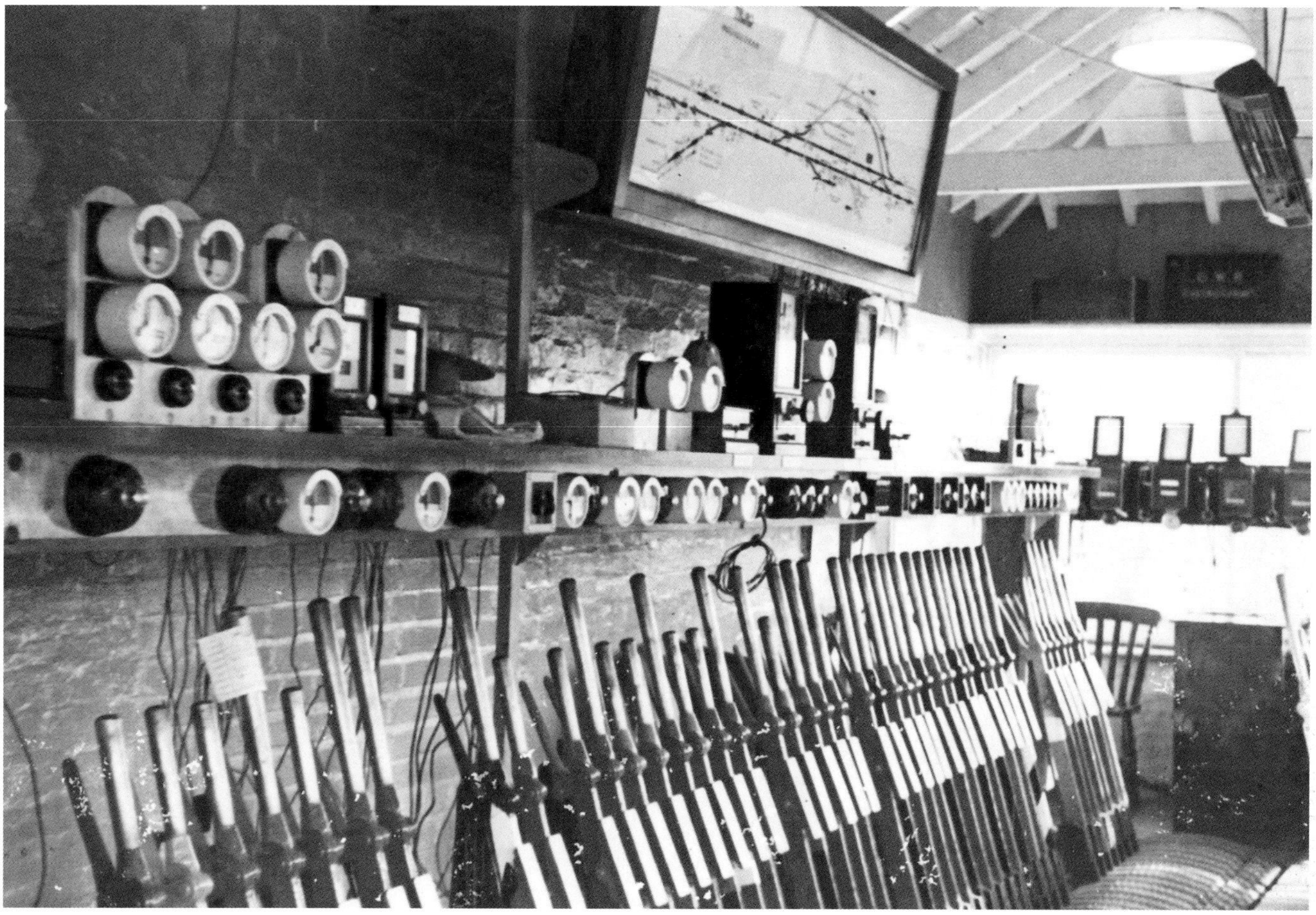

The Truro (East) Block Shelf in 1971. (RKM)

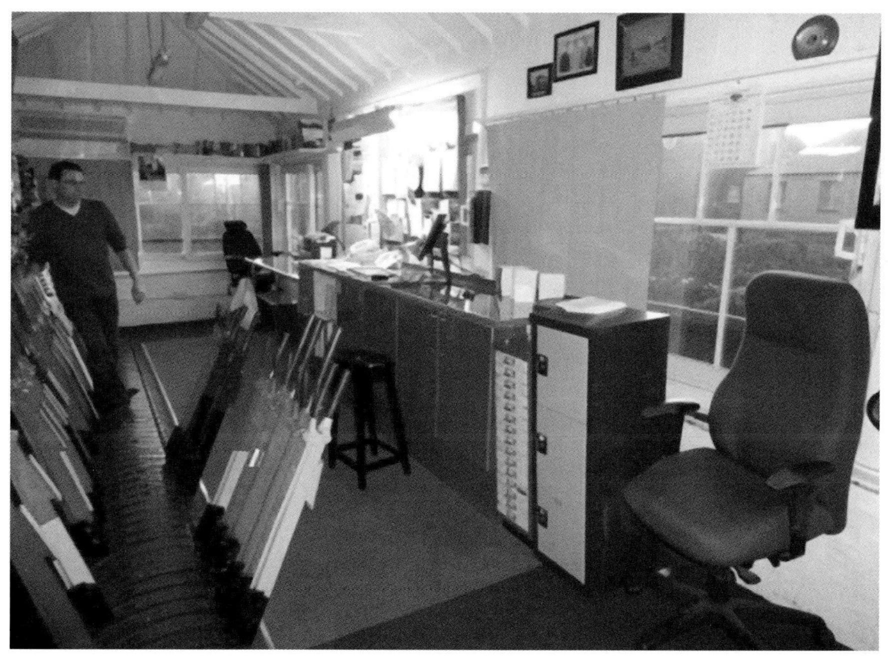

The refurbished Truro (Formerly East) Signalbox in 2012, having had extra levers and equipment added for the Penryn Loop enhancement two years earlier. The Signaller is Relief Craig Munday. (SFH)

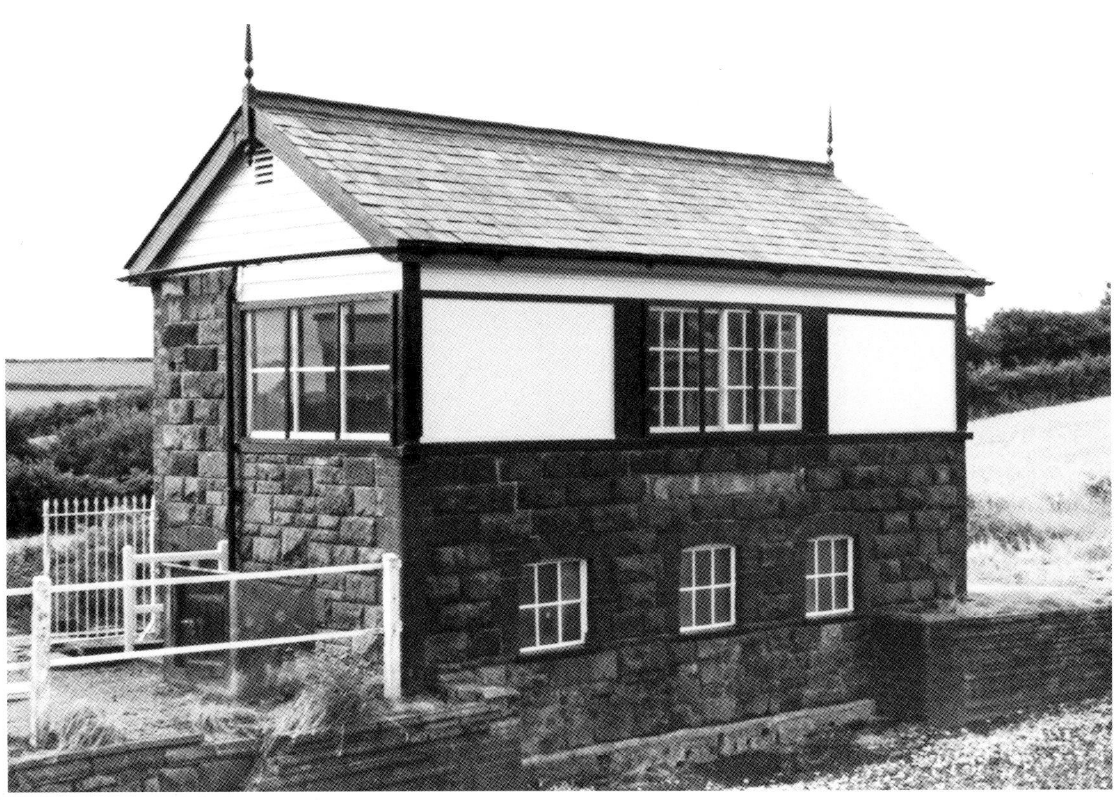

Burngullow box was a type 5 box opened c1895 to replace the original box. It controlled the main line and the branch to Drinnick Mill via Electric Key Token. Closed on 4 October 1986 when Par Panel was commissioned and the line towards Probus was singled. Like Newquay, it too was destroyed by vandals in a fire which I was also called out to. Empty, but ostensibly in good condition, it had just been donated to the Bodmin & Wenford Railway, and was awaiting dismantling when the vandals struck in 1996. Picture is July 1988. (GP)

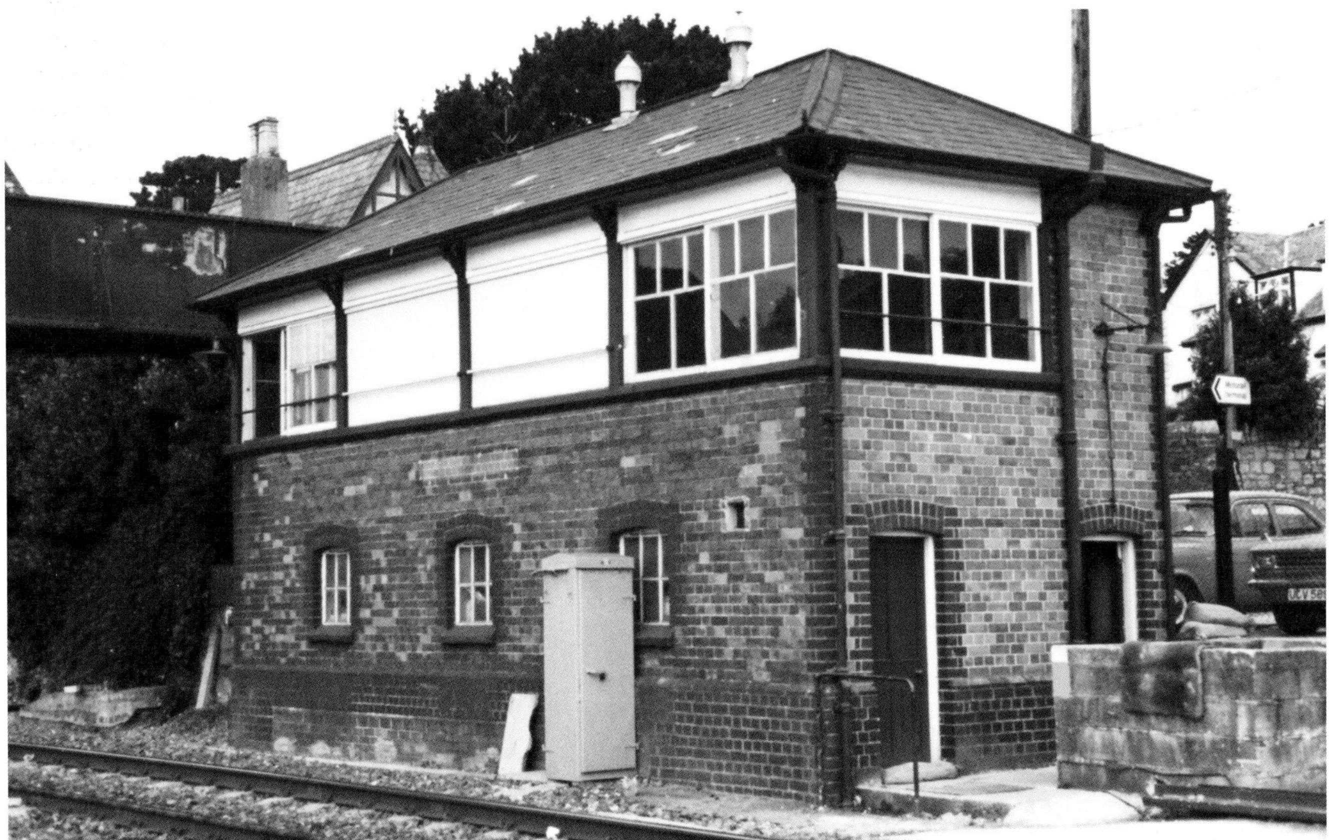

St Austell box is shown here in August 1983, three years after it had closed. Built c1905 as a type 7C box, it survives today, semi-derelict and the subject of many attempts to preserve it. In a poor state generally, and the only remaining decommissioned box left in Cornwall, its future remains uncertain. (GP)

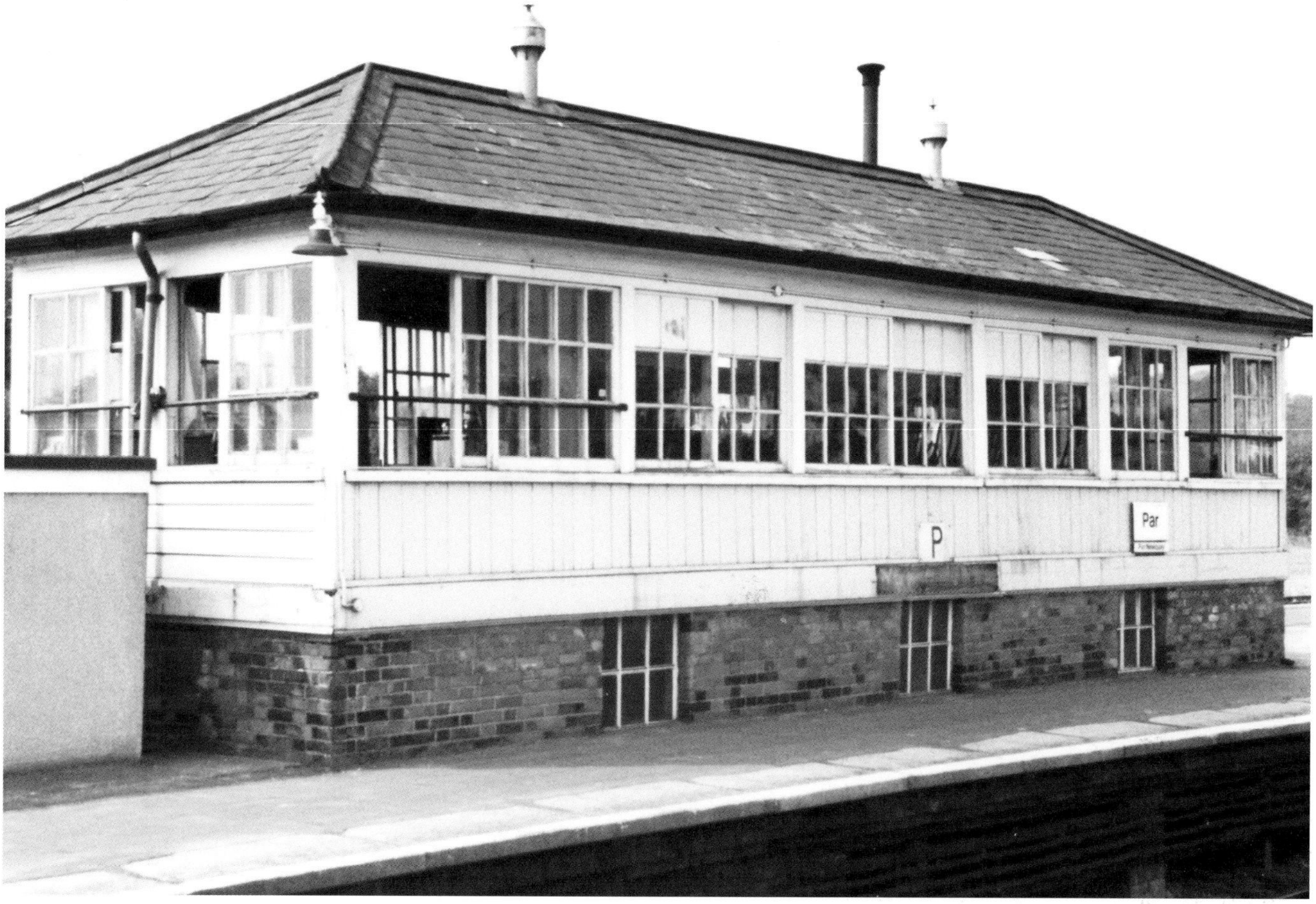

Par Signalbox is the oldest in the West Country that is still in use and is unclassified. It has been extended at least once in 1893, though may have other modifications that are undated, as evidenced inside. The box is probably dated to c1879 but the layout is actually very little altered to its pre-WW2 condition, although some minor rationalisation has occurred. Its 56 lever frame still has 50 working levers and of course the Panel which was added in October 1986, to control the track towards Truro. The single line section which was commissioned in the same year has since been reinstated to double track in 2004. It has TCB/AB mixed regulations to Truro, Absolute Block (AB) regulations to Lostwithiel, with an Intermediate-Block-Section at Treverrin, and AB regulations to St Blazey, which is the only location on the 'Western' where there has never been a signalbox between the two boxes. Picture was taken in Sept 1991. (GP)

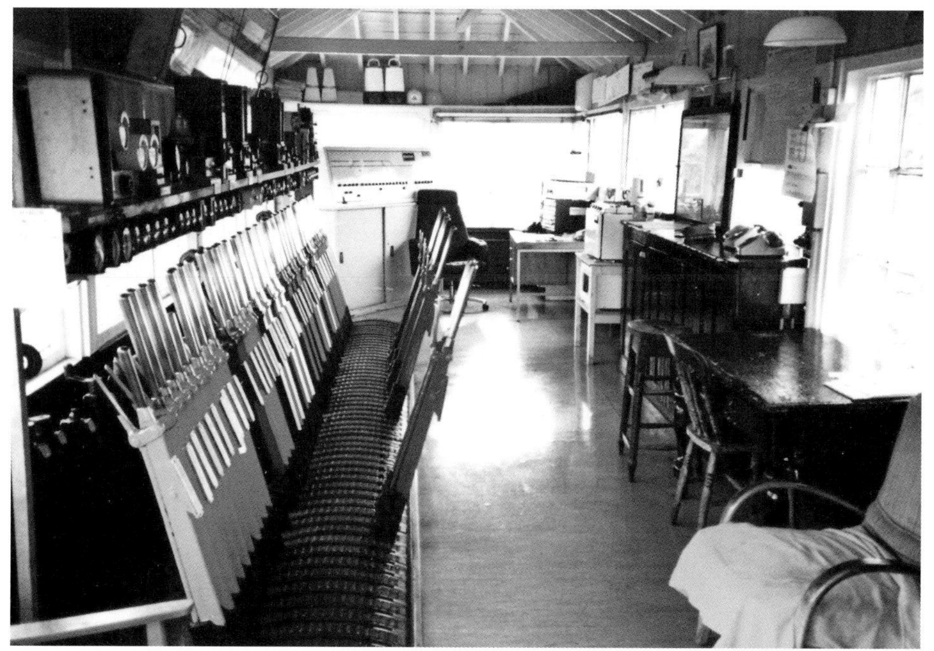

Par frame (circa 2000 in the picture) shows the 56 lever frame with only six levers not used. Par frame is the most complete (not the largest) ex-G.W.R. frame still in existence on the national network. It has a mixture of mechanical and electro-mechanical levers. The west end has a panel controlling the lines between Par and Truro, including the junction at Burngullow. The panel was modified in 2004 after the single-line section between Burngullow and Probus was reinstated to a double track section. The modified panel can be set to run automatically on the main lines, but must be reset to manual to enter Burngullow. (GP)

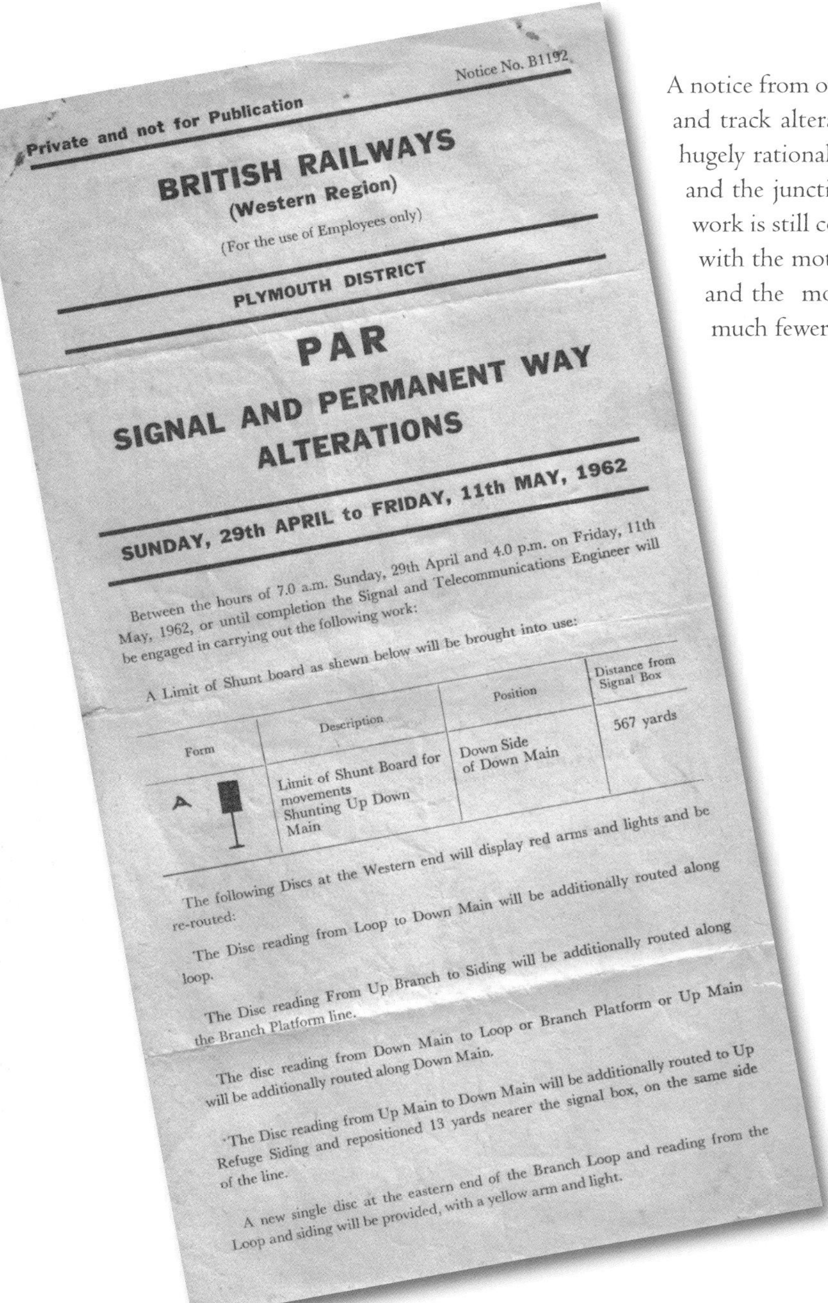

Notice No. B1192.

Private and not for Publication

BRITISH RAILWAYS
(Western Region)
(For the use of Employees only)

PLYMOUTH DISTRICT

PAR

SIGNAL AND PERMANENT WAY ALTERATIONS

SUNDAY, 29th APRIL to FRIDAY, 11th MAY, 1962

Between the hours of 7.0 a.m. Sunday, 29th April and 4.0 p.m. on Friday, 11th May, 1962, or until completion the Signal and Telecommunications Engineer will be engaged in carrying out the following work:

A Limit of Shunt board as shewn below will be brought into use:

Form	Description	Position	Distance from Signal Box
A	Limit of Shunt Board for movements Shunting Up Down Main	Down Side of Down Main	567 yards

The following Discs at the Western end will display red arms and lights and be re-routed:

The Disc reading from Loop to Down Main will be additionally routed along loop.

The Disc reading From Up Branch to Siding will be additionally routed along the Branch Platform line.

The disc reading from Down Main to Loop or Branch Platform or Up Main will be additionally routed along Down Main.

The Disc reading from Up Main to Down Main will be additionally routed to Up Refuge Siding and repositioned 13 yards nearer the signal box, on the same side of the line.

A new single disc at the eastern end of the Branch Loop and reading from the Loop and siding will be provided, with a yellow arm and light.

A notice from over fifty years ago describes signalling and track alterations at Par, which in 2012, is not hugely rationalised from then. Still a busy location and the junction for the Newquay line, the track-work is still considered a flexible layout. Of course with the mothballing of much of St Blazey Yard, and the movements to and from the depot are much fewer than they used to be.(SL)

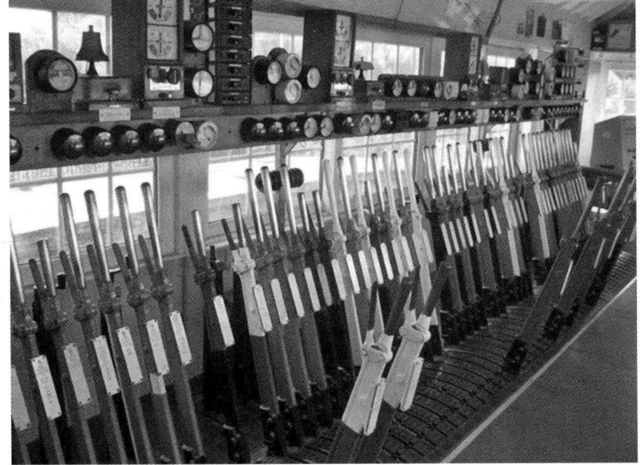

A modern day view of Par Signalbox block-shelf and lever-frame. The extensive and comprehensive equipment in Par makes it one of the most complex, traditional signalboxes still in use, although I can say, as a previous Signalman here, it was usually, though not always, a pleasure to work there, even though it was a busy place. It was the mini-panel on the west end that gave the most trouble, though not nearly as much now, as it used to do, before the single line was redoubled in 2004.

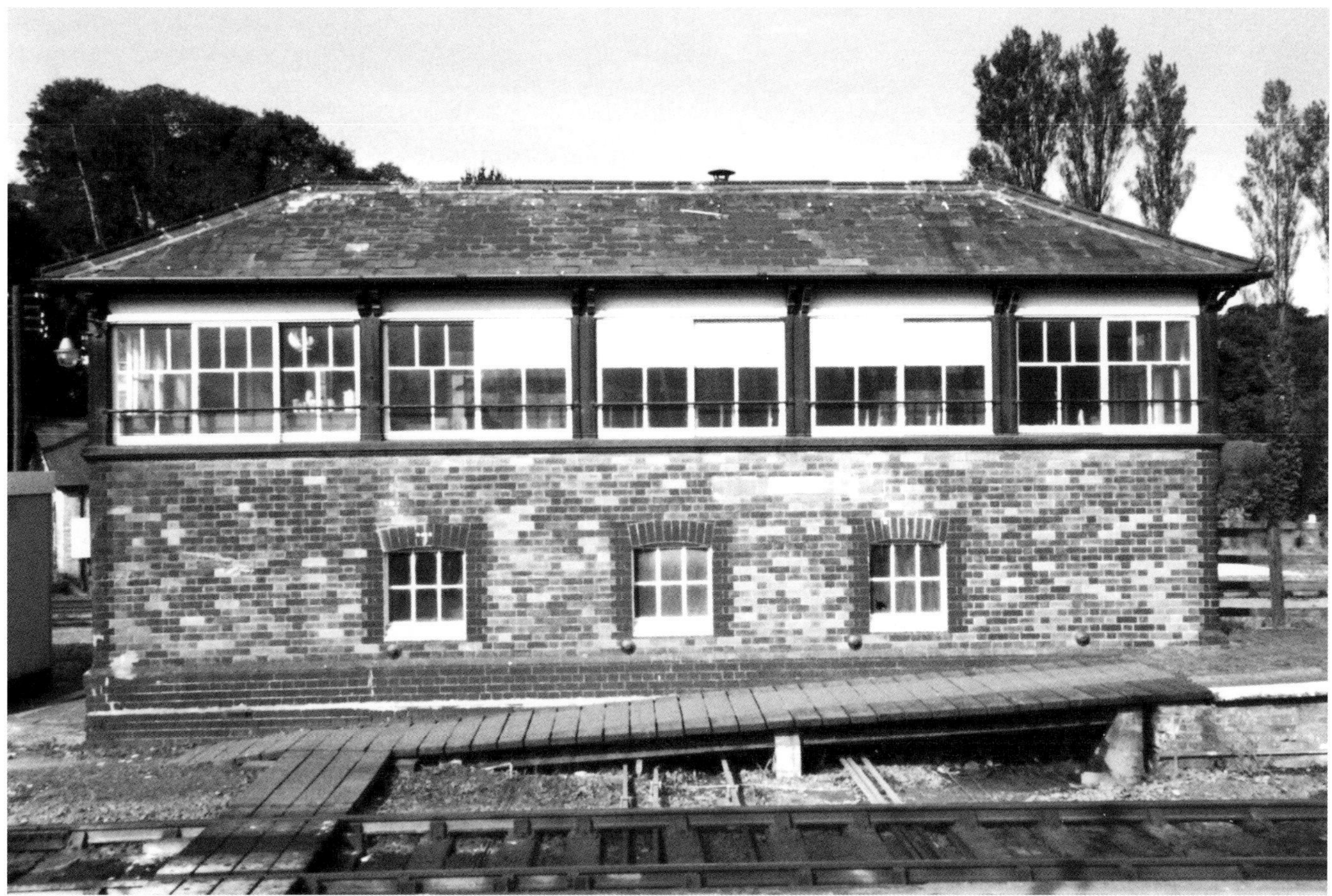

St Blazey Signalbox is a type 7D dating from 1908. Cosmetically restored and repainted in 2008 to celebrate its centenary, it has suffered from subsidence since it opened. It once controlled the busy adjacent yard and the signalling is AB to Par and ETB to Goonbarrow Junction. The drastically rationalised layout and almost redundant depot mean that this is now a quiet location, though it does still have a token catcher on the Up side, for freight trains to return the token (carried in a hoop) so as to avoid stopping with 1800+ ton trains. The Up refuge siding (Ballast Siding) is clipped out of use due to poor condition. Once used by the Royal Train, it was a hairy moment when we started to back the train into it and heard the creaks and bangs as the little-used track complained at having the heavy, armoured coaches roll over it. Last used by any train almost ten years ago, it will not form part of the new signalling at Didcot. St Blazey yard is home to stored class 60s and stored wagons and redundant clay wagons (CDAs) awaiting breaking up, but supplying a valuable source of spares for the remaining CDA fleet. Our office, which is behind the box was once the ticket office for the long closed St Blazey Station. This picture is from May 1993. (GP)

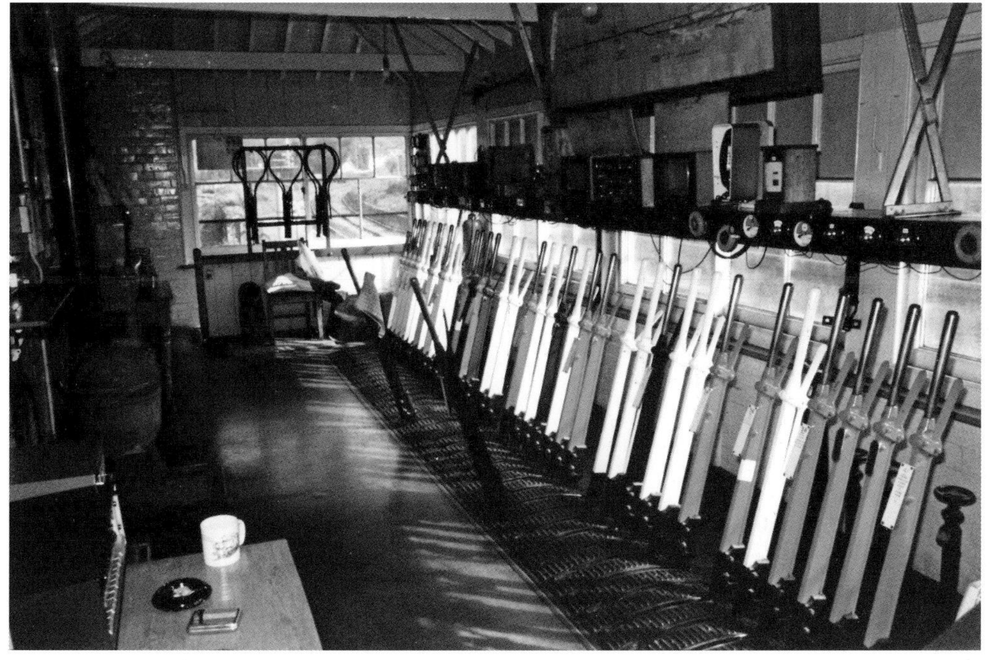

St Blazey Signalbox frame has 41 levers of which only one is shortened and the remaining 22 are the only ones still in use. Lever 1 is a combined colourlight Distant and home signal painted half yellow and half red to reflect this dual role. (GP)

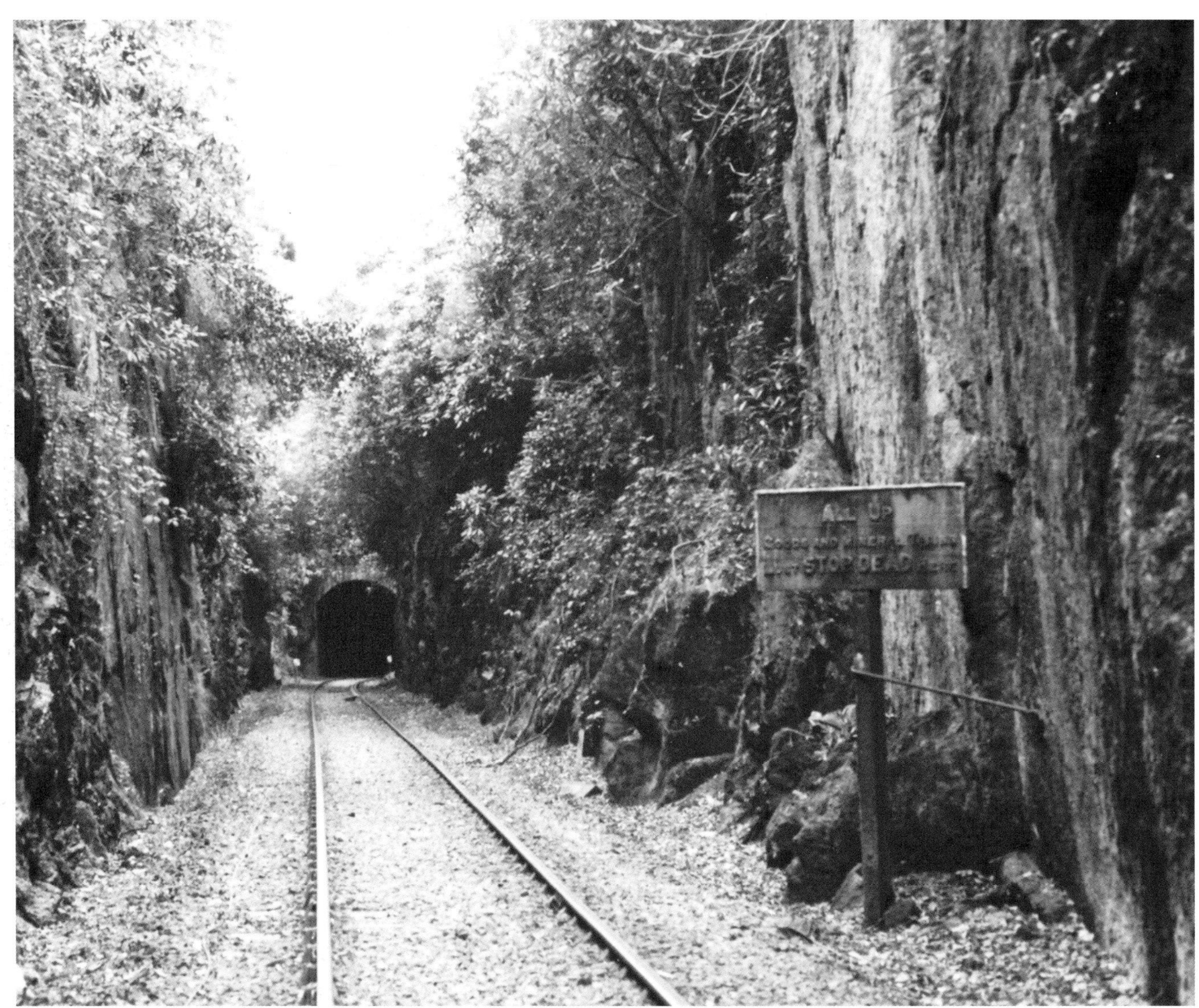

An interesting and rarely seen view of Luxulyan Tunnel looking in the Up direction, so therefore facing south. The sign on the right was in situ until a few years ago, when, after some engineering work in the area, it disappeared. The gradient drops away sharply as you exit the short tunnel, and it was on the sharp left-hand bend here about twenty years ago that an HST travelling towards Newquay, (Down) came to grief on poor track dynamics and sparked a major incident. A few more feet to the left and it would have been a worldwide headline as the train would have toppled down the embankment into the valley below. The excellent buck-eye coupling did a superb job in keeping the train intact and upright. (GP)

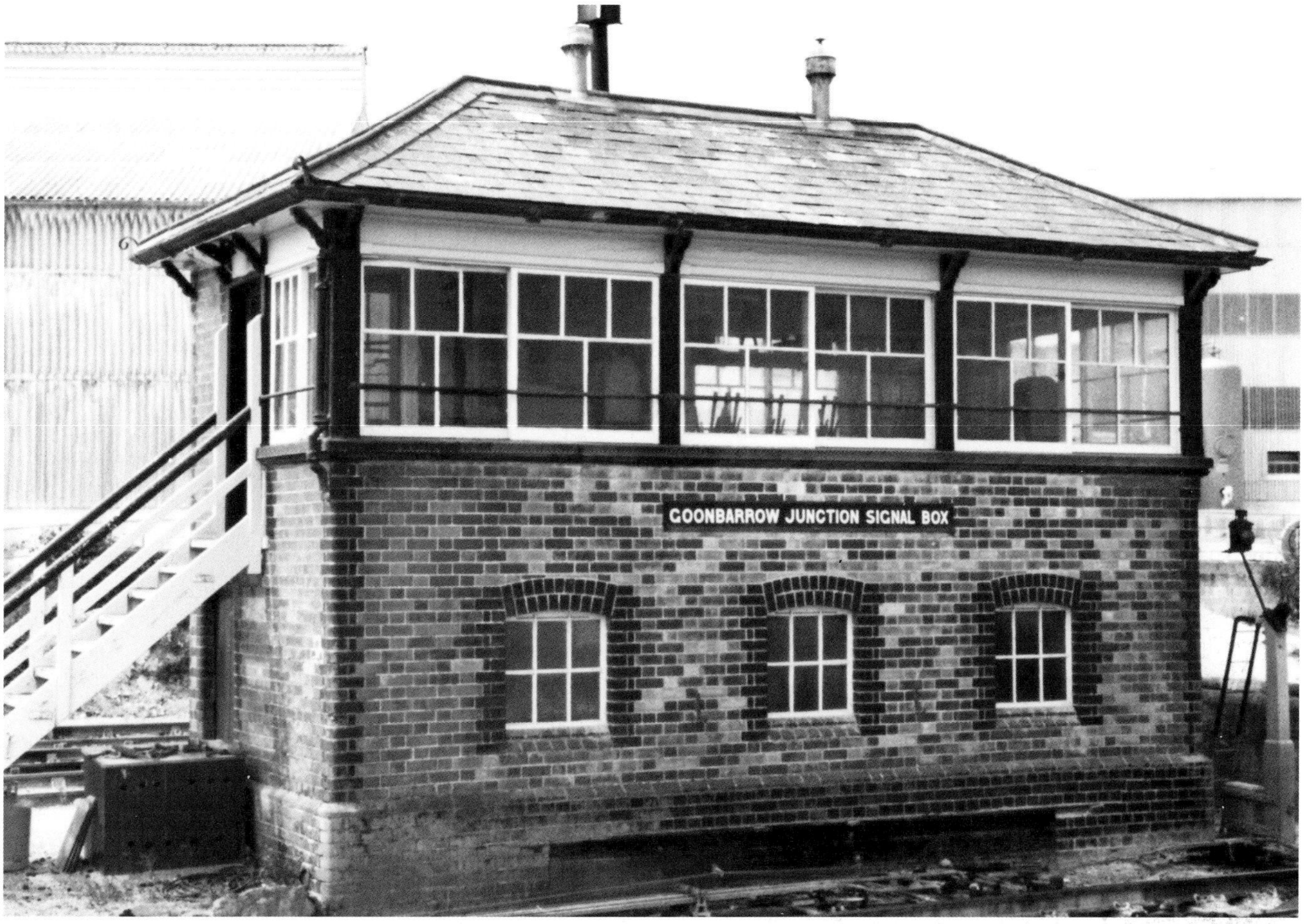

In 2013 Goonbarrow Junction Signalbox is, strictly speaking, no longer a junction, but merely the point where clay trains gain entry and exit to Imerys Rocks Works. The truncated branch line to the former Goonbarrow Branch is used as a headshunt for trains within the yard. Goonbarrow box still has a comprehensive track layout, but the Up refuge is clipped out of use and the former line to Carbis Wharf is truncated just short of Molinnis AOCL Crossing at Bugle. Recent housing developments in the former yards at Bugle have left a tract of land wide enough for a track bed on the former route to Carbis. Goonbarrow box is a type 7D opened c.1909 to replace an earlier one. Electric Token Block Regulations (ETB) apply to St Blazey and One-Train-Working-With-Train-Staff (OTWwTS) applies to Newquay, but uses an ETB token drawn from the former ETB machine. Plans exist that may result in closure before the mass resignalling scheme of 2019/20, that would see the box reduced to a Ground Frame and plain-lined with a point left in for the yard. This picture is from August 1983. (GP)

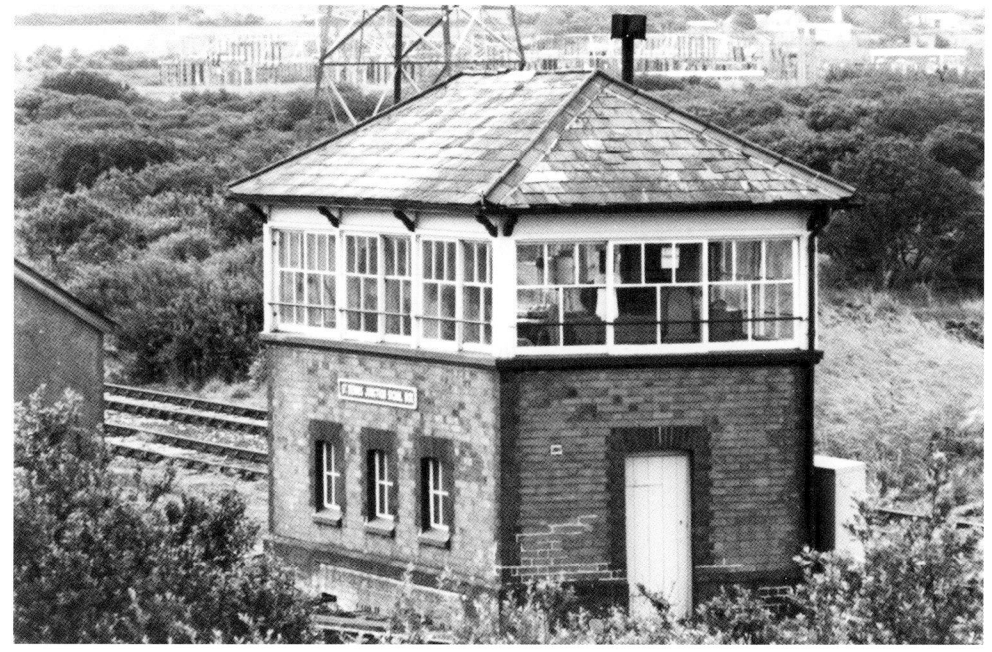

The former St Dennis box was a type 7B of 1900 vintage. It formerly controlled the lines to the Burngullow Branch, the Retew Branch, and The Spoil Tip and broke the long section between Goonbarrow and Newquay, after St Columb Road closed. Picture is from 1983. (GP)

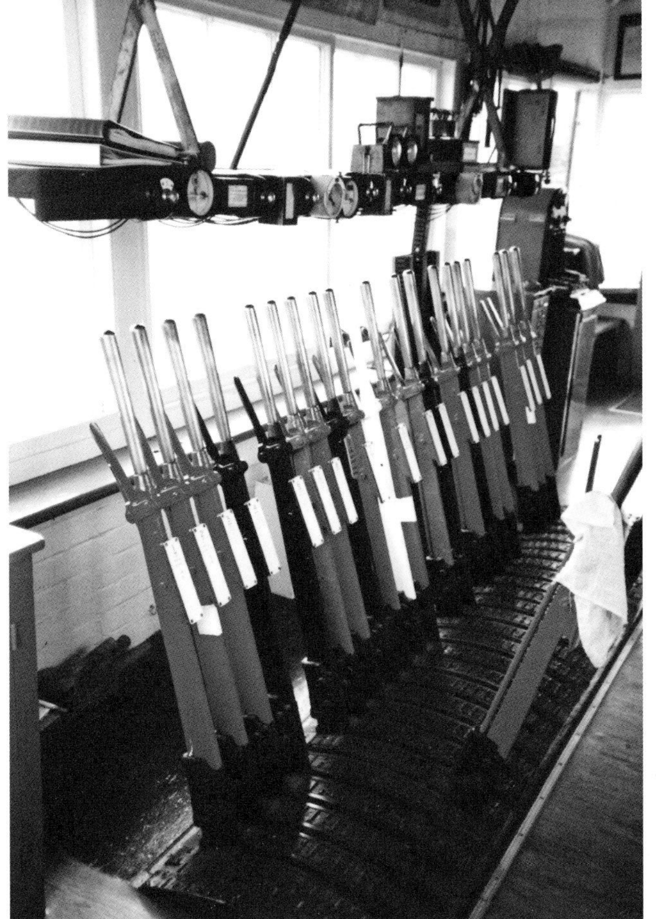

Goonbarrow Junction Signalbox still has its original 25 lever frame, of which 21 still work. The frame at Goonbarrow is ostensibly still complete, and this is because the layout is very little changed over the years, there being very little rationalisation to date, though as mentioned elsewhere, a huge cloud currently hangs over this historic location. (GP)

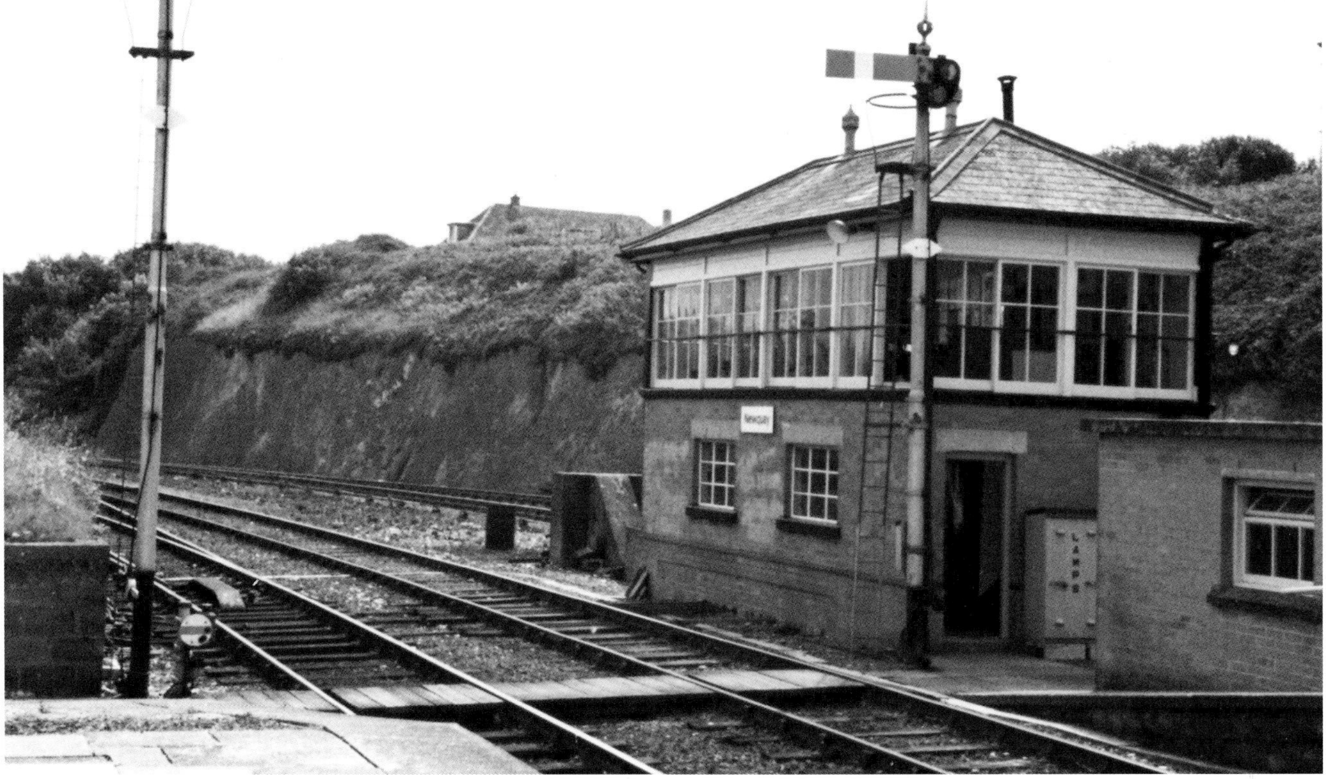

Newquay box was a type 12B opened on 20 March 1946, replacing and older structure. It was closed in October 1987 and stood empty but intact until it was burnt down by vandals in 1997. I attended that incident and watched it burn out. After the flames were out, the fire service thought that they had disturbed asbestos with the water jets. This turned out to be correct and an expensive clean- up operation was put in place to decontaminate the area. Picture is August 1983. (GP)

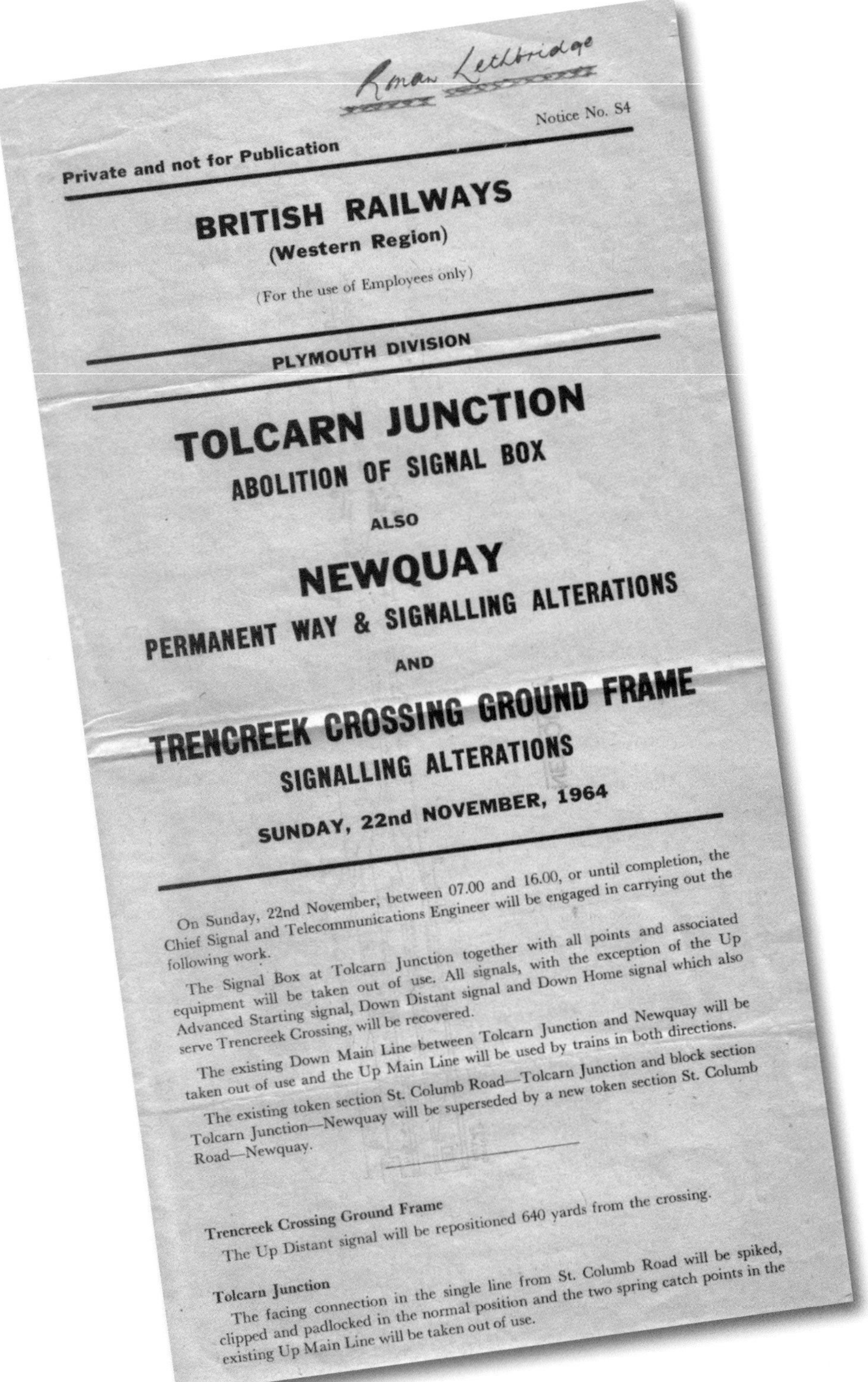

Roman Lethbridge

Notice No. S4

Private and not for Publication

BRITISH RAILWAYS
(Western Region)
(For the use of Employees only)

PLYMOUTH DIVISION

TOLCARN JUNCTION
ABOLITION OF SIGNAL BOX
ALSO
NEWQUAY
PERMANENT WAY & SIGNALLING ALTERATIONS
AND
TRENCREEK CROSSING GROUND FRAME
SIGNALLING ALTERATIONS

SUNDAY, 22nd NOVEMBER, 1964

On Sunday, 22nd November, between 07.00 and 16.00, or until completion, the Chief Signal and Telecommunications Engineer will be engaged in carrying out the following work.

The Signal Box at Tolcarn Junction together with all points and associated equipment will be taken out of use. All signals, with the exception of the Up Advanced Starting signal, Down Distant signal and Down Home signal which also serve Trencreek Crossing, will be recovered.

The existing Down Main Line between Tolcarn Junction and Newquay will be taken out of use and the Up Main Line will be used by trains in both directions.

The existing token section St. Columb Road—Tolcarn Junction and block section Tolcarn Junction—Newquay will be superseded by a new token section St. Columb Road—Newquay.

Trencreek Crossing Ground Frame

The Up Distant signal will be repositioned 640 yards from the crossing.

Tolcarn Junction

The facing connection in the single line from St. Columb Road will be spiked, clipped and padlocked in the normal position and the two spring catch points in the existing Up Main Line will be taken out of use.

An interesting and historic notice which refers to the closure of Tolcarn Junction Signalbox in 1964. Tolcarn was the Junction of the line from Chacewater, through Perranporth and Shepards and joined the line from Par at this location just before entering Newquay over Trenance Viaduct. This secondary route was used occasionally as a diversionary route when problems occurred or engineering work was taking place on the main line between Chacewater and Par. The Postal Train was a frequent user of this route due to its early schedule. (SL)

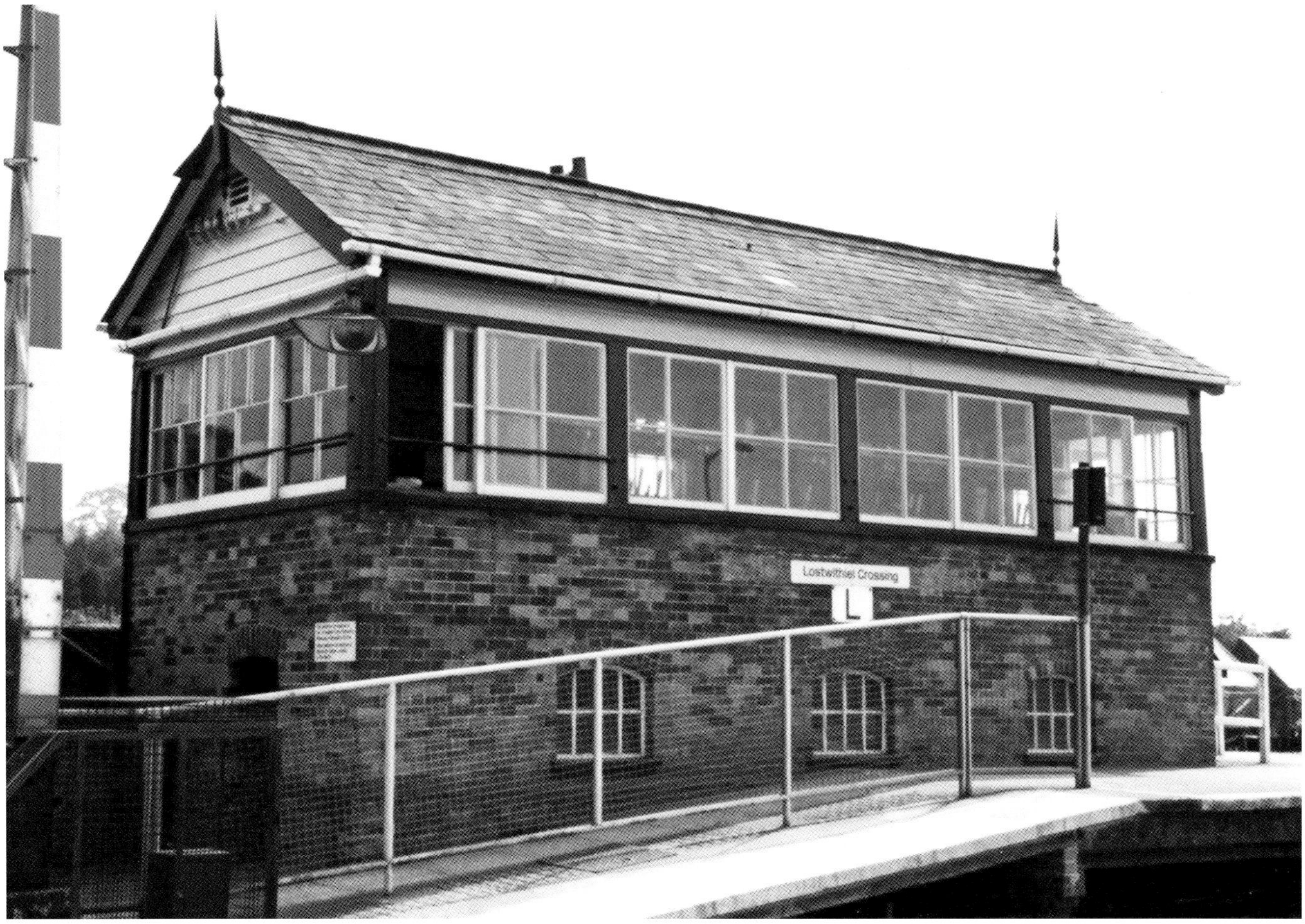

Lostwithiel was my first signalbox when I moved to Cornwall from Derbyshire, but due to an administrative error whilst I was moving, the vacancy there was filled again, and I was made redundant on day one! The type 5 box dates from 1893 and contains a 63 lever frame of which 38 are still used, plus a switch for the Intermediate Block Section (IBS) at Treverrin. It also controls the level-crossing directly outside the box. There is also a mini-panel controlling Largin area, which was installed in 1991. A formerly very busy location, but revised movements of Clay down the branch line to Fowey, means that Lostwithiel is a shadow of its former self, though it still has its moments. The signalling is by Absolute Block (AB) to Par, Track-Circuit-Block (TCB) to Liskeard and One-Train-Working-with-Train-Staff to Fowey. This picture dates from August 1983. (GP)

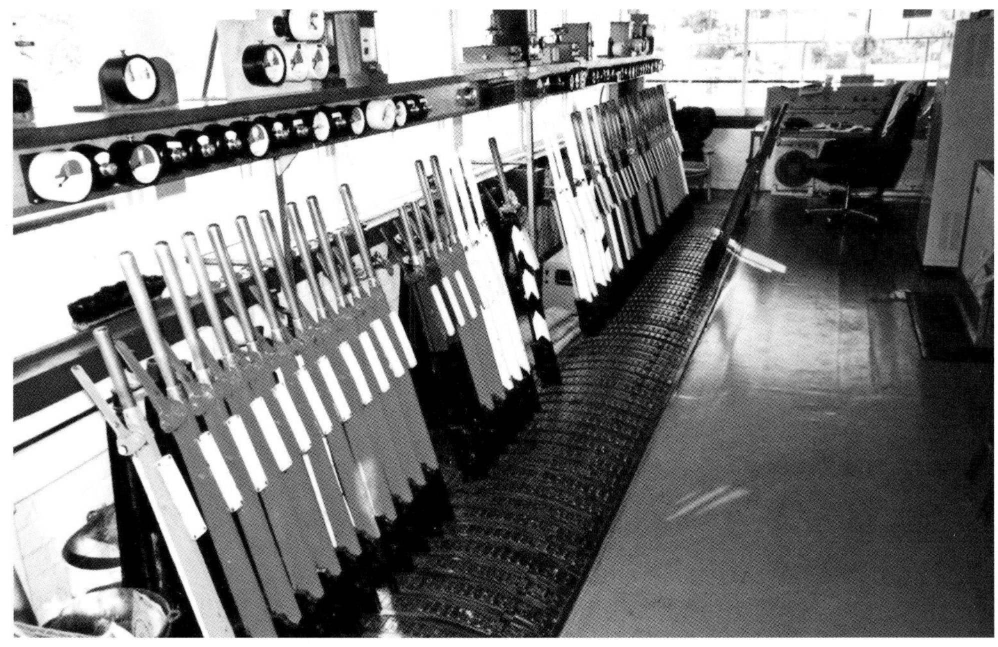

Lostwithiel frame has 63 lever spaces, but today only 38 work. The mini-panel adjacent to the east end of the frame, controls the line towards Bodmin, the single line over Largin, and onwards towards Liskeard, using three switches controlling the signals and three switches controlling the points. Additional switches control the ground frame release at Bodmin Parkway, and various alarms. (GP)

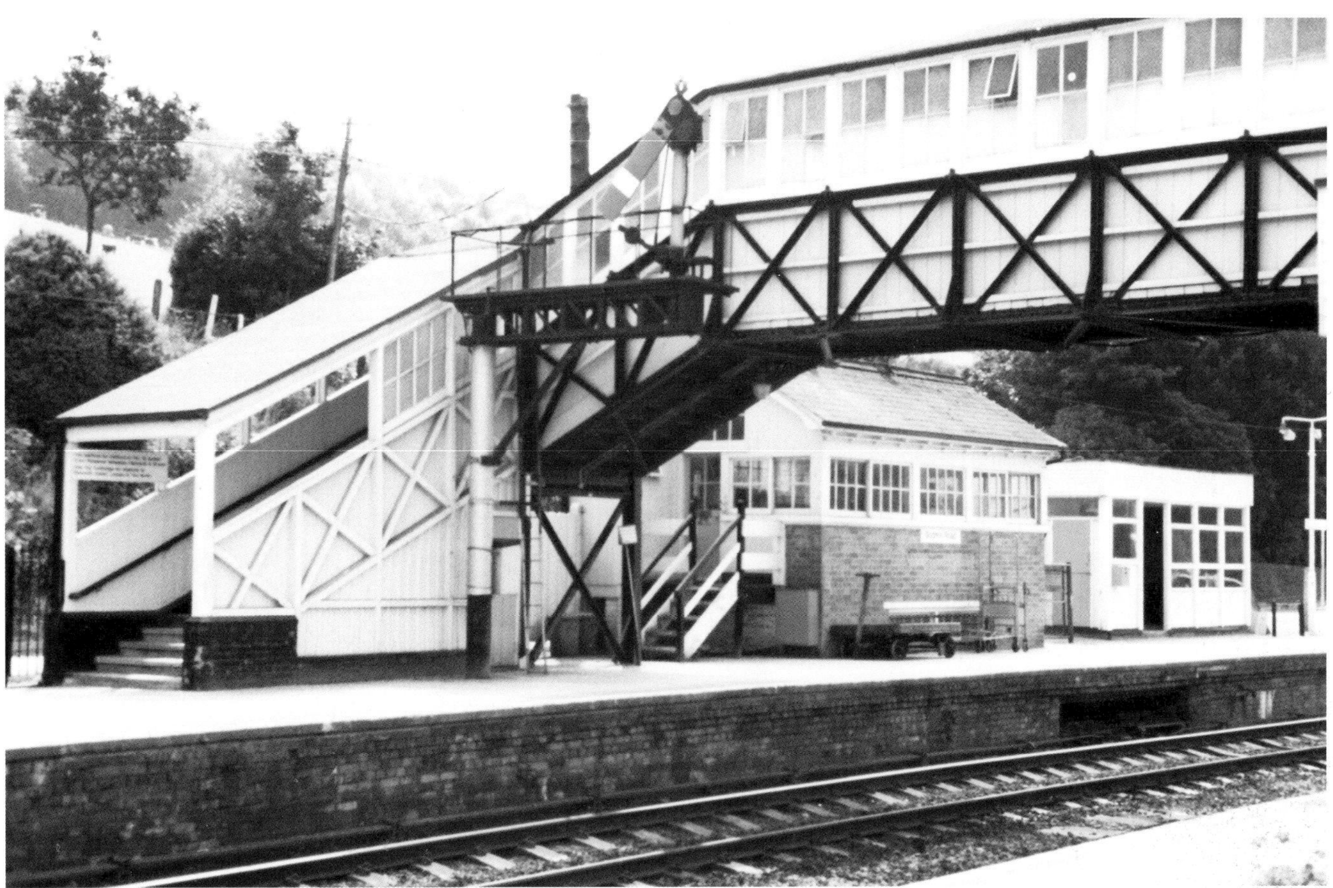

This 1983 picture of Bodmin Road (Parkway) was taken two years before its closure. Built in 1897 as a type 3 box and rebuilt c1928, it still stands and is currently in use as the Station Cafe. (GP)

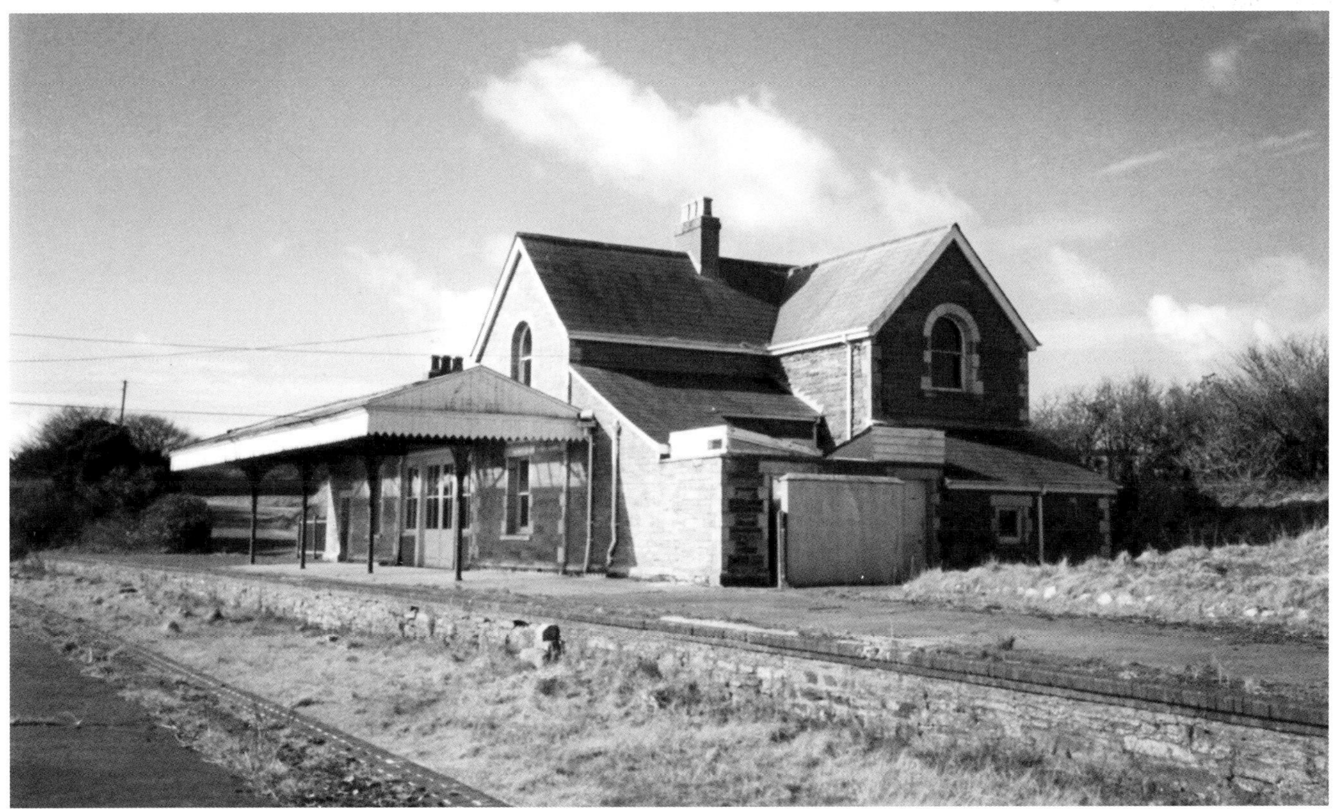

Here we see Camelford Station, in April 1988. Although ostensibly intact it had been closed to passengers for many years. (GP)

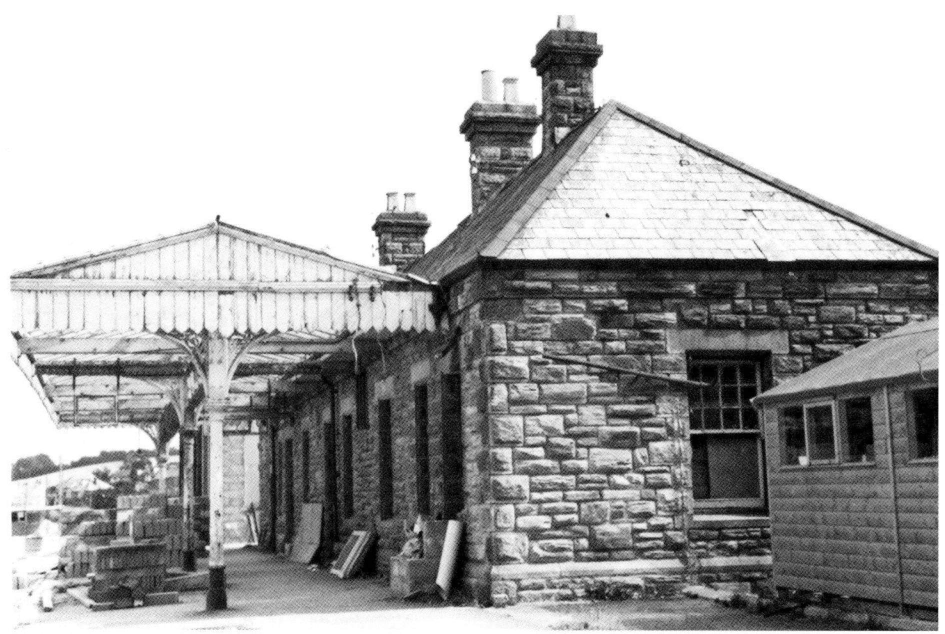

Wadebridge Station in August 1983, after closure to passengers and in what appears to be the start of the conversion into the 'John Betjeman Centre', in which guise it can still be found today. (GP)

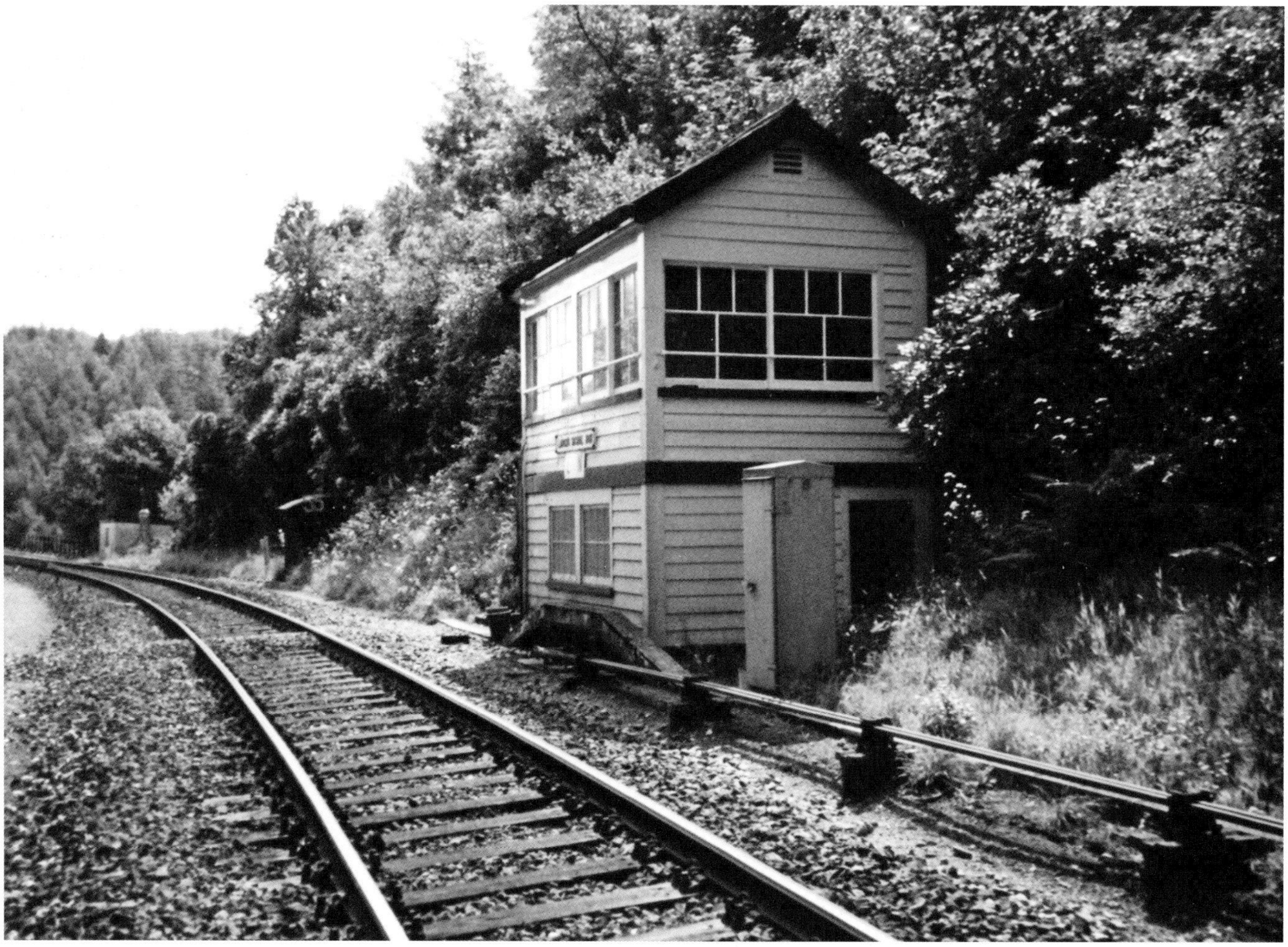

Here is a good picture of Largin Signalbox taken in July 1989, at which point it had two years life left. After closure on 14 December 1991, the control of the single-line over Largin and St Pinnock viaducts was transferred to a mini-panel in Lostwithiel box. This 1906 type 25B box originally controlled a double track section of track, but this was singled in May 1964 to avoid the costly relaying and strengthening of both viaducts, by the cash-strapped British Railways. Both viaducts have now been re-decked and strengthened, but there are at present no plans to reinstate the double track layout. At the East end of the layout is the ubiquitous 'Sand Drag', which has had the odd train or two in it over the years. This is still laid in GWR Bridge Rail, dating from c1900. (GP)

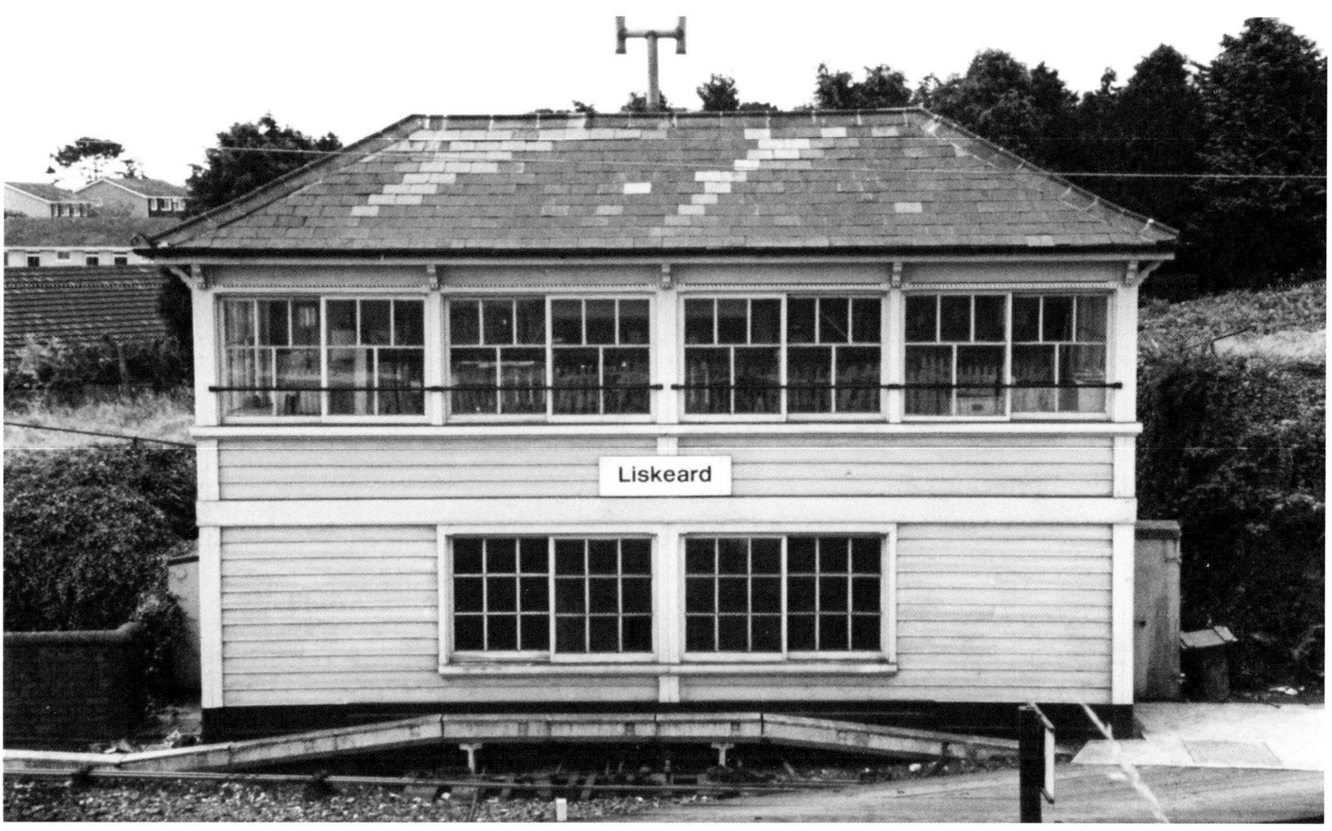

Liskeard signalbox is the only remaining operational all wooden ex-G.W.R. box still operational on the Bristol Area. Built as a type 27C it has recently received some renovation and refurbishment to arrest the rot that had started to take hold. Built in 1915, it controls the line to Coombe Junction, Moorswater and Looe as well as the main line west to Lostwithiel and the interface with Plymouth Panel to the east. Track-Circuit-Block regulations apply both ways on the main line and the line to Coombe Junction or Moorswater is by No-Signaller-Token regulations, whilst the line to Looe is by One-Train-Working-With-Train-Staff regulations. This picture is July 1985. (GP)

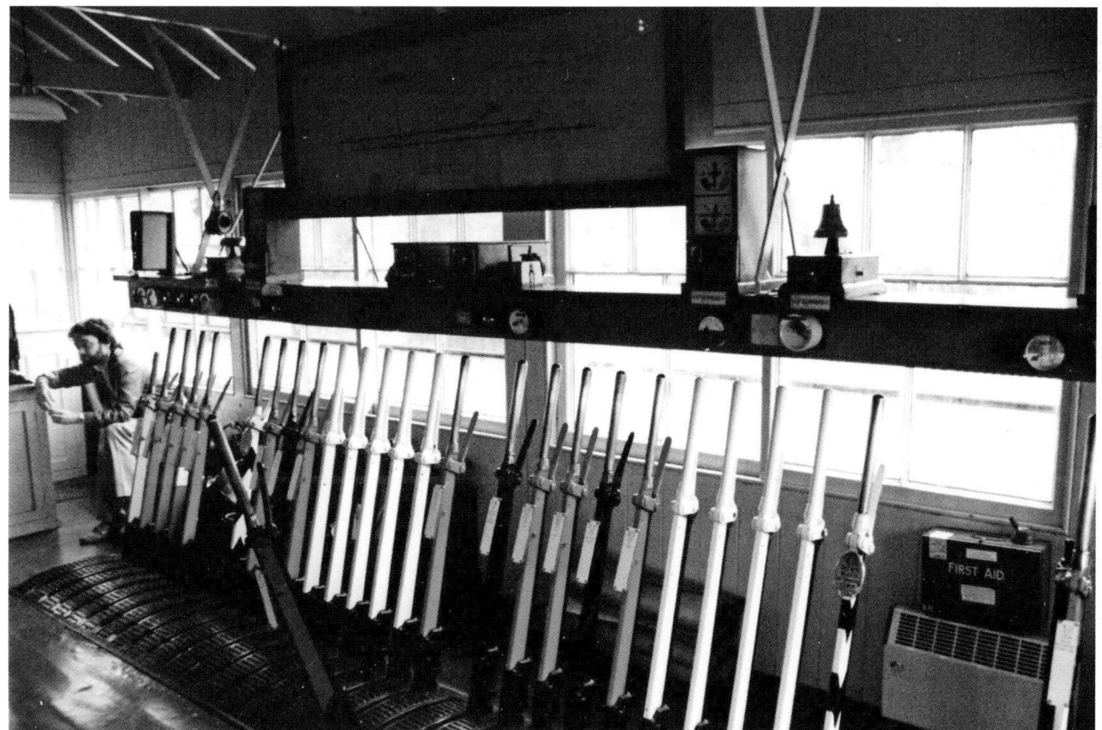

Liskeard Signalbox frame has 36 levers of which 19 still work, shared between both mechanical and electro-mechanical signals and points. The West end cross-over has been converted to power operation and number 5 signal was abolished when St Germans Signalbox closed. Number 4 signal was replaced with a colourlight and re-sited and the London end of the viaduct. (GP)

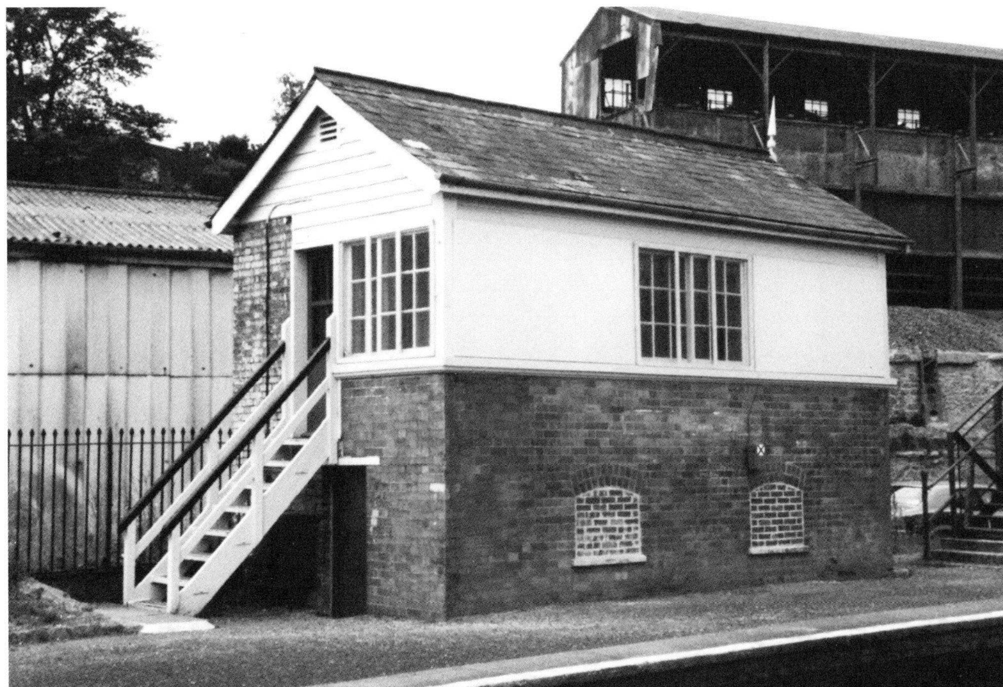

This picture of Menheniot box was taken in July 1985, twelve years after it had closed. As a type 5 box it had opened in 1892 and was demolished in 2007 after standing derelict for many years. (GP)

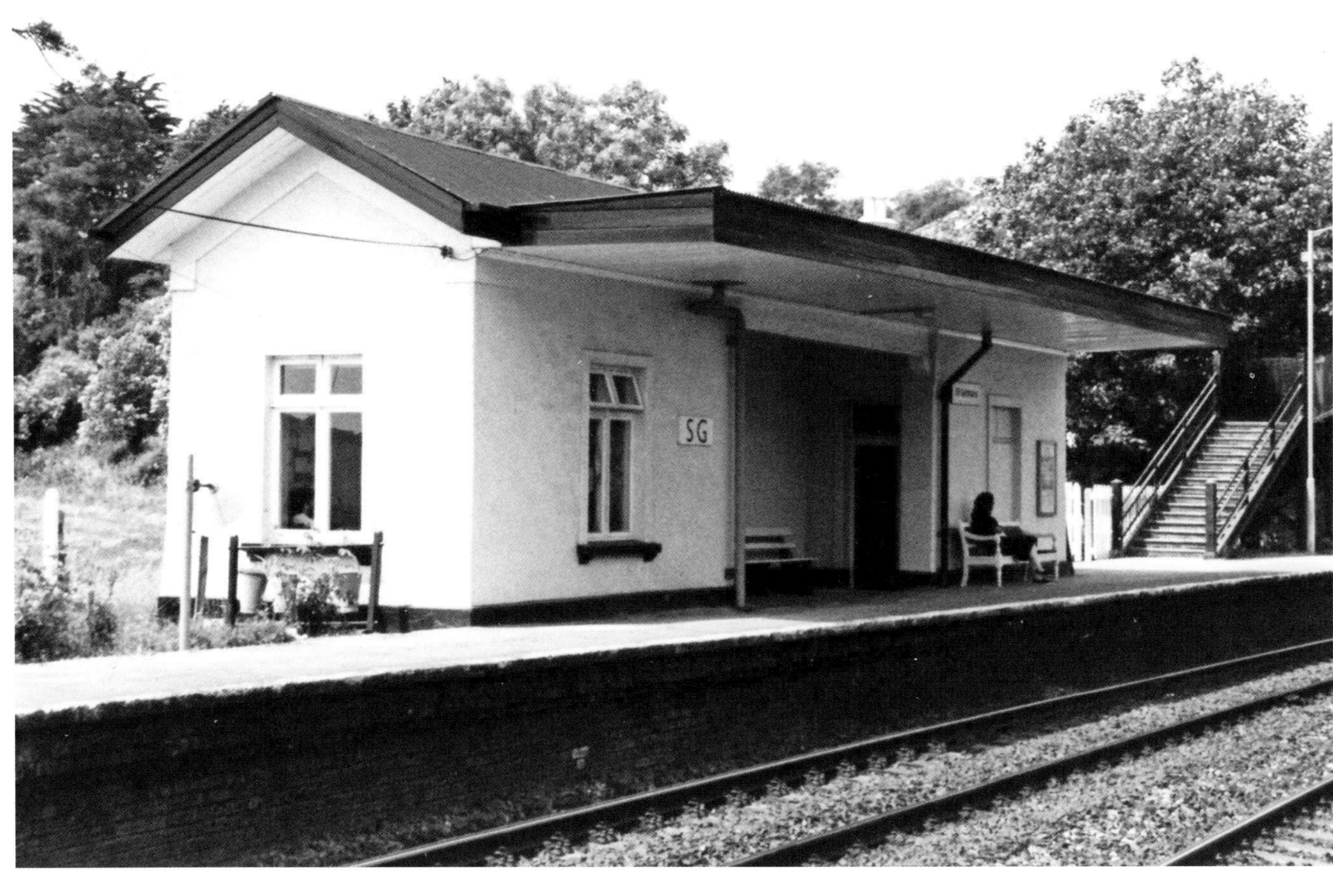

St Germans Signalbox was in the station building waiting-room nearest the camera, until it too was closed in April 1998, myself (as Duty MOM) being the final person to lock the door and change the locks. This makeshift and very much highbrid panel was meant to be a temporary arrangement when the original signalbox closed in May 1973. It lasted a staggering twenty-five years in this cramped room, together with a well, which was boarded over in the floor. After final closure the area was converted to Track-Circuit-Block signalling with axle-counters and transferred to Plymouth Panel, which interfaces with Liskeard signalbox. (GP)

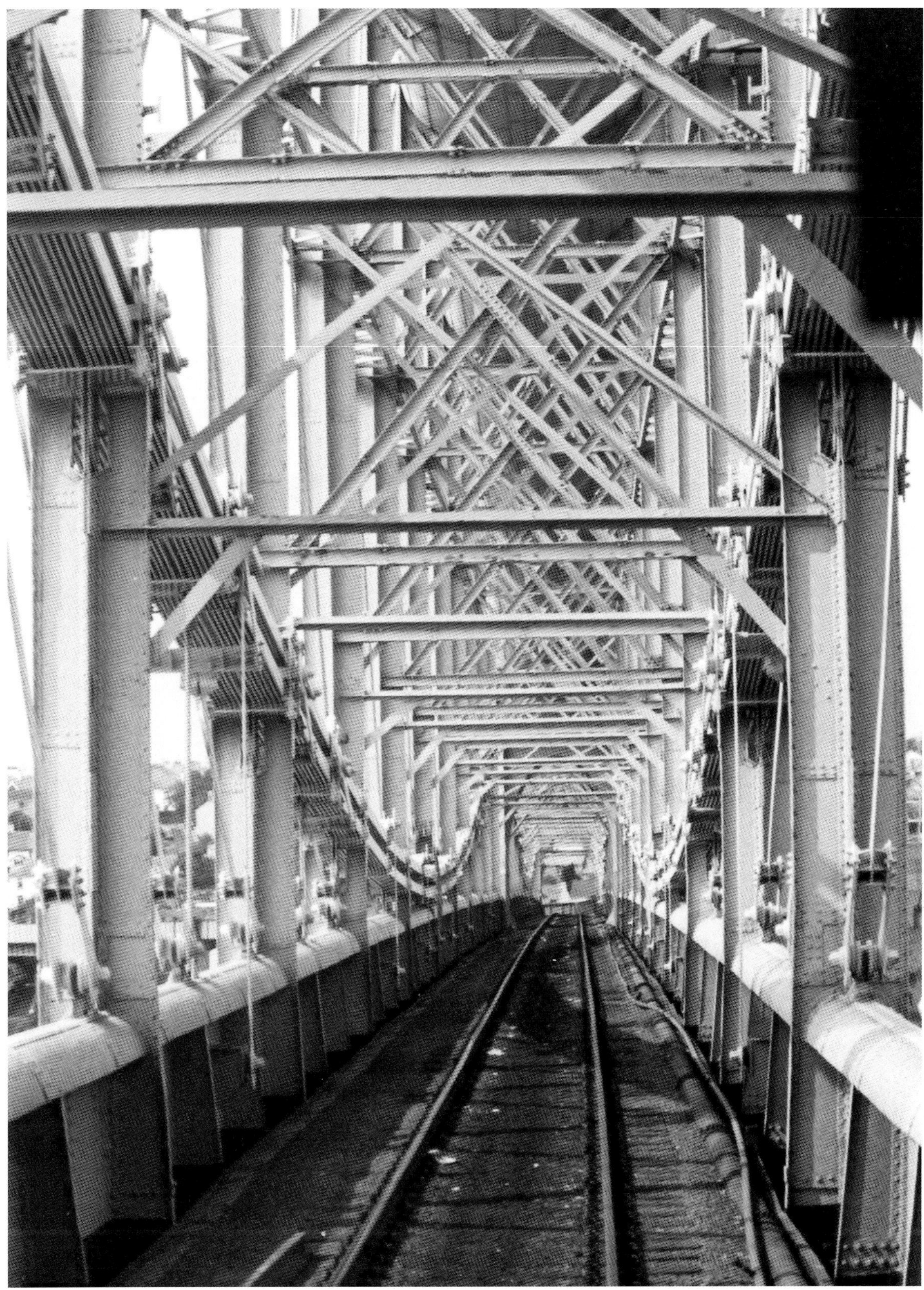

The awe inspiring and magnificent Royal Albert Bridge linking Devon with Cornwall. This grade I listed monument, is a fitting tribute to I.K. Brunel, and bears his name and date of completion. In 2009, prior to its 150 year celebrations, the ladders and footways that had blighted each end for many years were removed. Since then a major refurbishment has commenced which will remove some of the over-strengthening added by both the GWR and BR over the years. Built to the broad gauge, its original pattern Baulk Road timbers were reinstated about ten years ago, and the sleepers and ballast seen in the picture were removed. It can be seen from the picture that it climbs to the middle then drops away again. As a restricted structure, it is forbidden to access the structure whilst trains are running, but I have been fortunate to access it many times, the most recent being to check for a broken rail, or track-circuit fault, and before that to escort the RSPCA to rescue an injured Peregrine Falcon (a beautiful bird at close quarters). (GP)

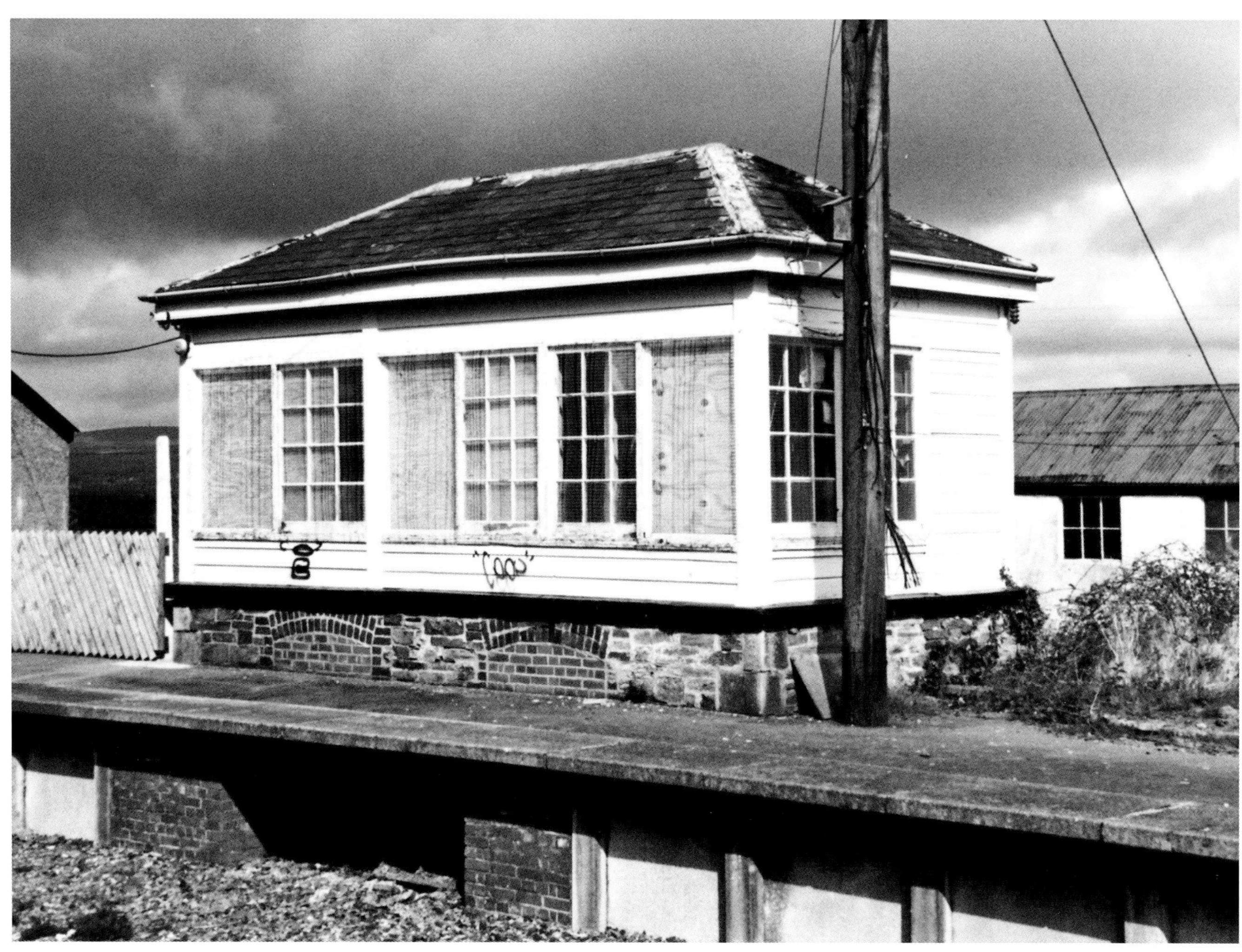

This is how the long time closed Bere Alston signalbox looked in April 1992. (GP)

CHAPTER 7

MISHAPS

LIKE ALL RAILWAYS throughout the world, occasionally things go wrong, which might result in a derailment or collision. Sometimes forces beyond the control of the railway will conspire to thwart the safety systems in place where the railway interfaces with the highway.

Here are a few pictures of just a small selection of some of the accidents and incidents my colleagues and myself have attended over the last twenty years or so, and a couple from before that period.

I have tried to steer away from allocating causes and blame for those illustrated here, although they were all thoroughly investigated, and the thinking within the railway now is slowly drifting towards the culture British Railways had of finding out what caused the incident and encouraging staff to be open about what they knew, so that measures can be put in place to prevent a reoccurrence. Since privatisation the drift towards blame has been steadily increasing, but it has had a negative effect on trust.

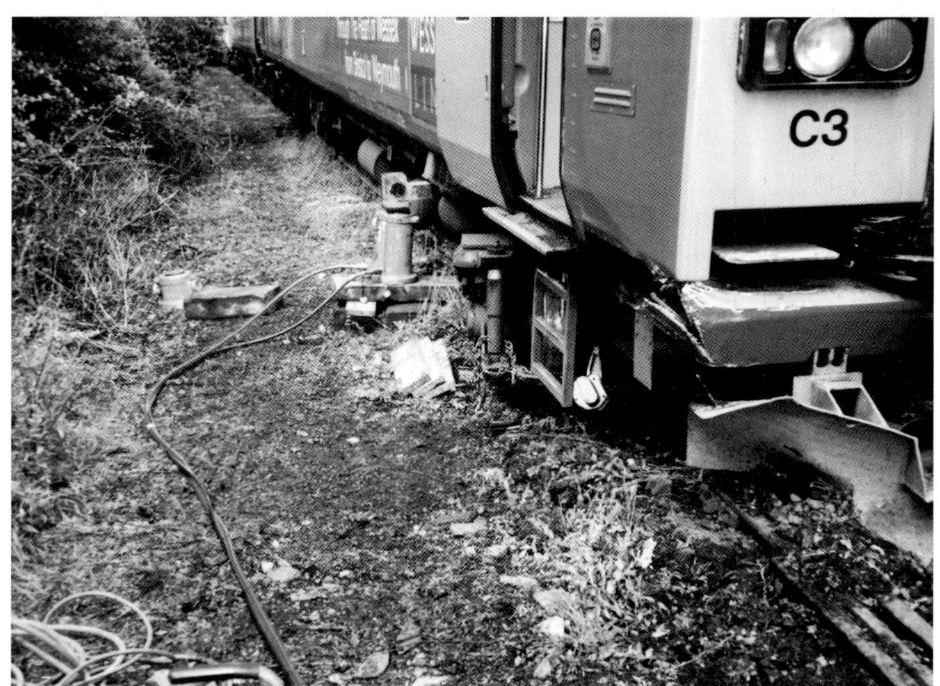

In 2002 an accident occurred at Par, in the Chapel Sidings, involving several units all coupled together. It was human error as the driver concerned overran the stop-blocks and planted the 153 unit, which was at the front of the train, over a capped mine shaft adjacent to the 'Chapel'. The recovery operation involved dragging the unit back to where the rails were still intact, and then re-railing. In BR days such 'minor' incidents were classed as mishaps, rather than accidents. The units were damaged, but all were returned to service after attention at Cardiff Depot. (SFH)

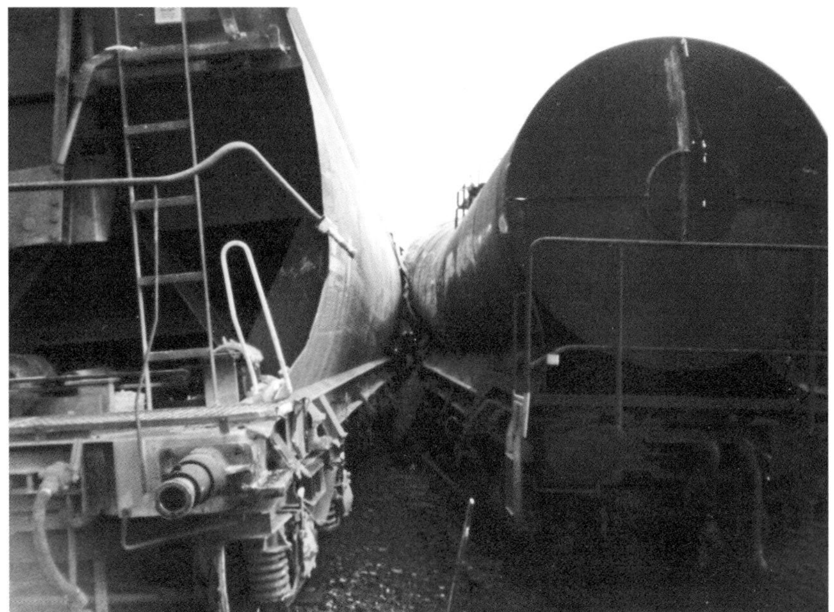

A 'fouling point' shunting collision took place in St Blazey Yard in 1998, involving a 'Silver Bullet' clay slurry tank and a 'Polybulk' tank, which caused considerable damage to both vehicles. (SFH)

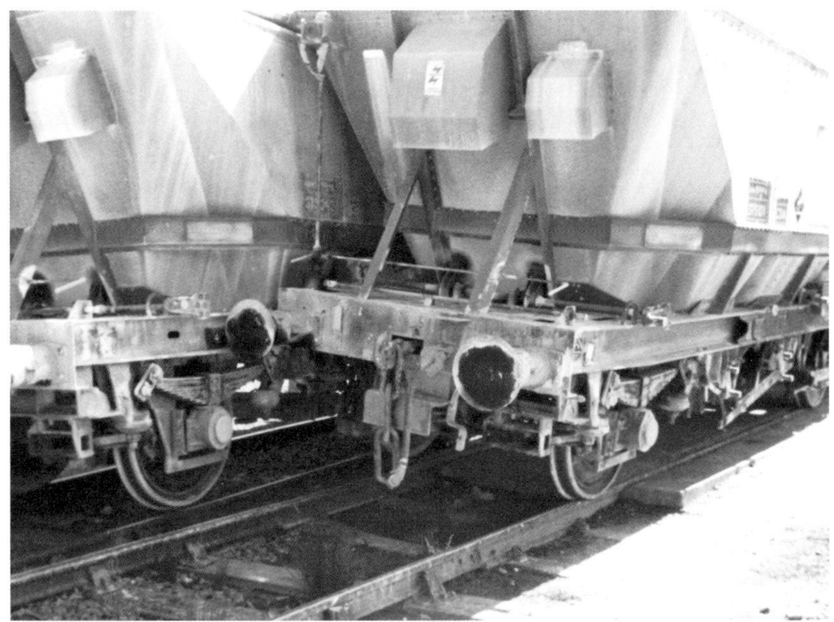

In 1997 another mishap occurred in Goonbarrow Yard and involved a shunting error, due to mis-communication, where two moving trains were shunted towards a common point. A little damage was sustained but all wagons returned to service shortly after. (SFH)

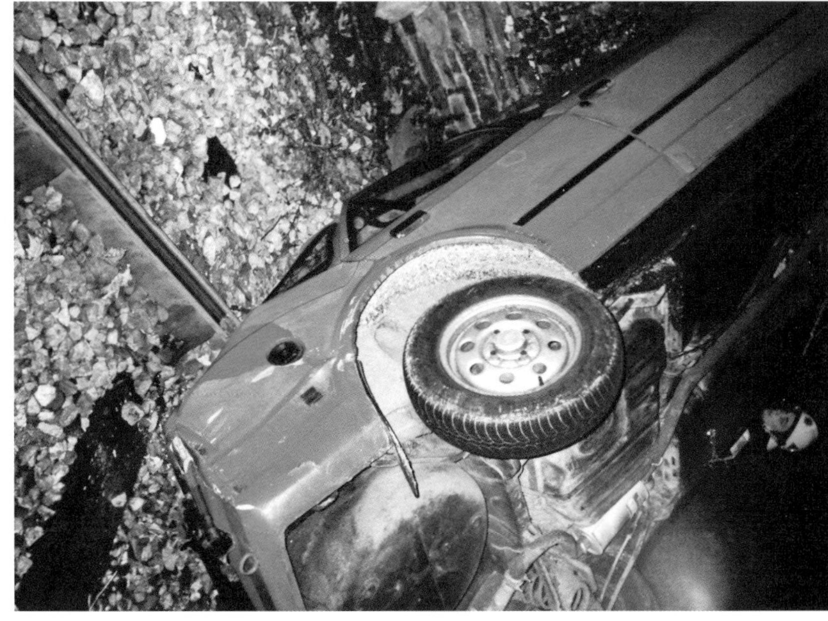

In 2000 a car skidded off the road in Looe after the driver lost control in the early hours. It landed on its roof not far from the station, but both occupants got out with only minor injuries. Vehicles crashing onto the railway are more common than you would imagine, there being four on the Looe line whilst I have been an MOM. The latest one I have attended was on 2 October 2012, on the St Ives line, when a driver lost control ascending the hill from Carbis Bay Beach and crashed onto the line adjacent to the bridge at the station. He also got out unhurt. (SFH)

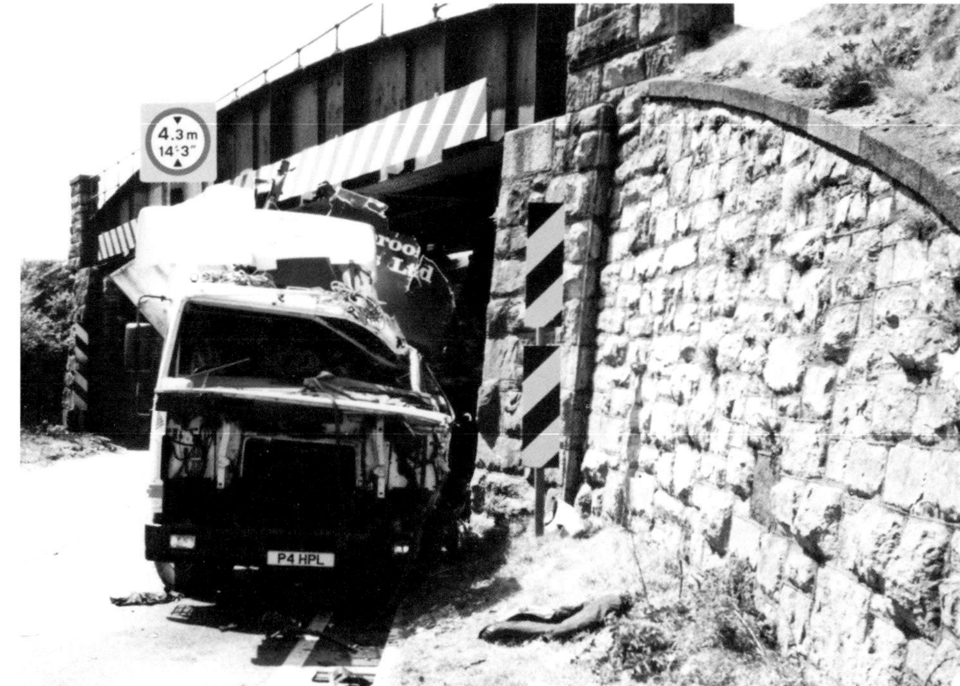

When the A30 still passed under the railway at the infamous Goss Moor iron bridge, accidents, usually attributed to over-height loads were almost a weekly event. In fact, I got to know some of the Police officers quite well, we attended together that often. Various schemes were installed to try and stop it, even a very expensive electronic beam and large visual display, but, just like level-crossing accidents, some drivers either miss the warnings or just think it does not apply to them! We have had one suicide using a car at this bridge, but of course I cannot show that picture here. The vehicle shown here, which was travelling towards Bodmin and carrying pallets, was slammed sideways at speed into the main granite structure and closed the road for several hours. (SFH)

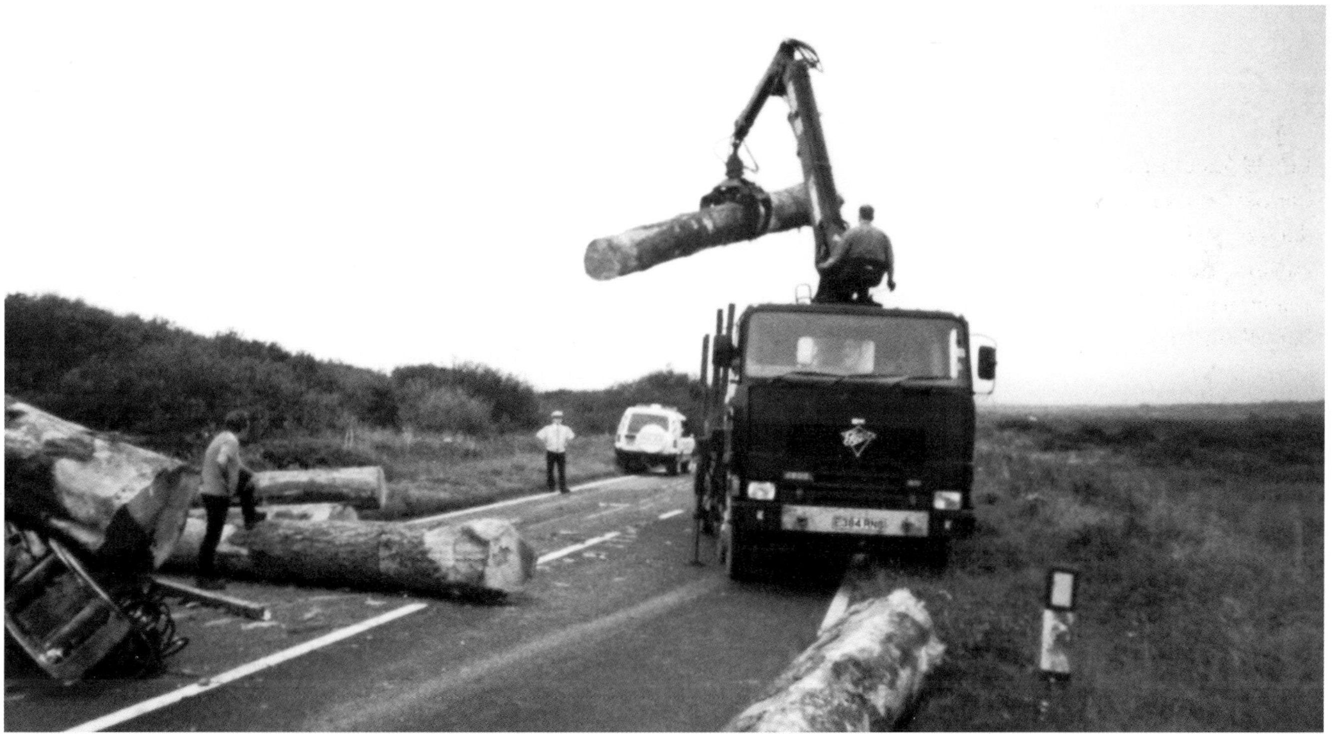

The most serious accident at 'The Iron Bridge' happened on the Friday before the August Bank Holiday Weekend in 1999, when an over-height , fully loaded 'log loader' articulated truck hit the bridge travelling towards Penzance. It hit the three inch bottom girder so hard that it tore it upwards, and apparently momentarily lifted the huge structure, which fortunately sat back on the bearings. As the truck rolled sideways it lost all its load of large logs which spilled down the opposite carriageway, and remarkably missed everything. The wrecked truck carried on up the embankment, before coming to rest on its side. The damage to the bridge was serious and the road was closed for twenty four hours on the busiest weekend of the year, causing traffic chaos for miles. This was the only time I have had a police escort to site as the Railway Incident Officer (RIO), as with the area grid-locked for miles I couldn't get there. Apparently it was this accident that finally drove on the need for a dual carriageway and the re-routing of the road away from the only low bridge left on the A30 for its whole length. (SFH)

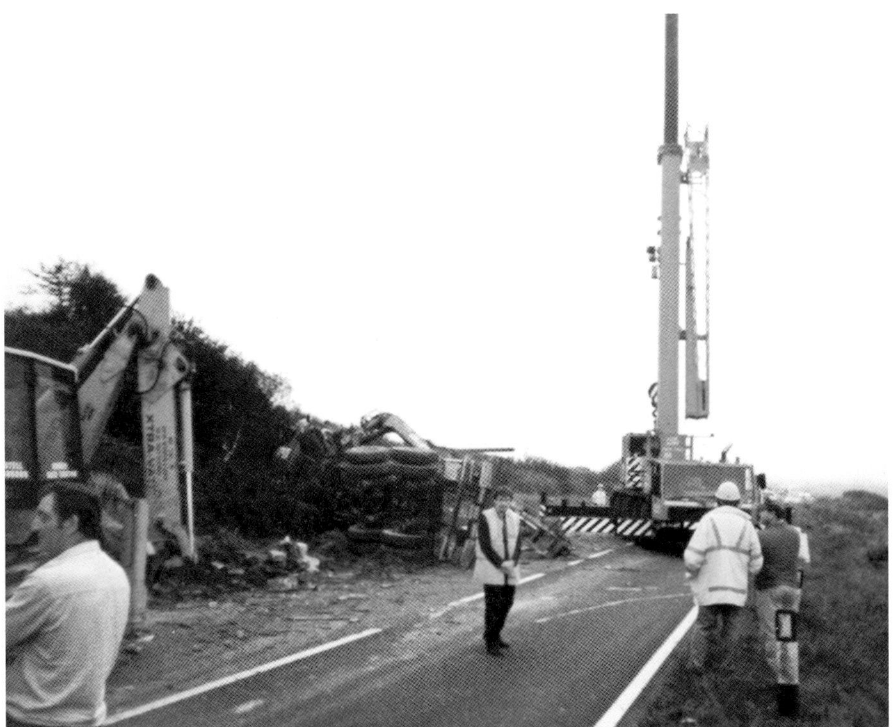

Another view of the Log truck. (SFH)

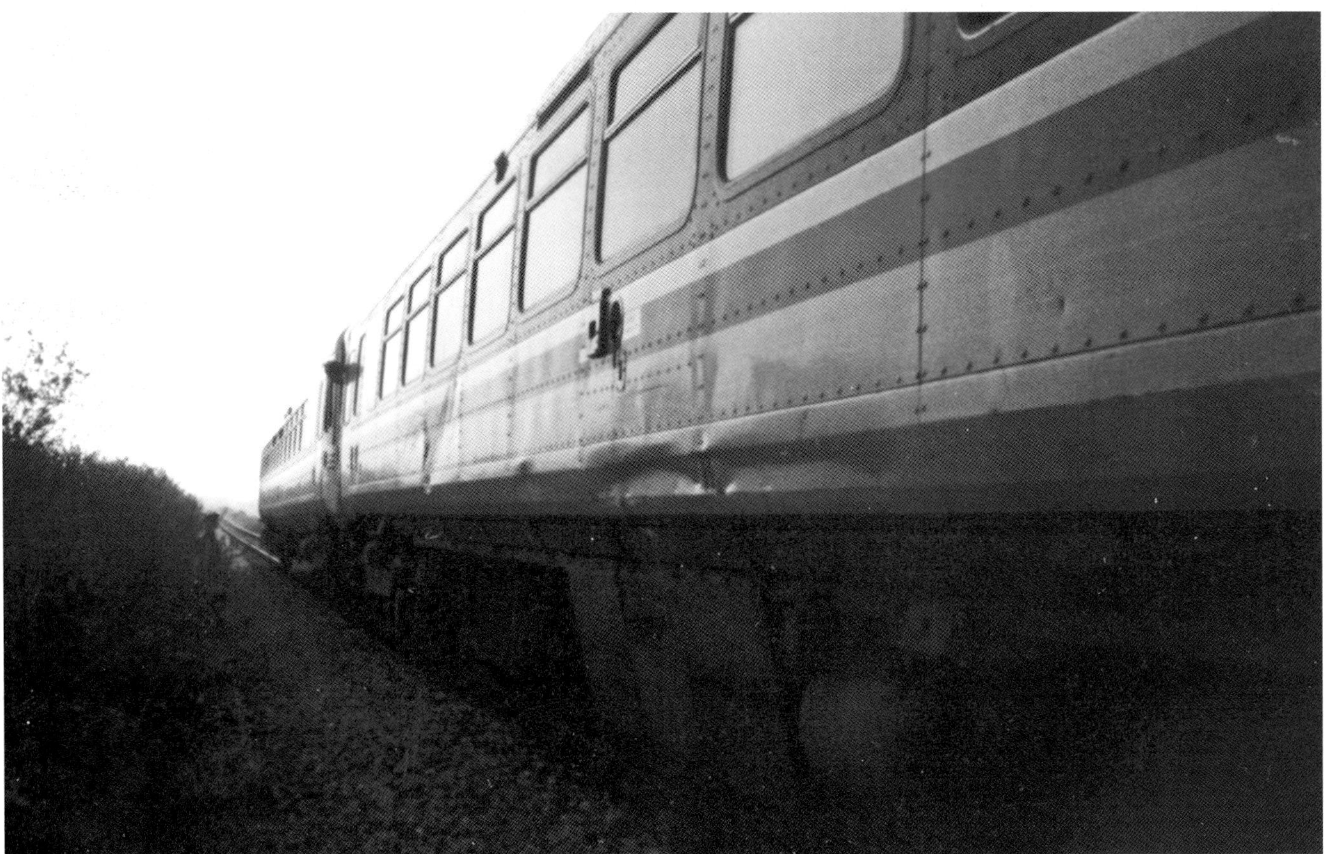

The most serious level-crossing accident I attended to date, was the car transporter at Tregoss Moor level crossing, just a few hundred yards from the ubiquitous iron bridge. The fully laden transporter turned on to the crossing, ignored the warning lights and drove into the path of the Down Newquay train, which momentarily derailed and re-railed, but stayed upright. The resultant impact closed the road and railway for forty-eight hours, whilst a specialist heavy crane was brought down by road overnight from Derbyshire, with a police escort. This huge crane had another smaller crane come with it to assemble the massive structure on site. The HGV driver was wholly to blame and the driver of the train was lucky to escape without serious injuries, although some passengers did sustain some minor injuries. The remarkable thing was just how well the class 153 stood up to the severe impact. It was rescued under my supervision by a fellow 153 and towed to St Blazey, where after inspection, it was taken by road for extensive rebuilding. (SFH)

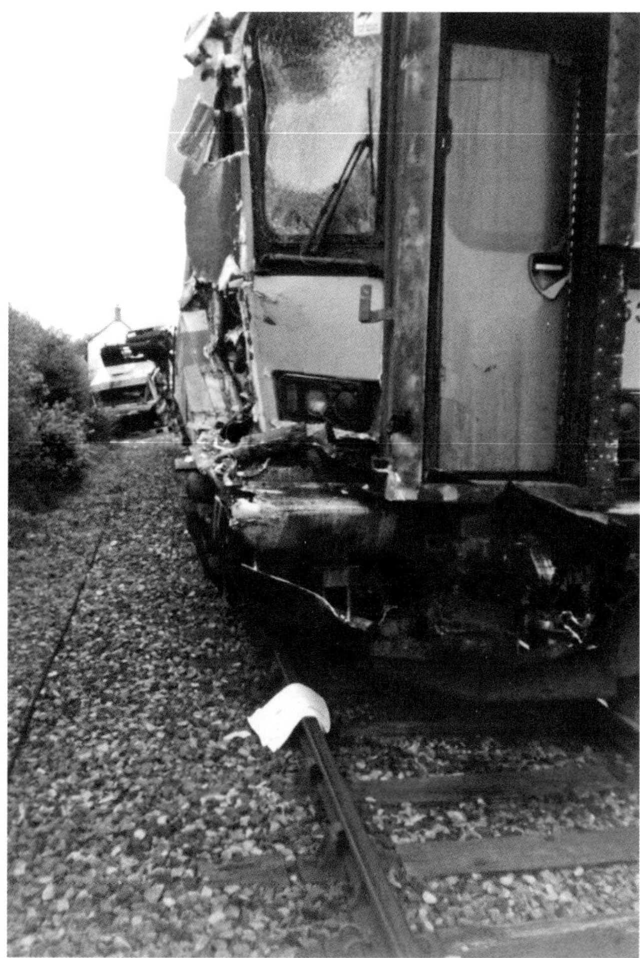

This is how 153308 looked after the terrible Tregoss Moor crossing collision. (SFH)

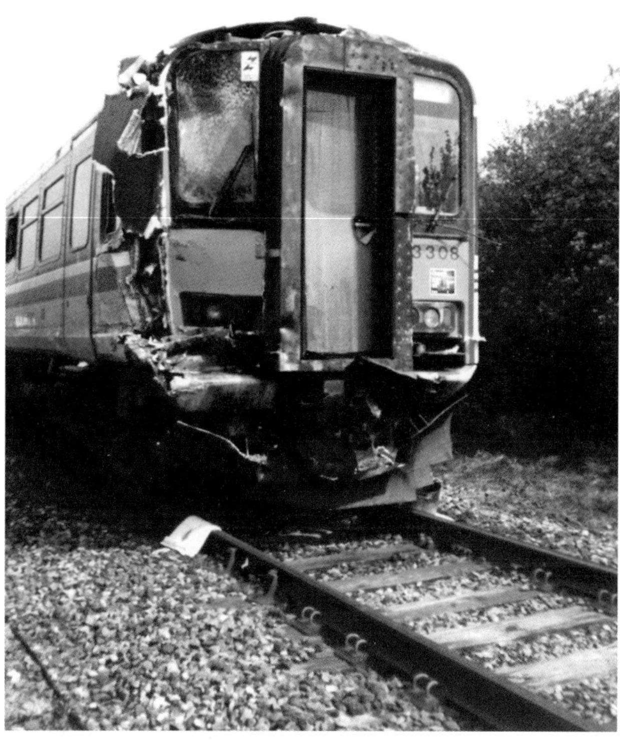

Another picture of 153308. (SFH)

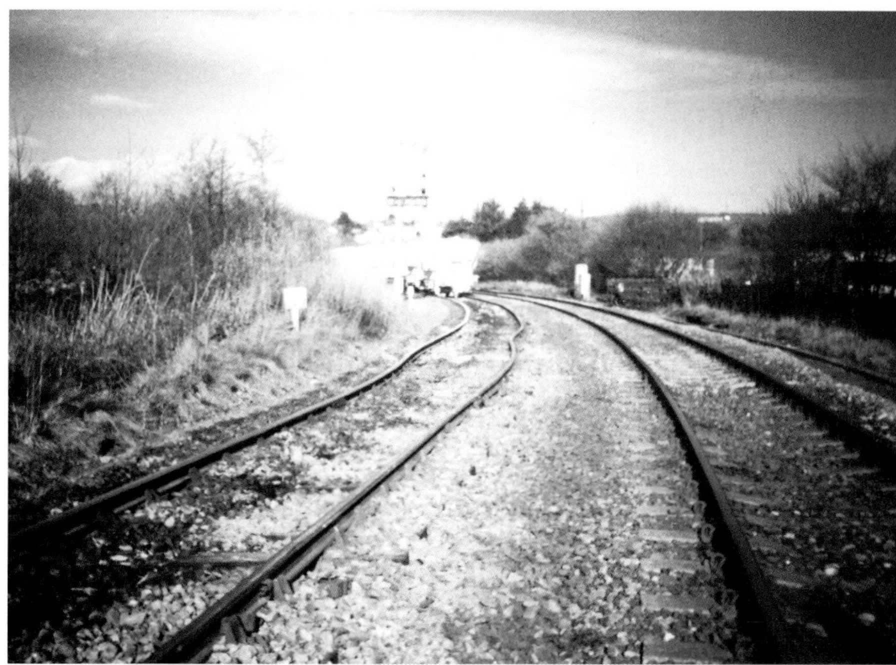

In 1998 a loaded CDA wagon, one of nineteen, spread the road as it rounded the curve on the Up line at St Blazey close to the river bridge, enroute to Lostwithiel . The track was in poor condition after years of underinvestment, and the resultant derailment involved most of the nineteen wagons, though not the locomotive. We operated Single-Line-Working over the next day or so, whilst the re-railing took place and after that a new track was laid. Whilst the use of CDAs were an improvement on the old wooden bodied wagons (clay hoods) that they had replaced in the 1980s, the problem with them (and still is), is the two axle design and loaded weight of forty-six tons. They place a severe strain on the track, especially on curves, pointwork and bridges. Although in 2013 the condition of the infrastructure is vastly improved on the condition BR maintained it in and that which RAILTRACK inherited, the underlying problem was lack of investment. (SFH)

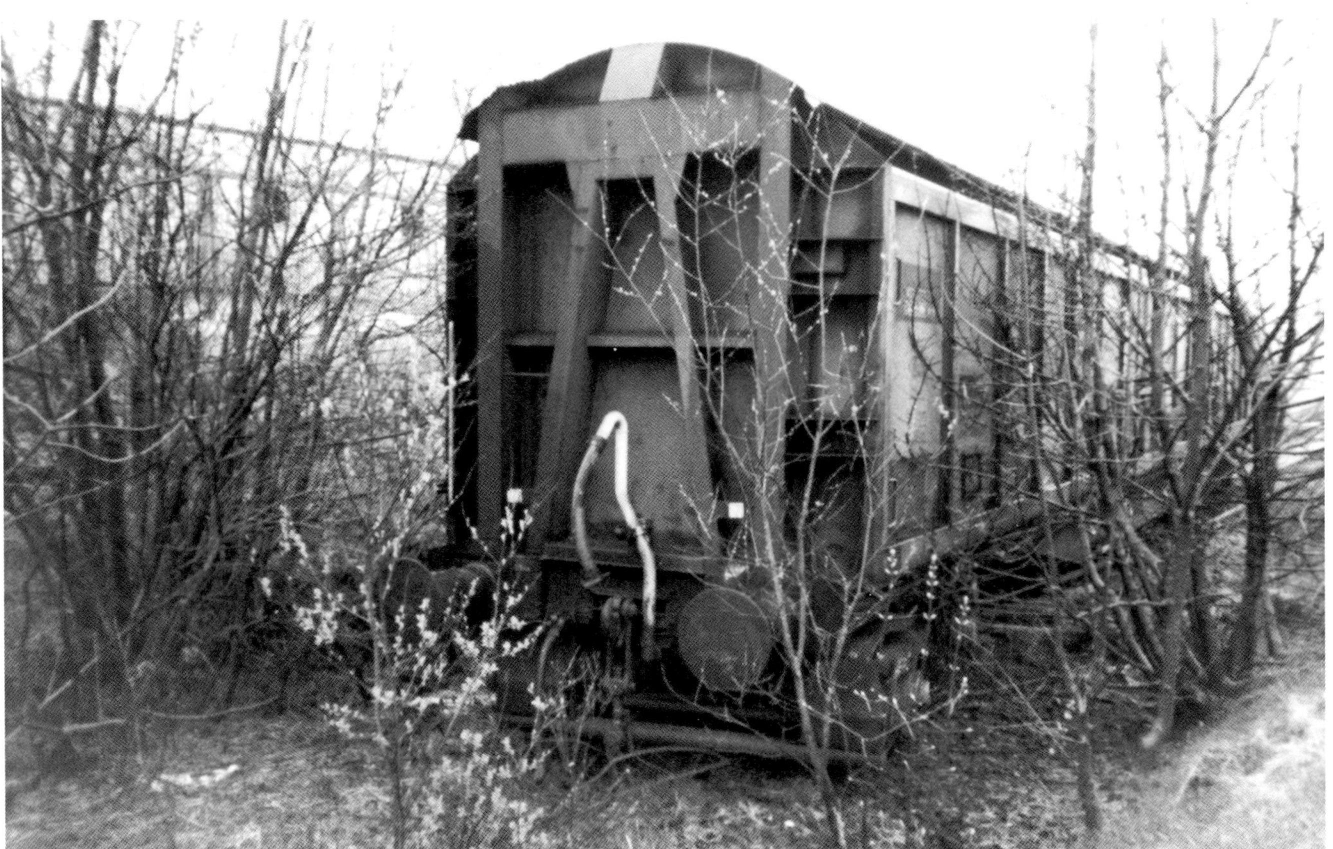

In 1997 a wagon ran away from the clay company sidings at Treviscoe and managed over a mile downhill before smashing through the stop-blocks at Parkandillack and trying to forge a way back to St Dennis Junction. The derailed Cargowagon ended up in the dirt fifty feet from where the track ended. (SFH)

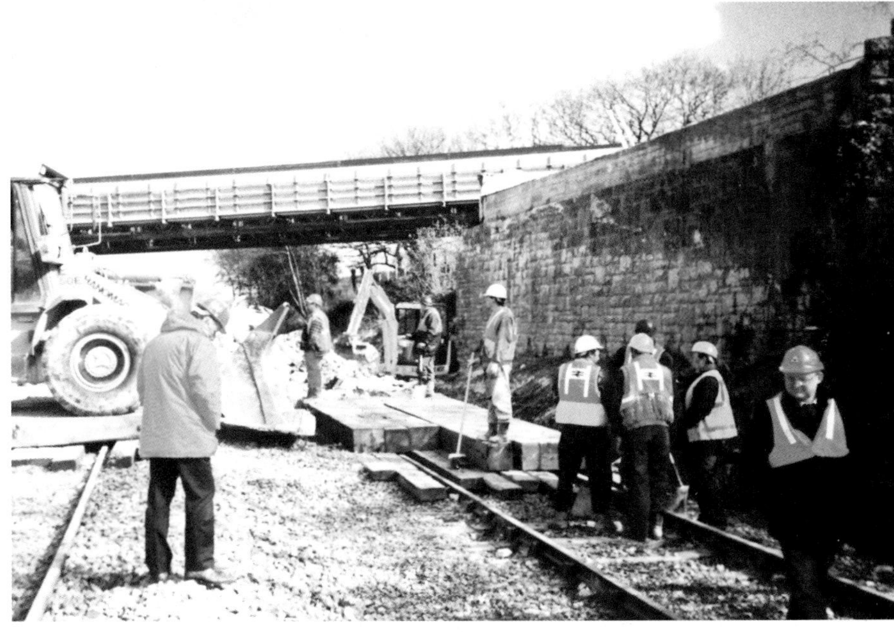

My first serious incident as an Inspector was just a couple of weeks after taking up the position, when a planned engineering job turned into a major incident at Lostwithiel. The 1930s built road bridge spanning the main line, both loops and the old Milk Siding was deemed to be unsafe due to 'concrete cancer' and after months of planning and a temporary structure being built at the side of it, it was scheduled for demolition using high explosives at midnight. The track was left in place and covered with several layers of heavy timbers and sleepers, to form a mat or cushion to absorb the impact as the pieces fell. Midnight came, the explosion was spectacular, and as the bridge legs shattered the two large sections of the bridge just dropped in the middle and stayed in their respective pieces. It was planned to have the shattered sections cut up before the Monday morning service started, but alas that was never going to be achieved. Even after the bridge was cut up over the next couple of days, the track under the matting, was wrecked, along with the signalling and cabling. We got the Down Loop back first, and as it was the least damaged, it was temporarily repaired and we put in SLW between Largin and Par at one train per hour. (SFH)

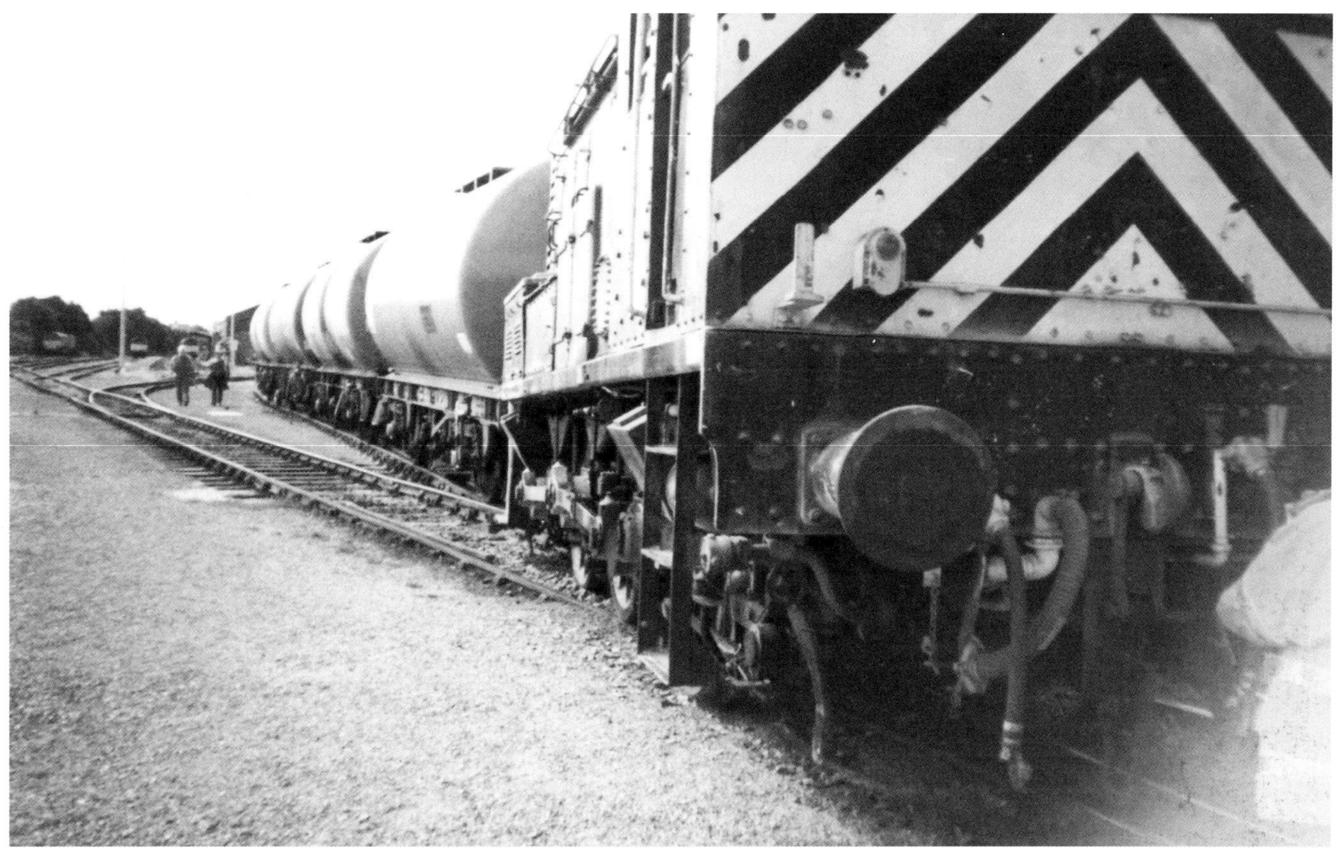

On a bright day in 1998, whilst both myself and the Senior Inspector Lawrie James, were just enjoying a cup of tea in the St Blazey office, Lawrie was watching the '08' loco shunting up and down the sidings, with ever increasing speed. Lawrie quipped "that if he continues at that speed he will fall off" and no sooner had the words left his mouth, than, in a spectacular cloud of dust, the loco fell off, all wheels. Embarrassment all round for the shunters and managers at EWS. A similar accident occurred the year after, when the same loco was propelling a rake of wagons from the Up main into the Ballast Siding opposite the signalbox. The loco derailed as it passed over the river bridge and footpath, but on this occasion the move was made at dead slow speed, and was fortunately captured on video by an enthusiast down in Cornwall on holiday. I eventually procured the film from the family who were staying at Hendra near Newquay, in exchange for a day on the clay trains, which he found to be a very acceptable deal. (SFH)

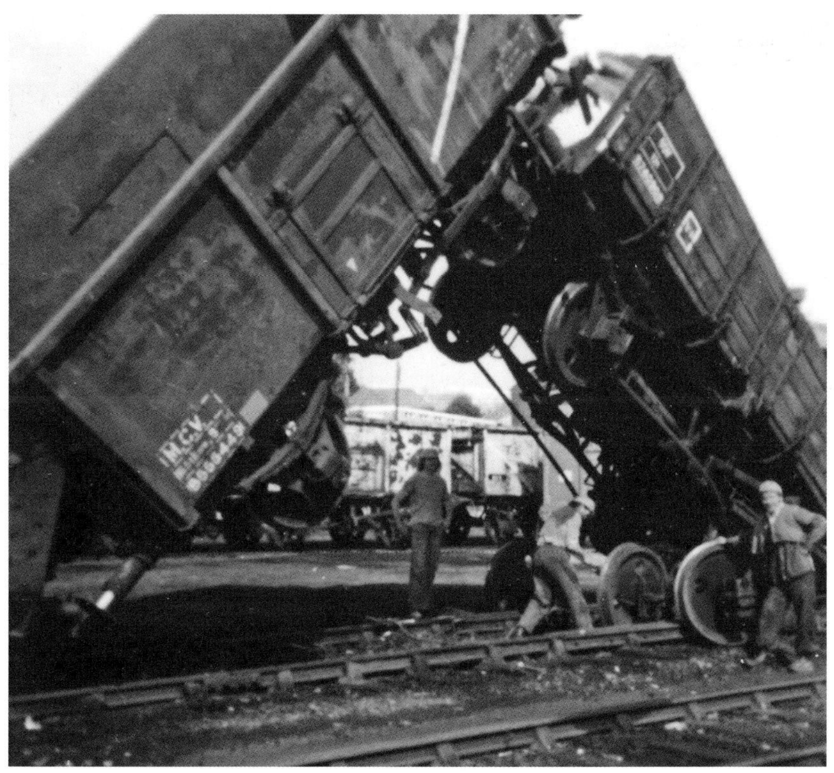

An interesting picture dated probably from the 1960s or 70s, but depicting a 'rough shunt' in what appears to be the old goods yard at St Austell. Health & Safety regulations plainly have not caught up yet, and these days such a scene is unthinkable. Back in the more practical days of British Railways the main aim was to get back to normality as quickly as possible so as not to inconvenience customers and passengers. As everyone worked for the same company there was no outside liability to consider and any delay was purely in-house. These days, whilst delay is a very high priority, the resultant enquiry and possible disciplinary, would have cost countless hours of the many staff investigating, med-screening and interviewing all those involved. (RKM)

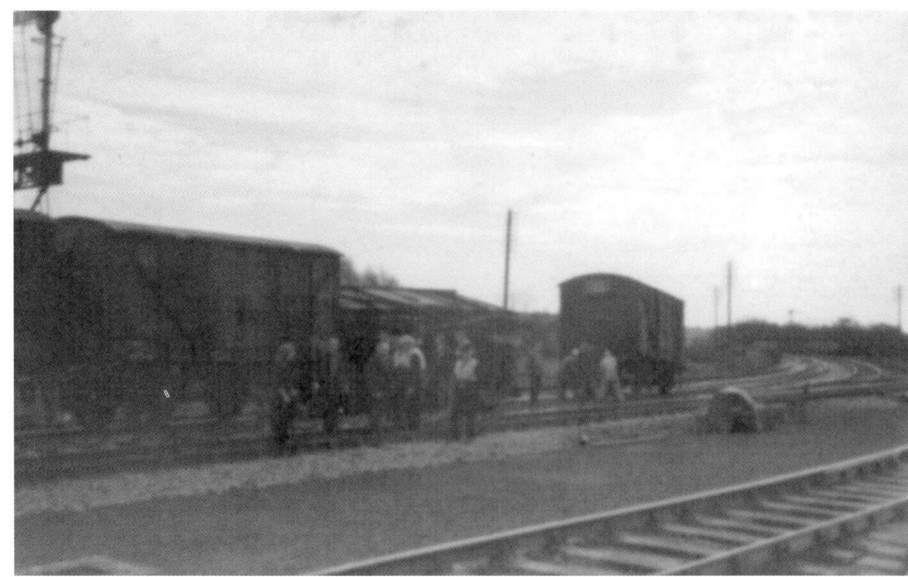

A poor quality picture, but worth including for its historic content. Derailments these days, are thankfully, less common, but prior to continuous braking (fitted) freights, vacuum braking and now air braking, derailments were common events and usually dealt with quickly. These days, because of the way the railway is set up, all derailments have to be investigated internally to establish cause and liability. If serious, or involving passenger stock, the RAIB (Rail Accident Investigation Branch) also need to be informed or will conduct the investigation themselves, and to placate the Department of Transport in its quest to prevent a reoccurrence. This minor derailment at St Blazey appears to be from the 1970s and involves short wheelbase vans, which were unstable, especially when empty. The breakdown crew will come from the adjacent depot and will have the stock re-railed and line opened in a couple of hours, whereas these days a derailment in Cornwall requires a road crew with a Bruff vehicle, or heavy breakdown crane to come from Cardiff or Old Oak Common. (SL)

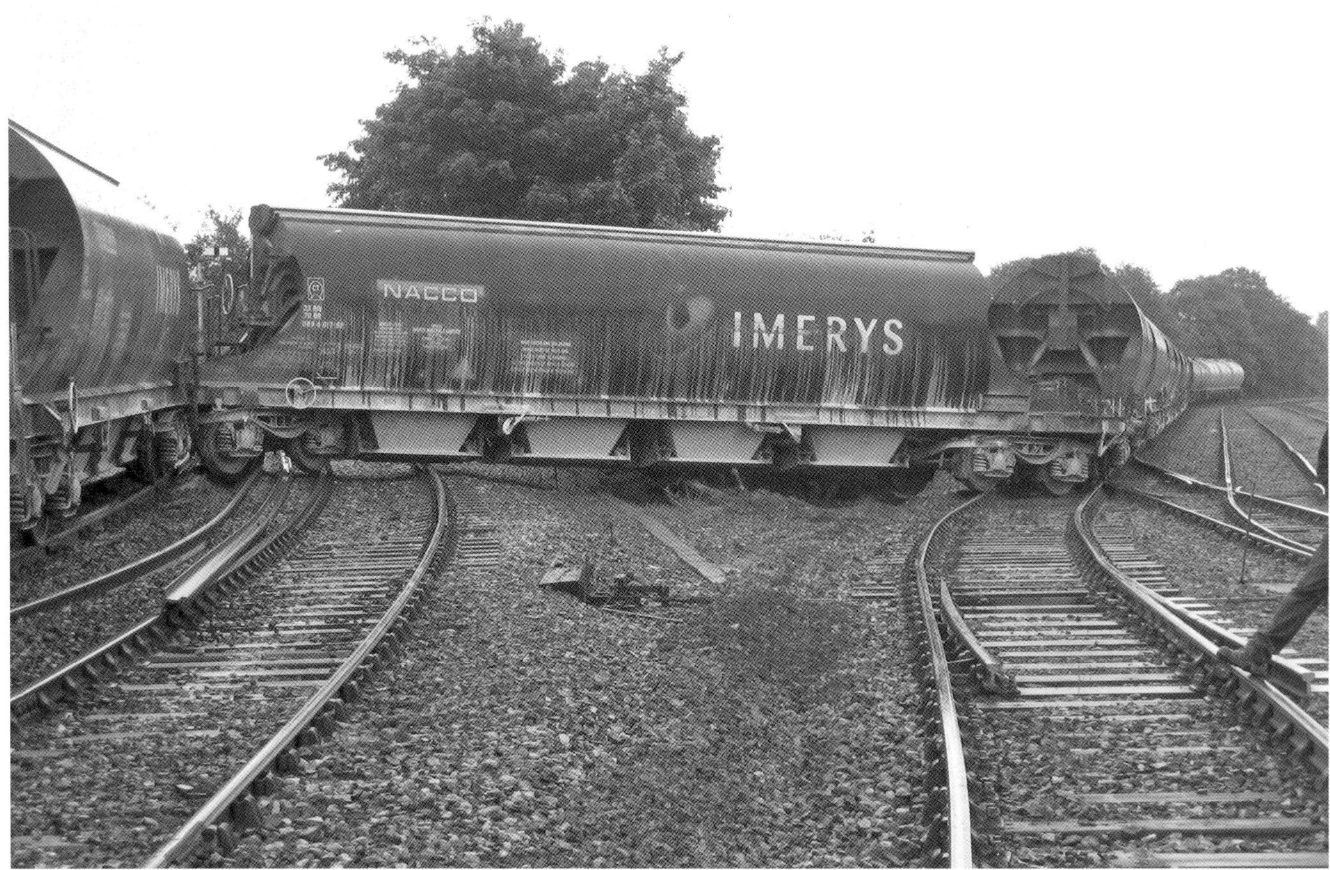

Early on the morning of 18 June 2010 a spectacular derailment took place at St Blazey whilst a particularly long train was propelling back into yard from the single-line/Down main. The result felled a ground position shunting signal and the signal protecting the exit from the yard, which is buried under the wagon. A full investigation took place and I attended later in the day to gather evidence on behalf of the signalman and RMT. (SFH)

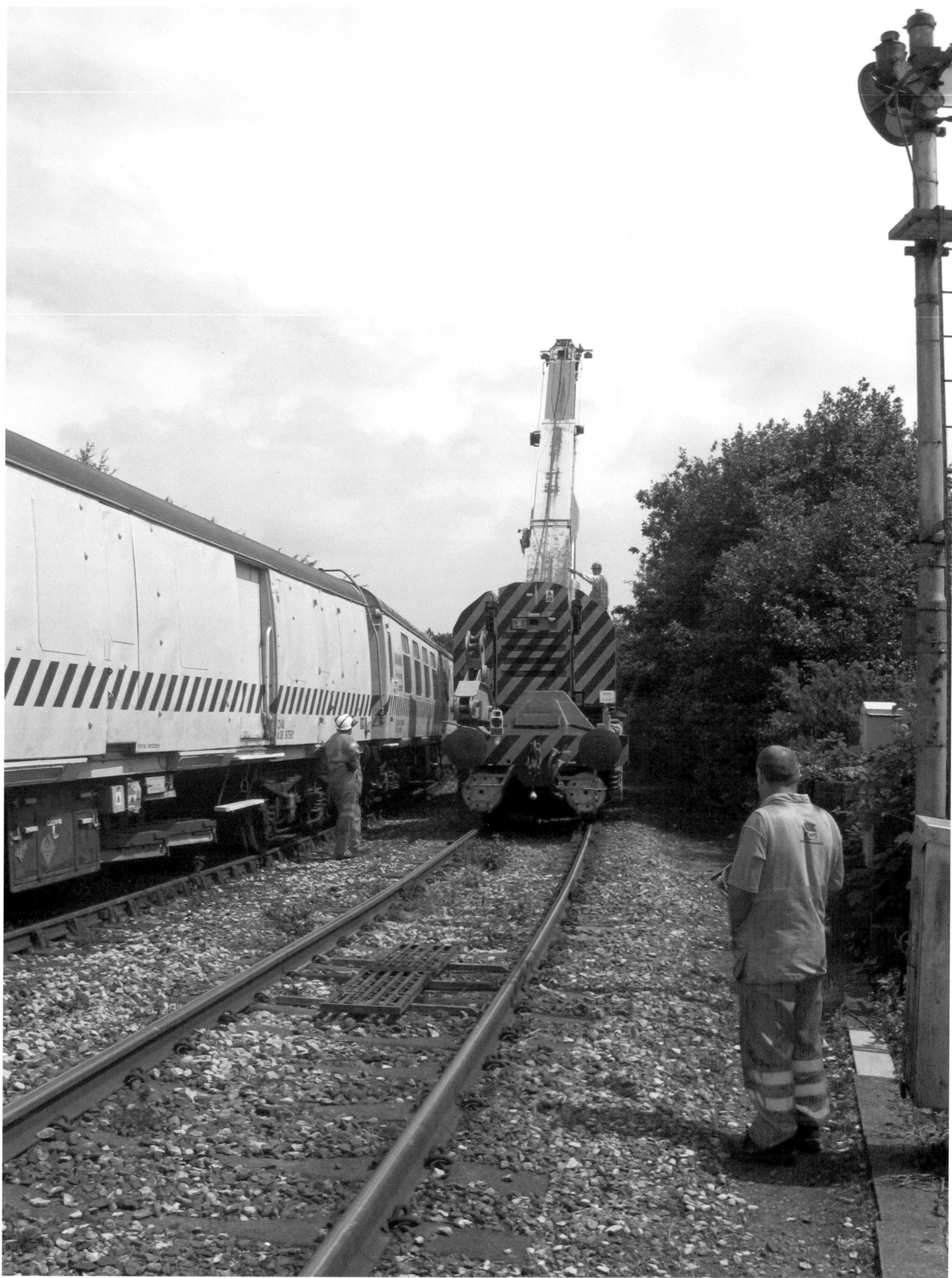

The Old oak Common Breakdown train is sat occupying both Up and Down lines between St Blazey And Par on 19 June 2010 after the destructive and potentially serious derailment at St Blazey on the previous day, the true cause of which has never been established. The Breakdown train came down as a Class 1 (Express) movement and had been given priority throughout its journey, because of the distance it had travelled and because the Cardiff crane was attending another incident elsewhere. (SFH)

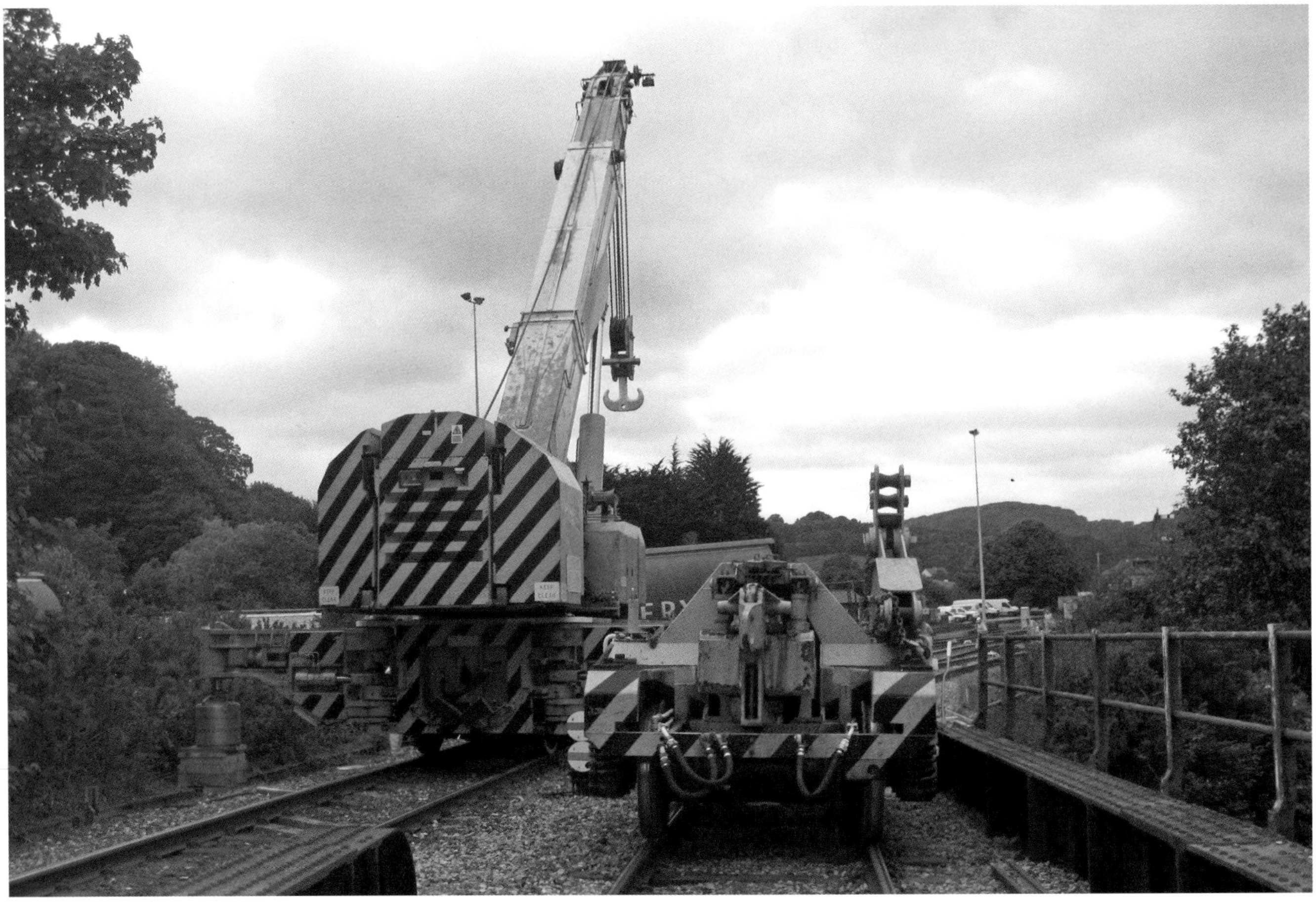

The crane is assembled and made ready for the first lift. (SFH)

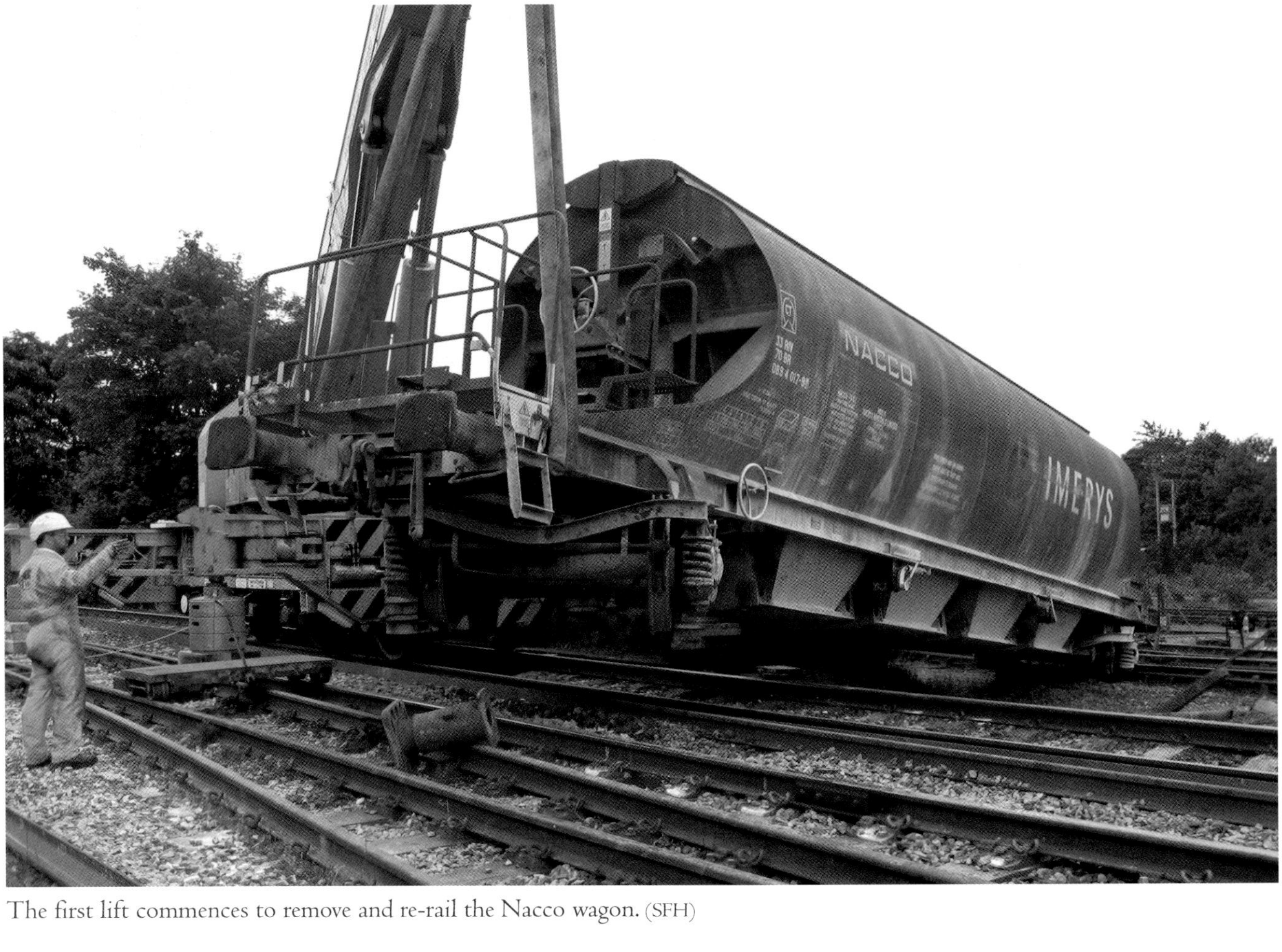

The first lift commences to remove and re-rail the Nacco wagon. (SFH)

In August 2007 a virtually brand new car jumped the lights at Quintrell Downs level crossing and collided with a Newquay bound class 153. No one aboard the train was injured, but the driver of the car and the two passengers were slightly injured. It was this accident that drove on the fitting of half-barriers to supplement the lights at this location, converting the crossing from AOCL to ABCL. (SFH)

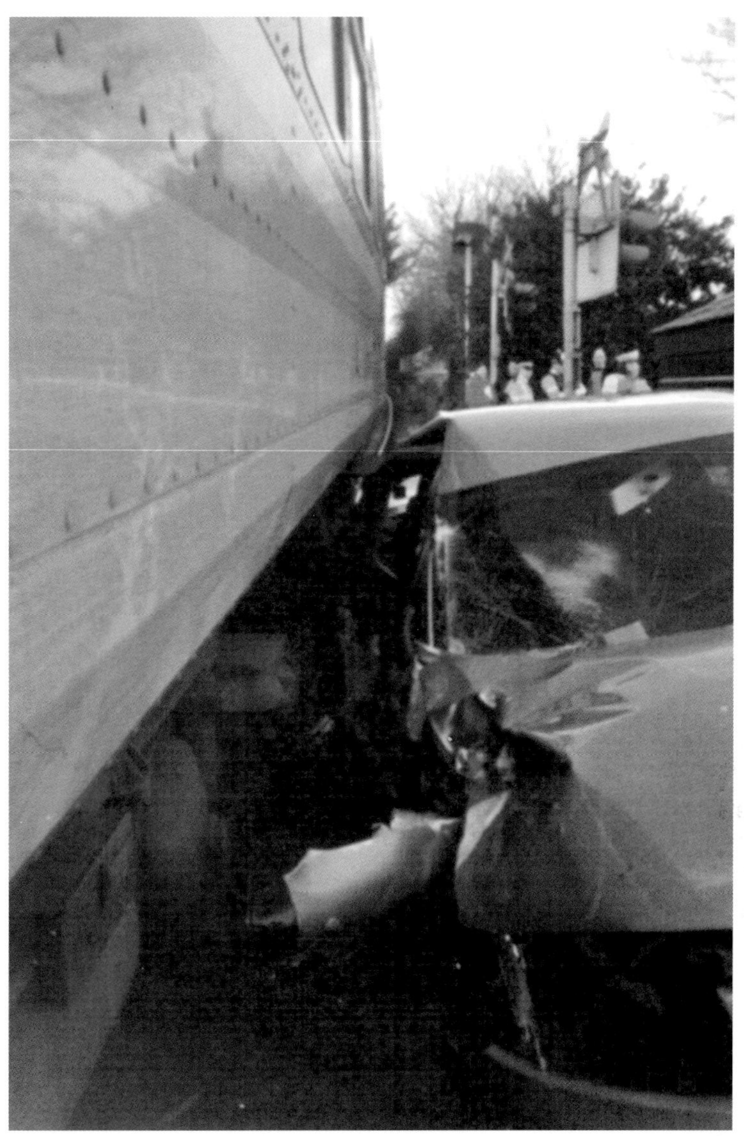

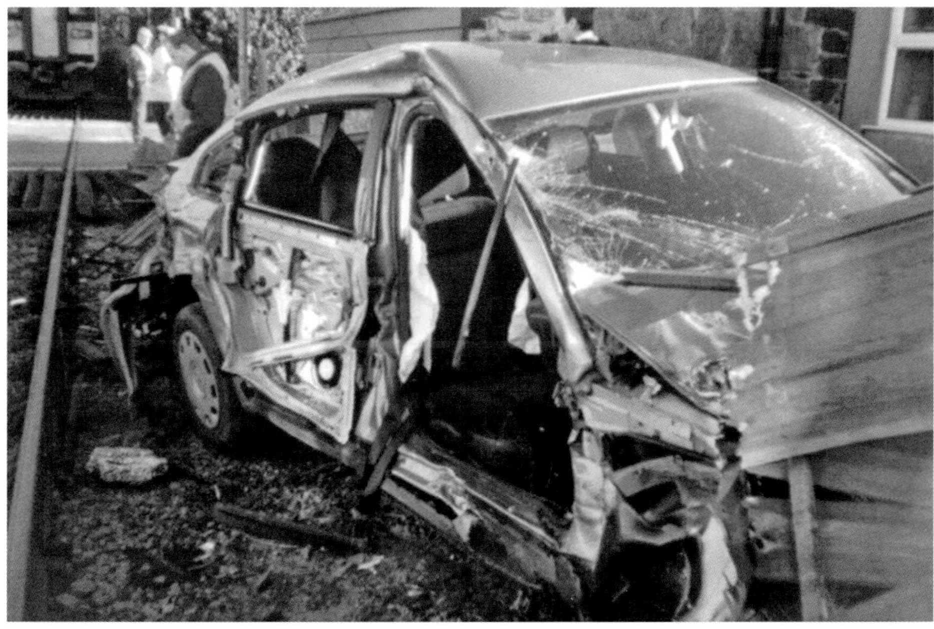

The car after the train was driven back across the crossing. (SFH)

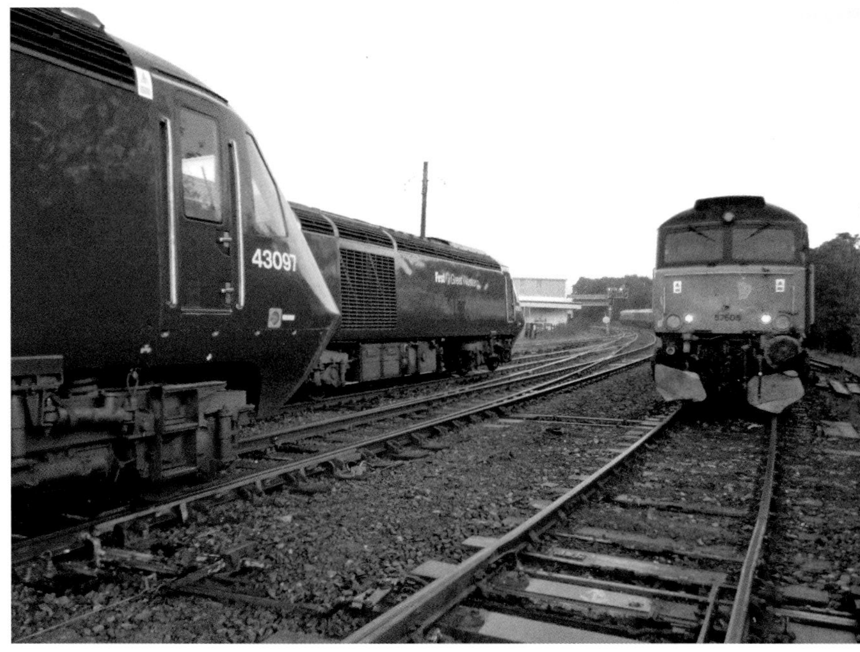

On 26 October 2011, early in the morning, a large oak tree fell across both lines near Lanhydrock , after the first up and down trains had passed but before the Down Sleeper, 'The Night Riviera' had passed through. The train was pulled by 57605 *'Totnes Castle'*, the train was travelling at line speed, and it was dark, wet and windy and the substantial third party owned tree, weighing several tons, was pushed aside and smashed up by the impact, which was heavy and sent a shock throughout the train. But for the fact it was a loco, and not a DMU or HST, the train stayed on the rails and no one was injured, though the train was badly damaged. I travelled out on an Up train to assess the damage and to get the train very slowly into Lostwithiel Down-Goods Loop after de-training the passengers onto buses and following trains. The services were disrupted but the picture depicts a rare event, in that we see two HSTs stopped at Lostwithiel along with the crippled *'Totnes Castle'* awaiting emergency repairs before going forward to Old Oak Common for rectification. It was built as D1856 in Crewe in August 1965, and was renumbered 47206 and named *'The Morris Dancer'*, before being rebuilt as a class 57 in January 2004.

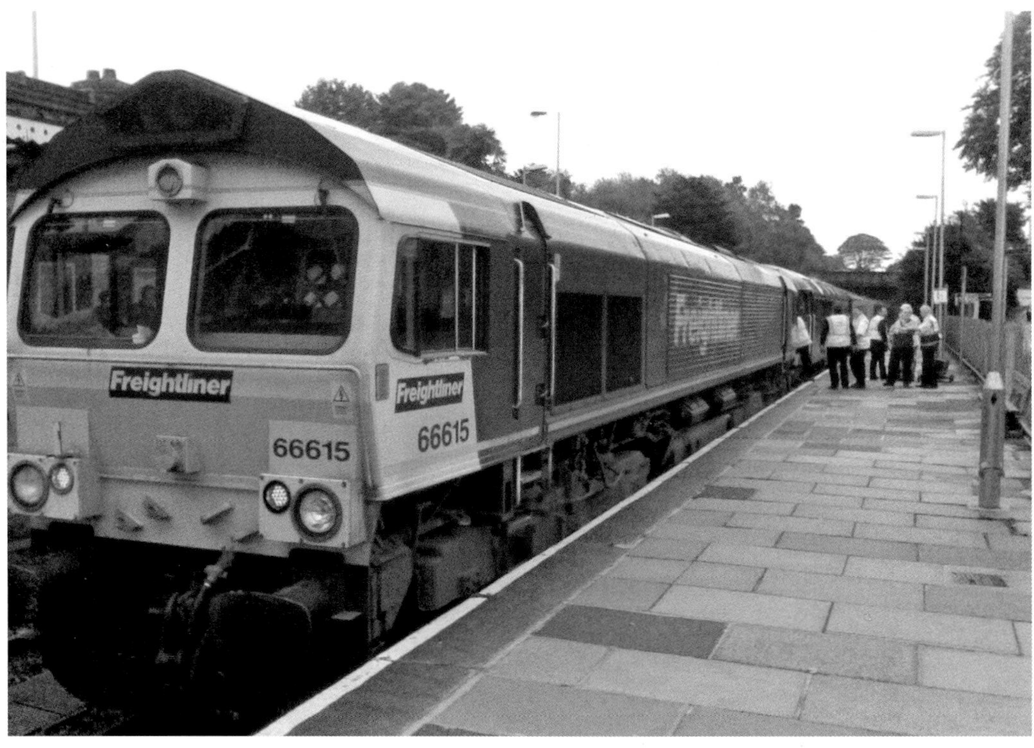

The 'Night Riviera' had suffered another problem during the previous summer, as it approached St Austell Station on the Down line, it suddenly had a full brake application, which turned out to be a fractured air pipe under the cab floor. With only one coach on the platform, the train-crew got everyone off and onto buses, but rectification, by the local travelling fitter, took several hours, and even the borrowing of Freightliner 66615 from its train at Burngullow, failed to get enough air pressure to release the brakes. Eventually after over four hours, the fitter made enough of a temporary repair to 57604 *'Pendennis Castle'* for it to be moved forward to clear the ground frame, which I operated to allow the train to be stabled in the old Up Siding, where the loco was detached and driven up to the stop-blocks behind the Up Platform. Here, over several hours a team of fitters repaired the fractured pipe. 57604 started out life as D1859, in August 1965 at BR Crewe. It became 47209, 47393 and 47209 again and previously carried the name *'Herbert Austin'*. (SFH)

CHAPTER 8

THE HSTs

WHEN I STARTED to compile this volume on Cornwalls Railways, I did not consider including any HST pictures, because I thought such apparently mundane trains was not what the reader wanted to see. However, on reflection, I consider that I was wrong. With the HST now in its fortieth year and still going strong with only four of the once one hundred and ninety-eight power cars having been scrapped, three of those due to serious collision damage.

They have had numerous owners, livery changes, modifications and upgrades since they first appeared in 1972, but the first production power cars which came into service in 1976 are still ostensibly the same in appearance today as when they were built, though the majority have been re-engined and have lost their loud, smokey Paxman-Valenta power units.

Arguably the most successful train British Railways ever built, the fact that most are still in service and refurbished to a good standard, is proof that they are both enduring and well designed. The mark 3 coach is probably the most well designed and strongest railway passenger coach made to this day, because it combined safety with comfort, though since they have been refurbished over and over again, the seating is perhaps not as comfortable and the leg room is less, as more seats are fitted in. There are also fewer tables and many buffet cars have been converted to seating coaches, but taking all that aside, it is still the preferred coach to travel in when making a journey, especially if the alternative is a Voyager!

So with all that said, here is a short chapter dedicated to the HST in Cornwall.

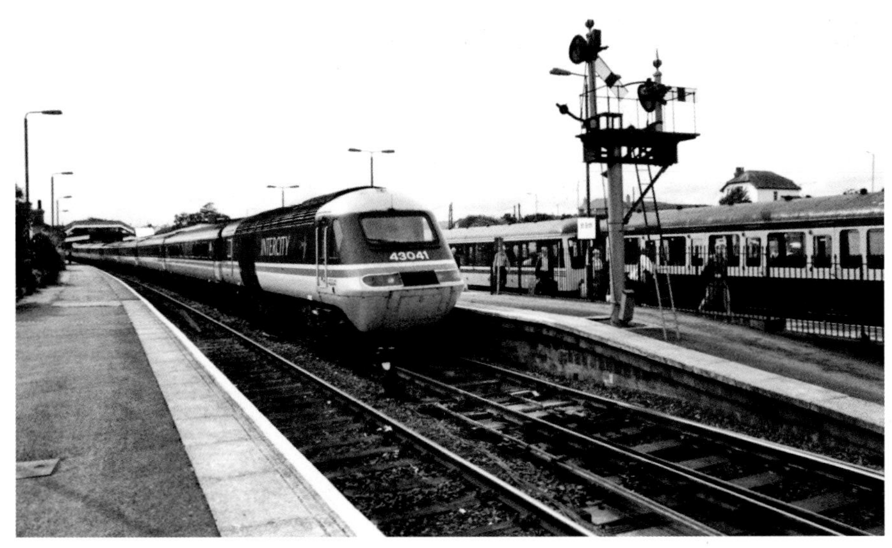

Another version of the 'Intercity' livery where the loco number was carried on the front and in this case 43041. The location is St Erth and the Branch Platform has at least two 'Bubble Cars' in it, which are probably strengthening the two or three car train on the St Ives line, as this is August 1992 and the branch line will be busy. (GP)

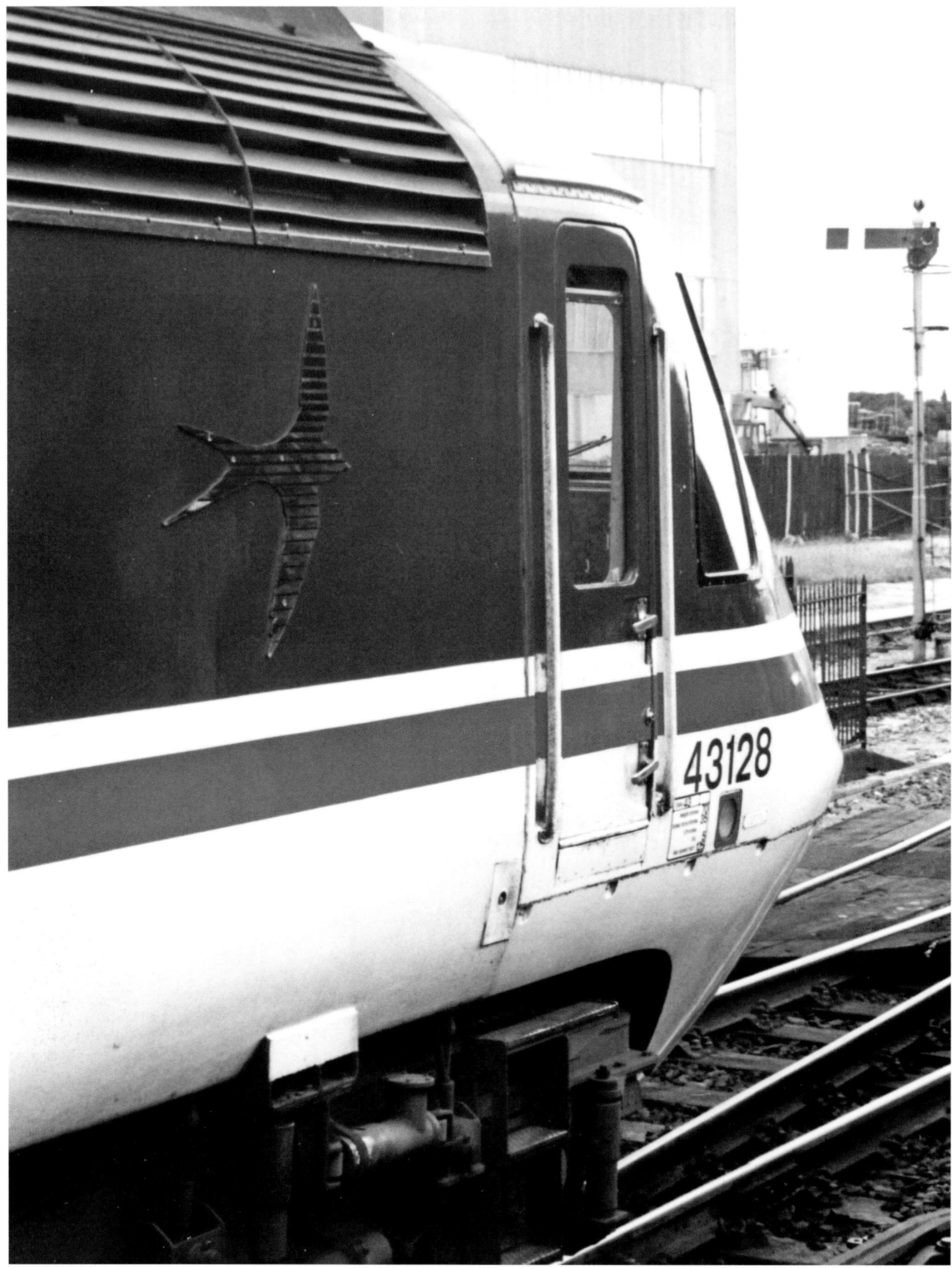

A study of the front end of HST number 43128 in St Erth in July 1992, shows the 'Intercity Swallow' and the number now on the cab side. (GP)

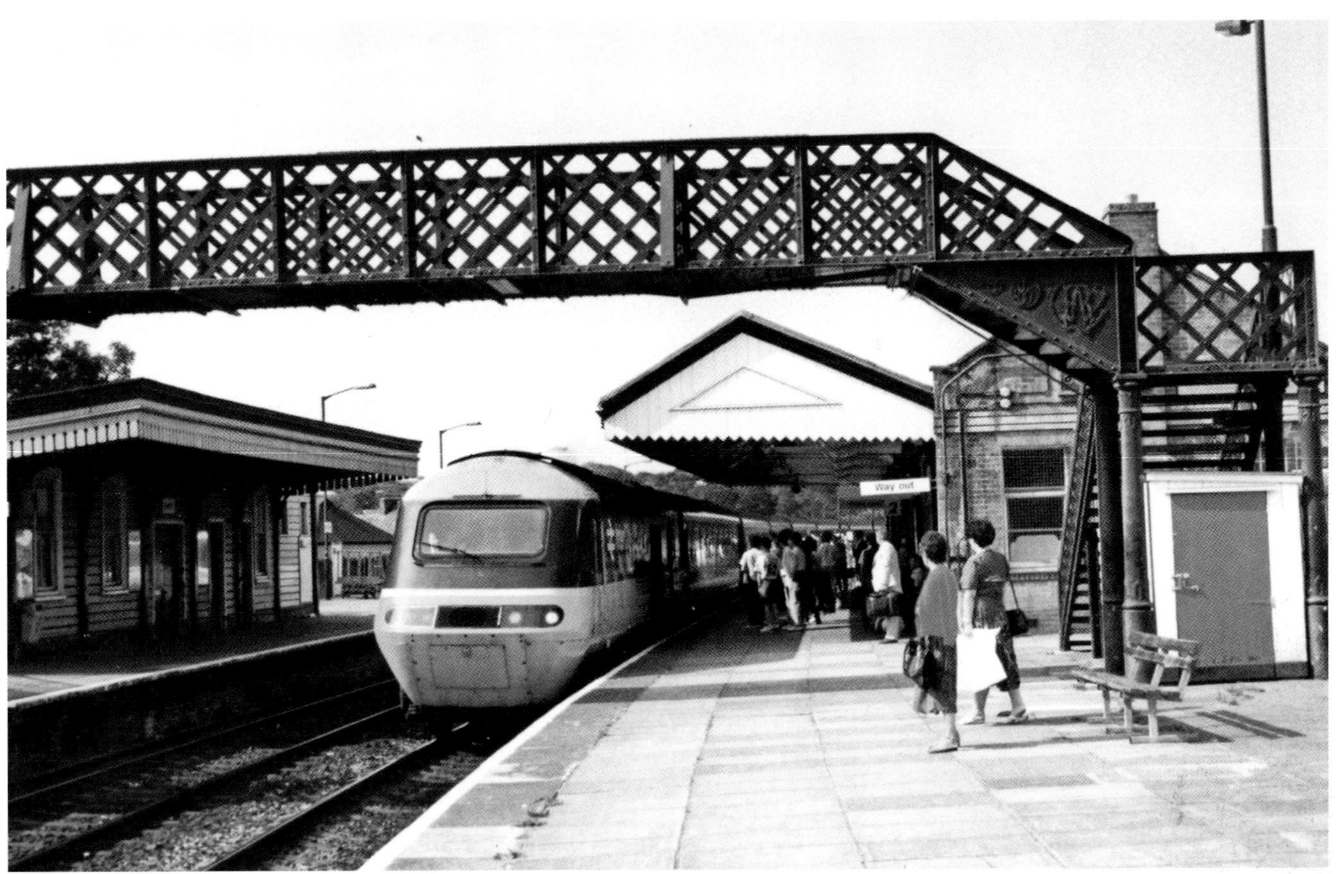

An Up HST is calling at Redruth on 25 July 1990. (GP)

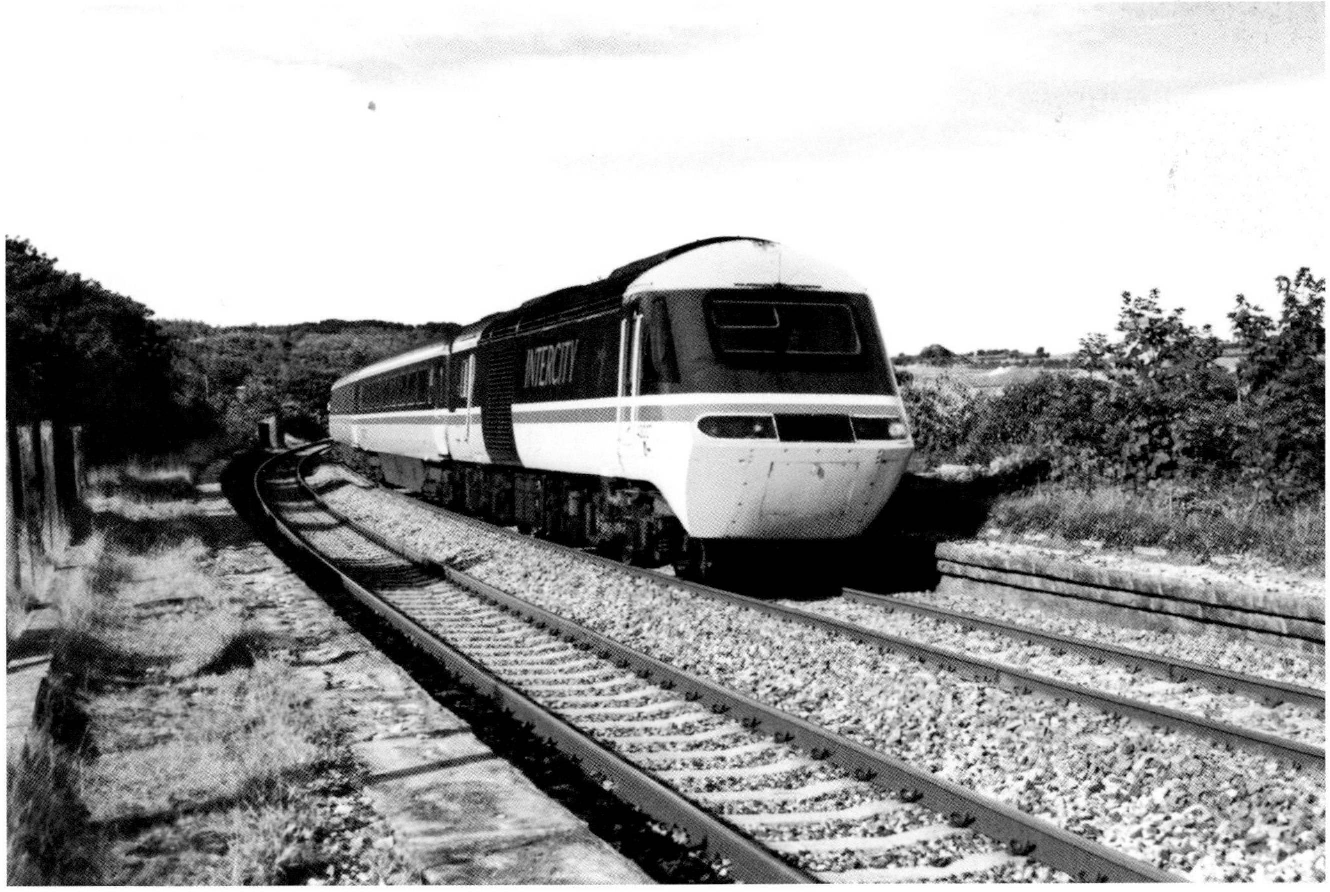

This photograph shows HST number 43007 passing Scorrier on the Up enroute for London Paddington on 19 August 1989. Now hired to Cross Country Trains and renumbered 43207. (GP)

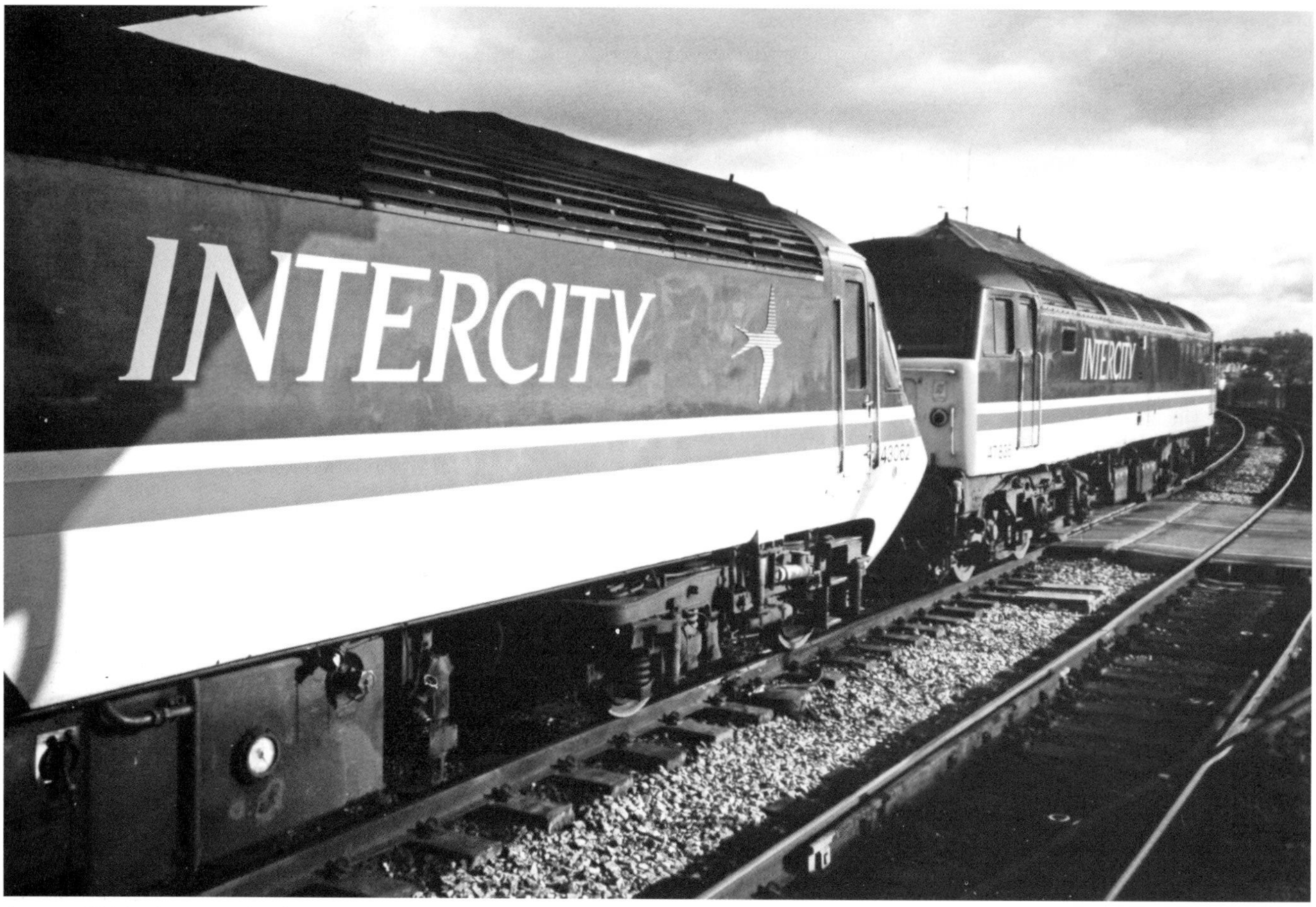

A circa 1992 photograph, shows an Up HST, number 43062 at Truro being assisted by 47836, in the days when an assisting loco and crew were easy to find and keeping the service to the public running was paramount to the Operating Department. These days, if an HST fails, (which is not as common as it was), and it can run on one engine, it will depart and be replaced or repaired en route, or if both engines fail, it is unlikely to be replaced unless the next set can be stepped up,. If all that fails it will be cancelled, because it is better for the performance figures if it does not run than if it ran late. 47836 was built as D1609 by BR at Crewe in August 1964, but subsequently became, 47030, 47618, 47836, 47618 (again), then finally 47780. It was withdrawn in April 2003 and cut up in August 2007. (GP)

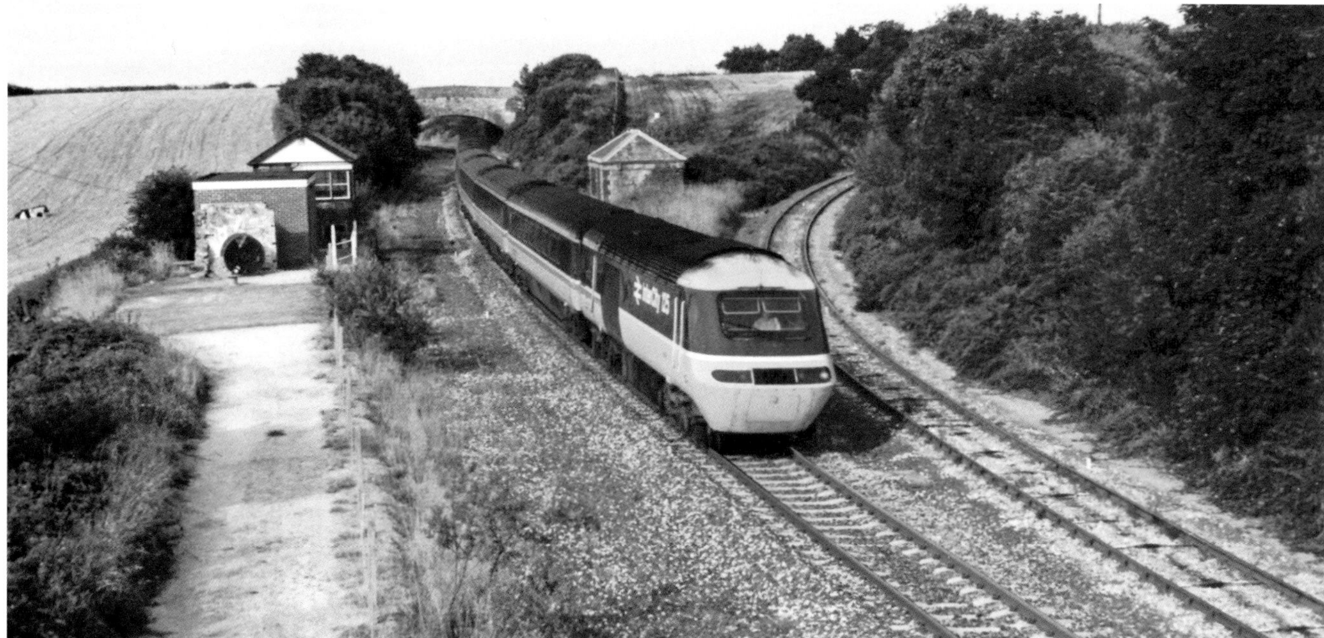

August 1989 is the date of this picture of an HST passing Burngullow Junction and Signalbox, which was disused, and a few years later would be burnt down by local vandals. This location is now a double line again after the redoubling project of 2004. The HST is in another version of the 'Intercity' livery. (GP)

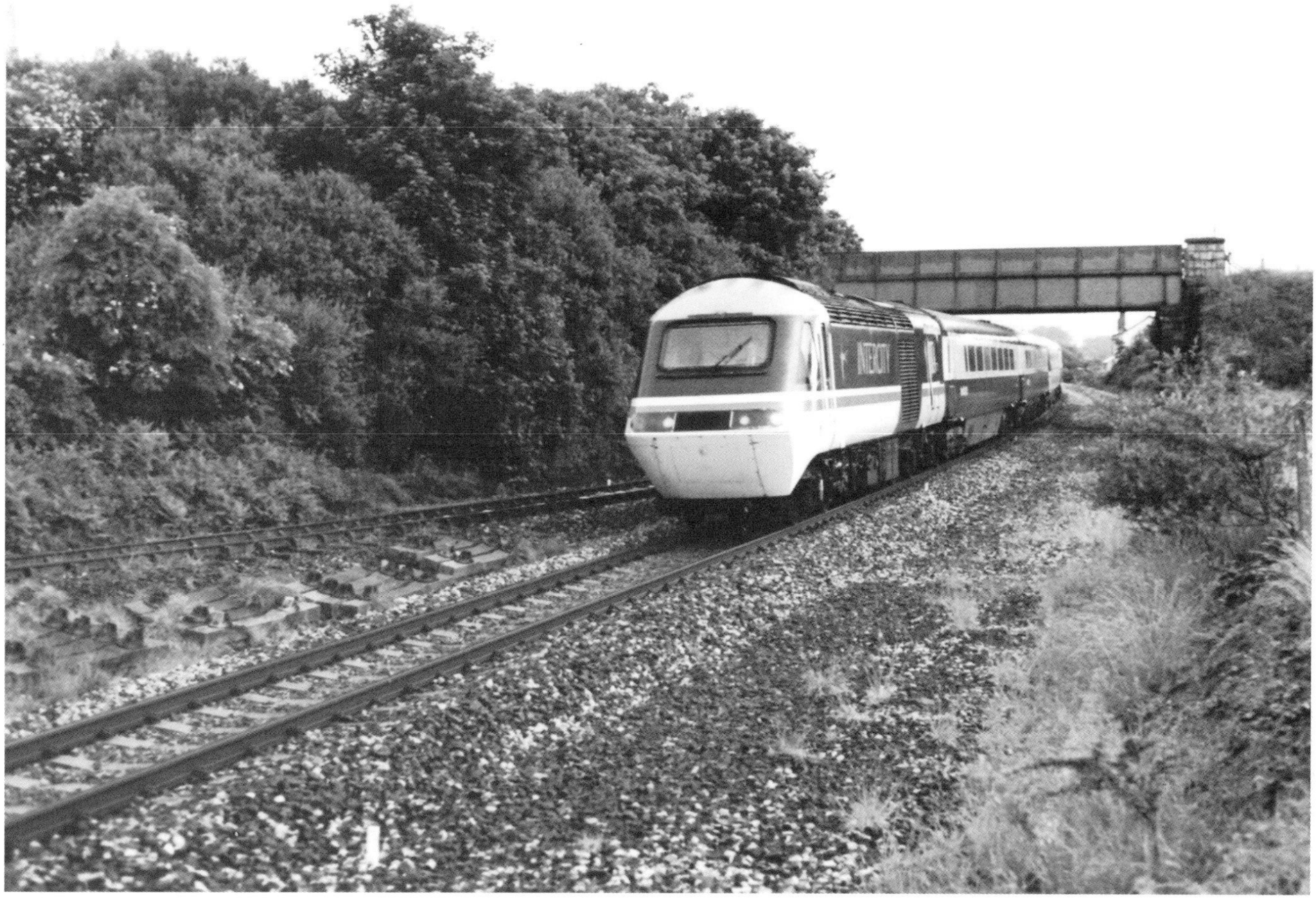

A down HST passing Burngullow old Signalbox and long closed Station in June 1989, whilst in mixed livery. (GP)

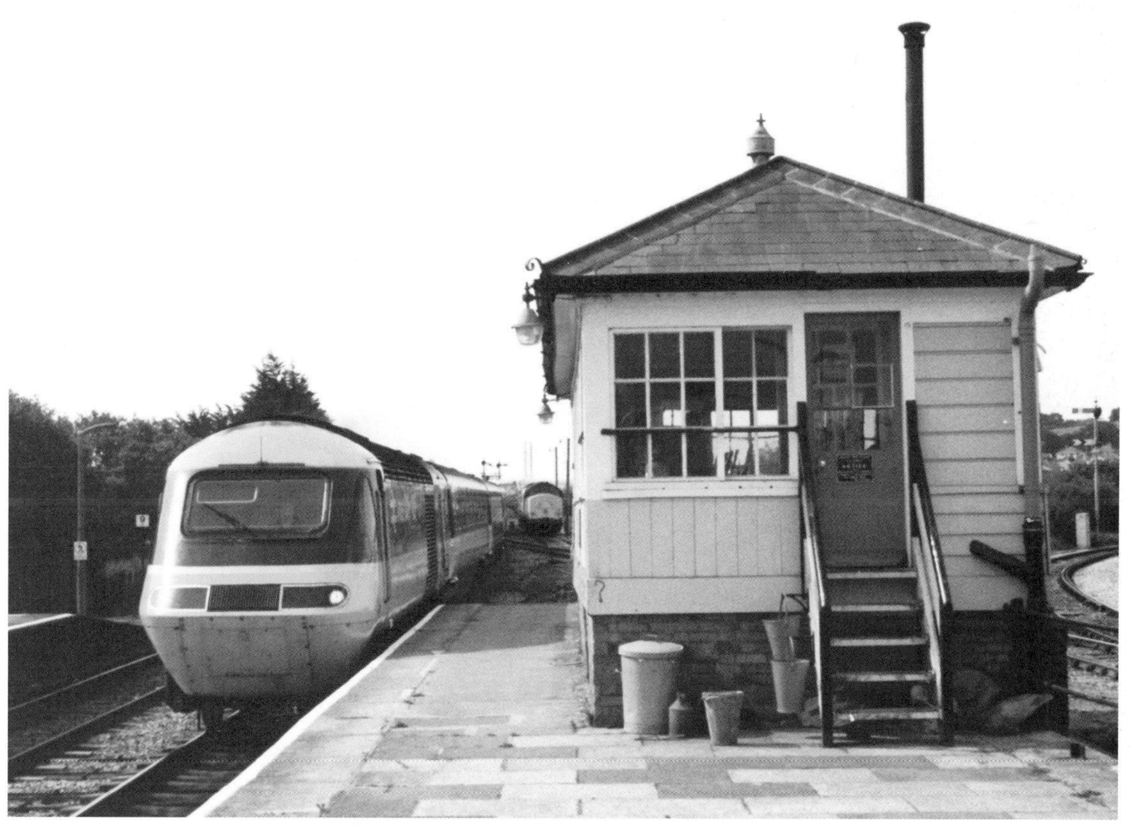

This picture is at Par Up Platform in June 1990. (GP)

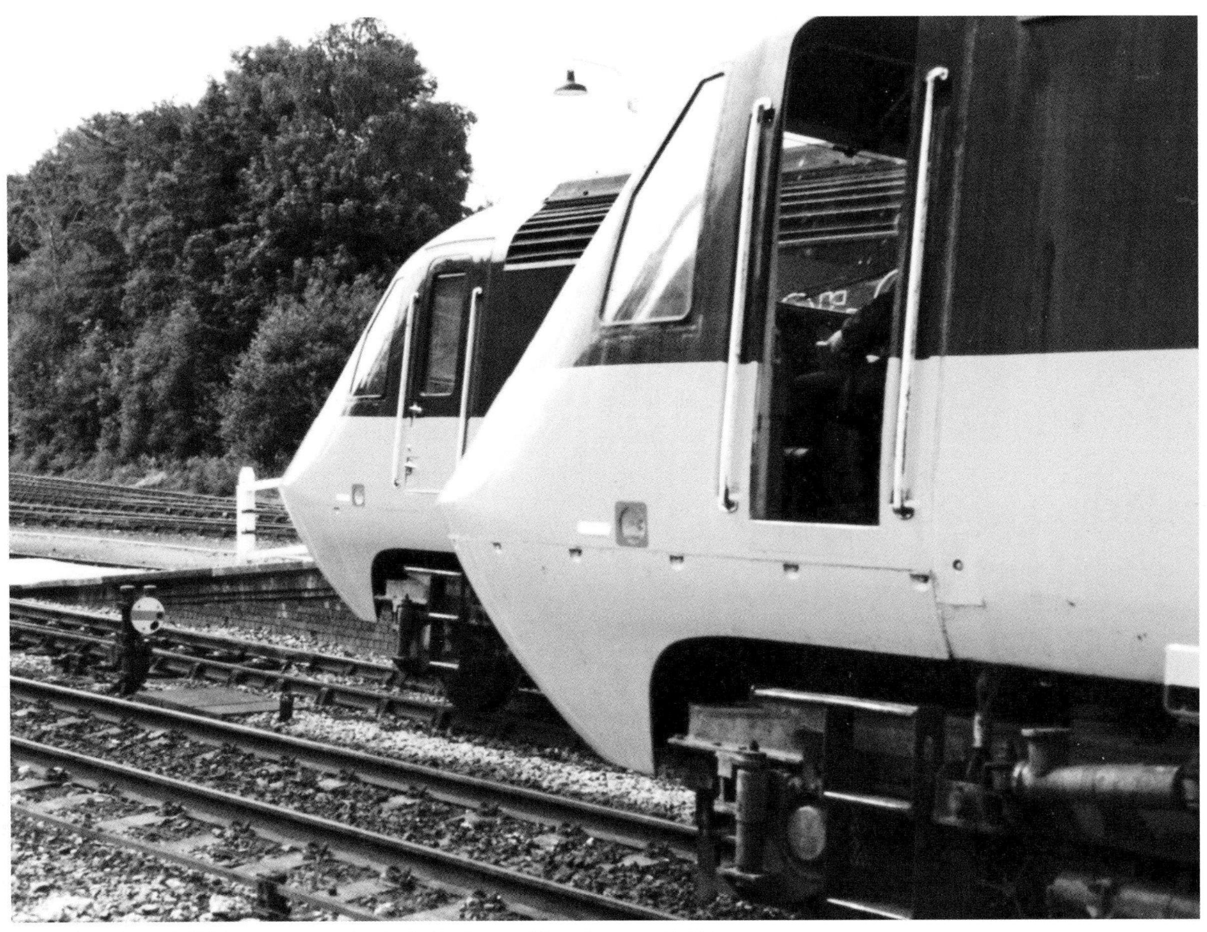

A study of two HSTs passing at Bodmin Parkway (Road) circa 1989. (GP)

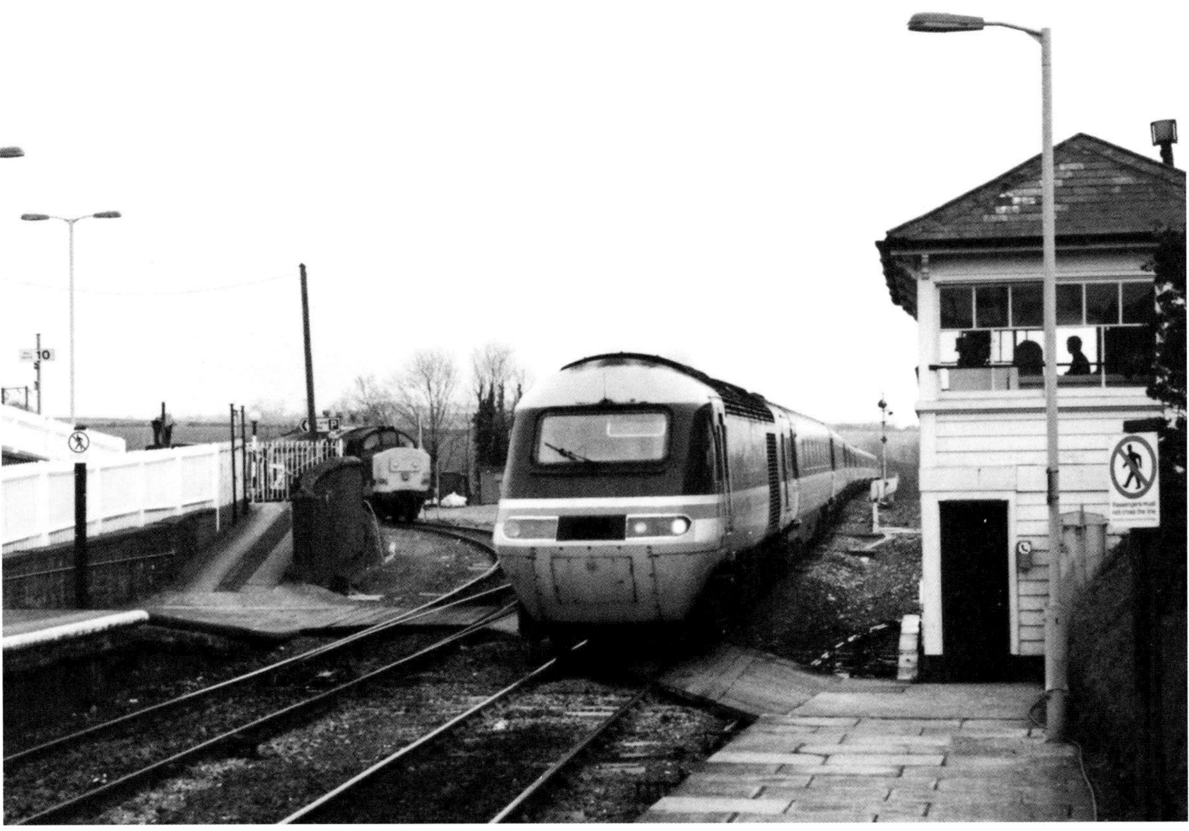

This April 1992 photograph shows an HST approaching Liskeard on the Down, whilst 37670 waits to follow it from Moorswater with Clay bound for Lostwithiel and Fowey. (GP)

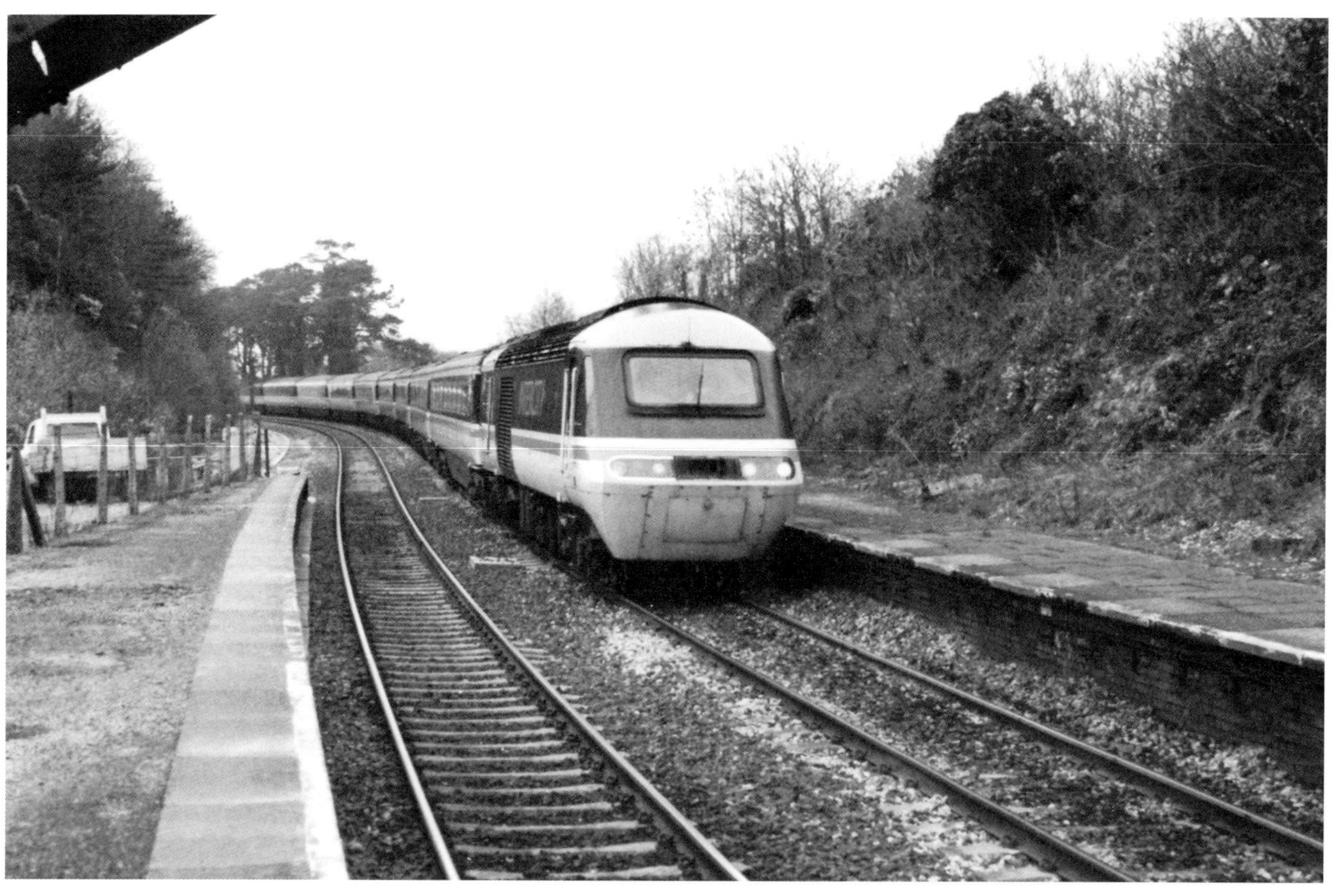

This photograph shows an HS passing through Menheniot Station on 9 April 1991, bound for Paddington. (GP)

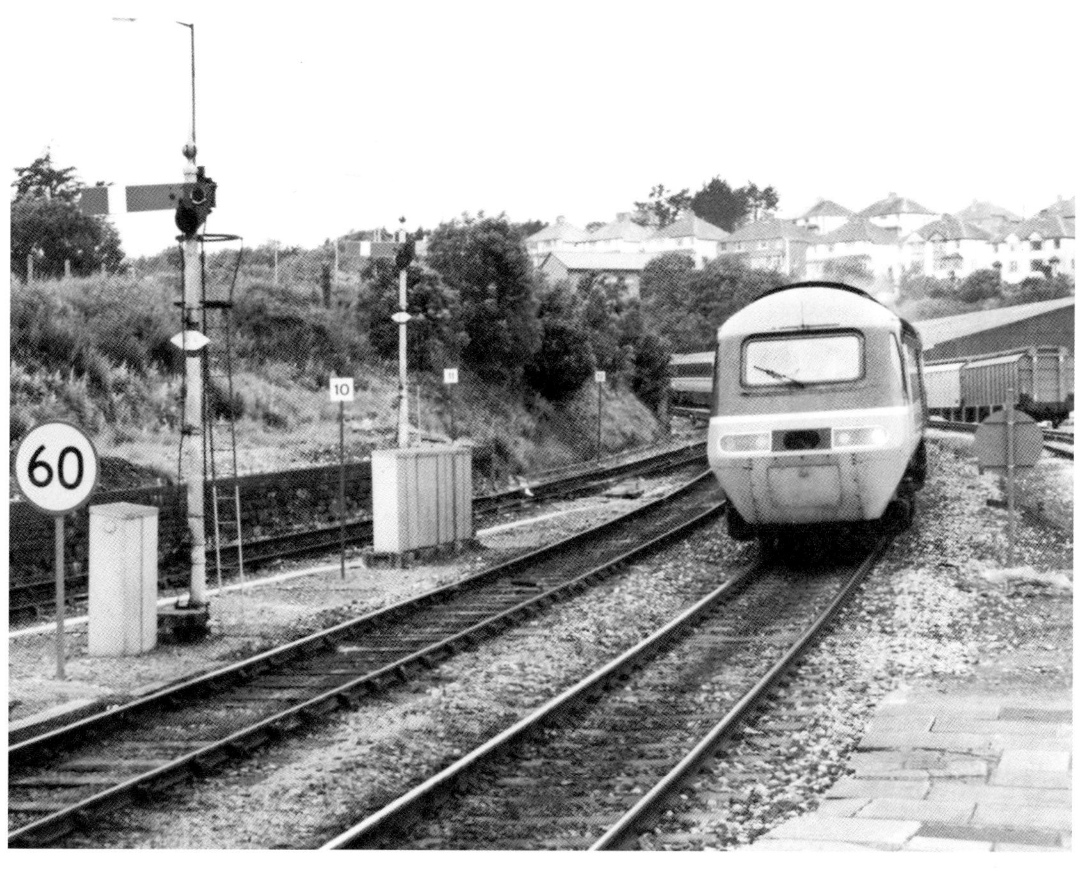

An HST is entering Truro bound for Paddington in May 1990 whilst still owned by British Rail. (GP)

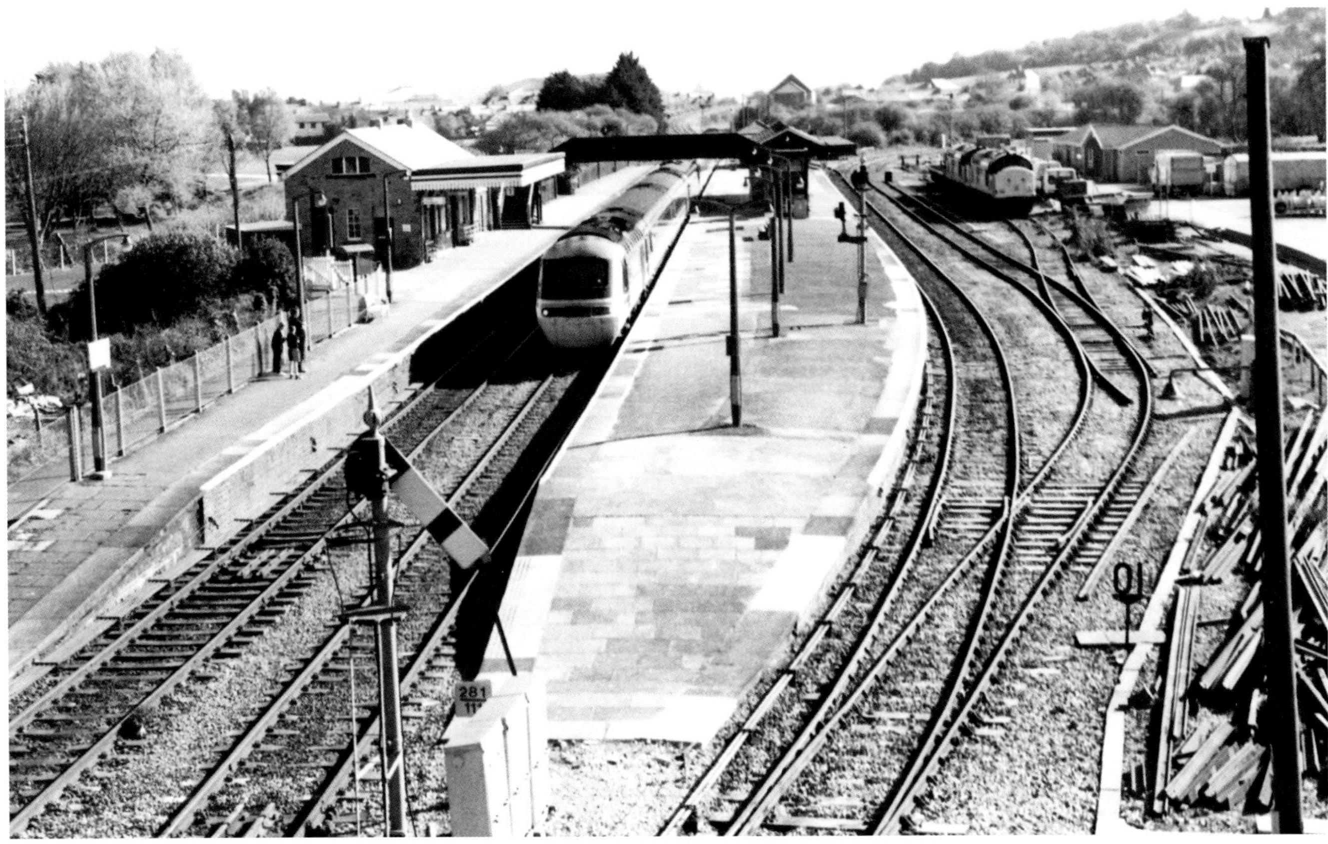

An HST is seen here entering Par Up Platform during the early 1990s. The livery is the 'Intercity Swallow'. In the Liner Siding are two class 37s. (GP)